Arms Transfers to the Third World, 1971–85

Arms Transfers to the Third World, 1971–85

Michael Brzoska and Thomas Ohlson

sipri
Stockholm International Peace Research Institute

Oxford · New York

OXFORD UNIVERSITY PRESS

1987

Oxford University Press, Walton Street, Oxford OX2 6DP
Oxford New York Toronto
Delhi Bombay Calcutta Madras Karachi
Petaling Jaya Singapore Hong Kong Tokyo
Nairobi Dar es Salaam Cape Town
Melbourne Auckland
and associated companies in
Beirut Berlin Ibadan Nicosia

Oxford is a trade mark of Oxford University Press

Published in the United States
by Oxford University Press, New York

© SIPRI 1987

British Library Cataloguing in Publication Data

Brzoska, Michael
Arms transfer to the Third World, 1971–85.
1. Munitions—Developing countries
2. Munitions   3. Developing countries—Commerce
I. Title   II. Ohlson, Thomas
III. Stockholm International Peace Research Institute
382'.456234   HD9743.D44
ISBN 0–19–829116–7

Library of Congress Cataloging in Publication Data

Brzoska, Michael
Arms transfer to the Third World, 1971–85.
Stockholm International Peace Research Institute.
Bibliography: p. Includes index.
1. Munitions—Developing countries.   I. Ohlson, Thomas
II. Stockholm International Peace Research Institute.
II. Title.
HD9743.D442B79   1987 382'.456234'091724   87–5579
ISBN 0–19–829116–7

Set by H Charlesworth & Co Ltd, Huddersfield
Printed and bound in Great Britain
by Biddles Ltd, Guildford and King's Lynn

Preface

The main purpose of this book is to give a comprehensive factual overview of the trade in major conventional weapons with Third World countries from 1971 to 1985. During this period the arms trade with the Third World boomed and reached unprecedented levels, both with respect to the number of actors on the supply and demand sides, and to the quality and quantity of weapons transferred.

SIPRI, since it began, has had a continuing project which deals with the arms trade. The thrust of the work in this project has, for good reasons, been concentrated on military developments in the Third World. The arms trade is the main route by which Third World countries build up their military arsenals. The other route is by building up domestic arms industries—this process was the subject of a recent SIPRI book: *Arms Production in the Third World*, published in 1986. Together, these two books present a complete picture of major-weapon procurement in the Third World. They provide the factual basis for continued study of the spread of conventional weapons in the Third World and of the political, military and economic frameworks within which weapons are being procured.

Other factors prompted the writing of this book. First, since the publication in 1971 of the SIPRI study *The Arms Trade with the Third World*, SIPRI data on arms transfers have been used extensively by political decision-makers, researchers, journalists, students and others throughout the world. Since there is a continuous flow of new information—also on arms deals made a long time ago—users of successive *SIPRI Yearbooks* have not always found in the annual arms trade registers and valuation statistics the most up-to-date information available at SIPRI. There is, therefore, a need to publish updated longer-term registers and valuation statistics at regular intervals. This was last done in the volume *Arms Trade Registers*, published in 1975 and effectively covering the period 1950 to 1973.

Second, price relations between weapon systems and between weapon categories tend to change over time. The SIPRI price system for evaluating the arms trade has been completely revised and a new base-year (1985) has been introduced (see appendix 8). This new price system is introduced in this book and will be used in subsequent *SIPRI Yearbooks*.

Third, the increasing importance of electronics in modern weapon systems has been a major feature of arms production (and thus of the arms trade) in the 1970s and early 1980s. SIPRI has, therefore, introduced a fifth weapon category—guidance and radar systems—in addition to those used earlier. This marks an attempt to adapt to the changing nature of the arms market so as to be able to cover as many as possible of the arms transfers that occur. Data problems are, however, immense (see appendix 9).

Finally, there were major structural changes in the arms market during the period under study. This book is therefore not simply a collection of data—it also attempts to describe these changes and the reasons behind them.

Arms Transfers to the Third World, 1971–85, gives a comprehensive overview of the flow of major conventional weapons during the period. It analyses both the main Third World recipients—describing the inflow of arms and the underlying factors and events—and the suppliers—their arms export bureaucracies, their degree of dependence on arms exports and shifts in their arms export policies. The factors that propel the arms trade with the Third World are assessed in a concluding chapter which also analyses the structural changes that have occurred in the arms market and their implications. Detailed statistics and arms trade registers for the period (in some cases from 1951) are appended.

Acknowledgement is due to Elisabeth Sköns, who prepared the bibliography in appendix 11. She also assisted, with Evamaria Loose-Weintraub, in the collection of data for appendices 1–7 and in the preparation of tables and figures. Finally, the editorial expertise of Billie Bielckus is gratefully acknowledged.

SIPRI   The authors
December 1986

Contents

Figures

Tables

Acronyms, abbreviations, and conventions

AA	Anti-aircraft
AAG	Anti-aircraft gun
AALS	Amphibious assault landing ship
AAM	Air-to-air missile
AAV	Anti-aircraft vehicle (gun-armed)
AAV(M)	Anti-aircraft vehicle (missile-armed)
AC	Aircraft/armoured car
AC carrier	Aircraft carrier
Acc to	According to
ADV	Air defence version
Adv	Advanced
AEV	Armoured engineering vehicle
AEW	Airborne early-warning system
AF	Air Force
ALCM	Air-launched cruise missile
Amph	Amphibious/amphibian
APC	Armoured personnel carrier
ARM	Anti-radar missile
ARV	Armoured recovery vehicle
ASEAN	Association of South East Asian Nations
AShM	Air-to-ship missile
ASM	Air-to-surface missile
ASROC	Anti-submarine rocket
ASSV	Assault vehicle
ASW	Anti-submarine warfare
ATM	Anti-tank missile
AV	Armoured vehicle
AWACS	Airborne early warning and control system
BL	Bridge-layer
Bty	Battery
CAF	Canadian Air Force
CIWS	Close-in weapon system
COIN	Counter-insurgency
CPS	Command post carrier
Displ	Displacement
DoD	Department of Defense (USA)
ECM	Electronic countermeasures
EW	Early warning
Excl	Excluding/excludes
FAC	Fast attack craft (missile/torpedo-armed)

FY	Fiscal year
GCC	Gulf Cooperation Council
GLCM	Ground-launched cruise missile
Grd	Ground
Hel	Helicopter
IAF	Italian Air Force
ICV	Infantry combat vehicle
IDS	Interdictor/strike version
Incl	Including/includes
Landmob	Land-mobile (missile)
LC	Landing craft (<600t displacement)
LS	Landing ship (>600t displacement)
LT	Light tank
LOA	Letter of Offer and Acceptance
LoO	Letter of Offer
MAP	Military Assistance Program
Mar patrol	Maritime patrol aircraft
MBT	Main battle tank
MCM	Mine countermeasures (ship)
MG	Machine-gun
MICV	Mechanized infantry combat vehicle
Mk	Mark
MoU	Memorandum of Understanding
MRCA	Multi-role combat aircraft
MRL	Multiple rocket launcher
MRS	Multiple rocket system
MSC	Minesweeper, coastal
MSO	Minesweeper, ocean
MT	Medium tank
NATO	North Atlantic Treaty Organization
OPEC	Organization of Petroleum Exporting Countries
OPV	Offshore patrol vessel
PAR	Precision approach radar
PC	Patrol craft (gun-armed/unarmed)
PDM	Point defence missile
Port	Portable
RAF	Royal Air Force (UK)
RAAF	Royal Australian Air Force
Recce	Reconnaissance (aircraft/vehicle)
RMAF	Royal Malaysian Air Force
RN	Royal Navy (UK)
SAAF	South African Air Force
SAM	Surface-to-air missile
SAR	Search and rescue
SC	Scout car

SEK	Swedish crowns
ShAM	Ship-to-air missile
ShShM	Ship-to-ship missile
ShSuM	Ship-to-submarine missile
SLBM	Submarine-launched ballistic missile
SPG	Self-propelled gun
SPH	Self-propelled howitzer
SShM	Surface-to-ship missile
SSM	Surface-to-surface missile
SuShM	Submarine-to-ship missile
TD	Tank destroyer (gun-armed)
TD(M)	Tank destroyer (missile-armed)
TG	Towed gun
TH	Towed howitzer
Trpt	Transport
UNITA	National union for the total independence of Angola
USCENTCOM	US Central Command
VIP	Very important person
WTO	Warsaw Treaty Organization
ZANU	Zimbabwean National Union

Conventions

Acronyms and abbreviations are listed in appendix 9 on sources and methods.

..	Data not available or not applicable
–	Negligible figure (<0.5)
( )	Uncertain data
billion	Thousand million

Region codes used in the appendices:

 8 Middle East
 9 South Asia
10 Far East and Oceania
12 North Africa
13 Sub-Saharan Africa, excluding South Africa
14 Central America
15 South America
16 South Africa

Superscript numbers refer to the lists of notes and references at the end of each chapter or appendix.

Chapter 1. The flow of arms: main trends

I. Overall growth

Between 1971 and 1985, major conventional weapons valued at $286 billion in constant (1985) US dollars were imported by countries in the Third World. That is almost four times the value recorded for the previous two decades: in the period 1951–70, $77 billion worth of major weapons were imported. Figure 1.1 illustrates some of the important dimensions of the arms trade with the Third World during 1971–85.

During the early and mid-1970s the trade in major weapons with the Third World was characterized by very high growth rates. The average annual growth rate between 1970 and 1977 was 13 per cent. During the late 1970s a decline was beginning to be seen: the average annual growth rate was down to 2 per cent in the period 1978–84. Despite this reduction of growth rates, it is clear that at no time in history were more major weapons supplied to the Third World than in the early 1980s.

However it is measured, the increase in the arms trade with the Third World in the 1970s was spectacular. As an illustration, figure 1.2 compares the trade in major weapons with the trade in all goods to the Third World. It shows that the growth in the transfer of major weapons was faster than the growth in general trade during most of the early and mid-1970s, while, in the late 1970s and early 1980s, index figures indicate generally lower growth rates.

II. The suppliers

The Soviet Union was the leading exporter of major weapons to the Third World during 1971–85, accounting for 36.6 per cent of total deliveries while the US share was 31.3 per cent. However, the USSR was not in the lead throughout the period: in the mid-1970s, US exports exceeded those of the USSR (see figure 1.3).

For each year and throughout the whole period the two superpowers were the dominant suppliers. Their average joint share during 1971–85 was approximately 68 per cent. There is a higher degree of concentration in the trade in major weapons than in the trade in any comparable category of manufactured goods, such as transport equipment, machinery or electrical products. This underlines the strong political element in the arms trade.

The combined share of the USSR and the USA, has, however, declined throughout the period (see table 1.1). The decline was small in the late 1970s, when the US share dropped as the Soviet share increased. It was more marked during the early 1980s, when both shares were decreasing.

Two groups of arms suppliers increased their shares of total arms sales to the Third World as the share of the superpowers declined (see table 1.1 and figure 1.4). The most important of these two groups was the group of traditional West European arms suppliers. Among these, France was most notable: French arms exports grew rapidly throughout the period studied. By the mid-1980s France was exporting considerably more major weapons than

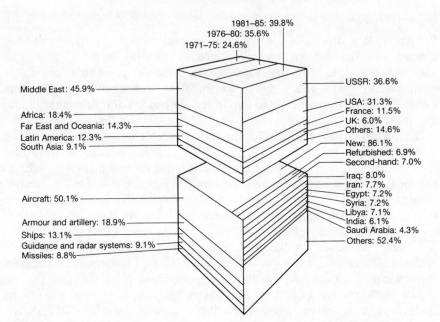

Figure 1.1. Some data on the trade in major weapons with the Third World, 1971–85

Shares are shown as percentages of the total trade in major weapons with the Third World 1971–85, US $286 b., at constant (1985) prices.
Source: SIPRI data base.

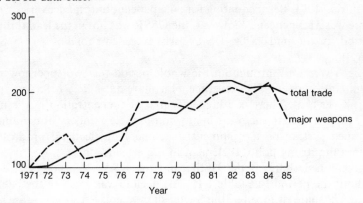

Figure 1.2. Volume index of the trade in major weapons with the Third World and total trade with the Third World, 1971–85

Sources: SIPRI data base and International Monetary Fund, *Direction of Trade Statistics Yearbook* (IMF: Washington, DC, annual).

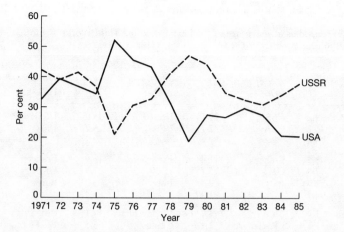

Figure 1.3. US and Soviet percentage shares in total exports of major weapons to the Third World, 1971–85

Figures are based on SIPRI trend indicator values in US $m., at constant (1985) prices.
Source: SIPRI data base.

any other West European country with comparable arms industries. The UK, Italy and FR Germany also belong to this group of traditional exporters.

The second group consists of newcomers to the arms market, particularly from the Third World (such as Israel and Brazil) but also from the European arms export periphery (e.g., Spain). Arms industries have been built up in more and more countries and these new producers have tried to establish themselves in the arms market.

Aside from the USA and the USSR some other countries experienced declining shares of major-weapon exports during the period, including Sweden, Switzerland and, in the late 1970s, China (see also appendix 4). Table 1.1 shows that the degree of concentration in arms supply to the Third World was lower in the early 1980s than in preceding periods, irrespective of whether the shares of the two, five or ten largest exporters are measured.

While the Soviet Union was the largest arms exporter—in terms of the value and quantity of weapons supplied—it was not the supplier with the highest number of recipients. Both the United States and France had more clients throughout the period, Soviet exports being concentrated towards comparatively fewer countries (see table 1.2).

III. The recipients

The regional pattern of major-weapon imports to the Third World is illustrated in figures 1.5 and 1.6. *The Middle East* was by far the leading importing region, accounting for almost half of total Third World major-weapon imports in 1971–85. The growth in imports to the Middle East was below the Third World

Table 1.1. Supplier shares in exports of major weapons to the Third World, 1971–85

Shares are expressed as a percentage of total exports to the Third World. Figures are based on SIPRI trend indicator values in US $m. at constant (1985) prices.

Supplier/period							
1971–75		1976–80		1981–85		1971–85	
USA	39.2	USSR	39.7	USSR	34.0	USSR	36.6
USSR	36.2	USA	32.7	USA	25.2	USA	31.3
Top 2	75.4		72.4		59.2		67.9
UK	8.5	France	11.4	France	13.9	France	11.5
France	7.8	UK	5.1	UK	5.3	UK	6.0
China	2.4	Italy	2.4	Italy	5.0	Italy	3.1
Top 5	94.1		91.3		83.4		88.5
FR Germany	1.2	China	1.7	FR Germany	4.1	China	2.6
Italy	1.1	FR Germany	1.1	China	3.5	FR Germany	2.3
Netherlands	0.7	Israel	1.0	Spain	1.6	Israel	0.9
Canada	0.5	Netherlands	0.9	Israel	1.2	Brazil	0.7
Sweden	0.3	Brazil	0.8	Brazil	1.1	Spain	0.7
Top 10	97.9		96.8		94.9		95.7
Total value:	**70 290**		**101 749**		**113 779**		**285 818**
(US $ m.)							

Source: SIPRI data base.

average during the second half of the 1970s, however, and its share declined slightly at that time. It rose again in the early 1980s, when overall growth rates declined in most other regions.

Major-weapon imports to *Africa* rose drastically in the late 1970s. Most of this increase is explained by high growth rates in North African countries such as Libya, Algeria and Morocco. Imports to some Sub-Saharan countries, such as Ethiopia and Nigeria, also increased. The shares of Africa as a whole dropped in the early 1980s, and imports of major weapons to South Africa declined throughout the period.

The high levels of major-weapon imports to the *Far East* in the early 1970s are explained by the Indo-China wars. Towards the end of the decade, a new increase accompanied the wars between Viet Nam and Kampuchea and between China and Viet Nam. The increase also partly resulted from reduced US involvement in the region, which generated higher import levels.

The pattern of imports to *South America* was rather stable throughout the period, while major-weapon imports by *Central American* countries increased in the early 1980s. *South Asian* imports—by India and Pakistan—rose faster than the Third World average from the late 1970s.

Given the huge arms flow to the Middle East, it is not surprising that countries in that region top the list of individual major-weapon importers (see table 1.3). The rank order of Middle Eastern countries has, however, varied considerably. Neither Iran—leading importer in 1971–75—nor Libya—topping the list in 1976–80—were among the top five importers in 1981–85.

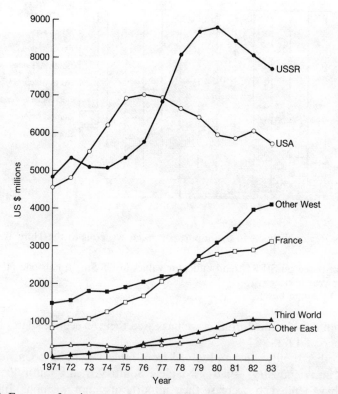

Figure 1.4. Exports of major weapons to the Third World by supplier, 1971–85

Figures are based on SIPRI trend indicator values in US $m. at constant (1985) prices, five-year moving averages.
Source: SIPRI data base.

Table 1.2. Average annual number of recipients per supplier of major weapons to the Third World, 1971–85

Supplier	Average annual number of Third World recipients		
	1971–75	1976–80	1981–85
USSR	16	24	24
USA	40	37	38
France	24	34	35
UK	22	21	19
Italy	10	13	17
China	6	7	9
FR Germany	5	12	11
Israel	3	6	7
Brazil	1	4	9
Spain	0	2	9

Source: SIPRI data base.

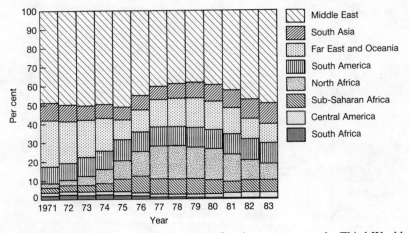

Figure 1.5. Regional shares in the imports of major weapons to the Third World, 1971–85

Figures are based on SIPRI trend indicator values in US $m. at constant (1985) prices, five-year averages.
Source: SIPRI data base.

Iraq, Saudi Arabia and Jordan have increased their respective shares through-out the period 1971–85.

Three other trends can be observed from table 1.3. First, countries with a growing arms industry—such as Israel, South Africa, South Korea and Brazil—have tended to decrease their imports of major weapons. India does not fit into this trend, largely because of the high share of licensed production in the Indian arms industry (production under licence is included in SIPRI's arms import statistics; see appendix 9).

Second, there is a high correlation between major-weapon imports and wars (see also chapter 2). High levels are recorded for Egypt, Syria and Israel in 1971–75 in connection with the 1973 war; Ethiopia ranks high in 1976–80 as a result of the war in the Horn of Africa; Argentinian and Syrian shares increased markedly in 1981–85, following the Falklands/Malvinas War and the 1982 war in the Lebanon.

Third, while the 25 leading Third World arms importers accounted for 89 per cent of total Third World imports in 1971–75, this share fell in the following period, illustrating the growing number of recipients in the 1970s. A narrowing of demand in the early 1980s has made this share grow slightly. The same trend can be observed when looking at the two, five or ten leading importers.

IV. Weapon categories

Throughout 1971–85 the most important weapon category in terms of values transferred to the Third World was *aircraft*, accounting for more than 50 per cent of the trade in major weapons (see figure 1.1). The relative share was slowly

Table 1.3. Leading Third World importers of major weapons, 1971–85

Shares are expressed as a percentage of total imports to the Third World. Figures are based on SIPRI trend indicator values in US $m. at constant (1985) prices.

Share of leading recipients for each period

1971–75		1976–80		1981–85		1971–85	
Iran	13.9	Libya	11.5	Iraq	13.3	Iraq	8.0
Egypt	10.5	Iran	10.3	Egypt	8.9	Iran	7.7
Top 2	24.4	*Top 2*	21.8	*Top 2*	22.2	*Top 2*	15.7
Syria	9.3	Iraq	5.5	Syria	8.8	Syria	7.2
Israel	9.1	India	5.0	India	7.6	Egypt	7.2
South Vietnam	6.7	Israel	4.9	Saudi Arabia	6.3	Libya	7.1
Top 5	49.5	*Top 5*	37.2	*Top 5*	44.9	*Top 5*	37.2
India	5.3	Viet Nam	4.4	Libya	5.0	India	6.1
Libya	4.0	Saudi Arabia	4.2	Argentina	3.6	Israel	5.3
North Vietnam	3.5	Syria	4.0	Israel	3.1	Saudi Arabia	4.3
Iraq	2.9	Algeria	3.3	Taiwan	2.3	Viet Nam	3.1
Brazil	2.8	South Korea	3.0	Pakistan	2.3	Argentina	2.5
Top 10	68.0	*Top 10*	56.1	*Top 10*	61.2	*Top 10*	58.5
South Africa	2.3	Egypt	2.9	Jordan	2.1	Algeria	2.0
Argentina	2.3	Peru	2.9	Venezuela	2.0	Pakistan	2.0
Pakistan	1.8	Morocco	2.6	Nigeria	1.9	Taiwan	2.0
Taiwan	1.8	Brazil	2.5	Cuba	1.9	South Korea	1.9
South Korea	1.7	Ethiopia	2.4	Algeria	1.8	Peru	1.9
North Korea	1.6	Jordan	1.9	Peru	1.7	Jordan	1.7
Saudi Arabia	1.5	Pakistan	1.8	Iran	1.6	Brazil	1.6
Venezuela	1.4	Taiwan	1.7	Viet Nam	1.6	South Vietnam	1.6
Singapore	1.3	Indonesia	1.6	Angola	1.4	Morocco	1.6
Chile	1.3	Kuwait	1.6	Morocco	1.3	Venezuela	1.5
Cuba	1.0	Argentina	1.6	Indonesia	1.2	Cuba	1.4
Peru	0.9	Thailand	1.2	UAE	1.2	Kuwait	1.3
Jordan	0.8	South Africa	1.1	Kuwait	1.2	Indonesia	1.2
Malaysia	0.8	Angola	1.0	South Korea	1.2	Ethiopia	1.2
Thailand	0.8	Cuba	1.0	Colombia	1.1	Nigeria	1.1
Top 25	89.3	*Top 25*	83.9	*Top 25*	84.4	*Top 25*	82.0
Total value: (US $m.)	**70 290**		**101 749**		**113 779**		**285 818**

Source: SIPRI data base.

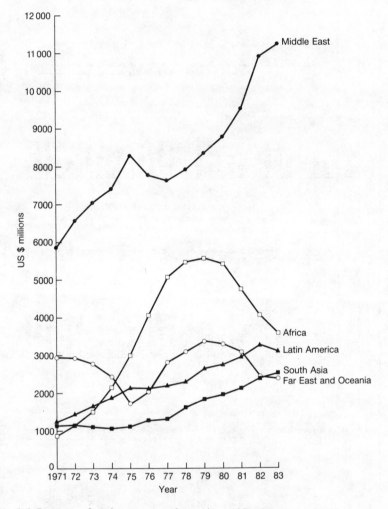

Figure 1.6. Imports of major weapons by region, 1971–85

Figures are based on SIPRI trend indicator values in US $m. at constant (1985) prices, five-year moving averages.
Source: SIPRI data base.

declining, however. Aircraft was still the most important weapon category in the early 1980s, but accounted for much less than 50 per cent of the total trade in major weapons. The reverse was true of *armour and artillery* and *ships* (see figure 1.7). These categories comprised much higher shares of weapon transfers in the early 1980s than in the early 1970s. Transfers of *missiles* and *guidance and radar systems* were roughly stable during the period studied, and their shares substantially smaller than those of the other weapon categories (for definitions of the weapon categories, see appendix 9).

The relative importance of the various weapon categories in the Third World

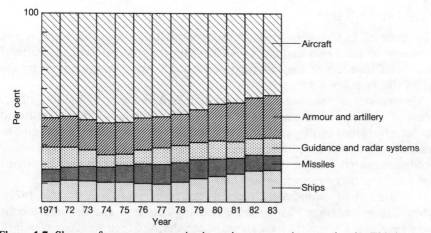

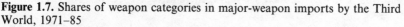

Figure 1.7. Shares of weapon categories in major-weapon imports by the Third World, 1971–85

Figures are based on SIPRI trend indicator values in US $m. at constant (1985) prices, five-year averages.
Source: SIPRI data base.

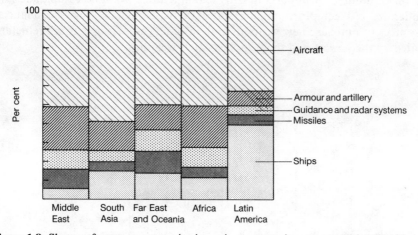

Figure 1.8. Shares of weapon categories in major-weapon imports to Third World regions, 1971–85

Figures are based on SIPRI trend indicator values in US $m., at constant (1985) prices.
Source: SIPRI data base.

regions is shown in figure 1.8. Aircraft was the main category of weapon imports to all regions; the importance of the other categories varies from region to region. Armour and artillery were the second most important category in the Middle East and Africa, while ships ranked second in Latin America and in the Far East. Missiles accounted for a comparatively large share of arms imports by the Middle East and the Far East.

V. Weapon status

The share of factory-new weapons in the arms trade with the Third World increased in the 1970s and early 1980s. More than 90 per cent of the total volume of transfers of major weapons was made up of new weapons by the mid-1980s (see figure 1.9).

The transfer of refurbished weapons increased in the mid- and late 1970s. Most of the refurbished weapons were ships: large numbers of US, British and Soviet refurbished ships were transferred during this time. Later, the volume of trade in refurbished weapons declined. One reason is that with increasing arms-production capabilities in the Third World, refurbishment can now be carried out locally in many recipient countries.

The transfer of second-hand weapons decreased sharply in the mid-1970s, when foreign exchange was available in many countries and the credit terms were generous. During the next 10 years, the share of used weapons remained more or less constant.

The highest share of factory-new major weapons was imported by the Middle East (see figure 1.10). The highest shares of refurbished and second-hand weapons are recorded for the Far East and Latin America. In both these regions a number of important arms manufacturers are able to upgrade and modernize old equipment. Some states in these regions lack the financial resources to purchase new weapons and, in some cases, suppliers are reluctant to deliver the newest and most sophisticated weapons.

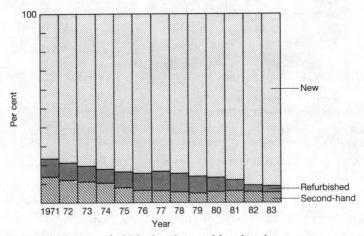

Figure 1.9. Shares of new, refurbished and second-hand major weapons exported to the Third World, 1971–85

Figures are based on SIPRI trend indicator values in US $m. at constant (1985) prices, five-year averages.
Source: SIPRI data base.

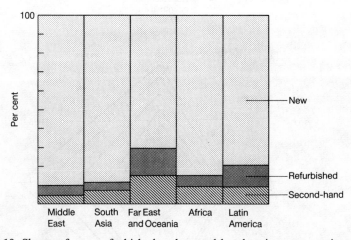

Figure 1.10. Shares of new, refurbished and second-hand major weapons imported by Third World regions, 1971–85

Figures are based on SIPRI trend indicator values in US $m. at constant (1985) prices. *Source*: SIPRI data base.

VI. Proliferation and diversification

Throughout the period studied, the arms trade—rather than, for example, the trade in military technology—remained the most important way of providing military capability to the Third World. Figure 1.11 shows that, of the various types of weaponry, diffusion was most pronounced for missiles. While less than 30 Third World countries had some type of missile in their inventories in 1970, the number had risen to 76 countries by 1985. Heavy armoured vehicles and major warships were also delivered to more countries than in any previous period. The number of countries deploying fighter aircraft increased less rapidly: a high number of countries already possessed such aircraft by 1971.

Arms transfers have a major bearing on the economic and technological relations between industrialized and Third World countries. They are also politically important. Tables 1.4 and 1.5 attempt to illustrate the importance of the political factor and its evolution during the period. The number of recipients for which one supplier was the predominant source of major weapons declined in the 1970s (see table 1.4). The decline in monopoly or near-monopoly supply was most pronounced for the USA; it also applied to the UK. The Soviet Union—with a smaller number of relatively more dependent recipients—maintained, or even increased, the level of monopoly supply, as did France (see also appendix 7).

Another illustration of the growing political fragmentation of the arms market is the number of recipients that import from both major power blocs. There was a small but visible increase in the number of countries receiving major weapons from both the USA and the USSR in the late 1970s. This trend was even stronger in cases where weapons were supplied by both the USSR and

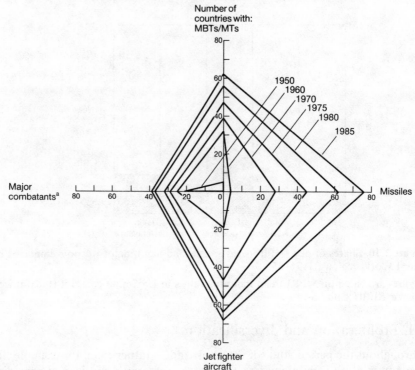

Figure 1.11. Numbers of countries in the Third World with selected weapon systems

Figures are based on SIPRI trend indicator values in US $m., at constant (1985) prices.
Source: SIPRI data base.
[a]Major combatants include submarines and surface-fighting ships of more than 800 t displacement.

Table 1.4. Number of Third World recipients with a high dependence on one supplier, by major suppliers 1971–85

Number of Third World recipients per supplier					Total Third World recipients
Level of dependence	USA	USSR	France	UK	
Dependence >90%					
1971–75	13	12	3	4	99
1976–80	6	11	2	6	107
1981–85	6	14	4	2	108
Dependence >66%					
1971–75	25	14	9	5	99
1976–80	16	19	7	7	107
1981–85	14	19	6	3	108
Dependence >50%					
1971–75	31	19	12	8	99
1976–80	21	20	12	8	107
1981–85	22	23	16	5	108

Source: SIPRI data base.

Table 1.5. Number of Third World countries importing major weapons from more than one supplier grouping, 1971–85

Joint supplier grouping	Number of recipients supplied														
	1971	1972	1973	1974	1975	1976	1977	1978	1979	1980	1981	1982	1983	1984	1985
USSR+USA	3	3	1	1	4	6	5	7	4	6	6	3	4	3	3
USA+NATO-Europe	24	20	21	23	26	25	27	30	21	29	32	29	31	26	18
USSR+NATO-Europe	5	4	4	3	5	11	10	13	14	12	11	7	9	7	9
USSR+Third World	0	0	2	2	1	3	3	3	9	5	5	3	3	4	2
USA+Third World	4	5	3	3	5	9	4	7	6	8	12	9	15	8	9
NATO-Europe+Third World	3	0	4	4	4	9	7	12	12	13	15	16	18	12	9

Note:
NATO-Europe: West European NATO-member countries
Third World: Third World countries
Source: SIPRI data base.

West European NATO countries. The new 'cold war' of the early 1980s—along with the poor economies of many recipient countries—again led to a reduction in the number of countries importing from opposing political blocs (see table 1.5).

VII. Summary

The arms trade with the Third World expanded rapidly in the early and mid-1970s. This expansion is largely explained by increased income in a number of recipient countries and by the many crises and conflicts in the Third World. The period saw many structural changes in the arms market: while the USA and the USSR were the dominant suppliers, their combined share declined throughout the period. Instead, the shares of West European suppliers, most notably France, and new exporters from the Third World rose. In addition shares of second-hand and refurbished weapons in Third World arms imports decreased in favour of more new and highly sophisticated weapon systems. Growth rates levelled off in the early 1980s in connection with the deterioration of the world economy and the debt crisis in the Third World. The import of major weapons, rather than production under licence or indigenous production, was the main factor explaining the unprecedented depth and width of Third World arms procurement during the period.

Chapter 2. Demand patterns

Some aggregate data on the large increase in Third World imports of major weapons during 1971–85 are discussed in chapter 1. This chapter provides an empirical description of the main trends within the various regions, based on statistical material collected by SIPRI and presented in the appendices. It could therefore most usefully be read in conjunction with these appendices, in particular, appendices 1, 2 and 7.

Attempts are made to identify some links between the main trends described and the overall framework of political, military and economic processes and events which help to explain them. Graphs are included which present details of arms deliveries prior to, during and after some of the wars that occurred during the period studied.

I. The Middle East

The Middle East is the most important arms-importing region in the Third World in both quantitative and qualitative terms. About 46 per cent of all major-weapon transfers to countries in the Third World went to the Middle East between 1971 and 1985 (see table 2.1). Countries in the region have sought the most modern weapon systems available and, more often than not, they have acquired them. The Iranian Air Force asked for the F-14 Tomcat fighter—the most modern fighter aircraft on the drawing board at the time—and received it even before the USA had deployed it in large numbers. The Saudi Arabian Government ordered AWACS early-warning aircraft in 1981 and gained US approval after a heated internal debate in the USA on whether it was prudent to allow this highly advanced aircraft to be exported to Saudi Arabia.

The Middle East was also the major driving force behind both the expansion of the arms market in the 1970s and early 1980s and the changes in the structure of the arms market that occurred during this period. There were three main ingredients. First, oil incomes had been high since 1973–74. Second, there had been numerous intense conflicts in the region. In some cases these led to war: notably the October War in 1973 between Israel and Egypt/Syria; clashes between Egypt and Libya in 1977; repeated wars in Lebanon involving Israel and Syria and, finally, the Iraq–Iran War. Third, there had been strong interest and increased involvement by the USA and the USSR in the region. Conflicts and the strategic position of the region, coupled with the low capacity of many oil-exporters to absorb capital relative to the amount of capital available for investments, had had a strong impact on the propensity to acquire modern weapons.

The USA has achieved friendly relations with both Israel and moderate Arab states such as Saudi Arabia, Jordan and Egypt (since the mid-1970s). The

Table 2.1. Imports of major weapons to Middle Eastern countries, 1971–85

Shares are based on SIPRI trend indicator values in US $m. at constant (1985) prices.

Country	Percentage of total exports of major weapons to the Third World, 1971–85	Index points, 5-year averages		
		1973	1978	1983
Iraq	8.0	100	272	743
Iran	7.7	100	107	19
Syria	7.2	100	62	154
Egypt	7.2	100	40	138
Israel	5.3	100	78	60
Saudi Arabia	4.3	100	394	668
Jordan	1.7	100	339	421
Kuwait	1.2	100	482	385
United Arab Emirates	0.9	100	169	299
Yemen, South	0.6	100	363	119
Oman	0.6	100	178	293
Yemen, North	0.5	100	12 363	3 295
Qatar	0.4	100	561	3 158
Lebanon	0.3	100	152	500
Bahrain	0.1	100	996	6 073
Middle East	45.9	100	112	160

Total value: 131 238

Source: SIPRI data base.

USSR lost its most important ally—Egypt—in 1973 and has had intermittent problems with another ally—Iraq. The most stable relationship has been that with Syria. Apart from sales, both superpowers have given large amounts of military aid to their clients in the Middle East. Nevertheless, recipients in the region are increasingly trying to diversify their arms sources in order to avoid dependence on a single superpower. During 1971–75, the combined US-Soviet share in arms supplies to the Middle East was 86 per cent. This share was down to 66 per cent by 1981–85.

Iraq was the leading importer of major weapons in the Middle East during 1971–85. In the first half of the 1970s the USSR was, more or less, the sole supplier of weapons to Iraq. From the mid-1970s relations between the USSR and Iraq deteriorated. One reason was that the USSR chose Syria as its main ally after Egypt had turned away from the Soviet Union. The Baath party leaderships in Syria and Iraq are bitterly opposed to each other. Another reason was alleged Soviet support for the illegal Iraqi communist party. The Iraqi armed forces began to look for other sources of supply and ordered aircraft and missiles from France and naval equipment from Italy.

Iraq was engaged in an arms race with Iran throughout the 1970s (see figure 2.1). Border tensions along the Shatt-al-Arab—among other things—led Iraq to attack Iran in 1980, in the hope of a quick victory against an enemy weakened by internal turmoil and arms resupply and maintenance problems.

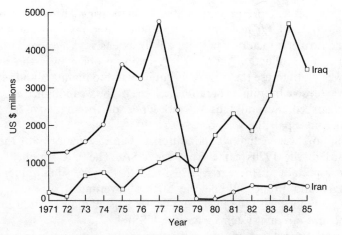

Figure 2.1. Imports of major weapons 1971–85: Iran and Iraq

Values are based on SIPRI trend indicator values in US $m., at constant (1985) prices.
Source: SIPRI data base.

The Iraqi armed forces fielded large numbers of sophisticated weapons from many sources against Iran. In the early stages of the war, Iraq was in a difficult position with respect to spare parts for its Soviet-made weapons. New sources were found in Eastern Europe, in China and, above all, in Egypt (Egypt had large stocks of Soviet weapons and Egypt also produces many Soviet-designed weapons). The import of weapons from Western and Third World countries was also increased. Main beneficiaries were the arms industries in France, Brazil and Italy. All in all, Iraq received some form of military support—weapons or otherwise—from more than 30 countries in the period 1981–85. The Soviet Union resumed large-scale deliveries to Iraq in 1983, while imports from Western countries—especially France—did not decline.

As long as the USSR was Iraq's main supplier in the 1970s, arms imports did not constitute a high direct cost to the Iraqi economy. The USSR gave high price rebates. Costs increased as the war dragged on and with the diversification of arms suppliers. The Soviet share of Iraqi major-weapon imports fell from 97 per cent in 1971–75 to 85 per cent in 1976–80 and, further, to 55 per cent during 1981–85.

Iraq's oil income, which financed the arms buildup in the 1970s, was not sufficient to cover the US $6–8 billion annual weapon bill in the 1980s. Arms imports have contributed to a deterioration of the Iraqi economy, despite substantial financial support from moderate Arab states.

The second-ranking importer of major weapons in the Middle East—and in the Third World—was *Iran*. The enormous buildup of the armed forces during the 1970s was greatly spurred by high oil incomes. Other factors contributing to the expansion of Iranian arms imports were the Shah's regional ambitions and US preparedness to give Iran the role of 'guardian of the Gulf'.

The procurement programme of the Iranian armed forces comprised new fighter aircraft, a large helicopter fleet, a blue-water navy, air defence systems, tanks and artillery. In addition, there was an extensive programme to build up a modern arms production industry.[1] A major problem was the shortage of manpower, both to use the weapons acquired and to maintain and repair them. Despite extensive training programmes, some of the weapons acquired were not easily absorbed. Several tens of thousands of foreign advisers helped to maintain and repair the weapons.

US support was virtually unconditional. The vast majority of the weapons purchased in the 1970s came from the USA. The UK supplied tanks and missiles, especially in the early 1970s, and there were some minor deliveries from Italy and France. While the Shah's government was staunchly pro-Western, relations with the East were good. This manifested itself in the order for some anti-aircraft systems from the USSR.

The arms-import programme did not directly damage the economy. However, there were extensive indirect effects. One was the diversion of qualified manpower from the civilian to the military sector. Another stemmed from the pull effect of the modern military sector, which generated a modern industrial and servicing sector in stark contrast to the traditional economy. The economic dualism and the close links between the Iranian military sector and the USA contributed to the popular opposition that eventually overthrew the Shah's rule.

One of the first actions of the post-Shah government was to cancel most of the ongoing arms-import programmes. When the US embassy was attacked in 1979, the USA and its allies stopped all deliveries of weapons and weapon-related items. Readiness levels were reduced.

The perception of low Iranian military preparedness was a major factor behind the Iraqi decision to attack. The Iranian armed forces, however, proved to be capable of stopping the Iraqi forces after some initial territorial losses. Tactics emphasizing manpower rather than sophisticated weapons (Iran has three times the population of Iraq) were employed. The modern arms purchased from the USA were not put to much use—instead, Iranian forces mostly relied on artillery and infantry weapons.

Since the Western countries by and large maintained their arms embargoes against Iran in the early 1980s, Iranian arms buyers had to look for other sources for most of the major weapons they wanted. Iranian arms procurement was often circuitous and reporting was sometimes speculative and unverifiable. However, the following patterns can be discerned: first, there were deliveries of mainly Soviet-made or Soviet-designed major weapons and spares from Libya, Syria, North Korea and China; second, there were deliveries of subsystems and spares for Iran's US-made inventory from Israel, the USA and Western Europe, mostly in a clandestine way via private arms dealers; and third, there were deliveries of civilian-labelled items which may be put to military use from countries such as FR Germany, Switzerland and the UK.

The level of *Syrian* arms imports has changed in conjunction with wars and with Soviet willingness to re-supply the Syrian armed forces. A steep rise is noted in connection with the 1973 war with Israel (see figure 2.2). Arms imports declined in the mid-1970s when war losses had been amply replaced with more modern weapons from the USSR. Imports increased again shortly thereafter and peaked in 1982 with the quick replacement of Syrian losses in the war in Lebanon. By the mid-1980s the Syrian armed forces were receiving the most modern Soviet equipment, such as T-72 tanks, SS-21 SSMs and SA-11/13 SAMs. MiG-29 fighters were on order.

As noted above, Syria became the Soviet Union's most important ally in the region. The Syrian economy would have been heavily burdened had not the USSR supplied weapons with high grant elements. Despite—or maybe because of—the high dependence on the USSR, Syria looked for other suppliers in the second half of the 1970s. Several types of missile and helicopter were delivered from France. This link weakened when France became an important supplier to Iraq.

Egypt was the first non-communist Third World customer for Soviet weapons after World War II. The Egyptian armed forces continued to receive large amounts of weapons throughout the 1960s and into the 1970s, making Egypt the most important Third World recipient of Soviet weapons. In the early 1970s political frictions with the USSR increased, leading to the expulsion of all Soviet military personnel from Egypt in 1972. The Soviet Union scaled down its weapon deliveries: few of the Egyptian losses in the 1973 war were replaced.

In the middle of the 1970s Egyptian hopes for refuelling the weapon arsenal rested with the moderate Arab states. Egypt's financial position did not allow large arms imports. The plan to create an Arab arms industry—the AOI—in Egypt with Saudi money, Western technology and Egyptian manpower was launched. Arms-import patterns changed again with the Camp David peace agreement and the Egypt-Israel Accord in 1979. The AOI faltered when Saudi Arabia and the other members withdrew funding in 1979. Subsequently, the USA committed itself to high levels of military and economic aid, and to

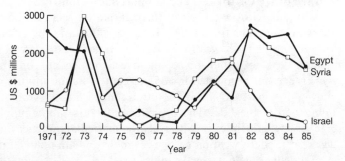

Figure 2.2. Imports of major weapons 1971–85: Egypt, Israel and Syria

Values are based on SIPRI trend indicator values in US $m., at constant (1985) prices.

Source: SIPRI data base.

massive deliveries of weapons. During 1981–85 the USA supplied about two-thirds of all Egyptian arms imports. France, China and Italy also supplied substantial amounts of weapons.

Israeli imports of major weapons have decreased since the mid-1970s, largely as a result of Israel's rapidly growing domestic arms production capabilities. The inflow of weapons in the early 1980s consisted mainly of highly advanced fighter aircraft and some types of warship. The Israeli arms industry received an important impetus in 1967 when France—up to the mid-1960s Israel's main arms supplier—declared an arms embargo on Israel.

As of the early 1970s, the Israeli arms industry grew rapidly, with technical know-how coming mainly from the USA. The United States also became Israel's predominant arms supplier and the financial backer of Israel's military effort. The 1973 war and its aftermath claimed a heavy toll on the Israeli economy. Domestic arms production has not lessened the problem. The USA has, through many channels, given large amounts of military aid to help finance the high Israeli military burden.

The relation between Israel and the USA was not without friction. Israeli armed forces have on several occasions used weapons supplied by the USA for purposes forbidden by the USA, for example, cluster bombs in the attack on Lebanon in 1982. Israel was highly dependent on the USA for the supply of weapons and know-how, but the USA had considerable difficulty in influencing Israeli decisions on military action.

Saudi Arabia was the main beneficiary of the oil price increases in the 1970s and much of that income has been used to build up modern military forces. Until the early 1970s, Saudi Arabia had no sizeable armed forces. Saudi military purchases in the 1970s and early 1980s reflect the lack of basic facilities. The emphasis was on the construction of barracks, military bases and training. Major purchases of highly advanced weapons, such as the F-15 fighter, the AWACS aircraft and the Shahine air defence system were made at large intervals in order systematically to build up modern and coherent armed forces. In the early 1980s the creation of a more heavily equipped navy was also initiated with the order for frigates and support ships from France.

Relations with the USA were close throughout the period. US advisers helped to draw up the plans for the Saudi arms buildup and the USA was the most important supplier of weapons. At the same time, however, Saudi decision-makers tried to avoid becoming overly dependent on the USA. Accordingly, France has accounted for 25 per cent of Saudi imports of major weapons during the past 10 years. More recently, Saudi Arabia ordered Tornado fighters from the UK. The diversification of weapon suppliers is a Saudi foreign policy principle, but it is also a matter of practical necessity: Saudi requests for modern weapon systems regularly create political problems in the USA and delivery is not always guaranteed.

Jordan is another country for which the USA was long the major arms supplier. Recently, however, the internal US policy debate has created even more problems for Jordan than for Saudi Arabia. Being closer to Israel and less well endowed with exportable raw materials, Jordan has had to rely on outside financial help for its weapon supply. US military aid decreased when Jordan did not sign a peace agreement with Israel similar to the Camp David agreement. Saudi Arabia then became Jordan's main financial backer. In the early 1980s, France and the UK were important suppliers. The fact that weapons were supplied and financed from sources close to the USA without US objections indicates that the USA was not trying to withhold weapons from the Jordanian armed forces but was merely concerned with domestic political opposition. Another factor in the intricate diplomatic game of arms supplies to Jordan is the Soviet Union. The USSR offered various weapon systems at low prices and, in a move evidently aimed at making the USA more malleable, the Jordanian Government ordered Soviet air defence weapons in 1984.

Kuwait has much more room to manoeuvre in its weapon acquisition policies. The foreign policy is decisively independent of East and West, and the country is rich in oil. The small armed forces received modern weapon systems from a large number of suppliers—including the USA, the USSR, France, the UK and Italy. In 1984 the USA refused to sell Stinger SAMs for fear that they might reach PLO guerrillas. The Kuwaiti Government responded by ordering similar weapons from the Soviet Union.

Other small and oil-rich countries in the region, such as the *United Arab Emirates* (UAE), *Oman*, *Qatar* and *Bahrain*, have policies similar to those of Kuwait, even if none of them have acquired weapons from the USSR. The Iraq-Iran War prompted these countries—together with Kuwait and Saudi Arabia—to better co-ordinate their arms-procurement policies under the umbrella of the Gulf Cooperation Council (GCC).

The two *Yemens* have at times been engaged in arms races with each other (see figure 2.3). There have been small border incidents, but in the early 1980s there was also talk of unifying the two countries. South Yemen is almost exclusively supplied by the Soviet Union, with which it has had a treaty of co-operation and friendship since 1980. North Yemen has also received many weapons from the USSR, but in 1979 the US Government judged a border incident serious enough to warrant immediate US support. President Carter invoked his presidential emergency authority to grant the supply of weapons to North Yemen. A few months later, the North Yemenite Government concluded a huge arms deal with the Soviet Union.

II. Africa

African arms imports increased dramatically in the second half of the 1970s (see table 2.2). This is true of both North Africa and Sub-Saharan Africa. Many African countries—independent for less than 20 years—had small armed forces with outdated weapons. Modernization programmes were initiated. A simultaneous growing awareness of Africa's strategic importance made the major powers more interested in the region. In addition, there were numerous conflicts, most notably in Southern Africa, the Horn of Africa and Western

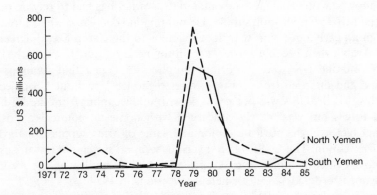

Figure 2.3. Imports of major weapons 1971–85: North and South Yemen

Values are based on SIPRI trend indicator values in US $m., at constant (1985) prices.
Source: SIPRI data base.

Table 2.2.   Imports of major weapons to selected African countries, 1971–85

Shares are based on SIPRI trend indicator values in US $m. at constant (1985) prices and do not add up to totals.

Country	Percentage of total exports of major weapons to the Third World, 1971–85	Index points, 5-year averages		
		1973	1978	1983
Libya	7.1	100	418	204
Algeria	2.0	100	1 258	781
Morocco	1.5	100	1 558	881
Ethiopia	1.1	100	1 063	212
Nigeria	1.1	100	257	810
South Africa	1.0	100	68	16
Angola	0.9	100	1 865	3 065
Mozambique	0.5	100	8 259	5 476
Somalia	0.5	100	52	101
Tunisia	0.3	100	548	1 853
Kenya	0.3	100	690	295
Tanzania	0.2	100	78	63
Sudan	0.2	100	562	934
Zaire	0.2	100	49	16
Gabon	0.2	100	323	283
Uganda	0.2	100	93	6
Cameroon	0.1	100	205	668
Zimbabwe (Until 1979: Rhodesia)	0.1	100	258	612
Africa (excl. Egypt)	18.4	100	363	238

Total value: 52 656

Source: SIPRI data base.

Sahara.[2] In the early 1980s arms imports decreased, mainly for economic reasons. The arms imports of the 1970s contributed to the difficult economic situation in many African countries.

Good relations were still maintained between some of the former colonial powers and their ex-colonies, especially where the transition to independence was relatively smooth. This was the case in most of the former French colonies and also, for example, in Kenya. A large proportion of the imports of the smaller African states was in the form of military aid. The Soviet Union gave such aid willingly—especially in the 1970s—and often in larger quantities than provided by the former colonial powers. The importance of China as an arms supplier to Sub-Saharan Africa declined following Chinese foreign policy changes in the early 1970s.

Libya's huge military buildup in the 1970s was made possible by high oil incomes and by the Soviet Union's choice of Libya as its main ally in North Africa. This made it possible for Libyan decision-makers to play an important role in the Middle East and in Africa. In both regions Libya became involved in wars: the 1973 war with Israel on the side of Egypt; the border skirmishes with Egypt in 1977; the Ugandan/Tanzanian war in 1978/79 and the civil war in Chad. Libya also became an important supplier of weapons to African governments, to Iran in the early 1980s and to some guerrilla movements.

The majority of weapons in the Libyan arsenals are of Soviet origin. Some West European countries were also important suppliers until early 1986, when an embargo was declared following alleged Libyan support for Arab terrorists operating in Western Europe. France, followed by Italy, was the major supplier in Europe—French deliveries were reduced after Libyan involvement in the civil war in Chad in the early 1980s. Libya was also a major customer for the Brazilian armoured-vehicle producer Engesa.

Libya imported such large amounts of weapons in the 1970s that it is inconceivable that the comparatively small Libyan armed forces could absorb them *in toto*. Some of the weapons may have been stored for future use by Libyan or other armed forces. The large stock of weaponry led to a drop in orders in the early 1980s. Another reason for the relative decrease of Libyan arms imports at this time was economic problems. There was also a more strained relationship with the USSR due to disagreements over the Lebanon War, the Iraq–Iran War and Libya's policy towards some other African countries.

Tunisia imported only small amounts of weapons until the early 1980s, but the growth rates were high. The main suppliers were the USA, France and Italy. In the early 1980s the armed forces were modernized with more advanced weapon systems. *Algeria* was not a major arms importer until 1978, when an arms race with Morocco developed (see below). The main supplier was the Soviet Union. In the early 1980s the Algerian armed forces continued their modernization with weapons supplied both by the USSR and by Western countries, mainly France. In 1985 the United States decided to supply Algeria with weapon systems. The long-term pre-eminence of the USSR as supplier of weapons to Algeria has given way to a much wider spectrum of weapon suppliers.

Morocco was one of the few states which by the 1960s already had weapon suppliers both in the West and in the East, but Soviet supplies ceased in the 1970s. The Moroccan Government opted for closer co-operation with the West, manifested, for instance, in Moroccan participation in the Shaba interventions in 1977–78. Arms imports to Morocco grew rapidly in the late 1970s in pace with Moroccan involvement in the Western Sahara conflict. Moroccan armed forces were modernized and expanded in order to hold the Western Saharan territory against the Polisario guerrillas fighting for an independent state. Algerian support for Polisario led to an arms race in North Africa (see figure 2.4). Morocco's main suppliers were the USA and France—some of the deliveries were in the form of military aid, but much had to be paid for. Financial assistance was given by Saudi Arabia, but the costs of the war were increasingly felt in the early 1980s. Arms imports dropped, while the high debt burden continued to drain the economy.

Another region smitten by conflict and high arms-import levels is the Horn of Africa. *Somalia* received large amounts of weapons from the Soviet Union in the early 1970s (see figure 2.5). In 1977, Somalian territorial claims resulted in a war with Ethiopia. The Soviet Union changed sides, stopped weapon deliveries to Somalia and started to supply Ethiopia. This shift was facilitated by the Ethiopian *coup d'etat* in 1974, which brought a Marxist-inspired military government to power. The USA—which had had Ethiopia as its favoured ally and main African base until then—started to support Somalia instead. The USSR continued to deliver weapons to Ethiopia in the 1980s, but on a lower level. The government used fresh supplies to fight several guerrilla movements, for example in the Eritrea region.

Kenya, bordering Somalia, increased its arms imports in the late 1970s in response to the war in the Horn. Unlike Ethiopia and Somalia, Kenya had to

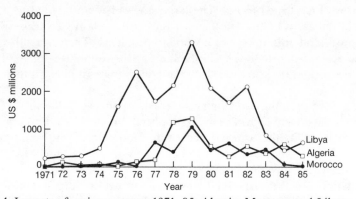

Figure 2.4. Imports of major weapons 1971–85: Algeria, Morocco and Libya

Values are based on SIPRI trend indicator values in US $m., at constant (1985) prices. *Source*: SIPRI data base.

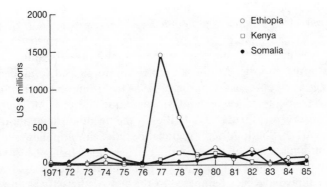

Figure 2.5. Imports of major weapons 1971–85: Ethiopia, Kenya and Somalia

Values are based on SIPRI trend indicator values in US $m., at constant (1985) prices.
Source: SIPRI data base.

pay for most of its arms imports. This contributed to the deterioration of the economy in the 1980s, which in turn led to reduced arms imports.

Among West African countries, *Nigeria* is the only one with large arms imports. Increased oil incomes enabled the armed forces to start a modernization programme in the early 1970s. From the late 1970s economic problems increased, but the modernization programme remained largely intact. A main reason for this was the delicate political balance between military and civilian interests. The military stepped down from power in 1979, only to take it back in 1983. One of the reasons given for the *coup d'etat* in 1983 was the high level of corruption and bribes in connection with arms import contracts. New sources for weapons were sought—including the USSR. Even though Nigeria's armed forces are small compared to those of Libya, Algeria, Ethiopia and South Africa, for example, they are by far the strongest in West Africa.

Another large Sub-Saharan country, *Zaire*, had to give up much of its regional power ambitions because of economic mismanagement and a drawn-out economic crisis. Arms imports were reduced—despite some military aid from various states, including North Korea—because of lack of funds and the tight control of the economy exercised by the International Monetary Fund.

Uganda's arms imports expanded in the early 1970s during the Amin regime. Military preparations put a heavy burden on the economy, which was only partly relieved by financial assistance from Libya and Saudi Arabia. In 1978 Ugandan forces intervened in Tanzania, only to be beaten back by Tanzanian and Ugandan anti-government forces. From the Ugandan defeat in 1979 and up to 1986 civil wars were fought, but with only a few major weapons. Neither side had the financial means to buy much more than small arms and ammunition.

Tanzania's arms procurement was rather small despite the war with Uganda:

indeed, the severe economic crisis of the early 1970s was deepened by the war. Tanzania depended on foreign military aid, mainly from China and the USSR.

In *Angola*, *Mozambique* and *Zimbabwe* the combat units of successful guerrilla movements were transformed into regular armed forces. Their weaponry was acquired from the former colonial masters and also through substantial arms imports. All three countries were pushed to modernize their armed forces as a consequence of their role as front-line states to South Africa, and the governments of Angola and Mozambique had to fight South African-supported insurgents. Insurgent activities in the neighbouring countries are an important part of South Africa's regional destabilization policy. Both Angola and Mozambique received the bulk of their weapons from the Soviet Union after independence in 1974 and 1975, respectively. Efforts to diversify the sources of supply have been hampered by the lack of alternatives, in view of the strained economic situation. Zimbabwe's main suppliers after independence in 1980 were China, North Korea and the UK. Most equipment has been given in the form of military aid. All three states have been heavily burdened by the costs of their military efforts. At the same time, the security situation for these countries is not conducive to any reductions of military spending.

South Africa's armed forces remain the dominant military force in Southern Africa despite substantial reductions in major weapon imports as a result of the UN embargoes of 1963 and 1977. The main reason for this is the buildup of a domestic arms industry, which provides the bulk of the weapons needed by the South African forces.

In the early 1970s a number of suppliers did not observe the voluntary embargo of 1963. Most prominent among these were France, Italy and Israel. In addition, many other governments did not include the transfer of know-how under the provisions of the embargo. South Africa was therefore able to build up its domestic arms industry step by step using foreign technology and components, while imports of advanced weapon systems, such as helicopters, fighter aircraft and fast patrol boats, continued.

The mandatory arms embargo of 1977 made arms imports much more difficult. In effect, arms could only be imported clandestinely, using private dealers willing to break national laws or using circuitous routes. However, there were still loopholes in the field of know-how, components and dual-use items and technology. These loopholes have been increasingly closed since the early 1980s by which time South Africa had improved the capacity for indigenous production of the components needed.

Nevertheless South Africa still lacks the capability to design and build new and sophisticated weapon systems. To some extent this weakness has been countered by the adoption of a military strategy based on the weapons that South Africa can produce. While in the mid-1970s South African strategists feared an attack by regular armed forces from Angola and/or Mozambique, the domestic problems of these countries had made such a scenario unlikely by the late 1970s. In the more likely event of a civil war, less sophisticated weapons are more suitable. Nevertheless the armed forces are pressing industry to design such weapons as helicopters and fighter aircraft, if only as demonstration objects to prove to the outside world the inefficiency of the embargoes. So far, these efforts have resulted in upgraded versions of weapons previously acquired abroad.

III. The Far East

After reaching high levels in the late 1960s and 1970s, arms imports by countries in the Far East stabilized in the early 1980s at about 10 per cent of total major-weapon imports by the Third World (see also table 2.3). Arms procurement in the region has been highly influenced by the level of conflict. The many conflicts represented a mix of historical and ethnic controversies, on the one hand, and political antagonism—fuelled by the USA and the USSR—on the other.

The Indo-China wars comprise one such set of conflicts: North and South Vietnam accounted for about 52 per cent of total regional arms imports during the first half of the 1970s. Viet Nam (post-1975) was the leading arms importer, even measured over the whole period 1971–85, largely due to its recurring conflicts with the People's Republic of China (PRC) and the Vietnamese involvement in Kampuchea. These conflicts spurred rearmament programmes

Table 2.3. Imports of major weapons to selected Far Eastern countries, 1971–85

Shares are based on SIPRI trend indicator values in US $m. at constant (1985) prices and do not add up to totals.

Country	Percentage of total exports of major weapons to the Third World, 1971–85	Index points, 5-year averages		
		1973	1978	1983
Viet Nam (incl. former North Vietnam)	3.1	100	180	72
Taiwan	2.0	100	141	216
South Korea	1.9	100	255	111
South Vietnam	1.6	100	..	..
Indonesia	1.2	100	513	419
North Korea	1.0	100	49	101
Thailand	1.0	100	222	205
Malaysia	0.9	100	168	189
Singapore	0.5	100	89	74
Kampuchea (until 1975: Cambodia)	0.2	100	73	8
Laos	0.1	100	328	407
Far East and Oceania	14.3	100	116	148
Total value: 40 974				

Source: SIPRI data base.

in the ASEAN (Association of South East Asian Nations) countries—these countries fear Vietnamese or Chinese regional dominance. Taiwan has throughout the period armed itself in preparation for a possible war with the People's Republic. On the Korean peninsula, another sub-regional arms race is underway.

In addition, domestic problems and guerrilla movements led to the acquisition of large numbers of counter-insurgency weapons in several countries in the region. In general, Far Eastern countries did not acquire—or were not granted—the most sophisticated weapon systems available. Because of the nature of the many conflicts, emphasis has been on weapons incorporating middle-level technology with a high military-use value. The level of sophistication was, however, significantly raised by the mid-1980s, with the introduction into the region of F-16 and MiG-23 fighter aircraft.

The USA and the USSR dominate arms supplies to the Far East which, like the Middle East, is a region highly torn by conflicts and wars. About 80 per cent of the total volume of major weapons supplied during 1971–85 came from these two countries, with the USA accounting for just over 50 per cent of the total. In common with all other regions, however, the importance of the two largest suppliers decreased in the 1980s, reflecting the commercialization of the arms market.

The USSR is the sole supplier of weapons to its close ally *Viet Nam*. Even if Viet Nam had wanted to diversify its arms supply sources, most Western countries would have refused to deliver any weapons because of Viet Nam's close relationship with the USSR and because of the continuing occupation of Kampuchea.

Taiwan—despite difficulties in finding willing suppliers—is the second-largest arms importer in the Far East. Taiwan is almost completely dependent on the USA for the supply of major weapons. Its substantial domestic arms-production capacity builds largely on licensed production of US weapons or reverse-engineering of basic US designs. However, because of improved relations with the PRC, US support for Taiwan is far from indiscriminate. In a joint US–Chinese communiqué in 1982, the USA promised progressively to reduce its arms sales to Taiwan. The Reagan Administration also agreed not to supply top-of-the-line weapons, such as F-16 or F-20 fighters, to Taiwan. In a move to reduce dependence on the USA, Taiwan has developed military co-operation with Israel, South Korea and, possibly, with South Africa.

South Korea is another example of a country with a high degree of dependence on the USA. This included direct arms imports and production under licence. Arms procurement depended largely on the perceived threat from North Korea, and the high level of arms production reflects efforts towards greater autonomy and the belief that a sophisticated military-industrial base promotes economic development.

There was a quantitive leap in the otherwise even growth of arms imports to South Korea in the second half of the 1970s (see figure 2.6). This resulted from the so-called Nixon Doctrine, which underlined the need for national military

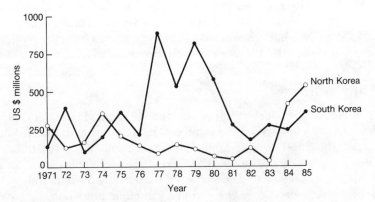

Figure 2.6. Imports of major weapons 1971–85: North and South Korea

Values are based on SIPRI trend indicator values in US $m., at constant (1985) prices.

Source: SIPRI data base.

capabilities of US allies in the Far East (see also chapter 3). Unlike in the case of Taiwan, US high technology was readily available to South Korea, as evidenced by the sale of F-16 fighters in 1981. South Korea was able to engage simultaneously in large-scale arms manufacturing, while continuing to import the most sophisticated equipment.

Having had two sources of arms supply—the USSR and China—has to some extent allowed *North Korea* to play one supplier against the other. Allegiances have shifted markedly. The USSR accounted for the mainstay of supplies in the early 1950s, then the situation reversed after the Korean War. In the 1960s, the USSR again became the predominant supplier. During the 1970s, the PRC recaptured some 25 per cent of the market, when Soviet foreign policy interests were mainly directed towards Europe and the Middle East. In the 1980s—when the Pacific region re-emerged as a key area in the global strategies of the superpowers—the Soviet hold on North Korea tightened again. Various diplomatic overtures in the mid-1980s resulted in the delivery of MiG-23 fighters, reportedly in exchange for Soviet rights to use North Korean airspace for reconnaissance missions.[3]

The British troop withdrawal from *Singapore* and *Malaysia* in the early 1970s and the US retreat from Indo-China in 1975 completely altered the strategic situation in South-East Asia. It also affected arms procurement patterns. Prior to the mid-1970s arms imports were generally on a low level in Singapore, Malaysia and the other ASEAN member states *Indonesia*, the *Philippines* and *Thailand* (*Brunei* became the sixth member in 1984). Arms were mainly purchased for counter-insurgency operations against local guerrillas. Quality-wise, the levels were also modest. After 1975, the ASEAN countries also had to consider external threats—such as Viet Nam's regional power position—and, consequently, the levels of arms imports rose dramatically. Indonesia emerged as the third largest arms importer in the Far East during 1981–85. Regional power ambitions are an additional explanation for this. Throughout the period 1971–85, ASEAN member states have been buying arms from the West, mainly from the USA, the UK, FR Germany, France and Italy.

IV. Latin America

South America continued throughout the 1970s and early 1980s to be characterized by a low level of arms imports in comparison to the Middle East, Africa and the Far East (see table 2.4). By the mid-1980s the trend was a downward one largely because of the huge external debt burden and the easing up of some intra-regional tensions after the shift to civilian rule in many countries. Nevertheless, over the period as a whole arms imports have been rather high considering the rapid buildup of domestic arms industries in many states.

Historically, South American—and Central American—defence policies have been largely dictated by the United States. US policy has concentrated on internal security and, throughout most of the period 1971–85, the USA refused to sell sophisticated weapons to the region. At the same time, at least the larger South American countries began to formulate security policies on a more independent basis. Partly as a result of the restrictive US policy, European suppliers entered the South American market in the late-1960s. The US share in the supply of major weapons dropped from 52 per cent in 1971–75 to 11 per

Table 2.4. Imports of major weapons to selected Latin American countries, 1971–85

Shares are based on SIPRI trend indicator values in US $m. at constant (1985) prices and do not add up to totals.

Country	Percentage of total exports of major weapons to the Third World, 1971–85	Index points, 5-year averages		
		1973	1978	1983
Argentina	2.5	100	100	255
Peru	1.9	100	453	292
Brazil	1.6	100	128	9
Venezuela	1.4	100	77	233
Cuba	1.3	100	141	306
Chile	1.0	100	81	124
Ecuador	0.8	100	435	447
Colombia	0.6	100	9	268
Mexico	0.3	100	73	277
Bolivia	0.1	100	165	77
El Salvador	0.1	100	31	382
Nicaragua	0.1	100	80	483
Latin America	12.3	100	138	188

Total value: 35 152

Source: SIPRI data base.

cent in 1981–85, while France, FR Germany, Italy and the UK steadily increased their shares.

In Central America, there was a marked increase in arms imports in the early 1980s, fuelled by the various intra- and international conflicts in the region. The arms flow was largely financed by outside military aid.

In *Argentina* the military government that came to power in 1976 expanded the modernization programme of the armed forces (see figure 2.7). Special emphasis was given to the Navy. The procurement programme included both imports and domestic production, mostly under licence from West German companies. From 1979 the economic situation worsened and arms imports and arms production became a burden for the balance of payments. In 1982— before the rearmament programme was completed—Argentina occupied the Falkland/Malvinas Islands. Some of the material lost in the war that followed was replaced, but the civilian government that came to power in 1983 tried to cut costs. A number of the weapons ordered—such as two of the four West German TR-1700 submarines—were offered for sale on the world market. Main suppliers to Argentina were FR Germany, France and the UK. The declining role of the USA as a supplier not only reflected the general US restrictiveness mentioned above, it also resulted from a partial arms embargo on Argentina in 1978 because of violations of human rights.

Some of *Chile's* most important arms suppliers, notably the USA and the UK (but not France) declared partial arms embargoes after the military coup in 1973. While curtailing some programmes, these declarations did not prevent the Chilean armed forces from receiving weapons from these countries. From 1978, the Chilean Government supported the establishment of a domestic arms industry. By the early 1980s the embargoes by, for example, the UK, Switzerland and FR Germany had lost much of their edge, and Chile began to modernize its armed forces despite severe economic problems. An attempt to

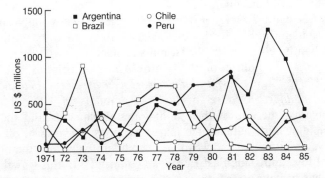

Figure 2.7. Imports of major weapons 1971–85: Argentina, Brazil, Chile and Peru Values are based on SIPRI trend indicator values in US $m., at constant (1985) prices.
Source: SIPRI data base.

buy Austrian tanks failed, however, owing to strong popular opposition after the Austrian Government had agreed to the sale. Israel and Spain also supplied both weapons and technology in the early 1980s.

Brazilian arms imports declined in the early 1980s. One reason was the economic crisis which hit Brazil after the mid-1970s. Another was that the domestic arms industry was capable of producing most of the weapons wanted by the Army and the Air Force. The Navy, which continued to demand weapons that had to be imported or produced under licence, was only allowed to order a few new ships (naval purchases largely explain the high import figures of the late 1970s).

Peru's armed forces were substantially modernized in the 1970s. The Air Force and the Army received weapons mostly from the USSR, while the Navy bought its weapons in the West, mainly from Italy. The high costs of the arms import programme contributed to the economic malaise of the country. In 1977 Peru became the first country in the Third World in which the International Monetary Fund (IMF) made a credit conditional on efforts to reduce the costs of military spending. The civilian government in power from 1979 has tried to cut costs. A licensed-production programme for Italian aircraft was cancelled and in 1986 the government reduced the order for Mirage-2000 fighters from 26 to 12. There was also a reorientation in the supply pattern, with West European companies substituting for the USSR in the delivery of several weapon categories.

Arms imports by *Colombia*, *Ecuador* and *Venezuela* increased in the early 1980s, mainly because of imports of warships from FR Germany and Italy. In addition, Venezuela bought modern fighter aircraft from the USA, and Ecuador bought similar aircraft from France. The Ecuadorean Air Force had initially intended to buy Israeli Kfir fighters, but the USA did not permit the resale of their engines.

Cuba, the most important arms importer in Central America, received almost all of its major weapons from the USSR. There was a significant increase in the early 1980s, reflecting heightened Cuban fears of US military measures against the country (see figure 2.8). Later in the 1980s, tensions between Nicaragua and the USA led to further deliveries of Soviet weapons to Cuba in the light of possible Cuban involvement in the isthmus conflict.

Arms imports by countries on the Central American isthmus rose rapidly in the early 1980s (see figure 2.8). *El Salvador*, *Honduras*, *Costa Rica* and, to some extent, *Guatemala* received relatively large amounts of US military aid—measured against the size of their military establishments and the levels of military spending—including some major weapons. *Nicaragua*, on the other hand, received military aid and weapons in comparatively large quantities from the USSR, Libya and some East European countries.[4] In this way the isthmus became rather heavily armed with major weapons during the 1980s, but the technological level of the weapons supplied was low. Neither the Soviet Union nor the United States had, by early 1986, introduced modern jet fighters or heavy tanks, despite repeated requests from their respective allies.

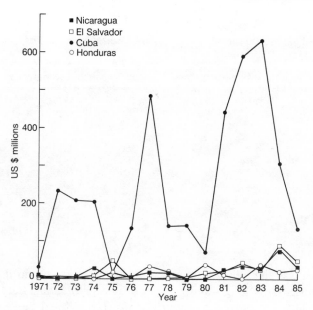

Figure 2.8. Imports of major weapons 1971–85: Cuba, El Salvador, Honduras and Nicaragua

Values are based on SIPRI trend indicator values in US $m., at constant (1985) prices. *Source*: SIPRI data base.

V. South Asia

During the period 1971–85 South Asia accounted for about 9 per cent of total Third World imports of major weapons (see table 2.5). South Asia is an exception to the low growth rates in Third World arms imports in the early 1980s. The demand for weapons in the region has been dominated by tensions first manifested during the process of decolonization in India and Pakistan. Indo–Pakistani relations are influenced by communal antagonism, cultural differences, military confrontation and superpower interests. New dimensions were added to this regional arms race after the Soviet invasion of Afghanistan and the emergence of a quasi-alliance pattern of sorts, pitting India and the Soviet Union against Pakistan, the United States and China. The action-reaction pattern of arms procurement rose to unprecedented levels in 1980 and has since risen further. Indian procurement decisions have often been influenced by political elements, flavoured by major-power grandeur, and economic factors, such as high technological aspirations. Procurement decisions in Pakistan have mostly been taken by military governments; they concentrated more on weapons of high military use. However, mutual threat perceptions and conflicting security needs have strengthened the case for those in both countries interested in acquiring sophisticated weapon systems. This was particularly obvious in the acquisition of front-line aircraft.

Table 2.5.   Imports of major weapons to selected South Asian countries, 1971–85

Shares are based on SIPRI trend indicator values in US $m. at constant (1985) prices and do not add up to totals.

Country	Percentage of total exports of major weapons to the Third World, 1971–85	Index points, 5-year averages		
		1973	1978	1983
India	6.1	100	136	231
Pakistan	2.0	100	141	199
Afghanistan	0.7	100	600	634
Bangladesh	0.2	100	81	107
South Asia	9.1	100	117	170
Total value: 26 107				

Source: SIPRI data base.

The USSR was the most important supplier to the region during 1971–85, mainly because of its long-standing relationship with India. Large-scale US deliveries to Pakistan started in the early 1980s. The UK—the leading supplier to the region in the 1950s and early 1960s—and France have throughout 1971–85 maintained the rank of second-tier suppliers, reflecting shifts in the relationship between the superpowers and the region as well as recurring attempts by India and Pakistan to diversify the sources for their arms supplies.

India accounted for two-thirds of South Asian arms imports during 1971–85; India is also—with Israel—the leading producer of major weapons in the Third World. The main reason for this arms buildup was the unstable relationship with Pakistan, which led to a war in 1971 (see figure 2.9). But there were other reasons. One was India's interest in maintaining its regional power status. Another was the growing interest of the superpowers *vis-à-vis* the Indian sub-continent, situated as it is between the two main hotspot regions during the 1970s, the Middle East and South-East Asia. During the 1980s the availability of finance was another important factor. Because of its introspective develop-ment policy, India was not hit as hard by the global recession as other Third World countries. The favourable balance of trade with the USSR was another element: the 'rouble mountain' in combination with India's efforts at diversifying its arms supplies, rendered India much leverage in negotiating favourable terms with the USSR.

India is the only country in the Third World to have been given the right to produce Soviet state-of-the-art weapons under licence. This began in the 1960s and from then on and up to the late 1970s India was heavily dependent on Soviet arms and technology for its most sophisticated weapons. Beginning in 1978–79, the last years of the Janata Government, and continuing into the 1980s, India began to order major weapons elsewhere. The main beneficiary of this was the British arms industry, with sales of Jaguar and Sea Harrier fighters, Sea King helicopters, Sea Eagle missiles and, most recently, the light aircraft

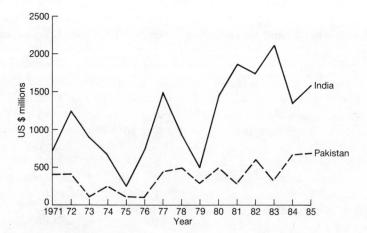

Figure 2.9. Imports of major weapons 1971–85: India and Pakistan

Values are base on SIPRI trend indicator values in US $m., at constant (1985) prices. *Source*: SIPRI data base.

carrier Hermes. France sold Mirage-2000 fighters and a wide assortment of missiles, while FR Germany received orders for light transport aircraft and submarines.

However, the USSR still accounted for two-thirds of arms sales to India. The orders for Mirages and Jaguars had no followers on the same scale; instead, the major deals of the mid-1980s were again with the USSR. They include, for example, licensed production of T-72M tanks, BMP-1/2 infantry combat vehicles and MiG-27 fighters. India was also scheduled to receive the latest Soviet fighter aircraft, the MiG-29, during 1986–87, possibly with assembly and licensed production to follow.

Pakistan received military aid from Britain and the USA from partition and until the early 1960s, when relations deteriorated as a result of the aid given by these two countries to India in its 1962 war with China. Three years later—after the 1965 Indo-Pakistani War—the USA imposed an embargo on both countries, a move which effectively favoured India because of Pakistan's earlier heavy dependence on US aid. Pakistan then turned to China and France. During the 1970s just over 40 per cent of Pakistani imports of major weapons came from China. Deliveries included all sorts of weapons, but the emphasis was on battle tanks and fighter aircraft, such as the T-59 and the F-6 (Chinese derivatives of basic Soviet designs). France, accounting for a similar share of deliveries to Pakistan in the 1970s, sold mainly Mirage fighters and associated missiles.

Successive US Administrations were reluctant to propel a regional arms race by selling the sophisticated weapons requested by the Pakistani generals. This changed in 1979: the presence of some 120 000 Soviet troops in Afghanistan was the major factor in the rapprochement between Pakistan and the USA. In

1981 the USA agreed to provide a $3.2 billion military aid package to Pakistan, including F-16 aircraft. By 1986, Pakistani military planners were considering the procurement of new US weapons following the termination of this aid programme in 1987. More F-16 fighters and missiles to arm them, as well as early-warning aircraft, are high on the shopping list.

The USSR has been more or less the sole supplier to *Afghanistan*. The volume has been rather small and a clear decrease is noted for the early 1980s. This is partly a result of the large Soviet presence after the invasion and partly a sign of Soviet fears that their weapons may end up in the hands of the Afghani resistance or, via Pakistan, in the West. In 1985, for example, Afghani pilots defected to Pakistan in two modern Soviet Mi-24 helicopter gunships.

Cost factors go a long way towards explaining the limited role of commercially-oriented West European arms suppliers in arms transfers to *Bangladesh*. The bulk of Bangladesh's major-weapon imports is for the Navy. This is also the case in *Sri Lanka*, where arms imports and military expenditures increased sharply in 1983 when internal fighting broke out between different ethnic groups. Imports by the Navy are intended to control the flow of refugees and guerrilla troops between Sri Lanka and India. Sri Lanka also imported counter-insurgency weapons, such as helicopters and light armoured vehicles.

VI. Summary

The demand for weapons in the Third World during 1971–85 was constrained mainly by the availability of funds. In the 1970s the increase in the price of oil and some other raw materials exported from the Third World generated an abundance of foreign exchange in many countries. This, in turn, made credits more readily available for those countries that did not themselves have any income from oil exports. In the late 1970s, credit financing of arms imports became widespread. The economic crisis of the late 1970s and the early 1980s was the main reason for the levelling out of Third World arms imports. High debt burdens have often been aggravated by weapon purchases.

The demand for weapons was mostly fuelled by conflicts. The period under observation has not been very peaceful. In addition to availability of funds and real and perceived conflicts, aspirations for power status and the internal standing of the military *vis-à-vis* other groups in society were important factors behind the growth in arms imports during 1971–85.

The major powers continued to play a major role as suppliers of arms and other forms of military aid, especially to crisis regions and to countries of strategic importance lacking the means to buy weapons. There was, however, a distinct trend among recipients to try to reduce single-source supply dependence through diversification. This development was facilitated by the general development of the arms market, with more and more producers pushing for exports.

The superpowers countered by making 'offers that could not be refused' when their strategic interests were overwhelming, for example in the case of the

Soviet–Indian relationship or US–Iranian links before 1979. By and large, though, the scope for strongly influencing the behaviour of recipients narrowed. This is also clearly underlined by cases of complete reversal of superpower allegiance despite previous sole-source arms supply as seen, for example, in Egypt and Ethiopia.

Notes and references

[1] See Schulz, A., 'Iran: an enclave arms industry' in Brzoska, M. and Ohlson, T. (eds), SIPRI, *Arms Production in the Third World* (Taylor & Francis: London, 1986). This book also contains case studies of the other Third World arms-producing countries mentioned in chapter 2.

[2] For an overview of the militarization process in Africa, see Luckham, R., 'Militarization in Africa', in SIPRI, *World Armaments and Disarmament, SIPRI Yearbook 1985* (Taylor & Francis: London, 1985).

[3] See Nations, R. 'Love boat to Wonsan', *Far Eastern Economic Review*, 29 Aug. 1985, pp. 22–23 and 'China's Korea fiasco', *Far Eastern Economic Review*, 26 Sep. 1985, p. 56.

[4] See Tullberg, R. and Millán, V., 'Security assistance: the case of Central America' in SIPRI, *World Armaments and Disarmament, SIPRI Yearbook 1986* (Oxford University Press: London, 1986).

Chapter 3. The suppliers

I. Introduction

This chapter describes arms exports and the changes in arms export policies that occurred in the respective supplier countries during 1971–85. A brief description of the flow of major weapons from each country is followed by an account of the major changes which took place in the institutional framework surrounding arms transfers.[1] Since arms export flows are affected both by the ability and the political will to export arms, some aspects of arms production and the main political issues concerning the countries' arms export policies are discussed.

While the subsections on the flow of arms from each country or group of countries only comment on the SIPRI data on the transfers of major conventional weapons, the other subsections refer to weapons in general or, rather, to weapons as defined in the specific national context (see also appendix 10). Readers especially interested in specific countries are referred to the literature mentioned in the footnotes and in the selective bibliography (appendix 11).

II. The Soviet Union

During 1971–85 the Soviet Union was the leading supplier of arms to the Third World.[2] From the early 1960s Soviet exports of major weapons have expanded in parallel to the expansion of the world arms market. At that time arms supplies were a major instrument of foreign policy and recipients were mainly allies, who received weapons at low cost or free of charge. In the 1970s arms exports became a major economic factor for the Soviet Union, in addition to being the most important instrument of foreign policy in many parts of the Third World. The level of arms deliveries to the Third World peaked in the late 1970s. By the mid-1980s political and economic factors—such as the structural changes in the arms market—had caused a slight decrease in the volume of Soviet arms exports.

The flow

The period between the early 1970s and the early 1980s was characterized by very high growth rates and Soviet exports of major weapons almost doubled. Statistics show however, that this growth occurred at a time when the arms exports of other countries also increased rapidly, and the Soviet share of the market was somewhat reduced by the early 1980s (see figure 3.1).

Soviet exports of major weapons are highly concentrated. Within individual five-year periods, one or two countries received 50 per cent or more of all Soviet

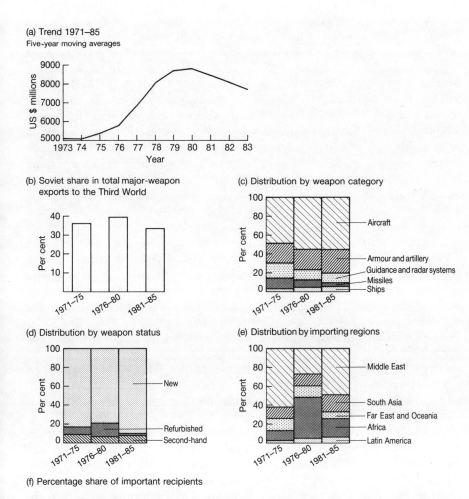

(a) Trend 1971–85
Five-year moving averages

(b) Soviet share in total major-weapon exports to the Third World

(c) Distribution by weapon category
— Aircraft
— Armour and artillery
— Guidance and radar systems
— Missiles
— Ships

(d) Distribution by weapon status
— New
— Refurbished
— Second-hand

(e) Distribution by importing regions
— Middle East
— South Asia
— Far East and Oceania
— Africa
— Latin America

(f) Percentage share of important recipients

Rank order	1971–75		1976–80		1981–85	
	Country	Share	Country	Share	Country	Share
1	Egypt	28	Libya	23	Syria	25
2	Syria	26	Iraq	12	Iraq	22
3	India	11	Viet Nam	11	India	15
4	N. Vietnam	9	India	10	Libya	9
5	Iraq	8	Syria	9	Cuba	5
6	Libya	7	Algeria	8	Viet Nam	5
7	N. Korea	3	Ethiopia	6	Angola	4
8	Cuba	3	S. Yemen	3	Algeria	3
9	Somalia	2	Peru	3	Afghanistan	3
10	S. Yemen	1	Cuba	2	N. Korea	2
Total of ten[a]		97		87		93

[a] Figures may not add up to totals due to rounding.

Figure 3.1. Soviet exports of major weapons to the Third World, 1971–85

Figures are based on SIPRI trend indicator values in US $m., at constant (1985) prices.

exports of major weapons to the Third World. There have been dramatic shifts among the leading importers of Soviet weapons, however. Whereas in the late 1960s and early 1970s, North Vietnam and Egypt were the major recipients, major weapon exports to both countries decreased in the early 1970s. After Egypt had broken its alliance with the Soviet Union in 1972, Syria and Iraq became the leading importers of Soviet weapons. Although the Middle East was the most important region for Soviet arms exports throughout, its relative importance declined in the late 1970s when Libya received large numbers of weapons from the Soviet Union and major deliveries of Soviet weapons went to Algeria, Ethiopia and Angola. Once supplies to Libya were reduced in the early 1980s, the largest shares were again going to Syria and Iraq: Soviet assistance helped resupply Syrian and Iraqi armed forces after their battles in Lebanon and the Iraq–Iran War.

Until the early 1970s, the Soviet Union exported mainly second-hand weapons drawn from its own armed forces or from stocks. Later, weapons were often provided to Third World customers at the same time as they were exported to WTO countries, or even before. The MiG-23 was transferred to Iraq, Syria, Egypt, Libya, Ethiopia and Cuba before other WTO countries received substantial numbers of this modern aircraft. India received the T-72 tank in the spring of 1979, before East European WTO countries. The same was true for the MiG-25—with sales to Algeria, India, Libya and Syria. The MiG-29 will be delivered to India and Syria before it reaches the Soviet forces in large quantities.

Only a handful of armed forces are thus privileged, however, the majority of recipients of Soviet weapons—the poor countries of Africa and Asia—still receive mostly second-hand weapons, sometimes in great numbers. The share of second-hand weapons in Soviet arms exports is comparatively high.

Soviet willingness to deliver large quantities of simple weapons at short notice gives the USSR an advantage over other suppliers when weapons are needed rapidly, and when the money is not available to purchase more sophisticated weaponry in the West. The Soviet Union has often supplied countries at war: for example, Egypt in the late 1960s and early 1970s, Syria in the early 1970s, Somalia before 1977 and Ethiopia after 1977, Angola and Mozambique in the late 1970s and early 1980s, and Iraq in the early 1980s. It has also supplied the poor countries in the world. In the period 1981–85, for example, 22 per cent of Soviet arms supplies to the Third World went to the low-income countries; the corresponding figure for the USA was 7 per cent.

Institutional framework

Little precise information is available about the decision-making apparatus and the rules employed to steer the flow of arms. Given the centralization of Soviet decision-making, it is probable that the Politbureau of the Communist Party of the Soviet Union must approve weapon sales in very important cases. Otherwise, decision-making is probably conducted in the Defence Council, which consists of a handful of Politbureau members, including the Minister of Defence. The Chairman of the Party is also the Chairman of the Defence Council, which, according to the 1977 constitution, is a state rather than a party institution. The State Committee of Economic Foreign Relations, which is directly responsible to the Defence Council, appears to be a key administrative agency in the handling of arms exports. Most offices of this committee are staffed by military officers. They handle routine decisions and co-ordinate policy with other parts of the administration, such as the Foreign Ministry, and the various ministries in charge of arms production. The institutional set-up ensures the predominance of the party, and gives most of the administrative power to the military.[3] The structure of decision-making is visible in the handling of talks about arms transfers with prospective recipient countries. While heads of state, foreign ministers or defence ministers—that is, mostly politicians—tend to head delegations from would-be recipients, the Soviet delegation is very often composed of high-ranking military officials. In important cases, however, it is the party chairman or some other high party official who leads the talks on the Soviet side.

Arms production

The Soviet Union has the largest arms industry in the world in terms of output and employees. Around two-thirds of the output of the aircraft and shipbuilding industries and one-third of the output of the machine-building and metalworking industries are devoted to arms production.[4]

Arms production is under tight state control. Some competition exists between various design bureaus in each of the weapon fields, but production is centrally co-ordinated. There are more than a hundred final assembly plants and several thousand installations which manufacture pre-products. Many plants also produce civilian goods, thus providing the Soviet Union with an emergency capacity in the event of war.

According to Western estimates the arms production capacity grew somewhat faster than the Soviet economy in the 1970s and early 1980s. At the same time procurement for the Soviet forces was, by and large, constant from about 1976 to 1984. The additional capacity from the arms production plants was partly used for exports, and partly redirected to the manufacture of civilian goods. It has been estimated that around 15 per cent of Soviet arms produced in the mid-1970s and early 1980s were exported.[5] Comparison of numbers of weapons exported and weapons produced (see table 3.1) gives the impression that more than 15 per cent of weapons produced in the USSR are exported. However, not all of the weapons exported came from current production lines. But the share of new weapons in Soviet arms exports increased in the 1970s, and stocks also have to be refilled.

Weapon exports made up a considerable part of Soviet foreign trade—between 10 and 15 per cent—in the 1970s and early 1980s. Since the weapon trade was concentrated towards member countries of the Warsaw Treaty

Table 3.1. US Defense Intelligence Agency estimates of the share of exports in Soviet arms production, by item, 1972–83

Figures are percentages.

	Average 1972–76	Average 1977–81	1982	1983
Armoured vehicles				
Heavy and medium tanks	27	17	16	11
Infantry combat vehicles[a]	3	6	18	12
Armoured personnel carriers[a]	43	18	20	–
Armoured reconnaissance vehicles	16	25	16	13
SP field artillery[b]	5	10	5	5
Towed field artillery[b]	33	20	4	7
Warships				
Major surface combatants	14	17	25	10
Minor surface combatants	17	37	36	22
Aircraft				
Fighters/fighter-bombers	33	36	36	26
Trainers	43	41	50	29
Helicopters[c]	9	27	25	22
Transports[c]	10	16	17	17

[a]The figure for production includes imports.
[b]Artillery over 100-mm calibre.
[c]Both civilian and military.
Source: Calculated from *Congressional Record*, US Senate, 10 August 1984, pp. S 10387–89.

Organization and the Third World, the ratios for these groups of countries were much higher. The Soviet arms trade with the Third World was more than sufficient to offset the otherwise negative trade balance with these countries. Statistics about Soviet arms exports are not indicative of the actual inflow of foreign currency, though. The value at which the weapons exported are entered into the accounts, or the extent to which the recipients actually pay these amounts, is not known. However, information from several recipient countries shows that up to the early 1970s most of the Soviet weapon exports were connected with long-term credits with soft terms (interest rates of between 2 and 2.5 per cent). These could be paid back over a period of 10 years, with goods delivered to the Soviet Union or in national currencies. The Soviet Union frequently granted rebates on what were already comparatively low prices for weapons and, furthermore, credits were in many cases turned into grants.

From the late 1960s there was a gradual change in Soviet policy. Increasingly, payment in hard currencies, US-dollars or other Western currencies was demanded, either in immediate cash or as repayment for credits. Prices for newer weapon systems tended to be higher and discounts lower. Countries with high oil incomes, such as Algeria, Iraq and Libya, or with access to countries with such incomes, for example Syria and South Yemen, were particularly victim to this changed attitude. Less privileged countries were offered better conditions, such as higher discounts and longer maturity periods for credits.

A number of purchasers of Soviet weapons had become highly indebted to the Soviet Union by the early 1980s. In 1985 Libya was estimated to owe $5 billion for weapons delivered earlier, and Peru was estimated to owe the Soviet Union $600 million. There were also old debts which the Soviet Union has most probably written off, such as $5 billion incurred by Egyptian arms imports before 1973. The inability of customers to pay contributed to the decline of Soviet weapon exports in the early 1980s.

Another effect of the Soviet demand for hard currency payments was a change in the trade pattern of recipients. Instead of being prompted into selling goods to the Soviet Union, they were encouraged to sell their export products on the world market. This led to a general decrease in trade in civilian goods with the Soviet Union, which in turn increased the importance of arms transfers as an instrument of Soviet Third World policy.

Political issues

There is hardly any political or academic discussion about arms export policy in the Soviet Union. It is therefore difficult to assess the aims and performance of Soviet arms export policy, but some features can be inferred from the Soviet literature on arms transfers, actual arms transfer patterns and Western debate on Soviet motives and behaviour.

One feature that emerges from Soviet statements is that possible recipients are seen as being divided into groups. The first such group comprises countries with which the Soviet Union is connected by treaties of friendship and co-operation (sometimes extended to mutual assistance). A second group is 'peaceful states which are legitimately apprehensive for their security, and are being threatened by aggressive forces armed by imperialism'.[6] A third group is made up of liberation movements, though deliveries to such groups have declined since the 1960s.

Another set of criteria stressed by Soviet authors is legalistic. The right of self-defence in the face of foreign aggression and the struggle against colonialism and racism, as enshrined in UN declarations, are some such legal principles. It was in line with these principles that the Soviet Union stopped the delivery of weapons, or threatened to stop the delivery of weapons, to some clients that went to war, such as Somalia in 1977, or Iraq in 1980. That the bulk of weapons has been delivered to countries that have signed friendship treaties with the Soviet Union is also in accordance with these principles (see table 3.2).

However, other features of the Soviet arms trade contradict these and other Soviet statements on the objectives and motives of arms exports. One such statement is that the Soviet Union does not seek financial or other advantages from its arms exports from recipients. But it is undeniable that the income from arms exports has become an important aspect of Soviet trade. The Soviet Union has also used the delivery of weapons in order to gain access to military facilities for its Navy and Air Force. Without access to such facilities in Africa, Asia and Cuba, the world-wide operation of the Soviet Navy and the resupply of weapons throughout the world would not be possible.[7]

Table 3.2. Soviet deliveries of major weapons to countries with which a treaty of friendship and co-operation has been signed

Country	Date of treaty	Percentage of Soviet deliveries of major weapons to the Third World		
		1981	1985	1981–85
Afghanistan	1978	0.2	5.2	2.5
Angola	1976	2.7	4.2	4.2
Ethiopia	1978	1.0	1.4	1.1
India	1971	18.2	12.4	15.2
Iraq	1972	12.3	29.3	21.5
Mozambique	1977	0.2	0.2	1.3
North Korea	1961	0.2	6.9	2.4
Syria	1980	22.2	21.5	25.1
Viet Nam	1978	10.6	4.2	4.7
Yemen, South	1980	1.8	0.2	1.0
Total		**69.4**	**85.5**	**79.0**

Source: SIPRI data base.

The Soviet Union has often taken the opportunity to deliver weapons even when the defence of a country was not at stake, for example, to Iran, Kuwait, Libya, Nigeria or Peru in the 1970s. The objective was clear: to show the Soviet presence and to give governments an alternative to buying from the USA or other Western states. The Soviet Union obviously views arms exports not only as an instrument to help strengthen the defence of independent states attacked by the 'forces of aggression and arbitrariness'[8] but also as an instrument in the 'world-wide struggle between imperialism and socialism', in other words between the USA and the Soviet Union. The military requirements of the Soviet Union and its great power rivalry with the USA (and the Western allies and China) have been overriding factors in shaping Soviet arms export policy.

As an instrument in the great power competition, arms exports have reflected the general relationship between the USA and the Soviet Union. There was a period in the early 1970s, at the height of *détente*, when the Soviet Union was prepared jointly with the USA to limit arms transfers to the Third World as long as its interests were not impaired.[9] At this time, though, the USA was shifting its Third World policy towards a greater reliance on the instrument of arms exports. In the late 1970s the situation was reversed: when the USA restrained its arms exports under the Carter Administration, the Soviet Union was delivering large amounts of weapons to crisis spots, such as Angola and Ethiopia. The Soviet involvement in Third World conflicts was an important element in ending *détente*. In the early 1980s Soviet and US arms export policies were again out of step when the Reagan Administration tried to push arms exports, while the Soviet Union—judging from the available data—was limiting its arms exports. It is difficult to explain these cycles. There was certainly an element of seizing the opportunity when US action in the Third World appeared cramped in the mid-1970s, and of stepping back when the USA began to take an aggressive posture *vis-à-vis* the Soviet Union in the early

1980s. The Soviet Union has taken into account that there are zones in the Third World where arms exports can run counter to its longer-term interests. The Allende Government in Chile 1970–73 did not receive large amounts of Soviet weapons, and the Soviet Union refrained from delivering advanced fighter aircraft to Nicaragua in the early 1980s. The Soviet Union has also refrained from delivering certain types of weapon where direct confrontation with US troops could lead to escalation of a local conflict, for example in the Korean peninsula and in the Middle East.

Because of the weakness of the USSR as a trading partner and aid giver, arms exports are the predominant instrument of Soviet foreign policy in many regions of the Third World. To ensure the success of this instrument, Soviet decision-makers have had to combine generosity in giving weapons away with control over arms transfers. One result of this approach was that Soviet offers of weapons and weapon deliveries were usually 'packaged', comprising various types of weapon system tailored to the current needs of a recipient. On the other hand, the share of weapon systems in export deals, as compared to spare parts, support equipment and infrastructure, was very high: according to one estimate it was 60 per cent as compared to 35 per cent for the USA.[10] This meant that recipients were more dependent on continuous supplies of spare parts from the Soviet Union to operate the weapons.

Another specific element of Soviet arms exports was that simple, rugged weapons were supplied to many recipients, while more sophisticated weapons were only delivered to a few customers. The yardstick was the Soviet objectives involved.[11] In cases where the customer had some leverage or where important Soviet foreign-policy issues were at stake, as in the cases of Algeria, India, Iraq, Libya and Syria, more sophisticated weapons were offered. Only India, though, has been favoured with offers to produce advanced Soviet weapons under licence. Soviet tanks and aircraft have been produced in India since the 1960s. But even in the case of the Indian armed forces control has been strict. Indian technicians training in the Soviet Union were reported to have received instruction in only rudimentary techniques, and written notes given to them were repeatedly retrieved upon completion of the course.[12]

In general, Soviet weapons have gained a reputation as being dependable, available in large numbers, rugged and useful against lightly armed enemies. On the other hand, if used against better-armed enemies, Soviet weapons have often gained little reputation. In the Ogaden War, Angola, Iraq and the Lebanon the performance of Soviet-produced weapons was poor. One reason was that the Soviet Union did not deliver its most advanced weapons in these cases. Strict control is kept over the technology delivered. Soviet reluctance to part with technology presented a dilemma of increasing dimensions because of the growing Third World demand for arms production technology in the 1970s and 1980s. The Soviet Union adapted its behaviour somewhat in the 1980s but it is unclear whether the decision-makers are prepared to make further concessions.

Another dilemma of Soviet arms export policy resulted from contradictions between ideology and great-power politics. The Soviet Union delivered weapons to a number of states that suppressed communist parties or popular movements fighting for socialist or communist ideas, such as Egypt before 1973, Libya, Guinea, Algeria and Peru. The Soviet Union toned down its support of the PLO in 1982 when this movement was fighting the heavily Soviet-supported Syrian troops in Lebanon. Soviet policy has come a long way from the 'two-camp theory' of the days of Stalin when it was claimed that states were either communist or capitalist. World-wide competition with the USA has led to a more differentiated view of the Third World. In addition, the Soviet Union has experienced the fall of governments it supported, as in Ghana and Indonesia in 1966, and Uganda in 1978, and the change of allegiance of governments it had supplied with weapons, such as Egypt and Sudan in 1972, Somalia in 1977 and Guinea in 1982. Great numbers of Soviet weapons remain in the hands of unfriendly governments. More importantly, though, Soviet leaders have lost faith in the reliability of radical Third World governments.[13]

The list of former Soviet arms export recipients that have turned away from the Soviet Union is long. This is an indication of the problems of relying on arms transfers as an instrument of foreign policy. There are other cases in which arms exports have helped to maintain a stable relationship, for example with Syria or India, and there are cases in which arms exports have given immediate political benefits to the Soviet Union, for example, when Iran was supported with weapons in the late 1960s and early 1970s, or when weapons were delivered to North Korea, a country shifting between Soviet and Chinese allegiance. In conclusion, the Soviet leadership must be taken to regard arms transfers as an unreliable, but indispensible, instrument of foreign policy.

III. The United States

The United States, together with the Soviet Union, dominated major-weapon supplies to the Third World during 1971–85. Arms exports are an integral part of US foreign policy; the dominant position of the USA in world affairs is reflected in the statistics on transfers of major weapons. However, because of their primary function as a policy instrument, US transfers of major weapons to the Third World have slowly decreased in parallel with commercialization of the arms market.

The flow

In the mid-1980s, US exports of major weapons to the Third World were at about the same level as in the early 1970s. Growth rates fluctuated widely in the interim: the annual delivery statistics reveal three peak periods (see appendix 4). The first peak occurred in 1972–73 when deliveries to South Vietnam were at their highest level. There were also massive transfers to Israel in connection with the 1973 war. The next peak is recorded for 1976–78 and is largely the result of the huge flow of major weapons to Iran at the time. The third peak period was in 1982–83, when many of the items promised to Egypt and Israel in connection with the 1979 Camp David Accords were delivered. This coincided with stepped-up deliveries to Pakistan and to Saudi Arabia which, together with Egypt, was the other key ally of the USA in the region after the fall of the Pahlavi regime in Iran.

Deliveries dropped markedly in 1979–80, illustrating the general effect of President Carter's attempt at unilateral restraint and the vacuum left in US arms sales after the halt in deliveries to Iran. There was another drop in 1984–85, reflecting the general slack in demand as well as the declining share of the USA in total exports of major weapons to the Third World (see figure 3.2).

In the 1950s and early 1960s US arms exports were primarily directed to countries in Latin America and the Far East; main recipients were Argentina, Brazil, Chile, South Korea and Taiwan. Iran became a major importer of US major weapons in the mid-1960s and deliveries to Israel increased markedly in the late 1960s. Since then, the Middle East has accounted for between one-half and two-thirds of all US major-weapon deliveries to the Third World. The Far East is the second most important recipient region, but its share is declining. US interests in certain countries in South Asia (e.g., Pakistan) and Africa (e.g., Kenya, Somalia and Sudan) explain the growing US share of exports to these regions in the 1980s.

A number of factors explain the changes in the distribution by weapon category during 1971–85 (figure 3.2). First, exports of aircraft had declined by the mid-1980s. Iran and Israel were the leading importers in 1971–75: both countries emphasized the acquisition of fighters and helicopters. Such aircraft, for example F-4 and F-5 fighters and various Bell helicopters, were produced in long series and were therefore comparatively cheap. In the late 1970s and in the 1980s the USA turned to the production of new generations of more complex and sophisticated aircraft. These became more expensive for recipients to buy and sometimes their delivery was refused by the USA. Certain countries therefore chose to upgrade existing inventories instead, others purchased fighters and helicopters from France and the UK, since better terms could be negotiated with these suppliers. In the case of Israel, domestic production of the Kfir design was stepped up.

Second, missiles, armour and artillery have increased their share of the market. From the mid-1970s recipients have tended to emphasize weapons over weapon platforms, partly as a result of the lessons of the 1973 war in the Middle East. Because it is ahead in missile technology the USA benefited from this tendency: exports of such guided systems as the Sidewinder and Sparrow air-to-air missiles, Hawk surface-to-air missiles and Harpoon anti-ship missiles increased dramatically from the mid-1970s. Similarly, the reputation of US armour and artillery benefited from the double advantages of documented war performance and relatively cheap unit prices due to long production runs.

(a) Trend 1971–85
Five-year moving averages

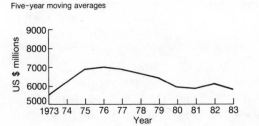

(b) US share in total major-weapon exports to the Third World

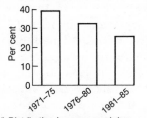

(c) Distribution by weapon category

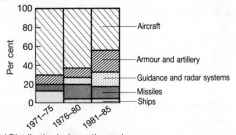

(d) Distribution by weapon status

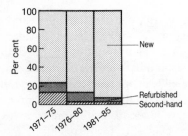

(e) Distribution by importing regions

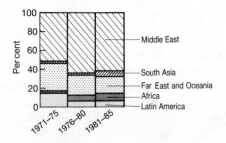

(f) Percentage share of important recipients

Rank order	1971–75		1976–80		1981–85	
	Country	Share	Country	Share	Country	Share
1	Iran	24	Iran	28	Egypt	23
2	Israel	22	Israel	15	Saudi Arabia	18
3	S. Vietnam	17	Saudi Arabia	9	Israel	13
4	Brazil	6	S. Korea	9	Taiwan	7
5	Taiwan	4	Jordan	6	Pakistan	5
6	S. Korea	4	Taiwan	5	S. Korea	4
7	Argentina	4	Egypt	3	Jordan	3
8	Saudi Arabia	3	Morocco	3	Venezuela	2
9	Thailand	2	Thailand	2	Thailand	2
10	Jordan	2	Kuwait	2	Morocco/UAE	2
Total of ten [a]	87		82		78	

[a] Figures may not add up to totals due to rounding.

Figure 3.2. US exports of major weapons to the Third World, 1971–85

Figures are based on SIPRI trend indicator values in US $m., at constant (1985) prices.

Institutional framework

US arms transfer programmes operate within a complex political and legal framework. Moreover, both programmes and legislation are often changed or amended following policy shifts in the executive branch or legislative measures in Congress.[14] This section briefly sets out the arms-transfer programmes in the mid-1980s, including some historical aspects, the factors in the early 1970s pushing for more Congressional control, the legislative framework, the decision-making process and the issue of financing.

By the mid-1980s arms-transfer programmes included three main components. First, Foreign Military Sales (FMS) which are government-to-government sales of defence articles or services. FMS is by far the largest programme. Commercial arms sales (CS) are direct contractor-to-recipient sales of military articles (as defined by the US Munitions List). The US Government does not normally function as an intermediary in these cases—CS transactions theoretically come to the government's notice only when the company applies for an export licence. Included as CS are also sales of manufacturing licences and technical assistance agreements. Until 1982 the Military Assistance Program (MAP) transferred defence articles and services to foreign countries on a grant basis. Since then, funds granted under MAP are merged with credits extended under the Arms Export Control Act and are used to finance FMS purchases. Some MAP funds were not merged with FMS accounts, such as MAP administrative expenses and funds used to close MAP orders made before

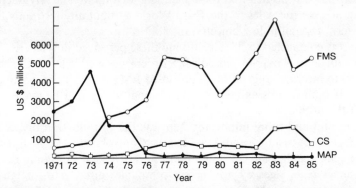

Figure 3.3. United States FMS, CS and MAP deliveries to the Third World, fiscal years 1971–85

Values are in US $m., at current (1985) prices.
Sources: FYs 1976–85: *Foreign Military Sales, Foreign Military Construction Sales and Military Assistance Facts*, Defense Security Assistance Agency (DSAA), US Department of Defense, 1985; FYs 1971–76: *Foreign Military Sales and Military Assistance Facts*, DSAA, US Department of Defense, Dec. 1980.
Notes: FY 1976: the estimate for 12 months is based on data for 15 months and the assumption of equal distribution of deliveries throughout the period. FY 1985: data are as of 30 Sep. 1985. FMS: Foreign Military Sales: CS: Commercial Sales: MAP: Military Assistance Program.

1982. Figure 3.3 shows the volume of deliveries under these three programmes during 1971–85.

Grant aid via MAP was predominant during the 1950s and the 1960s. MAP deliveries were to some extent reduced in the early 1960s and were increasingly replaced by FMS sales. In 1966 Military Assistance Service-Funded (MASF) was established to provide military aid on a grant basis to South Vietnam and other South East Asian countries participating in the Viet Nam War. MASF deliveries came directly from the Department of Defense (DoD) and were not channelled through the regular MAP network.

It has been suggested that US military assistance during the past two decades or so can be divided into the Viet Nam period (1964–73) and the Middle East period (1974–85).[15] During the changeover period, the debate over arms transfer policies and administrative control over arms transfers was intense in Congress. There were three main reasons for this. First, although Congress had authority over grant aid, it used to regularly approve MAP grants proposed by the executive branch. However, the conduct of the Viet Nam War led Congress to scrutinize proposed grants more closely than before. Second, in the early 1970s Congress had no authority over the rapidly expanding FMS programme: it did not vote on FMS deliveries, and there was no obligation to notify Congress of such sales. The size and qualitative nature of the vast sales to, for example, Iran was thus outside congressional control. Third, there were many revelations of bribery, inappropriate agent commissions, and so on, in connection with military sales during 1974–75, such as the Lockheed and Northrop scandals.[16] It was argued that these factors added up to a largely uncontrolled pushing of US arms sales to the Third World without any restraints based on longer-term foreign policy objectives.

Congress committed itself to rectifying these perceived deficiencies. The first step to gain control over proposed FMS orders was a 1975 legislation requiring the DoD to inform Congress of all proposed FMS transactions worth over $25 million. If both houses agreed, a congressional veto could be made within 20 days of the notification.

The second and more important step was the introduction of the International Security Assistance and Arms Export Control Act (AECA) in 1976. This Act brought together all legislation concerning US FMS programmes and CS programmes (e.g., sales by private US companies directly to foreign governments or service branches). The Act emphasized review procedures and public disclosure. One provision in the AECA was a dollar ceiling on commercial arms sales. This provided a check on the growing use of commercial military transfers by bringing them under FMS channels. The main tool in the Act for exercising control over arms sales is the right of Congress to veto certain proposed transfers, be they commercial or government-to-government. Other important provisions include requirements for quarterly and annual reports on military transfers from the President to Congress, a scaling-down of the arms-sales activities of US Military Assistance Advisory Groups (MAAGS) in foreign countries, reporting on agent fees and obligatory reporting on the perceived foreign policy net contributions from each major arms sale. Beyond these basic principles, a myriad of rules fall under the Act.[17] The AECA is regularly amended by Congress—the most substantial amendments occurred in 1981 as a result of the new guidelines for arms exports introduced by the Reagan Administration.

One change concerned the veto right. This right extends to three types of sale where certain dollar thresholds are met. First Congress can veto government-to-government (FMS) sales. Second, it can veto commercial sales made directly by US companies. Third, Congress can veto retransfers to a third country of items originally sold through FMS but not through commercial channels. The 1981 amendments to the AECA doubled the threshold dollar values for major defence equipment (from $7 million to $14 million) and for other defence articles (from $25 million to $50 million).

The 1981 amendments also created the Special Defense Acquisition Fund (SDAF) as a way of financing advance purchases of high-demand weapon systems and parts in anticipation of foreign orders. The reason was to shorten the time between order and delivery of such items without having to reduce US readiness levels by diverting material from US forces.[18]

The government's decision-making function with respect to arms exports is centred in the Department of State (DoS), but in reality this responsibility is shared with the DoD and a number of special agencies. Within the DoS, primary responsibility rests with the Bureau of Politico-Military Affairs (PM). The PM is, theoretically, the bureau in which the governmental review process of foreign requests for arms starts. Within the PM, commercial sales are supervised by the Office of Munitions Control (OMC), while the Office of Security Assistance and Sales (SAS) handles MAP and FMS transactions. Similarly, within the DoD, decision-making is the responsibility of the Office for International Security Affairs (ISA). ISA is also the main policy-making body within the DoD on matters concerning defence and foreign policy. The responsibility for administering FMS transactions once they are decided upon has been delegated to the Defense Security Assistance Agency (DSAA); the DSAA also has a say in the actual decision-making process. These four bodies—OMC, SAS, ISA and DSAA—are the key actors in the government review process. Other departments and agencies, such as the Arms Control and Disarmament Agency (ACDA), the Central Intelligence Agency (CIA), the National Security Council (NSC), the Treasury and the Commerce Department are also involved in reviewing requests for arms from abroad, especially in controversial or financially important cases.

Once the governmental review process has resulted in a formal approval, the DSAA prepares a Letter of Offer (LoO), which lists the buyer, the items to be sold, costs and so on. The LoO is then submitted to Congress for review. Congress must adopt a joint resolution of disapproval within 30 days in order to veto the sale or retransfer.[19] If Congress approves the sale, the LoO is sent to the prospective buyer for signature, the LoO thus becomes an LOA (Letter of Offer and Acceptance) and the material can then be delivered.

The congressional veto right is seldom used, for a number of reasons. First, and most important, arms sales are most often planned and implicitly decided upon long before the formal governmental and congressional review processes start. After years of informal negotiations, involving company officials and government and military officials from both sides, de facto commitments are created. It is argued that a congressional veto in such a situation would seriously damage US credibility and relations with the prospective buyer country. The anticipated view of Congress is a factor in the governmental decision-making process—the President may sometimes choose not to put a proposed sale before Congress in order to avoid an obvious defeat. This was the case, for example, with the planned sale of AWACS aircraft to Iran in 1977, the sale of additional F-15 fighters to Saudi Arabia in 1985 and the Jordan package of 1985, including fighters, missiles and armoury. Another impediment against vetoes is the fact that proposed sales are often 'packaged' in such a way that Congress finds it difficult to agree on vetoing a whole package when only one single component of the package is considered questionable. Also, US Presidents tend, in close cases, to utilize various methods of persuasion vis-à-vis individual congressmen, such as pointing out the importance of a particular sale to the employment situation in a certain constituency, and so on. The persuasive powers of President Reagan were, for example, instrumental in the sale of AWACS aircraft to Saudi Arabia in 1981.

Finally, with respect to financing, Third World governments may pay for arms either with cash, DoD direct credits or DoD guaranteed credits. In the mid-1980s the most common form of financing was a mix of various direct credit financing agreements: some loans at the prevailing Treasury rate, some at concessional rates, some loans for which repayment was waived and some grants under the MAP programme.[20] Repayments are scheduled in the loan arrangement. The normal repayment period is 12 years with a 1–2 year period of grace. Longer repayment periods have been authorized—mainly by the Reagan Administration—for some countries (e.g., Egypt, Israel and Sudan). The period has in these cases been extended to 20 years with a 2-year grace period. Repayments of large portions of the loans to Israel and Egypt have also been forgiven (i.e., turned into grants).[21]

Arms production

The US arms industry employed, by the late 1970s, around one-third of all US scientists and engineers and close to 10 per cent of the total manufacturing labour force.[22] A DSAA report from 1977 estimated that each billion dollars in foreign military sales created approximately 50 000 new jobs—an improbably high figure.[23] Arms exports accounted for around five per cent of total US exports in the early 1980s.

In the 1970s there was a tendency for prime contractors in the US arms industry to become increasingly dependent on foreign military sales, not only to maintain output levels and profits, but in some cases for survival (see table 3.3).

Table 3.3. Some US companies exporting major weapons to Third World countries

Figures are in US $m. at constant (1984) prices.

Company	FMS rank	DoD rank	Main export products	Total turnover	Value of military output [c]	Military output/total turnover (%)	Export share of military output (%) [e]		Exports of major weapons to Third World, 1971–85 [f]
							1976	1984	
McDonnell-Douglas[a]	1	1	Fighter aircraft, missiles, helicopters	9 662	8 788	91.0	50.0	12.5	10 404
General Dynamics	2	3	Fighter aircraft, tanks, missiles	7 880	7 013	90.0	..	15.1	5 186
Lockheed	8	4	Transport and maritime patrol aircraft	8 113	5 206	64.2	8.4	4.6	4 820
Bell Textron	..	28	Helicopters	3 220	980[d]	(30.0)	23.6	(18.0)	4 547
Northrop	11	26	Fighter aircraft	3 690	1 070[d]	(29.0)	46.6	17.0	3 831
Grumman	7	11	Fighter, early-warning and maritime patrol aircraft	(2 700)	2 659	98.5	23.6	9.0	3 565
Raytheon	5	9	Missiles, radars, guidance equipment	5 950	3 367	56.6	21.8	8.1	3 367
Boeing	3	5	Helicopters, missiles, transport aircraft	10 354	5 057	48.8	..	9.7	2 987
FMC	13	18	Armoured personnel carriers	3 500[b]	1 300[d]	(37.1)	32.5	(13.0)	2 596

[a] Including Hughes Aircraft Company.
[b] In 1982.
[c] DoD plus FMS contracts.
[d] FMS portion estimated.
[e] FMS contracts as a share of FMS + DoD contracts.
[f] SIPRI trend indicator values in US $m at constant (1985) prices.
( ) = estimated.
.. = not available or not applicable.

The surge in US arms sales in the early 1970s coincided with the reduction in military spending after the end of the Viet Nam War, thus partially offsetting the effects of the cut-backs on the arms industry. From a macro-economic standpoint, arms exports at the time contributed substantially to the propping up of the foreign-exchange account.

The rearmament programme, initiated by President Carter and carried through by the Reagan Administration, had the effect of lessening contractor dependence on foreign military sales. Table 3.3 lists the nine leading US arms manufacturers involved in exporting major weapons in fiscal year 1984. There are two main points to be made: first, with some important exceptions, these companies were not heavily dependent on military production in the mid-1980s (in some cases the civilian share of total output was larger than the military share); second, the export dependence in the military sector has decreased dramatically since the mid-1970s. This is mostly visible in the cases of Northrop, McDonnell-Douglas and Grumman, but it holds for all nine major-weapon contractors.

Clearly, the industry is interested in foreign sales—this interest is virtually open-ended, not least because foreign sales tend to be more profitable than sales to US armed forces.[24] While an econometric study from 1977 showed that the impact of widely fluctuating levels of sales on national economic aggregates was modest,[25] it can probably be concluded that the structural effects on the industrial level depend on a number of factors, most prominently: the level of domestic arms procurement. However, the US arms industry is, on the whole, less dependent on arms exports than its West European competitors.

Policy issues

In the USA, military transfers are an integral part of foreign policy—more so than in any other major-weapon exporting country except the Soviet Union. Various elements in the global situation, especially in the relationship with the USSR, and prevailing US perceptions of Soviet intentions shape arms-transfer policies. Different administrations try to implement their policies through changes in the legislative framework and the administrative routines. However, a combination of bureaucratic inertia and congressional action tends to some extent to level out the often dramatic differences that emerge from the rhetoric of various policy formulations on the executive level. The political and legal frameworks are therefore in a continuous state of flux. The pressure from external actors, such as industry or different lobbying groups (the 'Israeli' lobby, the 'OPEC' lobby, the 'Saudi' lobby, and so on) tends to be more even. The disparate policies as expressed in Presidential Directives are thus not always mirrored in statistics on weapon deliveries. The period 1971–85 divides itself into three periods with respect to policy issues: The Nixon-Kissinger policy, the Carter policy and the Reagan policy.

The Nixon-Kissinger policy

Two events in the early 1970s fundamentally changed the US attitude towards arms transfers; they also caused FMS deliveries to overtake MAP deliveries in 1973–74. First, there was the Viet Nam débâcle. Second, there were the developments in the Middle East. The British had announced their withdrawal from east of Suez by 1968—this took place in 1971. Then followed the October War in 1973 with the ensuing drastic rise in the price of oil. Finally, there was the related oil embargo against the United States which endangered US access to the strategic oil resources in the Gulf region. The so-called Nixon doctrine postulated—as a direct effect of the Viet Nam War—that the United States should furnish sufficient amounts of weapons to selected key Third World allies so that they could take care of their own defence. Direct US military involvement was to be avoided. This doctrine was also applied to the Middle East. Iran was selected to perform the function of regional policeman after the British withdrawal. Furthermore, arms sales to Iran and the Western-oriented Arab states contributed to the recycling of petrodollars, thus also improving the US balance of trade.

FMS sales to the Gulf countries rose by 2500 per cent between 1970 and 1976. During a trip to Teheran in May 1972, President Nixon and Special Adviser Henry Kissinger promised to sell the Shah of Iran any conventional weapon system in the US arsenal.[26] This led to the sale of 80 F-14 fighter aircraft and, along with other sales decisions, it prompted the above-mentioned congressional concern that FMS transfers were running out of control. Arms-transfer policies under Presidents Nixon and Ford indicate 'a strong tendency to use arms sales as a diplomatic instrument for immediate gain, with a rather *laissez-faire* or insouciant attitude towards the longer-term implications of the transfers for regional stability or the impact upon the recipient nation'.[27]

The Carter policy

In May 1977 President Carter issued a Presidential Directive (PD-13) setting out his policy for arms transfer restraint. The reason for this policy shift is not to be found exclusively in the perceived negative results from the previous policy; it should also be viewed as an offspring of the general foreign policy approach of the Carter Administration. US foreign policy under Presidents Nixon and Ford was largely conceived by Henry Kissinger. The Kissinger policy was marked by the concepts of superpower hegemony and '*realpolitik*'. The US-Soviet relationship was paramount; it decisively influenced all other interstate relations. The Carter Administration did not, at the outset, accept the view that global *détente* was an exclusive function of advances in US-Soviet relations. Instead, it saw fruitful co-operation between the USA, Western Europe and Japan as the most important guarantee for global stability: such co-operation would promote, first, Third World stability and economic development and, second, enhance *détente* with the USSR. In order to achieve this, the USA must restore the political and moral attraction it enjoyed in the late 1940s and the 1950s. This led the Carter Administration to conclude that economic and social problems were a greater threat to global stability than military problems. The need for rearmament and global security alliances were not, it was argued, the main driving force of international politics.

Against this background PD-13 stated that the unrestrained spread of conventional weaponry threatened stability in every region of the world and that, as the largest arms supplier, the United States bore a special responsibility to slow down the international arms trade. A number of specific controls were introduced to implement this policy of restraint, adding to the legislative measures in the AECA introduced during the Ford Administration. However, a number of key exceptions of a pragmatic nature were made. First, the controls should not apply to NATO, NATO members, Australia, Japan or New Zealand. Second, without specifically excepting Israel, PD-13 said that the USA would honour its responsibilities *vis-à-vis* Israel's security. Third, the controls would not be binding if extraordinary circumstances necessitated a presidential exception or if countries friendly to the USA needed advanced weaponry to offset regional imbalances. These disclaimers resulted in differences between policy as stated and implemented policy. The controls introduced by PD-13 are listed below and their implementation is assessed.

First, a ceiling was introduced. The value of US FMS transfers to non-exempt countries in constant 1976 dollars would not exceed FY 1977 levels and would be reduced further in subsequent years. This resulted in a dubious numbers game. With the treaty allies exempted, much of the total volume of arms transfers was excluded. Second, commercial sales were excluded and, finally, military services (training, technical assistance and construction works) were excluded, which left out another substantial part of the total. The net result was that, while total sales were actually rising, the ceiling (as defined) was met in FY 1978 and FY 1979, while in later years it was not.

Second, it would be prohibited to introduce newly developed, advanced weapon systems into regions that did not have them. This control was partially successful: the Administration refused to sell F-4Gs to Iran, F-4s to Taiwan, A-7s to Pakistan, F-5Es to Guatemala and Ecuador, and F-16s to South Korea. On the other hand, F-15s were sold to Israel and Saudi Arabia and F-16s to Egypt; it was proposed to sell AWACS aircraft to Iran and negotiations were also initiated to sell them to Saudi Arabia. The Camp David 'arms for peace' agreement and the need for strong ties with Saudi Arabia explain why most of the exceptions were in connection with arms sales to the Middle East.

Third, the USA would not develop or significantly modify advanced weapons solely for exports. The one major exception was the decision to allow the development of an intermediate fighter aircraft—the FX-fighter—for export, mainly as a replacement for the Northrop F-5A/E sold earlier.

Fourth, a prohibition against co-production agreements for certain weapon systems was introduced.[28] This prohibition was subject to more exceptions than any other. The Administration had to bow to market realities: purchasing countries often insist on some form of participation when expensive weapon systems are acquired.

Fifth, a prohibition against retransfers to third countries was imposed—retransfers were to be allowed only when the USA was prepared to supply the item directly to the third party. This prohibition was often implemented; it caused recipients to go elsewhere in many cases. For example, Ecuador bought French Mirage fighters when the USA denied delivery of Israeli Kfirs (because of its US engine) and India bought British Jaguars when Sweden could not export Viggen fighters (because the Viggen too has a US engine).

Sixth, DoS authorization would be required before US embassy or US military personnel abroad could engage in arms sales promotion activities. This aimed at avoiding unnecessary political friction, since the USA would not have to veto sales after promoters had raised hopes of prospective foreign customers.

PD-13 also indicated that human rights violations would be an important consideration in the decision-making process. Restrictions on arms sales and military assistance were primarily imposed on Latin American countries. Finally, the Directive stated that the USA would initiate negotiations with other suppliers to develop measures for multilateral action. The essence of the policy then was that by setting an example through unilateral restraint, the USA could induce allies and the USSR to follow. The European allies refused to restrain their arms sales efforts until an agreement was reached with the Soviet Union. Talks were held—the so-called CAT-talks—starting in December 1977, but they broke down about a year later, largely as a result of disagreements within the Carter Administration.

As a general assessment, Carter's policy of restraint was a failure. True, it did establish functional government procedures for handling arms transfer requests and it did turn down numerous requests for arms.[29] But the controls were not implemented in a systematic way. Furthermore, the perceived wish among Third World governments to disarm in order to improve economic and social development was overestimated, as was the will of other suppliers to impose restraints. The control mechanisms were compromised by their own inconsistencies and the repeated exceptions. Arms exports proponents found the policy naïve and overly restrictive. Those in favour of arms control found it weak and insufficient. The guidelines, undermined almost from the beginning, were effectively abandoned by President Carter in 1980 when he barred further reductions to non-exempt countries in the absence of agreed international restraint.

It is possible to identify specific policy reasons for every exception from the stated policy, but the final conclusion is that the basis for the entire foreign policy of the Carter Administration was eroded. It became impossible, therefore, for the arms export policy to successfully challenge the strong political, military and economic factors that always favour arms transfers as a key US foreign policy instrument.

The Reagan policy

During his electoral campaign, President Reagan criticized the Carter policy for having contributed to the deterioration of US strategic and military positions in the world. The specific foreign policy goals expressed by the Reagan Administration included enhancing the state of preparedness of US friends and allies and the revitalization of US alliances in order to contain perceived Soviet expansionism, especially in the Third World. There was widespread popular support for such a policy:

By the end of 1980, a series of events had shaken us out of our soul-searching and into a new, outward looking state of mind. The public had grown sceptical of detente and distressed by American impotence in countering the December 1979 Soviet invasion of Afghanistan. It felt bullied by OPEC, humiliated by the Ayatollah Khomeini, tricked by Castro, out-traded by Japan and out-gunned by the Russians. By the time of the 1980 presidential elections, fearing that America was losing control over its foreign affairs, voters were more than ever ready to exorcise the ghost of Vietnam and replace it with a new posture of American assertiveness.[30]

The Reagan arms transfer policy, presented in a White House document in July 1981, stemmed from the same philosophy as the US rearmament programme did: basic US interests, it was argued, were challenged by the USSR and this threatened stability in many regions vital to the USA. The new guidelines were more in the nature of a general repeal of the Carter policy than the elaboration of a new one. It presented broad aims and principles: arms transfer decision-making should be flexible and based on case-by-case judgements of each transfer's net contribution to US security, rather than on a specific set of rules. Arms transfers were firmly reinstated as a key foreign-policy instrument, especially with respect to the Third World. None of the restraining measures initiated by President Carter were kept, the basic idea was 'to see the world as it is, rather than as we would like it to be'.[31]

Since arms transfer decisions under the Reagan Administration are made on a case-by-case basis, the policy implementation is best described by some examples (with reference to the Carter Administration's controls). The sales of F-16 fighters to Pakistan, Singapore, South Korea, Thailand and Venezuela, the sale of AWACS aircraft to Saudi Arabia and the sale of E-2C Hawkeye early-warning aircraft to Egypt and Singapore all meant the introduction of highly advanced weapons which created significantly higher combat capabilities in these regions.

The approval of exports of Israeli Kfirs with US engines for Ecuador and South Korean M-101 howitzers for Uruguay, and the military assistance programmes to Chile, Guatemala, El Salvador and Honduras repealed the traditional US restraint towards Latin America, the retransfer prohibition and the human rights element. President Carter's so-called 'leprosy letter', instructing US Government representatives abroad not to promote foreign arms sales, was replaced by an instruction to vigorously assist private firms in their marketing efforts.

The general permissiveness with respect to arms transfers shown by the Reagan Administration led many US critics to describe the policy as, in effect, a 'non-policy'. With mounting congressional criticism, however, some of the major arms sales to the Third World had, by the mid-1980s, created major clashes between Congress and the President. The AWACS sale to Saudi Arabia, the sale of F-16s to South Korea and Venezuela and the proposed package to Jordan in 1985 exemplify this. Arms sales to China and the US-Taiwan relationship were also sensitive issues. This issue divided Congress and also, to some extent, the Administration in two camps. The main reason for selling weapons to the People's Republic of China was not the enhancement of Chinese military strength *per se*, but rather the effect such a relationship would have on the USSR (and the opening up of Chinese markets in general). On the other hand, it was argued, the 'China card' was a powerful instrument only as long as it was not being played. Furthermore, such sales would complicate the Reagan Administration's commitments to the security of Taiwan (see also chapter 2).

Finally, there seems to be at least one important difference between the Nixon-Ford-Kissinger policy and the Reagan policy. In the early 1970s arms were transferred as a substitute for direct US military presence. The Reagan policy continues to favour key allies, such as Egypt, Saudi Arabia and Pakistan, but also signals a preparedness to use US military force abroad, as witnessed by the strengthening of the USCENTCOM (US Central Command—formerly the Rapid Deployment Force), the buildup of base facilities in the Third World, the direct military actions against Grenada and Libya, and the threat of such actions against Cuba and Nicaragua.

The policy changes under President Reagan have not, however, led to significantly higher arms export levels. This underlines the importance of the basic factors of continuity mentioned above. It also, to some extent, reflects the relative unwillingness of US arms manufacturers to build too high hopes around a volatile international market. Finally and most importantly, it shows (as in the case of the Soviet Union) that the superpowers are at a disadvantage on the arms market in the mid-1980s. The changing climate—with decreased demand and increasing commercialization—tends to benefit suppliers that are less concerned with the political factors than are the USA and USSR.

IV. France

In the 1970s and 1980s French arms producers consolidated the position of France as the third largest exporter of major weapons to the Third World. There has been continuous growth, fuelled by the greater independence of recipient states from superpower domination and an increase in the income of a number of recipients, especially in the oil-rich Middle East. This growth was unaffected by a number of profound changes surrounding French arms export policies, for example, the embargoes on arms exports to Israel, in 1969, and South Africa, in 1977, and the nationalization of parts of the French arms industry from 1981. Neither did the historic election victory of the socialist and communist parties in 1981 change the course of arms exports in any dramatic way—despite election campaign announcements. The French arms industry is heavily dependent on arms exports and arms exports are of major importance for the entire French economy.

The flow

The aggregate total of French exports of major weapons has grown steadily—with growth rates of 13 per cent in the 1970s and 8 per cent in the first half of the 1980s. The French share in total exports of major arms to the Third World also grew steadily and reached 10 per cent in the early 1980s. France has begun to compete on an equal footing with the superpowers in many regions of the Third World—on a per capita basis France is the most important exporter of major weapons to the Third World (see figure 3.4).

While the expansion of French arms exporters has been steady, recipient patterns have changed. In the early 1960s, Israel was the most important customer for French weapons. At that time it was difficult for Israel to get weapons elsewhere. After the June war of 1967 relations between Israel and France cooled and in 1969, after French weapons delivered for defensive purposes were used in an attack on Beirut, the French Government declared an embargo on deliveries of weapons to Israel. Although the embargo was politically motivated, it facilitated the later expansion of arms exports to Arab states in the Middle East and Northern Africa. Libya, Iraq, Algeria and later Saudi Arabia and Syria became major customers of the French arms industry. The embargo against Israel remained in force.

Another important early customer was South Africa. After the voluntary UN arms embargo against South Africa in 1963, France became South Africa's most important supplier of weapons and arms production technology. While France was criticized by African and other Third World states for defying the UN embargo, the French position only changed slowly. It was claimed that only defensive weapons were delivered, but finally, in 1977, France succumbed to the mandatory UN arms embargo.

After the USA tried to limit arms exports to Latin America in the late 1960s, France became a major exporter of weapons to Latin American countries. The first jet fighters delivered to the continent were French Mirage-5s delivered in 1969–70. Since then many French fighter aircraft and missiles have followed, but the number of land and naval weapons delivered has been very limited.

French arms exports have been heavily concentrated towards the Arab countries in the Middle East and Africa (there were hardly any exports to the biggest importer in the Middle East in the 1970s, namely Iran). The largest deals of the French arms export industry were concluded with countries in the Middle East, for example, an oil barter deal with Iraq in 1977, worth $2.3 billion, and the Sawari and Al Thakeb deals with Saudi Arabia amounting to $2 billion and $4 billion respectively in 1980 and 1984. Fluctuations in the oil market in the early 1980s only marginally affected French arms exports. France's position as a supplier was strengthened by the ups and downs of the arms export policies of the USA and the USSR. Another boost to French arms exports was the performance of French weapons in wars, especially the sinking of British warships in the Falklands/Malvinas War by French Exocet missiles.

The bulk of French exports of major weapons continue to come from the

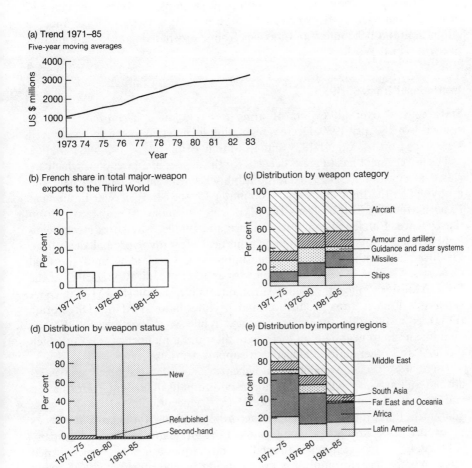

(a) Trend 1971–85
Five-year moving averages

(b) French share in total major-weapon exports to the Third World

(c) Distribution by weapon category

(d) Distribution by weapon status

(e) Distribution by importing regions

(f) Percentage share of important recipients

Rank order	1971–75		1976–80		1981–85	
	Country	Share	Country	Share	Country	Share
1	South Africa	23	Morocco	13	Iraq	21
2	Libya	16	Libya	9	Saudi Arabia	11
3	Venezuela	6	Pakistan	8	Argentina	7
4	Pakistan	6	Saudi Arabia	8	Egypt	6
5	UAE	6	Egypt	8	India	5
6	Egypt	6	Indonesia	7	Qatar	5
7	Malaysia	5	Iraq	5	Libya	5
8	Argentina	5	South Africa	5	Jordan	5
9	Zaire	3	UAE	4	Nigeria	4
10	Colombia	3	Kuwait	4	Peru	4
Total of ten[a]		79		71		72

[a] Figures may not add up to totals due to rounding.

Figure 3.4. French exports of major weapons to the Third World, 1971–85

Figures are based on SIPRI trend indicator values in US $m., at constant (1985) prices.

aircraft industry, despite growing exports of warships, armoured vehicles and missiles. Fighter aircraft produced by Dassault, such as the Mirage and the Alpha Jet, and helicopters and missiles from Aérospatiale are to be found all over the Third World.

Institutional framework

State control over all export of arms is based on a *décret-loi*—order in council—of 18 April 1939. Decrees regulating such details as the goods covered were issued on 14 August 1939 and 12 March 1973.

The government has to grant licences for the export of all weapons which are classified as war material. Final responsibility lies with the Prime Minister, who is advised by the Inter-ministerial Committee for the Study of War Equipment Exports (the CIEEMG). The CIEEMG, which includes representatives from the Defence, Foreign, Economic, Finance and Budget Ministries meets regularly to discuss potential and ongoing arms deals. It is involved in all deals from the first stages of contacts between suppliers and recipients until the final deliveries. There is close co-operation with another organization located at the Prime Minister's office: the General Armaments Delegation (DGA). The DGA supervises French arms production and its International Affairs Directorate (DAI) is responsible for arms exports. While it is possible for French manufacturers to negotiate on their own, there are a number of ways in which the DAI and other state organizations support arms exports.

There are special armaments attachés in most large French embassies abroad. In Paris, at the DAI, desk officers co-ordinate all incoming information and pass it on to the arms producers. In the negotiation phase, the state guarantees that production will occur according to French standards and backs up export risks through the state-owned Foreign Trade Insurance Company (COFACE). If the weapons requested are not required for the French armed forces, companies can apply for pre-financing by the government's Foreign Trade Bank (BFCE). The negotiation process as such can be conducted or supported by a number of marketing companies which, while outside the state apparatus, are either fully or partly state-owned. There are companies for the export of material from the aerospace industry (OGA, founded 1921, OFEMA 1977), for ground material (SOFEMA, 1939 and 1974) and naval material (SOFREXAN). These organizations are also in charge of the main exhibitions of French weapons: the aerospace exhibition at Le Bourget (Paris Air Show—organized since 1909), the ground material exhibition at Satory (1968) and the Bourget naval exhibition (1968). In some cases, the different organizations specialize on different countries, for example, on the Indian subcontinent, OGA covers Pakistan and Bangladesh while OFEMA is responsible for sales to India.

The DGA also supports companies in securing loans, either from commercial banks and backed up by COFACE, or via direct government credits. Most credits are given at commercial rates also applicable for civilian goods plus an extra charge of up to 2 per cent for the services of the DGA. Credits are only given in exceptional cases, when the competition is very tough or when there is a clear French foreign policy interest. In such cases French military or economic assistance is given to soften the terms of the deal. Egypt, for example, received Mirage-2000 fighters with a $1 billion loan at an interest rate of 7.75 per cent in 1981, when 9–10 per cent was the more normal rate.[32] Since 1982, the BFCE and COFACE have renegotiated the Iraqi debt for arms (totalling more than $5 billion in the mid-1980s) several times.

One important element of French sales strategy is the combination of arms deliveries with training of personnel, either in France or by French military personnel or arms contractors in the recipient country. In 1983, for example, about 3500 foreign trainees attended French military schools and about 3500 French advisors worked in foreign countries.[33] Another element of sales support was added by the DAI in the late 1970s: the co-ordinated delivery of spare parts and repairs. There are now specialized state-run companies performing this task in the ground material and naval fields, while OGA and OFEMA share this responsibility in the case of aircraft. If necessary, the resources of the DGA, the arms-producing companies and the armed forces can be pooled to meet the requirements of the recipient and the selling company.

The French marketing system has been changed and expanded a number of times. When Giscard d'Estaing came to power in 1973 more emphasis was put on co-ordinating sales between the armed forces and the arms-producing companies. After 1981 the Mitterrand Government strengthened the training and after-sales elements. In 1983, when sales figures were lower than expected (see figure 3.5), the head of the DGA, Marc Cauchie, spoke of a 'world-wide crisis' in arms exports and demanded a review of the sales organization.[34] The reorganization led to a strengthening of the power of the desk officers in the DAI and a reorientation of sales efforts. It was felt that concentration on

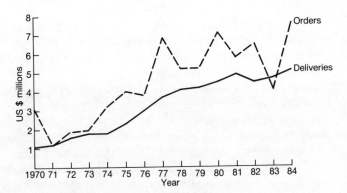

Figure 3.5. French arms exports: some official data, 1970–84

Figures are in US $b., at constant (1985) prices.
Source: Délégation Générale pour l'Armement.

exports to the Middle East was very risky and that efforts to sell to other industrialized countries, especially the USA, should be strengthened.

Arms production

Arms production has occupied an important position in the French economy since the 1960s, both because of its size and because of its importance as a policy tool. A high proportion of the arms produced are exported; this proportion has grown throughout the 1970s and 1980s. Official figures show that in the early 1980s about 300 000 persons were employed directly in arms production, that is, 5.6 per cent of the industrial labour force.[35] The number of persons whose jobs depended, directly or indirectly, on arms production has been estimated to be as high as one million.[36] (Although this figure is probably too high, it has been used in the political debate.)

The buildup of the arms industry in the 1960s was motivated by the French policy of independence. The aim was an arms industry capable of supplying all types of weapon to the French armed forces and also capable of injecting technological advances into civilian industry. It was planned that arms production be conducted by state-owned enterprises, such as Aéro-spatiale, GIAT or DTCN, or by private companies working together with the state, such as Dassault or Matra. Close co-operation was achieved through the DGA.

With the expansion of French arms exports in the early 1970s, arms exports gained importance in their own right. They became a major component of the French foreign exchange balance, and a major source of employment. In the early 1980s close to 5 per cent of all French exports, or 15 per cent of all exports of capital goods, were arms. More than 100 000 persons were directly employed producing arms for export.[37] Despite early efforts to decrease reliance on foreign production of arms and pre-products, co-operation exists with arms producers in other NATO-member countries and there are substantial imports of pre-products, for example electronics from the USA.[38]

Arms production has been concentrated in a few industrial sectors. Within the aircraft and space industry, 70 per cent of total output in 1984 was military, and 42 per cent of these products were exported. In electronics and informatics the corresponding shares were 62 per cent and 30 per cent.[39] There is also a high degree of concentration when it comes to arms-producing companies (see table 3.4). The state plays a very important role and there are state arsenals under the direction of the DGA (DTCN and GIAT) and nationalized companies (such as Aérospatiale). After 1981, the government increased the number of state-controlled companies (Matra, Dassault, Thomson-CSF). Although in 1986 the conservative government announced that it would privatize some of these companies, the state sector will continue to dominate arms production in France.

The contribution of arms exports to lowering the cost of arms for the French armed forces has turned out to be less important than expected in the 1960s.

Table 3.4. Some French companies exporting major weapons to Third World countries

Name	Export weapons produced	Turnover in arms production 1983 ($m.)	Rank among French arms producers	Share of exports in arms production (%)	Exports of major weapons to Third World, 1971–85 ($m.)[a]
Avions Marcel Dassault-Bréguet Aviation	Fighter aircraft, transport aircraft	1 600	4	70	7 800
Aérospatiale	Helicopters, missiles, training aircraft	1 900	2	50	3 160
DTN	Warships	1 650	3	5	2 650
GIAT	Tanks, armoured vehicles	1 000	5	40	500
Matra	Missiles	550	8	75	700
Panhard	Armoured vehicles	90	18	95	500
Thomson	Radars	2 000	1	60	1 170

[a] SIPRI trend indicator values in US $m. at constant (1985) prices.
Source: SIPRI data base and Dussauge, P., *L'industrie française de l'armement* (Economica: Paris, 1985).

One reason for this is that much of French research and development went into nuclear weapons, which are not exported. Another is that many of the weapons exported by French companies have been designed especially for the export market, like the Mirage-5 aircraft, or the F-2000 frigates, or have even been developed with financial assistance from other countries, like the Crotale missile that was developed with South African assistance (an improved version, the Shahine missile, was later developed with Saudi assistance). Also, French arms exports consist mainly of weapons that have been in series production for a longer time, such as the various helicopters built by Aérospatiale or the armoured vehicles from GIAT, Panhard and Renault, and for which it is difficult to charge R&D costs. Finally, the increasing competition on the world market for weapons has made it more and more difficult to be competitive. The DGA therefore had to exempt deals from the provision that R&D costs should be recovered from the customers.[40]

France has manoeuvred itself into a difficult position with respect to the economics of arms exports. Both for employment and for foreign exchange, arms exports have become a major factor. While economic studies show that more employment and foreign exchange could be gained from the export of civilian goods than from the export of arms, this is no viable short-term alternative for an industry that is stronger in exporting arms than civilian goods.[41]

Political issues

French governments of various political persuasions have maintained that arms exports are not predominantly driven by economic incentives, but are first and foremost part of French foreign policy. A typical statement reads as follows:

Because its arms exports afford friendly independent states the capacity to exercise their legitimate right to security without the political constraints generally tied to similar support from the superpowers, France offers a '*third route*', highly appreciated by a great number of states, and particularly the youngest among them.[42]

The roots of this argument can be found in Gaullist anti-superpower rhetoric of the 1960s, but it has been used by successive French governments. Outside observers, on the other hand, have attached much greater importance to the economic incentives for French arms exports.[43] As elsewhere, there is in France a mixture of both economic and political considerations.

An instructive set of examples of French arms export policy are the various embargoes the French Government has declared. An embargo is an anti-commercial measure which not only closes business with a certain customer, but can also harm the whole arms export business as other customers lose confidence in the security of their deliveries (embargoes were declared against Israel in 1969, South Africa in 1977, Libya in 1981, Chile in 1981 and Argentina in 1982). For all the embargoes declared, political motives have outweighed commercial interests. But in some cases the balance was close: in the case of

Libya deliveries of some items, such as fast attack craft and spare parts for Mirage fighters, continued while Libyan forces helped armed groups in Chad fight the Chad Government, which was backed by France. In the case of Argentina France was the first Western country to lift the embargo in August 1982. Chile was allowed to receive a replacement Mirage fighter in 1984, while the embargo was officially maintained.

There are also cases in which French embargoes might have been expected but did not occur, such as against South Africa until 1977. The continuation of French supplies to Iraq during the Iraq–Iran War, which started with an Iraqi invasion of Iranian territory, has led to much international and domestic criticism. Because of its arms-for-oil deals, and the large Iraqi arms debt to France, France has been banking on an Iraqi victory since the beginning of the war, supplying large amounts of weapons and in 1983 going so far as to lease Super Etendard fighters to the Iraqi armed forces until newly-built Mirage fighters arrived. The Super Etendards were borrowed from the French Air Force.

Expectations that the socialist government would change the arms export policy once it was in power were high. While still in opposition, both the communist and the socialist parties had criticized the arms export policy as a whole and specific deals. During the election campaign, socialist politicians declared that the arms business would be 'moralized', that no sales would be made to 'fascist or racist' regimes and that sales should be re-oriented towards Western recipients. Shortly after re-election, the government announced that all existing contracts would be honoured, except the delivery of armoured vehicles to Chile. In addition, an embargo was declared on further exports of weapons to Chile and it was decided that licences would no longer be granted for exports of certain types of weapon to other countries, such as Argentina and Libya.

There had also been some earlier attempts by the socialist party to extend parliamentary control over arms sales. In 1978, Jean-Pierre Cot and Charles Hernu, both later to become ministers in the first left-wing cabinet, had put forward a proposal that arms sales be put under parliamentary control. In November 1981 then Defence Minister Hernu announced that parliament would receive biennial reports on arms transfers and would also be informed about the conclusion of major deals.[44] Instead of parliamentary control, there was to be more information to the parliament.

Efforts to sell to Western industrialized countries were indeed increased after the left-wing parties came into power, but this was not combined with reduced arms sales to Third World countries.

The socialist government was able to continue French arms export policy without much political opposition. While it had been useful to oppose the arms export policies during the election campaign, the economic importance of arms exports put a formidable barrier on all efforts to limit sales. The conservative government which came into power in 1986 saw no reason to change the arms export policy inherited from its socialist predecessor.

V. The United Kingdom

The relative importance of the UK as an arms exporter dropped in the 1970s. While the UK was the next most important exporter of major weapons after the USA and the USSR in 1970, it lost this position to France soon afterwards. In the early 1980s exports of major weapons from the UK were on the level of those from Italy and FR Germany. The British arms industry profited less than other West European suppliers from the expansion of the arms market in the early 1970s. Behind this relative decline lay the changed role of Britain in the world, the position of the British arms industry at the high-technology end of the market and the restraint shown by the labour government between 1974 and 1979. The British share of exports of major weapons increased in the mid-1980s because of a massive sales drive by the conservative government which came into power in 1979.

The flow

British exports of major weapons to the Third World reached a high level in the early 1970s at which time the main customer was Iran (see figure 3.6). Other important recipients were former British colonies, such as India, Oman and Nigeria. The British arms industry still benefited from close ties between the British armed forces and armed forces in former colonies and also from the major role which the UK had played in the Middle East in the 1960s and 1970s.

British exports of major weapons have remained more or less at this level, with a slightly upward trend towards the early 1980s. When the world market for weapons expanded explosively in the mid-1970s, the British share in total Third World arms imports declined. This was mainly because Britain had little part in the increase in arms imports by the Middle East and North Africa. Whereas the Middle East was the most important buyer region for the UK throughout the entire period from 1971 to 1985, the share of British weapons in Middle Eastern imports is relatively low. During the 1970s, Iran remained an important customer for British weapons, but in 1979 the UK declared an embargo on exports to Iran. Large orders were placed by Jordan and Egypt in the late 1970s and Saudi Arabia became an important customer again in 1985, ordering a package of fighter and training aircraft valued at $3.2 billion. The most important single customer for British major weapons over the entire period 1971–85 was India, taking delivery of artillery, ships and aircraft and producing a number of British weapons under licence (figure 3.6). The UK also supplied weapons to Pakistan, though at a much lower level.

British exports of major weapons to South America grew in the 1970s, mainly because of exports of ships to a number of countries, such as Brazil and Argentina. Chile, a traditional importer of British weapons, was among the most important recipients despite an embargo on British sales to Chile between 1974 and 1980.

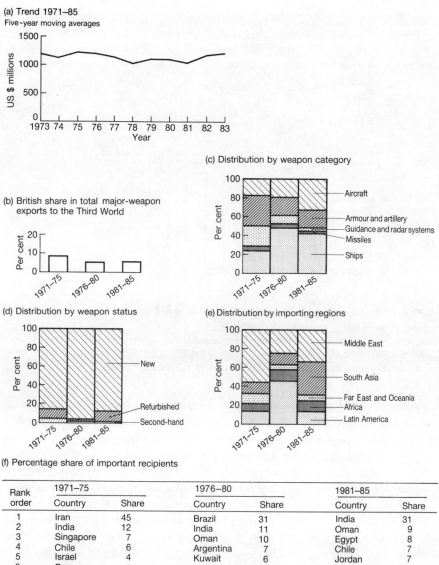

(a) Trend 1971–85
Five-year moving averages

(b) British share in total major-weapon exports to the Third World

(c) Distribution by weapon category

(d) Distribution by weapon status

(e) Distribution by importing regions

(f) Percentage share of important recipients

Rank order	1971–75		1976–80		1981–85	
	Country	Share	Country	Share	Country	Share
1	Iran	45	Brazil	31	India	31
2	India	12	India	11	Oman	9
3	Singapore	7	Oman	10	Egypt	8
4	Chile	6	Argentina	7	Chile	7
5	Israel	4	Kuwait	6	Jordan	7
6	Oman	3	Kenya	5	Nigeria	6
7	Brazil	3	Nigeria	5	Argentina	5
8	Nigeria	2	Ecuador	4	Pakistan	3
9	South Africa	2	Iran	3	Indonesia	3
10	Malaysia	2	Singapore	2	Iran	3
Total of ten[a]		85		82		83

[a] Figures may not add up to totals due to rounding.

Figure 3.6. British exports of major weapons to the Third World, 1971–85

Figures are based on SIPRI trend indicator values in US $m., at constant (1985) prices.

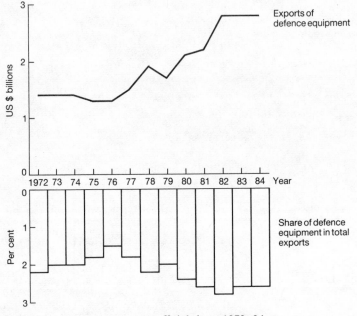

Figure 3.7. British arms exports: some official data, 1972–84

Values are in US $b., at constant (1985) prices.
Sources: British Ministry of Defence, *Statement on the Defence Estimates* (Her Majesty's Stationary Office: London, annual); International Monetary Fund, *International Financial Statistics* (IMF: Washington, DC, monthly).

The sales drive initiated by the Thatcher Government which gained power in 1979 did not immediately result in a large expansion of British exports of major weapons, but there was a definite increase in the export of other types of weapon, support equipment, and so on (see figure 3.7).

The government has encouraged the development of weapons especially designed for export and British procurement agencies are asked to bear in mind that weapons for the British armed forces should also be attractive to foreign customers. British companies are very active in the field of modernization and upgrading: for example, they offer upgrading kits for Soviet ships, tanks and artillery.

Institutional framework

The export of items which have military uses is controlled by the government under the Export of Goods (Control) Order. The licences are granted by the Department of Trade (formerly the Board of Trade). The Ministry of Defence (MoD), the Foreign and Commonwealth Office (FCO) and other ministries have to be consulted in the decision-making process. There are no legal rules, only general guidelines for policy. In practice, it is the MoD which dominates arms sales policy.[45] Since 1966, the Defence Sales Organization (DSO, in 1986 renamed Defence Export Services Organization), within the MoD, has been charged with facilitating British arms exports and working closely together with arms manufacturers. Its role has been described as a lubricant between the various government agencies, the customers and British companies. At the same time, the MoD has interests in limiting arms exports for security reasons. British weapons are not to fall into the hands of unfriendly states and secrets embodied in weapons have to be preserved. There is a secretariat within the MoD which works out the MoD position on arms sales. The FCO has a similar secretariat. Opinions from these two and other ministries concerned are then either referred to the Department of Trade by the MoD secretariat for approval of licence, if the ministries concur, or are discussed at interministerial meetings up to cabinet level in important cases. While the DSO has been in charge of marketing British weapons, companies owned by the government have been used to oversee actual weapon deals. The most important of these has been International Military Services (IMS). The IMS, which grew out of similar operations with other names, can act like a normal company, thereby shielding the government from political inconvenience, while at the same time guaranteeing the customer a close connection with the British Government. The IMS and its predecessors were heavily involved in arms sales to the Middle East, especially to Iran.

One aspect of arms sales which has become more and more important is the financing of deals. Only very few weapons are given away as military aid and many potential customers are short of cash. Bank loans are used to finance arms deals. The risk can be underwritten by the Export Credits Guarantee Committee after review by the Treasury. The criteria of credit-worthiness are the same as for civilian exports. Development aid cannot be used for financing arms exports. IMS and DSO are experienced in making packages, which include arms and, for example, goods as repayments from the recipient. In the sale of Tornado and other aircraft to Saudi Arabia in 1985, the major part of the Saudi payment was agreed to be in the form of oil, which is to be marketed by British companies. This way conditions can be made more attractive for the customer.

The traditional good relations between British armed forces and those in the Third World are of advantage for British weapon suppliers. Not only do active and retired officers have many contacts, there is also considerable knowledge of British weapon systems throughout the Third World. British expertise, both in military training and in the maintenance and repair of weapons, has spread freely to the Third World. In Saudi Arabia, for example, throughout the 1970s, a detachment of around 3000 employees of British Aerospace was engaged in building up the country's air defences. The military academy at Sandhurst has a high standing and is only one of the places where officers and soldiers from Third World countries are educated. This is another way in which the government supports arms sales, in addition to high-level political support, arms fairs and the operation of the DSO.

Arms production

Arms production is an important economic activity in the UK. According to official statistics, more than 700 000 jobs were supported directly and indirectly by arms production. This is equal to about 3.6 per cent of the total labour force in the early 1980s.[46]

Research and development for the armed forces takes up a large share of total government-sponsored R&D—more than 50 per cent in the early 1980s. Although there are no institutional requirements, the spin-off of technological advances from military to civilian technology is expected to stimulate the economy.[47] The very high level of military R&D has enabled the British arms industry to remain at a high technological level in a number of crucial areas. It is in general the most advanced in Western Europe and in some fields, such as electronics and tank protection, it is even more advanced than US industry. British weapons have a tendency to be sophisticated and expensive. This latter feature has been picked out as a factor contributing to the decline in the British share of exports of major weapons to the Third World. The development of weapons tailored for exports was one of the central elements of the export drive of the early 1980s.

Arms exports are an important part of the output of arms-producing industries. The share of arms exports in total arms production has fluctuated between 25 and 30 per cent throughout the 1970s and dropped slightly below 25 per cent in the mid-1980s with post-Falklands/Malvinas War expansions of the British procurement budget. More than three-quarters of British arms exports go to Third World countries.[48] Arms exports provided employment for about 80 000 persons directly and an additional 50 000 or so indirectly in the early 1980s.

Arms production is especially important in the aerospace sector, involving over 60 per cent of total output, in the electronics sector, with almost 30 per cent and in shipbuilding, with around 50 per cent. Although a large number of firms are involved in arms production, a few prominent major companies comprise the core of the arms industry and many of them have been active in the sector for a long time (table 3.5). There have been many changes of ownership, both as companies grew and swallowed others and as a result of government action.

The labour government that came to power in 1974 wanted to nationalize the major companies in the traditional areas of arms production. This affected primarily the aerospace sector. Aside from Westland (producing helicopters and hovercraft) the major factories were united under the umbrella of British Aerospace. Naval shipyards became part of the naval division of British Shipbuilders. In addition the government already had control over the Royal Ordnance Factories (ROF), the former army arsenal, and Rolls Royce, the engine manufacturer. Except for the important companies in the electronics sector, such as GEC, EMI, Smith, Plessey and Racal, the government had control of the armaments sector. But there is no evidence that this changed the outlook of the companies towards arms exports.

Table 3.5. Some British companies exporting major weapons to Third World countries

Name	Export weapons produced	Turnover in arms production, c. 1983, in $m.	Rank among British arms producers c. 1983	Share of exports in arms production c. 1983 (%)	Exports of major weapons to Third World, 1971–85[a]
British Shipbuilders	Warships	(750)	3	(30)	3 245
British Aerospace	Fighter aircraft, training aircraft, transport aircraft, missiles	(2 400)	1	(55)	2 633
Royal Ordnance Factories	Armoured vehicles, artillery	650	4	42	1 015
Vickers	Armoured vehicles	(100)	12	. .	736
Westland	Helicopters, hovercraft	(300)	7	(60)	728
Short Brothers	Transport aircraft, missiles	(100)	11	(60)	413

[a]SIPRI trend indicator values in US $m. at constant (1985) prices.
. . = not available.
Source: SIPRI data base.

The new conservative government in 1979 started a programme of reprivatization, including not only the companies nationalized earlier, but also Rolls Royce and Royal Ordnance Factories. In the mid-1980s, the arms production sector was almost totally in private ownership.

Although arms exports are quite important for employment and also for the balance of trade (see figure 3.7), the economic importance of arms exports was played down by successive British governments. Instead, the contribution of exports to lowering the costs of weapons for the British armed forces was stressed. It is in exactly this respect, however, that the economic contribution of arms exports is doubtful. Because of the composition of British arms exports, the recoupment of R&D expenditures via the sale of weapon systems to foreign customers is limited.[49] Nevertheless the production of arms for exports does keep personnel employed in arms production even when the demand from the British armed forces is low. Another important motive for British arms exports is to broaden the arms-industrial base and to maintain the industrial capacity to produce almost all types of weapon system.

Political issues

The UK was the first West European country to follow the lead of the USA in the 1960s in commercializing arms exports, by creating the DSO as a marketing operation in charge of trying to sell as many British weapons as possible. This took place in 1966, under a labour government. Although the basic attitude towards arms exports has not changed under successive governments, there were some differences in details.

The governments have based their position on the perception of a Third World of free nations needing to defend themselves with the help of weapons. The head of the DSO in 1978, when Labour was in power, expressed it in this way: 'The present Government's stated attitude towards requests for exports of defence equipment is based on the respect for the right of other countries, as sovereign states, to protect their independence and to exercise their right of self-defence.'[50] It is line with this reasoning that the British Government, unlike those of the USA and the USSR, does not use arms exports as a major instrument of foreign policy. Of course there is the DSO, with its various arms exhibitions, the annual British Defence Equipment Catalogue and the floating arms exhibitions travelling around the world. But the main role of the government is to receive notifications about possible deals from the companies or the DSO sales agents and to decide whether or not to grant a licence. If there are no strong reasons against granting such a licence, then the fact that a country requests weapons—plus the economic gains for the British economy—are enough for government support. A number of problems have arisen with respect to this seemingly simple arms export policy.

First, the mixture of control and marketing invested in the Ministry of Defence creates a dilemma. The MoD has strong interests in exporting arms in order to strengthen the arms industry. Its inclination towards control is limited to not undermining the British and Western position towards the Soviet Union and other countries that are considered unfriendly. There are cases in which the countervailing body, the FCO, has been overruled or by-passed, for example in the various deals with the Shah of Iran in the late 1970s.[51] The predominance of the MoD also means that British military policies are co-ordinated with those of the USA. The latent integration of British arms sales in a larger framework of Western policy towards the Third World contradicts the basic premise of supplying weapons to all nations wanting to defend themselves.

Second, in practice it is often very hard to decide whether countries will only use weapons in self-defence. An obvious counter-example was the Argentinian attack on the Falkland/Malvinas Islands in April 1982. Until March of that year the UK had supplied Argentina with military materials, including detailed maps of the islands. The use of weapons for internal repression is part of the same problem. British companies have special expertise in this area (partly as an outgrowth of weapons designed for use by the British armed forces in Northern Ireland). The labour governments have been reluctant to sell weapons that could be used for internal repression and have not granted licences in a number of cases, ranging from Chile to Uganda. The conservative governments have taken a different stand, allowing exports of such items to Pakistan and Indonesia, though not to Chile.

Third, recipient countries do not interpret deliveries as pure commercial transactions but as some kind of political commitment, and this view is shared by countries which have unfriendly relations with the recipients. The UK supplies a number of Middle Eastern countries, but not Israel. It was a major supplier to Iran, but not to Iraq. There is an embargo on exports to Taiwan, mostly because of the British interest in good relations with China. Arms exports are part of foreign policy, even if the government would prefer it otherwise.

There have only been slight differences in outlook between various governments with respect to the willingness to participate in efforts to limit the arms trade. The labour government voiced favour for such efforts if the co-operation of suppliers and recipients could be obtained. The conservative government was also in support of multilateral arms control in principle, but insisted that the only safe and sensible approach to restraint in international trade in military equipment is one which involves both suppliers and recipients on the basis of regional agreements.[52] Since 1974, all governments have been willing to observe the UN embargo against South Africa, which had not been the case with previous conservative governments. There continued, however, to be a string of accusations that British military material reached South Africa, including spare parts for tanks and military radars.[53] Some of the material had reached South Africa illegally, while in other cases the government maintained that the material in question was civilian. The British arms export regulations exclude some items which are classified as military in the USA, for example.

This was evident when the US Government complained about deliveries of spare parts and other items to Iran in the early 1980s.[54]

Since Britain ceased to be a global colonial power, the arms export policy has been fairly consistent despite changes of government, despite various restructurings of the arms industry, including nationalization and privatization, and despite a number of major problems—for example when British weapons were turned against British forces in the Falklands/Malvinas War, or when the cancellation of Iranian orders after the fall of the Shah led to economic problems in the arms industry. There has been a growing promotion apparatus, headed in practice by the Prime Minister and lubricated by the perceived economic and political gains. On the other hand, there has been selective control and restraint—sometimes less, sometimes more—to countries at war, or close to war, and countries violating human rights.

VI. Italy

Italian arms exports grew at high rates during the 1970s. Italy became one of the group of second-string suppliers of major weapons. Exports from Italy are concentrated in a few areas in which the relatively small Italian arms industry has acquired comparative advantages. There have been very few restrictions on arms-exporting companies, allowing deliveries to many trouble-spots in the Third World. In the 1980s, the growth in exports of major weapons came to a halt because of increasing competition from other exporters producing weapons on a similar technological level.

The flow

Major weapon exports from Italy grew at an average annual rate of 21 per cent between 1971 and 1985. Most of the growth occurred in the second half of the 1970s, when the average annual rate was as high as 36 per cent. In the early 1980s the growth curve levelled out.

In the 1950s and 1960s Italy had been a minor supplier of ships and aircraft to Middle Eastern and African countries. During the Viet Nam War, when US companies were working at full capacity, Italian aircraft produced under licence were ordered by many armed forces, particularly in the Middle East. The most important customer in the early 1970s, though, was South Africa, which was producing various Italian aircraft under licence, most notably the Impala. Italy officially declared that it would follow the UN embargo of 1977 against South Africa and deliveries of weapon systems came to a halt (deliveries of parts for the production of Impalas in South Africa continued into the early 1980s).

While exports of aircraft continued to increase steadily, the major export increases of the second half of the 1970s came in the naval field. Corvettes, frigates, destroyers and other ships were sold to a number of Latin American, African and Middle Eastern countries; these regions were the major recipients

(a) Trend 1971–85
Five-year moving averages

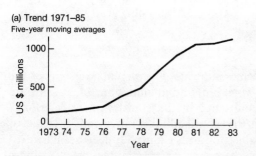

(b) Italian share in total major-weapon exports to the Third World

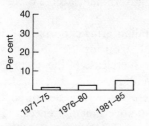

(c) Distribution by weapon category

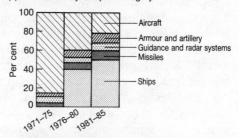

- Aircraft
- Armour and artillery
- Guidance and radar systems
- Missiles
- Ships

(d) Distribution by weapon status

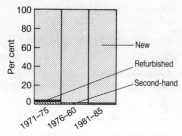

- New
- Refurbished
- Second-hand

(e) Distribution by importing regions

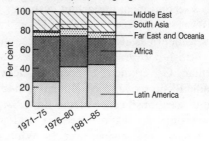

- Middle East
- South Asia
- Far East and Oceania
- Africa
- Latin America

(f) Percentage shares of important recipients

Rank order	1971–75		1976–80		1981–85	
	Country	Share	Country	Share	Country	Share
1	South Africa	30	Peru	23	Venezuela	25
2	Iran	18	Libya	20	Libya	21
3	Brazil	17	Iran	12	Iraq	15
4	Venezuela	7	Venezuela	11	Ecuador	8
5	Zambia	7	Thailand	6	Peru	8
6	Libya	6	Somalia	5	Thailand	5
7	Argentina	3	Brazil	4	Nigeria	4
8	Morocco	3	Argentina	3	Egypt	3
9	Philippines	3	Tunisia	3	Argentina	2
10	India/Zaire	1	Egypt	2	Somalia	1
Total of ten[a]		95		90		92

[a] Figures may not add up to totals due to rounding.

Figure 3.8. Italian exports of major weapons to the Third World, 1971–85

Figures are based on SIPRI trend indicator values in US $m., at constant (1985) prices.

of Italian major weapons (see figure 3.8). With the expansion of ship exports, deliveries of missiles and electronic systems for ships also grew substantially.

Institutional framework

Pre-World War II government decrees stipulate government oversight of the exports of weapons of war (*armi da guerra*) and ammunition. Light arms are controlled by extra regulations administered by the Ministry of the Interior.[55]

The Ministry of Foreign Trade is the central administrative body involved in reviewing applications from companies for arms exports. If deals seem controversial, decisions are made by an interministerial committee which includes representatives from the Ministries of Defence, Foreign Affairs and Finance. Their considerations are based on an unpublished government decree of 1975 (*Decreto ministeriale* 20 Mar. 1975, no. 5544).

It can be inferred from what is known about Italian arms exports that, in practice, hardly any restrictions are exercised. In 1979, during the US-hostage crisis in Iran, deliveries to Iran were stopped. After the release of the hostages, deliveries resulting from unfulfilled contracts were resumed, but no new contracts for major weapons were concluded. There were deliveries of small arms and spare parts, though—but probably without government licences.[56] In early 1986, a partial embargo was placed on deliveries to Libya, which had been Italy's second most important customer for major weapons in the early 1980s. This was in answer to an urgent US call to stop deliveries to Libya. The Italian Government has also had to take account of other pressures, for example from the British Government during the Falklands/Malvinas War, or the West German Government concerning deliveries of German-designed tanks to Middle Eastern countries. (Italian arms exports are also legally restricted in the case of weapons licenced from the USA, see below.)

Not only are export permits seldom refused, some arms exports have occurred without proper licences. While it is in the nature of the issue that not much information is available, it seems that substantial amounts of exports of small arms, mines, ammunition, spare parts, and so on, bypass the Italian Government.[57]

Several attempts have been made in the Italian parliament to strengthen control over arms exports, notably in the late 1970s during the boom phase of Italian arms exports and again in the mid-1980s. None of the initiatives of the late 1970s led anywhere. In 1985 the Defence Minister introduced a law to regulate arms exports that would give more controlling power to the Foreign Ministry. This law did not foresee much more publicity about arms exports, nor parliamentary influence on decision-making (by the time of writing, no decision had been made). While there is little government restriction, there is also little government support for arms exports. There is no government sales agency corresponding to those of France and the UK (the one major arms exhibition — the naval expo in Genoa — is organized by private industry) and there is no special financial support for the export of weapons. The absence of a government marketing infrastructure was criticized by the arms-producing companies in the early 1980s. In response the government has set up a joint government–industry committee to study possible reforms in the structure of arms production, the promotion of exports, and so on. For the time being, marketing is carried out by the companies.

Arms production

Italy spends comparatively little money on the procurement of weapons—about one-quarter of the British or West German investment. The amount spent on R&D is even lower. Here the ratio to the UK was about 1:20 in the early 1980s. The financial manoeuvring space for the domestic arms industry is therefore very small.

In the 1950s and 1960s, two strategies were pursued to build up an arms industry despite these limits. One was to build US weapons under licence, the other was to design rather simple weapons. The export expansion of the 1970s was largely built on these foundations. Weapons produced under US licence, such as helicopters and electronic components, and simple designs of training and transport aircraft, small arms, mines, ammunition and explosives, provided the bulk of exports up to the mid-1970s. The speciality of Italian arms exports since then, the sale of warships, can be traced to the deliberate policy of converting civilian shipyards to warship production. In response to the crisis in shipbuilding resulting from increased competition from East Asian shipyards and the fall of freight rates in the early 1970s, the government launched a major naval re-equipment programme in 1975. While the programme had to be extended and changed several times for financial reasons, it provided the Italian naval industry with a major impetus.

With the expansion of arms exports and the relatively much slower growth of domestic arms procurement, the Italian arms industry has become highly dependent upon exports. This dependence was in the range of 70 per cent of output in the late 1970s, and still over 50 per cent in the early 1980s. These percentages are higher than for any other of the major exporters of weapons. About 90 per cent of exports go to Third World countries (see also table 3.6).

The whole arms industry employed about 80 000 persons directly and another 40 000 indirectly in the early 1980s (the number of persons employed indirectly is low if compared with other major exporters, since many pre-products and components are imported). This was equal to about 2.5 per cent of total employment in Italy. The contribution of arms exports to the foreign trade balance is on a similar level. The share of arms exports in total exports was around 2 per cent in the early 1970s, grew to around 3 per cent at the turn of the decade and has since returned to a level of just over 2 per cent.[58]

In the early 1980s, 60 per cent of the aerospace industry, over 40 per cent of shipbuilding and about 15 per cent of the electronics industry depended on military orders.[59] While the share for the aircraft industry was similar to that in other Western countries, the share for shipbuilding was exceptionally high.

Table 3.6. Some Italian companies exporting major weapons to Third World countries

Name	Export weapons produced	Turnover in arms production, 1983 in US $m. (1985 prices)	Rank among Italian arms producers	Share of exports in arms production, 1983 (%)	Exports of major weapons to Third World, 1971–85[a]
Fincantieri	Warships	400	6	53	2 800
OTO-Melara	Armoured vehicles, missiles, missile guidance	730	2	55	950
Aermacchi	Training aircraft, attack aircraft	130	9	60	610
Aeritalia	Transport aircraft	500	4	65	580
Agusta	Helicopters	460	4	80	570

[a]SIPRI trend indicator values in US $m. at constant (1985) prices.
Sources: SIPRI data base and Rossi, S.A., 'The Italian defence industry with respect to international competition', *Defence Today*, no. 77–78, 1984.

Most of the arms production is carried out by a number of large state holdings. For these holdings, as well as for the largest producer, the private FIAT company, arms do not constitute the major part of production. There are a number of smaller producers, though, some of them subsidiaries of foreign arms producers (Oerlikon, Contraves) which are dependent on arms production to a much greater extent. The rather complex and diverse structure of the Italian arms industry was seen as one major reason for its stagnating competitiveness on the world market in the early 1980s. Efforts were started to reorganize the state sector, reducing some of the competition among state-owned companies (such as that between Aeritalia and Agusta) and combining efforts more closely with some private firms.

One consequence of the way in which the Italian arms industry was built up is that most of the weapons offered are in what could be called the middle level of technology. Only in some areas, such as naval guns, mines or naval electronics are Italian companies in the forefront of technology. In the 1970s, this profile of the Italian arms industry helped its exports. Customers were looking for modern weapons, but were reluctant to opt for too advanced technology. In the 1980s, the structure of the arms market changed to the disadvantage of many Italian arms producers. On the one hand, the competition from 'below', from other, 'new' producers such as Spain, Israel and Brazil has increased considerably. On the other hand, traditional exporters from the 'high end' (from France, the UK, the USA) have tried to scale down weapon systems in order to gain orders.

The Italian response has been to try to increase the technological level of the arms industry. A major ingredient in this effort are joint projects with arms producers in other West European countries. In addition, one objective of the reform of arms production initiated in the early 1980s was to increase the funding for R&D.

Political issues

The justification given for a liberal stance on arms exports is basically economic. Arms exports provide employment and contribute to the trade balance. In addition, it is argued that arms exports sustain, and have indeed expanded, the Italian arms industry beyond the level that could be achieved by Italian orders. In this way arms exports provide a safety margin in times of crisis.[60] This last argument has to be weighed against the high dependence of Italian arms production on foreign components. It is also doubtful whether much contribution can be made to the R&D efforts of individual companies, given the competitive nature of the arms business. It seems more likely that some of the R&D spent by the Italian Government for development of weapons for the Italian armed forces has helped the companies to increase exports. This seems to be the case in shipbuilding, for example, where the 1975 programme helped to improve the weapons offered on the world market, or as regards armoured vehicles from OTO Melara, where production for the Italian armed forces preceded exports of similar weapons.

Critics of the Italian Government's arms export policy have focused their attention on the moral aspects. Italian weapons have often gone to crisis areas, for example, to both Iraq and Iran in the early 1980s, and to customers which had difficulties in obtaining weapons from other Western suppliers, such as South Africa in the early 1970s and Libya in the early 1980s. The then Defence Minister, Giovanni Spadolini, said in 1984 that there was a need to 'moralize' arms exports.[61] As a first step critics have proposed to sharpen control in order to be able to then apply some criteria which follow from a discussion on the moral and political aspects of arms production. The public interest in these issues is rather high.[62]

The high content of foreign imports and foreign technology in Italian arms production has imposed some restrictions on Italian arms exports. The USA has repeatedly refused to allow exports of components originating in the USA to be exported to third countries, for example, in 1980 Libya was denied the G-222 transport aircraft, since the plane has US-made engines. The Italian response was to re-equip the aircraft to use British engines. In general, the Italian arms industry has tried to substitute dependence on US companies by dependence on West European companies. West European companies are much less likely to be bound by their respective governments when it comes to the delivery of components and technology. The one counter-example is that of the West German Government pressuring West German companies not to participate in the scheme to produce a derivative of the Leopard-1 tank in Italy for delivery to Middle Eastern countries. OTO Melara instead had to opt for more Italian components and a design called the OF-40 tank (which still resembles the Leopard to a considerable extent). Otherwise, though, Italy has become the place to go for West European companies when the restrictions in their own countries might hamper exports. The two Swiss-owned companies Oerlikon and Contraves are examples of this approach. It would of course be possible for the West European governments concerned to control delivery of technology and components to Italy, in the same way as the USA, in order to impose their stricter rules on the less strict exporter Italy instead of seeing their rules undermined by and reduced to the lower level of Italian arms transfer control.

VII. The People's Republic of China

China was a minor though important supplier of weapons in the 1960s. It supported a large number of guerrilla movements in the Middle East, Africa and Asia, and sent weapons to some neighbouring states such as North Korea, North Vietnam and Pakistan. While the support of bordering states (excluding Viet Nam after 1974) continued in the 1970s and 1980s, the number of guerrilla movements that received Chinese weapons decreased from the early 1970s. In the late 1970s, Chinese exports of weapons started to increase and a new market was found in the Middle East. Available information indicates that China became one of the important exporters of major weapons once more. While in the past weapons had mostly been given away, by the late 1970s customers in the Middle East and elsewhere had to pay for what they received. Arms exports became regarded as a vital source of income and a major export drive, using conventional marketing methods such as advertisements and trade fairs, was started in 1984. Changes in the Chinese arms export policy reflect changes in the country's foreign and industrial policies.

The flow

Information about Chinese arms exports is scanty. This has been the case since the 1950s, when exports started with deliveries to North Korea and North Vietnam, but was recently newly highlighted by alleged Chinese deliveries of aircraft and armoured vehicles to the Middle East. According to various reports, large amounts of Chinese-produced weapons have reached both Iraq and Iran since the war started in 1980. While some reports imply direct Chinese deliveries, others suggest that various circuitous routes have been used, for example via Egypt and Jordan for deliveries to Iraq and via North Korea for deliveries to Iran. Official Chinese sources have invariably denied supporting either side through the delivery of major weapons. In line with SIPRI policy as described in the appendix on sources and methods, SIPRI has adopted reports that seemed to come from various independent sources without being able to verify them independently. The information remains scanty and it would be useful if the Chinese Government would supply more and reconcilable information about its arms exports.

With all the necessary reservations as to the accuracy of the data, two periods can be distinguished with respect to Chinese exports of major weapons for the 1970s and 1980s. During the first period, which lasted until about 1977, China contributed about 2 per cent of the total exports of major weapons to the Third World (see figure 3.9). The majority of deliveries were to states in South East Asia and South Asia with which China had friendly relations. China ceased to support guerrilla movements in these areas. In Africa, where guerrilla movements had enjoyed substantial Chinese support in the 1960s, deliveries from China remained important for only a few customers in the 1970s, such as Tanzania, Zambia, Zaire, Congo and the ZANU (Zimbabwean National Union) liberation movement.

During the second period the level of Chinese arms exports increased with the addition of a number of customers in the Middle East, notably Egypt but also Sudan and Somalia, and, reportedly, later Iraq and Iran. The Chinese share in total exports of major weapons increased to an estimated 3.5 per cent in the early 1980s. China became one of the major exporters of weapons to the Third World.

The types of weapons sold did not change much during the 1970s and early 1980s. Most of them were copies of Soviet weapons designed in the 1950s and earlier and there were also some Chinese-designed armoured vehicles and ships. The low technological level of Chinese weapons exported was an advantage as

(a) Trend 1971–85
Five-year moving averages

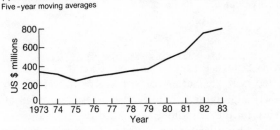

(b) Chinese share in total major-weapon exports to the Third World

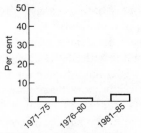

(c) Distribution by weapon category

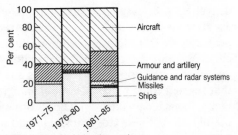

(d) Distribution by weapon status

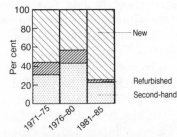

(e) Distribution by importing regions

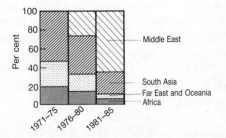

(f) Percentage share of important recipients

Rank order	1971–75		1976–80		1981–85	
	Country	Share	Country	Share	Country	Share
1	Pakistan	45	Pakistan	32	Egypt	31
2	N.Korea	16	Egypt	26	Iran	28
3	Tanzania	15	Kampuchea	10	Pakistan	18
4	N. Vietnam	12	N. Korea	9	Iraq	6
5	Bangladesh	8	Bangladesh	8	Bangladesh	5
Total of 5[a]		95		85		88

[a] Figures may not add up to totals due to rounding.

Figure 3.9. Chinese exports of major weapons to the Third World, 1971–85

Figures are based on SIPRI trend indicator values in US $m., at constant (1985) prices.

long as the recipients were mostly guerrilla movements or regular armed forces lacking high technological competence. When arms exports to Middle Eastern countries were increased from 1978, the weapons exported were much the same as those exported to Asian and African countries earlier. Technological advances are a pre-condition, though, for further expansion of arms exports. China has sought the co-operation of foreign companies in France, FR Germany, Israel, Italy, the UK and the USA to upgrade Chinese weapon systems with Western electronics.[63]

Arms production

It is not clear from the outside who decides about Chinese arms exports. Since arms exports are an element of foreign policy, as well as industrial and military policy, involvement of the respective ministries in charge is probable. But the final decision in all likelihood lies with the Central Military Commission of the Chinese Communist Party's Central Committee (with identical membership to the State Military Commission). This Commission exercises political control over the military forces as well as the arms production factories. Although little is known about arms exports and associated decision-making in China, somewhat more is known about Chinese arms production. The level and structure of arms production have been debated intensely at various points in time. This is unsurprising given the size of the armaments sector. It is estimated to produce around 10 per cent of the total industrial output of China and to employ somewhere between 2 and 6 million people. This would be equivalent to 5–15 per cent of the industrial workforce.[64]

During and after the Chinese Cultural Revolution of the late 1960s, the arms industry was in a privileged position, being able to expand on the basis laid with Soviet help in the 1950s. In 1971, this privileged position was questioned both from within the armed forces and by the 'conservative' wing of the party leadership. This debate became known as the 'electronics versus steel' controversy. It posed those in favour of expanding and modernizing the arms industry to meet the US challenge against those advocating priority for the overall development of heavy industry to compete with the Soviet Union in the long term. It ended with a victory of the 'steel' side, and only shortly predated the downfall of then Defence Minister Lin Biao, nominated to succeed Chairman Mao, and the reopening of diplomatic channels with the USA. The output of the arms industries did not expand further. Around 1975, military industrial directives were changed. In early 1975, Premier Zhou Enlai presented to the Fourth National People's Congress a plan to modernize the economy, which later became known under the heading of the 'four modernizations'. The military sector was only fourth on the list of modernizations but, still, efforts were made to raise the technological level. One hotly debated issue was whether foreign technology should be imported for this purpose. Some technology eventually was imported, for example, helicopters from France and aircraft engines from the UK. Some of the arms deals of the time were also motivated by the wish to import foreign technology, for example the trading of modern Soviet fighter aircraft (MiG-23), in the possession of the Egyptian armed forces, against spare parts and aircraft produced in China.

After the ousting of the 'gang of four', the expansion of arms production in China was once more given lower priority and, according to available estimates, halted.[65] The power struggle was over and the new civilian leadership gradually took more control of the military sector and arms production. The bureaucracy in charge of arms production was changed several times in efforts to bring it in line with the demands—first voiced at the Third Plenum of the eleventh Party Congress in December 1978—for rationalization, greater efficiency and higher profitability in arms production. Gradually, the economic accountability of the branches of the arms industry increased vis-à-vis the central management. The various ministries formerly in charge of arms production were supplemented with corporations dealing with imports and exports of weapon systems (see table 3.7). While arms production remains an activity guided by national security interests, arms-producing firms have been expected to work in a commercial way since the early 1980s.

Arms-producing establishments reacted in various ways to ride the tide of changes. The surplus capacity that had grown during the 1970s could either be used to produce civilian goods or to expand arms exports. In a first phase after 1978, arms industries mainly increased their output of civilian goods. This was made easier by the economic planning goal of increasing the output of light industrial products, such as bicycles and household consumer goods. In the mid-1980s, it was estimated that around 40 per cent of the output of the designated arms industries, integrated in the arms industrial sector, was for civilian markets in China.[66] Arms exports were also increased, but the real push for arms exports came only later, probably during the Iraq–Iran War. From about 1984 arms exports have become a major activity for the arms-producing industries via their commercial outlets (see table 3.7). These corporations have participated in arms exhibitions all over the world, staged their own arms exhibitions in China and advertised in international arms trade journals. Whether their activities are still strictly controlled by the Central Military Commission, or some other political body, is not known. Neither is it known to what extent the various corporations act as private enterprises within China, since they remain significant for China's national security.

One indication of the behaviour of Chinese arms-producing corporations and the willingness to abandon political control is the creation of marketing companies outside China. The National Aviation Technology Import–Export Corporation has set up a joint company with Lucas Aerospace of the UK, to market an improved version of the F-7 (similar to the Soviet MiG-21) aircraft, with Western electronics. The company is based in Hong Kong and is not under Chinese political control. The same is true of the Singapore Aircraft Industry, a company that has been given the task of marketing other Chinese aircraft world-wide. Other such companies either have been set up or are in the process of being set up.

Table 3.7.   Structure of the Chinese conventional arms production sector

Output responsibility	In charge		Associated corporation
	before May 1982	after May 1982	
Co-ordination of production and procurement	National Defence Industries Office/ National Defence Science and Technology Commission (NDSTC)	NDSTC	Xinshidai Corp.
Aircraft	Third Ministry of Machine-Industry (Third MMI)	Ministry of Aviation Industry	National Aviation Technology Import-Export Corp. (CATIC)
Electronics	Fourth MMI	Ministry of Electronics Industry	China Electronics Import-Export Corp. (CEIEC)
Ordnance	Fifth MMI	Ministry of Ordnance	China North Industries Corp. (NORINCO)
Shipbuilding	Sixth MMI	China State Shipbuilding Corp. (CSSC)	
Missiles	Seventh MMI	Ministry of Space Industry	China Precision Machinery Import-Export Corp. (CPMIEC)
Space	Eighth MMI (founded 1979, merged with Seventh MMI in 1981)		China Great Wall Industries

Sources: Jammes, S., 'China' in Ball, N. and Lietenberg, M. (eds), *The Structure of the Defence Industry* (Taylor & Francis: London, 1983), pp. 268–69; *Jane's Defence Weekly*, 3 Aug. 1985, pp. 215–21.

The recent Chinese export drive is based on commercial motives. While Chinese arms seem to have been supplied to customers free of charge up until the late 1970s, most customers now have to pay for them. The prices seem to vary and are low in comparison to those of Western equipment.[67] From US data on Chinese arms production, it can be calculated that exports have constituted around 10 per cent of production in the recent past, and have amounted to about 6 per cent of total Chinese exports.[68] If these figures are reliable and reflect monetary income from arms sales, arms production for export has become a major industrial activity for China.

Political issues

Three main strands of Chinese arms export policy, though sometimes competing, have persisted alongside each other over the years.

The first and, until recently, most important is the support of friendly states in the region. North Korea and North Vietnam were the first recipients of Chinese military aid. Later Pakistan, as a counterweight to Soviet-supplied India, became a mainstay of Chinese regional policy. From 1983, Thailand has also become a recipient of Chinese weapons. While North Korea and North Vietnam could be judged to be in the same political camp as China, some later recipients certainly have not been. Pakistan received most of its Chinese tanks and aircraft when it was an Islamic military dictatorship. Thailand is firmly Western-oriented.

The first strand of Chinese arms export policy has at times been at odds with the second, the support of revolutionary movements in the Third World. During its heyday in the 1960s this policy extended to a large number of countries in Africa, Asia and the Middle East, including anti-government guerrilla movements in Thailand. The support of such movements lay in the internationalist ideology of communist China, but it also served the more narrow purpose of national security since it went almost exclusively to anti-Soviet movements. Some elements of the support of progressive movements can still be seen in Chinese arms export policy, for example, in the support of the government in Zimbabwe that emerged from the ranks of the Chinese-supported ZANU guerrilla. In other cases of weapon deliveries to countries far from China the motives are less clear, as for example in the case of Zaire or Tanzania. It can be speculated that anti-Soviet rivalry still plays a role, for example when Somalia received Chinese weapons after the break with the Soviet Union in 1977. The only guerrilla movements known to receive strong support in the mid-1980s were Afghan and Kampuchean groups. Given their ideological persuasions, the Chinese support can not only be attributed to the internationalist attitudes of the Chinese communists but must be seen in the context of the first strand of Chinese arms export policy, that of regional policy.

The third strand of Chinese arms export policy was the latest to be introduced. It is based on the commercialization of the arms industry and the search for profits. The fact that most sales in this category have gone to the Middle East does not follow from Chinese foreign policy priorities, but from demand patterns in the international arms market. Like other new low-cost suppliers China has had to export most of its weapons to crisis spots—in this case, available reports indicate, the Iraq–Iran War. Chinese arms export policy has come a long way from the 1960s to the 1980s. The long-standing policy of not selling weapons has been reversed. Chinese arms-producing companies are among the ones using capitalistic marketing channels most aggressively, whereas before they were advising communist guerrilla leaders.

Despite these drastic changes and increases in the level of arms exports, little is known of the possible internal debate about arms export policy in China, or of criticism about the predominance of commercial incentives over political control for at least a part of Chinese arms exports. The changes in arms export policy were embedded in overall changes in foreign policy that from the early 1970s postulated less Chinese involvement in the affairs of other countries, and changes in the military-industrial sector, which in turn were part of a general reorientation of industrial policy towards more economic accountability and commercialism of production units. This reorientation did not exclude arms-producing companies.

VIII. The Federal Republic of Germany

Between the mid- and late 1970s the Federal Republic of Germany emerged as one of the leading exporters of weapons. Up to the late 1960s, arms exports were limited because the arms industry was small and mainly supplied the West German *Bundeswehr*. In the early 1970s, a strictly restrictive arms export policy was adopted. Although this was successively relaxed from the mid-1970s because of economic and political pressures, FR Germany is still more restrictive than allied countries such as France or the UK. Joint ventures with companies in these countries have further eroded the West German restrictive position.

The flow

In the mid-1980s FR Germany was one of the more important suppliers of major weapons to the Third World—in a league with the UK and Italy. Compared with the West German share in world exports of civilian manufactured goods, however, the West German share in global arms exports was comparatively low. There had been rapid growth, from a low level, in the late 1970s and early 1980s. Most of the major weapons traded were ships—submarines, fast attack craft, support ships, frigates and corvettes. The major customers were Argentina, Nigeria, Colombia and Kuwait (see figure 3.10), West German exports going mainly to regions and countries outside the major markets of the 1970s (i.e., the Middle East and North Africa).

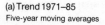

(a) Trend 1971–85
Five-year moving averages

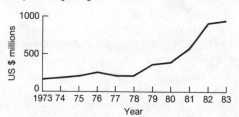

(b) West German share in total major-weapon
exports to the Third World

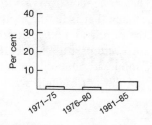

(c) Distribution by weapon category

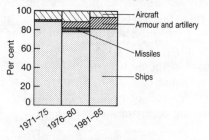

(d) Distribution by weapon status

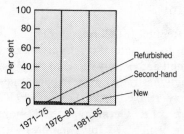

(e) Distribution by importing regions

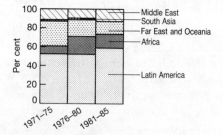

(f) Percentage shares of important recipients

Rank order	1971–75		1976–80		1981–85	
	Country	Share	Country	Share	Country	Share
1	Singapore	27	Ecuador	25	Argentina	40
2	Argentina	23	Malaysia	14	Nigeria	14
3	Colombia	16	Venezuela	14	Colombia	11
4	Iran	8	UAE	8	Malaysia	9
5	Brazil	6	Peru	7	Kuwait	6
6	Ecuador	6	Nigeria	7	Indonesia	4
7	Nigeria	3	Chile	4	Chile	4
8	Israel	2	Ghana	4	UAE	4
9	Ghana	2	Sudan	2	Peru	4
10	Zambia	2	Philippines	2	Bahrain	2
Total of ten[a]		96		89		98

[a] Figures may not add up to totals due to rounding.

Figure 3.10. West German exports of major weapons to the Third World, 1971–85
Figures are based on SIPRI trend indicator values in US $m., at constant (1985)
prices.

Institutional framework

West German export legislation distinguishes between weapons of war which are controlled by the *Kriegswaffenkontrollgesetz* (War Material Control Act) of 1961 and other weapons which are controlled under the *Aussenwirtschaftsgesetz* (Foreign Trade Act). The War Material Control Act stipulates that weapons of war may not be exported (a) to countries at war or close to war; (b) in disobedience of international law; or (c) if a 'peace-breaking action' might be expected from the recipient of the weapons. The export of weapons and other weapon-related goods falling under the Foreign Trade Act can be limited if the government so decides for similar reasons to those given in the War Material Control Act. The Foreign Trade Act stipulates that any restriction has to be balanced against economic interests.[69] Both laws are administered by the Ministry of Economics for the government. In politically important cases the *Bundessicherheitsrat* (National Security Council) decides. In practice, the advice of the Foreign Ministry is important. There are few known cases of divergent views on arms exports by various ministries.

In order to establish internal rules for the interpretation of the laws, political guidelines were drawn up by the government in 1971 and revised in 1982.

The 1971 guidelines said that only in exceptional cases should weapons of war be exported to countries outside the NATO alliance. No weapons of war should be exported to 'areas of tension'. The export of weapons other than weapons of war should be restricted. The 1982 guidelines did not mention the term 'area of tension'. Instead, they stated that the export of weapons of war should only be allowed if vital interests of the Federal Republic would benefit from such an export. Economic interests alone could not be considered sufficient. In addition, the domestic conditions within a prospective recipient country should be taken into account. The 1982 guidelines also introduced a new group of goods not previously mentioned, goods close to weapons of war *(kriegswaffennahe Rüstungsgüter)*. These included licences to produce weapons of war and are to be controlled in the same way as weapons of war.

In cases of co-production of weapons the West German Government has tried to reach agreements with the foreign governments involved on how to handle exports. A West German veto was written into agreements with the UK and Italy about the MRCA Tornado aircraft (in May 1983 the conservative Kohl Government relinquished this right). In an agreement with France from 1971, regulating the exports of French/German co-produced missiles and aircraft, the French Government only agreed to consult the West German Government, which had no right to veto sales from France.

There is no government marketing support for arms exports. Export credit schemes can only be used to guarantee the export of arms if the government gives special permission.

Arms production

The economic importance of arms exports is low. Less than 1 per cent of total exports and less than 3 per cent of exports to the Third World consist of exports of weapons of war. If other weapons are included these shares increase somewhat though they remain substantially below the levels of British, French or Italian exports.[70] The share of exports in total arms production is also lower than the same share in other West European countries. Estimates range from 10 to 20 per cent. The economic importance of the arms industry as a whole is also low. Less than 2 per cent of all persons employed in manufacturing industry are engaged in arms production.

In some regions arms production is of higher importance, such as around Munich, around Kassel, in Kiel, Bremen and Hamburg. Here arms production is part of regional policy and domestic procurement and export policy are used as instruments of economic policy. The manufacturing sector most dependent on arms production is the aircraft industry with a military share of more than 50 per cent. In shipbuilding the share has increased from less than 5 per cent in the early 1970s to around 20 per cent in the early 1980s. In other sectors such as electronics or automobile production it is around 2 per cent.

The sector of the arms industry which has been most successful in obtaining export licences from the government has been the shipbuilding industry (see table 3.8). Two arguments put forward by the shipbuilding industry carried strong weight with the administration: first, that ships were seldom used in wars in the Third World and, second, that shipbuilding was in a severe economic crisis and employment was at stake. Other sectors of the arms industry, such as the tank-building industry and the aircraft industry, have also tried to use the employment argument but with much less success. They were not part of a pronounced sectoral crisis.

Another strategy used by the arms industry to expand its export business was co-production of weapons with companies in other countries. Examples of such co-production are the HOT and Milan ATMs and the Alpha Jet aircraft. The federal government tolerated such activities as long as the companies involved could argue that money could be saved for the defence budget.

Given the different treatment of weapons of war and other weapons, the export of weapons-related material flourished earlier than the trade in major weapons. For example, engines produced by MTU propel the majority of fast attack craft built since the 1970s, tank engines built by MTU are to be found in Brazilian, Korean and Indian tanks, and gearshafts for tanks very often come from FR Germany.

Political issues

One of the aims of the socialist/liberal government that took power in 1969 was to limit the export of arms. The then Defence Minister, Helmut Schmidt, was a driving force behind these limitations, giving earlier political embarrassments as

Table 3.8. Some West German companies exporting major weapons to Third World countries

Company	Export weapons produced	Turnover in arms production 1983 ($m.)	Rank among West German arms producers	Exports of major weapons to Third World, 1971–85[a]
Blohm & Voss	Frigates, destroyers corvettes	300	10	870
Howaldtswerke-Deutsche Werft AG.	Submarines, corvettes	400	6	870
Fr. Luerssen Werft	FACs, PCs, MCMs	110	19	700
Thyssen Industrie AG.	APCs, ACs, submarines	275	11	510
Dornier	Light-planes, jet trainers	250	12	410
Messerschmidt-Bölkow-Blohm	MRCA Tornado, helicopters, ATMs	1 290	1	390

[a]SIPRI trend indicator values in US $m. at constant (1985) prices.

a major reason. But he had to compromise with the Foreign Ministry, led by Walter Scheel, which was in favour of keeping arms exports as a foreign policy instrument. The 1971 guidelines reflect this compromise.

Shipbuilding and co-production were practically exempted from such efforts at limitation. In the mid-1970s when the arms business boomed and the economic crisis in FR Germany deepened, the arms industry strengthened its argumentative pressures for a less restrictive arms export policy. It was suppported by requests from various governments in the Middle East, notably the Iranian and the Saudi Arabian. On the other hand, public opinion and the ranks of the governing parties were opposed to a further slackening of export regulations.

The public debate continued throughout the late 1970s and early 1980s. The federal government kept tabs on the delivery of some weapon systems, most notably tanks, but allowed the transfer of blueprints to produce German weapons, whose export was not allowed, in an attempt not to offend customers such as the Shah of Iran or the Argentinian Government. The debate reached its peak during the winter of 1980–81, when it became publicly known that the Saudi Arabian Government insisted that Chancellor Schmidt had agreed to the sale of Leopard tanks and that a licence had been granted to produce submarines for export to Chile, whose government had been consistently condemned by the West German Government for its human rights violations.

The debate resulted in the 1982 guidelines, which were generally considered to be a relaxation of the earlier stricter rules, though the government insisted that this was not the case.

The new conservative/liberal government that took power in October 1982 had not—by 1986—changed the 1982 guidelines despite some pressure from within its leadership to do so. So far it has found the guidelines flexible enough to accommodate its own arms export policy, which reflects the same dilemma and interest group pressures as those of the former government. Major changes have been the dropping of veto provisions in some co-production agreements, the general exemption of the ASEAN region from case-to-case scrutiny of licensing and a generally more favourable attitude towards arms exports. Also, the government reversed a decision made in May 1982 by the former government to give information on pending arms transfer decisions to a parliamentary body.

Public debate on arms transfers has lingered on, from time to time fuelled by newspaper reports about imminent deals and government decisions. The periodic Saudi requests for West German tanks are a constant source of news. In the autumn of 1983, Chancellor Kohl denied Saudi Arabia Leopard-2s but promised any other tank that the country might be interested in. An agreement on military co-operation was concluded between FR Germany and Saudi Arabia. The opposition parties, the Social Democrats and the Greens, have introduced a number of proposals to tighten arms exports regulations again.

IX. Other Western industrialized suppliers

NATO-member countries with smaller procurement budgets than, say, the Federal Republic of Germany and the UK, cannot maintain an arms industry capable of producing a wide range of weapons. But as part of an alliance with large arms exporters anxious to sell to them, these countries can try to specialize and trade certain products and components. All the smaller NATO-member countries with sizeable industries have done this. They have specialized in one or several areas within the field of arms production in which they have traditionally been producers or have acquired expertise: Belgium in the field of small arms and ammunition, Canada in transport aircraft, Greece in ammunition, the Netherlands in both transport aircraft and shipbuilding, Norway in shipbuilding and ship electronics, Spain in shipbuilding and aircraft, and Turkey in ammunition. Australia and Japan, while not members of NATO, are in similar positions since they are allied to the USA.

The existence of a competitive—albeit specialized—arms-production sector raises the question of exports. As with a broader-based arms-production industry, national demands are too small to maintain a sufficient research and production capacity. The capacity problem can be reduced if the major alliance partners can be persuaded to buy products from the countries concerned, but there will still be commercial pressure to export outside the alliance. While this pressure will be less than in countries with the strategic aim of maintaining a broad-based arms industry, it can be augmented by arguments about employment within the arms-producing sector and about technological spin-offs into the civilian industry.

Differing restraints on arms exports in the smaller Western producer countries have led to different levels of arms exports, despite the rather similar positions with respect to the structural pressures to export.

Belgium has a rather large arms-production sector. All in all, an estimated 100 000 people work directly or indirectly for the arms industry.[71] The region around Liège has long been a centre for arms manufacture and FN Herstal carried on this tradition, employing almost 10 000 people in the manufacture of small arms, guns, aircraft engines, and so on. Ninety per cent of the output is exported to more than 80 countries each year.[72] Poudre Réunis Belge (PRB), the ammunition manufacturer, is of equal economic importance. Its products are exported to an even larger number of countries. Since most Belgian weapon exports consist of small arms and ammunition, they do not show up in SIPRI's statistics on the trade in major weapons (see figure 3.11). In the category of major weapons, only a few armoured vehicles and used aircraft have been exported.[73]

Belgium has few restrictions on arms exports. While all exports require licences from the Ministry of Economics, there are strong indications that control is less stringent than in most other NATO countries. Licences for small arms are granted in most cases, except for exports to countries under embargo by the UN, the EEC or NATO. The list of trouble spots in which weapons of

(a) Trend 1971–85
Five-year moving averages

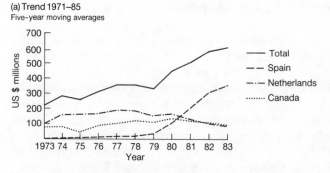

(b) Arms export shares and number of Third World customers, 1971–85

Supplier	Percentage share of Third World arms imports in world	in group	Number of Third World customers
Spain	0.67	31.9	26
Netherlands	0.66	31.7	22
Canada	0.51	24.6	28
Australia	0.10	4.9	10
Belgium	0.04	2.0	4
Portugal	0.04	1.8	8
Turkey	0.04	1.7	1
Japan	0.03	1.3	4
Denmark	—	0.2	1
Greece	0	0	0
Iceland	0	0	0
Luxembourg	0	0	0
Norway	0	0	0
Total	2.08	100.0	

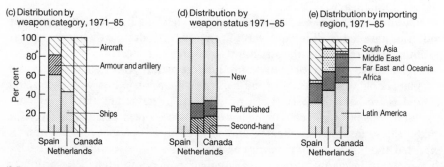

(c) Distribution by weapon category, 1971–85

(d) Distribution by weapon status 1971–85

(e) Distribution by importing region, 1971–85

(f) Percentage shares of important recipients, 1971–85

Rank order	Spain Country	Share	Netherlands Country	Share	Canada Country	Share
1	Egypt	35	Peru	34	Peru	22
2	Morocco	16	Indonesia	19	Venezuela	21
3	Mexico	13	Iran	9	Egypt	8
4	Argentina	11	Argentina	9	Ecuador	6
5	Iraq	7	Nigeria	6	Kenya	6
Total of 5[a]		82		75		63

[a] Figures may not add up to totals due to rounding.

Figure 3.11. Other industrialized Western countries: exports of major weapons to the Third World, 1971–85

Based on SIPRI trend indicator values in US $m., at constant (1985) prices.

Belgian origin can be found is long; this is partly the result of a reportedly extensive illegal arms trade conducted via companies in Belgium.[74] There has been much discussion on Belgian arms export policy both within and outside parliament. The main issues have been alleged deliveries to South Africa (the design for South Africa's main armoured personnel carrier, the Ratel, originated in Belgium; there was also Belgian involvement in the delivery of technology to produce the G-5 155-mm howitzer) and to regimes that violate human rights (e.g., when tanks were delivered to Uruguay in 1982). In several instances, initiatives were taken to tighten legislation and to introduce some form of parliamentary control,[75] but the government refused to make changes. It regarded the provision in the relevant law of 19 July 1968, that arms export policy must take into account 'the general principles of law and humanity as accepted among civilized nations', as both sufficient and effective in regulating Belgian arms exports.[76]

Canada also has a comparatively large arms industry. According to estimates by the Defence Ministry, total employment (direct and indirect) stood at 240 000 in the early 1980s.[77] Arms production is concentrated in a few sectors, namely the aircraft industry, electronics and shipbuilding. In addition, arms production is regionally concentrated in areas with structural unemployment problems.

Canadian arms production is closely intertwined with that of the USA and there is a series of agreements on the sharing of arms production between the two countries. Most of the weapons in the inventory of the Canadian armed forces are purchased in the USA or built under US licence in Canada. Canadian exports of parts for weapon systems for the US forces' inventory or for export out of the USA provide a rough balance in trade of weapons-related material. About three-fifths of arms produced in Canada are exported to the USA.

Direct exports of major weapons to Third World countries have been entirely in one sector: transport aircraft. De Havilland and Canadair, for example, have specialized in the production of various types of small transport aircraft for both civilian and military use. These aircraft have been sold to a large number of countries in Africa, Asia and, especially, Latin America. It can be debated whether or not such aircraft should be classed as weapons. The Canadian Government does not treat them as such, although their export requires a licence from the Ministry of Economics. While rather strict guidelines exist for other weapon systems, forbidding exports to countries at war or close to war and to countries whose policies are considered to be 'wholly repugnant to Canadian values'—transport aircraft and certain electronic systems are restricted only in exceptional cases. The main reason for this is employment in the industries concerned.

Criticism of Canadian arms exports has focused both on this special treatment of transport aircraft and on the 'US connection'.[78] Canadian-built components, such as aircraft engines made by Pratt & Whitney, are exported all over the world via the USA. There is also a clear connection between US orders to Canadian arms producers and exports to the Third World: when US orders were up, as in the late 1960s (the Viet Nam War) or the early 1980s (the Reagan buildup), capacities were fully employed. When US orders decreased, Canadian firms had to seek export orders to fill capacities.

Greece is only a minor arms producer employing less than 20 000 persons in the early 1980s.[79] Until the early 1970s, there was only limited production of ammunition and some ships. When some countries stopped supplying weapons to the military government that came to power in 1967, plans were made to broaden the military-industrial base. The democratic governments have continued on this path, subsidizing the establishment of production facilities for aircraft, small arms and armoured vehicles, with extensive help from US, West German, French and Austrian companies. The expansion has been curtailed by lack of finances, however. Exports have been limited to small arms and ammunition. Pyrcal, the largest Greek arms producer, and state-owned like the majority of arms manufacturers, exports around 70 per cent of its output of ammunition, mostly to Middle Eastern countries. The socialist government that came to power in 1982 has tried to strengthen control over the arms industry through further nationalizations, and has taken a positive attitude towards the expansion of arms exports. In 1984 and early 1985 the government negotiated large deliveries of weapons to Libya. Sums of up to $1.5 billion were mentioned in the press.[80] However, this spur to Greek arms exports remained largely fictitious because of the arms embargo against Libya in early 1986, declared after political pressure from the USA.

Arms exports have been heatedly debated in the *Netherlands*. In the 1970s, the main discussion points were deliveries to Indonesia, Iran, South Africa and Taiwan. In the cases of Indonesia, Iran and Taiwan, the respective navies had chosen Dutch warships at a time when ship construction in the Netherlands was in deep crisis. In the case of South Africa, the discussion evolved around deliveries of electronic components which were put to military use.[81]

There has been less discussion about the goods that constitute the bulk of Dutch exports as measured by SIPRI: transport aircraft. As mentioned above, it is debatable whether such unarmed transport vehicles constitute major weapons and whether they should be included in SIPRI statistics (and indeed it has been debated in the Netherlands).[82] That major-weapon exports are concentrated in this category should be kept in mind when the Dutch arms trade is analysed.

According to Dutch statistics, exports of military material are small, but not negligible. In addition to ships and aircraft, electronic products and ammunition are exported. Export orders grew from about $200 million in the early 1970s to about $500 million in the early 1980s—about 0.8 per cent of total exports at both points in time. During the 1970s and early 1980s arms exports made up about one-third of total arms production, and the share of Third World orders in the total arms export business has fluctuated largely around 40 per cent. Arms production employed about 30 000 persons directly or indirectly.[83] Arms exports are controlled by the government under the import–export law of 1962, supplemented by lists of goods subject to control, which are frequently changed. There are no legal criteria, but the government has outlined its policy through reports, answers in parliament and in political debates. The major criteria are (a) the type of material to be exported; (b) the internal and external situation of the recipient country (no weapons are delivered to a country at war); (c) international embargoes; (d) the creation of precedent; and (e) employment in the arms industry. The latter consideration is not intended to be a major one.[84] Licences are first reviewed by the Economics Ministry, but it falls to the Ministry of Foreign Affairs to judge the crucial political aspects. The views of the Defence Ministry and the Ministry for Development Co-operation (since 1973) are also heard, when appropriate. There is no legal role for parliament in the decision-making. Initiatives by members to establish such a role have been consistently rejected by the majority in parliament. On the other hand, arms export issues are frequently discussed in parliament. In two votes in late 1980 and early 1981, the majority in parliament urged the government not to licence the export of two submarines to Taiwan. The government went ahead with the export licence but stated that it would be the last delivery to Taiwan. When there was a new order for four submarines in 1984, the government refused to grant a licence. The main reason was the relationship to China, an important Dutch trading partner. The interests of the Dutch shipbuilding industry in producing these ships were judged to be secondary.

Norway is unique among NATO-member countries with respect to arms exports to the Third World. Since the end of the 1950s there has been a clear policy not to export weapons to the Third World. Although a diversified arms industry was built up during the 1960s this policy has been adhered to, and no Norwegian exports of major weapons to the Third World are recorded in the SIPRI arms trade registers for 1971 to 1985. In the late 1960s, after its initial buildup, the Norwegian arms industry was faced with a lack of orders. Instead of trying to export to the Third World, the decision was made to try and expand exports to other NATO countries and to non-aligned countries in Europe and to switch production capacities from military to civilian use.[85] By the end of the 1970s Norway had become a major exporter of weapons to other industrialized countries, especially in the fields of electronics and naval equipment. With more than 10 000 persons employed, the arms industry has become an important economic factor in Norway. Nevertheless, it seems very unlikely that the restrictive export policy with respect to the Third World will be changed. When in 1984 the then commander of the armed forces, General Sven Hauge, offered to discuss the sale of Norwegian military material with Chinese officials, it stirred a political controversy in Norway.[86]

Spain's exports increased substantially in the late 1970s and early 1980s. Previously ranked among the small producers, Spanish arms production companies had advanced to seventh position among exporters of major weapons to the Third World by the early 1980s. This sharp increase in arms exports was facilitated by a number of outside factors, such as the growing demand from the Middle East and the re-emergence of the black and grey markets in the 1980s. But they were mostly the result of Spanish policy.

In 1977, a major reform of the defence sector was initiated. A Ministry of Defence was formed, superseding ministries for the three services. A central procurement agency was created, followed later by an Armaments Advisory Board with members from the Defence Ministry, the armed forces and the arms industries.

The institutional changes were accompanied by a new armaments policy, in which arms exports played a major role. Since the inventory of the Spanish armed forces was to be thoroughly modernized, large outlays were required for R&D and for production. The expansion of arms exports was seen as a means of broadening the financial base of the arms industry. With the production of more modern weapons the chances for exports on the world market were also expected to grow. In addition, it was hoped that increased arms production and arms exports would provide additional employment and a technological boost for Spanish industry. Arms exports became a key variable both in transforming the military from a political force, oriented towards internal threats, into a modern professional army as well as in industrialization policy.

The traditional market for Spanish weapons had been Latin America, and it continued to be an important recipient region (see figure 3.11). Most of the growth in arms exports in the late 1970s and early 1980s was otherwise accounted for by sales to the Middle East.

The machinery for controlling arms exports did not grow in parallel with the exports. All exports have to be given a go-ahead by an interministerial committee (*Junta Interministerial Reguladora de Comercio de Armas y Explosivos*), but there is general agreement that insufficient control is exercised.[87] In a number of cases the government has denied granting export licences for arms shipments from Spain. In 1978, a freighter supposedly carrying weapons for the IRA (Irish Republican Army) was stopped by British authorities. In the same year, the Nicaraguan opposition claimed that weapons had been delivered to the Somoza Government. In the early 1980s, there were persistent reports that Spanish weapons had been delivered to Iran.[88] However, there were also cases in which the government stopped sales efforts by the arms industry. In 1982 it was reported that Bazán was negotiating the sale of warships to South Africa. This was prohibited by the government which is committed to the UN embargo of 1977 (although exports of 'light weapons' were allowed).[89] There have been several attempts to strengthen control over arms exports. In 1978, socialist politicians wanted to establish parliamentary control over arms exports.[90] In 1985, the socialist government reviewed the arms export policy but did not establish parliamentary control.

Despite some pre-election rhetoric, the socialist government has not tried to stop the export drive. Instead, since gaining power in 1982 it has been determined to expand arms exports for the same reasons as led to the initiation of the export drive: control of the military via modernization of the armed forces (partly financed through arms exports) and expansion of employment and technology imports. Efforts to start joint production with West European arms-producing companies have been increased. Spain is now partner in a number of joint projects such as the European Fighter Aircraft (with FR Germany, Italy and the UK). A number of licence agreements have also been made. Arms exports have become an economic factor of some importance: about 30 000 persons were employed through arms exports in the early 1980s.[91]

Arms production in *Portugal* is very limited, employing less than 4000 persons. The most important branches are production of ammunition, small arms, small ships and armoured vehicles. Until the early 1980s, exports consisted mainly of ammunition to some Latin American and African countries. Then, the share of weapon sales in total exports rose markedly, largely due to deliveries of small arms and ammunition to Iraq and Iran. Statistics for Portugal in the SIPRI arms trade registers are comparatively high because of the transfers of Portuguese equipment to the armed forces of Angola and Mozambique at the time of independence.

The *Turkish* arms industry employs about 50 000 persons. The main sector is the production of ammunition, although efforts have been made to build up shipbuilding and aircraft industries with West German and US aid. The ammunition industry exports actively, mostly to other NATO countries, but also to the Middle East. The volume of exports was around $30 million per year in the early 1980s.[92] The SIPRI statistics show exports of ships to Libya. The Turkish Defence Ministry, which up to the mid-1980s controlled all arms production in the country, had tried to expand co-operation in arms production several times during the 1970s and early 1980s, primarily with Egypt and Saudi Arabia. Because Turkey and Egypt were short of funds and Saudi Arabia showed little interest, the projects remained at the planning stage.

Being allied to the United States, *Australia* and *Japan* are in a similar position to the NATO-member countries. In both countries most of the weapons in the armed forces are of US design and are either imported directly or produced under licence. The local arms industries are sizeable, employing about 30 000 persons in Australia[93] and 80 000 in Japan.[94]

There have been some exports of major weapons from Australia (see figure 3.11), mostly comprising transport aircraft produced by the Government Aircraft Factories. In addition, naval missiles and some ships have been exported. Australia has a role as a regional power in South East Asia and the Western Pacific and exports weapons mainly to neighbouring countries.

The Japanese arms industry has achieved a high technological status. A major reason for this is that the arms manufacturers are at the same time the most important heavy engineering companies in Japan, and can use their impressive civilian capabilities also in the military field. None of the big arms producers, such as Mitsubishi or Kawasaki, has more than 10 per cent of its output in the military field. These companies would be able to increase arms production substantially, if they were allowed to export.

It has been Japanese policy not to allow the export of arms. In 1967, the government under Prime Minister Sato announced three principles that would guide government arms export policy: no sales to communist countries, no sales to countries subject to a UN embargo and no sales to countries at war or likely to become engaged in armed conflicts. Whereas other countries expanded arms exports while stating similar principles, in Japan they were increasingly interpreted as not allowing exports of arms to any country. Exports of military goods decreased and were limited to unarmed ships and aircraft. In the early 1970s, during the Third World's arms import boom, the pressure on the government to allow more arms exports increased. But the political forces opposing arms exports, which are to be found in the various socialist parties, the orthodox Buddhist party and to some extent in the liberal party—ruling throughout the period under review—prevailed. In 1976 the rules were restated and expanded to include arms production technology.

The strict Japanese restraint is based on a moralistic interpretation of history and a desire to eradicate the image of Japan as a militaristic nation making profit from wars. The Japanese restraint is all the more remarkable since Japan is one of the leading exporters of civilian goods in the world. These civilian exports also tend to erode the Japanese policy, since it becomes more and more difficult to distinguish between civilian and military goods. The SIPRI arms trade registers contain some, though few, entries for Japan as an exporter. The entries concern helicopters, transport aircraft and supply ships. All these goods were classified as non-military by the producers and the government, although they were destined for military customers. Co-operation with the USA might also threaten Japanese restraint. In 1983, the Japanese Government ruled that the US-Japanese Defense Treaty overruled the above-mentioned arms export rules and, therefore, military exports to the USA were permissible. In the future Japanese components may be exported to the Third World via incorporation into US weapons.

X. Other Eastern industrialized suppliers

Arms production in the Warsaw Treaty Organization (WTO) is much more centralized than in NATO. Almost all production of heavy armaments for the armed forces of WTO member countries is carried out in the Soviet Union. WTO arms production policies are undoubtedly affected by the Soviet Union's interest in controlling its allies. But there are other considerations which make arms production unattractive in the smaller WTO countries. Their economic potential is too small to sustain independent arms industries and the large production runs that can be achieved in the Soviet Union allow lower prices for the WTO as a whole.

Militarily, the main advantage of centralization of arms production is the high degree of standardization of weapon systems that has been achieved in the WTO.[95] This centralization increased during the 1960s and 1970s. In the 1950s and into the 1960s, both Czechoslovakia and Poland had sizeable capacities for the production of fighter aircraft and main battle tanks of Soviet design. In the 1970s, the Polish industry concentrated on the production of landing ships, small aircraft and helicopters, mostly of Soviet design, while the Czech industry was responsible for supplying training aircraft and small transport aircraft to a number of other WTO member countries. The division of labour within the WTO also entailed ammunition production in Czechoslovakia, Bulgaria and Romania in exchange for the delivery of heavy weapons from the Soviet Union. In the late 1970s and early 1980s, Romania, Bulgaria and, probably, Czechoslovakia expanded their production facilities for small arms and ammunition, mostly for exports to the Third World in response to the increased demand for weapons in the 1970s. Tank production was restarted in several countries in the late 1970s.

It is very difficult to estimate the sizes and the economic importance of arms industries in East European WTO member countries. In the *German Democratic Republic* and *Hungary*, there is little production of armaments. In Bulgaria, Romania and Poland, arms production employs somewhere between 20 000 and 50 000 persons directly and indirectly. Production of small arms of Soviet design and ammunition dominates *Bulgarian* production. *Romania*'s arms production differs from that of other WTO-member countries in that there is production of aircraft under licence from Western industrialized countries and in co-production with Yugoslavia in addition to production under Soviet licences. *Polish* arms production is marked by the production of small fixed-wing aircraft and helicopters. *Czechoslovakia* has the second largest arms industry among WTO member countries, after the Soviet Union. Total employment is between 50 000 and 100 000 (direct and indirect). In addition to training and transport aircraft, the production of armoured vehicles, small arms and ammunition is important.[96]

Given the sizes and areas of specialization of their arms industries, it is no surprise that smaller WTO member countries do not figure prominently in the SIPRI arms transfer statistics (see figure 3.12). There are some retransfers of Soviet weapons, especially to Iraq in the early 1980s, and some deliveries of aircraft and armoured vehicles from Czechoslovakia, ships and helicopters from Poland and aircraft built under British and French licences from Romania. Other Western sources give considerably higher estimates, which are plausible if they include deliveries of small arms and ammunition.[97] Czechoslovakia and Bulgaria, in particular, are important exporters of Soviet-designed small arms and ammunition. More than 9 per cent of total Bulgarian exports in 1982 were reported to be of such weapons, but there is no way to substantiate this figure, said to be from an internal Bulgarian source.[98] For all these countries, the majority of exports go to other WTO countries. Exports to the Third World are important, however, especially to countries in the Middle East. Almost half of the Bulgarian exports of arms in 1982 were reportedly sent to the Third World,[99] and 24 per cent of the exports of the Polish aircraft-exporting company (PZL) were directed towards countries in the Middle East in 1983.[100]

Not only is it very difficult to get information about the quantity of arms exported from the East European WTO member countries, it is even more difficult to assess how decisions are made about them. A question constantly discussed is whether they are co-ordinated with the Soviet Union or whether decisions are made by the individual governments. Cases can be found to support both propositions, as well as the hypothesis that arms are exported without any political oversight. When the Soviet Union cut back its deliveries

(a) Trend 1971–85
Five-year moving averages

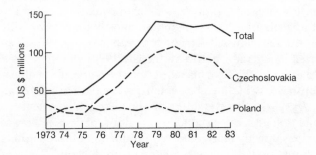

(b) Arms export shares and number of Third World customers, 1971–85

| Supplier | Percentage share of Third World arms imports | | Number of Third World customers |
	in World	in group	
Czechoslovakia	0.31	64.7	11
Poland	0.12	23.8	8
Romania	0.04	7.5	7
Hungary	0.01	2.7	1
German DR	0.01	1.0	1
Bulgaria	—	0.3	2
Total	0.48	100.0	

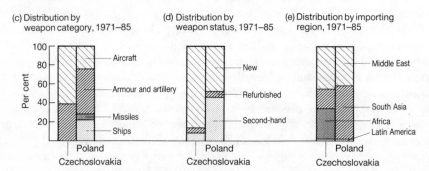

(c) Distribution by weapon category, 1971–85

(d) Distribution by weapon status, 1971–85

(e) Distribution by importing region, 1971–85

(f) Percentage shares of important recipients, 1971–85

| Rank order | Czechoslovakia | | Poland | |
	Country	Share	Country	Share
1	Syria	28	India	57
2	Libya	24	Iraq	31
3	Iraq	18	S. Yemen	6
4	India	17	Syria	4
5	Afghanistan	6	Madagascar	1
Total of 5[a]		93		99

[a] Figures may not add up to totals due to rounding.

Figure 3.12. Other industrialized Eastern countries: exports of major weapons to the Third World, 1971–85

Based on SIPRI trend indicator values in US $m., at constant (1985) prices.

to Iraq after the beginning of the Iraq–Iran War in 1980, exports from the East European suppliers increased dramatically. This was a case of substituting for direct Soviet deliveries. A division of labour is very visible with respect to training. Much of the military training in countries in Sub-Saharan Africa using Soviet military equipment, for example, has been carried out by advisors from the German Democratic Republic.[101] On the other hand, there are cases of arms deliveries that were not in the interests of the Soviet Union, for example, small arms were shipped from Bulgaria to South Africa in 1979.[102] Romania, which is a special case because of its more independent foreign policy, reportedly delivered spare parts and even weapon systems of Soviet origin to Egypt after the break in Soviet-Egyptian ties.[103]

XI. Neutral and non-aligned industrialized suppliers

There are at least two reasons why neutral and non-aligned European countries are in a special position with respect to arms exports. First, the laws of neutrality impose certain restrictions on arms exports. Specifically, this means that the states should not actively export arms to war combatants unless such support is justified by other provisions of international law, for example, the Charter of the United Nations, which states the right of nations to defend themselves. Second, small non-aligned states find it even harder to keep up with the pace of technological advances in military technology than large states, or states that are members of alliances. They cannot remain independent of foreign arms supplies over the whole range of armaments, even if they are prepared to pay a considerable price for domestic arms production. Arms exports are then seen as an attractive supplement to domestic demand that can help sustain a larger arms industry and diminish the cost burden for domestic arms procurement.

The politics of arms production and arms exports vary greatly among the different countries. Sweden and Switzerland try to remain independent in at least some areas of arms production, while recognizing that imports have to be made in others. Yugoslavia does not attempt to produce weapons at such a high technological level, but has a broad basis for the production of less advanced weapons. Austria and Finland have small arms industries that only produce in selected areas. In all these countries there are strong pressures to export weapons and, except in Yugoslavia, there is also much political discussion about arms transfers.

Up to the mid-1970s, *Austrian* arms exports were very limited and confined to small arms and ammunition. At that time two large engineering companies—Steyr-Daimler-Puch and Voest-Alpine—expanded their arms production to include armoured vehicles and artillery. Exports began to grow and became important both for these and other, smaller companies and for the Austrian economy. There are no official Austrian statistics on arms exports, but they reportedly reached a total of more than $400 million or a share of more than 1 per cent of total exports in the late 1970s.[104] Employment in arms production was estimated at more than 20 000 persons (direct and indirect) in the early 1980s.[105]

There was strong political support for the expansion of arms production by exports in the late 1970s. The main reason was that exports would make weapons for the Austrian forces cheaper. In 1977, a special law on arms exports was adopted. It gave prime responsibility for licensing the exports of all arms to the Ministry of the Interior, which has to receive clearances from the Ministry of Defence and the Foreign Ministry. The Chancellery is also heard. The main criteria for not granting a licence are the neutral status of Austria, its foreign policy interests and security considerations. Although these provisions cannot be interpreted as forbidding arms exports to NATO- or WTO-member countries, almost all arms exports have gone to the Third World (see figure 3.13). The political support for the expansion of arms exports began to waiver when it became known that Austrian weapons had been exported illegally and that the customers included both states involved in war fighting, such as Morocco, as well as states violating human rights, such as Guatemala and Bolivia before 1980. In 1980, there was intense political discussion about the delivery of tanks to Chile. The export licence was revoked because of strong opposition from within the ruling social democratic party, the liberal party, the Catholic Church and some trade unions.[106] In 1985, licence for a new order for more tanks by Morocco was refused. In the same year there were criminal investigations into alleged supplies of Austrian weapons both to Iraq and to Iran.

In 1982 the waivering political support manifested itself in the adoption of a revision in the 1977 law. A clause was introduced forbidding exports to states violating human rights. The extreme secrecy surrounding Austrian arms exports was also lifted to some extent by providing for an annual report to an all-party advisory body on foreign policy (*Aussenpolitischer Rat*). The more restrictive political climate contributed to a decrease in orders for the Austrian arms industry. In the early 1980s, it entered a crisis. While the arms industry increased its efforts to sell, the government tried to find alternatives to arms production and studied conversion proposals.

Finland has a rather small arms industry, employing less than 10 000 people (directly and indirectly). Arms exports are also small, amounting to less than $10 million according to official figures in 1985.[107] There were no exports of major weapons in the period under review. Arms exports were not a political issue until the mid-1980s when various allegations of the involvement of Finnish companies in covert deliveries of ammunition and explosives to the Middle East were made. The allegations were by-products of Swedish investigations into illegal arms sales from Swedish arms manufacturers.

Controversies in the mid-1980s concerning *Swedish* arms exports originate from one of the cornerstones of Swedish security policy, namely that Sweden shall be non-aligned in peacetime and neutral in wartime. The dilemma is that while Sweden, on the one hand, probably cannot maintain its broadly-based arms industry unless parts of the output are allowed to be exported, on the other hand it is argued that every arms sale is a potential threat to neutrality.

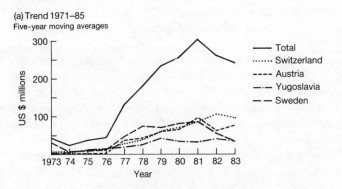

(a) Trend 1971–85
Five-year moving averages

Legend:
—— Total
········ Switzerland
---- Austria
—·— Yugoslavia
— — Sweden

US $ millions (y-axis: 100, 200, 300)
Year (x-axis: 1973 74 75 76 77 78 79 80 81 82 83)

(b) Arms export shares and number of Third World customers, 1971–85

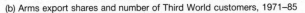

Supplier	Percentage share of Third World arms imports in world	in group	Number of Third World customers
Switzerland	0.25	30.4	27
Sweden	0.24	29.9	14
Austria	0.21	25.6	9
Yugoslavia	0.11	13.4	8
New Zealand	0.01	0.7	4
Total	0.81	100.0	

(c) Distribution by weapon category, 1971–85

Per cent (0, 20, 40, 60, 80, 100)
Labels: Aircraft, Armour and artillery, Missiles, Ships, Guidance and radar systems
Switzerland | Sweden | Yugoslavia | Austria

(d) Distribution by weapon status, 1971–85

Labels: New, Refurbished, Second-hand
Switzerland | Sweden | Yugoslavia | Austria

(e) Distribution by importing region, 1971–85

Labels: Middle East, South Asia, Far East and Oceania, Africa, Latin America
Switzerland | Sweden | Yugoslavia | Austria

(f) Percentage share of important recipients, 1971–85

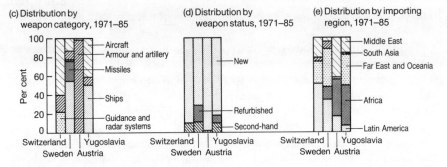

Rank order	Switzerland Country	Share	Sweden Country	Share	Austria Country	Share	Yugoslavia Country	Share
1	Colombia	19	Malaysia	23	Jordan	41	Indonesia	32
2	Iraq	10	Chile	21	Morocco	21	Libya	32
3	Mexico	9	Singapore	12	Argentina	10	Iraq	16
4	Chile	7	Trinidad	12	Tunisia	8	Ethiopia	8
5	Iran	7	Pakistan	9	Bolivia	7	Honduras	6
Total of 5[a]		52		77		87		95

[a] Figures may not add up to totals due to rounding.

Figure 3.13. Industrialized neutral and non-aligned countries: exports of major weapons to the Third World, 1971–85

Based on SIPRI trend indicator values in US $m., at constant (1985) prices.

Historically, Sweden is committed to a restrictive arms export policy. State-ments by Swedish politicians since the 1950s have emphasized restrictions well beyond the provisions in the Law of Neutrality. The role of Sweden as a mediator in international conflicts and an advocate of disarmament have further underlined Sweden's image as a restrictive arms exporter.

Although Sweden spends relatively more of its national income on defence (close to 3 per cent in 1985) than Austria and Finland (just over 1 per cent each), the domestic demand is limited. The two largest arms producers in Sweden, Bofors and the state-owned FFV, export about 60 and 30 per cent of their arms production, respectively. More than 40 000 people are employed in arms production.[108]

According to SIPRI's statistics, Sweden is a minor arms exporter, accounting for only 0.3 per cent of total exports of major weapons to the Third World during 1971–85 (see figure 3.13). This is to some extent misleading since Sweden—along with, for example, Austria, Belgium, Czechoslovakia and Switzerland—exports a disproportionately large amount of items not covered by the SIPRI statistics. According to the official Swedish statistics, annual arms exports during the early 1980s were in the area of $300 million or about 1 per cent of total Swedish exports. In the period 1983–85, about 41 per cent of Swedish arms exports were to countries in the Third World (the main recipients are listed in table 3.9). The main export items include anti-aircraft guns, mines, torpedoes, ammunition and electronics. Export levels are expected to rise considerably in the second half of the 1980s, largely due to a sizeable order from India covering howitzers and associated equipment initially valued at well over one billion dollars.

All Swedish arms exports are exceptions from a prohibition in principle, most recently expressed in the arms export law of 1983. Exceptions are granted by the government on a case-by-case basis. In routine cases, the decision is taken by the War Materials Inspectorate (*Krigsmaterielinspektionen*) while, in more controversial cases, the decision is taken by the foreign trade minister and/or the government. According to the most recent guidelines on how to apply the law, an advisory function also rests with the Foreign Policy Committee (*Utrikesnämnden*); and a special parliamentary committee is also to be consulted before major decisions are taken. Swedish policy prohibits arms exports to (*a*) states involved in armed conflict with another state or states with armed domestic conflicts; (*b*) states in which tensions may lead to armed conflict; and (*c*) states in which the exported equipment may be used in the oppression of human rights. The arms export law, with guidelines, restricts the sale of production licences in the same manner as it restricts direct weapon sales. Finally, all recipients are obliged to sign so-called end-use certificates, that is, they have to promise not to re-export the Swedish-made equipment to another country.

The controversies around Swedish arms exports have so far only centred indirectly on procedural matters, although the criticism has been made that items of strategic importance or with dual-use capabilities are not classified as

Table 3.9.   Swiss and Swedish arms exports according to the official statistics

(a) Value of exports

Year	Exports by Switzerland		Exports by Sweden	
	in Sfr m.	in US $m. (constant 1985)	in SEK m.	in US $m. (constant 1985)
1975	369	192	536	162
1976	492	257	502	139
1977	513	266	695	176
1978	426	229	905	351
1979	426	220	1 671	383
1980	340	168	2 078	280
1981	511	239	1 697	233
1982	471	203	1 588	209
1983	377	162	1 658	203
1984	392	164	2 178	267

(b) Largest customers in the Third World, percentage share of total:

Switzerland	1975–79	Switzerland	1980–84	Sweden	1983–85
Iran	11.7	Nigeria	14.2	Singapore	10.7
Ghana	3.2	Singapore	1.4	Nigeria	10.1
Singapore	1.1	United Arab		Malaysia	4.7
		Emirates	0.9	India	4.5
				Brazil	2.3

Note: Detailed statistics for Switzerland are available from 1975; and for Sweden from 1983.
Sources: Krigsmaterielinspektionen; Sonderstatistik Kriegsmaterial-Exportstatistik der Monatsstatistik des Aussenhandels; $-values: calculated from IMF International Financial Statistics.

weapons.[109] The main debate is on the recipients, and in this context two types of arms deal have been identified. In the first, Swedish arms manufacturers have delivered arms in violation of the law and without the knowledge of the government. By mid-1986 several such cases were being investigated by Swedish police and customs authorities, including the alleged smuggling of Bofors RBS-70 missiles to Bahrain and Dubai via Singapore and covert deliveries of gunpowder, chemicals and ammunition to countries in the Middle East. In the second type of deal, licences have been granted by the government when the recipient could be judged to fall into the categories of countries to which exports are not allowed. Indonesia is the main case in point.

Despite the intense public debate, by mid-1986 there were no signs that the government would drastically alter its policy. Proposals such as the one put forward by Ambassador Inga Thorsson to use arms export taxes as a way of funding conversion efforts in Sweden were not received favourably. As long as critics cannot invalidate the argument that arms exports are economically vital and a necessity for Sweden's security policy, current levels of restriction are likely to be raised only marginally.

Switzerland faces the same dilemma as Sweden and tries to balance domestic pressures to export with public demand for a restrictive arms export policy. The Swiss arms-production industry is smaller than that in Sweden, employing about 30 000 persons (directly and indirectly).[110] Most of the export sales go to other industrialized countries, both in Western Europe and in North America. According to official statistics, the share of Third World recipients is less than one-third of the total. Having reached more than $250 million in the mid-1970s, this total had dropped to less than $170 million in 1984 (see table 3.9). The share in total Swiss exports was about 1.3 per cent in 1981 and 0.7 per cent in 1984. Official exports exclude some material destined for the armed forces, such as light aircraft. It is also suspected that material delivered to countries such as Italy and the UK (countries in which Swiss companies have subsidiaries producing weapons), is then shipped on to other countries in the Third World.[111] SIPRI statistics include small aircraft if they are sold to armed forces and therefore SIPRI statistics and Swiss statistics differ as regards main recipients.

Both the problem of whether small aircraft should be considered as weapons or not and of Swiss companies having foreign subsidiaries have been debated in Switzerland. The current legal framework was established in 1972, after a popular referendum aimed at outlawing all arms exports to the Third World had only just failed to gain a majority of votes. The government then adopted a restrictive law, forbidding exports to areas with armed conflicts, or a risk for armed conflict or where there were dangerous tensions. The law also stipulates that weapon deliveries should not violate Swiss attempts to further the cause of human rights and to help the development of the Third World. The Swiss law is probably the most restrictive in the world.

Swiss arms manufacturers responded by increasing exports not regulated by the law and by building up political pressure to change the law. Oerlikon-Bührle increased production in its British and Italian subsidiaries (i.e., in countries with less restrictive export laws) and Mowag began to sell licences to produce weapons instead of complete weapon systems. Mowag-designed armoured vehicles are produced in Chile, although there has been an arms embargo against the country since 1974. The political efforts of the arms industry to change the law on the basis of the economic advantages of arms sales, were to some extent honoured in 1978 by the adoption of a resolution in both chambers of parliament asking the government to interpret the law in a less restrictive way and specifically to exclude small aircraft from its provisions.[112] Such aircraft have gone to a number of countries in the Third World, including Iraq and Iran during their war against each other. These aircraft can be armed, but are not armed when they leave Switzerland and have therefore consistently not been classified as war material by special inquiry commissions and the Swiss Government.

Yugoslavian arms exports are difficult to assess as there is very little information available. Information from various sources is most contradictory, even allowing for the large margins to be expected in the secretive business of arms supply.

SIPRI statistics of the trade in major weapons contain some deliveries of ships (mostly training frigates with light armament), training aircraft, and light armoured vehicles to a number of countries in the Middle East and Asia. Judging from these statistics, Yugoslavia was only a very minor arms exporter, though there was a rising trend in the late 1970s (see figure 3.13). US Government figures give a different picture. According to these figures, which include deliveries of small arms, military vehicles, ammunition, light artillery, spare parts and machinery for the production of armaments, Yugoslavian arms exports have grown from a level of around $30 million in the early 1970s to more than $400 million in the early 1980s (in constant 1982 prices).[113] Evidence from arms producers suggests that there is a substantial export of small arms, ammunition and parts from Yugoslavia. Zavodi Crvena Zastava, the largest Yugoslavian arms production company, is an important producer of artillery, small arms, and military vehicles. Iskra, another large arms producer, specializes in weapon parts, such as laser range-finders. Other important companies are the aircraft producer SOKO and the various shipyards. All in all, employment adds up to 60 000–70 000.[114]

Even higher arms export figures are given in Yugoslavian sources. The Defence Ministry gives figures in annual reports to the parliament, which are quoted in the Western press. According to these figures, arms exports had reached $1 billion in 1981, $1.7 billion in 1982, $2.4 billion in 1983 and $2.5 billion in 1984.[115] These figures imply that between 20 and 25 per cent of all Yugoslavian exports in the early 1980s consisted of arms. Such figures are implausible. Not only are they not reconcilable with Yugoslavian foreign trade statistics,[116] they also imply a much wider spread of Yugoslavian arms than can be actually detected and they contradict other official figures about arms production in Yugoslavia. If the share of exports in total production does not exceed one-third,[117] then total exports cannot be higher than a maximum of $400 million, given the Yugoslavian military expenditures of about $2.5 billion in the early 1980s.[118] The Yugoslav figures could include the re-export of material originating in other countries, both in the West and the East, but even if allowance is made for extensive re-export, the figures seem inflated.

Yugoslavia is unique among the countries surveyed in this section in that there is no opposition to arms exports. On the contrary, the increase of arms exports is an official aim of the government. In the Law on Economic and Other Relationships in the Production and Transportation of Armaments and Military Equipment of 1979, Article 45 states that the government (the Federal Executive Council) 'will establish…measures and mechanisms for regular and supplementary stimulation of exports of products for special services and other forms of economic relations.'[119] The 1979 legal reform, which centralized arms production and arms exports, put the Federal Secretariat of National Defence in charge of the control and promotion of arms exports. The Secretariat supervises the activities of the individual companies, the association of arms manufacturers (INVOJ) and the state trading agency.

The main reasons given for the expansion of arms exports is the support of the non-aligned movement in the world. It is consistent with this policy that Yugoslavia mainly exports to Third World countries. The weapons exported are of Yugoslavian, Eastern and Western design and often incorporate technology from various sources. Another justification for arms exports is the necessity to maintain a wide arms-production base, independent of the great powers.[120] The timing of the expansion of arms exports and the main customers (reportedly Libya, Iraq, Egypt)[121] indicate that the Yugoslavian arms industry has benefited much from the arms boom of the late 1970s. Economic incentives were important in shaping the expansive arms export policy.

XII. Third World suppliers

Arms production in the Third World, negligible up to the early 1960s, has grown dramatically since then.[122] Post World War II arms production started in Argentina and North Korea, and these countries were the most important producers in the 1950s. From then on, large-scale arms production was introduced in more and more countries, such as India and South Africa in the early 1960s, Brazil and Israel in the late 1960s, South Korea and Taiwan in the early 1970s and Indonesia and Singapore in the late 1970s.

In some cases, arms export earnings were an important factor behind the growth of the arms industries. The best documented case is that of Brazil. In most cases, however, the main motives for setting up an arms industry were political. Domestic arms production was either intended to counter the effects of real or anticipated embargoes—as in the cases of Chile, Israel and South Africa—or it was an attempt to live up to the rhetoric of greater independence from the major industrialized arms suppliers—as in the cases of Argentina and India. Commercial and economic considerations were secondary: governments were prepared to spend money for political reasons. Under such conditions, arms production was allowed to be uneconomical, even if the prospect of export earnings may have increased the general attraction of arms production.

Arms exports from Third World countries have grown with arms production. During 1971-75, the export share of Third World countries in total Third World major-weapon imports was 1.1 per cent. For the following five years, 1976-80, the share was 2.9 per cent, while—in the five-year period 1981-85—it had risen to 4.9 per cent. Brazil and Israel are by far the most important exporters of major weapons from the Third World (see figure 3.14). The Third World arms suppliers can be divided into two categories: those that mainly export indigenously produced weapons and those that primarily or exclusively re-export major weapons previously imported from elsewhere else. This section first discusses countries in the first category.

Israel co-operates very closely in security matters with the United States. Throughout 1971-85 the USA was almost the exclusive supplier of weapons to Israel. Within this framework of dependency, consecutive Israeli governments have tried to establish political and military manoeuvring space by building up

(a) Trend 1971–85
Five-year moving averages

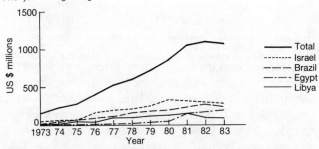

(b) Arms export shares and number of Third World customers, 1971–85

Supplier	Percentage share of Third World arms imports		Number of Third World customers
	in World	in group	
Israel	0.92	28.7	24
Brazil	0.71	22.1	25
Egypt	0.35	10.9	14
Libya	0.35	10.8	11
Jordan	0.18	5.6	6
S. Korea	0.18	5.6	7
Singapore	0.09	2.9	10
South Africa	0.07	2.2	5
N. Korea	0.06	1.8	8
Syria	0.05	1.7	2
Iran	0.04	1.3	5
India	0.03	0.9	6
Cuba	0.03	0.9	3
Iraq	0.02	0.7	3
Indonesia	0.02	0.7	5
Others	0.10	3.3	
Total	3.2	100.0	

(c) Distribution by weapon category, 1971–85

(d) Distribution by weapon status, 1971–85

(e) Distribution by importing region, 1971–85

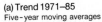

(f) Percentage share of important recipients

Rank order	Israel		Brazil		Egypt		Libya	
	Country	Share	Country	Share	Country	Share	Country	Share
1	Taiwan	27	Iraq	33	Iraq	82	Syria	52
2	South Africa	27	Libya	31	Sudan	11	Uganda	19
3	Argentina	14	Chile	8	Somalia	4	Iran	13
4	Colombia	6	Colombia	4	Morocco	1	Iraq	8
5	Chile	5	Paraguay	3			Nicaragua	4
Total of 5[a]		78		79		97		96

[a] Figures may not add up to totals due to rounding.

Figure 3.14. Third World suppliers: exports of major weapons to the Third World, 1971–85

Based on SIPRI trend indicator values in US $m., at constant (1985) prices.

an arms industry. Arms production is closely supervised by the government and most of the major companies are government-owned. Control also extends to the private sector. Co-operation between the armed forces and the arms industry is so close that some observers speak of an Israeli 'military-industrial complex'.[123] While the prime motive for the expansion of arms production activities in Israel was the demand from the Israeli armed forces, resulting from insecure foreign supplies, arms exports—which started to grow in the mid-1970s—served two important functions. First, they offered a means of breaking Israel's increasing diplomatic isolation. Second, arms exports earned foreign exchange.[124] On the other hand, since Israel's edge compared with the Arab countries is traditionally in superior technology (and the capacity to put it to efficient use), arms exports are closely scrutinized for security reasons. The most sophisticated weapons were not exported, while arms exports to Arab countries in the geographical vicinity of Israel were forbidden.

Consequently, the weapons on which the growth in Israeli arms exports was based were naval equipment (less relevant for the Arab–Israeli conflict), transport aircraft, older types of fighter aircraft, small arms and certain electronics equipment. Tanks were not exported at all and other armoury or artillery only rarely. The main customers were countries in Latin America and a few countries in Africa and Asia. Total arms exports reportedly amounted to $750–1000 million annually in the early 1980s. This was equal to 16–20 per cent of total exports. A small share of the total arms exports was imported by the USA and some West European countries.

There were some controversies concerning arms exports. Deliveries to Argentina during the military dictatorship in the late 1970s were criticized in Israel due to harassment of Jews in Argentina at the time. There was concern about Israeli support to ring-wing governments in Central America, such as the Somoza Government in Nicaragua. Israel also had strong military ties with South Africa, despite the mandatory UN embargo.[125] Since 1980 weapons and spare parts were supplied to the Khomeini regime in Iran. These deliveries were justified on the grounds that, according to the majority view in the Israeli Government, Iraq should be seen as a greater enemy in the long run than Iran.

A crucial aspect of Israeli arms exports is the relationship with the United States. Not only does the USA have the power to veto many of Israel's weapons from being exported since they include US components. Israel is also dependent on the USA both financially and strategically. This dependence became an issue with respect to arms transfers during the time of the Carter Administration. On the one hand, some Israeli exports—such as the sale of the Kfir to Ecuador—were not allowed by the USA. On the other hand, Israel stepped in and seemingly substituted for the USA by supplying some governments in Central America, such as Guatemala and Nicaragua, when the USA stopped deliveries because of human rights violations in these countries. The same was true for Israeli deliveries to Iran in the early 1980s.

The current status of the *Brazilian* arms industry as one of the ten largest exporters of major weapons in the world can be traced back to government decisions made in the late 1960s. At that time, arms production was singled out as one of the industrial sectors which could earn the foreign exchange needed to fuel the economy. Because of earlier efforts to increase the number of Brazilian engineers and technicians, there was a sufficient supply of manpower. In order to avoid US embargoes on components or technology, the use of US technology was limited to components which were not under strict control by the US Government. Given the large number of foreign multinational companies in Brazil, it was natural to use as many components as possible from these producers. This way the import content could be kept low, while at the same time customers could be offered the international service networks of big multinational companies for parts like engines, electronics, and so on. The government encouraged private Brazilian companies to enter arms production, but kept control over this sector which was judged to be strategic for both political and economic reasons. Thus foreign companies, while important suppliers of components, did not become involved in the final assembly and sale of Brazilian major weapons. After the early 1970s, when some Brazilian designs had been thoroughly tested (for example, in the border clash between Libya and Egypt in 1977), exports of transport and training aircraft and armoured vehicles grew fast. The main customers were some countries in the Middle East, most notably Iraq and Libya. Cheap, rugged Brazilian weapons became an alternative to supplies from industrialized countries for a large number of Third World recipients. The way was paved for other Third World producers trying to export on the world market. In addition to armoured vehicles and aircraft, production of missiles and artillery was started. The one sector lagging behind was shipbuilding which was never part of the general arms export drive.

Employment in arms production was estimated at about 100 000 persons in the early 1980s. More than 70 per cent of production was for export. Reliable export figures are hard to get—Brazilian industry regularly claims very high figures in order to stress its importance for the economy. The authority for foreign trade transactions, CACEX (*Carteira de Comercio do Banco do Brasil S.A.*), through which all arms exports are authorized, also reports high figures.[126] Nevertheless, it can be assumed that total Brazilian exports were close to $1 billion per year in the early 1980s. This was equal to about 4–5 per cent of total Brazilian exports, making arms production one of the most important earners of foreign exchange. It is no wonder, then, that the government has tried to support arms exports as much as possible. In addition to export subsidies, there are marketing aids, such as a catalogue of Brazilian weapons put out by the Foreign Ministry and diplomatic assistance in negotiating with customers. Still, the Brazilian Government has to take account of US political pressure. In October 1983, the government decided to endanger further deliveries to Libya by complying with a US demand to seize a Libyan aircraft transporting weapons to Nicaragua via Brazil.

US leverage over Brazilian arms exports could increase if more US components and technology were used. Parts of the armed forces, more interested in getting modern weapon systems than in arms exports, succeeded in getting the

Brazilian Government to sign a Memorandum of Understanding with the USA in 1984 to facilitate military co-operation. The Brazilian arms industry objected since agreement could result in increased US leverage over Brazilian arms exports.

South Korea is a late-comer among the Third World arms producers and exporters. The development of the mostly private arms industry was intimately connected with relations between South Korea and the United States. As long as the United States freely supplied the South Korean armed forces with weapons, there was no incentive to produce more than a limited supply of some small arms and munitions. When US policy towards South East Asia began to change in the early 1970s, arms production became a strategic goal of the South Korean Government. Although South Korea has a strong civilian industrial base, US assistance was needed in setting up the arms industry. Most of the weapons produced are of US origin.[127] The USA has on occasion protested against the extensive re-engineering of US artillery weapons and other items in South Korea.

With respect to arms exports, this makes it difficult to distinguish between South Korean and US weapons. Despite some controversies with the USA about deliveries, for example, of artillery to Jordan in 1982, South Korea has reportedly become an important exporter of small arms and ammunition. Artillery and ships are also exported. All in all, exports have been reported at a level of up to $250 million in the early 1980s. Most of the customers are in the ASEAN area, but odd exports have been made to a number of countries in South America, Africa and other Asian countries.

The total value of *Singapore*'s arms exports by the mid-1980s is estimated at around $200 million annually. According to official government policy, Singapore is not allowed to sell weapons to Communist countries or countries subject to UN embargoes. The production capacity of Singapore's arms industry far exceeds the domestic demand, but the real extent of Singapore's arms exports is hard to identify. However, there are two basic export categories: sales of finished weapons (such as naval vessels, small arms and munitions) and sales of components, spare parts and services (such as aircraft overhaul or the refurbishment of armoured vehicles). Similarly, there are three basic channels for arms exports (*a*) from private companies; (*b*) from the state-owned (MoD) Sheng-Li holding company through Unicorn International (the marketing company in the Sheng-Li group); and (*c*) from countries or companies outside Singapore, often with Unicorn as middleman. The privately owned exporters are often organized under Western multinational companies in order to exploit the comparatively low labour costs and advantageous commercial regulations. The Sheng-Li group is responsible for most of Singapore's arms exports in both of the above-mentioned categories. The third export channel is shrouded in much secrecy. However, it is clear that Unicorn, on the one hand, has agreements with a number of foreign arms producers to market their products in Asia and elsewhere. In addition, Unicorn is sometimes used by foreign companies to re-route weapons intended for customers not approved by their respective governments. Thus, Bofors of Sweden delivered RBS-70 missiles to Bahrain and Dubai via Unicorn in 1979–80.

South Africa began systematically to build up a broad-based arms industry when it became clear that its major suppliers might declare an arms embargo in the early 1960s. The UN voluntary arms embargo that came in 1963 furthered South African arms production by making it more difficult to obtain complete major weapon systems from at least some suppliers, while not limiting the flow of arms production technology. When the mandatory arms embargo was declared in 1977, South Africa had an arms production base that was capable of producing most of the weapons required by the South African armed forces. South African efforts then turned increasingly to the production of components, such as electronic parts and engines, in order to be able to withstand an even more far-reaching embargo. Domestic demand left little room for weapon exports until the early 1980s. At that time Armscor, the state-owned coordinating company for arms production, got into a difficult situation: the weapons that could be produced in South Africa were in sufficient stock with the armed forces, while those weapons (such as maritime surveillance aircraft, fighter aircraft or helicopters) that the South African armed forces would have wanted to buy were too costly or complex to design and produce. Exports were an obvious way out, and an expensive export campaign was started. Only some exports to a few Latin American and African countries, such as Chile, Paraguay and Morocco, were reported. The political opposition against the South African apartheid regime made extensive South African exports impossible. In December 1984 this was codified in a UN Security Council resolution requesting all states to refrain from buying South African weapons.[128]

North Korea, together with Argentina, was the most important Third World arms producer in the 1950s. While the basic aim—a higher degree of self-sufficiency of the armed forces—was the same, the industrial and technological strategy chosen was rather different. The emphasis in North Korea was on production of ammunition, small arms, artillery and small ships. In the beginning, all designs were of Soviet origin; later some items were designed domestically. Despite some efforts in the 1970s to include the production of more sophisticated weaponry such as submarines and fighter aircraft, the arms industry has maintained its early profile. Exports are therefore confined to small arms, ammunition, artillery and small ships of domestic production and the re-export of weapons supplied from China and the Soviet Union. It is very difficult to get hard information about North Korean arms exports. Until the late 1970s, North Korea was known as an avid, though not very resourceful, supplier of military expertise, small arms and the odd piece of artillery and naval equipment, both to governments and guerrilla movements throughout the world. This activity was decreased and was substituted by more concentrated programmes, for example in Zimbabwe and Zaire, that included the transfer of major weapons. In addition, in the early 1980s North Korea reportedly became a major supplier to Iran. Annual exports of $500 million and more have been mentioned for the early 1980s. Given North Korea's arms production profile, these large deliveries, if they really occurred, can only have been retransfers of Soviet and Chinese major weapons. What North Korea might have added from its own production are small arms and ammunition, especially for artillery.

Given its position as one of the two foremost arms producers in the Third World, *India* is a very minor arms supplier. The Indian arms industry, employing as many people as, for example, that of FR Germany, or between 250 000 and 300 000 people, was set up in response to a need for greater self-sufficiency in the military field. Although the high goals have not been met, the arms industry utilized its capacity with the production for domestic use of Soviet-, Western- and indigenously-designed tanks, armoured vehicles, aircraft and missiles. The extensive use of foreign licences was one factor limiting Indian arms exports: the licensers were unwilling to allow further spread of their weapon designs. Another factor was the restrictive Indian arms export policy. Arms exports were limited to a few unarmed ships and aircraft to countries in South Asia.[129]

Egypt is the main representative of the second category of Third World major-weapons suppliers—the re-exporters. However, Egypt not only re-exports weapons, it also exports domestically-produced and designed equipment as well as weapons built under licence. Egyptian weapons are sold to other Middle Eastern countries (e.g., Iraq) and to some countries in Africa (notably Somalia, Sudan and Zaire). There are three main reasons for Egypt's emergence as a leading Third World arms supplier in the 1980s. First, sales to Iraq serve the purpose of reintegrating Egypt in the Arab fraternity; second, sales to neighbouring countries in Africa are part of the US–Egyptian regional containment policy towards Libya; and third, Egypt has unique know-how and experience in the region in the reverse-engineering, manufacture and overhaul of Soviet weapons, which abound in many countries in the region.

Egypt's domestic production consists of two different lines of production. One—for small arms, ammunition and components, but also for some missile types—was established in the 1960s with Soviet help. It continued after the breakdown of Soviet–Egyptian relations in the mid-1970s. At this time the other line was started with an ambitious plan to set up an Arab arms industry in Egypt. This plan fell through with the signing of the Camp David Accords in 1979. Egypt instead went ahead on its own with assembly and licenced production of aircraft, vehicles and missiles of West European and US origin. The arms industry employs up to about 100 000 people. Before the Iraq–Iran War, most of the output was for domestic use. Since 1980 a large part of total production has gone to Iraq, including weapons from Brazil, China, France and Romania which are sent to Iraq via Egypt or from Egyptian licensed production.

Jordan was also an important resupplier of weapons to Iraq, while *Syria* and *Libya* sent weapons to Iran. Libya also delivered Soviet and East European weapons to some countries in Africa and to Nicaragua.

By the mid-1980s Third World arms producers were hampered in their arms export efforts by the structure of demand. The types of weapon they can best produce—simple and unsophisticated items, such as small arms and ammunition—represent only a small market when compared to the market for more sophisticated major-weapon systems. The competition at this lower end of the market has become more intense with the attempts of more and more countries to copy the Brazilian model. The dilemma, then, is that what can be efficiently produced is not much in demand, while products much in demand cannot be produced.

The increasing level of re-exports raises a number of important issues, especially with respect to the resupplier's relationship with the original producer. Re-exports may be the result of instructions or tacit approval from the original supplier—in which case the re-exporter functions as a proxy. They may also be an expression of a more independent foreign and economic policy, even in the absence of a domestic arms industry.

Political limitations are—with a few exceptions such as Israel and India— most often absent in the Third World. This undermines the possibilities for arms control in the field of conventional weapons. Arms supply patterns in connection with the Iraq–Iran War illustrate the lack of control by many Third World arms-exporting countries, irrespective of whether they export from their own production or from earlier imports.

Notes and references

[1] For a description of earlier laws, administrative procedures and government approaches concerning arms transfers, see SIPRI, *The Arms Trade with the Third World* (Almqvist & Wiksell: Stockholm, 1971).

[2] Data on Soviet arms exports are surrounded by a high degree of uncertainty. Such data are not derived from Soviet sources, but come mainly from reports from the recipient countries, newsletters and journals and intelligence services.

[3] See *Prospects for Multilateral Arms Export Restraint*, a staff report prepared for the use of the Committee on Foreign Relations, US Senate (US Government Printing Office: Washington, DC, 1979), p. 20; Holloway, D., *The Soviet Union and the Arms Race* (Yale University Press: New Haven, 1983), pp. 109–115.

[4] See Holloway, D., 'The Soviet Union', in Ball, N. and Leitenberg, M. (eds), *The Structure of the Defence Industry* (Croom Helm: London, 1983), pp. 56–62.

[5] Holloway (note 4), pp. 67–72.

[6] Kozyrev, A., *The Arms Trade: A New Level of Danger* (Progress Publishers: Moscow, 1985), p. 25.

[7] Buildup of a Soviet blue-water navy and large transport fleet during the late 1960s and early 1970s and arms transfers reinforced each other: deliveries world-wide were made possible and access to bases could be negotiated.

[8] Kozyrev (note 6), p. 179.

[9] Krause, J., 'Soviet military aid to the Third World', *Aussenpolitik*, vol. 34, no. 4 (1983), pp. 399–400.

[10] Wharton Econometric Forecasting Associates, *Soviet Arms Trade with the Non-Communist Third World in the 1970s and 1980s*, Special Report, Washington, DC, 1984, p. 28.

[11] See Roberts, C. A., 'Soviet arms-transfer policy and the decision to upgrade Syrian air defences', *Survival*, vol. 25, no. 4 (1983), pp. 158–62.

[12] Ali, S., 'The Soviet connection'; *Far Eastern Economic Review*, 7 Mar. 1985, p. 36.

[13] See the discussion of Soviet Third World debate in Hough, J. F., *The Struggle for the Third World: Soviet Debates and American Options* (Brookings Institution: Washington, DC, 1986).

[14] For thorough descriptions of US arms transfer programmes and the relevant legislation, see *US Military Sales and Assistance Programs: Laws, Regulations and Procedures*, House of Representatives, Committee on Foreign Affairs, CRS report for the Subcommittee on Arms Control, International Security and Science, 99th Congress, 1st Session (US Government

Printing Office: Washington, DC, July 1985); Hammond, P., Louscher, D., Salomone, M. and Graham, N., *The Reluctant Supplier: US Decisionmaking for Arms Sales* (OGH Publishers: Cambridge, MA, 1983).

[15] See Grimmett, R., *An Overview of United States Military Assistance Programs*, CRS Report No. 85–92F (Library of Congress: Washington, DC, 1985).

[16] For an overview of these irregularities, see Lydenberg, S., *Weapons for the World—Update* (Council on Economic Priorities: New York, 1977).

[17] See *US Military Sales* (note 14), pp. 65–72.

[18] In the mid-1980s numerous changes and additions in the legislative framework were made as a result of the Reagan Administration's concerns about the trend towards offsets in connection with arms sales as well as the risks involved in supplying sensitive military and dual-use technology to other countries. With respect to offsets, the US DoD negotiated offset arrangements between US arms industries and other countries in connection with FMS sales until May 1978. At that time a DoD directive stated that the government should withdraw from such negotiations mainly on the grounds that they were pure business judgements and that the responsibility for fulfilling the offset should lie with the contractor, not the government. In 1984 a Defense Production Act extension introduced a provision stating concern about the lack of data on the effect of offsets on US technology leadership, defence preparedness and employment. Federal agencies conducting the ensuing investigations into the extent and effects of offsets included the Office of Management and Budget, the International Trade Commission and the Departments of Defense, Labor and Commerce. On technology transfers, a 1985 Pentagon study claimed that more than 5000 Soviet weapon projects had benefited from research data and technology obtained from the USA and its allies. US measures in the mid-1980s to counter this include (*a*) new regulations for the control of commercial exports of defence articles (ITAR), (*b*) a revised Export Administration Act (EAA) including a merger of the Commodity Control List (CCL) with the updated Military Critical Technology List (MCTL) and (*c*) a Senate provision requiring the Administration to notify Congress of upgrades in the technology or mission capability of equipment sold under FMS, if the upgrades are made after approval for the sale.

[19] The 30-day review and the legislative veto do not apply to commercial sales to NATO, NATO members, Australia, New Zealand or Japan. For FMS sales to these recipients, the review period is 15 days. In 1983 the Supreme Court ruled that a one-House concurrent resolution was unconstitutional; since then, the AECA veto has required a joint resolution of disapproval in both houses, plus a two-thirds majority in both houses to overrule a presidential veto.

[20] Guaranteed loans were extended by the Federal Financing Bank at cost plus an administrative fee. In the mid-1980s the government did not extend any such loans. This change to the exclusive use of direct loans was intended to make the budgeting of FMS financing more realistic and viable, since guaranteed loans did not appear as appropriated funds or as obligational authority: they were 'off-budget'.

[21] The AECA requires foreign military sales to be self-supporting. This is done through the imposition of an administrative fee of 3 per cent on all FMS transactions. The levelling-out of arms orders in the 1980s has caused a downturn also in these administrative funds and, by 1985, the DoD and DoS bureaucracies handling arms transfers were faced with a need for substantial personnel cuts.

[22] These figures are derived from Gansler, J., *The Defense Industry* (MIT Press: Cambridge, MA, 1980). They represent average estimates for the 10-year period up to 1980. By and large, more recent data indicate that the levels given are still valid approximations.

[23] This figure would indicate that about one-third of total employment in the military sector depends on arms exports. The DSAA estimate should perhaps be seen in the light of the US recession at the time as well as the low levels of military spending. A more conservative estimate from the US Bureau of Labor Statistics gives the figure of about 257 000 people dependent on arms exports in 1975 (or 10–15 per cent of the military-industrial labour force). These and other estimates are discussed in Pierre, A., *The Global Politics of Arms Sales* (Princeton University Press: New Jersey, 1982), pp. 68–71.

[24] A DoD study from 1976, entitled 'Profit '76', indicated that foreign military sales were about 2.5 times as profitable as military sales to the US Government. More recent data suggest that the difference was smaller by the mid-1980s. There are obviously also measurement problems involved since foreign sales include training, support and infrastructure not needed in sales to

the US armed forces. See also DeSouza, P., 'The other side of the defense coin', *Defense & Foreign Affairs*, vol. 11, no. 3 (Mar. 1983), pp. 20–23.

[25] *Study of the Economic Effects of Restraints in Arms Transfers*, A Treasury report to the US Senate, Committee on Foreign Relations, Annex 2, 95th Congress, 1st Session (US Government Printing Office: Washington, DC, July 1977).

[26] *US Military Sales to Iran*, US Senate, Committee on Foreign Relations, A State Report to the Subcommittee on Foreign Assistance, 94th Congress, 2nd Session (US Government Printing Office: Washington, DC, July 1978), p. vii. For an initiated discussion of US arms transfer policy and behaviour towards Iran, see Klare, M., *American Arms Supermarket* (University of Texas Press: Austin, 1984), pp. 108–26.

[27] See Pierre (note 23), p. 48. For a completely different assessment of the Nixon-Ford-Kissinger arms transfer policy, see Sorley, L., *Arms Transfer under Nixon—A Policy Analysis* (University Press of Kentucky: Lexington, MA, 1983), pp. 33–50.

[28] In the United States, the term co-production includes production under licence of the weapon or parts thereof, as well as joint production of weapons or components and various forms of industrial offset arrangements in connection with sales.

[29] Pierre (note 23), pp. 55–56.

[30] Yankelovich, D. and Kagan, L., 'Assertive America', *Foreign Affairs*, vol. 59, no. 3 (1981), pp. 696–713.

[31] *Conventional Arms Transfer Policy* (The White House: Washington, DC, 9 July 1981).

[32] de Brigantini, G., 'France's exports: foreign sales drive much of France's aerospace policy', *Armed Forces Journal International*, vol. 122, no. 4 (Nov. 1984), p. 72.

[33] Isnard, J., 'Marketing weapon systems: an analysis of France's export apparatus', *Defence & Armament*, no. 20, June 1983, p. 41.

[34] Isnard, J., 'La France veut accroître ses exportations d'armes', *Le Monde*, 19 Jan. 1984.

[35] These figures are taken from *Armament in France* (French Ministry of Defence: Paris, 1985), pp. 7–8.

[36] This figure was given, for example, by then Defence Minister Hernu in an interview with *Le Figaro* in Sep. 1982, quoted in Kolodziej, E., 'French arms trade: the economic determinants', in SIPRI, *World Armaments and Disarmament: SIPRI Yearbook 1984* (Taylor & Francis: London, 1984), p. 380.

[37] Kolodziej estimates the direct employment from arms exports to be 130 000–140 000, while the official figures are around 100 000 to 110 000 for the early 1980s, see Kolodziej (note 36), pp. 387–89.

[38] One econometric study gave the result that for each billion francs of French arms exports 315 million francs of pre-products had to be imported, mostly in the armaments sector: Aben, J., 'Commerce de guerre ou commerce de paix: un dilemma pour les relations entre la France et le Tiers Monde', *Défense Nationale*, vol. 41, no. 2 (1985), pp. 65–69.

[39] Figures taken from Dussauge, P., *L'industrie française de l'armement* (Economica: Paris, 1985), p. 25.

[40] According to DGA rules, repayment for R&D costs (which can be up to 30 per cent for items to be produced under licence) can be forgiven, if so decided by the DGA; see Dussauge (note 39).

[41] Aben (note 38) has calculated that civilian exports to Third World countries are 9–13 per cent more beneficial to the foreign trade balance and 5–10 per cent more beneficial for employment than arms exports of the same amount.

[42] *Armament in France* (note 35), p. 23.

[43] See for example Kolodziej (note 36).

[44] Assemblée nationale, Proposition de loi no. 536, 29 June 1978; there is also a law of 30 June 1952 which envisages the availability of information from a parliamentary commission about arms transfers, which has never been put into use; see Chatillion, G., 'La France et le Tiers Monde: problèmes d'armements', *Défense Nationale*, vol. 39, no. 7 (1983), pp. 78–79.

[45] In-depth descriptions of the control apparatus are given in: Pearson, F. S., 'The question of control in British defence sales policy', *International Affairs*, vol. 28, no. 2 (1983), and Edmonds, M., 'The British Government and arms sales', *ADIU-report*, vol. 4, no. 6 (1982). British government documents outlining policy include: 'Procedures used by Her Majesty's Government in arms sales decisions', mimeo, London, ca. 1978 and, Foreign and Commonwealth Office, 'Foreign policy aspects of overseas arms sales', Memorandum to the Select Committee on Foreign Affairs, FCO/FCA/12/81, London, 1981.

[46] Some employment figures are given in the yearly Defence Statistics, Secretary of State for

Defence, *Statement on the Defence Estimates*, vol. 2 (Her Majesty's Stationary Office: London, annual). For an overview see Pite, C., 'Employment and defence', *Statistical News*, no. 51, Nov. 1980.

47 Statistics on military R&D can be found in *SIPRI Yearbooks*. In a report on the electronics industry, where one would expect spin-off to be comparatively high, a government commission found only very limited spin-off: see *Civil Exploitations of Defence Technology, Report to the Electronics Economic Development Committee* by Sir Ieuan Maddock and Observations by the Ministry of Defence (National Economic Development Office: London, Feb. 1983).

48 Some figures on arms trade, including a geographical breakdown, can be found in recent Defence Statistics (note 46).

49 A comparison of arms exports and R&D-intensive sectors of arms production showed that arms exports are not concentrated in such sectors. In addition, the tough competition on the arms export market makes it difficult to recoup R&D costs. See Taylor, T., 'Research note: British arms exports and R&D costs', *Survival*, vol. 22, no. 6 (1980), pp. 259–62.

50 Ellis, R., 'Defence sales', *Journal of the Royal United Services Institute for Defence Studies*, June 1979, p. 3.

51 Pearson (note 45), p. 227.

52 Taken from comparison of the two government documents mentioned in note 45.

53 Such claims have repeatedly been made by the Anti-Apartheid movement, see e.g., *How Britain Arms Apartheid* (Anti-Apartheid-Movement: London, 1985).

54 The US Government has complained repeatedly that parts classified as non-lethal have been allowed to go to Iran. Such parts have reportedly included spares for jet engines and even Phantom aircraft, see e.g., *Guardian*, 22 Feb. 1984.

55 For an overview of old regulations see SIPRI (note 1); for newer developments see *Archivio Disarmo*, 'La legge sul commercio de materiale bellico', Codice LI, no. 1 (10 Nov. 1982), Rome.

56 Melega, G., 'Al mercato dei missili' *L'espresso*, 14 July 1955.

57 See note 56.

58 Data are taken from Rossi, S. G., 'The Italian defence industry with respect to international competition', *Defence Today*, no. 77–78, 1984, and de Briganti, G., 'Italian defense industry's status threatened', *Armed Forces International Journal*, vol. 122, no. 10 (May 1985), pp. 109–13; see also di Falco, M., 'The volume of trade', *Defence Today*, no. 93/94, 1986.

59 See Rossi (note 58), p. 408.

60 See e.g., Ministry of Defence, *White Paper 1985*, Rome 1985, pp. 73–77, 183–87.

61 *Neue Züricher Zeitung*, 29 Sep. 1984.

62 See e.g., *Archivio Disarmo*, 'Industria militare Italiana: esportazioni (II)', Codice IB, no. 13 (5 May 1986), Rome.

63 On Chinese efforts to acquire Western arms technology see SIPRI, *World Armaments and Disarmament: SIPRI Yearbook 1985* (Taylor & Francis: London, 1985), p. 356; and Shambaugh, D. L., 'China's defence industries: indigenous and foreign procurement', in H. B. Goodwin (ed.), *The Chinese Defense Establishment: Continuity and Change in the 1980s* (Westview Press: Boulder, CO, 1985), pp. 69–79.

64 Data are taken from Jammes, S., 'China', in Ball and Leitenberg (note 4), p. 26.

65 See *The Allocation of Resources in the Soviet Union and China*, Statement before the Subcommittee on International Trade, Finance, and Security Economics of the Joint Economic Committee, US Congress (US Government Printing Office: Washington, DC, annual).

66 See Jammes (note 64); a detailed account of changes in the late 1970s and early 1980s can be found in Latham, R. J., 'People's Republic of China: the restructuring of defense-industrial policies', in Katz, S. (ed.), *Arms Production in Developing Countries* (Lexington Books: Lexington, MA, 1984). The figure is from *Peace* (Journal of the Chinese People's Association for Peace and Disarmament), vol. 1, no. 2 (1986), p. 18.

67 See Segal, G. and Gilks, A., 'China and the arms trade', *Arms Control*, vol. 6, no. 3 (1985), pp. 258–63.

68 See US Congress (note 65) and CIA data on China's arms exports based on import statistics of China's trade partners as reported in *Government Business Worldwide Report*, 2 Dec. 1985.

69 An overview of the legal situation is given in Mammitzsch, T., *Die rechtlichen Grenzen von Rüstungsproduktion und Rüstungshandel* (Haag und Herchen: Frankfurt, 1980).

70 Figures for the West German arms industry are taken from Brzoska, M., 'The Federal Republic of Germany', in Ball and Leitenberg (note 4).

71 This figure is taken from Vanstralen, W., 'Attention, matière explosive', *Tendances*, 30 Sep. 1982.

[72] Information on the Belgian arms industry can be found, e.g., in Fabrimetal, *Introducing Defense Industry of Belgium* (Fabrimetal: Brussels, 1984); *Military Technology*, no. 14, 1981; and *Military Technology*, no. 2, 1986.

[73] On export data and their problems see, e.g., Adam, B., 'Un acroissement sans précédent des commandes d'armes belges', *Gyroscope*, no. 1, 1982.

[74] On illegal exports see, e.g., Ralet, O., *Illegale Vapenhandel* (EPO: Berchem, 1982) and Pierard, P. F., 'Le trafic clandestin d'armes légéres', *Gyroscope*, no. 2, 1982.

[75] On legal initiatives see, e.g., Gautier, C., 'Les exportations d'armes et le laxisme de loi belge', *Gyroscope*, no. 2, 1982; and Schoonbroodt, E., 'Détention et trafic d'armes légères en Belgique: aspects législatifs', *Dossier 'notes et documents'*, no. 93, Feb. 1986.

[76] See Gautier (note 75); own translation.

[77] Defence Estimates 1984/5, *Statements of Minister of National Defence* before the House of Commons Standing Committee on External Affairs and National Defence, Ottawa, 1984, p. 54. This figure seems to be high if compared to the employment figures in the relevant companies.

[78] For a critical review of Canadian arms exports see Regehr, E., *Making a Killing: Canada's Arms Industry* (McClelland and Steward: Toronto, 1975).

[79] *Military Technology*, vol. 7, no. 10, 1984, Supplement p. 45; total employment: SIPRI estimate.

[80] *Defense & Foreign Affairs Daily*, 8 Feb. 1985.

[81] See Faltas, S., *Nederland in de wapenhandel*, Cahier voor vredesvraagstukken nr. 20 (Interkerkelijk Vredesberaad: Den Haag, 1978).

[82] See Rozemond, S. and van der Mey, L. M., 'Het NIVV, de SIPRI-cijfers en de Nederlandse wapenexport', *Transaktie*, vol. 10, no. 3 (1981).

[83] Figures are taken from van der Mey, L. and Kerstens, B., 'Het Nederlands wapenexportbeleid in cijfers', in Colijn, C. and van der Mey, L. (eds), *De Nederlandse wapenexport: Beleid en praktijk, Indonesië, Iran, Taiwan* (Statsutgiverij, 's-Gravenhage, 1984). The total employment figure is a SIPRI estimate.

[84] See Colijn, C. and Rusman, P., 'Het Nederlands wapenexportvergunningenbeleid', Colijn and van der Mey (note 83).

[85] See Wicken, O., 'Arms and expertise: industrial policy and military exports in Norway', *Defence Analysis*, vol. 1, no. 2 (1985).

[86] *Defense & Foreign Affairs Daily*, 15 May 1984.

[87] *El Pais*, 7 Apr. 1985.

[88] There were several US complaints that US weapons had been shipped to Iran via Spain, see e.g., *El Pais*, 24 May 1984.

[89] *El Pais*, 16 Mar. 1982.

[90] *El Pais*, 27 Oct. 1978.

[91] This figure is calculated from data given in Leal, J., 'La industria militár española', *Tecnologia Militár*, vol. 6, no. 1 (1984), pp. 49–59.

[92] Bachard, D., 'Low profile belies efficient performance', *Financial Times*, 19 Dec. 1983.

[93] This is a rough estimate based on information given in Ministry of Defence, *Defence Report 1984–5* (Australian Government Publishing Service: Canberra, 1985), pp. 59–66.

[94] A rough estimate based upon information given in: Hori, Y., 'The defence industry of Japan', *Military Technology*, no. 11, 1983; Tanaka, N., 'The economy: military and non-military aspects', *Bulletin of the Atomic Scientists*, no. 2, 1984; Horiguchi, Y., 'Problems and possibilities—Japan's defence industries', *Pacific Defence Reporter*, vol. 10, no. 8 (1984).

[95] See, e.g., Tiedtke, S., 'Czechoslovakia', in Ball and Leitenberg (note 4).

[96] Employment figures are rough estimates, based on figures for individual producers, estimates of exports and procurement and other available material.

[97] See the collection in Dupres, L., *Les ventes d'armes et la coopération militaire Est-Sud*, Université de Paris I, Centre d'economie internationale des pays socialistes, Jan. 1985; and Snitch, T. H., 'East European involvement in the world's arms market' in US ACDA, *World Military Expenditures and Arms Transfers 1972–1982* (Government Printing Office: Washington, DC, 1984).

[98] *Wall Street Journal*, 10 Aug. 1984.

[99] See Wharton Econometric Forecasting Associates, *Centrally Planned Economies. Current Analysis*, vol. 4, no. 58, 2 Aug. 1984.

[100] *Interavia*, no. 6 (1986), pp. 635–40.

[101] See, e.g., 'Wir haben euch Waffen und Brot geschickt', *Der spiegel*, 3 Mar. 1980.

[102] See, e.g., Paul, B., '"Bulgarian Connection" to illicit arms trade is found', *Wall Street Journal*, 10 Aug. 1984.

[103] This has been denied by the Romanian Government in the past, see, e.g., *Frankfurter Allgemeine Zeitung*, 27 Dec. 1979. In 1983, Romania agreed to supply Egypt with 200 T-55 tanks. Deliveries were reportedly stopped after 60 tanks had been delivered when it became clear that the tanks were shipped on from Egypt to Iraq.

[104] See statistics given in Pilz, P., *Die Panzermacher: Die österreichische Rüstungsindustrie und ihre Exporte* (Verlag für Gesellschaftskritik: Wien, 1982) p. 2; Ohlson, T. and Loose-Weintraub, E., 'The trade in major conventional weapons', SIPRI, *World Armaments and Disarmament: SIPRI Yearbook 1983* (Taylor & Francis: London, 1983) pp. 280–88.

[105] See Pilz (note 104), pp. 20–21.

[106] See Schallamon, M., 'Programmorientierung und Pragmatik in der Aussenpolitik der SPÖ, untersucht am Beispiel des gescheiterten Panzerexportgeschäfts nach Chile 1980', *Österreichische Zeitschrift für Politikwissenschaft*, vol. 13, no. 2 (1984).

[107] *Interavia Air Letter*, 20 June 1986.

[108] See *In Pursuit of Disarmament*, Report by the Special Expert Inga Thorsson, Foreign Ministry (Liber: Stockholm, 1985).

[109] See Hagelin, B., *Kullorna rullar* (Ordfront: Stockholm, 1985).

[110] See Eckart, R., 'Armee und Wirtschaft', *Wirtschaftsrevue*, no. 5, 1976; *Wehrtechnik*, no. 10, 1978.

[111] The official Swiss statistic is reviewed in Frei, H. and Tobler, R., 'Kriegsmaterial-Exportstatistik 1975–1982', *Waffenplatz Schweiz*, Beiträge zur schweizerischen Rüstungsindustrie und Waffenausfuhr (Arbeitsgemeinschaft für Rüstungskontrolle und Waffenausfuhrverbot: Berne, 1983).

[112] Quoted in Waffenplatz Schweiz (note 111), p. 154.

[113] US Arms Control and Disarmament Agency, *World Military Expenditures and Arms Transfers* (US Government Printing office: Washington, DC, several years).

[114] Nichol, J. P., 'Yugoslavia', in Katz (note 66), pp. 347–79 gives an overview of companies involved; employment: SIPRI estimate.

[115] *Financial Times*, 21 Dec. 1984; *DMS Intelligence*, 4 Feb. 1985, *Frankfurter Rundschau*, 22 Apr. 1986.

[116] *Defense and Foreign Affairs*, Mar. 1985, p. 2 reports that 29 per cent of arms production was exported in 1984, according to Yugoslavian reports.

[117] See, e.g., the detailed overview in Bjoanić, M., 'SPFY foreign trade in 1985 and forecast in 1986', *Review of International Affairs*, vol. 37, no. 858 (Jan. 1986).

[118] SIPRI, *World Armaments and Disarmament: SIPRI Yearbook 1986* (Oxford University Press: Oxford, 1986), p. 234.

[119] Quoted in Nichol (note 114), p. 350.

[120] These are criteria for successful local arms production stressed in Bekić, D., 'Armaments of developing countries', *Review of International Affairs*, vol. 33, no. 774–75 (1982), p. 27.

[121] See the collection of information in Nichol (note 114), pp. 352–54.

[122] This section builds on the country studies in Brzoska, M. and Ohlson, T. (eds), *SIPRI, Arms Production in the Third World* (Taylor & Francis: London, 1986). Unreferenced data are taken from this source.

[123] See, for example, Kraar, L., 'Israel's own military-industrial complex', *Fortune*, vol. 97, no. 5 (1978); Mintz, A., 'The military-industrial complex: the Israeli case', *Journal of Strategic Studies*, vol. 6, no. 3 (Sep. 1983).

[124] Klieman, A., *Israel's Global Reach: Arms Sales as Diplomacy* (Pergamon-Brassey's: Washington, DC, 1985).

[125] On Israeli-South African relations, see Adams, J., *The Unnatural Alliance* (Quartet Books: London, 1984). Factual information in this book is, however, often unverifiable.

[126] The various estimates are discussed in *Latin America Weekly Review*, 18 Oct. 1985.

[127] See Nolan, J., *Military Industry in Taiwan and South Korea* (Macmillan: London, 1985).

[128] UN Security Council Resolution no. 558, 13 Dec. 1984.

[129] The Indian Government was highly embarrassed when it became clear that ex-Indian Army Centurion tanks in 1978–79 had, unintentionally, ended up in South Africa via arms dealers in Jordan and Spain.

Chapter 4. Structure and dynamics: an assessment

With the facts and figures contained in the SIPRI data base as a starting point, the first three chapters of this book illustrate the ups and downs of the arms trade during the past 15 years. Going beyond this descriptive approach, this chapter sets out to analyse changes in the framework and structure of the arms market during the period 1971–85. For both recipient and supplier countries it examines the driving forces that have determined the volume and composition of arms transfers to the Third World. Generalizations are obviously not applicable to all countries. Nevertheless, certain overall factors are relevant for such a great number of the supplier and recipient countries covered in this book that they can be considered substantially to shape the arms trade with the Third World.

The first section presents a schematic overview of the factors that propel the arms trade with the Third World. Section II divides the post-World War II arms transfer history into phases and analyses the main features of each phase. Some aspects of the relationship between arms trade and economic crisis are dealt with in section III, while the final section discusses some possible future developments in the arms trade with the Third World.

I. The forces propelling the arms trade

There is a close interaction between the various factors which give impetus to the arms trade with the Third World, and they are not always easily definable as separate determinants of specific arms transfers. From an analytical viewpoint, it is nevertheless valuable to list these factors, both on the supply and the demand side.

On the supply side, the incentives to export weapons are multiple. They can be grouped into two basic categories: political and economic incentives. They operate on three different levels: international, national and sub-national (or industrial), as illustrated:

	Political	Economic
International	I	II
National	III	IV
Sub-national	V	VI

Starting at the global level, the political factors are shaped by the East-West conflict and the struggle for political and ideological hegemony in the world (I). This basic determinant mainly steers arms exports from the USSR and the USA, but other suppliers, such as France or Sweden, use global rationales by pointing out that their weapons come free of political or other strings. Arms sales are seen as a means of establishing or maintaining influence in a region or a country, or to prevent other countries from becoming influential. At the same time, weapons are also commodities that—at least since the 1970s—have to be paid for. Arms transfers represent a considerable part of the global economic exchange (II).

At the national level, such factors as the influence on the military élites of the recipient, burden sharing, and access to transit rights, facilities and spares come into play. Furthermore, the longer production runs resulting from arms exports are claimed to ensure stable employment and provide a surge capacity in case of war (III). Economically, one aim is to ensure the stability of civilian markets and the inflow of necessary raw materials. Arms transfers may open doors for civilian exports; conversely, it is argued that restrictions on arms transfers would cause hidden losses to the economy. Though chiefly belonging to the national level, this argument is also sometimes used—by the superpowers on behalf of their alliance partners—on the global economic level. Furthermore, it is also argued that the longer production runs lower domestic procurement costs and help recoup some of the outlays on military research and development. Finally, it is suggested that arms exports, at least in the short term, help to improve the balance of payments (IV). In times of pressures to economize on domestic procurement spending, these political and economic arguments at the national level become very powerful.

Political incentives are few on the sub-national or industrial level. It may be argued that some companies, for example large multinational corporations involved in arms production, may share the political incentives felt at one or both of the other levels (V). Otherwise, the pressures to export arms are, at this level, purely economic (VI). In the West, for example, there are specific structural differences between the arms industry and the ideal of free market enterprise. Weapon prices do not normally fall with reduced demand; instead they tend to rise. Added demand from abroad contains the price rises and firms remain competitive. Another difference is that supply does not adjust to demand in all cases, because of the need for excess capacity in an emergency. Arms exports help to finance this excess capacity. Second, arms exports are a profitable business: even when weapons are sold on favourable credit terms, the export earnings are normally guaranteed by the supplier's government. Third, in many arms industries exports account for a substantial part of the turnover, and with the relatively high barriers to entry and exit in arms production this comprises yet another strong and built-in pressure to export. Many companies entered the arms business in the 1970s when demand boomed and they found it difficult to move back to civilian production in times of general slack in civilian markets.

When economic constraints in the recipient countries caused a slow-down in the arms trade with the Third World in the 1980s, arms manufacturers intensified their marketing efforts. This reinforced a tendency for arms industries to dissociate themselves from their respective governments. From an arms control perspective there is an important point to be made here: the various determinants listed above do not always pull in the same direction. There is an inherent tendency towards a collision of interests between political and economic factors. This has most often occurred in countries with restrictive arms export policies—such as FR Germany and Sweden—taking the form of a clash between the government and industry; but it also happened in the USA when President Carter attempted to restrain US arms exports in the late 1970s.

The pressures to import arms can be identified on levels similar to those for the pressures to export. At the regional or sub-regional level, there is the almost automatic pressure arising from circular arms procurement patterns and regional arms races. They key phrase is 'enhancement of national security'. This ill-defined proposition not only relates to legitimate security concerns, but is also used to legitimize both preparation for counter-attack and the acquisition of weapon arsenals for international repression.

Other factors at the national level include a desire to enhance political prestige, regime stabilization and the proposition that the import of modern weapons is good for industrialization and development. At the sub-national level, military élites often have vested interests and exert a major influence on arms procurement decisions, while inter-service rivalry is a related factor which can lead to excessive arms imports.

The obvious restraining factor on the demand side is cost. When measured against the security needs of a country plagued by economic problems, the cost of modern weapons may be prohibitive, particularly if the weapons are of little relevance for any likely conflict. Another restraining factor of a different character is the increasing substitution of domestic arms production for arms imports. The choice of this more ambitious alternative to importing arms directly is most often determined by a wish for greater political and military independence.

II. A structural analysis

On the basis of statistics and the inherent structural elements, the post-World War II arms trade with the Third World can be roughly divided into four phases. The first phase, which preceded the period under observation in this book, continued until about the mid-1960s. In this phase, there were few arms suppliers. The USA, the only industrialized country whose production capacity was wholly intact after the war, started to supply its allies—mainly in Europe but also in the Third World—with weapons. Britain delivered some surplus equipment to its colonies in the Third World. The Soviet Union also supplied its allies and, from the mid-1950s, began to deliver weapons to non-aligned countries in the Third World. US-Soviet competition for influence in the world was thus broadened to include the Third World. Weapon deliveries in this phase were characterized by the giving away of used weapons to allies and other friendly states, often with political and economic strings attached.

The second phase—which essentially covers the 1970s—began in the mid-1960s with two important changes. The first was a change from gifts to sales: instead of giving them away, some supplier countries (notably the United States) began to sell weapons. At the same time, the weapons became more sophisticated: recipients who could pay demanded more in terms of quality than those who received gifts. The other trend was a major change in the structure of the arms market. On the demand side, European imports decreased and a larger part of the total flow of weapons was directed towards the Third World. An important reason for this was that West European arms industries had been rebuilt. On the supply side, competition on the arms market increased when new producers sought new markets. These markets were found in the Third World, where the demand for weapons increased as a result of conflicts and the process of decolonization. These structural changes set the stage for the boom in the early 1970s.

The arms boom in the early 1970s

As the statistics show, the arms trade expanded in an unprecedented manner in the 1970s. This is explained by various factors and events in the early 1970s. One such factor was the rise in the price of oil. Another was the October War in the Middle East in 1973, which not only generated large arms imports by Middle Eastern countries but also caused imports to rise in other regions. A third factor was the changed attitude of the superpowers with respect to arms transfer policy. The Nixon Administration in the USA formulated a policy based on massive transfers of arms to friendly and often regionally dominant states, rather than more direct forms of military involvement. The Soviet Government began to view arms transfers as a source of income and not only as an instrument of foreign policy. The arms boom was also supported by a procurement cycle. Many Third World countries had received large amounts of obsolete weapons in the 1940s and 1950s in the form of military aid. The demand to replace these weapons arose in the early 1970s, not least because of the demonstration effect on other regions of the supply of sophisticated weapons to the Middle East. Technological developments also lay behind this demand, such as guided conventional munitions and the integration of more and more electronics into weapon systems. Rich Third World countries, especially in the Middle East and North Africa, were attracted by these modern technologies and had the means to procure them.

The expansive phase of the early 1970s was still marked by the elements of the classical hierarchial system—despite the function of the arms trade as an instrument used by Western suppliers to recycle oil money and by Eastern suppliers to gain hard currency. The world was rather tidily, if dangerously, divided into spheres of interest and dependence. Both efforts by Third World governments to break up the world hierarchy and efforts by industrialized countries to strengthen it were reflected in the arms market of the early 1970s. The struggle for a new economic order, led by the Organization of Petroleum-Exporting Countries (OPEC), gave many Third World countries the means to buy weapons as symbols of greater political importance. At the same time it was in the political interests of major powers to transfer weapons, and all producers had an economic interest in selling arms.

The interim phase of the late 1970s/early 1980s

As noted in chapter 1, arms imports continued to increase—though with much lower growth rates—in the late 1970s and into the early 1980s. Much of this continued trend can be attributed to the dynamics of the time lags inherent in political processes. The dynamics of several local or regional arms races escalated towards the end of the 1970s, for example between Iraq and Iran, India and Pakistan or Argentina and Chile. The lead times connected with arms sales also increased with the boom in the first half of the 1970s.

The vicious circle of militarization was often evident in this period. Militarization can best be described as an interactive process of increasing influence of the military on all levels of society.[1]

Militarization was fuelled by economic crises and the weakness of civilian political institutions. During the 1970s—and especially in the second half of the decade—such militarization processes could be observed in a number of Third World countries. In fact, only states with stable political structures, such as India, seemed to escape the trend towards militarization that accompanied the worsened economic situation in the Third World in the late 1970s. Modern weapon systems have a central position in the process of militarization. Their contribution to military preparedness may, however, be contradictory, as witnessed by the case of Iran.

At the same time, West European countries were, in the late 1970s, in danger of becoming entrapped in a different vicious circle. The trend towards more producers—and thus more exporters—continued. Financial rewards from arms exports during the boom in the early 1970s attracted more and more producers into the armaments sector, both in traditional West European producer countries and in other countries such as Austria, Greece and Spain. At the same time, governments tended to place fewer weapon orders with their domestic arms industries as a result of economic restrictions and accelerating costs for advanced weapon systems. Nevertheless, these governments continued anxiously to protect their arms industries. Arms exports became more important for providing income, and competition increased. Governments increasingly found the economic forces behind the export pressures so strong that they approved arms deals which for political reasons they would rather have prevented.

While the political demand for weapons in the Third World remained high, the means available for their acquisition diminished. There was no new international economic order. Raw material prices—at the time excepting oil—began to fall. Many Third World governments realized that the increase in earnings in some countries had decreased the earnings in others: this deepened the world-wide economic crisis. Borrowing became widespread, also for weapon purchases.[2] Government budgets and foreign exchange accounts were stretched beyond the limit in order to keep up with the plans of the early 1970s. Arms imports added a substantial share to the debt burden of many countries and they contributed to the destruction of the dream for a new and more just economic order.[3] In the late 1970s, the Third World was more firmly in the grip of multinational institutions and banks than ever before. The symbols of greater political room for manoeuvre—modern weapon systems—extracted a high price.

In the United States the Carter Administration attempted to counter these developments in a systematic way. One view held by the Carter Administration was that the costs of the huge arms buildup in the Third World had a crippling effect on economic development. This required efforts to limit arms transfers to the Third World, both in the interests of the recipients and of the United States. Another factor was that unlimited tranfers of arms—including the technology to produce arms—threatened to undermine the positions of the superpowers in the Third World. This line of thought supported efforts to limit arms transfers.

Little is known about the Soviet attitude towards arms transfer control at the time.[4] But the Soviet willingness to discuss arms transfer limitations with the USA, despite lamentations from many of its allies in the Third World, indicated that the ideas put forward in the USA were not entirely alien to Soviet policy-makers.

However, the Carter Administration underestimated the political importance many Third World governments attached to their arms import programmes; it also underestimated the commercial interests of arms producers, both in the USA and in Western Europe. The US Administration retreated: talks with the Soviet Union ceased, arms were given to those demanding them and, at the same time, plans were drawn up to return to a policy of greater reliance on the direct use of force, as witnessed by the buildup of the Rapid Deployment Force. There are indications that the USSR also adapted its Third World arms transfer policy, giving more priority to direct military involvement (e.g., Afghanistan, Ethiopia).

Some features of the mid-1980s

In the current phase, the effects of the developments described have culminated in what can be labelled the fourth phase of post-World War II arms trade with the Third World. Growth rates in the international market for arms have been low for some time and there has been a trend towards a buyer's market. The leverage of recipients has, as a rule, been increasing. This is primarily the result of the concurrence of fierce competition among a growing number of suppliers, and budgetary constraints among the recipients. This fourth phase of the arms trade with the Third World has been characterized by a number of features.

First, there has been a great number of offset deals. While arms transfers were previously usually concluded on straightforward cash or credit terms, it has become difficult for a seller to avoid offset arrangements with the arms recipient. Such arrangements have included joint production, licensed production, sub-contracting in the purchasing country for components and spare parts, transfer of research and development capabilities, marketing rights, maintenance contracts for regional users of the weapon and imports of other industrial goods from the weapon recipient by the supplier country.

Second, there is the related issue of financing. In many cases success in the race for contracts has been determined by the financial conditions. A case in point is that of the 1982 'Al Thakeb' air defence deal between France and Saudi Arabia, in which French debts to Saudi Arabia were written off as payment for the development and production of the missiles and launchers.

Both industrial offsets and financing agreements have generated resource flows in addition to the arms flows; both have been expressions of the growing tendency for suppliers to subsidize their own arms exports.

Third, there have been frequent reports about the intensity of competition for contracts. The new Nigerian military government, for example, which claimed irregularities in arms purchases to be one of the reasons for taking power in late 1984, found that bribes had been handed out on a regular basis in connection with arms imports. In India, suspicions were raised about irregularities in the purchase of 155-mm towed howitzers.

Fourth, there is the case of 'export' weapons. In Western Europe, many weapons have been tailor-made to the specifications of Third World recipients—this has been a commercial success for the arms industries in France, FR Germany and Italy. In the USSR and the USA the term 'export' weapons had a different meaning: it referred to weapons with downgraded capabilities. The US FX fighter is one example; the USSR also tried to export less capable versions of its frontline aircraft and tanks. Third World customers have been sceptical: they have demanded, and often received, state-of-the-art aircraft such as the F-16. Clients of the Soviet Union have also preferred more advanced systems when they could afford them: the USSR sold its newest fighter, the MiG-29, to Syria and India even before it was deployed in substantial numbers with the Soviet Air Force. In the case of India, the Indian Government could capitalize on Soviet fears the India would continue to diversify its arms imports and move away from the Soviet Union.

Fifth, there has been an increasing demand from cost-conscious recipients for modernization of existing stocks of weaponry. The suppliers have responded to this: there is an increasing flow of enhanced components, upgrading and modernization kits, and so on in order to prolong the life of aircraft, armoured vehicles and other weapons in the inventories of the armed forces.

Finally, the increasing leverage of recipients is illustrated by the fact that certain countries, for example Jordan, Kuwait and Nigeria, have all bought weapons from both the USA and the USSR in recent years. Sellers' leverage is no longer the trademark of the arms trade with the Third World, at least not all the time. If one superpower declines to supply certain equipment, customers may—if political allegiances or economic prerequisites do not make it impossible—simply turn to the other superpower.

Among the most commonly evoked explanations for the structure of the arms market in the mid-1980s and the much lower growth rates are excess supply, more arms production within the Third World and market saturation due to the high import levels during the 1970s. The most important explanation, however, is obviously economic.

III. The arms trade and economic crisis

Among the reasons given for the recent stagnation in the arms market, the economic crisis in almost all Third World countries is the most prominent one. It is also highly plausible: less growth in GNP and government income erodes the financial basis for military expenditures—and thus, for arms imports. This can also be seen from the trends for arms imports and economic indicators in the late 1970s and early 1980s. However, arms transfers have not moved in parallel with economic indicators: in the 1970s arms imports grew faster and in the 1980s they decreased faster than the economic indicators.

Further, table 4.1 shows that the relation between various economic aggregates and arms imports also depends on different levels of economic activity. In the low-income group, imports of major conventional weapons are comparatively small—not much larger than the share of world military expenditures. In this group of countries, military spending goes largely on salaries to the armed forces. For the two groups of middle-income Third World countries the situation is different: the shares in world-wide imports of major weapons are much higher than their respective shares in global military spending. The group of high-income oil exporters have huge military expenditures, but—relative to the other Third World groupings—they use more of their military expenditures on the buildup of military infrastructure than on imports of major weapons.

On the basis of these and other data,[5] a kind of substitution cycle can be deduced with respect to growing income: first, expenditures on personnel are being substituted by expenditures on weapons that have to be imported. Then, direct imports of weapons are increasingly being supplemented by imports of support equipment and arms production technology and, finally, imports are substituted by growing domestic production (this last stage refers mainly to the group of industrial market economies in table 4.1). This crude trend is modified by factors such as the size of the armed forces, depth and type of industrialization, security environment and political decisions. Furthermore, and importantly, there is no mechanistic overall progress in national income. The evidence from recent years indicates that—even in times of an expanding world economy—growth rates can be very different in different countries. Some advance, others lag behind. The size and composition of the arms market are influenced by such movements, since the two middle-income groups are the most prolific arms importers. If this differentiation process in connection with

Table 4.1. Shares in world economic and military sectors by economic regions, 1983

Economic regions	Percentage of world population	Percentage of world GNP	Percentage of total world imports	Percentage of world military spending	Percentage of world-wide imports of major weapons, 1981–85
Low-income economies (per capita GNP <$440)	50.4	5.0	3.1	7.5	9.9
Lower middle-income economies (per capita GNP $440–$1639)	14.4	4.1	6.1	2.3	19.6
Upper middle-income economies (per capita GNP >$1639)	10.8	8.5	13.2	3.1	26.7
High-income oil exporters	0.4	1.8	3.8	5.0	10.8
Industrial market economies	15.7	66.8	65.0	52.4	25.4
East European non-market economies	8.3	13.7	8.8	24.7	7.5

Sources: World Bank, World Development Report 1985 (Oxford University Press: New York, 1985); SIPRI data base.

global economic growth works to their disadvantage, this would decrease the probability of an increase in arms imports even if the world economic situation as a whole were to improve.

A more general argument in support of this last proposition can also be found in the growing awareness in the Third World—enhanced by the bad performance of the world economy in the 1980s—that security (national and regional) not only includes the absence of foreign intervention and domination by military means, but also some minimum level of economic and social well-being.

Also in the economic field, there are the above-mentioned links between arms imports and debt burdens. Military credits were available on easier terms than in any civil sector during much of the 1970s. Creditor governments were willing to take risks, largely due to their ambition to prop up their indigenous arms industries. At the time, the IMF was also reluctant to suggest cuts in military spending even in cases where drastic cuts in general government spending was recommended. The military sector was often exempted from the general policy conditions made in connection with IMF loans. What makes military debts particularly burdensome is that no help in generating funds for the repayment of the accumulated debt will come from the unproductive military sector.

IV. Possible future developments

The levelling-out of the arms trade with the Third World in the 1980s is largely explained by short-term economic conditions and long-term procurement factors. It can therefore be argued that the volume of arms transfers will increase again if, or as, the world economy re-establishes an upward momentum (with the possible disclaimers mentioned above) and when weapons become outdated again. Also, weapons are used: the number of conflicts has not decreased during the 1980s. The Iraq–Iran War and other recent wars have clearly shown that the fear of horizontal escalation does not prevent suppliers from transferring arms. Such fears are often disregarded; instead, factors in favour of arms transfers prevail.

Another argument supporting continued high levels of military transfers is the structure of the arms market itself. The private, civilian sectors of the economies in both supplying and receiving countries are increasingly getting drawn into arms transfers through the offset arrangements, the transfers of civil and dual-use technology and so on that are part and parcel of arm transfers today.

Finally, and closely linked to the above argument, the size and dynamics of the world military industries pushing for sales of their products must be considered. The immediate conclusion seems to be that as long as arms production and military R&D are conducted on anything approaching the current levels, then there will also be strong pressures to trade weapons and weapon technology. The market will—at least in the short run—continue to be guaranteed by national security needs and regional instabilities.

The described changes in the arms market are part of the general trend towards the commercialization and internationalization of industrial production. This trend is not without contradictions, however, especially with respect to arms production. National subsidizing policies of an almost mercantilistic nature are used to prop up the competitiveness of domestic arms industries on the world market. Exports that are subsidized in this manner may, in the long run, decrease 'national welfare'. Given other favourable economic and political developments in the international system, it may therefore be premature to discard entirely as wishful thinking the proposition that arms suppliers may take steps to reduce the pressures to export arms.

Even in the absence of immediate positive signs towards arms trade reduction from the actors on the market, a simple extrapolation of current trends indicates that the *magnitude* of the total flow of arms and arms technology will grow only marginally in the late 1980s or early 1990s. With respect to the *content* of the arms flow, it is useful to distinguish between two types of trend. There will probably be a continued reduction in the flow of finished weapon systems in favour of more licensed production, technology tranfers and so on to well-endowed and/or strategically important Third World countries. For many customers among the poorer countries, transfers of complete weapon systems at a less sophisticated level and modernization packages will—given economic realities—be the rule.

The *originators* of the arms flow, that is, the suppliers, will not increase in number as much as they have up to the present. Some new producers will certainly appear, and the Third World share in total exports to the Third World will continue its slow increase. But limitations regarding production capabilities, the size of domestic markets and factors of scale in general set a ceiling for the number of countries that can enter into large-scale arms production. Unless they change their attitudes (an inheritance from the first phase in international arms transfers after World War II) and cease to attach strings to arms transfers, the USA and the USSR will continue to lose market shares to other suppliers. This will continue to be most valid in the case of the USA, since the Soviet Union has a larger number of clients for which—due to lack of finance or political choice—alternatives to supplies from socialist countries will not be available.

Finally, a note on the structure of the future arms transfer system is appropriate. Even if a new global division of labour is developing—as in the civil sector of international trade—this system will remain a hierarchical one, but with changes within. True, it can be argued that at least those countries able to pay now have a set of choices and that, for them, arms exporters have lost much of their inherent political leverage. Some privileged importers/producers in the Third World will move upwards in the hierarchy. But, by virtue of the size of their military industries, their overwhelming dominance in high-technology areas and the huge sums spent on research and development, the largest industrial countries will still continue to dominate the system in the future.

Notes and references

[1] See Skjelsbaek, K., 'Dimensions and modes of militarism', in Huldt, B. and Lejins, A. (eds), *Militarism and Militarization*, the Swedish Institute of International Affairs, Conference Papers 3; Brzoska, M., 'The concept of Third World militarization' in *Viertelsjahresberichte der Friedrich-Ebert Stiftung*, no. 95, 1984.

[2] Tullberg, R., 'Military-related debt in non-oil developing countries, 1972–82' in SIPRI, *World Armaments and Disarmament, SIPRI Yearbook 1985* (Taylor & Francis: London, 1985); and Brzoska, M., 'The military-related external debt of Third World countries', *Journal of Peace Research*, vol. 20, no. 3 (1984).

[3] For an early statement on the incompatibility between a continuation of existing arms transfer patterns and a new international economic order, see Lock, P., 'New international economic order and armaments', in Jahn, E. and Sakamoto, Y. (eds), *Elements of World Instability* (Campus: Frankfurt, 1981).

[4] See Krause, J., *Sowjetische Militärhilfepolitik gegenüber Entwicklungsländern* (Nomos: Baden-Baden, 1985); Kozyrev, A., *The Arms Trade: A New Level of Danger* (Progress: Moscow, 1985).

[5] See the discussion and the individual country studies in Brzoska, M. and Ohlson, T. (eds), SIPRI, *Arms Production in the Third World* (Taylor & Francis: London, 1986).

Appendices

Appendix 1. Register of the trade in major conventional weapons with Third World countries, 1971–85

The sources and methods for the data collection are explained in appendix 9, and the conventions, abbreviations and acronyms used are given in the front of the book. The entries are made alphabetically, by recipient and supplier, in chronological order by year of order and, finally, alphabetically by weapon designation.

Recipient code/ Recipient	Supplier	No. ordered	Weapon designation	Weapon description	Year of order	Year(s) of delivery	Total delivered	Comments
5 Afghanistan	Czechoslovakia	(10)	L-29 Delfin	Jet trainer	1978	1978	(10)	
		(20)	L-39 Albatross	Jet trainer	1978	1979-82	(20)	
	USA	(100)	FIM-92A Stinger	Port SAM	1986	1986	(100)	Unconfirmed; reportedly delivered for Afghani resistance
	USSR	10	An-26 Curl	Lightplane	1978	1978	10	
		(30)	Mi-24 Hind-C	Hel	1978	1978	(30)	
		(4)	Mi-8 Hip	Hel	(1970)	1971	(4)	
		(35)	Mi-8 Hip	Hel	1979	1979-80	(35)	
		24	MiG-19PF	Fighter	(1979)	1979	(24)	
		(10)	MiG-21F	Fighter	1978	1978	(10)	
		(40)	MiG-23BN	Fighter/grd attack	(1983)	1984-85	(40)	Unconfirmed whether part of Afghani AF
		(15)	Su-17 Fitter-C	Fighter/grd attack	1982	1982	(15)	1 squadron to replace Su-7s
		(30)	Su-7 Fitter	Fighter	(1970)	1971-72	(30)	
		(10)	Su-7BM	Fighter/bomber	1978	1978	(10)	
		(10)	Su-7U Moujik	Jet trainer	(1970)	1971-72	(10)	
		(40)	BMP-1	MICV	(1979)	1980	(40)	
		(20)	BRDM-1	SC	(1979)	1979	(20)	
		(200)	BTR-60P	APC	(1978)	1979-81	(200)	
		(200)	D-30 122mm	TH	(1978)	1978-81	(200)	
		(20)	PT-76	LT	1979	1979	(20)	
		(150)	T-34	MT	1978	1978-79	(150)	
		(200)	T-54	MBT	1978	1978-79	(200)	
		(200)	T-55	MBT	1978	1978-79	(200)	
		(100)	T-62	MBT	(1973)	1975-76	(100)	
		..	T-62	MBT	1979	1979	(50)	
		(20)	ZSU-23-4 Shilka	AAV	(1974)	1976	(20)	
		7	SA-3 SAMS	Mobile SAM system	(1978)	1979	(7)	

Recipient	Supplier	No.	Weapon designation	Weapon description	Year of order	Year of delivery	No. delivered	Comments
15 Algeria	Brazil	..	EE-9 Cascavel	AC	(1986)			Negotiating package incl Urutu APCs, trucks and technology transfers; total value: approx $400 m
	Canada	2	CL-215	Amphibian	(1978)	1978	(2)	Unconfirmed
	Egypt	:	Walid	APC	(1978)	1978	(20)	In addition to 2 previously acquired
	France	5	SA-330 Puma	Hel	1974	1975	5	
		..	BRDM-1	SC	(1982)	1982	(100)	Unconfirmed
		:	D-74 122mm	TG	(1981)	1981	(50)	
		55	M-3	APC	1982	1983-84	(55)	
		(4 000)	VP-2000	APC	1983	1984-85	(1 500)	
			Milan	ATM	(1982)	1982	(50)	Supplier unconfirmed
	Netherlands	(8)	F-27 Mk-400	Transport	1974	1976	(8)	
		(2)	F-27 Mk-600	Transport	1976	1977	(2)	
		2	F-28 Mk-3000	Transport	1978	1979	2	For Navy
	Romania	(6)	SA-316B	Hel	(1983)	1984	(6)	Reportedly ordered
	UK		Hawk	Jet trainer/strike	(1985)			
		2	Kebir Class	PC	1981	1982-83	2	Delivered prior to licensed production of 4 additional PCs in Algeria
	USA	2	Type 84M	Support ship	1981	1984	2	Similar to ships ordered by Oman; order incl 2 PCs; total value: $124 m
		6	C-130H Hercules	Transport	(1980)	1980-82	6	Order incl 2 C-130H-30 Super Hercules
		6	C-130H Hercules	Transport	1982	1983	6	
		2	C-130H-30	Transport	1982	1983	2	
		3	C-130H-30	Transport	(1983)	1984	3	Recipient unconfirmed
		1	King Air A-100	Transport	(1978)	1978	1	Supplier unconfirmed
		(6)	L-100-30	Transport	(1984)	1984	(6)	Originally supplied to Air Algeria
		3	Queen Air B-80	Transport	(1978)	1978	3	Supplier unconfirmed
		12	Sierra	Trainer	(1978)	1978-79	12	
		5	Super King Air	Transport	(1978)	1978	5	Supplier unconfirmed
		6	T-34C-1	Trainer	1979	1979	6	To replace Gomhouriah trainers
	USSR	:	Mi-24 Hind-D	Hel	(1977)	1979-80	(18)	First shown in military parade Nov 1979
		:	Mi-24 Hind-D	Hel	(1980)	1981-82	(12)	
		(40)	Mi-4 Hound	Hel	(1972)	1973	(40)	
		(4)	Mi-6 Hook	Hel	(1972)	1972	(4)	
		(12)	Mi-8 Hip	Hel	(1972)	1972	(12)	
		:	MiG-21FL	Fighter	1977	1978	(24)	
		:	SA-3 SAMS	Mobile SAM system	(1983)	1983-84	(10)	Arming MiG-21s
		(240)	AA-2 Atoll	AAM	1978	1978-79	(240)	
		(200)	AT-3 Sagger	ATM	(1975)	1976-77	(200)	
		(40)	SA-3 Goa	Landmob SAM	(1978)	1978	(40)	
		(80)	SA-3 Goa	Landmob SAM	(1983)	1983-84	(80)	

Recipient code/ Recipient	Supplier	No. ordered	Weapon designation	Weapon description	Year of order	Year(s) of delivery	Total delivered	Comments
		..	MiG-21MF	Fighter	1977	1978	(24)	
		(40)	MiG-23	Fighter/interceptor	(1978)	1978-79	(40)	
		(12)	MiG-25	Fighter/interceptor	(1978)	1979	(12)	
		(9)	MiG-25R	Recce	1978	1978-79	(9)	
		(30)	Su-20 Fitter-C	Fighter/grd attack	(1977)	1977-78	(30)	
		20	Su-7BM	Fighter/bomber	(1973)	1974	20	
		(150)	BM-21 122mm	MRS	1976	1977-83	(150)	
		..	BMP-1	MICV	(1978)	1979-82	(331)	First shown in military parade Nov 1979
		6	BRDM-2 Gaskin	AAV(M)	(1978)	1979	(6)	
		..	BRDM-2 Spigot	TD(M)	1980	1981-82	(20)	
		..	BTR-40	APC	(1978)	1978	(100)	
		..	BTR-50P	APC	(1979)	1979	(100)	
		..	BTR-60P	APC	(1978)	1979-81	(91)	First shown in military parade Nov 1979
		..	D-20 152mm	TH	(1982)	1982	(20)	
		..	D-30 122mm	TH	(1982)	1983-85	(150)	
		..	D-74 122mm	TG	(1978)	1979	(100)	
		..	JSU-122	SPG	(1978)	1978	(50)	
		..	JSU-152	SPG	(1972)	1972-73	(15)	
		..	M-1974 122mm	SPH	(1983)	1983	(20)	
		..	M-46 130mm	TG	(1982)	1982	(20)	
		(50)	T-55	MBT	(1981)	1982	(50)	
		..	T-62	MBT	1977	1978-84	(300)	
		..	T-72	MBT	(1979)	1979-82	(100)	First shown in military parade Nov 1979
		..	ZSU-23-4 Shilka	AAV	(1978)	1979-81	(47)	First shown in military parade Nov 1979
		..	ZSU-57-2	AAV	(1979)	1980-82	(45)	
		..	FROG L	Mobile SSM system	(1975)	1976-79	(20)	Unconfirmed
		..	SA-6 SAMS	Mobile SAM system	(1980)	1980	(5)	
		..	SA-8 SAMS	Mobile SAM system	(1978)	1979-80	(8)	
		2	SA-N-4 L	ShAM launcher	(1977)	1980-82	2	Arming 2 Koni Class frigates
		4	SA-N-4 L	ShAM launcher	(1979)	1980-83	4	Arming 4 Nanuchka Class corvettes
		1	SA-N-4 L	ShAM launcher	(1982)	1984	(1)	Arming third Koni Class frigate
		9	SSN-2 Styx L	ShShM launcher	1975	1976-81	9	Arming 9 Osa-2 Class fast attack craft
		(8)	SSN-2 Styx L	ShShM launcher	1979	1980-83	8	Arming 4 Nanuchka Class corvettes
		..	AA-2 Atoll	AAM	(1977)	1978-79	(360)	Arming MiG- and Sukhoi fighters
		..	AT-3 Sagger	ATM	(1976)	1976-80	(500)	
		..	AT-4 Spigot	ATM	(1980)	1981-82	(200)	Arming BRDM-2 APCs
		..	AT-5 Spandrel	ATM	(1980)	1981-82	(200)	Arming Hind-D helicopters
		..	AT-6 Spiral	ATM	(1980)	1981-82	(48)	
		..	FROG-4	Landmob SSM	(1975)	1976-79	(60)	Unconfirmed

Supplier	No. ordered	Weapon designation	Weapon description	Year of order	Year(s) of delivery	No. delivered	Comments
	..	SA-6 Gainful	Landmob SAM	(1980)	1980	(15)	First shown in military parade Nov 1979
	..	SA-8 Gecko	Landmob SAM	(1978)	1979-80	(32)	
	..	SA-9 Gaskin	Landmob SAM	(1978)	1979	(100)	
	(24)	SA-N-4	ShAM	(1977)	1980-82	(24)	Arming 2 Koni Class frigates
	(24)	SA-N-4	ShAM	(1979)	1980-83	(24)	Arming 4 Nanuchka Class corvettes
	(12)	SA-N-4	ShAM	(1982)	1984	(12)	Arming third Koni Class frigate
	(108)	SSN-2 Styx	ShShM	1975	1976-81	(108)	Arming 9 Osa-2 Class fast attack craft
	(48)	SSN-2 Styx	ShShM	(1979)	1980-83	(48)	Arming 4 Nanuchka Class corvettes
	2	Koni Class	Frigate	(1977)	1980-82	2	
	1	Koni Class	Frigate	(1982)	1984	(1)	Armed with SA-N-4 ShShMs
	4	Nanuchka Class	Corvette	(1979)	1980-83	4	
	9	Osa-2 Class	FAC	1975	1976-81	9	
	1	Polnocny Class	LS	1976	1976	1	
	2	Romeo Class	Submarine	(1982)	1982-83	2	
Yugoslavia	..	G-4 Super Galeb	Jet trainer	(1986)			Negotiating
12 Angola							
Algeria	4	Nord-262A-2M	Mar patrol	1980	1980	4	For mar patrol and transport duties
China	(25)	T-59	MBT	1974	1975	(25)	Originally delivered via Zaire; for FNLA
	1	Shanghai Class	PC	(1975)	1975	1	
Czechoslovakia	..	OT-62	APC	(1975)	1976	(50)	Supplier unconfirmed
France	4	AS-365N	Hel	1985			Ordered with Gazelle helicopters; option on 3 more
	6	SA-316B	Hel	(1979)	1980	6	Delivered Oct 1980
	6	SA-342K Gazelle	Hel	1985			Part of Mar 1985 order incl 4 AS-365Ns; total cost: $47 m
	(72)	HOT	ATM	1985	1985		Arming Gazelle helicopters
Netherlands	1	F-27 Maritime	Mar patrol	1980	1980	1	Handed over at independence
Portugal	(27)	AOP-9	Lightplane	(1974)	1975	(27)	Handed over at independence
	(2)	C-45 Expeditor	Transport	(1974)	1975	(2)	Handed over at independence
	3	C-47	Transport	(1974)	1975	3	Handed over at independence
	(2)	Do-27	Transport	(1974)	1975	(2)	Handed over at independence
	(4)	G-91R-3	Fighter/grd attack	(1974)	1975	(4)	Handed over at independence
	(6)	Noratlas 2501	Transport	(1974)	1975	(6)	Handed over at independence
	(12)	SA-316B	Hel	(1974)	1975	(12)	Handed over at independence
	2	SA-316B	Hel	1983	1983	2	
	..	AML-90	AC	(1974)	1974	(5)	Left behind at independence
	..	M-3	APC	(1974)	1974	(10)	Left behind at independence
	1	Alfange Class	LC	(1975)	1975	(1)	Handed over at independence
	5	Argos Class	PC	(1975)	1975	(5)	Handed over at independence
	1	Flower Class	Frigate	(1975)	1975	1	Handed over at independence
	..	BN-2A Defender	Lightplane	1976	1978-79	(8)	
Romania	..	SA-316B	Hel	(1982)	1983-84	12	Fitting out probably done in France
Spain	8	C-212-200	Transport	(1984)	1985-86	8	

Recipient code/ Recipient	Supplier	No. ordered	Weapon designation	Weapon description	Year of order	Year(s) of delivery	Total delivered	Comments
	Switzerland	4	PC-6	Lightplane	1976	1976	4	
		(25)	PC-7	Trainer	1982	1983-85	(13)	
	USA	1	C-130H Hercules	Transport	(1980)	1980	1	
		(100)	FIM-92A Stinger	Port SAM	1986	1986	(100)	Unconfirmed; reportedly delivered via Zaire; for UNITA
	USSR	(12)	An-12 Cub-A	Transport	(1982)	1983-85	(12)	
		..	An-2	Transport	(1978)	1979	(6)	
		1	An-2	Transport	(1982)	1983	1	
		..	An-26 Curl	Lightplane	(1977)	1977	(6)	
		(30)	An-26 Curl	Lightplane	(1982)	1983-86	(30)	
		(4)	An-32 Cline	Transport	(1983)	1984	(4)	
		19	Mi-8 Hip	Hel	(1977)	1978	19	
		..	Mi-8 Hip	Hel	(1982)	1983-85	(42)	Unconfirmed
		3	MiG-15UTI	Fighter/trainer	(1976)	1977	3	
		..	MiG-17F	Fighter	(1976)	1977	(20)	
		(40)	MiG-21MF	Fighter	(1975)	1976-77	(40)	
		(70)	MiG-21bis	Fighter	(1982)	1983-85	(22)	
		(23)	MiG-23	Fighter/interceptor	(1982)	1982-84	(23)	Unconfirmed; acc to South African report
		5	Su-22 Fitter-J	Fighter/grd attack	(1984)	1984	(5)	
		(6)	Su-22 Fitter-J	Fighter/grd attack	(1985)	1985	(6)	Unconfirmed
		(4)	Yak-40 Coding	Transport	(1980)	1981	(4)	In military use with civilian markings
		(100)	BM-21 122mm	MRS	(1975)	1976-77	(100)	
		(200)	BRDM-2	SC	(1976)	1977-78	(200)	
		..	BRDM-2	SC	(1977)	1977-78	(200)	Some possibly BRDM-1 version
		(20)	BRDM-2 Gaskin	AAV(M)	(1983)	1983-85	(17)	Some upgraded BTR-50 version
		..	BRDM-2 Spigot	TD(M)	(1980)	1982	(10)	
		150	BTR-60P	APC	(1977)	1977-78	(150)	
		..	D-30 122mm	TH	(1981)	1983	(40)	
		..	M-1974 122mm	SPH	(1979)	1980-81	(100)	
		..	M-1974 122mm	SPH	(1980)	1982	(40)	Unconfirmed
		..	M-46 130mm	TG	(1976)	1976	(40)	
		(60)	PT-76	LT	(1976)	1976-77	(60)	
		(4)	SA-13 TELAR	AAV(M)	(1984)	1985	(2)	2 delivered with 72 SA-13s each
		85	SU-100	TD	(1980)	1981	(40)	
		150	T-34	MT	(1976)	1976-77	(85)	
		..	T-54	MBT	(1974)	1977-78	(150)	
		..	T-62	MBT	(1980)	1981-85	(175)	Some possibly upgraded T-55 version
		(20)	ZSU-23-4 Shilka	AAV	(1977)	1978-79	(20)	
		..	ZSU-23-4 Shilka	AAV	(1980)	1981-83	(30)	

Country	No.	Designation	Description	Year ordered	Year delivered	No. delivered	Comments
	(20)	ZSU-57-2	AAV	(1977)	1978-79	(20)	
	(33)	SA-2 SAMS	Mobile SAM system	1979	1980-81	(8)	
	(16)	SA-3 SAMS	Mobile SAM system	(1980)	1981-85	(25)	
	(8)	SA-6 SAMS	Mobile SAM system	1979	1980-84	(16)	
	6	SA-8 SAMS	Mobile SAM system	(1983)	1983-85	(8)	Unconfirmed
	6	SSN-2 Styx L	ShShM launcher	1981	1982-83	6	
	(72)	AA-2 Atoll	AAM	1975	1976	(72)	Arming MiG-17/21s
	..	AA-2 Atoll	AAM	1983	1983	(100)	Arming MiGs
	..	AT-3 Sagger	ATM	1977	1977-78	(1 000)	
	..	AT-4 Spigot	ATM	(1980)	1982	(30)	Unconfirmed
	(288)	SA-13 Gopher	Landmob SAM	(1984)	1985	(144)	Unconfirmed; for 4 SA-13 TELAR vehicles
	..	SA-2 Guideline	Landmob SAM	1979	1980-81	(40)	Unconfirmed; maybe confused with SA-3s also reportedly used in southern Angola
	(165)	SA-3 Goa	Landmob SAM	(1980)	1981-85	(120)	Unconfirmed
	..	SA-6 Gainful	Landmob SAM	(1979)	1980-84	(84)	SA-2/6 sites in Angola destroyed prior to South African attack Aug/Sep 1981
	..	SA-7 Grail	Port SAM	(1976)	1976-78	(6 000)	Unconfirmed; reportedly manned by Soviet personnel
	(96)	SA-8 Gecko	Landmob SAM	(1983)	1983-85	(96)	
	(240)	SA-9 Gaskin	Landmob SAM	(1983)	1983-85	(216)	Arming 6 Osa-2 Class fast attack craft
	(72)	SSN-2 Styx	ShShM	(1981)	1982-83	(72)	Armed with SSN-2 Styx missiles
	6	Osa-2 Class	FAC	(1981)	1982-83	6	
	3	Polnocny Class	LS	1977	1979	1	
	5	Shershen Class	FAC	(1976)	1977-83	5	Armed with torpedoes
7 Argentina	57	Cuirassier	LT/TD	1981	1981	57	Originally intended for Chile
Belgium	5	BDX	APC	(1979)	1980	5	For evaluation
Brazil	3	EMB-111	Mar patrol	1982	1982	3	Delivered during Falkland/Malvinas conflict
	(44)	EMB-312 Tucano	Trainer	(1986)			Negotiating; last 35 for local assembly
	12	EMB-326 Xavante	Trainer/COIN	1982	1983	12	Total cost: $60 m
	(10)	EE-9 Cascavel	AC	1982	1982	(10)	Evaluation quantity
	(50)	SA-7 Grail	Port SAM	1983	1983	(50)	For marine infantry
Bulgaria	(12)	AS-332	Hel	1983	1984-85	(12)	
France	9	Alouette-3	Hel	1970	1972-74	9	For naval transport fleet
	2	Mirage-3D	Jet trainer	1970	1972	2	
	(3)	Mirage-3D	Jet trainer	(1982)	1983	(3)	
	12	Mirage-3E	Fighter/bomber	1970	1972-73	12	Armed with R-530 AAMs
	14	Mirage-3E	Fighter/bomber	(1972)	1974-75	(14)	
	7	Mirage-3E	Fighter/bomber	1977	1980	7	
	5	SA-315B Lama	Hel	1972	1973	5	
	(7)	SA-315B Lama	Hel	(1973)	1974-75	7	In addition to 5 ordered 1972
	9	SA-316B	Hel	1980	1981	9	

Recipient code/ Recipient	Supplier	No. ordered	Weapon designation	Weapon description	Year of order	Year(s) of delivery	Total delivered	Comments
		12	SA-330J Puma	Hel	1978	1979	12	In addition to 12 delivered 1979
		12	SA-330J Puma	Hel	1980	1981	12	
		14	Super Etendard	Fighter/strike	1979	1982-83	14	Armed with Exocet ShShMs and Magic AAMs
		(24)	AML-90	AC	(1968)	1969-71	(24)	
		60	AMX-13	LT	(1970)	1971	60	
		32	AMX-13	LT	(1972)	1973	(32)	
		30	AMX-13	LT	1973	1974	(30)	
		24	AMX-155 Mk-F3	SPH	(1969)	1969-73	24	
		(6)	AMX-30 Roland	AAV(M)	1981	1982-83	(6)	
		36	ERC-90 Lynx	AC	1979	1982-83	(36)	Ordered Oct 1979; for border defence against Chile
		60	ERC-90 Sagaie	AC	1981	1983-84	(60)	
		2	VBC-90	AC	1980	1980	2	Test vehicles; planned licensed production later cancelled
		8	MM-38 L	ShShM launcher	(1974)	1977-81	8	Arming 2 Type 42 destroyers
		2	MM-38 L	ShShM launcher	1977	1978	2	Arming 1 Sumner Class destroyer
		2	MM-38 L	ShShM launcher	1977	1978	2	Arming 1 Gearing Class destroyer
		4	MM-38 L	ShShM launcher	1978	1978	(4)	
		(2)	MM-38 L	ShShM launcher	1979	1981	2	Arming 1 D'Orves Class corvette
		(6)	MM-40 L	ShShM launcher	1980	1985	(2)	Arming 6 Meko-140 frigates
		(8)	MM-40 L	ShShM launcher	(1980)	1983-84	(8)	Arming 4 Meko-360 destroyers
		(28)	AM-39 Exocet	AShM	1979	1982-83	(28)	Arming 14 Super Etendard fighters
		20	AS-11	ASM	1973	1974	20	Arming Alouette-3 helicopters
		30	AS-12	ASM/AShM	1973	1974	30	Arming Alouette-3 helicopters
		(1 000)	HOT	ATM	1980	1980-84	(1 000)	Current status uncertain
		24	MM-38 Exocet	ShShM	(1974)	1977-81	(24)	Arming 2 Type 42 destroyers
		6	MM-38 Exocet	ShShM	(1977)	1978	6	Arming 1 Gearing Class destroyer
		6	MM-38 Exocet	ShShM	1977	1978	(6)	Arming 1 Sumner Class destroyer
		12	MM-38 Exocet	ShShM	1978	1978	(12)	Arming 2 D'Orves Class corvettes
		6	MM-38 Exocet	ShShM	1979	1981	(6)	Arming 1 D'Orves Class corvette
		(72)	MM-40 Exocet	ShShM/SShM	1980	1985	(24)	Arming 6 Meko-140 frigates
		(96)	MM-40 Exocet	ShShM/SShM	(1980)	1983-84	96	Arming 4 Meko-360 destroyers
		(60)	R-530	AAM	(1971)	1972-73	(60)	Arming Mirage-3 fighters
		(30)	R-530	AAM	(1980)	1981-83	(30)	Arming Super Etendard and other fighters
		(90)	R-550 Magic	AAM	(1980)	1981-83	(90)	Arming Super Etendard and other fighters
		(72)	Roland-1	Landmob SAM	1981	1982-83	(72)	
		2	D'Orves Class	Corvette	(1978)	1979	2	Originally built for South Africa, but embargoed; armed with Exocet ShShMs
		1	D'Orves Class	Corvette	1979	1981	1	New construction; in addition to 2 delivered 1979

Country	Qty	Weapon	Type	1978	1983-84	Qty	Comments
Germany, FR	4	Meko-360 Type	Destroyer	1978	1983-84	4	Armed with Aspide ShAMs and MM-40 Exocet ShShMs
	2	TNC-45	FAC	1970	1974	2	Further 2 projected units were cancelled
	2	Type 209/1	Submarine	1969	1974	2	Built in sections for assembly
	2	Type TR-1700	Submarine	1977	1984-86	2	Prior to licensed production of 4
Israel	1	B-707-320C	Transport	(1985)	1986	(1)	For electronic intelligence duties
	16	Mirage-3C	Fighter	1981	1981	(16)	In addition to 36 delivered 1979
	36	Nesher	Fighter	1978	1978-79	36	Total cost: $185 m
	22	Nesher	Fighter	(1981)	1982	22	
	(10)	Shoet Mk-2	APC	(1984)	1984	(10)	Unconfirmed
	(100)	Shafrir-2	AAM	(1977)	1978	(100)	Arming Dagger; unconfirmed
Italy	4	Dabur Class	PC	1976	1978	4	
	18	A-109 Hirundo	Hel	1977	1978-79	(18)	
	3	G-222	Transport	1972	1978	(3)	
	8	MB-326GB	Jet trainer	1971	1972	8	
	10	MB-339A	Jet trainer	1980	1981	10	
	2	S-61R	Hel	(1983)	1984	(2)	
	(3)	SH-3D Sea King	Hel	(1984)	1986	(3)	3-5 reportedly delivered
	(15)	Palmaria 155mm	SPH	(1983)			Possibly order for turret only; (for adaption on TAM chassis)
Korea, South	4	Aspide/Albatros	ShAM/ShShM launcher	(1979)	1983-84	(4)	Arming 4 Meko-360 destroyers
	2	SHORAR	Tracking radar	(1986)			
	(96)	Aspide	AAM/SAM/ShAM	(1979)	1983-84	96	Arming 4 Meko-360 destroyers
	1	LC-3800 Type	LC	1982	1985	1	
	1	Tacoma Type	LS	1982	1985	(1)	Ordered from Hyundai Shipyard
Libya	(120)	SA-7 Grail	Port SAM	1982	1982	(120)	Identity of seller unconfirmed
Netherlands	1	F-27 Mk-1000	Transport	(1970)	1971	1	
	2	F-27 Mk-1000	Transport	1974	1976	2	
	1	F-27 Mk-400M	Transport	1979	1979	1	VIP version
	2	F-27 Mk-500	Transport	(1980)	1981	2	
	2	F-27 Mk-600	Transport	1971	1971	2	
	5	F-28 Mk-5000	Transport	1976	1978	5	
Peru	10	Mirage-5	Fighter	1982	1982	10	Delivered during Falkland/Malvinas conflict
Spain	12	C-212-200	Transport	1984			
	5	Halcon Class	OPV	1979	1982-83	5	
Sweden	50	RB-53 Bantam	ATM	1975	1977	50	
	(50)	RBS-70	Port SAM	(1983)	1984	(50)	
Switzerland	4	PC-6	Lightplane	(1968)	1971	4	For Navy
	3	PC-6	Lightplane	1978	1978	3	For Army
UK	2	Canberra B-I-12	Bomber/interdictor	(1970)	1970-71	2	
	10	Canberra B-I-8	Bomber/interdictor	(1970)	1970-71	10	

Recipient code/ Recipient	Supplier	No. ordered	Weapon designation	Weapon description	Year of order	Year(s) of delivery	Total delivered	Comments
		1	HS-125	Transport	(1971)	1971	1	
		2	Lynx	Hel	1977	1978	2	On 2 Type-42 destroyers; first ordered 1973; final contract 1977
		5	Skyvan-3M	Transport	1971	1971	5	For SAR duties
		2	Seadart L	ShShM/ShAM launcher	1970	1977-81	2	Arming 2 Type 42 destroyers
		44	Sea Dart Mk-1	ShAM/ShShM	(1970)	1977-81	44	Arming 2 Type 42 destroyers
		1	Type 42	Destroyer	1970	1977	1	Armed with Exocet ShShMs and Sea Dart ShAMs; one more ship to be licence-produced
	USA	16	A-4B Skyhawk	Fighter/bomber	1970	1972	16	
		16	A-4B Skyhawk	Fighter/bomber	1975	1976	16	
		25	A-4P Skyhawk-2	Fighter/bomber	(1973)	1975	25	For use on aircraft carrier
		1	C-130E Hercules	Transport	(1970)	1972	1	
		(5)	C-130H Hercules	Transport	(1974)	1975-76	5	In addition to 1 delivered 1972
		3	CH-47C Chinook	Hel	(1977)	1980	3	To operate in 1980 Antarctic mission
		2	Citation-1	Transport	1977	1978	2	
		3	DC-6	Transport	(1970)	1971	3	
		(12)	HU-16D Albatros	Mar patrol/ASW	(1970)	1971-72	(12)	
		2	KC-130H	Tanker/transport	(1978)	1979	2	Total cost $29.5 m
		1	King Air A-100	Transport	(1970)	1971	1	
		2	King Air E-90	Trainer	1978	1979	1	Ordered via US Navy; total cost: $10 m
		3	L-100-20	Transport	(1982)	1983	3	
		3	L-188 Electra	Transport	1973	1974-75	3	For Navy
		4	L-188 Electra	Transport	(1982)	1983	4	Total costs: $10.2 m
		4	Learjet-35A	Mar patrol/trpt	(1976)	1977-78	4	
		1	Learjet-35A	Mar patrol/trpt	1980	1981	1	Delivered May 1981
		1	Learjet-35A	Mar patrol/trpt	1981	1982	1	
		4	Merlin-3A	Transport	1977	1977	2	
		41	Model 182	Lightplane	(1970)	1972-76	(41)	For air ambulance duties
		12	Model 185	Lightplane	(1970)	1971	12	
		(18)	Model 205 UH-1H	Hel	(1967)	1970-71	18	
		7	Model 207	Lightplane	(1974)	1975-76	7	
		5	Model 207	Lightplane	1976	1976	5	Including spares
		8	Model 212	Hel	1978	1978	8	
		2	Model 212	Hel	(1982)	1983	2	
		6	Model 500M	Hel	(1972)	1974	6	
		5	Navajo	Lightplane	(1972)	1973-75	5	
		1	Queen Air B-80	Transport	(1970)	1971	1	Ordered for Navy

No.	Weapon designation	Description	Year of order	Year of delivery	No. delivered	Comments
1	RC-47 Skytrain	Transport/recce	(1976)	1978	1	
4	S-2E Tracker	Fighter/ASW	1977	1978	4	
(5)	S-55 Chickasaw	Hel	(1970)	1972	(5)	For naval transport fleet
2	S-58	Hel	1971	1973	2	
4	S-61 D-4	Hel	1971	1972	4	
2	S-61R	Hel	1974	1975	2	Ex-US
4	SP-2H Neptune	Mar patrol/ASW	(1969)	1970-72	4	Ex-US
4	SP-2H Neptune	Mar patrol/ASW	1977	1977-78	4	
2	Sabreliner	Transport	1975	1975	2	One for VIP transport
2	Super King Air	Transport	1975	1975	2	
8	Super King Air	Transport	(1976)	1976-77	8	Total cost : $10 m
16	T-34C-1	Trainer	1977	1978	16	
6	T-41D Mescalero	Lightplane	1976	1976	6	
1	Turbo Porter	Transport	(1970)	1971	1	For transport and liaison
(100)	M-101-A1 105mm	TH	(1971)	1972-73	(100)	
55	M-113	APC	(1970)	1973	55	In addition to 75 APCs delivered 1972
(100)	M-114 155mm	TH	(1969)	1970-71	(100)	
(100)	M-18	TD	(1970)	1970-72	100	
(100)	M-5 Stuart	LT	1970	1971-72	(100)	
167	AN/PPS-15	Surveillance radar	(1973)	1974-76	(167)	
3	AN/TPS-43	3-D radar	(1976)	1977	(3)	
..	AN/TPS-44	Surveillance radar	(1980)	1981	(6)	
2	Balao Class	Submarine	1971	1971	2	Ex-USA; one ship hit during Falklands/Malvinas conflict Apr 1982
2	Fletcher Class	Destroyer	1971	1971	2	Ex-US Navy
1	Gearing Class	Destroyer	1973	1973	1	Ex-US Navy; Exocet ShShMs added 1977-78
4	LSM Type	LC/minelayer	1971	1971	4	Ex-US Navy
2	Sumner Class	Destroyer	1972	1972	2	Ex-US Navy; Exocet ShShMs on one 1977-78
2	Sumner Class	Destroyer	1974	1974	2	Ex-US Navy; Exocet ShShMs on one 1977-78
4 Bahamas						
3	Protector Class	PC	1985	1986	(3)	
2	Vosper 103 Type	PC	1976	1978	2	1 sunk by Cuban aircraft 1980
8 Bahrain						
Egypt						
..	Fahd	APC	(1984)			Unconfirmed order for unspecified number
France						
(23)	AML-90	AC	(1979)	1980	(23)	
(110)	M-3	APC	(1977)	1978-81	(110)	
2	MM-38 L	ShShM launcher	1979	1983-84	2	On 2 TNC-45 FACs
(24)	MM-38 Exocet	ShShM	1979	1983-84	(24)	Arming 2 TNC-45 FACs
Germany, FR						
2	Bo-105C	Hel	1977	1977	2	For police
1	Bo-105C	Hel	1978	1978	1	For police
2	FPB-38	PC	1979	1981-82	2	
2	TNC-45	FAC	1979	1983-84	2	Armed with 4 Exocet ShShMs
2	Type 62-001	Corvette	1985		2	

Recipient code/ Recipient	Supplier	No. ordered	Weapon designation	Weapon description	Year of order	Year(s) of delivery	Total delivered	Comments
	Italy	2	AB-212	Hel	(1981)	1982	2	
	Sweden	161	RBS-70	Port SAM	(1978)	1979	161	Total cost incl 14 aiming units: SEK 30 m; purchased by Unicorn International in Singapore on behalf of Bahrain
	UK	(20)	AT-105 Saxon	APC	(1979)	1981	(20)	Unconfirmed
		(8)	Ferret FV-703	Recce AC	(1971)	1972	(8)	
		(8)	Saladin FV-601	AC	(1971)	1972	(8)	
		2	Shorland	AC	(1970)	1971	2	
		3	Guardian Class	OPV	1984	1986	(3)	
	USA	4	F-4E Phantom	Fighter	1985	1986	(4)	Originally offered in 1982; delayed for financial reasons; total cost incl 2 F-5Fs and 60 AIM-9P AAMs: $114 m
		4	F-5E Tiger-2	Fighter	1985	1985-86	6	
		6		Fighter	(1986)			US LoO June 1985; in addition to 6 F-5s ordered earlier in 1985
		2	F-5F Tiger-2	Jet trainer	1985	1985	(2)	
		3	Model 269A	Hel	1972	1973-74	3	
		1	Model 500C	Hel	1973	1974	1	For police
		(2)	Model 500D	Hel	(1975)	1977	(2)	
		(54)	M-60-A3	MBT	1986			US LoO; total cost: $90 m
		60	AIM-9P	AAM	1985	1986	(60)	Arming F-5E/F fighters
		2 000	BGM-71A TOW	ATM	(1982)	1983-84	(2 000)	
3 Bangladesh	China	(12)	BT-6	Trainer	1979	1979	(12)	Delivered Oct 1979
		36	F-6	Fighter	(1974)	1975-76	(36)	Incl some FT-6 trainers
		(10)	F-6	Fighter	(1980)	1983	(10)	
		4	MiG-15UTI	Fighter/trainer	(1974)	1975	4	
		36	T-59	MBT	(1980)	1980-81	(36)	
		(20)	Type 54 122mm	SPH	1983	1984	(20)	
		4	Hai Ying-2 L	ShShM launcher	(1983)	1983	4	Arming 4 Hegu Class FACs
		(24)	Hai Ying-2	ShShM/SShM	(1983)	1983	(24)	Arming 4 Hegu Class FACs
		(2)	Hainan Class	PC	(1980)	1982-83	2	Option on more
		4	Hainan Class	PC	(1984)	1984-85	4	In addition to 2 delivered 1982-83
		4	Hegu Class	FAC	(1983)	1983	4	Equipped with ShShMs; option on more
		4	P-4 Class	FAC	(1982)	1983	4	
		(6)	Romeo Class	Submarine	(1980)	1980-82	(1)	
		8	Shanghai Class	PC	(1980)	1984	8	
	France	6	Super Magister	Jet trainer	1977	1977	6	
		4	Super Magister	Jet trainer	(1980)	1980	4	Attrition aircraft

(Recipient continued from previous page)

Supplier	No. ordered	Weapon designation	Weapon description	Year of order	Year of delivery	No. delivered	Comments
India	5	Super Magister	Jet trainer	(1985)	1985	5	
	3	An-12 Cub-A	Transport	(1971)	1972	3	
	4	DHC-3 Otter	Transport	(1970)	1971	4	
	1	DHC-4 Caribou	Transport	(1970)	1971	1	
	4	SA-316B Chetak	Hel	(1972)	1973	4	
	(30)	Model 56 105mm	TH	(1971)	1971	(30)	
	2	Abhay Class	PC	(1972)	1973-74	2	
Japan	1	Shamjala Class	PC	1981	1982	2	
Pakistan	(10)	M-24 Chaffee	LT	1971	1971	(10)	
	1	Town Class	PC	1978	1978	1	Sunk in 1971 Indo-Pakistani War; salvaged by Bangladeshi Navy
Singapore	2	PB-46 Type	PC	(1983)	1984	2	For fishery protection
UK	2	Wessex	Hel	1973	1973	2	Gift
	1	Leopard Class	Frigate	(1977)	1978	1	
	1	Leopard Class	Frigate	(1981)	1982	1	In addition to 1 delivered 1978
	2	Salisbury Class	Frigate	1976	1976	1	
USA	2	Model 206L	Hel	(1981)	1981	2	
	6	Model 212	Hel	1976	1977	6	
	(4)	Model 212	Hel	(1980)	1981	(4)	
	2	Model 337	Trainer	(1985)	1985	(2)	Seller unconfirmed
USSR	(50)	M-101-A1 105mm	TH	(1981)	1982	(50)	Seller unconfirmed
	1	An-24 Coke	Transport	(1972)	1973	1	
	3	An-26 Curl	Lightplane	(1981)	1981	3	
	6	Mi-8 Hip	Hel	(1973)	1974	6	
	10	MiG-21MF	Fighter	(1972)	1973	10	
	2	MiG-21UTI	Jet trainer	(1973)	1973	2	
	1	Yak-40 Codling	Transport	(1973)	1974	1	For VIP transport
	(15)	T-54	MBT	(1973)	1975	(15)	Via Egypt
	(15)	T-55	MBT	(1973)	1975	(15)	Via Egypt
	(72)	AA-2 Atoll	AAM	(1972)	1973	(72)	Arming MiG-21s
Yugoslavia	2	Kraljevica Cl	PC	(1974)	1975	2	
4 Belize							
UK	2	BN-2A Defender	Lightplane	1982	1983	2	For maritime patrol
4 Benin							
France	2	AS-350 Ecureuil	Hel	(1983)	1984-85	2	Gift
	3	C-47	Transport	1982	1982	3	Delivered May 1982
	1	SN-601 Corvette	Transport	(1979)	1979	1	
	.:	M-20	AC	(1981)	1982		
Indonesia	(6)	F-27 Mk-600M	Transport	(1981)	1982	(6)	Unconfirmed
Korea, North	(2)	P-4 Class	FAC	1978	1978	(2)	
Libya	1	Falcon-50	Transport	(1979)	1981	1	Also reported as Falcon-20
USA	1	Model 337	Trainer	(1971)	1972	1	
USSR	2	An-26 Curl	Lightplane	(1978)	1979	2	

Recipient code/ Recipient	Supplier	No. ordered	Weapon designation	Weapon description	Year of order	Year(s) of delivery	Total delivered	Comments
		..	BRDM-2	SC	(1982)	1983	(6)	
		..	BRDM-2 Gaskin	AAV(M)	(1983)	1983	(2)	
		..	SA-9 Gaskin	Landmob SAM	(1983)	1983	(24)	
15 Bolivia	Argentina	12	IA-63 Pampa	Jet trainer/strike	(1986)		(36)	Negotiating first export order
	Austria	36	Cuirassier	LT/TD	(1978)	1979-80	(20)	For Army and paramilitary forces
		20	Steyr-4K 7FA	APC	(1975)	1976-77	18	
	Brazil	18	122A Uirapuru	Trainer/COIN	(1973)	1974	6	
		6	HB-315B Gavaio	Hel	1981	1981-82	3	
		3	HB-315B Gavaio	Hel	1984	1984	8	
		3	HB-315B Gavaio	Hel	1985			Total cost: $3.8 m
		8	S-11	Trainer	(1973)	1974	(24)	
		(24)	EE-11 Urutu	APC	(1977)	1979-80	(30)	
		(30)	EE-9 Cascavel	AC	(1977)	1979-80	(15)	
	Canada	15	T-33A	Jet trainer	(1973)	1974	5	Total cost including spares
		5	T-33A	Jet trainer	1977	1978	(12)	
	France	(12)	Mirage-5	Fighter	(1983)	1983	6	12 Mirage-3/5s reportedly delivered
		6	SA-315B Lama	Hel	(1979)	1981	18	Total cost incl spares: $6.2 m; ex-Canadian AF; refurbished in France
		18	T-33A	Jet trainer	1984	1985-86	6	
	Israel	6	IAI-201 Arava	Transport	1975	1976	6	
	Italy	6	SF-260C	Trainer/COIN	1978	1979	6	
	Netherlands	7	F-27 Mk-400M	Transport	1979	1980-81	(7)	Embargo for last 2 lifted Mar 1981
	Spain	6	CV-440	Transport	(1971)	1972	6	
	Switzerland	36	PC-7	Trainer	1977	1978-81	(36)	
	Taiwan	6	C-47	Transport	1979	1979	6	Designation unconfirmed; also reported as C-46 Commando
	USA	12	T-6 Harvard	Trainer	1979	1979	12	
		2	C-130H Hercules	Transport	(1973)	1975	2	
		1	C-130H Hercules	Transport	1976	1977	1	To replace 1 C-130H lost in accident
		1	C-130H Hercules	Transport	1977	1978	1	
		12	C-47	Transport	(1973)	1975	12	
		(3)	F-86F Sabre	Fighter	(1972)	1973	(3)	
		1	King Air A-100	Transport	(1973)	1973	1	
		1	L-100-30	Transport	1979	1980	1	
		1	L-188 Electra	Transport	1974	1975	1	
		8	Model 185	Lightplane	(1970)	1975		
		8	Model 185	Lightplane	(1972)			
		6	Model 205 UH-1H	Hel	(1970)	1973	6	

Recipient	Supplier	No. ordered	Weapon designation	Weapon description	Year of order	Year of deliveries	No. delivered	Comments
	Venezuela	7	Model 207	Lightplane	(1980)	1982	7	Designation unconfirmed
		1	Model 210T	Lightplane	(1981)	1982	1	
		1	Model 414	Lightplane	(1972)	1973	1	
		2	Model 421C	Trainer	(1974)	1976	2	
		1	Sabreliner	Transport	1980	1982	1	For VIP transport
		2	Super King Air	Transport	1974	1976	2	Version 200
		6	T-41D Mescalero	Lightplane	(1970)	1972	6	
		2	Turbo Centurion	Lightplane	(1972)	1973	2	
		1	Turbo Porter	Transport	(1974)	1975	1	
		9	F-86K Sabre	Fighter	(1973)	1975	9	Licence-produced in USA
4 Botswana	Canada	1	DHC-6	Transport	(1982)	1982	1	Supplier unconfirmed
	France	2	AS-350 Ecureuil	Hel	(1984)	1985	2	
	UK	·	BN-2A Defender	Lightplane	(1977)	1977	3	First aircraft in AF
		3	BN-2A Defender	Lightplane	(1979)	1979	3	
		2	BN-2A Islander	Transport	1984	1984	2	
		6	Bulldog-120	Trainer	1980	1980	6	
		1	Skyvan-3M	Transport	1978	1979	2	
		·	Trislander M	Transport	1984	1985	1	
		2	Shorland	AC	(1980)	1980	(10)	Supplier unconfirmed
	USA	6	Model 152	Lightplane	(1978)	1979	2	Unconfirmed
		2	Model 206B	Hel	(1986)		6	
		(25)	V-150 Commando	APC	(1980)	1981-82	(25)	
		(12)	V-150 Commando	APC	(1986)			Unconfirmed
	USSR	(100)	SA-7 Grail	Port SAM	(1981)	1981	(100)	
11 Brazil	Australia	4	Ikara L	ShShM launcher	1972	1976-78	4	Arming 4 Niteroi Class frigates
		40	Ikara-3	ShSuM	1972	1976-78	40	Arming 4 Niteroi Class frigates
	France	6	AS-332	Hel	1985	1985	6	For Navy; reduced from 10; possibly from Brazilian production line
		20	AS-332	Hel	1986			For AF; 6 used Brazilian Pumas will be part of payment
		11	AS-350 Ecureuil	Hel	1985	1985	11	For Navy; reduced from 15
		40	AS-350 Ecureuil	Hel	1985	1985	40	For AF; renegotiated Dec 1985
		4	Mirage-3B	Jet trainer	(1972)	1973	4	
		4	Mirage-3D	Jet trainer	1977	1980	4	
		2	Mirage-3D	Jet trainer	1982	1984	2	
		12	Mirage-3E	Fighter/bomber	1972	1972-73	12	Replacing losses
		(12)	Mirage-3E	Fighter/bomber	(1986)			Formal proposals from France and Israel
		6	SA-330 Puma	Hel	1980	1981	6	Offset to French order for Xingu trainer
		4	AMX-30 Roland	AAV(M)	1972	1977	4	Armed with Roland SAMs
		8	MM-38 L	ShShM launcher	1970	1978	8	Arming 2 Niteroi Class frigates
		(8)	MM-40 L	ShShM launcher	1984			Arming 2 corvettes under construction

Recipient code/ Recipient	Supplier	No. ordered	Weapon designation	Weapon description	Year of order	Year(s) of delivery	Total delivered	Comments
		(2)	TRS-2052/3/6	Early warning radar	(1978)	1978-79	(2)	Part of DACTA surveillance system
		(60)	AM-39 Exocet	AShM	1985			Arming 6 AS-332 helicopters on order
		576	AS-11	ASM	1972	1974-75	576	Arming Xavantes
		576	AS-12	ASM/AShM	1972	1976-77	576	Arming Xavantes
		24	MM-38 Exocet	ShShM	1970	1979-80	24	Arming 2 Niteroi Class frigates produced under licence
		(24)	MM-40 Exocet	ShShM/SShM	1984			Arming 2 corvettes under construction
		72	R-530	AAM	(1972)	1973	(72)	Arming Mirage-3s
		(48)	Roland-2	Landmob SAM	1972	1977	(48)	Arming AMX-30s; partly locally assembled
	Germany, FR	6	Schuetze Class	MCM	1969	1971-75	6	Aratu-Class; armed with guns; displacement: 230t
		1	Type 209/3	Submarine	1982			Order incl 1 submarine for licensed production; also designated Type 1400
	Israel	8	Model 205 UH-1D	Hel	(1982)	1982	8	From Israeli surplus stocks
	Italy	(12)	SH-3D Sea King	Hel	1981	1983-84	12	
		3	SH-4	Hel	(1972)	1973	(3)	Prior to start of licence production
	Korea, South	26	F-5E Tiger-2	Fighter	(1986)			Incl some F-5F trainers
		38	M-44 155mm	SPH	1981	1981	38	
	Sweden	..	BOFI 40mm	Mobile AA-system	1985			Unspecified number for delivery 1986-87; total value: SEK 200 m
	UK	1	Giraffe	Fire control radar	(1985)	1985	1	For evaluation
		9	BAC-111	Transport	(1974)	1975-76	(9)	In addition to 2 in service
		10	HS-125	Transport	1973	1974-77	10	For radio and VIP duties
		6	HS-748-2	Transport	1973	1974	6	
		9	Lynx	Hel	1975	1977-78	9	Arming Niteroi Class frigates
		2	Wasp	Hel	1973	1973	2	Arming 2 Gearing Class destroyers
		7	Wasp	Hel	1977	1977-79	7	Arming Gearing and Sumner Class destroyers
		4	Wasp	Hel	(1979)	1980	4	From Royal Navy surplus stocks
		5	Seacat L	ShAM launcher	1972	1972	5	Arming 5 Sumner Class destroyers
		36	Seacat L	ShAM launcher	(1973)	1976-80	36	Arming Niteroi Class frigates
		(40)	Sea Skua	AShM	1985			Arming Lynx helicopters
		(24)	Seacat	ShAM/ShShM	1972	1972	24	Arming 5 Sumner Class destroyers
		360	Seacat	ShAM/ShShM	(1973)	1976-80	360	Arming Niteroi Class frigates
		4	Niteroi Class	Frigate	1970	1976-78	4	
		3	Oberon Class	Submarine	1969	1973-77	3	
		1	Oberon Class	Submarine	1972	1977	1	Delivery of 2nd delayed due to fire
	USA	3	B-707-320C	Transport	1985	1986	(3)	In addition to 2 previously ordered
		2	B-737-200C	Transport	1975	1976	2	

No. ordered	Weapon designation	Description	Year of order	Year(s) of delivery	No. delivered	Comments
4	B-737-200L	Transport	1975	1976	4	
11	C-130E Hercules	Transport	1975	1976-78	(11)	
5	C-130H Hercules	Transport	1974	1975	5	
36	F-5E Tiger-2	Fighter	1973	1975	36	Total cost incl 6 F-5Fs: $72.9 m
6	F-5F Tiger-2	Jet trainer	1973	1975	6	Total cost: $ 72.9 m incl 36 F-55Es
:	HH-13	Hel	(1970)	1973-74	(34)	For training
2	KC-130H	Tanker/transport	1977	1978	2	
22	Model 205 UH-1H	Hel	1973	1974	22	
14	Model 205 UH-1H	Hel	(1974)	1975	14	In addition to 22 previously acquired
(20)	Model 205 UH-1H	Hel	1984	1985	(10)	US Army surplus; total cost: $14m
3	Model 206A	Hel	1975	1976	3	For VIP transport
18	Model 206B	Hel	(1973)	1974	18	
16	Model 206B	Hel	(1985)	1986	16	For Navy
1	Model 412	Hel	(1985)	1986	1	
4	OH-6A Cayuse	Hel	(1973)	1975	4	
8	S-58	Hel	(1973)	1973	8	To support oil drilling operations
6	S-61B	Hel	1968	1969-72	6	For SAR duties
6	SH-3D Sea King	Hel	1973-74		6	For coastal defence and AC carrier
2	SH-3D Sea King	Hel	1971	1973	2	
25	T-37C	Jet trainer	(1971)	1972	25	
12	UH-60A	Hel	(1986)		(11)	Total cost: $90 m
11	VC-60 Lodestar	Transport	(1973)	1975-78	(11)	
16	LVTP-7A1	Amph ASSV	1983	1985	(16)	Amphibious; for Brazilian Marines
(50)	M-101-A1 105mm	TH	(1974)	1980	(50)	
(50)	M-108 105mm	SPH	(1980)	1971-72	(50)	
(100)	M-113	APC	(1970)	1974-75	(100)	
(70)	M-113	APC	(1974)	1978	(70)	
(100)	M-113	APC	(1976)	1973	(100)	
(90)	M-114 155mm	TH	(1973)	1972	(90)	
(100)	M-114 155mm	TH	(1980)	1971-73	(100)	
(50)	M-3-A1 Stuart	LT	(1970)	1972	(50)	
(100)	M-3-A1 Stuart	LT	(1971)	1971-73	(100)	
30	M-3-A1 Stuart	LT	(1974)	1974	30	
20	M-3-A1 Stuart	LT	(1977)	1978	(20)	
(25)	M-4 Sherman	MT	(1970)	1971	(25)	
(65)	M-7 105mm	SPH	(1980)	1981	(65)	
9	Hawk SAMS	Mobile SAM system	(1976)	1977-80	(9)	
120	AGM-65A	ASM	1973	1976	(120)	Arming 36 F-36s
120	AIM-9J	AAM	1975	1975	120	Arming 36 F-5Es
24	Asroc	ShSuM	1973	1973	24	Arming 2 Gearing Class destroyer
486	MIM-23A Hawk	Landmob SAM	(1976)	1977-80	(486)	
3	Fletcher Class	Destroyer	1967	1972-73	3	2 originally loaned
2	Gearing Class	Destroyer	1973	1973	2	Armed with ASROC ShSuMs and Wasp hel

Recipient code/ Recipient	Supplier	No. ordered	Weapon designation	Weapon description	Year of order	Year(s) of delivery	Total delivered	Comments
		7	Guppy-2 Class	Submarine	1972	1972-73	7	Ex-US Navy
		4	LCU 1610 Class	LC	1974	1975-78	4	Loaned May 1971, purchased 1973
		1	LCU-501 Class	LC	1973	1973	1	MAP loan 1962; purchased Dec 1977
		1	LST 511-1152	LS/minelayer	1962	1977	1	Ex-US Navy
		1	Parish Class	LS	1973	1973	1	Ex-USA; armed with Seacat SAMs
		5	Sumner Class	Destroyer	1972	1972-73	5	
4 Brunei	France	(3)	MM-38 L	ShShM launcher	1976	1978-79	(3)	On 3 Waspada Class FACs
		(18)	MM-38 Exocet	ShShM	1976	1978-79	(18)	Arming 3 Waspada Class FACs
		(24)	SS-12	ShShM	(1970)	1972	(24)	For one Soloven Class FAC delivered 1967
	Germany, FR	6	Bo-105C	Hel	1979	1981	6	Follow-on batch of 6 units for COIN duties; unconfirmed
	Italy	2	SF-260 Warrior	Trainer/COIN	(1981)	1982	2	
	Singapore	3	Waspada Class	FAC	1976	1978-79	3	Armed with 2 MM-38 Exocet ShShMs; hull identical to Venezuelan Constitution Class
	UK	1	HS-748-2	Transport	1970	1971	1	Transferred to local airline 1981
		24	AT-104	APC	(1971)	1972-76	(24)	For internal security
		16	FV-101 Scorpion	LT	1976	1978	16	
		1	Samson FV-106	ARV	(1980)	1981	(1)	Delivery year unconfirmed
		2	Sultan FV-105	CPC	(1980)	1981	(2)	Delivery year unconfirmed
		1	Rapier SAMS	Mobile SAM system	1979	1983	(1)	
		(12)	Rapier	Landmob SAM	1979	1983	(12)	1 bty ordered; incl Blindfire radar; total cost: $82 m
	USA	1	Model 205A-1	Hel	(1971)	1972	1	
		3	Model 206A	Hel	(1970)	1971	3	Replacing Wessex helicopters as trainers
		4	Model 212	Hel	1973	1974	4	Delivered 1979 via Heliorient in Singapore; in addition to 4 in service
		3	Model 212	Hel	1979	1979	3	Replacing 3 old Model 212s
		3	Model 212	Hel	1981	1982	3	
		3	Model 212	Hel	1982	1983	3	
		1	S-76 Spirit	Hel	1980	1981	1	For VIP use
15 Burkina Faso	Brazil	:	EE-9 Cascavel	AC	(1981)	1983	(10)	Unspecified number reportedly delivered
	France	2	AS-365	Hel	(1983)	1983	2	For VIP use
		2	Nord-262A-1	Transport	(1973)	1974	2	Second delivered Nov 74
		:	M-3	APC	(1974)	1975	(5)	
	UK	1	HS-748M	Transport	1976	1977	1	Delivered Sep 1977
		1	HS-748M	Transport	1981	1981	1	In addition to 1 in service

4 Burma

Supplier	No.	Designation	Role	Year of order	Year(s) of delivery	No. delivered	Comments
USA	..	Ferret FV-701	Recce AC		1971	(6)	Supplier unconfirmed
USSR	..	M-56	TD	(1983)	1983	(10)	
USSR	..	MiG-17	Fighter/strike	(1984)	1984	(6)	Delivered via Algeria and Benin by Aug 1984; may be MiG-21
Italy	12	SF-260 Warrior	Trainer/COIN	1975	1975-76	(12)	Ordered Jul 1979
	9	SF-260M	Trainer	1979	1980	(9)	Designation unconfirmed
	3	SF-260M	Trainer	(1981)	1981	3	Unconfirmed
	(4)	SF-260M	Trainer	(1984)	1985	(4)	Delivery year uncertain
Japan	4	Aiyar Maung Cl	LC	(1968)	1972	(4)	
	2	Sinde Class	LC	(1975)	1978	2	
Switzerland	7	PC-6	Lightplane	(1975)	1976-78	(7)	
	8	PC-7	Trainer	1977	1978-79	(8)	
	9	PC-7	Trainer	1979	1980-81	9	
	(11)	PC-9	Trainer	1985	1986	(4)	
USA	1	Citation-2	Transport	1982	1982	1	Delivered Aug 1982
	4	FH-227	Transport	1978	1978	4	For AF; supplier unconfirmed; refurbished in Thailand
	18	Model 205 UH-1H	Hel	(1974)	1975	18	
	4	T-33A	Jet trainer	(1971)	1972	4	
	12	T-37C	Jet trainer	(1970)	1971	12	
	5	T-37C	Jet trainer	(1975)	1976	5	

8 Burundi

Supplier	No.	Designation	Role	Year of order	Year(s) of delivery	No. delivered	Comments
Egypt	(20)	Walid	APC	(1981)	1982	(20)	Dates and number ordered unconfirmed
France	3	Model 150	Lightplane	(1972)	1973	3	
	2	SA-342L Gazelle	Hel	(1983)	1984	2	
	6	AML-60	AC	1982	1983	(6)	
	12	AML/D-90 Lynx	Recce AC	1982	1983	(12)	Partly financed by France; deal incl AML-60 and M3 vehicles
Italy	9	M-3	APC	1982	1983	(9)	
	3	SF-260 Warrior	Trainer/COIN	(1981)	1981	3	
UK	..	Shorland	AC	(1983)	1983	(6)	
USSR	..	BRDM-1	SC	(1980)	1980	(20)	Unconfirmed

4 Cameroon

Supplier	No.	Designation	Role	Year of order	Year(s) of delivery	No. delivered	Comments
Canada	3	DHC-4 Caribou	Transport	(1970)	1971	3	For VIP transport
	2	DHC-5D Buffalo	Transport	1982	1982	2	
	4	DHC-5D Buffalo	Transport	(1983)	1984-85	4	Replacing crashed aircraft
	1	DHC-5D Buffalo	Transport	1985	1985	(1)	
China	..	Shanghai Class	PC	1975	1976	2	Unconfirmed
Egypt	..	M-46 130mm	TG	(1982)	1983	(10)	Military aid
France	6	Alpha Jet	Jet trainer/strike	(1984)	1984	(6)	NG version
	3	SA-316B	Hel	(1972)	1974	3	For VIP use

Recipient code/ Recipient	Supplier	No. ordered	Weapon designation	Weapon description	Year of order	Year(s) of delivery	Total delivered	Comments
		2	SA-316B	Hel	(1978)	1978	2	
		1	SA-330 Puma	Hel	(1971)	1973	1	
		4	SA-342K Gazelle	Hel	1980	1982	4	Ordered Dec 1980
		(5)	Super Magister	Jet trainer	(1973)	1976	(5)	From French surplus stocks
		2	Super Magister	Jet trainer	1979	1979	2	Order including spares; in addition to 6 received earlier
		(2)	Super Magister	Jet trainer	(1980)	1980	(2)	Unconfirmed
		..	M-20	AC	(1982)	1983	(10)	
		1	MM-40 L	ShShM launcher	1981	1983	(1)	Arming 1 P-48 Class FAC
		(12)	AS-12	ASM/AShM	1980	1982	(12)	Arming 1 Gazelle helicopter
		..	HOT	ATM	1980	1982	(12)	
		8	MM-40 Exocet	ShShM/SShM	1981	1983	(8)	Arming 1 P-48 Class FAC
		..	Milan	ATM	(1981)	1982–84	(148)	6 launchers and 12 missiles delivered 1982; additional deliveries under new military co-operation programme
	Gabon	1	P-48 Type	PC/FAC	1974	1975	1	In addition to 1 delivered 1976
		1	P-48 Type	PC/FAC	1981	1983	1	Larger than same type built for Gabon
	Germany, FR	1	Leon M'Ba Class	PC	(1972)	1974	1	For maritime patrol
		3	Do-128-6	Transport	1981	1981–82	3	
		4	Do-228-200	Transport	(1985)			
		2	Do-28D-1	Transport	1979	1979	2	
	Israel	2	IAI-202 Arava	Transport	(1985)			
	Switzerland	1	BN-2A Defender	Lightplane	1985	1985	1	Gift
		1	PC-6	Lightplane	1985	1985	1	Gift
		1	PC-7	Trainer	1985	1985	1	Gift
	UK	2	HS-748M	Transport	1976	1978	2	
	USA	1	B-727-200	Transport	(1979)	1979	1	For VIP use
		2	C-130H Hercules	Transport	1976	1977	2	
		1	C-130H-30	Transport	1982	1982	1	
		..	C-47	Transport	(1972)	1973–74	(5)	
		..	Gulfstream-2	Transport	(1970)	1972	1	For VIP
		..	M-3	APC	(1978)	1979	(10)	
		24	V-150 Commando	APC	1981	1985	24	
3 Cape Verde	China	2	Shanghai Class	PC	(1975)	1975	2	
	USSR	2	An-26 Curl	Transport	1982	1982	2	First aircraft in service
		(8)	BRDM-2	SC	(1982)	1983	(8)	Unconfirmed
		3	Shershen Class	FAC	(1979)	1979	(3)	Probably delivered without torpedo tubes

15 Central African Republic

Supplier	No.	Weapon designation	Description	Year of order	Year of delivery	No. delivered	Comments
Argentina	12	IA-58A Pucara	COIN	(1986)	1976	(1)	Negotiating
Denmark	1	Caravelle	Transport	(1975)	1980	(4)	Sold by private company; for VIP use
Egypt	:	BRDM-2	SC	(1979)	1984	1	Supplier unconfirmed
France	1	AS-350 Ecureuil	Hel	(1984)	1978	2	
	2	Rallye-235GT	Lightplane	1977	1980	(1)	
	1	SN-601 Corvette	Transport	(1980)	1983	5	Delivered Apr 1983
Libya	5	VAB	APC	(1983)	1982	4	
	4	BTR-152	APC	1982	1981	(22)	Unconfirmed
	(22)	Ferret FV-701	Recce AC	(1980)	1982	4	
	4	T-55	MBT	1982	1982	4	
UK	1	Baron 95-B55	Lightplane	(1972)	1973	(1)	Unconfirmed
	..	Ferret FV-701	Recce AC	(1972)	1973	(10)	Unconfirmed

4 Chad

Supplier	No.	Weapon designation	Description	Year of order	Year of delivery	No. delivered	Comments
France	1	A-1 Skyraider	Fighter	(1974)	1976	(5)	Out of service by 1980
	1	C-130H Hercules	Transport	(1983)	1984	(1)	
	1	C-212-200	Transport	1983	1983	1	
	:	C-47	Transport	(1975)	1976	(7)	Unconfirmed
	1	Caravelle	Transport	(1976)	1976	(1)	Supplier unconfirmed
	(3)	DHC-4 Caribou	Transport	(1974)	1975	(3)	Ex-French for long-range transport
	5	Model 337	Trainer	(1974)	1975	5	For liaison and supply
	10	Noratlas 2501	Transport	(1970)	1971	(10)	
	2	PC-7	Trainer	(1984)	1985	2	Taken over from French company CIPRA; armed with twin 20mm gun
	10	S-58	Hel	(1970)	1971	(10)	
	1	SA-316B	Hel	(1972)	1973	(1)	
	10	SA-318C	Hel	(1970)	1971	(10)	Ex-Armee de L'Air
	4	SA-330 Puma	Hel	1976	1976	4	
	1	SA-341H Gazelle	Hel	(1976)	1976	(1)	Unconfirmed
	(10)	AML-60	AC	(1973)	1974	(10)	
	(10)	AML-60	AC	(1980)	1981	(10)	Unconfirmed
	(10)	AML-60	AC	(1981)	1982	(10)	
	(16)	AML-90	AC	(1981)	1982	(16)	
	4	ERC-90 Lynx	AC	(1982)	1983	4	
	:	M-3	APC	(1981)	1982	(10)	Unconfirmed
	(20)	M-3	APC	(1983)	1983	(20)	Military assistance
	1	F-27 Mk-600	Transport	1985	1986	1	
Libya	(4)	SF-260 Warrior	Trainer/COIN	(1986)	1986	(4)	Ex-Libyan AF; delivered to GUNT forces
	(5)	BM-13-16 132mm	MRS	(1980)	1981	(5)	
	(5)	BM-21 122mm	MRS	(1980)	1981	(5)	
	:	BRDM-2	SC	(1982)	1982	(10)	
	(6)	D-30 122mm	TH	(1980)	1981	(6)	
Switzerland	2	PC-6	Lightplane	1976	1976	2	Unconfirmed

Recipient code/ Recipient	Supplier	No. ordered	Weapon designation	Weapon description	Year of order	Year(s) of delivery	Total delivered	Comments
	USA	1	C-130H Hercules	Transport	1983	1984	1	
		6	V-150 Commando	APC	1985	1986	6	
		(1)	Hawk SAMS	Mobile SAM system	(1986)	1986	(1)	Unconfirmed
		(30)	FIM-43A Redeye	Port SAM	1983	1983	(30)	
		(100)	FIM-43A Redeye	Port SAM	(1986)	1986	(100)	Emergency MAP
		(30)	FIM-92A Stinger	Port SAM	1983	1983	(30)	
		(27)	MIM-23B Hawk	Landmob SAM	(1986)	1986	(27)	Unconfirmed
15 Chile	Brazil	3	EMB-110	Transport	1976	1976	3	Total cost: $3.9 m
		6	EMB-111	Mar patrol	1977	1978	(6)	First export order; for Navy
		2	EMB-120	Transport	1982			To replace C-47 Dakotas
		10	Universal-1	Trainer	1974	1975	10	Also for COIN duties; 5 re-transferred to Paraguay 1983
		(100)	EE-11 Urutu	APC	1979	1980	(100)	
		(200)	EE-9 Cascavel	AC	1980	1981-82	(200)	
	Canada	1	DHC-5D Buffalo	Transport	(1979)	1980	1	
		6	DHC-6	Transport	(1977)	1978	6	
	France	3	AS-332	Hel	(1982)	1983	3	
		1	Mirage-3D	Jet trainer	1984	1984	1	Replacing lost aircraft
		16	Mirage-50	Fighter/MRCA	1979	1980	(16)	Designation also reported as Mirage-5; possibly 20-22 delivered
		(30)	Mirage-50	Fighter/MRCA	(1986)			Negotiating
		5	PBY-5A Catalina	Mar patrol/ASW	1973	1973	5	Ex-French Air Force
		7	SA-315B Lama	Hel	(1970)	1972	7	
		15	SA-315B Lama	Hel	(1974)	1975-76	15	
		2	SA-316B	Hel	(1971)	1972	2	Arming 2 Leander Class frigates
		(15)	SA-319B	Hel	(1977)	1977-78	(15)	Radar-equipped
		10	SA-330 Puma	Hel	(1973)	1974	10	
		10	SA-330L Puma	Hel	1976	1977	10	
		3	SA-330L Puma	Hel	1980	1981	(3)	
		47	AMX-13-105	LT	1976	1977	47	
		12	AMX-155 Mk-F3	SPH	(1976)	1978	12	
		50	AMX-30B	MBT	(1980)	1981	(21)	Delivery of last 29 vetoed by Mitterrand Government; Chile may have returned 21
		6	Crotale SAMS	Mobile SAM system	1981	1983	6	
		4	MM-38 L	ShShM launcher	(1970)	1974-75	4	Arming 2 Leander Class frigates
		4	MM-38 L	ShShM launcher	(1972)	1973-74	4	Arming 2 County Class destroyers
		(2)	MM-38 L	ShShM launcher	1981	1984	(1)	
		150	AS-11	ASM	1974	1975	150	

Supplier	No.	Weapon designation	Weapon description	Year of order	Year(s) of delivery	No. delivered	Comments
	150	AS-11	ASM	1976	1977	150	Arming 30 Puma helicopters
	150	AS-12	ASM/AShM	1974	1975	150	Arming 30 Puma helicopters
	150	AS-12	ASM/AShM	1976	1977	150	After modernization of 2 Almirante Class destroyers 1972-75
	(32)	MM-38 Exocet	ShShM	(1970)	1974-75	(32)	
	24	MM-38 Exocet	ShShM	(1972)	1973-74	24	Arming 2 Leander Class frigates
	(8)	MM-38 Exocet	ShShM	1981	1981		Arming 2 County Class destroyers
	(300)	Milan	ATM	(1972)	1977-80	(300)	
	(108)	R-440 Crotale	Landmob SAM	1981	1983	(108)	
	(128)	R-530	AAM	1979	1980	(128)	For 16 Mirage-50s; designation unconfirmed
Germany, FR	6	Bo-105	Hel	(1975)	1976	6	For paramilitary forces
	(50)	Bo-105CB	Hel	1985	1985		Both civil and military versions; assembly planned
Israel	1 900	Mamba	ATM	(1977)	1979	1 900	Via Switzerland; delivered Feb 1979
	2	Type 209/3	Submarine	1980	1984	2	
	(80)	M-4 Sherman	MT	(1981)	1982	(80)	
	12	Gabriel L	ShShM launcher	1979	1979-81	12	Arming 2 Reshef Class FACs
	(150)	Gabriel-1	ShShM	1979	1979-81	(150)	Arming 2 Reshef Class FACs
	2	Shafrir-2	AAM	1976	1977-78	2	Arming F-5Es and Mirage-50s
	1	Reshef Class	FAC	1979	1979-81	1	Armed with Gabriel ShShMs
Netherlands	16	F-27 Maritime	Mar patrol	1980	1981-83	16	
Spain	16	C-101 Aviojet	Jet trainer	1984	1984		First 4 delivered complete; next 12 assembled in Chile
	1	C-101 Aviojet	Jet trainer	(1986)	(1986)	1	In addition to 16 for assembly
	(6)	C-212-200	Transport	1978			Unconfirmed
	10	C-212A Aviocar	Transport	1970	1978	10	For Army and Navy
Sweden	1	Tre Kronor Cl	Cruiser	(1970)	1971	1	Ex-Swedish Navy 'Gota Lejon'
Switzerland	10	PC-7	Trainer	1979	1980	10	
	15	MR-8	APC	(1972)	1973	15	
UK	3	Canberra PR-57	Bomber/recce	(1981)	1982	3	Ex-British Royal Navy
	9	Hunter FGA-74	Fighter	1971	1971	9	
	8	Hunter FGA-74	Fighter	(1973)	1973	8	
	12	Hunter FGA-9	Fighter/grd attack	1982	1982	12	
	3	Sea Vampire T22	Fighter	1971	1973	3	
	4	Seacat L	ShAM launcher	1973	1973-74	4	Arming 2 Leander Class frigates
	4	Seacat L	ShAM launcher	1981			Arming 2 County Class destroyers
	(50)	Blowpipe	Port SAM	(1983)	1983	(50)	
	(2)	Sea Eagle	AShM	(1985)	1986	(2)	At least 2 delivered; on T-36 Halcons
	16	Seacat	ShAM/ShShM	1971	1973-74	16	Arming 2 Leander Class frigates
	(16)	Seacat	ShAM/ShShM	1981			Arming 2 County Class destroyers
	2	County Class	Destroyer	1981	1982-84	2	

Recipient code/ Recipient	Supplier	No. ordered	Weapon designation	Weapon description	Year of order	Year(s) of delivery	Total delivered	Comments
	USA	2	Leander Class	Frigate	1971	1973-74	2	
		2	Oberon Class	Submarine	1972	1976	2	
		34	A-37B Dragonfly	Fighter/COIN	1974	1975-77	34	
		2	B-727	Transport	(1979)	1981	2	For VIP transport
		1	C-130E Hercules	Transport	(1971)	1971	1	
		1	C-130E Hercules	Transport	1972	1972	1	
		1	Citation-1	Transport	1972	1973	1	
		4	DC-6	Transport	(1980)	1982	4	
		18	F-5E Tiger-2	Fighter	1973	1976	18	Incl 3 F-5Fs
		1	FH-1100	Hel	(1972)	1973	1	For paramilitary forces
		1	King Air A-100	Transport	(1969)	1971	1	
		2	King Air C-90	Trainer	(1973)	1976	2	
		1	King Air C-90	Trainer	(1984)	1984	1	
		2	Learjet-35A	Mar patrol/trpt	(1971)	1973	2	For paramilitary forces
		4	Metro-2	Transport	(1974)	1976	4	
		(10)	Model 205 UH-1D	Hel	1981	1981	(10)	
		14	Model 310	Lightplane	(1970)	1972	14	For paramilitary forces
		3	Model 337	Trainer	(1978)	1980	3	
		18	Model R172K	Lightplane	1978	1978	18	
		..	Navajo	Lightplane	(1978)	1980	4	
		6	S-55T	Hel	1976	1977	6	
		8	T-37B	Jet trainer	1972	1974	8	
		12	T-37B	Jet trainer	(1974)	1974	12	
		75	M-113	APC	1969	1970-71	(75)	
		55	T-54	MBT	(1974)	1975	55	Shipped via Yugoslavia and Algeria; incl 1 300 tank grenades
		(36)	AGM-65A	ASM	1974	1976	(36)	Arming15 F-5Es
		(42)	AIM-9E	AAM	1974	1976-78	(42)	Arming 15 F-5Es and Mirage-50s
		2	Sumner Class	Destroyer	(1974)	1974	2	Ex US Navy
11 Colombia	Australia	2	C-130A Hercules	Transport	1984			
	Brazil	(76)	EE-11 Urutu	APC	1981	1983-84	(76)	
		120	EE-9 Cascavel	AC	1981	1983-84	120	
	France	14	Mirage-5	Fighter	1971	1973	14	Armed with R-530 Matra AAMs
		2	Mirage-5D	Jet trainer	1971	1973	2	Armed with R-530 Matra AAMs
		2	Mirage-5R	Recce	1971	1973	2	Armed with R-530 Matra AAMs
		27	SA-315B Lama	Hel	(1972)	1972-75	(27)	For SAR duties
		8	MM-40 L	ShShM launcher	(1980)	1983-84	(8)	Arming 4 FS-1500 Class frigates
		(18)	AS-11	ASM	1974	1975	(18)	

Supplier	No.	Weapon designation	Weapon description	Year of order	Year of delivery	No. delivered	Comments
	18	AS-12	ASM/AShM	1974	1975	(18)	
	(32)	MM-40 Exocet	ShShM/SShM	(1980)	1983-84	(32)	Arming 4 FS-1500 Class frigates
	(108)	R-530	AAM	1971	1973	(108)	Arming 18 Mirage-5s
Germany, FR	4	Bo-105C	Hel	(1983)	1984-85	4	On 4FS-1500 Type frigates
	4	FS-1500 Type	Frigate	1980	1983-84	4	Armed with Exocet and Seasparrow ShShMs
	2	Type 209/1	Submarine	1970	1975	2	
Israel	3	IAI-201 Arava	Transport	(1979)	1980	3	
	12	Kfir-C2	Fighter/MRCA	1981	1982	12	
Italy	(4)	Aspide/Albatros	ShAM/ShShM launcher	(1980)	1983-84	4	Armed with AAMs and ASMs
Netherlands	1	F-27 Mk-1000	Transport	1970	1971	1	Arming FS-1500 Class frigates
	2	F-27 Mk-600	Transport	1983	1984	2	
Spain	5	C-212-200	Transport	1984		(6)	Total cost: $14.5 m
Switzerland	6	PC-6	Lightplane	(1981)	1983	6	
	6	PC-6	Lightplane	1983	1984-85	6	
	(10)	Skyguard SAMS	Mobile SAM system	1982	1983-84	(10)	For AIM-7F Sparrow SAMs
UK	4	HS-748-2A	Transport	1972	1973	4	
	1	HS-748-2A	Transport	1980	1981	1	
	10	A-37B Dragonfly	Fighter/COIN	(1978)	1980	10	
	15	A-37B Dragonfly	Fighter/COIN	1982	1983-84	(15)	
	1	C-130H Hercules	Transport	(1983)	1984	(2)	
	1	DC-7	Transport	(1971)			
	3	HS-748-2A	Transport	1980	1981	3	In addition to 6 in service
	(3)	King Air C-90	Trainer	(1972)			
	12	Model 205 UH-1H	Hel	1981	1982	12	
	1	Model 212	Hel	(1970)	1971	1	
	2	Model 212	Hel	(1985)	1985	2	
	8	Model 300C	Hel	(1983)	1984	8	
USA	2	Model 412	Hel	(1985)	1985	2	
	10	Model 500C	Hel	1976	1977	10	
	2	Model 500E	Hel	(1984)	1985-86	(2)	
	6	Model 500MD	Hel	(1982)			Incl fully integrated control station
	6	Model 530MG	Hel	(1984)	1985-86	(6)	
	12	T-33A	Jet trainer	1977	1978	12	
	6	T-34B Mentor	Trainer	1977	1977	6	
	6	T-38 Talon	Jet trainer	(1977)	1978	6	
	12	M-3-A1 Stuart	LT	(1975)	1977	12	
	240	AIM-7F Sparrow	AAM	1982	1983-84	(240)	For Skyguard air defence system
	(64)	Seasparrow	ShAM/ShShM	(1980)	1983-84	(64)	Arming FS-1500 Class frigates
	2	Asheville Class	Frigate	(1982)	1984	2	Leased by Navy; for coastal patrol
	1	Dealey Class	Frigate	1972	1972	1	Ex-USA
	2	Sumner Class	Destroyer	1972	1972-73	2	

4 Comoros

| France | 4 | VLRA | Recce AC | (1982) | 1982 | 4 | |

Recipient code/Recipient	Supplier	No. ordered	Weapon designation	Weapon description	Year of order	Year(s) of delivery	Total delivered	Comments
	Italy	(5)	SF-260 Warrior	Trainer/COIN	1977	1978	(5)	
	USA	(2)	C-47	Transport	1977	1978	(2)	
		1	Model 402C	Lightplane	1978	1979	1	
13 Congo	Angola	1	Noratlas 2501	Transport	1979	1979	1	Unconfirmed
	China	(8)	BTR-60P	APC	(1980)	1981	(20)	Supplier unconfirmed
		(10)	M-1938 122mm	TG	(1971)	1972	(8)	Supplier unconfirmed
		(10)	M-1944 100mm	TG	(1970)	1971	(10)	Supplier unconfirmed
		(4)	PT-76	LT	(1971)	1972	(4)	Supplier unconfirmed
			T-59	MBT	(1977)	1978	(15)	
		(14)	T-62	LT	(1970)	1971	(14)	
		(10)	Type 55	APC	(1971)	1972	(10)	Supplier unconfirmed
		(10)	Type 55	APC	(1982)	1983	(10)	Supplier unconfirmed
		:	Type 56	APC	(1976)	1977	(25)	Supplier unconfirmed
	Cuba	:	MiG-15	Fighter/grd attack	(1980)	1980	(1)	Unconfirmed
		(8)	MiG-17	Fighter/strike	(1980)	1980	(8)	Unconfirmed; number also reported as 30
	Czechoslovakia	(4)	L-39 Albatross	Jet trainer	(1982)	1983	(4)	Unconfirmed
	France	1	Noratlas 2501	Transport	1981	1981	1	Military assistance
		:	Noratlas 2501	Transport	1985	1985	(2)	
		:	Nord-262A-1	Transport	1976	1978	(2)	
		1	SA-330L Puma	Hel	(1980)	1981	(1)	Unconfirmed
		1	SA-360 Dauphin	Hel	(1984)	1985	1	Designation unconfirmed; possibly SA-365
	Netherlands	1	F-27 Mk-1000	Transport	1974	1975	1	For VIP transport
	Spain	3	Piranha Class	PC	1981	1982-83	3	Derivative of Barcelo Class
	USSR	2	An-24 Coke	Transport	1978	1978	2	In addition to 3 in service
		(3)	Il-14	Transport	(1969)	1971	(3)	
		2	Il-18	Transport	(1969)	1971	2	
		(6)	BM-21 122mm	MRS	(1978)	1979	(6)	
		(25)	BRDM-2	SC	(1978)	1978	(25)	
		(3)	ZSU-23-4 Shilka	AAV	(1984)	1984	(3)	Unconfirmed
		2	Shershen Class	FAC	(1979)	1979	2	Delivered Dec 1979
14 Costa Rica	Panama	2	Model 204 UH-1B	Hel	(1978)	1979	2	
	Spain	3	C-212-200	Transport	(1983)			Reportedly on order
	USA	3	DHC-3 Otter	Transport	(1974)	1975	3	
		1	FH-1100	Hel	(1974)	1975	1	
		3	Model 500E	Hel	(1984)	1985	3	
		6	PA-28 Cherokee	Lightplane	(1972)	1973	6	
		2	S-58	Hel	1974	1975	2	

Recipient / Supplier	No.	Designation	Type	Order	Delivery	No.	Comments
4 Côte d'Ivoire	2	T-41A	Lightplane	(1984)	1985	(2)	Reportedly on order
	(3)	M-113-A2	APC	(1984)			
	1	Swift 105 Type	PC	(1977)	1979	1	For Coast Guard
	2	Swift 105 Type	PC	(1984)	1985	(2)	For Coast Guard
France	4	AS-365	Hel	(1979)	1979	4	
	6	Alpha Jet	Jet trainer/strike	1977	1980-81	(6)	Replacing lost aircraft
	1	Alpha Jet	Jet trainer/strike	1983	1984	1	
	3	Model F337	Trainer	(1970)	1971	(3)	
	7	SA-330 Puma	Hel	1973	1974	3	
	7	ERC-90 Sagaie	AC	(1979)	1980	7	
	..	M-3	APC	(1973)	1974	(5)	Delivered Apr 1980
	..	M-7 105mm	SPH	(1971)	1972	(10)	Designation unconfirmed
	6	M3-VDA	AAV	(1979)	1980	(6)	
	13	VAB	APC	1978	1980	13	
	2	MM-38 L	ShShM launcher	(1981)	1981	(24)	
	..	MM-38 Exocet	ShShM	(1981)	1981	1	Fitted to Patra Class
	..	Batral Class	LC	1974	1977	1	Can operate Alouette-3
	1	P-48 Type	PC/FAC	1975	1976	1	
	2	Patra Class	PC/FAC	1977	1978	2	MM-38 Exocet ShShMs installed 1981
Netherlands	1	F-27 Maritime	Mar patrol	1978	1978	1	
	2	F-27 Mk-1000	Transport	1975	1977	2	
	2	F-27 Mk-400	Transport	(1970)	1971	2	
USA	(2)	C-130H Hercules	Transport	(1985)	1979	6	Reportedly ordered
	6	F-33C Bonanza	Trainer	(1978)		1	
	1	Gulfstream-3	Transport	1981	1981		
5 Cuba — Czechoslovakia	(4)	L-39 Albatross	Jet trainer	(1982)	1983	(4)	Unconfirmed
Poland	(2)	Mi-2 Taurus-2	Hel	(1983)	1983	(2)	
USSR	25	An-26 Curl	Lightplane	(1977)	1978-79	(25)	Unconfirmed
	(2)	An-32 Cline	Transport	(1983)	1983	(2)	Unconfirmed
	(4)	Mi-14 Haze	Hel	(1983)	1983	(4)	Unconfirmed
	(10)	Mi-17 Hip-H	Hel	(1982)	1983-84	(10)	
	..	Mi-24 Hind-D	Hel	(1981)	1982	(12)	Unspecified number delivered Mar 1982
	(25)	Mi-8 Hip	Hel	(1967)	1968-72	(25)	
	60	MiG-21MF	Fighter	(1970)	1972-74	(60)	
	30	MiG-21bis	Fighter	(1980)	1981-83	(30)	
	15	MiG-23	Fighter/interceptor	(1977)	1977	(15)	
	20	MiG-23BN	Fighter/grd attack	(1980)	1981-84	(20)	
	25	MiG-23M	Fighter/interceptor	(1980)	1981-83	(25)	
	(2)	MiG-23U	Jet trainer	(1980)	1981	(2)	
	..	BMP-1	MICV	(1980)	1981-85	(125)	
	(100)	BRDM-1	SC	(1974)	1975-78	(100)	Unconfirmed

Recipient code/ Recipient	Supplier	No. ordered	Weapon designation	Weapon description	Year of order	Year(s) of delivery	Total delivered	Comments
		(30)	BRDM-2 Sagger	TD(M)	1981	1982-84	(30)	
		..	BTR-152	APC	(1984)	1985	(50)	Replacements
		..	BTR-60P	APC	(1984)	1985	(50)	Replacements
		(50)	D-1 152mm	TH	(1985)	1985	(50)	
		(100)	D-20 152mm	TH	(1971)	1972-74	(100)	
		(150)	D-30 122mm	TH	(1975)	1976-78	(150)	
		(100)	M-46 130mm	TG	(1975)	1976-78	(100)	
		(50)	M-46 130mm	TG	(1985)	1985	(50)	
		(20)	PT-76	LT	(1984)	1985	(20)	Replacements
		..	SU-100	TD	(1984)	1985	(50)	
		(100)	T-55	MBT	1981	1983	(100)	Unconfrimed
		(60)	T-62	MBT	(1980)	1981	(60)	
		(100)	T-62	MBT	(1983)	1983	(100)	Unconfirmed
		..	T-62	MBT	(1984)	1985	(20)	Replacements
		(50)	ZSU-23-4 Shilka	AAV	(1974)	1975-77	(50)	
		(12)	SA-3 SAMS	Mobile SAM system	1976	1977-78	(12)	
		(12)	SA-6 SAMS	Mobile SAM system	(1982)	1982-83	(12)	
		1	SA-N-4 L	ShAM launcher	1979	1981	1	Arming Koni Class frigate
		1	SA-N-4 L	ShAM launcher	(1982)	1984	1	Arming second Koni Class frigate
		6	SSN-2 Styx L	ShShM launcher	1972	1972-74	6	Arming 6 Osa-1 Class FACs
		13	SSN-2 Styx L	ShShM launcher	(1976)	1976-82	13	Arming 13 Osa-2 Class FACs
		360	AA-2 Atoll	AAM	(1970)	1972-74	(360)	Arming MiG-21MFs
		450	AA-2 Atoll	AAM	(1980)	1981-84	(450)	Arming MiG-21/23s
		120	AA-8 Aphid	AAM	(1980)	1981-84	(120)	Arming MiG-23s; unconfirmed
		500	AT-3 Sagger	ATM	1979	1980-81	(500)	
		200	AT-3 Sagger	ATM	(1981)	1982-84	(200)	On BRDM-2s
		400	SA-2 Guideline	Landmob SAM	1976	1976-77	(400)	
		216	SA-3 Goa	Landmob SAM	1976	1977-78	(216)	
		140	SA-3 Goa	Landmob SAM	(1982)	1982	(140)	Delivered Dec 1982
		450	SA-6 Gainful	Landmob SAM	(1982)	1982-86	(450)	Part of air defence deal incl SA-3s
		400	SA-7 Grail	Port SAM	1975	1976-77	(400)	
		18	SA-N-4	ShAM	1979	1981	(18)	Arming Koni Class frigate
		18	SA-N-4	ShAM	(1982)	1984	(18)	Arming second Koni Class frigate
		48	SSN-2 Styx	ShShM	(1972)	1972-74	(48)	Arming 6 Osa-1 Class FACs
		104	SSN-2 Styx	ShShM	(1976)	1976-82	(104)	Arming 13 Osa-2 Class FACs
		2	Foxtrot Class	Submarine	1978	1979-80	2	
		1	Foxtrot Class	Submarine	(1982)	1984	1	
		1	Koni Class	Frigate	(1979)	1981	1	
		1	Koni Class	Frigate	(1982)	1984	1	

No.	Recipient	Supplier	Designation	Type	Order	Delivery	No. del.	Comments
6			Osa-1 Class	FAC	1972	1972-74	6	
13			Osa-2 Class	FAC	1976	1976-82	13	
2			Polnocny Class	LS	(1981)	1982	2	
2			Sonya Class	MSC	(1979)	1980	2	
1			Sonya Class	MSC	(1984)	1985	1	
6			Turya Class	Hydrofoil FAC	1978	1979-81	6	
3			Turya Class	Hydrofoil FAC	(1982)	1983	3	
1			Whiskey Class	Submarine	(1978)	1979	1	
10			Yevgenia Class	MSC	(1976)	1977-82	10	
2			Yevgenia Class	MSC	(1984)	1984	2	
4	Djibouti	France	AS-350 Ecureuil	Hel	(1982)	1983	2	
1			Alouette-2	Hel	1979	1979	1	French military aid
1			Alouette-2	Hel	(1985)	1985	(1)	
1			Model 172	Lightplane	1980	1980	1	
1			Noratlas 2501	Transport	1979	1979	1	Replacing 1 delivered 1979
1			Noratlas 2501	Transport	1980	1980	1	French military aid
1			Noratlas 2501	Lightplane	(1985)	1985	(1)	Delivered Mar 1980
1			Rallye-235GT	Lightplane	1980	1980	1	
(2)		Iraq	AML-90	AC	(1979)	1979	(2)	MAP
100			VLRA	Recce AC	1983	1983-84	100	
1			Mystere-20	Transport	1980	1980	1	Unconfirmed
(12)			BRDM-2	SC	(1979)	1980	(12)	Unconfirmed
(12)		Spain	BTR-60P	APC	(1979)	1980	(12)	French military aid
2			C-212-200	Transport	1985	1985	2	
4	Dominican Republic	France	AS-365	Hel	(1978)	1978	1	
2		USA	Model 205 UH-1H	Hel	1981	1982	2	From USAF surplus stocks
(8)			Model 205 UH-1H	Hel	(1983)	1983	(8)	
2			Model 205A-1	Hel	1976	1977	2	
7			Model 500	Hel	(1970)	1972	7	
12			T-34B Mentor	Trainer	1981	1982	12	Replacing T-6 Texan trainers
(12)			M-41	LT	(1983)	1984	(12)	Unconfirmed
(8)			V-150 Commando	APC	(1979)	1980	(8)	
3			Cohoes Class	OPV	(1976)	1976	3	
3			Osprey Class	PC	(1982)	1982	3	
15	Ecuador	Brazil	EE-9 Cascavel	AC	1981	1983	(28)	
(28)		Canada	DHC-5D Buffalo	Transport	1974	1976	2	Incl spares
2			DHC-5D Buffalo	Transport	(1979)	1980	1	Ordered in addition to 1 delivered 1980
4			DHC-5D Buffalo	Transport	1981	1981-82	(4)	
1			DHC-5D Buffalo	Transport	1985			
3			DHC-6	Transport	1974	1975	3	

Recipient code/ Recipient	Supplier	No. ordered	Weapon designation	Weapon description	Year of order	Year(s) of delivery	Total delivered	Comments
	France	6	DHC-6	Transport	(1981)	1982	6	
		3	DHC-6	Transport	1985			
		8	Alouette-3	Hel	1973	1974	8	
		2	Mirage F-1B	Jet trainer	1977	1979	2	Ordered instead of Kfir-C2
		(16)	Mirage F-1C	Fighter/interceptor	1977	1980-82	(16)	Ordered instead of Kfir-C2
		6	Mirage-5	Fighter	(1978)	1979	6	
		5	SA-315B Lama	Hel	1974	1976	5	
		9	SA-316B	Hel	(1970)	1972	9	
		2	SA-319B	Hel	1973	1975	2	
		2	SA-330 Puma	Hel	(1974)	1975	2	
		(4)	SA-342L Gazelle	Hel	(1981)	1982	(4)	Previously unannounced order
		3	Super Magister	Jet trainer	1978	1978	3	
		13	AML-60	AC	(1969)	1971	(13)	
		(9)	AML-60	AC	(1980)	1982	(9)	In addition to 15 in service
		(14)	AML-90	AC	(1969)	1971	14	
		(9)	AML-90	AC	(1980)	1982	(9)	In addition to 14 in service
		40	AMX-13	LT	(1970)	1971-72	(40)	
		40	AMX-13	LT	1974	1975	40	In addition to 40 purchased 1971-72
		40	AMX-13	LT	(1976)	1978	40	In addition to 80 delivered 1972-75
		6	AMX-155 Mk-F3	SPH	1974	1975	6	Self-propelled howitzer
		25	AMX-VCI	MICV	(1982)	1984	25	
		3	MM-38 L	ShShM launcher	(1974)	1976-77	3	Arming 3 TNC-45 FACs
		6	MM-40 L	ShShM launcher	1979	1982-84	6	Arming 6 Esmeraldas Class corvettes
		12	MM-38 Exocet	ShShM	(1974)	1976-77	12	Arming 3 TNC-45 FACs
		(18)	MM-40 Exocet	ShShM/SShM	1979	1982-84	(18)	Arming Esmeraldas Class corvettes
		72	R-550 Magic	AAM	1974	1977-78	72	
		108	Super-530	AAM	1977	1979-82	108	Arming 18 Mirage F-1s
	Germany, FR	10	UR-416	APC	(1970)	1971	10	
		3	TNC-36	FAC	(1970)	1971	3	Armed with Gabriel ShShMs in 1980-81
		3	TNC-45	FAC	(1974)	1976-77	3	Arming Exocet ShShMs
		2	Type 209/2	Submarine	1974	1978	2	Total cost: $66 m
	Israel	6	IAI-201 Arava	Transport	1974	1974-75	(6)	For Army
		3	IAI-201 Arava	Transport	1975	1975-77	3	
		3	Gabriel L	ShShM launcher	(1980)	1981	3	Arming 3 Manta Class FACs
		(12)	Gabriel-2	ShShM	(1980)	1981	(12)	Arming 3 Manta Class FACs
	Italy	12	SF-260M	Trainer	(1977)	1977	12	Replacing T-34s and T-6s
		6	Aspide/Albatros	ShAM/ShShM launcher	1979	1982-84	(6)	Arming 6 Esmeraldas Class corvettes
		(72)	Aspide	AAM/SAM/ShAM	1979	1982-84	(72)	Arming 6 Esmeraldas Class corvettes
		6	Esmeraldas Cl	Corvette	1979	1982-84	6	Similar to Libyan Wadi (Assad) Class

Country	No.	Type	Role	Date	Date	No.	Notes
Netherlands	1	F-28 Mk-3000	Transport	(1985)	1986	1	
	1	F-28 Mk-4000	Transport	1985	1971	1	
Portugal	3	DC-6	Transport	(1970)	1972	3	Formerly operated by civilian airline
Switzerland	1	PC-6	Lightplane	(1970)	1972	1	
UK	1	B-727	Transport	(1984)	1984	1	
	4	BAC-167	Trainer/COIN	1971	1973	4	Aircraft originally destined for Sudan; may have been cancelled in favour of more T-33s
	8	BAC-167	Trainer/COIN	1972	1972	8	
	4	BAC-167	Trainer/COIN	1974	1974	4	
	6	BAC-167	Trainer/COIN	(1985)	(1985)	6	
USA	3	HS-748-2	Transport	1970	1971	3	
	2	HS-748-2	Transport	1974	1975	2	
	12	Jaguar	Fighter	1974	1977-78	12	Arming R-530 Magic AAMs
	1	Skyvan-3M	Transport	1970	1971	1	
	250	Blowpipe	Port SAM	(1975)	1976-78	(250)	
	12	A-37B Dragonfly	Fighter/COIN	1975	1976	12	
	3	B-720-047B	Transport	(1972)	1973	3	
	1	B-727-200	Transport	(1979)	1980	1	
	1	B-737-200C	Transport	(1979)	1981	1	
	2	C-130H Hercules	Transport	1976	1978	2	Replacement for 2 C-130Hs lost 1979
	1	C-130H Hercules	Transport	1979	1980	1	
	1	Citation-1	Transport	1970	1971	1	
	1	L-100-30	Transport	1982	1984	1	
	4	L-188 Electra	Transport	(1975)	1976	4	Ex-surplus airline stocks
	4	L-188 Electra	Transport	1976	1978	4	
	3	Learjet 25B	Transport	1974	1975	3	
	24	Model 150	Lightplane	(1973)	1978	4	
	4	Model 204 UH-1B	Hel	(1975)	1977-78	3	For SAR duties
	3	Model 212	Hel	(1976)	1975	2	
	2	Navajo	Lightplane	(1973)	1974	1	
	1	Queen Air B-80	Transport	(1973)	1981	(1)	
	1	Super King Air	Transport	1980	1977-78	(20)	Ex US reserves; refurbished to AT-33 standard before transfer
	(25)	T-33A	Jet trainer	1985	1980	3	
	20	T-34C-1	Trainer	1975	1977-78	18	
	3	T-34C-1	Trainer	(1979)	1980	(25)	For Navy; total cost incl 1 Super King Air
	18	T-41D Mescalero	Lightplane	1970	1970-71	44	
	(25)	M-101-A1 105mm	TH	(1971)	1973	6	
	44	M-163 Vulcan	AAV	(1978)	1981	15	
	6	M-198 155mm	TH	(1979)	1980		
	15	M-3	APC	(1973)	1975		

Recipient code/ Recipient	Supplier	No. ordered	Weapon designation	Weapon description	Year of order	Year(s) of delivery	Total delivered	Comments
		(15)	M-56	TD		1980	(15)	
		1	Gearing Class	Destroyer	1978	1978	1	
		1	LST 511-1152	LS/minelayer	1977	1977	1	Ex-US; transfer after extensive refit
15 Egypt	Brazil	10	EMB-312 Tucano	Trainer	1983	1984	10	To be followed by local assembly of 110, of which approx 80 for transfer to Iraq
	Canada	1	EE-11 Urutu	APC	(1983)	1983	1	For evaluation
		1	EE-9 Cascavel	AC	(1983)	1983	1	For evaluation
		10	DHC-5D Buffalo	Transport	1981	1982	10	Ordered Nov 1981
	China	40	F-6	Fighter	1976	1979	40	Delivered in exchange for some MiG-23s for Chinese examination
		(50)	F-6	Fighter	1981	1982-84	(50)	In addition to 40 delivered 1979; assembled in Egypt
		(110)	F-7	Fighter	1980	1980-85	(110)	Last 80 assembled in Egypt
		(4)	Hai Ying-2 L	ShShM launcher	(1983)	1984	(4)	Arming 2 Jianghu Class frigates
		6	Hai Ying-2 L	ShShM launcher	(1984)	1984	6	Arming 6 Hegu Class FACs
		(24)	Hai Ying-2	ShShM/SShM	1983	1984	(24)	Arming 2 Jianghu Class frigates
		(72)	Hai Ying-2	ShShM/SShM	(1984)	1984	(72)	Arming 6 Hegu Class FACs
		(2)	Hainan Class	PC	(1982)	1983	2	
		6	Hainan Class	PC	1983	1984	6	In addition to 2 delivered 1983
		6	Hegu Class	FAC	(1984)	1984	6	Delivered Sep 1984
		(2)	Jianghu Class	Frigate	1983	1984-85	2	
		:	Luda Class	Destroyer	(1985)			Unconfirmed
		2	Romeo Class	Submarine	(1980)	1982	2	In addition to 2 delivered 1982
		2	Romeo Class	Submarine	1982	1984	2	3rd pair of ex-Chinese Navy submarines
		2	Romeo Class	Submarine	(1984)	1985	(2)	Prior to local assembly/production of 37
	France	8	Alpha Jet	Jet trainer/strike	1981	1982-83	(8)	Ordered Dec 1981, total cost: $1000 m
		20	Mirage-2000	Fighter/strike	1981		(20)	Option on 16-20 more taken up 1984 but still under discussion; assembly in Egypt possible
		(20)	Mirage-2000	Fighter/strike	(1986)	1986		
		38	Mirage-5SD	Fighter	1973	1973-75	(38)	Bought on US refusal to sell F-4; Saudi Arabia funding; order incl Crotale and AMX-30; 32 fighters and 6 trainers
		14	Mirage-5SD	Fighter	1975	1977	14	8 fighters and 6 recce
		14	Mirage-5SD	Fighter	(1977)	1980	14	Ordered Jun 1980
		16	Mirage-5SD	Fighter	1980	1983	(16)	
		2	Mystere-20	Transport	(1974)	1975	2	For VIP transport
		4	SA-342K Gazelle	Hel	(1973)	1974	4	

Supplier	No.	Weapon	Type	Order date	Delivery date	No. delivered	Comment
	60	SA-342L Gazelle	Hel	1975	1976-78	(60)	At least 24 with HOT ATMs, 12 with AS-12 ASMs and 12 with 20mm cannon
	(16)	Crotale SAMS	Mobile SAM system	1976	1979-80	(16)	
	12	Crotale SAMS	Mobile SAM system	1982	1982-83	(12)	
	(4)	Crotale SAMS	Mobile SAM system	(1984)	1985	(4)	Third order
	6	Otomat-2 L	ShShM launcher	1978	1980-81	6	Coastal defence version
	..	Tiger	Point defence radar	(1980)	1981	(3)	
	(40)	AM-39 Exocet	AShM	1982	1982-83	(40)	Ordered Aug 1982
	(60)	ARMAT	ARM	1984	1985	(20)	Arming Mirage-2000s
	(112)	AS-12	ASM/AShM	(1973)	1974-76	(112)	Arming 24 Westland Commandos
	(72)	AS-12	ASM/AShM	1975	1977-78	(72)	Arming 12 Gazelle helicopters
	..	AS-30L	ASM	1983	1985	(50)	Arming Mirage-2000s
	(288)	HOT	ATM	1975	1976-78	(288)	Arming 24 Gazelle helicopters ordered 1975
	(2 400)	HOT	ATM	(1976)	1978-80	(2 400)	
	(288)	HOT	ATM	1981	1984-85	(288)	Arming 24 of 36 Gazelle helicopters ordered 1981
	(4 000)	Milan	ATM	(1975)	1976-79	(4 000)	First customer of coastal defence system
Italy	60	Otomat-2	ShShM	1978	1980-81	(60)	
	384	R-440 Crotale	Landmob SAM	1976	1979-81	(384)	
	(144)	R-440 Crotale	Landmob SAM	1982	1982-83	(144)	
	..	R-440 Crotale	Landmob SAM	(1984)	1985	(48)	Third order
	(114)	R-530	AAM	1974	1975-76	(114)	Arming 38 Mirage-5s
	(42)	R-530	AAM	(1977)	1980	(42)	Arming 14 Mirage-5s
	(180)	R-550 Magic	AAM	1977	1980-83	(180)	Arming Mirage-5s
	..	R-550 Magic	AAM	1983	1985	(60)	Arming Mirage-2000s
	..	Super-530	AAM	1983	1986	(60)	Arming Mirage-2000s
	15	CH-47C Chinook	Hel	1980	1982	15	
	4	S-61R	Hel	1981	1983	4	
	2	Aspide/Albatros	ShAM/ShShM launcher	(1983)	1984	2	Arming 2 F-30 Class frigates
	6	Otomat-1 L	ShShM launcher	1977	1978-79	(6)	On October Class FACs
	6	Otomat-1 L	ShShM launcher	1978	1981-82	(6)	For Ramadan Class FACs
	(18)	Skyguard SAMS	Mobile SAM system	1982	1985-86	(8)	18 btys comprising 2 twin 35mm AAGs and 2 quadruple Sparrow launchers
	(48)	Aspide	AAM/SAM/ShAM	(1983)	1984	48	Arming 2 F-30 Class frigates
	(36)	Otomat-1	ShShM	1977	1978-79	(36)	Arming 6 October Class FACs
	(72)	Otomat-1	ShShM	1978	1981-82	(72)	Arming 6 Ramadan Class FACs
Netherlands	2	Alkmaar Class	Minehunter	(1986)			Tripartite type; negotiating; total cost approx $80 m
Romania	200	T-55	MBT	1983	1983-84	(60)	Romanian designation: M-77 or TR-77; deliveries stopped due to Egyptian re-exports to Iraq
Saudi Arabia	1	C-123 Provider	Transport	(1980)	1981	1	Transferred from Saudi Arabia

Recipient code/ Recipient	Supplier	No. ordered	Weapon designation	Weapon description	Year of order	Year(s) of delivery	Total delivered	Comments
Spain		600	BMR-600	ICV	1982	1984-85	(600)	
		2	F-30 Class	Frigate	1982	1984	2	Option on 2 more; rapid delivery due to diversion to Egypt of last 2 ships for Spanish Navy
UK		4	S-70 Class	Submarine	(1986)			Negotiating
		32	Commando Mk-2	Hel	1975	1977-79	(32)	Financed by Saudi Arabia; small number updated with EW equipment 1981
USA		6	SH-3D Sea King	Hel	(1973)	1975-76	6	Ordered via Saudi Arabia
		(600)	Beeswing	ATM	1975	1976-77	(600)	
		6	Ramadan Class	FAC	1978	1981-82	6	
		1	B-720-047B	Transport	(1975)	1975	1	For VIP use
		1	B-737-100	Transport	(1979)	1981	1	
		(6)	C-130H Hercules	Transport	1976	1976-77	6	2 equipped for ECM duties
		14	C-130H Hercules	Transport	1978	1979-81	(14)	
		3	C-130H Hercules	Transport	1981	1982	3	
		6	Commuter-1900	Transport	(1985)			
		4	E-2C Hawkeye	AEW	1983	1985-87	(4)	For electronic surveillance Total cost for 4 aircraft: $689 m; remaining 2 for delivery 1987 along with 5th aircraft ordered 1984
		1	E-2C Hawkeye	AEW	1985	1987	(1)	Total cost: $50 m
		40	F-16A	Fighter/strike	1980	1982-83	(40)	Incl a few F-16B trainers
		34	F-16C	Fighter/strike	1982	1986	(8)	Agreement in principle for a total of 150 aircraft; total cost incl 6 F-16D trainers: $1.2 b
		6	F-16D	Fighter/trainer	1982	1986	(6)	
		35	F-4E Phantom	Fighter	1979	1979-80	(35)	
		3	Gulfstream-3	Transport	(1983)	1985	3	For VIP use
		(20)	UH-12	Hel	1979	1982	(20)	
		79	M-106-A1	APC	1982	1982	79	
		100	M-109-A2 155mm	SPH	1982	1984-85	(100)	
		48	M-109-A2 155mm	SPH	1985	1986-87	(48)	In addition to 100 supplied in 1984
		400	M-113-A2	APC	1979	1980-82	(400)	
		570	M-113-A2	APC	1980	1982-83	(570)	Second batch brings total to 1100
		472	M-113-A2	APC	(1984)	1985-87	(472)	US LoO Mar 1984; total cost incl M-125s, M-577s and M-548s: $157 m
		41	M-125-A1	APC	1979	1982	41	
		19	M-125-A2	APC	1984	1986	(19)	US LoO Mar 1984
		42	M-198 155mm	TH	1983	1986	(18)	US LoO Oct 1983
		54	M-548	APC	1979	1980-81	(54)	

No.	Weapon designation	Weapon description	Year of order	Year(s) of deliveries	No. delivered	Comments
33	M-548	APC	1984	1986-87	(33)	US LoO Mar 1984
34	M-577-A1	CPC	1979	1982-83	(34)	US LoO Mar 1984
13	M-577-A2	CPC	1984	1986	(13)	
439	M-60-A3	MBT	1980	1981-84	(439)	In addition to 439 already on order; deal incl 23 M-88-A1 ARVs
220	M-60-A3	MBT	1982	1984-85	(220)	
94	M-60-A3	MBT	1985			Exempted from temporary US ban on arms sales to Middle East imposed Jan 1985
86	M-88-A1	ARV	1980	1981-83	(86)	
23	M-88-A1	ARV	1982	1984-85	(65)	
56	M-88-A1	ARV	1984	1983	(52)	Total cost: $63 m
52	M-901 TOW	TD(M)	1986	1986		Improved ATM-version of M-113-A1
2	AN/TPQ-37	Tracking radar	1979			
72	I-Hawk SAMS	Mobile SAM system	1982	1982-84	(72)	
24	I-Hawk SAMS	Mobile SAM system	1983	1985-86	(24)	
(10)	I-Hawk SAMS	Mobile SAM system	(1985)			Third order
26	M54 Chaparral	Mobile SAM system	(1983)	1983	(13)	
4	RGM-84A L	ShShM launcher	1980	1984	4	Arming 2 F-30 Class frigates
600	AGM-65A	ASM	1979	1980-84	(600)	Arming F-4s and F-16s
70	AIM-7E Sparrow	AAM	1979	1979-80	(70)	Arming F-4E Phantoms
424	AIM-7M Sparrow	AAM/SAM	(1984)	1985-86	(192)	To arm Skyguard air defence system
350	AIM-9E	AAM	1979	1979-80	(350)	Arming F-4E Phantoms
300	AIM-9L	AAM	1982	1983	300	Delivered Apr 1983
150	AIM-9L	AAM	1983	1984-85	(150)	In addition to 300 delivered Apr 1983
(1 856)	BGM-71A TOW	ATM	1980	1980-81	(1 856)	
2 400	BGM-71A TOW	ATM	1981	1982-83	(2 400)	Improved version
216	MIM-23B Hawk	Landmob SAM	1979	1982-84	(216)	Order incl 24 launch units in 4 btys; in addition to 12 btys ordered 1979
72	MIM-23B Hawk	Landmob SAM	1982	1985-86	(72)	
(120)	MIM-23B Hawk	Landmob SAM	(1985)	1986		Third order
483	MIM-72F	SAM/ShAM	1983	1984	(240)	Total cost incl 26 towed launchers: $160 m
18	RGM-84A Harpoon	ShShM	(1983)		18	US LoO Sep 1983; arming 2 F-30 Class frigates; total cost: $40 m
USSR						
20	Mi-6 Hook	Hel	(1969)	1971	20	
80	Mi-8 Hip	Hel	(1969)	1970-71	80	
(25)	Mi-8 Hip	Hel	1973	1973	(25)	
20	MiG-15	Fighter/grd attack	(1970)	1971	(20)	
(35)	MiG-17	Fighter/strike	(1970)	1971	(35)	
(50)	MiG-17	Fighter/strike	1973	1973	(50)	
(30)	MiG-19	Fighter/grd attack	1973	1973	(30)	
25	MiG-21F	Fighter	(1970)	1972	25	
(150)	MiG-21MF	Fighter	(1971)	1972-73	(150)	

Recipient code/Recipient	Supplier	No. ordered	Weapon designation	Weapon description	Year of order	Year(s) of delivery	Total delivered	Comments
		(20)	MiG-23BN	Fighter/grd attack	1973	1976	(20)	16 MiG-23BNs and 4 MiG-23Us
		(20)	Su-20 Fitter-C	Fighter/grd attack	(1970)	1972	(20)	Including some swing-wing version
		(140)	Su-7 Fitter	Fighter	(1967)	1967-72	(140)	
		(25)	Tu-16B Badger-B	Bomber	(1970)	1971-72	(25)	
		(100)	BM-21 122mm	MRS	(1967)	1971-72	(100)	
		(250)	BMP-1	MICV	(1971)	1968-72	(250)	
		(650)	BTR-60P	APC	(1969)	1973-74	(650)	
		(25)	K-61	APC	(1972)	1970-73	(25)	
		(200)	PT-76	LT	(1965)	1972	(200)	
		(800)	T-54	MBT	(1967)	1966-73	(800)	
		(50)	T-54	MBT	(1972)	1967-72	(50)	
		(550)	T-55	MBT	(1967)	1973	(550)	
		(750)	T-62	MBT	(1971)	1969-73	(750)	
		(150)	ZSU-23-4 Shilka	AAV	(1967)	1972-75	(150)	
		(20)	FROG L	Mobile SSM system	(1969)	1967-73	(20)	
		(100)	SA-2 SAMS	Mobile SAM system	(1969)	1971	(100)	
		(200)	SA-3 SAMS	Mobile SAM system	(1969)	1970-72	(200)	
		(50)	SA-6 SAMS	Mobile SAM system	(1971)	1970-71	(50)	
		(12)	Scud-B L	Mobile SSM system	(1972)	1972-73	(12)	
		..	Straight Flush	Fire control radar	(1970)	1971	(5)	Unconfirmed
		(1 910)	AA-2 Atoll	AAM	(1967)	1967-73	(1 910)	Arming MiG-21s
		(288)	AA-2 Atoll	AAM	1973	1974-76	(288)	Arming MiG-23s
		(25)	AS-5 Kelt	ASM	(1969)	1971-72	(25)	Arming Tu-16s
		(300)	AT-1 Snapper	ATM	(1971)	1972-73	(300)	
		(400)	AT-3 Sagger	ATM	(1971)	1972-73	(400)	
		(60)	FROG-7	Landmob SSM	(1969)	1971	(60)	Approx. 12 launchers
		(750)	SA-2 Guideline	Landmob SAM	(1969)	1970-72	(750)	
		(1 200)	SA-3 Goa	Landmob SAM	(1969)	1970-71	(1 200)	
		(500)	SA-6 Gainful	Landmob SAM	(1971)	1972-73	(500)	
		(2 400)	SA-7 Grail	Port SAM	(1970)	1972-74	(2 400)	
		(60)	SCUD-B	Landmob SSM	(1972)	1973	(60)	
		3	Polnocny Class	LS	1972	1973-74	3	
		12	SO-1 Class	PC	(1961)	1962-71	(12)	
		7	T-43 Class	MSO	(1955)	1956-71	(7)	
		2	Whiskey Class	Submarine	1971	1972	2	Replacing 2 older ones
		4	Yurka Claps	MSO	(1969)	1970-71	4	
4 El Salvador	France	6	Rallye-235GT	Lightplane	(1981)	1981	6	
		3	Super Magister	Jet trainer	1977	1978	3	

		Qty	Designation	Type	(Ordered)	Delivered	Qty	Comment
	Israel	(12)	AML-90	AC	(1979)	1980-81	(12)	Supplier unconfirmed
		(12)	AMX-13	LT	1974	1974	(12)	Ex-Austrian; refurbished in France
		4	IAI-201 Arava	Transport	1973	1974-75	4	
		18	MD-450 Ouragan	Fighter/bomber	1973	1975	18	In addition to 3 from France
		6	Magister	Jet trainer	(1974)	1975	6	Probably in storage or cannibalized
	USA	(18)	Mystere B-2	Bomber	(1981)	1981-84	(18)	
		14	A-37B Dragonfly	Fighter/COIN	1982	1982	14	
		3	A-37B Dragonfly	Fighter/COIN	1984	1985	3	Delivered Jan 1985
		7	AC-47	Transport	(1984)	1984-85	(7)	To replace old C-47s
		1	C-118A	Transport	(1970)	1971	1	
		3	C-123 Provider	Transport	1982	1982	3	
		1	C-130H Hercules	Transport	(1983)	1984	1	Transferred to replace 1 C-123 Provider
		5	C-47	Transport	(1973)	1974	5	Ex-USAF surplus
		1	FH-1100	Hel	(1970)	1971	1	
		10	Model 205 UH-1H	Hel	1980	1980-81	10	
		12	Model 205 UH-1H	Hel	1982	1982-83	12	
		10	Model 205 UH-1H	Hel	1983	1984	10	
		25	Model 205 UH-1H	Hel	1984	1984-85	(25)	
		10	Model 205 UH-1H	Hel	1985	1985-86	(10)	6 UH-1H and 4 UH-1M with night vision equipment
		(6)	Model 300C	Hel	(1986)	1986	(6)	
		4	Model 321	Lightplane	1982	1982	4	Also designated O-2 or Model 337
		1	Model 500	Hel	(1978)	1979	(1)	
		2	Model 500	Hel	(1982)	1983	2	
		4	Model 500MD	Hel	1985	1985	4	Gunship version; in addition to 2 AC-47s also delivered as gunships
		4	T-41A	Lightplane	1973	1974	4	
		(6)	M-102 105mm	TH	(1983)	1984	(6)	
		10	M-113	APC	(1978)	1979	(10)	
		10	M-113-A2	APC	(1983)	1984	(10)	
		(6)	M-114 155mm	TH	1981	1982	(6)	
		5	M-3-A1 Stuart	LT	1983	1984	(5)	
	Yugoslavia	(14)	M-56 105mm	TH	(1982)	1982	(14)	Unconfirmed
4 Equatorial Guinea	Spain	3	C-212A Aviocar	Transport	1980	1981	3	
	USSR	(1)	Yak-40 Codling	Transport	(1979)	1979	(1)	
		10	BRDM-2	SC	(1979)	1980	(10)	
		10	BRDM-2	SC	(1981)	1982	(10)	
		10	BTR-152	APC	(1979)	1980	(10)	Unconfirmed
		10	BTR-152	APC	(1980)	1980	(10)	
		1	P-6 Class	FAC	1977	1978	1	
4 Ethiopia	Canada	2	DHC-6	Transport	(1980)	1981	2	Delivered Jun 1981; uncertain whether sold or leased

Recipient code/ Recipient	Supplier	Weapon designation	No. ordered	Weapon description	Year of order	Year(s) of delivery	Total delivered	Comments
	Czechoslovakia	T-33A	(5)	Jet trainer	(1972)	1972	(5)	Unconfirmed
		L-39 Albatross	10	Jet trainer	(1983)	1984	10	
	France	AML-60	(56)	AC	(1971)	1972	(56)	
		SS-12	4	ShShM	(1975)	1976	(4)	Unconfirmed
	Germany, FR	EDIC/EDA Type	:	LC	(1976)	1977	(1)	
		Do-28D-1	2	Transport	1974	1975	2	
		Do-28D-2	2	Transport	1978	1979	2	
		Model F337	1	Trainer	1970	1971	1	
		Model F337	1	Trainer	(1971)	1971	(1)	MAP
	India	SA-316B Chetak	10	Hel	(1984)	1984	10	
	Iran	AGM-12B Bullpup	(36)	ASM	1974	1975-76	(36)	Arming ex-Iranian AF F-5As; unconfirmed
	Italy	SF-260TP	(11)	Trainer	(1985)			In addition to 10 received earlier; also for civilian use
	Libya	T-55	(90)	MBT	(1983)	1984	(90)	Delivered Jan 1984
	Netherlands	Dokkum Class	1	MSC	1973	1973	1	
	Romania	SA-316B	(10)	Hel	(1984)	1984	(10)	Unconfirmed
	USA	C-119 Packet	(17)	Transport	(1970)	1970-71	(17)	
		DHC-3 Otter	4	Transport	1974	1975	4	
		F-5A	(3)	Fighter	(1970)	1971	(3)	
		F-5E Tiger-2	(6)	Fighter	1974	1974	(6)	Unconfirmed
		T-33A	2	Jet trainer	1972	1972	2	
		M-101-A1 105mm	(52)	TH	(1970)	1971	(52)	Delivery schedule unconfirmed
		M-109-A1 155mm	(12)	SPH	1974	1975	(12)	
		M-113-A1	(90)	APC	1973	1974-75	(90)	Delivery schedule unconfirmed
		M-114-A1	(12)	Recce AC	(1970)	1971	(12)	
		M-60-A1	(72)	MBT	1973	1974-76	(72)	
		V-150 Commando	(12)	APC	(1975)	1976	(12)	
	USSR	Swift Type	(4)	PC	1976	1977	(4)	
		An-12 Cub-A	2	Transport	1977	1977	2	
		An-12 Cub-A	:	Transport	(1982)	1982	(10)	Unspecified number delivered
		An-26 Curl	(6)	Lightplane	1976	1977	(6)	
		Mi-14 Haze	2	Hel	(1983)	1984	2	For ASW duties
		Mi-24 Hind-D	:	Hel	(1980)	1980	(10)	
		Mi-24 Hind-D	(12)	Hel	(1982)	1982	(12)	
		Mi-6 Hook	(10)	Hel	1977	1978	(10)	
		Mi-8 Hip	(15)	Hel	1977	1978	(15)	
		Mi-8 Hip	:	Hel	(1980)	1980	(10)	Designation unconfirmed
		Mi-8 Hip	(12)	Hel	1982	1982	(12)	
		MiG-17F	(17)	Fighter	(1977)	1977-78	(17)	

No.	Designation	Type	(Year ordered)	Year delivered	No. delivered	Comments
(50)	MiG-21MF	Fighter	(1977)	1977	(50)	
12	MiG-21MF	Fighter	(1982)	1982	(12)	
:	MiG-23	Fighter/interceptor	(1977)	1977	(20)	
(6)	Su-20 Fitter-C	Fighter/grd attack	(1982)	1982	(6)	Unconfirmed
:	Yak-40 Codling	Transport	(1984)	1984	(1)	
(50)	BM-21 122mm	MRS	(1977)	1978-79	(50)	
(20)	BMD-20 200mm	MRS	(1978)	1978	(20)	
(100)	BMP-1	MICV	(1977)	1977	(100)	
40	BRDM-1	SC	(1976)	1977	(40)	Designation unconfirmed; possibly paid for by Libya
(50)	BRDM-2	SC	(1977)	1977	(50)	
(100)	BTR-152	APC	(1977)	1977-78	(100)	
(100)	BTR-60P	APC	(1980)	1977	(100)	Designation unconfirmed
(200)	BTR-60P	APC	(1977)	1980-81	(200)	Designation unconfirmed
:	D-20 152mm	TH	(1977)	1977	(100)	Unconfirmed
:	D-30 122mm	TH	(1977)	1977	(150)	
(150)	JSU-122	SPG	(1978)	1979	(10)	Unconfirmed
:	M-46 130mm	TG	1977	1977	(30)	USSR reportedly got on black market
:	M-47 Patton	MBT	1977	1977	(100)	Unconfirmed
35	S-23 180mm	TG	(1976)	1977	(31)	Reportedly paid for by Libya
:	T-34	MT	(1977)	1977-78	(115)	
:	T-34	MT	(1977)	1977-79	(300)	
:	T-54	MBT	1977	1977-82	(320)	
(20)	T-55	MBT	(1977)	1977	(20)	Unconfirmed
(50)	T-62	MBT	(1980)	1980	(50)	Designation unconfirmed
(40)	T-62	MBT	(1977)	1978	(40)	Unconfirmed
(50)	T-72	MBT	1985	1985	(50)	
:	T-72	MBT	(1977)	1978	(20)	
:	ZSU-23-4 Shilka	AAV	(1977)	1978	(10)	
25	ZSU-57-2	AAV	(1977)	1977-78	25	
:	SA-3 SAMS	Mobile SAM system	1977	1977-78	(2 000)	
:	AT-3 Sagger	ATM	(1977)	1977-78	(500)	
2	SA-3 Goa	Landmob SAM	(1977)	1977-78	(3 000)	
4	SA-7 Grail	Port SAM	1978	1978	2	
1	Mol Class	FAC	1978	1978-81	4	
1	Osa-2 Class	FAC	(1982)	1983	1	
1	Petya-2 Class	Frigate	(1984)	1984	1	In addition to 1 delivered 1983
1	Petya-2 Class	Frigate	1981	1981	1	Delivered Dec 1981
(50)	Polnocny Class	LS	(1982)	1983	1	In addition to 1 delivered 1981
1	Polnocny Class	LS	(1977)	1977	(50)	Unconfirmed
	M-47 Patton	MBT				
Yugoslavia	Kraljevica Cl	PC	1974	1975	1	

Recipient code/ Recipient	Supplier	No. ordered	Weapon designation	Weapon description	Year of order	Year(s) of delivery	Total delivered	Comments
15 Gabon	Brazil	3	EMB-110	Transport	1980	1980	3	
		1	EMB-111	Mar patrol	1980	1981	1	For maritime patrol
		11	EE-11 Urutu	APC	(1981)	1983-84	(11)	
		15	EE-3 Jararaca	SC	1981	1984	(15)	
		36	EE-9 Cascavel	AC	1981	1983-84	(36)	
	France	2	AS-350 Ecureuil	Hel	(1985)			
		(6)	Mirage-3B	Jet trainer	1975	1978	(6)	
		6	Mirage-5	Fighter	1983	1984-85	(6)	
		3	Mirage-5R	Recce	(1983)	1985	(3)	Total cost: $2.6 m
		1	Mystere-20	Transport	1975	1975	1	
		1	SA-316B	Hel	1973	1975	1	In addition to 1 previously acquired
		1	SA-330 Puma	Hel	(1973)	1974	(1)	
		2	SA-330 Puma	Hel	1975	1976	2	
		(2)	SA-330 Puma	Hel	1979	1980	(2)	
		..	SA-342L Gazelle	Hel	(1985)			3 armed with HOT ATMs; part of package incl aircraft, missiles and ships
		8	AML-60	AC	1980	1980	8	Ordered May 1980
		10	AML-90	AC	1980	1980	10	
		4	ERC-20 Kriss	Recce/AAV	1985			
		(6)	ERC-90 Sagaie	AC	(1983)	1984	(6)	Part of new armoured squadron
		6	ERC-90 Sagaie	AC	1985			
		:	M-3	APC	(1982)	1983	(6)	
		(8)	VCR-6	APC	(1983)	1984	(8)	Part of new armoured squadron
		75	VP-2000	APC	1982	1984	(75)	
		(12)	VXB-170	APC	(1973)	1974	(12)	
		(72)	HOT	ATM	1985			
		(100)	Milan	ATM	(1985)			
		(12)	SS-12	ShShM	1976	1978	(12)	Arming 3 Gazelle helicopters
		1	Batral Class	LC	(1983)	1984	1	
		1	Omar Bongo	FAC	1976	1978	1	Arming Omar Bongo Type
		2	P-400 Class	PC/FAC	1984			
	Italy	1	ATR-42	Transport	(1985)			For Presidential Guard
	Netherlands	2	F-27 Mk-1000	Transport	1975	1976	2	
	Senegal	1	Manga Class	LC	(1974)	1976	1	
	South Africa	..	Eland-90	AC	(1981)	1982	(10)	Unconfirmed; reportedly also Eland-60 version; may have been confused with AML-90 and AML-60 also in service
	Spain	2	Pelicano Class	LC	1981	1982	(2)	Ordered Aug 1981; delivery not confirmed

Recipient	Supplier	No. ordered	Designation	Description	Year of order	Year of delivery	No. delivered	Comments
	USA	(4)	A-1 Skyraider	Fighter	(1977)	1978	(4)	Supplier unconfirmed
		1	C-130H Hercules	Transport	1977	1977	1	
		1	Gulfstream-2	Transport	(1971)	1971	(1)	
		1	Gulfstream-2	Transport	(1975)	1975	1	
		2	L-100-20	Transport	1980	1980	1	
		1	L-100-30	Transport	1973	1976	2	Incl spares support, training
		1	L-100-30	Transport	1981	1973	1	Delivered Sep 1981; for AF
		1	L-100-30	Transport	1982	1981	1	In addition to 3 in service
		4	T-34C-1	Trainer	1982	1982	1	
		..	M-7 105mm	SPH	(1977)	1982	4	
		6	V-150 Commando	APC	(1977)	1978	(6)	Unconfirmed
		(15)	V-150 Commando	APC	(1985)	1978	(6)	
		1	Swift 105 Type	PC	(1974)	1975	(1)	Supplier unconfirmed
7 Gambia	Switzerland	1	BN-2A Defender	Lightplane	(1980)	1981	1	
	UK	1	Skyvan-3M	Transport	(1980)	1981	1	
4 Ghana	France	4	SA-316B	Hel	1973	1974	4	
	Germany, FR	(6)	Dela Class	PC	(1973)	1975	2	Originally 6 ordered; only 2 delivered due to bancrupcy of producer
	India	2	FPB-45	PC	1976	1979-80	2	
		2	PB-57 Type	PC	1976	1980	2	
		(5)	HTT-34	Trainer	(1985)	1986	1	
	Italy	8	MB-326L	Jet trainer	1976	1978	(5)	
		6	SF-260TP	Trainer	1982	1983	8	
	Netherlands	1	F-27 Mk-400	Transport	1973	1974	(6)	
		1	F-28 Mk-3000	Transport	(1975)	1975	1	
	Switzerland	(100)	Piranha	APC	(1979)	1979-80	(100)	Both 4x4 and 6x6 versions
	UK	8	BN-2A Islander	Transport	1971	1973	8	
		(12)	Bulldog-120	Trainer	(1971)	1973-74	(12)	
		6	Skyvan-3M	Transport	1973	1974	6	
	USA	(1)	Gulfstream-2	Transport	(1979)	1979	(1)	
		2	Model 212	Hel	(1970)	1972	2	
4 Guatemala	France	3	Super Magister	Jet trainer	(1978)	1979	3	
	Israel	8	AMX-13	LT	(1972)	1974	8	
		10	IAI-201 Arava	Transport	1974	1975-76	10	
		1	IAI-201 Arava	Transport	(1982)	1983	1	
		10	RBY-1	Recce AC	(1976)	1977-78	(10)	
	Switzerland	12	PC-7	Trainer	1978	1979-81	(12)	
	USA	8	A-37B Dragonfly	Fighter/COIN	(1971)	1973	8	
		(6)	A-37B Dragonfly	Fighter/COIN	(1975)	1976	(6)	
		3	C-118A	Transport	1974	1975	3	

Recipient code/ Recipient	Supplier	No. ordered	Weapon designation	Weapon description	Year of order	Year(s) of delivery	Total delivered	Comments
		2	F-27 Mk-400	Transport	(1983)	1984	2	Ex-Nigerian; Dutch refurbishing
		6	Model 205 UH-1D	Hel	(1970)	1971	6	
		(6)	Model 205 UH-1H	Hel	(1974)	1976	(6)	
		6	Model 206B	Hel	(1980)	1981	6	In civilian markings
		6	Model 206L	Hel	(1980)	1982	6	
		3	Model 212	Hel	(1980)	1981	3	Total cost incl 3 Model 212s: $10.5 m; Congress not informed of delivery
		6	Model 412	Hel	(1980)	1981-82	(6)	
		(15)	M-113	APC	(1971)	1973	(15)	
		7	V-150 Commando	APC	1974	1975	7	
3 Guinea	China	..	M-1938 122mm	TG	(1979)	1979	(20)	
		..	M-46 130mm	TG	(1982)	1982	(20)	Unconfirmed
		..	T-63	LT	(1983)	1983	(20)	Unconfirmed
		..	Type 54 122mm	SPH	(1982)	1982	(10)	
		6	Shanghai Class	PC	(1973)	1973-76	6	
	Czechoslovakia	(3)	L-39 Albatross	Jet trainer	(1973)	1973	(3)	
	Egypt	(50)	Walid	APC	1983	1983-84	(50)	Order includes mortars, machine-guns, rifles and ammunition
	France	(1)	Model F337	Trainer	1980	1980	(1)	
		(2)	SA-316B	Hel	(1971)	1972	(2)	
		1	SA-330 Puma	Hel	1979	1979	(1)	
		1	SA-342K Gazelle	Hel	(1979)	1979	(1)	
		(1)	UH-12	Hel	(1983)	1983	(1)	Unconfirmed
	Spain	1	C-212A Aviocar	Transport	(1984)	1984	1	Gift
	USSR	2	An-24 Coke	Transport	(1983)	1984	2	
		(3)	MiG-21UTI	Jet trainer	(1977)	1977	(3)	
		(7)	Yak-18	Trainer	1973	1973	(7)	
		1	Yak-40 Codling	Transport	(1983)	1983	(1)	
		(10)	BRDM-1	SC	(1980)	1980	(20)	Unconfirmed
		(10)	BRDM-2	SC	1970	1971	(10)	
		..	BRDM-2	SC	(1982)	1982	(5)	
		..	BRDM-2 Gaskin	AAV(M)	(1982)	1982	(5)	
		..	BTR-50P	APC	(1981)	1982	(10)	
		..	BTR-60P	APC	(1983)	1983	(10)	
		..	PT-76	LT	(1977)	1977	(20)	
		..	T-55	MBT	(1974)	1974	(10)	
		..	SA-9 Gaskin	Landmob SAM	(1982)	1982	(60)	
		6	P-6 Class	FAC	(1965)	1965-72	6	Unconfirmed

Country	Supplier	Qty	Equipment	Type	(Order)	Delivery	No.	Notes
		4	Shershen Class	FAC	(1978)	1978–79	4	Transferred to Navy Jul 1979
		1	T-58 Class	MSO	(1978)	1979	1	
13 Guinea Bissau	Angola	1	Do-27	Transport	1980	1980	1	
		1	HS-748-2	Transport	(1978)	1978	(1)	
		1	Mystere-20	Transport	1980	1980	1	
		1	Yak-40 Codling	Transport	1980	1980	1	
	China	20	Type 56	APC	(1983)	1984	20	
	Czechoslovakia	10	L-39 Albatross	Jet trainer	(1981)	1982–83	(10)	
	France	1	Model F337	Trainer	1978	1978	1	Gift; also designated Alouette-2
		1	SA-318C	Hel	1984	1984	1	Handed over at independence
	Portugal	1	C-47	Transport	(1976)	1976	(1)	Handed over at independence
		:	Do-27	Transport	(1976)	1976	(3)	Handed over at independence
		2	SA-316B	Hel	(1976)	1976	2	Handed over at independence
	USSR	6	An-26 Curl	Lightplane	(1980)	1981	6	Unconfirmed
		1	Mi-8 Hip	Hel	(1977)	1978	1	
		12	MiG-21MF	Fighter	(1977)	1977–78	(12)	
		:	BRDM-2	SC	(1980)	1980	(10)	
		:	BRDM-2 Gaskin	AAV(M)	(1982)	1982	(3)	
		(100)	SA-7 Grail	Port SAM	(1984)	1984	(100)	
		:	SA-9 Gaskin	Landmob SAM	(1982)	1982	(36)	
		4	P-6 Class	FAC	(1975)	1975–76	4	
		2	Shershen Class	FAC	(1979)	1979	2	
15 Guyana	Brazil	1	EMB-110	Transport	1985	1985	1	
		1	Model 412	Hel	1985	1985	1	
		:	EE-11 Urutu	APC	(1984)	1984	(30)	For border defence against Venezuela
		6	EE-9 Cascavel	AC	(1981)			
	France	2	SA-319B	Hel	(1972)	1974	2	
	Korea, North	5	Sin Hung Class	FAC	(1980)	1980	(5)	Probably without torpedoes
	Netherlands	1	Kimbla Class	LC	(1980)	1981	1	Landing craft
	UK	8	BN-2A Islander	Transport	1971	1971–77	8	
		4	Skyvan-3M	Transport	(1984)	1984	1	
		4	Shorland	AC	(1970)	1971	4	
			Type 32m	PC	1976	1977	1	
	USA	1	King Air C-90	Trainer	(1973)	1975	1	For VIP duties
		1	Model 185	Lightplane	(1970)	1971	1	Designation unconfirmed
		2	Model 206B	Hel	1974	1976	2	
		3	Model 212	Hel	(1975)	1976	3	For transport
	USSR	25	SA-7 Grail	Port SAM	(1981)	1982	(25)	In service
		1	DHC-6	Transport	(1982)	1983	1	
4 Haiti	Canada	3	DHC-2 Beaver	Lightplane	(1975)	1977	3	

Recipient code/ Recipient	Supplier	No. ordered	Weapon designation	Weapon description	Year of order	Year(s) of delivery	Total delivered	Comments
	Italy	4	S-211	Trainer	1983	1985	4	
		6	SF-260TP	Trainer	1982	1983	6	
	UK	1	BN-2A Islander	Transport	(1983)	1983	1	
	USA	1	Baron 95-B55	Lightplane	(1974)	1975	1	
		(3)	C-47	Transport	(1983)	1983	(3)	
		1	F-33C Bonanza	Trainer	(1983)	1983	1	Designation unconfirmed
		3	Model 150	Lightplane	(1973)	1974	3	
		2	Model 300C	Hel	(1977)	1978	2	
		8	Model 337	Trainer	1973	1974	8	
		1	Model 402B	Lightplane	(1975)	1974	1	
		2	Model 500C	Hel	(1977)	1976	2	
		3	S-55 Chickasaw	Hel	(1972)	1973	3	
		4	S-58	Hel	(1974)	1975	4	
		(5)	M-113	APC	(1970)	1971	(5)	Unconfirmed
		6	V-150 Commando	APC	(1976)	1978	6	
15 Honduras	Brazil	(12)	EMB-312 Tucano	Trainer	(1984)	1985-86	(12)	
	Israel	2	IAI-201 Arava	Transport	1976	1976	2	
		12	Mystere B-2	Bomber	(1976)	1977	12	
		(6)	Mystere-4A	Fighter/interceptor	1977	1978	(6)	
		(2)	Westwind 1124	Transport	(1976)	1978	(2)	
		14	RBY-1	Recce AC	(1976)	1978	(14)	
		(20)	Shafrir-2	AAM	(1977)	1979	(20)	Possibly arming Super Magisters or Mysteres; unconfirmed
	Morocco	8	T-28S Fennec	Trainer/strike	1978	1978	8	
	Spain	(4)	C-101 Aviojet	Jet trainer	1983	1984-85	(4)	Option on 4 more
	UK	2	Jetstream-31	Transport	(1986)			
	USA	16	FV-101 Scorpion	LT	1978	1981	16	Ordered Mar 1978; delivered Apr 1981
		5	A-37B Dragonfly	Fighter/COIN	(1974)	1975	5	
		(10)	A-37B Dragonfly	Fighter/COIN	1982	1983-84	(10)	
		6	A-37B Dragonfly	Fighter/COIN	(1984)			Order incl 36 105mm howitzers
		2	C-130H Hercules	Transport	(1983)	1983	2	On loan
		6	F-51 Mustang	Fighter	(1970)	1971	6	
		4	F-86F Sabre	Fighter	(1976)	1977	4	
		1	L-188 Electra	Transport	(1976)	1977	1	
		6	Model 204 UH-1B	Hel	(1985)	1985	6	
		10	Model 205 UH-1H	Hel	(1980)	1980	10	
		(1)	Model 205 UH-1H	Hel	(1985)	1985	(1)	At least 1 delivered
		(8)	Model 300	Hel	1983	1984-85	(8)	

Supplier	No.	Weapon designation	Weapon description	Year of order	Year of delivery	No. delivered	Comments
	5	Model 412	Hel	1985	1986	5	Option on 6 more
	5	Model 412	Hel	1986	1986	(5)	In addition to 5 ordered Nov 1985
	(1)	Model 500	Hel	(1983)	1985	1	Designation unconfirmed
	1	S-76 Spirit	Hel	(1980)	1981	1	
	5	T-41D Mescalero	Lightplane	(1972)	1973	5	
	8	M-101-A1 105mm	TH	1974	1975	8	
	(4)	M-101-A1 105mm	TH	(1979)	1980	(4)	
	(12)	M-102 105mm	TH	1982	1982	(12)	
	(36)	M-102 105mm	TH	(1984)			Pending congressional approval
Yugoslavia	1	Swift 105 Type	PC	(1976)	1977	1	
	2	Swift 105 Type	PC	(1979)	1980	2	
	6	CL-13 Sabre	Fighter	(1979)	1980	6	Canadian-built F-86 Sabre; private deal; seller unconfirmed

11 India

Supplier	No.	Weapon designation	Weapon description	Year of order	Year of delivery	No. delivered	Comments
Australia	5	N-24A Nomad	Transport	1977	1977	5	Mainly for civilian use
Czechoslovakia	(300)	OT-62	APC	(1967)	1969-72	(300)	For Navy
	(300)	OT-64	APC	(1969)	1971-74	(300)	
	225	T-54	MBT	(1967)	1968-71	(225)	
France	27	AS-365N	Hel	(1986)	1986-87	(27)	
	12	Breguet Alize	Fighter/ASW	1977	1978	12	
	40	Mirage-2000	Fighter/strike	1982	1985-86	(40)	36 fighters and 4 trainers
	9	Mirage-2000	Fighter/strike	1986			In addition to 40 ordered 1982
	..	MM-38 L	ShShM launcher	(1983)			To arm new Indian missile corvettes
	..	AM-39 Exocet	AShM	(1986)			Negotiating; to arm 6 Jaguars; competing with British Sea Eagle AShM
	..	MM-38 Exocet	ShShM	(1983)			To arm new missile corvettes
	(240)	Magic-2	AAM	(1984)	1986-87	(240)	Arming 40 Mirage-2000s
	(1 800)	Milan	ATM	(1980)	1982-84	(1 800)	Licensed production from 1985
	(558)	R-550 Magic	AAM	(1979)	1981-87	(558)	Arming 93 Jaguar fighters
	(48)	R-550 Magic	AAM	(1983)	1983-84	(48)	Arming Sea Harriers
	(186)	R-550 Magic	AAM	(1984)			Arming 31 Jaguar fighters
	(240)	Super-530	AAM	(1984)	1986-87	(240)	Arming 40 Mirage-2000s
Germany, FR	2	Type 1500	Submarine	(1981)	1986	(1)	Licensed production to follow
Italy	(50)	Model 56 105mm	TH	(1969)	1971	(50)	Some probably shipped on to Bangladesh
Netherlands	..	Flycatcher	Mobile AA-system	1985	1985		Assembly planned
Poland	50	TS-11 Iskra	Jet trainer	1975	1976-77	(50)	Ordered instead of L-39
	(200)	T-54	MBT	(1971)	1972-73	(200)	
	4	Polnocny Class	LS	(1973)	1975-76	4	
	4	Polnocny Class	LS	(1984)	1985-86	2	In addition to 6 in service
Sweden	(400)	FH-77 155mm	TH	1986			Total cost incl ammunition, vehicles and other support: $1.2 b; for delivery over 5 years; licensed production to follow
UK	5	BN-2A Defender	Lightplane	(1975)	1976	5	

Recipient code/ Recipient	Supplier	No. ordered	Weapon designation	Weapon description	Year of order	Year(s) of delivery	Total delivered	Comments
		4	BN-2A Defender	Lightplane	(1980)	1980	4	In addition to 5 delivered 1976
		6	BN-2A Defender	Lightplane	(1983)	1983	6	In addition to 9 in service
		12	Canberra B-15	Bomber	(1968)	1970-71	12	
		10	Canberra B-I-12	Bomber/interdictor	(1968)	1970-71	10	
		5	Hunter F-6	Fighter	(1970)	1972	5	
		40	Jaguar	Fighter	(1979)	1981-82	(40)	18 delivered on loan from RAF in 1980; 8 returned 1982; 1 to Oman; 1 crashed; rest offered to Indian AF
		8	Jaguar	Fighter	(1982)	1982	8	
		6	SH-3D Sea King	Hel	(1970)	1971	6	
		6	SH-3D Sea King	Hel	(1972)	1973-74	6	
		5	SH-3D Sea King	Hel	1977	1978	5	
		6	Sea Harrier	Fighter/strike	1979	1983-84	6	For use on AC carrier 'Vikrant'
		10	Sea Harrier	Fighter/strike	1985			Total cost incl 1 trainer: $230 m
		2	Sea Harrier T-4	Fighter/trainer	1979	1984	2	
		1	Sea Harrier T-4	Fighter/trainer	1985			
		12	Sea King HAS-5	Hel	1983	1984-86	(12)	Contract signed Jun 1983; option on 8 more; to be armed with Sea Eagle AShMs; total value: approx $125 m
		20	Sea King HAS-5	Hel	1985			In addition to 12 ordered 1983; to carry Sea Eagle AShMs; total cost: $80 m
		(75)	Abbot 105mm	SPG	(1968)	1969-71	(75)	
		(24)	Sultan FV-105	CPC	(1979)	1980-81	(24)	
		10	Seacat L	ShAM launcher	1972	1972-81	10	Arming Nilgiri Class frigates
		(10)	Tigercat SAMS	Mobile SAM system	1983	1972-73	(10)	Unconfirmed
		(84)	Sea Eagle	AShM	1985			Arming 12 Sea King helicopters; follow-on orders expected; for delivery 1987
			Sea Eagle	AShM				To arm Sea Harriers
		(160)	Seacat	ShAM/ShShM	1972	1972-81	(160)	Arming Nilgiri Class frigates
		(120)	Tigercat	Landmob SAM	(1971)	1972-73	(120)	
		1	Hermes Class	AC carrier	1986			Total cost approx $74 m
	USA	2	B-737-100	Transport	1977	1978	2	For Navy
		2	B-737-200L	Transport	1980	1983	2	
		10	Model 300	Hel	1969	1971-72	10	
	USSR	95	An-32 Cline	Transport	1980	1984-86	(57)	Delivery rate: 2/month; some Western avionics integrated
		20	Il-20	Transport	(1985)			Unconfirmed
		4	Il-38 May	Mar patrol/ASW	1975	1977	4	For Navy
		(20)	Il-76 Candid	Transport	(1984)			Possibly Il-76 Mainstay AEW version; order may be reduced to 8

No.	Designation	Description	(Year of order)	Year(s) of delivery	No. delivered	Comments
5	Ka-25 Hormone	Hel	(1977)	1980	5	On 3 Kashin Class destroyers
(18)	Ka-27 Helix	Hel	(1984)	1985	(3)	Helix-A version
(100)	Mi-17 Hip-H	Hel	(1984)	1984-86	(50)	Replacing Mi-8s
12	Mi-24 Hind-D	Hel	(1982)	1983	(12)	Unconfirmed
(10)	Mi-26 Halo	Hel	(1985)			Reportedly ordered
(80)	Mi-8 Hip	Hel	1979	1980-81	(80)	40 delivered 1980; additional batch arrived early 1981
20	Mi-8 Hip	Hel	1971	1971	20	In addition to 140 licence-produced
75	MiG-21FL	Fighter	(1971)	1972-73	(75)	
(20)	MiG-21MF	Fighter	(1971)	1972	(20)	
(75)	MiG-21bis	Fighter	1976	1976-77	(75)	
80	MiG-23BN	Fighter/grd attack	(1979)	1980-83	(80)	
40	MiG-23M	Fighter/interceptor	1983	1983-84	(40)	
15	MiG-23U	Jet trainer	(1979)	1980-82	(15)	
(8)	MiG-25R	Recce	(1980)	1981	(8)	8 delivered in first batch; others reportedly ordered and delivered Aug 1984
(40)	MiG-29	Fighter	1986			Originally requested Aug 1984
(3)	Tu-142 Bear	Recce/ASW	(1984)	1985	(1)	Bear-F version for maritime recce and ASW duties
(150)	BM-21 122mm	MRS	(1974)	1975-77	(150)	Unconfirmed
(300)	BMP-1	MICV	(1982)	1983-85	(300)	Licensed production to follow
(12)	BRDM-2 Gaskin	AAV(M)	(1981)	1981-83	(12)	Unconfirmed
(250)	BTR-152	APC	(1971)	1972-73	(250)	
(200)	BTR-50P	APC	(1977)	1978-79	(200)	
(25)	BTR-60P	APC	(1979)	1980	(25)	
(550)	D-30 122mm	TH	(1969)	1970-74	(550)	
(600)	M-46 130mm	TG	(1967)	1968-75	(600)	India also produces the Catapult SPG based on Vijayanta chassis and M-46 gun
(40)	S-23 180mm	TG	(1974)	1975-76	(40)	
225	T-55	MBT	(1967)	1968-71	(225)	
(450)	T-55	MBT	1971	1972-74	(450)	
(300)	T-72	MBT	1980	1981-83	(300)	
(60)	ZSU-23-4 Shilka	AAV	(1975)	1977	(60)	
(6)	FROG L	Mobile SSM system	(1980)	1982	(6)	Unconfirmed; FROG-7
(20)	SA-2 SAMS	Mobile SAM system	(1967)	1969-72	(20)	
(25)	SA-3 SAMS	Mobile SAM system	1977	1977-78	(25)	
(36)	SA-6 SAMS	Mobile SAM system	1976	1977-79	(36)	Some 180 launchers in approx 36 btys
:	SA-8 SAMS	Mobile SAM system	(1982)	1984-86		Reportedly operational early 1984
(6)	SA-N-1 L	ShAM launcher	(1977)	1980-83	6	Arming 3 Kashin Class destroyers
3	SA-N-4 L	ShAM launcher	1975	1977-78	3	Arming 3 Nanuchka Class corvettes
3	SA-N-4 L	ShAM launcher	(1978)	1983-86	3	Arming Godavari Class frigates
8	SSN-2 Styx L	ShShM launcher	(1970)	1971	8	Arming 8 Osa-1 Class FACs

Recipient code/Recipient	Supplier	No. ordered	Weapon designation	Weapon description	Year of order	Year(s) of delivery	Total delivered	Comments
		8	SSN-2 Styx L	ShShM launcher	1975	1976-77	(8)	Arming 8 Osa-2 Class FACs
		3	SSN-2 Styx L	ShShM launcher	(1976)	1977-78	3	Arming 3 Nanuchka Class corvettes
		3	SSN-2 Styx L	ShShM launcher	(1977)	1980-83	3	Arming 3 Kashin Class destroyers
		(3)	SSN-2 Styx L	ShShM launcher	(1978)	1983-86	3	Arming 3 Godavari Class frigates
		(480)	AA-5 Ash	AAM	1980	1980-83	(480)	Arming MiG-23s
		(320)	AA-7 Apex	AAM	(1979)	1980-83	(320)	Arming MiG-23s
		80	AA-7 Apex	AAM	(1984)	1986	(30)	Arming MiG-29s
		(240)	AA-8 Aphid	AAM	(1983)	1983-84	(240)	Arming 40 MiG-23Ms
		160	AA-8 Aphid	AAM	(1984)	1986	(30)	Arming MiG-29s
		(1 200)	AT-3 Sagger	ATM	1980	1981-84	(1 200)	Possibly on BRDM-2 vehicles
		(20)	FROG-7	Landmob SSM	1980	1982	(20)	Probably version 7; unconfirmed
		(480)	SA-2 Guideline	Landmob SAM	(1967)	1969-72	(480)	
		(500)	SA-3 Goa	Landmob SAM	1977	1977-78	(500)	
		(1 050)	SA-6 Gainful	Landmob SAM	1976	1977-79	(1 050)	
		(400)	SA-7 Grail	Port SAM	1981	1982-83	(400)	
		(250)	SA-8 Gecko	Landmob SAM	(1982)	1984-86	(250)	Reportedly operational early 1984
		(300)	SA-9 Gaskin	Landmob SAM	(1981)	1981-83	(300)	Mounted on modified BTR-40 chassis
		(72)	SA-N-1	ShAM	(1977)	1980-83	(72)	Arming 3 Kashin Class destroyers
		(36)	SA-N-4	ShAM	1975	1977-78	(36)	Arming 3 Nanuchka Class corvettes
		(36)	SA-N-4	ShAM	(1978)	1983-86	(36)	Arming 3 Godavari Class frigates
		(40)	SSN-2 Styx	ShShM	(1970)	1971	(40)	Arming 8 Osa-1 Class FACs
		(40)	SSN-2 Styx	ShShM	1975	1976-77	(40)	Arming 8 Osa-2 Class FACs
		(36)	SSN-2 Styx	ShShM	(1976)	1977-78	(36)	Arming 3 Nanuchka Class corvettes
		(36)	SSN-2 Styx	ShShM	(1977)	1980-83	(36)	Arming 3 Kashin Class destroyers
		(36)	SSN-2 Styx	ShShM	1978	1983-86	(36)	Arming Godavari Class frigates
		8	Foxtrot Class	Submarine	(1967)	1968-74	8	
		3	Kashin Class	Destroyer	1976	1980-83	3	Modified Kashin Class
		3	Kashin Class	Destroyer	1982			In addition to 3 previously delivered; further 3 projected Apr 1984
		(2)	Kresta-2 Class	Cruiser	(1982)			Unconfirmed
		3	Nanuchka Class	Corvette	1975	1977-78	3	Total of 8 reportedly to be delivered
		(3)	Nanuchka Class	Corvette	1982			In addition to 3 in service
		6	Natya Class	MSO	(1977)	1978-80	6	
		6	Natya Class	MSO	1982	1985-87	(4)	In addition to 6 delivered earlier
		8	Osa-1 Class	FAC	(1970)	1971	8	
		8	Osa-2 Class	FAC	1975	1976-77	(8)	
		10	Petya-2 Class	Frigate	(1967)	1969-74	10	
		1	T-58 Class	MSO	(1970)	1971	1	Converted to submarine rescue ship
		(5)	Tarantul Class	Corvette	(1985)			Unconfirmed

Country	No.	Designation	Type	(1983)	1983-84	No.	Comments
11 Indonesia	6	Yeygenia Class	MSC			6	
Australia	2	C-47	Transport	1971	1973	2	Military aid
	16	CA-27 Sabre	Fighter	1972	1973	16	Ex-RAAF; gift valued at A$10 m
	8	Model 47G-3	Hel	(1978)	1978	8	Ex-Australian Army
	6	N-22B Nomad	Mar patrol	1977	1978	6	For Navy
	6	N-22L Nomad	Mar patrol	1973	1975-76	6	For Navy; military aid
	6	N-22L Nomad	Mar patrol	1980	1981-82	6	For Navy
	2	Attack Class	PC	(1972)	1973-74	2	
	3	Attack Class	PC	(1981)	1982-83	3	
France	3	C-160F Transall	Transport	1979	1982	3	Ordered Sep 1979
	6	SA-330L Puma	Hel	1977	1978	6	Followed by licensed production of 7
	..	AMX-10 PAC-90	MICV/SPG	1981	1981	(5)	Transited via Singapore
	40	AMX-13	MICV	1981	1979	40	Number and delivery schedule uncertain
	200	AMX-VCI	LT	(1979)	1977-78	(200)	
	(100)	VPX-110	MICV	(1976)	1981	(100)	
			TD	1980		(10)	
	(3)	MM-38 L	ShShM launcher	(1982)	1979-80	(3)	Arming 3 Fatahillah Class frigates
	(4)	MM-38 L	ShShM launcher	(1977)	1979-80	(4)	Arming 4 PSMM-5 Class FACs
	(2)	MM-38 L	ShShM launcher	1975	1981-84	(2)	
	(4)	MM-38 L	ShShM launcher	1976	1978-79		On 4 PSMM-5 Class FACs
	(20)	TRS-2230/15	Air defence radar	(1978)	1979-80	(20)	
	(36)	MM-38 Exocet	ShShM	(1982)	1979-80	(36)	Arming 3 Fatahillah Class frigates
	(48)	MM-38 Exocet	ShShM	1982	1979-80	(48)	Arming 4 PSMM-5 Class FACs
	24	MM-38 Exocet	ShShM	1977	1981-84	(24)	Arming 2 frigates from Yugoslavia
	(48)	MM-38 Exocet	ShShM	(1986)			Arming 4 PSMM-5 Class FACs
Germany, FR	2	PB-57 Type	PC	1982	1984	2	Delivered prior to licensed production
	2	Type 209/2	Submarine	1977	1981	2	Modified enlarged version
	2	Type 209/2	Submarine	(1986)		2	Negotiating; in addition to 2 in service; total of 6 planned
Israel	14	A-4E Skyhawk	Fighter/bomber	1979	1980	14	From Israeli surplus stocks; total cost incl 2 TA-4Hs: $25.8 m; some sources report USA as seller
Korea, South	2	TA-4H Skyhawk	Jet trainer	1979	1980	2	
	4	PSMM-5 Type	FAC	1976	1979-80	4	Armed with 4 MM-38 Exocet ShShMs
	4	PSMM-5 Type	FAC	1982		4	In addition to 4 in service; armed with Exocet ShShMs
	4	Tacoma Type	LS	1979	1981		Designed to carry 3 Puma helicopters; copy of US LST-542 Type
Malaysia	2	Tacoma Type	LS	1981	1982	2	
	12	Pioneer-2	Lightplane	(1970)	1971	12	
Netherlands	8	F-27 Mk-400M	Transport	1975	1976	8	
	8	F-27 Mk-500	Transport	(1974)	1975	8	Ex-RMAF; in exchange for pilot training

Recipient code/ Recipient	Supplier	No. ordered	Weapon designation	Weapon description	Year of order	Year(s) of delivery	Total delivered	Comments
		10	Wasp	Hel	1981	1981-82	10	
		2	Alkmaar Class	Minehunter	1985			First export order of Tripartite design; for delivery 1987-88
		3	Fatahillah Cl	Frigate	1975	1979-80	3	Arms: 4 Exocet ShShMs and Bofors guns
		4	Van Speijk Cl	Frigate	(1986)			Negotiating
	New Zealand	(2)	Airtourer-150	Lightplane	(1970)	1972	(2)	
	Sweden	(150)	RBS-70	Port SAM	(1981)	1982	(150)	
	Switzerland	20	AS-202 Bravo	Trainer	1980	1981	20	
	UK	8	Hawk	Jet trainer/strike	1978	1980-81	8	Mk-53
		4	Hawk	Jet trainer/strike	1980	1981	4	In addition to 8 ordered 1978; Mk-53
		5	Hawk	Jet trainer/strike	1982	1983	5	In addition to 12 in service; Mk-53
		3	Hawk	Jet trainer/strike	1983	1984	(3)	In addition to 17 ordered earlier; Mk-53
		(600)	FV-101 Scorpion	LT	(1986)			Negotiating
		(25)	Rapier SAMS	Mobile SAM system	1984			Total value: $128 m; offsets for Indonesian electronics industry
		(20)	Rapier SAMS	Mobile SAM system	1985			Repeat order; total value incl missiles: approx $100 m
		(300)	Improved Rapier	Landmob SAM	1984			
		(240)	Improved Rapier	Landmob SAM	1985			Total value: $100 m
		3	Tribal Class	Frigate	1984	1985-86	3	Ex-UK Navy; refurbished before delivery
	USA	16	A-4E Skyhawk	Fighter/bomber	1981	1982	16	In addition to 16 from Israel
		4	B-26 Invader	Bomber	(1970)	1971	4	
		1	B-707-320C	Transport	(1981)	1982	1	From Pelita Air Services to AF
		3	B-737-200C	Transport	1981	1982-83	3	2 for AEW; 1 for VIP transport
		2	C-130B Hercules	Transport	(1975)	1976	2	
		2	C-130H Hercules	Transport	1980	1981	2	For maritime patrol
		5	C-130H-30	Transport	1979	1980-81	5	Last 3 reported as stretched version
		4	C-130H-30	Transport	1981	1982	(4)	Incl 2 mar patrol version C-130H-MP
		21	C-47	Transport	1970	1973-74	(21)	
		8	F-16A	Fighter/strike	(1986)			Negotiating; 4 F-16As and 4 F-16Bs
		14	F-51 Mustang	Fighter	(1970)	1971	14	
		12	F-5E Tiger-2	Fighter	1977	1980	12	Total cost incl 4 F-5Fs: $108 m
		4	F-5F Tiger-2	Jet trainer	1977	1980	4	
		2	HU-16B Albatros	Mar patrol/ASW	(1975)	1977	2	
		2	King Air A-100	Transport	1975	1977	2	Ex-USAF; private US seller
		1	L-100-30	Transport	1979	1980	1	Ordered for civilian use; first aircraft diverted to AF
		16	Model 205 UH-1H	Hel	1978	1978	16	For Army
		2	Model 206B	Hel	1975	1976	2	

No.	Weapon designation	Weapon description	Year of order	Year of delivery	No. delivered	Comments
5	Model 207	Lightplane	(1970)	1971	5	Ordered Dec 1982; delivered Sep 1983
6	Model 212 UH-1N	Hel	1982	1983	6	Ordered Dec 1982; delivered Jul 1983
9	Model 300C	Hel	1982	1983	9	
4	Model 310	Lightplane	(1971)	1972	4	Delivered prior to licensed production
6	Model 412	Hel	1983	1983	6	
3	Model 47G	Hel	1975	1976	3	
21	Musketeer Sport	Lightplane	1975	1976-77	(21)	
16	OV-10F Bronco	Trainer/COIN	1975	1976-77	16	
(6)	PA-38 Tomahawk	Trainer	(1983)	1983	(6)	Delivered via Singapore
10	S-55 Chickasaw	Hel	(1970)	1972-73	(10)	
16	T-33A	Jet trainer	(1971)	1972	16	Delivered via Australia
16	T-34C-1	Trainer	1978	1978	16	
9	T-34C-1	Trainer	1983	1984	9	
..	T-41A	Lightplane	(1980)	1981	(5)	Unannounced order
22	Commando Ranger	APC	(1983)	1983	22	Total cost incl 28 Scouts: $9.6 m
28	Commando Scout	Recce AC	(1983)	1983	28	
133	M-101-A1 105mm	TH	(1981)	1982	(133)	
(40)	M-102 105mm	TH	(1971)	1973-76	(40)	Unconfirmed
100	M-113	APC	(1976)	1978	100	Designation unconfirmed
60	V-150 Commando	APC	(1977)	1978-79	(60)	Delivery schedule uncertain
(96)	AIM-9J	AAM	1977	1980	96	Arming 16 F-5E/F Tiger-2 fighters
(48)	AIM-9P	AAM	(1986)			To arm 8 F-16A/Bs on order
1	Arcadia Class	Support ship	(1970)	1971	1	Ex-US Tidewater; renamed Duma; gun-armed
6	Bluebird Class	MSC	1970	1971	6	Deleted 1976
4	Claud Jones Cl	Frigate	(1972)	1973-74	4	Torpedo-armed
1	Jetfoil	Hydrofoil FAC	1980	1982	1	For evaluation
4	Jetfoil	Hydrofoil FAC	1983	1984-86	(4)	In addition to 1 in service; total cost: $150 m; option on 6 more and licensed production of 36
Yugoslavia						
3	LST 511-1152	LS/minelayer	(1969)	1970-71	3	In addition to 7 or more received before
1	LST 511-1152	LS/minelayer	(1971)	1971	1	Leased after service in Vietnam war
1	Training ship	Frigate	1978	1981	1	
1	Training ship	Frigate	(1981)	1984	(1)	
3 Iran						
China						
(80)	F-6	Fighter	(1981)	1982-84	(80)	Part of deal incl T-59 tanks and artillery reportedly worth $1.3 b; unconfirmed; possibly via N. Korea
12	F-6	Fighter	(1985)	1985-86	(9)	Unconfirmed; reportedly part of $1.6 b deal allegedly signed Mar 1985
..	T-59	MBT	(1981)	1982-84	(300)	Part of larger deal; Iran reportedly has given China access to Soviet weapons captured from Iraq; unconfirmed

Recipient code/ Recipient	Supplier	No. ordered	Weapon designation	Weapon description	Year of order	Year(s) of delivery	Total delivered	Comments
		200	T-59	MBT	(1985)	1985-86	(200)	Incl in $1.6 b deal; unconfirmed
		(300)	Type 59/1 130mm	TG	(1981)	1982-84	(300)	
		(100)	Type 59/1 130mm	TG	(1985)	1985-86	(100)	Incl in $1.6 b deal; unconfirmed
		(100)	Type-60 122mm	TG	(1985)	1985-86	(100)	Incl in $1.6 b deal; unconfirmed
		(300)	Type-63 107mm	MRS	(1982)	1982-85	(300)	
		(6)	CSA-1 SAMS	Mobile SAM system	(1985)	1985-86	6	Unconfirmed
		(130)	CSA-1	SAM	(1985)	1985-86	(130)	Incl in $1.6 b deal; unconfirmed
		(300)	Hong Ying-5	Port SAM	(1985)	1985-86	(300)	Incl in $1.6 b deal; unconfirmed
Ethiopia		(10)	F-5A	Fighter	(1984)	1984	(10)	Unconfirmed; 7-20 F-5A/Bs reportedly delivered to Iran 1984 or earlier
	France	8	Mystere-20	Transport	1975	1975-76	8	Order date Jan 1975
		16	Super Frelon	Hel	(1969)	1971	16	Total cost: $28 m
		(120)	AS-12	ASM/AShM	1974	1976-79	(120)	
		(500)	SS-11	ATM	(1969)	1970-71	(500)	
		(500)	SS-12	ShShM	(1969)	1970-71	(500)	
		12	Combattante-2	FAC	1974	1977-81	12	France lifted embargo on last 3
		2	Bandar Abbas Cl	Support ship	1972	1974	2	
	Germany, FR	6	Type 209/3	Submarine	1985			Originally ordered in 1979; cancelled same year; order reopened for delivery after end of Iraq-Iran War
	Italy	(85)	AB-205	Hel	1970	1972-76	(85)	For all services
		114	AB-206A	Hel	(1968)	1969-76	(114)	For AF, Navy, Army and Gendarmerie
		5	AB-212	Hel	(1970)	1971	5	For AF
		(20)	AB-212ASW	Hel	1974	1976-79	(20)	
		16	CH-47C Chinook	Hel	(1970)	1971-73	(16)	For AF and Army; 4 direct from USA
		26	CH-47C Chinook	Hel	(1974)	1976-77	26	Several supplied by Boeing, USA, due to production delays in Italy
		50	CH-47C Chinook	Hel	1977	1978-81	(23)	20 cancelled 1979; 7 vetoed by USA
		2	S-61A-4	Hel	1976	1977	2	For AF
		20	SH-3D Sea King	Hel	(1974)	1976-81	(20)	
		4	Seakiller-2 L	ShShM launcher	(1966)	1971-72	4	
		(60)	Sea Killer	ShShM	1966	1971-72	(60)	On SAAM Class frigates
		100	Seakiller/Marte	AShM	(1978)	1978-82	(100)	
	Korea, North	(60)	F-6	Fighter	(1985)			Unconfirmed
		(150)	T-62	MBT	(1981)	1982-83	(150)	Unconfirmed
		: :	SA-2 SAMS	Mobile SAM system	(1985)	1985	(10)	Unconfirmed
		: :	SA-2 Guideline	Landmob SAM	(1985)	1985	(60)	Unconfirmed
		(130)	EE-9 Cascavel	AC	1980	1980	(130)	Delivered Nov 1980
Libya		(60)	T-54	MBT	1981	1981	(60)	

	(65)	T-55	MBT	1981	1981	(65)	MAP; incl T-54/55 MBTs, field guns and small arms
	(65)	T-62	MBT	1981	1981	(65)	
Netherlands	(5)	SS-12 L	Mobile SSM system	(1983)	1984	(5)	Unconfirmed
	(15)	Scaleboard	Landmob SSM	(1983)	1984	(15)	Unconfirmed
	8	F-27 Mk-400	Transport	1974	1976-81	(8)	
	16	F-27 Mk-600	Transport	(1969)	1971-77	16	13 for AF, 2 for Navy and 1 for Army
Switzerland	15	PC-6	Lightplane	(1982)	1982-84	(15)	
	(80)	PC-7	Trainer	(1983)	1983-84	(41)	Delivery suspended after 41 aircraft
Syria	(200)	BMP-1	MICV	(1981)	1982-83	(200)	
	(120)	T-55	MBT	(1982)	1982	(120)	Syria and Libya supplied at least 350
	(100)	T-62	MBT	(1982)	1982	(100)	MBTs late 1981-early 1982
UK	..	Scud-B L	Mobile SSM system	(1984)	1984-86	(24)	
	..	SCUD-B	Landmob SSM	(1984)	1984-86	(120)	
	764	Chieftain-3	MBT	1971	1971-75	764	Incl some ARVs
	250	FV-101 Scorpion	LT	1976	1977-78	250	
	(100)	Ferret FV-703	Recce AC	(1972)	1974-75	(100)	
	(300)	Fox FV-721	AC	1972	1974-75	(300)	
	(20)	Sultan FV-105	CPC	(1977)	1979	(20)	Unconfirmed
	(36)	DN-181 Rapier	Mobile SAM system	1974	1975	(36)	
	(48)	Rapier SAMS	Mobile SAM system	1970	1972-73	(48)	
	4	Seacat L	ShAM launcher	(1966)	1971-72	4	On SAAM Class frigates
	(25)	Tigercat SAMS	Mobile SAM system	(1967)	1971-72	(25)	
	(1 248)	Rapier	Landmob SAM	1970	1972-73	(1 248)	
	(936)	Rapier	Landmob SAM	(1966)	1971-72	(936)	On SAAM Class frigates
	(36)	Seacat	ShAM/ShShM	(1972)	1974	(36)	
	(500)	Swingfire	ATM	(1967)	1971-72	(500)	
	(225)	Tigercat	Landmob SAM	1972	1974	(225)	25 systems delivered
	2	Hengam Class	LS	1972	1974	2	Originally 4 ships ordered
	2	Hengam Class	LS	1977	1984-85	2	Gun-armed support ship; displacement:
	1	Kharg Type	Support ship	1974	1985	1	10 900t; can carry 3 helicopters
	4	SAAM Class	Frigate	1966	1971-72	4	Armed with Seakiller ShShMs and Seacat ShAMs
USA	(15)	B-707-320C	Transport	(1971)	1975-78	(15)	
	16	B-747-100B	Transport	1975	1976-78	16	
	43	C-130H Hercules	Transport	(1969)	1970-75	43	
	38	CH-47C Chinook	Hel	(1976)	1976-78	(38)	
	17	Commander 680	Transport	(1970)	1970-76	17	Incl some Commander 690s
	80	F-14A Tomcat	Fighter/strike	1974	1976-78	80	
	45	F-33C Bonanza	Trainer	1971	1972-77	45	

Recipient code/Recipient	Supplier	No. ordered	Weapon designation	Weapon description	Year of order	Year(s) of delivery	Total delivered	Comments
		32	F-4E Phantom	Fighter	1970	1971	32	
		102	F-4E Phantom	Fighter	1972	1973-75	102	
		36	F-4E Phantom	Fighter	1974	1977	36	
		91	F-5A	Fighter	1963	1964-71	91	
		21	F-5B	Fighter/trainer	1963	1964-71	21	
		139	F-5E Tiger-2	Fighter	1972	1973-76	139	
		28	F-5F Tiger-2	Jet trainer	1975	1976-77	28	
		202	Model 209 AH-1J	Hel	1972	1974-77	202	
		314	Model 214A	Hel	1972	1975-78	314	
		2	Model 214B	Hel	1975	1977	2	
		39	Model 214C	Hel	1976	1976-78	39	
		6	P-3C Orion	Mar patrol/ASW	(1972)	1975	6	
		12	RF-4E Phantom	Recce	1974	1975	12	For Navy
		6	RH-53D	Hel	1975	1976-77	6	
		1	S-62A	Hel	1975	1975	1	
		(50)	M-107 175mm	SPG	(1972)	1973	(50)	
		(50)	M-109-A1 155mm	SPH	(1972)	1973	(50)	
		(50)	M-110 203mm	SPH	(1972)	1973	(50)	
		100	M-113-A1	APC	1976	1978	100	
		(2)	RGM-84A L	ShShM launcher	1974	1978	(2)	For first Kaman Class FAC
		2	RIM-66A L	ShAM launcher	(1970)	1974	2	On 2 Sumner Class destroyers
		1	RIM-66A L	ShAM launcher	1974	1976	1	On 1 Battle Class destroyer
		2 850	AGM-65A	ASM	(1971)	1972-77	(2 850)	
		(72)	AGM-84A Harpoon	AShM	(1972)	1975	(72)	Arming 6 P-3F Orions
		424	AIM-54A Phoenix	AAM	1974	1976-78	(424)	Arming 80 F-14 Tomcats
		(680)	AIM-7C Sparrow	AAM	(1970)	1971-76	(680)	Arming F-4Es
		(546)	AIM-9B	AAM	(1963)	1964-71	(546)	Arming F-5As
		(680)	AIM-9J	AAM	1970	1971-77	(680)	Arming F-4Es
		(1 000)	AIM-9J	AAM	(1972)	1973-77	(1 000)	Arming F-5E/Fs
		(640)	AIM-9J	AAM	1975	1976-78	(640)	Arming F-14A Tomcats
		(500)	BGM-71A TOW	ATM	(1970)	1971-73	(500)	For Army
		(2 880)	BGM-71A TOW	ATM	1972	1974-77	(2 880)	Arming AH-1J Cobra helicopters
		634	FGM-77A Dragon	ATM	(1975)	1976	634	
		10 000	FGM-77A Dragon	ATM	1977	1977-78	(10 000)	
		9	RGM-84A Harpoon	ShShM	1974	1978	9	Intended to arm 12 Combattante-2 (Kaman) Class FACs; only 9 delivered out of 222 ordered when deal cancelled 1979
		(32)	RIM-66A/SM-1	ShAM/ShShM	(1970)	1974	(32)	Arming 2 Sumner Class destroyers
		(24)	RIM-66A/SM-1	ShAM/ShShM	1974	1976	(24)	Arming 1 Battle Class destroyer

15 Iraq

Supplier	No.	Weapon designation	Weapon description	Year of order	Year(s) of deliveries	No. delivered	Comments
USSR	1	Amphion Class	Support ship	1970	1971	1	Transferred on loan 1971; purchased 1977
	2	Gearing Class	Destroyer	1974	1975-77	2	Scrap value; bought for spares
	2	Sumner Class	Destroyer	(1970)	1974	2	Seller unconfirmed
	(100)	M-46 130mm	TG	(1976)	1976-77	(100)	
	100	ZSU-23-4 Shilka	AAV	1976	1977-78	(100)	
	2 000	SA-7 Grail	Port SAM	1976	1977-78	(2 000)	
	(1 000)	SA-9 Gaskin	Landmob SAM	1976	1977-78	(1 000)	
Argentina	20	IA-58A Pucara	COIN	(1986)		(6)	
Brazil	(6)	Astros-II SS-30	MRS	(1983)	1984	(6)	
	(22)	Astros-II SS-30	MRS	(1984)	1985	(22)	
	(38)	Astros-II SS-30	MRS	(1985)			
	(150)	EE-11 Urutu	APC	1979	1980-82	(150)	Ordered in 3 batches
	(350)	EE-11 Urutu	APC	1982	1983-84	(350)	Total cost incl EE-3 Jararaca: $250 m
	(300)	EE-3 Jararaca	SC	1982	1984-85	(300)	
	(750)	EE-9 Cascavel	AC	(1979)	1980-83	(750)	Ordered in 4 batches
	26	EE-9 Cascavel	AC	(1984)	1985	26	May incl some Urutu vehicles; deal also incl Astro rockets and MRLs; cost: $30 m
China	(100)	Cobra-2000	ATM	(1980)	1981	(100)	Designation unconfirmed
	(250)	T-59	MBT	(1981)	1982-83	(250)	Unconfirmed
	(50)	T-69	MBT	(1982)	1983-84	(50)	Unspecified number delivered
	(70)	Type 531	APC	(1982)	1983-84	(70)	Unspecified number delivered
Czechoslovakia	24	L-29 Delfin	Jet trainer	1979	1980	24	
	24	L-39 Albatross	Jet trainer	1973	1978	24	
	(200)	OT-64	APC	(1980)	1981	(200)	
Egypt	(80)	EMB-312 Tucano	Trainer	(1983)	1985	(10)	From Brazil and from Egyptian licensed production
	(10)	EMB-312 Tucano	Trainer	(1983)	1985		
	(40)	F-6	Fighter	(1983)	1983	(40)	
	..	F-7	Fighter	(1983)	1983-85	(80)	Chinese version of MiG-21 assembled in Egypt
	(250)	T-55	MBT	1981	1981-83	(250)	Several hundred delivered
	(200)	T-55	MBT	1983	1983-84	(60)	Built in Romania; transferred via Egypt until Romanian half of deliveries
	(100)	Walid	APC	(1979)	1980	(100)	Dates and number ordered unconfirmed
	(100)	AT-3 Sagger	ATM	1981	1981	(100)	Possibly Swingfire
France	..	Alpha Jet	Jet trainer/strike	(1986)			Negotiating; assembly in Egypt possible
	36	Mirage F-1C	Fighter/interceptor	1977	1981	36	Armed with Magic AAMs; incl 6 trainers
	24	Mirage F-1C	Fighter/interceptor	1979	1983-84	(24)	Armed with Magic AAMs and AM-39 Exocet AShMs; incl 4 trainers
	29	Mirage F-1C	Fighter/interceptor	1982	1984-85	(29)	Incl 6 trainers; armed with Magic AAMs
	24	Mirage F-1C	Fighter/interceptor	1985	1986	(24)	In addition to 89 acquired earlier
	(8)	Mirage-5D	Jet trainer	(1984)	1984	(8)	

Recipient code/ Recipient	Supplier	No. ordered	Weapon designation	Weapon description	Year of order	Year(s) of delivery	Total delivered	Comments
		2	Mystere-20	Transport	(1975)	1975-76	2	
		16	SA-316B	Hel	(1969)	1971	16	Armed with AS-11s
		(44)	SA-316B	Hel	(1974)	1975-77	(44)	Armed with AS-12s
		3	SA-330 Puma	Hel	1975	1976	3	For VIP transport
		20	SA-330L Puma	Hel	1979	1980-81	(20)	
		20	SA-342K Gazelle	Hel	1975	1976-77	(20)	Armed with HOT ATMs
		20	SA-342K Gazelle	Hel	(1978)	1980-81	(20)	Armed with HOT ATMs
		5	Super Etendard	Fighter/strike	1983	1983	(5)	Diverted from French order for 71; armed with AM-39 Exocet AShMs; down-graded before delivery; returned Sep 1985
		10	Super Frelon	Hel	1976	1976-80	(10)	Armed with AM-39 Exocet AShMs
		3	Super Frelon	Hel	(1980)	1981	3	
		(110)	AMX-10RC	Recce AC	1978	1981	(110)	
		(150)	AMX-30 Roland	AAV(M)	1981	1982-85	(60)	At least 30 delivered by 1983
		85	AMX-30-155 GCT	SPG	1982	1983-85	(85)	
		100	AMX-30B	MBT	(1978)	1979	(100)	
		50	ERC-90 Sagaie	AC	(1978)	1980	(50)	Unconfirmed
		(200)	ERC-90 Sagaie	AC	(1981)	1982-84	(200)	
		(200)	M-3	APC	(1981)	1982-84	(200)	
		100	VCR-6	APC	(1978)	1979-81	(100)	
		(60)	AM-39 Exocet	AShM	1978	1979-80	(60)	Armed with HOT ATMs
		..	AM-39 Exocet	AShM	1983	1983-85	(446)	
		..	ARMAT	ARM	(1984)	1985	(12)	Arming Super Etendards and Mirages
		(192)	AS-11	ASM	(1969)	1970-71	(192)	Unconfirmed
		(264)	AS-12	ASM/AShM	(1974)	1975-77	(264)	Arming Alouette-3 helicopters
		(200)	AS-30L	ASM	(1984)	1985-86	(200)	Arming Alouette-3 helicopters
		360	HOT	ATM	1976	1980-81	(360)	Unconfirmed; to arm Mirage F-1s
		(267)	R-530	AAM	1977	1981-85	(267)	Arming Gazelle helicopters
		(534)	R-550 Magic	AAM	1977	1981-85	(534)	Arming Mirage F-1s
		(600)	Roland-2	Landmob SAM	1981	1982-85	(600)	Arming Mirage F-1s
		(200)	SS-11	ATM	1979	1980-81	(200)	
German DR		(50)	T-55	MBT	1980	1981	(50)	Surplus; incl some T-54s
Germany, FR		(6)	BK-117	Hel	(1984)	1984-85	(6)	Refurbishment of electronics in Austria
		(23)	Bo-105	Hel	(1978)	1979-83	(23)	
Hungary		(200)	Fug-70	SC	(1980)	1981	(200)	
Italy		2	A-109 Hirundo	Hel	1984	1984-85	(2)	On 2 Wadi Class corvettes; total cost incl 5 AB-212ASW helicopters: $164 m
		5	AB-212ASW	Hel	1984	1985-86	(5)	On 4 Lupo Class frigates
		6	S-61A-4	Hel	(1980)	1982	6	For VIP transport

Country	No.	Weapon designation	Description	Year of order	Years of deliveries	No. delivered	Comments
	(10)	Aspide/Albatros	ShAM/ShShM launcher	(1981)	1984-86	(10)	Arming Lupo and Wadi Class
	(14)	Otomat-2 L	ShShM launcher	(1981)	1984-86	(14)	Arming Lupo and Wadi Class
	(224)	Aspide	AAM/SAM/ShAM	(1981)	1984-86	(224)	Arming 4 Lupo Class frigates and 6 Wadi Class corvettes
	(60)	Otomat-2	ShShM	(1981)	1984-86	(60)	Arming 4 Lupo Class frigates and 6 Wadi Class corvettes
Jordan	4	Lupo Class	Frigate	1981	1985-86	(4)	Order incl 6 Wadi Class corvettes and 1 Stromboli Class support ship
	1	Stromboli Class	Support ship	1981	1984	1	Commissioned Mar 1984
	6	Wadi Class	Corvette	1981	1984-85	6	Iraqi designation: Assad Class
	(20)	F-6	Fighter	(1983)	1984	(20)	Unconfirmed; Chinese F-6 assembled in Egypt reportedly transferred via Jordan
Kuwait	(200)	GHN-45 155mm	TH/TG	(1982)	1983	(200)	Unconfirmed
	(200)	GHN-45 155mm	TH/TG	(1984)			
	(50)	Khalid	MBT	1982	1982-83	(50)	Military aid
	(100)	M-109 155mm	SPH	(1980)	1981-83	(100)	Seller unconfirmed
	(30)	M-114 155mm	TH	(1980)	1981	(30)	Seller unconfirmed
	(50)	Chieftain-5	MBT	(1984)	1984	(50)	Unconfirmed
Libya	(400)	EE-9 Cascavel	AC	(1982)	1983	(400)	
Poland	300	T-55	MBT	(1980)	1981	(300)	
	(200)	SA-6 Gainful	Landmob SAM	(1985)	1985-86	(200)	Sale approved by the USSR; replacement for losses in the war with Iran
Spain	24	Bo-105CB	Hel	(1981)	1982-83	(24)	Unconfirmed
	:	BMR-600	ICV	(1981)	1982-85	(200)	Delivery from CASA confirmed by MBB 1984
Sudan	10	MiG-21MF	Fighter	1979	1979	10	Unconfirmed
Switzerland	48	AS-202 Bravo	Trainer	1979	1979-81	(48)	Purchased for spares
	(52)	PC-7	Trainer	(1981)	1981-82	(52)	
	(50)	Roland	APC	1980	1981	(50)	Seller unconfirmed
UK	3	BN-2A Islander	Transport	1970	1971	3	For photographic survey
	58	Saboteur	APC	1982	1982-83	(58)	Commercial deal; may be for civil use
USA	45	Model 214ST	Hel	1985	1985	(10)	
	30	Model 300C	Hel	(1981)	1983	30	
	30	Model 500D	Hel	(1981)	1983	30	Possibly for civilian use
	24	Model 530MG	Hel	1985	1985	24	
USSR	(4)	An-12 Cub-A	Transport	1976	1977	(4)	
	(2)	An-24 Coke	Transport	1976	1977	(2)	
	2	An-26 Curl	Lightplane	1976	1977	2	
	16	Il-76 Candid	Transport	(1980)	1980-84	(16)	At least 12 in civilian markings
	(2)	Mi-24 Hind-C	Hel	(1975)	1976	(2)	
	(10)	Mi-24 Hind-C	Hel	(1983)	1984	(10)	
	(40)	Mi-24 Hind-D	Hel	(1977)	1979-80	(40)	
	(25)	Mi-4 Hound	Hel	(1969)	1970-71	(25)	Unspecified number delivered
	(15)	Mi-6 Hook	Hel	(1972)	1973	(15)	

Recipient code/ Recipient	Supplier	No. ordered	Weapon designation	Weapon description	Year of order	Year(s) of delivery	Total delivered	Comments
		12	Mi-8 Hip	Hel	(1970)	1971	12	
		(90)	Mi-8 Hip	Hel	(1975)	1976-79	(90)	
		(30)	Mi-8 Hip	Hel	(1983)	1984	(30)	Unconfirmed
		(36)	MiG-21F	Fighter	(1967)	1968-71	(36)	
		(15)	MiG-21F	Fighter	(1973)	1973	(15)	War replacements
		(40)	MiG-21MF	Fighter	(1973)	1974	(40)	
		(61)	MiG-21bis	Fighter	(1983)	1984	(61)	Version uncertain; unconfirmed
		(20)	MiG-23	Fighter/interceptor	(1974)	1976	(20)	
		70	MiG-23BN	Fighter/grd attack	1976	1977-78	(70)	Part of deal estimated at $2500 m; reportedly guaranteed by Saudi Arabia
		50	MiG-23BN	Fighter/grd attack	1984	1984-85	(50)	Part of large deal signed May 1984
		(25)	MiG-25	Fighter/interceptor	1979	1980-81	(25)	
		..	MiG-25	Fighter/interceptor	1984	1984-85	(30)	
		(8)	MiG-25R	Recce	1979	1982	(8)	
		(80)	Su-20 Fitter-C	Fighter/grd attack	(1973)	1974-81	(80)	
		(30)	Su-20 Fitter-C	Fighter/grd attack	(1983)	1985	(30)	Unconfirmed
		(12)	Su-7 Fitter	Fighter	(1972)	1973	(12)	
		(30)	Su-7 Fitter	Fighter	(1982)	1984	(30)	
		2	Tu-124	Transport	(1970)	1971	2	
		2	Tu-134	Transport	(1976)	1978	2	For VIP transport
		12	Tu-22 Blinder-A	Bomber	(1972)	1973	12	
		(100)	BM-21 122mm	MRS	(1978)	1979-80	(100)	
		(200)	BM-21 122mm	MRS	(1982)	1983-84	(200)	
		(100)	BMP-1	MICV	(1973)	1974-75	(100)	
		(250)	BRDM-2	SC	(1966)	1967-73	(250)	
		..	BRDM-2 Gaskin	AAV(M)	1982	1982-85	(20)	
		(250)	BTR-50P	APC	(1968)	1969-73	(250)	
		(250)	BTR-60P	APC	(1970)	1971-75	(250)	
		(100)	D-30 122mm	TH	1980	1982-84	(100)	
		(200)	M-1955 100mm	TG	(1973)	1973-76	(200)	
		(50)	M-1973 152mm	SPG	(1979)	1980	(50)	USSR delivered 122/152mm SPHs; designations unconfirmed
		(50)	M-1974 122mm	SPH	1979	1980	(50)	
		(200)	PT-76	LT	(1983)	1984	(200)	Delivered Aug 1984
		(50)	T-54	MBT	(1981)	1982-83	(50)	
		(300)	T-55	MBT	1973	1974-75	(300)	
		(100)	T-55	MBT	(1981)	1982-83	(100)	Transferred via Saudi Arabia; possibly also some T-54s
		(200)	T-55	MBT	1984	1984-85	(200)	Part of large deal signed May 1984

No. ordered	Weapon designation	Description	Year of order	Years of deliveries	No. delivered	Comments
(100)	T-62	MBT	1973	1974-75	(100)	
600	T-62	MBT	1976	1977-80	(600)	
(300)	T-62	MBT	(1982)	1982-83	(300)	Supply of T-62/72s resumed in 1982
(300)	T-62	MBT	1984	1984-85	(300)	Part of large deal signed May 1984
50	T-72	MBT	(1979)	1979	50	Delivered Aug 1979
(400)	T-72	MBT	1980	1982-83	(400)	
:	T-72	MBT	1984	1984-85	(600)	Part of large deal signed May 1984
(200)	ZSU-23-4 Shilka	AAV	1973	1973-76	(200)	
(100)	ZSU-57-2	AAV	(1970)	1971-73	(100)	
(6)	SA-3 SAMS	Mobile SAM system	1971	1972-73	(6)	On ZIL trucks
:	SA-6 SAMS	Mobile SAM system	1979	1980-85	(40)	
:	SA-8 SAMS	Mobile SAM system	(1982)	1982-85	(24)	
(6)	SS-21 L	Mobile SSM system	(1984)	1985	(6)	
(6)	SSN-2 Styx L	ShShM launcher	1971	1972-74	(6)	Arming 6 Osa-1 Class FACs
8	SSN-2 Styx L	ShShM launcher	1973	1974-77	8	Arming 8 Osa-2 Class FACs
(2)	Scud-B L	Mobile SSM system	1974	1975	(2)	
(918)	AA-2 Atoll	AAM	(1962)	1963-73	(918)	Arming MiG-21s
(840)	AA-2 Atoll	AAM	(1975)	1976-85	(840)	Arming MiG-23s
(330)	AA-2 Atoll	AAM	(1979)	1980-85	(330)	Arming MiG-21s and MiG-25s
(36)	AS-4 Kitchen	ASM	(1972)	1973	(36)	Arming 12 Tu-22s
(24)	AS-4 Kitchen	ASM	(1983)	1984	(24)	Unconfirmed
(36)	AS-6 Kingfish	ALCM	(1983)	1984	(36)	Unconfirmed
(500)	AT-3 Sagger	ATM	(1974)	1976	(500)	
(90)	SA-2 Guideline	Landmob SAM	(1970)	1971	(90)	
(108)	SA-3 Goa	Landmob SAM	(1971)	1972-73	(108)	
(135)	SA-6 Gainful	Landmob SAM	1976	1977	(135)	
:	SA-6 Gainful	Landmob SAM	1979	1980-85	(400)	
:	SA-8 Gecko	Landmob SAM	(1982)	1982-85	(288)	
:	SA-9 Gaskin	Landmob SAM	1982	1982-85	(160)	On BRDM-2 (BTR-40PB Gaskin) vehicles
(12)	SCUD-B	Landmob SSM	1974	1975	(12)	On order in addition to 12 in service
(6)	SCUD-B	Landmob SSM	(1978)	1980	(6)	
(18)	SS-21	SSM	(1984)	1985	(18)	
(24)	SSN-2 Styx	ShShM	(1971)	1972-74	(24)	Arming 6 Osa-1 Class FACs
(96)	SSN-2 Styx	ShShM	(1973)	1974-77	(96)	Arming 8 Osa-2 Class FACs
(6)	Osa-1 Class	FAC	1971	1972-74	(6)	
8	Osa-2 Class	FAC	1973	1974-77	8	At least 4 sunk by 1983
4	Polnocny Class	LS	1976	1977-79	4	One sunk by Iranian Harpoon ShShM 1980
3	Yevgenia Class	MSC	1974	1975	3	
1	Training ship	Frigate	1978	1981	1	Similar to ship delivered to Indonesia

Yugoslavia

7 Israel

Austria	S-65A	Hel	1981	1981	2	
Germany, FR	Do-27	Transport	(1975)	1976	(23)	
	Do-28D-1	Transport	(1973)	1974	15	

Recipient code/ Recipient	Supplier	No. ordered	Weapon designation	Weapon description	Year of order	Year(s) of delivery	Total delivered	Comments
	UK	4	BN-2A Islander	Transport	(1973)	1974	4	Some from the Netherlands
	USA	(400)	Centurion	MBT	(1969)	1970-73	(400)	Modernized in Israel
		(400)	Centurion	MBT	1974	1974-75	(400)	
		3	Type-206	Submarine	1972	1977	3	
		53	A-4E Skyhawk	Fighter/bomber	(1973)	1973	53	War replacement; from US Marine Corps
		(101)	A-4N Skyhawk-2	Fighter/bomber	(1971)	1972-74	(101)	
		(20)	AS-365N	Hel	1986			12-20 ordered
		5	B-707-320C	Transport	(1973)	1975	5	Also designated 707-131; tanker version
		7	B-707-320C	Transport	1976	1977-79	(7)	For transport and ECM duties
		1	B-707-320C	Transport	(1982)	1983	1	For ECM duties
		12	C-130E Hercules	Transport	(1973)	1973	12	
		4	C-130H Hercules	Transport	(1970)	1971-74	4	
		8	C-130H Hercules	Transport	(1975)	1976-78	(8)	
		4	E-2C Hawkeye	AEW	1976	1977-78	4	
		40	F-15A Eagle	Fighter	(1975)	1976-82	40	
		11	F-15A Eagle	Fighter	1982			
		75	F-16A	Fighter/strike	1978	1980-82	(75)	Total cost: $2700 m of which half grant and half credit; for delivery 1985-88
		75	F-16C	Fighter/strike	1983	1985-86	(35)	
		93	F-4E Phantom	Fighter	(1968)	1969-71	93	
		85	F-4E Phantom	Fighter	(1971)	1972-73	85	
		45	F-4E Phantom	Fighter	(1973)	1974-75	45	
		2	G-134 Mohawk	Recce	(1974)	1975	2	Ex-USAF; version OV-1E
		2	KC-130H	Tanker/transport	1975	1976-77	2	
		(20)	Model 206B	Hel	(1971)	1972	(20)	
		(6)	Model 209 AH-1G	Hel	1974	1975	(6)	Equipped with TOW ATMs
		12	Model 209 AH-1S	Hel	1977	1977-78	(12)	
		18	Model 209 AH-1S	Hel	1981	1982	(18)	Armed with TOW ATMs
		(10)	Model 209 AH-1S	Hel	(1985)	1985	(10)	
		(12)	Model 212	Hel	1975	1976-77	(12)	
		30	Model 500MD	Hel	1978	1980-81	(30)	Gunship version; armed with TOW
		32	Queen Air B-80	Transport	(1974)	1974-75	(32)	
		6	RF-4E Phantom	Recce	(1968)	1971	6	
		12	RF-4E Phantom	Recce	1974	1976-78	12	
		4	RU-21E	Recce	(1979)	1980	4	
		12	S-61R	Hel	1975	1976-77	12	
		(6)	S-65A	Hel	(1973)	1973	(6)	During Oct war 1973
		7	S-65A	Hel	1974	1975-77	7	
		2	SA-366	Hel	(1985)	1985	2	Ex-US Coast Guard; for evaluation; requirement for 16-20

No.	Designation	Type	(Ordered)	Delivered	No.	Comment
3	Stratofreighter	Transport	(1971)	1971-73	3	Ex-USAF
(4)	Super King Air	Transport	(1983)	1983	(4)	Equipped for battlefield surveillance
25	TA-4H Skyhawk	Jet trainer	1971	1972-73	25	Version uncertain
(90)	M-101-A1 105mm	TH	(1967)	1969-71	(90)	
(200)	M-107 175mm	SPG	(1968)	1968-73	(200)	
(100)	M-109-A1 155mm	SPH	1976	1977-78	(100)	
200	M-109-A1 155mm	SPH	1979	1982-83	(200)	
(60)	M-110 203mm	SPH	(1967)	1968-71	(60)	
(100)	M-113-A1	APC	(1969)	1970-71	(100)	
700	M-113-A1	APC	1976	1977-79	(700)	
800	M-113-A2	APC	(1979)	1981-82	(800)	
(240)	M-48 Patton	MBT	(1967)	1968-71	(240)	
(200)	M-48 Patton	MBT	1973	1973	(200)	Replacing war losses
56	M-548	APC	1979	1981-82	(56)	
98	M-577-A1	CPC	1979	1981-82	(98)	
(150)	M-60	MBT	(1969)	1970-73	(150)	
(150)	M-60	MBT	(1973)	1973	(150)	Replacing war losses
(100)	M-60-A1	MBT	1973	1974	(100)	
(450)	M-60-A1	MBT	1975	1975-76	(450)	
125	M-60-A1	MBT	1976	1977	125	
300	M-60-A3	MBT	1979	1980-85	(300)	
(15)	M-728	AEV	1977	1977-78	(15)	
(24)	M-730 Chaparral	AAV(M)	1972	1973-74	(24)	
25	M-88-A1	ARV	1979	1981-82	(25)	
:	AN/PPS-15	Surveillance radar	(1972)	1973	(20)	
(6)	I-Hawk SAMS	Mobile SAM system	1979	1980-84	(6)	
(12)	Lance SAM	Mobile SSM system	1974	1976	(12)	
:	RGM-84A L	ShShM launcher	1978	1979-85	(15)	Arming Reshef- and Aliya Class FACs
(8)	RGM-84A L	ShShM launcher	(1980)	1982-84	(8)	Arming 2 Flagstaff Class FACs
(550)	AGM-12B Bullpup	ASM	(1968)	1969-73	(550)	Arming F-4 Phantoms
(210)	AGM-12B Bullpup	ASM	(1973)	1974-76	(210)	Arming A-4 Skyhawks
(300)	AGM-45A Shrike	ARM	(1969)	1970-71	(300)	
(300)	AGM-45A Shrike	ARM	1973	1973	(300)	Airlifted during October War 1973
(200)	AGM-45A Shrike	ARM	(1974)	1975	(200)	
(200)	AGM-45A Shrike	ARM	1978	1978	(200)	
(200)	AGM-65A	ASM	1973	1973	(200)	Airlifted during October War 1973
(360)	AGM-65A	ASM	(1974)	1976	(360)	
(600)	AGM-65A	ASM	1979	1980-82	(600)	
(1 338)	AIM-7C Sparrow	AAM	(1968)	1969-75	(1 338)	Arming F-4 Phantoms
320	AIM-7E Sparrow	AAM	(1975)	1976-82	(376)	Arming F-15s
170	AIM-7F Sparrow	AAM	1978	1979	(170)	
150	AIM-7M Sparrow	AAM/SAM	1983	1986-87	(150)	Arming F-15s; total cost: $52 m

Recipient code/ Recipient	Supplier	No. ordered	Weapon designation	Weapon description	Year of order	Year(s) of delivery	Total delivered	Comments
		336	AIM-9D	AAM	(1971)	1972-73	(336)	Airlifted during October War 1973
		(2 000)	AIM-9D	AAM	1973	1973	(2 000)	Arming 25 F-15s
		300	AIM-9J	AAM	1975	1976-79	(300)	
		600	AIM-9L	AAM	1979	1980-81	(600)	US LoO Mar 1983
		200	AIM-9L	AAM	1983	1985-86	(200)	Airlifted during October War 1973
		(500)	BGM-71A TOW	ATM	1973	1973	(500)	Arming M-113 APCs and Cobra helicopters; also in infantry version
		(3 000)	BGM-71A TOW	ATM	1974	1975-76	(3 000)	
		(96)	BGM-71A TOW	ATM	1977	1977-78	(96)	
		(144)	BGM-71A TOW	ATM	1981	1982	(144)	Arming 18 Model 209 Cobras
		(2 000)	FGM-77A Dragon	ATM	(1975)	1977	(2 000)	
		5 000	FGM-77A Dragon	ATM	1980	1980-81	(5 000)	
		(500)	FIM-43A Redeye	Port SAM	1974	1975	(500)	Has probably received more; possibly local production of warhead
		(110)	MGM-52C Lance	Landmob SSM	1974	1976	(110)	Airlifted during October War 1973
		(100)	MIM-23B Hawk	Landmob SAM	1973	1973	(100)	
		100	MIM-23B Hawk	Landmob SAM	1979	1980	100	Replacement missiles
		200	MIM-23B Hawk	Landmob SAM	1982	1983-84	(200)	
		(288)	MIM-72A	Landmob SAM	(1972)	1973-74	(288)	At least 100 ordered to complement Gabriel; AShM version for F-4s probably also ordered
		..	RGM-84A Harpoon	ShShM	(1978)	1979-85	(140)	
		(24)	RGM-84A Harpoon	ShShM	(1980)	1982-84	(24)	Arming 2 Flagstaff-2 Class FACs
		12	Dabur Class	PC/FAC	1973	1975-76	12	Delivered prior to licensed production
		1	Flagstaff-2 Cl	Hydrofoil FAC	1977	1982	1	Delivered prior to licensed production
		3	LSM Type	LC/minelayer	(1971)	1972	3	
4 Jamaica	UK	1	BN-2A Defender	Lightplane	1976	1977	1	
	USA	1	BN-2A Islander	Transport	1973	1974	1	
		3	Duke B60	Lightplane	1975	1975	3	
		1	King Air A-100	Transport	1974	1974	1	
		3	Model 206A	Hel	(1970)	1971	3	
		2	Model 206B	Hel	(1980)	1981	2	
		3	Model 212	Hel	1975	1975	3	
		1	Model 337	Trainer	(1976)	1977	1	
		10	V-150 Commando	APC	(1977)	1978	10	
		1	Sewart Type	PC	(1972)	1974	1	

15 Jordan

Supplier	No.	Weapon designation	Weapon description	Year of order	Year(s) of delivery	No. delivered	Comments
Argentina	200	GHN-45 155mm	TH/TG	(1986)	1982-83	(200)	Turrets to be made in Israel; unconfirmed
Austria	(200)	GHN-45 155mm	TH/TG	1982	1985	(100)	Unspecified number deployed in Iraq
Egypt	:	Fahd	APC	(1984)	1985	(10)	Unconfirmed
France	2	Falcon-50	Transport	(1984)	1982	2	Financed by Saudi Arabia
	2	Mirage F-1B	Jet trainer	1979	1982	2	Financed by Saudi Arabia
	17	Mirage F-1C	Fighter/interceptor	1979	1982	17	
	17	Mirage F-1C	Fighter/interceptor	(1982)	1983	17	In addition to 17 in service
	(12)	Mirage F-1C	Fighter/interceptor	(1986)			Negotiating
	(100)	R-530	AAM	1979	1982	(100)	Arming Mirage F-1Cs
	(100)	R-530	AAM	(1982)	1983	(100)	Arming Mirage F-1Cs
	(100)	R-550 Magic	AAM	1979	1982	(100)	Arming Mirage F-1Cs
	(100)	R-550 Magic	AAM	(1982)	1983	(100)	Arming Mirage F-1Cs
	:	SATCP Mistral	Port SAM	(1984)			Unconfirmed
Iran	30	F-5A	Fighter	1974	1974-75	30	May have been sold by Egypt
	4	F-5B	Fighter/trainer	(1974)	1974-75	4	
Iraq	(3)	An-12 Cub-A	Transport	(1983)	1983	(3)	Captured from Iran and given to Jordan
	36	M-60-A1	MBT	1980	1980	36	
Italy	:	Spada	Mobile SAM system	(1986)			Negotiating
	:	Aspide	AAM/SAM/ShAM	(1986)			Negotiating
Spain	16	C-101 Aviojet	Jet trainer	1986	1987	(8)	
	1	C-212-200	Transport	1985			
	3	C-212A Aviocar	Transport	1974	1975-76	3	
	2	CN-235	Transport	1985			Option taken Jun 1985
UK	5	Bulldog-125	Trainer	1974	1974	5	
	(5)	Bulldog-125	Trainer	1975	1975	(5)	
	5	Bulldog-125	Trainer	1976	1976	5	
	5	Bulldog-125	Trainer	1980	1981	5	
	5	Bulldog-125	Trainer	1981	1982	5	
	(100)	Centurion	MBT	(1972)	1973-74	(100)	
	278	Khalid	MBT	1979	1981-84	(278)	Also designated FV-4030/2; originally ordered by Iran and designated Shir-1
	(248)	Khalid	MBT	(1986)			Negotiating
	(14)	Tigercat SAMS	Mobile SAM system	(1969)	1969-70	(14)	
	(1 500)	Blowpipe	Port SAM	(1986)			Paid for by Saudi Arabia
USA	(1 500)	Javelin	Port SAM	(1986)			May order as result of US withdrawal of offer to sell Stinger SAMs
	(555)	Tigercat	Landmob SAM	(1969)	1970-71	(555)	Reportedly negotiating
	3	C-119 Packet	Transport	(1971)	1972	3	
	2	C-130B Hercules	Transport	1973	1973	2	
	2	C-130B Hercules	Transport	1976	1976-77	2	Total cost: $16 m; Saudi funding
	2	C-130H Hercules	Transport	1977	1978-79	2	
	1	C-130H Hercules	Transport	(1982)	1982	1	Ex-US

Recipient code/ Recipient	Supplier	No. ordered	Weapon designation	Weapon description	Year of order	Year(s) of delivery	Total delivered	Comments
		(22)	F-104A	Fighter	1966	1969-73	(22)	Ex-Taiwanese
		5	F-104B	Fighter	1966	1969-73	5	Ex-Taiwanese
		57	F-5E Tiger-2	Fighter	1974	1975-80	(57)	
		6	F-5F Tiger-2	Jet trainer	1974	1975-77	(6)	
		6	F-5F Tiger-2	Jet trainer	1979	1981	6	
		4	Model 205 UH-1H	Hel	(1975)	1976	4	
		24	Model 209 AH-1S	Hel	1982	1985-86	(24)	Armed with TOW ATMs
		8	Model 500D	Hel	1980	1981	8	
		12	PA-28 Cherokee	Lightplane	(1985)	1985	12	For Royal Air Academy
		6	PA-34 Seneca-2	Lightplane	(1985)	1985	6	For Royal Air Academy; may be version 3
		18	S-76 Spirit	Hel	1980	1980-82	(18)	
		2	Sabreliner	Transport	(1977)	1979	2	
		8	T-37B	Jet trainer	(1975)	1976	8	
		(30)	M-102 105mm	TH	(1973)	1974	(30)	
		(56)	M-109-A1 155mm	SPH	1974	1975-76	(56)	
		78	M-109-A2 155mm	SPH	1980	1983-85	(78)	Status of deal uncertain
		(12)	M-110 203mm	SPH	1978	1980	(12)	
		(29)	M-110-A2 203mm	SPH	1980	1982	(29)	
		(200)	M-113-A1	APC	(1968)	1972-74	(200)	
		(700)	M-113-A1	APC	1976	1976-79	(700)	
		81	M-113-A2	APC	1980	1982-83	(81)	Ordered Jan 1980
		(20)	M-114 155mm	TH	1973	1974	(20)	
		(20)	M-114 155mm	TH	(1977)	1979	(20)	
		(50)	M-114-A1	TH	(1973)	1974	(50)	
		(22)	M-115 203mm	Recce AC	(1975)	1977	(22)	
		100	M-163 Vulcan	AAV	1974	1977	100	Paid for by Saudi Arabia
		(20)	M-44 155mm	SPH	(1973)	1974	(20)	
		(100)	M-48 Patton	MBT	1976	1977-78	(100)	
		(35)	M-52 105mm	SPH	(1969)	1970-71	(35)	
		(20)	M-59 155mm	TG	1972	1974-75	(20)	
		82	M-60-A1	MBT	1976	1977-78	82	
		200	M-60-A3	MBT	1980	1982-85	(200)	
		..	AN/TPQ-36	Tracking radar	(1982)	1983-84	(9)	
		..	AN/TPS-32	3-D radar	(1984)			
		14	I-Hawk SAMS	Mobile SAM system	1976	1977-78	(14)	
		100	M-167 Vulcan	Mobile AA-system	1976	1977-78	(100)	
		(342)	AIM-9J	AAM	1974	1975-80	(342)	Arming F-5E/Fs
		(340)	AIM-9P	AAM	1979	1981-82	(340)	Arming F-5E/Fs
		(6 000)	BGM-71A TOW	ATM	1973	1974-77	(6 000)	Unconfirmed

	No.	Weapon designation	Weapon description	Year of order	Year(s) of delivery	No. delivered	Comments
	(200)	BGM-71A TOW	ATM	(1980)	1981-82	(200)	Arming 24 Model 209 Cobras
	(192)	BGM-71A TOW	ATM	1981	1985-86	(192)	
	(100)	FGM-77A Dragon	ATM	(1975)	1976	(100)	
	(310)	FGM-77A Dragon	ATM	1980	1981	(310)	
	(300)	FIM-43A Redeye	Port SAM	(1975)	1977-78	(300)	
	(532)	MIM-23B Hawk	Landmob SAM	1976	1977-78	(532)	For 12 I-Hawk SAM systems
	222	MIM-23B Hawk	Landmob SAM	(1986)	1984		Unspecified number ordered
USSR	..	BRDM-2 Gaskin	AAV(M)	1984	1983	(16)	Transferred via Iraq
	..	ZSU-23-4 Shilka	AAV	1983			Unconfirmed
	..	ZSU-23-4 Shilka	AAV	(1984)	1983	(20)	Transferred via Iraq
	..	SA-8 SAMS	Mobile SAM system	1981			Unspecified number ordered
	..	SA-8 SAMS	Mobile SAM system	1984	1983	(100)	Transferred via Iraq
	..	SA-7 Grail	Port SAM	(1981)			Unconfirmed
	..	SA-7 Grail	Port SAM	1984	1983	(320)	Transferred via Iraq
	..	SA-8 Gecko	Landmob SAM	(1981)			
	..	SA-8 Gecko	Landmob SAM	1984			
	..	SA-9 Gaskin	Landmob SAM	1984			
11 Kampuchea							
Australia	6	C-47	Transport	(1971)	1972	6	5 ex-RAAF; 1 ex-Jet Air; military aid
China	3	F-4	Fighter	(1978)	1978	3	MiG-17 copy
	16	F-6	Fighter	(1978)	1978	16	MiG-19 copy; military aid
	33	BRDM-1 Sagger	TD(M)	1978	1978	33	Military aid package; unconfirmed
	(100)	T-60	LT	(1977)	1978	100	
	(200)	Hong Jian-73	ATM	(1978)	1978	(200)	Copy of At-3 ATM; designation and number unconfirmed
USA	24	A-37B Dragonfly	Fighter/COIN	(1973)	1974	24	Promised after cessation of US bombing in Aug 1973; delivery unconfirmed
	8	AC-47	Transport	(1972)	1973	8	Military aid
	5	Bird Dog	Lightplane	(1972)	1972	5	Military aid
	(35)	Bird Dog	Lightplane	(1973)	1973	(35)	Probably transferred from S. Vietnam
	(40)	C-123 Provider	Transport	(1972)	1973-74	(40)	Previously operated in Viet Nam
	20	C-47	Transport	(1970)	1971-72	20	Military aid
	(3)	DHC-3 Otter	Transport	(1973)	1973	(3)	Probably transferred from S. Vietnam
	32	Model 185	Lightplane	(1971)	1972	32	Military aid
	14	Model 205 UH-1H	Hel	1971	1973	14	US military aid; part of COIN programme
	15	Stallion	Lightplane	(1972)	1971	15	Probably refurbished; military aid
	66	T-28D Trojan	Trainer/COIN	(1970)	1972-73	66	Military aid
	14	T-28D Trojan	Trainer/COIN	(1971)	1974	14	Delivery unconfirmed
	20	T-28D Trojan	Trainer/COIN	(1973)	1970-72	20	Military aid
	8	T-41D Mescalero	Lightplane	(1969)	1973	8	Military aid
	30	M-109-A1 155mm	SPH	(1972)	1973	30	Military aid
	(50)	M-113-A1	APC	(1972)	1973	(50)	Military aid
	(50)	M-48 Patton	MBT	(1972)	1973	(50)	Military aid

Recipient code/Recipient	Supplier	No. ordered	Weapon designation	Weapon description	Year of order	Year(s) of delivery	Total delivered	Comments
	USSR	5	LCU-501 Class	LC	1961	1962-73	5	Ex-US Navy; seller unconfirmed
		(3)	Mi-24 Hind-D	Hel	(1985)	1985	(3)	First aircraft in re-established AF
		2	Mi-8 Hip	Hel	1980	1980	2	Delivered Jun 1980
		(10)	PT-76	LT	(1983)	1983	(10)	Unconfirmed
		(10)	T-54	MBT	(1983)	1983	(10)	Unconfirmed
		1	Turya Class	Hydrofoil FAC	(1984)	1984	(1)	
4 Kenya	Canada	2	DHC-4 Caribou	Transport	(1970)	1972	2	
		6	DHC-5D Buffalo	Transport	1976	1977-78	6	
	France	18	SA-330L Puma	Hel	1977	1978-81	(18)	
		2	SA-342K Gazelle	Hel	(1982)	1983	(2)	Unconfirmed
		(7)	AML-60	AC	(1970)	1971	(7)	
		(8)	AML-90	AC	(1970)	1971	(8)	
		(12)	M-3	APC	(1979)	1979	(12)	
		2	Otomat-2 L	ShShM launcher	1984	1986	(2)	
			Milan	ATM	(1980)	1980	(100)	
	Germany, FR	(24)	Otomat-2	ShShM	1984	1986	(24)	Arming 2 Type 56M FACs on order from UK
		(8)	Do-28D-2	Transport	1978	1978	(8)	
		(50)	UR-416	APC	(1977)	1978-80	(50)	
	Israel	(4)	Gabriel L	ShShM launcher	(1981)	1981-84	(48)	Arming 4 Brooke Marine PCs
			Gabriel-2	ShShM	(1981)	1981-84	(48)	Arming 4 Brooke Marine PCs
	UK	6	BAC-167	Trainer/COIN	(1970)	1971	6	Unconfirmed
		6	BAC-167	Trainer/COIN	1977	1978	6	Unconfirmed
		(5)	Bulldog-103	Trainer	(1972)	1972	(5)	
		9	Bulldog-103	Trainer	1977	1978	9	
		12	Hawk	Jet trainer/strike	1979	1980	(12)	Mk-52
		3	Hunter FGA-9	Fighter/grd attack	1973	1974	3	
		3	Hunter T-75	Fighter	1973	1973	3	
		(8)	Ferret Swingfr	TD(M)	(1978)	1979	(8)	
		(8)	Fox FV-721	AC	1975	1976	(8)	
		70	Light Gun 105mm	TG	(1981)	1983-84	(70)	
		39	MBT Mk-3	MBT	1977	1979-80	(39)	36 MBTs and 3 ARVs
		42	MBT Mk-3	MBT	1980	1981-83	(42)	38 MBTs and 4 ARVs
		(8)	Shorland	AC	(1980)	1980	(8)	
		:	Swingfire	ATM	(1978)	1979	(1 920)	
		3	Type 32m	PC	(1974)	1975	3	Missiles fitted 1981-83
		1	Type 37.5M	FAC	(1974)	1974	1	Missiles fitted in 1981
		2	Type 56M	PC	1984	1986	(2)	Similar to Omani Province Class
	USA	10	F-5E Tiger-2	Fighter	1976	1977-78	10	

Recipient	Supplier	No. ordered	Weapon designation	Weapon description	Year of order	Year of delivery	No. delivered	Comments
		2	F-5F Tiger-2	Jet trainer	1976	1978	2	In addition to 2 in service
		2	F-5F Tiger-2	Jet trainer	1980	1982	2	
		32	Model 500MD	Hel	(1979)	1980-81	32	15 equipped with TOW ATMs, 15 gunships and 2 trainers
		8	Model 500MD	Hel	(1984)	1985	(8)	Part of $3 m aid package
		2	Navajo	Lightplane	(1971)	1973	2	
		1	Navajo	Lightplane	1980	1980	1	For VIP transport
		:	M-109 155mm	SPH	(1980)	1980	(12)	Unconfirmed
		(60)	BGM-71A TOW	ATM	1979	1981	(60)	Arming Model 500MD hel
3 Korea, North	China	(40)	BT-6	Trainer	(1977)	1978	(10)	Delivered Sep 1982
		(20)	Q-5 Fantan-A	Fighter/grd attack	(1982)	1982	(40)	Unconfirmed number and year of delivery
		(20)	T-59	MBT	(1972)	1973	(20)	Unconfirmed number and year of delivery
		(50)	T-62	LT	(1971)	1972	(20)	Unconfirmed number and year of delivery
		(100)	Type 531	APC	(1972)	1973-74	(50)	Unconfirmed number and year of delivery
		(50)	Type 54 122mm	SPH	(1977)	1978-79	(100)	Unconfirmed number and delivery year
		(100)	Type 59/1 130mm	TG	(1980)	1981	(50)	Unconfirmed number and delivery year
		(50)	Type 63 130mm	MRS	(1981)	1982-85	(100)	Unconfirmed number and delivery year
		:	Type-66 SPH 152	SPH	(1972)	1973	(50)	Unconfirmed number and year of delivery
		(6)	Crow Slot	Early warning radar	(1973)	1974-75	(20)	Unconfirmed
		7	Hainan Class	PC	(1974-75)	1975-78	6	Followed by licensed production of 8
		(23)	Romeo Class	Submarine	(1973)	1973-75	7	Total number unconfirmed
		(40)	Shanghai Class	PC	(1967)	1967-78	(23)	
	USA	(40)	Model 300	Hel	(1984)	1984	(40)	85 Hughes Model 300/500 helicopters supplied illegally
	USSR	(45)	Model 500E	Hel	(1984)	1984	(45)	Number and delivery period uncertain
		(90)	An-2	Transport	(1966)	1967-74	(90)	
		65	MiG-21F	Fighter	(1967)	1968-71	65	In addition to 130 in service
		(24)	MiG-21MF	Fighter	(1973)	1974	(24)	
		(50)	MiG-23	Fighter/interceptor	(1984)	1985	(16)	
		28	Su-7 Fitter	Fighter	(1969)	1971	28	In response to S. Korean F-4 Phantoms
		(800)	BM-21 122mm	MRS	(1965)	1966-80	(800)	
		(50)	BMP-1	MICV	(1972)	1973	(50)	Unconfirmed number and year of delivery
		(250)	BTR-152	APC	(1965)	1965-71	(250)	
		250	BTR-40	APC	(1965)	1965-71	(250)	
		(50)	T-55	MBT	(1970)	1972-73	(50)	
		(20)	T-62	MBT	(1970)	1971	(20)	
		(100)	ZSU-23-4 Shilka	AAV	(1970)	1971	(100)	
		:	FROG L	Mobile SSM system	(1970)	1971-74	(19)	Unconfirmed number and year of delivery
		(50)	SA-2 SAMS	Mobile SAM system	(1971)	1984-85	(50)	Unconfirmed number and year of delivery
		(30)	SA-3 SAMS	Mobile SAM system	(1984)	1984-85	(30)	For Frog-5s and Frog-7s
		(14)	SSN-2 Styx L	ShShM launcher	(1970)	1970-73	(14)	To counter S. Korean purchase of F-16s
		(15)	SSN-2 Styx L	ShShM launcher	(1979)	1980-84	(15)	On Osa and Komar Class FACs

Recipient code/ Recipient	Supplier	No. ordered	Weapon designation	Weapon description	Year of order	Year(s) of delivery	Total delivered	Comments
		(2)	Scud-B L	Mobile SSM system	(1984)	1985	(2)	Unconfirmed
		(390)	AA-2 Atoll	AAM	(1967)	1968-71	(390)	Arming MIG-21 fighters
		(144)	AA-2 Atoll	AAM	(1973)	1974	(144)	Arming MIG-21 fighters
		(200)	AA-2 Atoll	AAM	(1983)	1985	(128)	Reportedly arming MiG-23s
		(40)	FROG-5	Landmob SSM	(1969)	1971	(40)	
		(20)	FROG-7	Landmob SSM	(1971)	1972-73	(20)	
		60	FROG-7	Landmob SSM	(1973)	1974	60	
		(450)	SA-2 Guideline	Landmob SAM	(1984)	1984-85	(450)	To counter S. Korean purchase of F-16s
		(180)	SA-3 Goa	Landmob SAM	(1984)	1985	(180)	Reportedly some 30 launchers deployed around Pyongyang; unconfirmed
		(200)	SA-7 Grail	Port SAM	(1971)	1972-73	(200)	Unconfirmed
		(12)	SCUD-B	Landmob SSM	(1984)	1985	(12)	To arm Osa and Komar class FACs
		(44)	SSN-2 Styx	ShShM	(1969)	1970-73	(44)	For Sohung/Soju Class FACs and 1 Najin Najin Class frigate
		(50)	SSN-2 Styx	ShShM	(1979)	1980-84	(50)	
		(3)	Samlet	GLCM	(1970)	1971	(3)	Unconfirmed
		6	Komar Class	FAC	(1970)	1970-72	(6)	Armed with Styx ShShMs
		(8)	Osa-1 Class	FAC	(1970)	1970-73	(8)	Armed with Styx ShShMs
		4	Shershen Class	FAC	(1973)	1973-74	4	Torpedo-armed
15 Korea, South	Brazil	(30)	T-37C	Jet trainer	(1983)	1983	(30)	From surplus
	France	(2)	MM-38 L	ShShM launcher	(1973)	1974	(2)	For 2 Wildcat Class FACs
		(12)	MM-38 L	ShShM launcher	1977	1978	(12)	Unspecified number reportedly procured
		(12)	MM-38 Exocet	ShShM	(1973)	1974	(12)	Arming 2 Wildcat Class FACs
		(50)	MM-38 Exocet	ShShM	(1977)	1978	(50)	Unspecified number reportedly procured
	Germany, FR	2	Type 209/3	Submarine	(1986)			Negotiating
	Indonesia	10	CN-235	Transport	1986			For delivery from 1988
	UK	2	HS-748M	Transport	1976	1977	2	For VIP transport
	USA	27	A-37B Dragonfly	Fighter/COIN	1976	1976	27	
		1	B-707-320C	Transport	(1985)	1985	1	For VIP use
		(10)	C-123 Provider	Transport	(1976)	1977	(10)	Unspecified number delivered in 1977
		6	C-123 Provider	Transport	(1979)	1980	6	
		6	C-130H Hercules	Transport	1977	1979	6	
		11	C-54 Skymaster	Transport	(1976)	1977	(11)	Delivery year uncertain
		(2)	CH-47C Chinook	Hel	(1985)	1985	(2)	Unconfirmed
		30	F-16C	Fighter/strike	1981	1986	(8)	Total cost incl 6 F-16Ds: $931 m
		6	F-16D	Fighter/trainer	1981	1986	(2)	
		18	F-4D Phantom	Fighter/interceptor	(1971)	1972	18	Leased in return for F-5s 1972-75
		6	F-4D Phantom	Fighter/interceptor	1982	1982	6	Compensation for attrition losses

No.	Designation	Type	Order year	Delivery year	No. delivered	Comments
37	F-4E Phantom	Fighter	1977	1977-79	37	US surplus; replacing losses
4	F-4E Phantom	Fighter	1985	1985	4	
72	F-5E Tiger-2	Fighter	1972	1972	72	Cost of 54 F-5Es and 6 F-5Fs: $205 m
54	F-5E Tiger-2	Fighter	1975	1974-77	(54)	
6	F-5F Tiger-2	Jet trainer	1975	1978-81	6	
14	F-5F Tiger-2	Jet trainer	1978	1977	14	Bringing total to 20
67	Model 205 UH-1H	Hel	(1978)	1979	67	
20	Model 205 UH-1H	Hel	1984	1980	20	For Army
2	Model 206B	Hel	(1984)	1985	2	For Navy
(8)	Model 209 AH-1J	Hel	(1976)	1984	(8)	For Army
21	Model 209 AH-1S	Hel	(1985)	1977	21	US LoQ; total cost incl spares and training: $178 m; armed with TOW ATMs
2	Model 212 UH-1N	Hel	(1970)	1972	2	
14	Model 321	Lightplane	(1974)	1975	14	Birddog O-2
3	Model 412	Hel	(1984)	1984	3	
34	Model 500MD	Hel	1976	1977-78	34	Delivered prior to licensed production
20	Model 500MD	Hel	1983	1977		Could be for local production
24	OV-10F Bronco	Trainer/COIN	1976	1985	24	Purchased via USN; total cost incl 733 Sidewinder AAMs: $58.2 m
24	OV-10F Bronco	Trainer/COIN	(1985)	1971	(7)	In addition to 24 in service
1	PL-2	Lightplane	(1969)	1980	1	
16	S-2E Tracker	Fighter/ASW	(1979)	1963-73	16	For Navy
17	S-55 Chickasaw	Hel	(1962)	1971-77	17	
7	T-33A	Jet trainer	(1970)	1972	7	
20	T-41D Mescalero	Lightplane	(1971)	1984	20	
42	LVTP-7A1	Amph ASSV	1982	1971	(42)	
(50)	M-107 175mm	SPG	(1970)	1980-81	(50)	
37	M-109-A2 155mm	SPH	1978	1971	(37)	Ordered Aug 1978
(50)	M-110 203mm	SPH	(1970)	1971	(50)	
(100)	M-113-A1	APC	(1970)	1966-71	(100)	
(300)	M-115 203mm	TH	(1965)	1970-71	(300)	
(250)	M-48-A2	MBT	(1970)	1981	(250)	
(50)	M-48-A5	MBT	1980	1973-75	(50)	
(250)	M-577-A1	CPC	(1972)	1972	(250)	
(70)	M-60	MBT	(1971)	1978	(70)	
15	M-88	ARV	1977	1984	15	
21	M-88-A1	ARV	1981	1985-86	(21)	
12	AN/TPQ-36	Tracking radar	(1985)	1971	(12)	
(2)	Honest John	Mobile SSM system	(1970)	1978	(2)	
(3)	Honest John	Mobile SSM system	1977	1978	(3)	Unconfirmed number and delivery year
(1)	I-Hawk SAMS	Mobile SAM system	1977	1980	(1)	
(5)	I-Hawk SAMS	Mobile SAM system	(1978)	1978	(5)	Unconfirmed number and delivery year
(70)	M-167 Vulcan	Mobile AA-system	(1976)		(70)	Unconfirmed number and delivery year

Recipient code/ Recipient	Supplier	No. ordered	Weapon designation	Weapon description	Year of order	Year(s) of delivery	Total delivered	Comments
		(15)	Nike Hercules L	Mobile SAM system	1976	1977	(15)	
		(4)	RGM-84A L	ShShM launcher	(1974)	1977-78	(4)	Arming 4 indigenous PSMM-5s
		(1)	RGM-84A L	ShShM launcher	(1976)	1977	(1)	For one PSMM-5 Class FAC received 1975
		1	RGM-84A L	ShShM launcher	(1980)	1980	(1)	Arming 1 Ulsan Class frigate
		(8)	RGM-84A L	ShShM launcher	(1981)	1983	(8)	Arming 2 Gearing Class destroyers
		(3)	RGM-84A L	ShShM launcher	(1985)	1985	(1)	Arming 3 Ulsan Class frigates
		(4)	RIM-66A L	ShAM launcher	(1974)	1975	(4)	
		(200)	AGM-65A	ASM	1977	1980-83	(200)	Probably for F-5E fighters
		341	AIM-7E Sparrow	AAM	1978	1979	341	For F4E Phantom fighters to be delivered from 1979
		733	AIM-9J	AAM	1972	1974-77	733	For 72 F-5E delivered 1974-77
		600	AIM-9L	AAM	1975	1978-81	(600)	Arming F-5E aircraft
		(680)	AIM-9L	AAM	(1979)	1982-86	(680)	For licence-produced F-5E/F fighters; unconfirmed
		1 800	BGM-71A TOW	ATM	1979	1980-82	(1 800)	For ground units and Model-500MD hels
		(504)	BGM-71C I-TOW	ATM	(1985)			To arm 21 Model 209 Cobra helicopters
		(732)	FIM-92A Stinger	Port SAM	1986			Total cost incl 133 launch units: $57 m
		(9)	Honest John	Landmob SSM	(1970)	1971	(9)	
		(18)	Honest John	Landmob SSM	1977	1978	(18)	Sale approved by US Gov in Apr 1977
		48	MIM-23B Hawk	Landmob SAM	1977	1978	48	
		265	MIM-23B Hawk	Landmob SAM	(1978)	1980	265	Total cost incl 723 rocket motors: $68 m
		170	MIM-23B Hawk	Landmob SAM	1982	1984-85	(170)	
		(298)	MIM-23B Hawk	Landmob SAM	(1983)			Unconfirmed
		45	Nike Hercules	Landmob SAM	1976	1977	45	One battalion taken over from US Army
		(48)	RGM-84A Harpoon	ShShM	(1974)	1977-78	(48)	Arming 4 indigenous PSMM-5 FACs
		(12)	RGM-84A Harpoon	ShShM	(1976)	1977	(12)	For one PSMM-5 Class FAC received 1975
		(24)	RGM-84A Harpoon	ShShM	(1980)	1980	(24)	Arming 1 indigenous Ulsan Class frigate
		(48)	RGM-84A Harpoon	ShShM	(1981)	1983	(48)	For 2 Gearing Class destroyers
		(72)	RGM-84A Harpoon	ShShM	(1985)	1985	(24)	Arming 3 indigenous Ulsan Class frigates
		(32)	RIM-66C/SM-2	ShAM/ShShM	(1974)	1975	(32)	On 3 PSMM-5 Class FACs received from USA and for one Asheville Class PC received in 1971
		1	Asheville Class	PC	(1971)	1972	1	Standard ShShMs fitted in 1975-76
		8	Bluebird Class	MSC	(1957)	1959-75	8	Built especially for transfer under MAP
		1	CPIC Type	PC/FAC	(1972)	1975	1	Followed by licensed production; local designation: Kilurki (Sea Dolphin) Class
		2	Diver Class	Support ship	(1977)	1978-79	2	
		1	FS-330 Type	Support ship	(1970)	1971	1	
		2	Gearing Class	Destroyer	(1970)	1972	2	Ex US Navy; loaned 1972; purchased 1977

Country	No.	Item	Type	Order	Delivery	In service	Comment
	3	Gearing Class	Destroyer	1975	1977-78	3	In addition to 2 in service
	2	Gearing Class	Destroyer	(1979)	1981	2	In addition to 5 in service
	4	PSMM-5 Type	FAC	(1974)	1975	4	Followed by licensed production; 3 with Standard ShAMs and 1 with Harpoon ShShMs
	2	Sumner Class	Destroyer	(1971)	1973	2	Ex US-Navy
	1	Tonti Class	Tanker	(1981)	1982	1	Ex US Navy
	1	YO Type	Support ship	(1970)	1971	1	Ex US Navy
15 Kuwait							
Argentina	20	IA-58A Pucara	COIN	(1985)		2	Total cost: $120 m; option on 40 more
France	6	AS-332	Hel	1983			Cost incl AM-39 Exocet AShMs: $95 m
	2	Mirage F-1B	Jet trainer	1973	1976	(1)	Attrition aircraft
	1	Mirage F-1B	Jet trainer	(1984)	1985	18	
	18	Mirage F-1C	Fighter/interceptor	1974	1976-77	(13)	
	(13)	Mirage F-1C	Fighter/interceptor	1983	1984-85		Ordered Mar 1983; armed with Super-530 AAMs; total cost: $400 m
	(12)	SA-330 Puma	Hel	1974	1975-76	(12)	
	24	SA-342K Gazelle	Hel	1974	1975-77	(24)	
	(3)	SA-342K Gazelle	Hel	(1976)	1977	(3)	
	(3)	SA-342L Gazelle	Hel	(1981)	1983	(3)	
	34	AMX-13-90	LT	(1983)	1983	34	Incl other AMX-13 versions; unconfirmed
	(10)	AMX-155 Mk-F3	SPH	(1974)	1975	(10)	
	10	AMX-155 Mk-F3	SPH	1982	1983	10	
	(8)	MM-40 L	ShShM launcher	1980	1983-85	(8)	
	12	AM-39 Exocet	AShM	1983			
	..	ARMAT	ARM	1983			To arm 6 AS-332 Super Pumas
	(504)	HOT	ATM	1974	1975-77	(504)	To arm 6 AS-332 Super Pumas
	(500)	Harpon	ATM	(1974)	1975	(500)	Arming Gazelle and Puma helicopters
	(96)	MM-40 Exocet	ShShM/SShM	1980	1983-85	(96)	Total cost including SS-11
	(120)	R-530	AAM	1974	1976-77	(120)	Arming 6 TNC-45 and 2 Type 57 FACs
	(120)	R-550 Magic	AAM	1974	1976-77	(120)	Arming Mirage F-1s
	(1 200)	SS-11	ATM	(1974)	1975	(1 200)	Arming Mirage F-1s
	(78)	Super-530	AAM	1983	1986-87	(78)	Arming 13 Mirage F-1Cs
Germany, FR	2	PB-57 Type	PC	1980	1983-84	2	
	6	TNC-45	FAC	1980	1984-85	(6)	Armed with MM-40 Exocet ShShMs
Singapore	3	Type 27M	LC	1970	1971-75	3	
	3	Type 32M	LC	1978	1979	3	Ordered in addition to 3 in service
UK	6	BAC-167	Trainer/COIN	(1970)	1971	6	
	12	Hawk	Jet trainer/strike	1983	1985-86	(12)	Mk-64 trainer/ground attack version; total cost: $105 m
	(30)	AT-105 Saxon	APC	(1980)	1982	(30)	Unconfirmed
	160	Chieftain-5	MBT	1977	1978-79	(160)	
	(100)	Chieftain-5	MBT	(1986)			Negotiating
	(100)	FV-101 Scorpion	LT	(1983)	1984	(100)	Unconfirmed whether in service

Recipient code/ Recipient	Supplier	No. ordered	Weapon designation	Weapon description	Year of order	Year(s) of delivery	Total delivered	Comments
	USA	70	MBT Mk-1	MBT	(1969)	1970-72	(70)	
		(10)	Sultan FV-105	CPC	(1983)	1984	(10)	Unconfirmed
		4	Loadmaster Type	LC	1982	1985	4	
		30	A-4M Skyhawk-2	Fighter/bomber	1974	1977-78	30	
		2	DC-9	Transport	1975	1976	2	
		2	L-100-20	Transport	(1970)	1971	2	
		4	L-100-30	Transport	1981	1983	(4)	
		6	TA-4K Skyhawk	Jet trainer	1974	1977-78	6	
		(100)	M-113	APC	(1973)	1974-75	(100)	
		(188)	M-113-A2	APC	1982	1984-85	(100)	
		56	M-901 TOW	TD(M)	1982	1984-85	(56)	
		20	V-150 Commando	APC	1984	1985	(20)	Cost incl 62 V-300 Commandos: $40 m
		62	V-300 Commando	APC	1984	1985-86	(62)	
		..	AN/TPS-32	3-D radar	(1978)	1978-79	(6)	
		(8)	I-Hawk SAMS	Mobile SAM system	1974	1977-78	(8)	
		300	AIM-9H	AAM	1975	1977-78	300	Arming Skyhawk fighters
		(3 150)	BGM-71A TOW	ATM	1973	1974-76	(3 150)	
		4 840	BGM-71C I-TOW	ATM	1982	1984-85	(2 000)	Cost incl M-901s and M-113s: $97 m
		(240)	MIM-23B Hawk	Landmob SAM	1974	1977-78	(240)	
	USSR	..	FROG L	Mobile SSM system	1978	1979-80	(5)	
		..	SA-6 SAMS	Mobile SAM system	1978	1979-80	10	Deliveries unconfirmed
		..	SA-8 SAMS	Mobile SAM system	(1984)	1984-85	(8)	Displayed Feb 1980; also designated Luna
		..	FROG-7	Landmob SSM	(1978)	1979-80	(100)	
		..	FROG-7	Landmob SSM	(1984)			Unconfirmed
		..	SA-6 Gainful	Landmob SAM	1978	1979-80	(90)	Total cost incl SA-7s: $100 m
		..	SA-7 Grail	Port SAM	1979	1979-80	(500)	
		..	SA-7 Grail	Port SAM	1984	1984-85	(200)	
		(96)	SA-8 Gecko	Landmob SAM	(1984)	1984-85	(96)	Deliveries unconfirmed
11 Laos	Australia	3	C-47	Transport	(1970)	1971	3	
	USA	(5)	C-47	Transport	(1971)	1972-73	(5)	Transferred from S. Vietnam
		7	Model 172	Trainer	(1971)	1972-73	(7)	
		24	S-58	Hel	(1971)	1972-73	(24)	
		14	Stallion	Lightplane	(1972)	1973	14	
		(20)	M-113-A1	APC	(1969)	1970-71	(20)	Transferred from S. Vietnam
	USSR	(6)	An-2	Transport	(1976)	1976	(6)	
		6	An-24 Coke	Transport	1976	1976-77	6	
		3	An-26 Curl	Lightplane	1978	1978	3	

	No.	Designation	Type	(Order)	Delivery	No. del.	Comments
	10	C-123 Provider	Transport	(1973)	1973-74	(10)	Delivery year uncertain
	6	Mi-8 Hip	Hel	1976	1976-77	6	Unspecified number reportedly delivered in 1976-77
	10	MiG-21F	Fighter	1976	1977	10	
	4	MiG-21F	Fighter	(1981)	1981	4	Gift
	(20)	MiG-21F	Fighter	(1982)	1983	(20)	
	(12)	MiG-21F	Fighter	(1985)	1985	(12)	In addition to some 20 delivered 1983
	2	MiG-21UTI	Jet trainer	1976	1977	2	
	2	Yak-40 Coding	Transport	1976	1977	2	
	(35)	BTR-60P	APC	(1980)	1981-82	(35)	Unconfirmed; some sources report BTR-152
	(10)	D-30 122mm	TH	(1982)	1983	(10)	Unconfirmed
	(10)	M-46 130mm	TG	(1984)	1985	(10)	Unconfirmed
	(15)	T-54	MBT	(1973)	1975	(15)	Unconfirmed; Could be PT-76 tanks
	15	T-55	MBT	(1973)	1975	(15)	Unconfirmed; could be PT-76 tanks
	(3)	ZSU-57-2	AAV	(1983)	1984	(3)	Unconfirmed
	:	SA-2 SAMS	Mobile SAM system	(1983)	1984	(3)	Unconfirmed
	:	SA-3 SAMS	Mobile SAM system	(1983)	1984	(3)	Unconfirmed
	(60)	AA-2 Atoll	AAM	1976	1977	(60)	Arming MiG-21 fighters
	:	SA-2 Guideline	Landmob SAM	(1983)	1984	(27)	Unconfirmed
	:	SA-3 Goa	Landmob SAM	(1983)	1984	(18)	Unconfirmed
	:	SA-7 Grail	Port SAM	(1983)	1984	(20)	Unconfirmed
4 Lebanon France	7	Alouette-3	Hel	1972	1973-74	7	
	6	SA-330L Puma	Hel	1978	1980-82	(6)	
	(6)	SA-330L Puma	Hel	1982	1984	(6)	Part of $75 m military aid package
	10	SA-342K Gazelle	Hel	1982	1984	(10)	Possibly armed with HOT ATMs
	6	SA-342L Gazelle	Hel	1979	1980	6	
	4	Super Magister	Jet trainer	(1972)	1973	4	Ex-West German Luftwaffe
	22	AMX-13	LT	(1970)	1972	22	
	13	AMX-13	LT	(1981)	1982	13	
	30	M-3	APC	(1971)	1973	30	
	5	VAB	APC	1982	1983	5	
	(85)	VAB	APC	1983	1983-84	(85)	
	(200)	Milan	ATM	1978	1979	(200)	
	(100)	SS-11	ATM	(1975)	1975	(100)	
	(96)	SS-11	ATM	1979	1980	(96)	Arming SA-342 Gazelle helicopters
	(96)	SS-12	ShShM	1979	1980	(96)	Arming SA-342 Gazelle helicopters
	(60)	SS-12	ShShM	1982	1984	(60)	Arming some of Gazelle helicopters delivered 1984
Italy	2	EDIC/EDA	LC	(1982)	1985	2	
	6	AB-212	Hel	(1972)	1973-74	6	
	6	AB-212	Hel	1979	1980	6	
Jordan	(40)	M-48 Patton	MBT	(1982)	1983	(40)	Deal may cover up to 100 MBTs

Recipient code/Recipient	Supplier	No. ordered	Weapon designation	Weapon description	Year of order	Year(s) of delivery	Total delivered	Comments
	Syria	18	D-74 122mm	TG	(1985)	1985	(18)	For Amal militia; unconfirmed
		(10)	M-1938 122mm	TG	(1982)	1982	(10)	Unconfirmed
		(10)	M-46 130mm	TG	(1982)	1982	(10)	Unconfirmed
		(50)	T-54	MBT	(1985)	1985	(50)	For Amal militia
	UK	6	Bulldog-125	Trainer	1975	1975	6	
		6	Hunter FGA-74	Fighter	1975	1975-77	6	
		(100)	Saladin FV-601	AC	(1978)	1979-80	(100)	
		(100)	Saracen FV-603	APC	(1978)	1979-80	(100)	
	USA	18	M-101-A1 105mm	TH	(1979)	1982	18	Designation unconfirmed
		(50)	M-113	APC	(1970)	1971-72	(50)	Cost: $3 m
		26	M-113-A2	APC	1979	1982	26	
		102	M-113-A2	APC	1983	1984	(102)	
		(24)	M-114 155mm	TH	(1982)	1983	(24)	Unconfirmed
		93	M-125-A2	APC	1983	1983	(93)	
		12	M-198 155mm	TH	1982	1982-83	(12)	
		34	M-48-A5	MBT	(1982)	1983	34	In storage
		68	M-48-A5	MBT	1983	1984	(68)	In storage
		35	M-48-A5	MBT	1984	1984	(35)	All 137 M-48s in storage
		25	M-577-A2	CPC	1983	1984	(25)	
		13	M-578	ARV	1979	1982	13	
		35	M-60-A3	MBT	(1984)			US LoO 1984
		2	AN/TPQ-36	Tracking radar	(1983)	1983	(2)	Left behind by US Marines
		(1 000)	BGM-71A TOW	ATM	1974	1975-76	(1 000)	Delivered Aug 1980 with 3000 M-16 rifles
		100	BGM-71A TOW	ATM	(1979)	1980	100	
	USSR	(15)	BTR-60P	APC	(1970)	1972	(15)	Designation unconfirmed
4 Lesotho	Germany, FR	1	Bo-105L	Hel	(1980)	1980	1	Unconfirmed
	Italy	1	Do-27	Transport	1980	1980	1	Unconfirmed
		1	Do-28B-1	Lightplane	1980	1980	1	
		2	AB-412 Griffon	Hel	(1982)	1984	(2)	Delivery blocked by South Africa since May 1984; unconfirmed whether final destination yet reached
	Poland	1	Mi-2 Taurus-2	Hel	(1983)	1984	1	Seller unconfirmed
	UK	2	Skyvan-3M	Transport	1978	1979	2	
9 Liberia	India	..	HJT-16 Kiran-2	Jet trainer	(1986)			Negotiating sale of small number
		6	SA-316B Chetak	Hel	(1986)			Negotiating
	Israel	3	IAI-201 Arava	Transport	1983	1984	(3)	
		3	IAI-201 Arava	Transport	(1984)	1985	(3)	In addition to 3 delivered 1984

	No.	Weapon designation	Weapon description	Year of order	Year of delivery	No. delivered	Comments
USA	2	C-47	Transport	1975	1976	2	
	2	Model 172	Trainer	(1975)	1976	2	
	1	Model 185	Lightplane	1975	1976	1	
	1	Model 207	Lightplane	(1975)	1976	1	
	(10)	Model 337	Trainer	1977	1978	(10)	
	(8)	M-101-A1 105mm	TH	(1972)	1972	(8)	
	(10)	M-3	APC	(1981)	1981	(10)	Unconfirmed
Austria	(20)	GHN-45 155mm	TH/TG	(1985)	1985	(20)	Unconfirmed
Brazil	(8)	EMB-111	Mar patrol	(1986)			Negotiating
	25	EMB-121 Xingu	Transport	(1986)			Negotiating
	(100)	EMB-312 Tucano	Trainer	(1986)			Negotiating for 100-150 aircraft
	(30)	Astros-II SS-40	MRS	1978	1979-81	(750)	
	(700)	EE-11 Urutu	APC	(1986)			Negotiating
	..	EE-11 Urutu	APC	1973	1976-78	(700)	
	(700)	EE-9 Cascavel	AC	(1986)			Negotiating
	..	EE-9 Cascavel	AC	(1986)			Negotiating
	..	EE-T1 Osorio	MBT	(1986)			Negotiating
Czechoslovakia	30	L-39Z Albatross	Jet trainer	1978	1979-80	(30)	
	12	Let L-410	Transport	(1983)	1984	12	
	6	Let L-410	Transport	1985			Ordered Jun 1985
	(30)	Dana 152mm	SPH	(1981)	1983-84	(30)	
	(36)	M-51 130mm	MRS	(1975)	1976-77	(36)	
	..	M-53/59	AAV	(1979)	1980	(50)	
	..	OT-62	APC	(1978)	1978	(50)	
	30	OT-64	APC	(1977)	1978	30	
	(36)	RM-70 122mm	MRS	(1979)	1981-82	(36)	
France	4	MS-880 Rallye	Lightplane	(1977)	1977	4	Delivered via Malta
	38	Mirage F-1C	Fighter/interceptor	1975	1978-79	(38)	
	10	Mirage-3B	Jet trainer	(1971)	1971-74	(10)	Some loaned to Egypt in 1973
	32	Mirage-3E	Fighter/bomber	(1971)	1971-74	(32)	Some loaned to Egypt in 1973
	(10)	Mirage-3R	Recce	(1971)	1971-74	(10)	Some loaned to Egypt in 1973
	58	Mirage-5	Fighter	(1970)	1971-74	(58)	Some loaned to Egypt in 1973
	1	Mystere-20	Transport	(1970)	1971	1	
	4	SA-316B	Hel	(1970)	1971-72	(4)	
	40	SA-342K Gazelle	Hel	(1978)	1981-82	(40)	
	9	Super Frelon	Hel	(1970)	1972	9	
	20	Super Magister	Jet trainer	(1970)	1971	20	
	24	Crotale SAMS	Mobile SAM system	(1970)	1974-80	(24)	
	(216)	Milan	ATM	(1979)	1979	(100)	
	..	R-440 Crotale	Landmob SAM	1972	1974-80	(216)	Unconfirmed
	..	R-530	AAM	(1975)	1979	(76)	Arming Mirages; status of deal uncertain
	..	R-550 Magic	AAM	1972	1975		To arm Mirage

7 Libya

Recipient code/ Recipient	Supplier	No. ordered	Weapon designation	Weapon description	Year of order	Year(s) of delivery	Total delivered	Comments
		232	R-550 Magic	AAM	1975	1977-78	232	Arming Mirage F-1s
		(100)	SS-11	ATM	1974	1975	(100)	Reserve missiles
		(48)	SS-12	ShShM	1974	1975	(48)	
		10	Combattante-2G	FAC	1977	1982-84	10	Delivery of last FAC suspended until Jan 1984 due to Libyan intervention in Chad
	Greece	2	PS-700 Class	LS	(1975)	1977-78	2	Libyan designation: Ibn Ouf Class
	Italy	:	Steyr-4K 7FA	APC	(1986)			Negotiating
		1	AB-212	Hel	1978	1980	1	Ordered Dec 1978
		1	AB-212	Hel	(1980)	1981	1	In addition to 1 delivered 1980
		3	AB-47G	Hel	(1970)	1971	(3)	
		20	CH-47C Chinook	Hel	(1974)	1975-77	(20)	
		24	CH-47C Chinook	Hel	(1975)	1976-77	(24)	
		20	G-222L	Transport	(1979)	1981-84	(20)	
		1	S-61A-4	Hel	1976	1977	1	For VIP use
		80	SF-260 Warrior	Trainer/COIN	1977	1978-79	110	Bringing total on order to some 300
		(60)	SF-260 Warrior	Trainer/COIN	1981	1982-83	(60)	
		200	Lion	MBT	1978	1980-82	(200)	Ex-Italian
		170	M-113	APC	(1972)	1972-73	(170)	
		210	Palmaria 155mm	SPH	1981	1982-85	(210)	
		(60)	Type 6616	AC	1979	1981	(60)	On order; status of deal uncertain
		(1)	Aspide/Albatros	ShAM/ShShM launcher	(1982)	1983	(1)	
		56	Otomat-1 L	ShShM launcher	1977	1979-83	56	
		4	Otomat-2 L	ShShM launcher	(1982)	1984	(4)	
		:	Otomat-2 L	ShShM launcher	(1985)			
		(32)	Aspide	AAM/SAM/ShAM	(1982)	1983	(32)	Arming frigate 'Dat Assawari'
		168	Otomat-1	ShShM	1977	1979-83	(168)	Arming 10 Combattante-2G Class FACs and 4 Wadi Class corvettes
		(12)	Otomat-2	ShShM	(1982)	1984	(12)	Arming frigate 'Dat Assawari' after retrofit in Italy
		:	Otomat-2	ShShM	(1985)			To arm 4 new Wadi Class corvettes
		4	Wadi Class	Corvette	1974	1979-81	4	Renamed Assad Class
		4	Wadi Class	Corvette	(1985)			
	Portugal	:	Chaimite	APC	(1978)	1978	(50)	
	Spain	4	S-70 Class	Submarine	(1986)			Spanish offer renewed
	Turkey	20	C-107 Class	LC	(1979)	1979-81	(20)	Unconfirmed orders for up to 30 more
		14	SAR-33	PC	1980	1982-83	(14)	West German design; for customs service
	UK	40	Ferret FV-712	Recce AC	(1977)	1978	40	
		10	Saracen FV-603	APC	(1977)	1978	10	
		(2)	Seacat L	ShAM launcher	(1972)	1973	(2)	On 'Dat Assawari'

USA						
(18)	Seacat	ShAM/ShShM	(1972)	1973	(18)	2 triple launchers on 'Dat Assawari'
1	SAAM Class	Frigate	1968	1973	1	Called Dat Assawari; retrofitted 1980-83
8	C-130H Hercules	Transport	1973	1976-77	(8)	Embargoed since 1974
2	C-130H Hercules	Transport	(1980)	1981	2	Via circuitous routes
1	Jetstar-2	Transport	1978	1978	1	Via private dealer
:	King Air A-100	Transport	(1974)	1975	1	
1	Model 421C	Trainer	1978	1978	1	Via private dealer
1	S-61A Sea King	Hel	(1976)	1977	1	For VIP use
:	M-46 130mm	TG	(1972)	1972-74	(275)	
USSR						
(3)	An-26 Curl	Lightplane	(1983)	1983-84	3	Unconfirmed
(15)	An-26 Curl	Lightplane	(1985)	1985	(15)	Replacing aircraft destroyed during US Apr attack
3	Il-76 Candid	Transport	1986	1986	3	
(12)	Mi-14 Haze	Hel	(1982)	1982-83	(12)	For ASW; number unconfirmed; first deliveries outside WTO
26	Mi-24 Hind-D	Hel	(1978)	1978-80	(26)	Libya first non-WTO customer
12	Mi-8 Hip	Hel	1975	1976	12	
(25)	MiG-23	Fighter/interceptor	1976	1976-78	(25)	
:	MiG-23	Fighter/interceptor	(1978)	1979-82	(100)	
29	MiG-23BN	Fighter/grd attack	(1974)	1975	29	Incl 5 trainer
15	MiG-23U	Jet trainer	1976	1976-78	(15)	
:	MiG-25	Fighter/interceptor	1977	1979-82	(60)	
(6)	MiG-25R	Recce	1978	1978	(6)	
:	MiG-25U	Jet trainer	1977	1979	(5)	
(35)	Su-22 Fitter-J	Fighter/grd attack	(1974)	1975	(35)	
12	Tu-22 Blinder-A	Bomber	1975	1979	12	Unconfirmed
(24)	Tu-22 Blinder-A	Bomber	1970	1972	24	
(15)	BMP-1	MICV	1977	1978	(15)	
(60)	BRDM-1	SC	1977	1978	(60)	
:	BRDM-1 Swatter	TD(M)	(1984)	1984	(10)	
:	BRDM-2 Gaskin	AAV(M)	(1979)	1979	(10)	
:	BTR-50P	APC	1977	1978	(60)	
(100)	BTR-60P	APC	1974	1975	(100)	Unconfirmed
(60)	BTR-60P	APC	(1977)	1978	(60)	
:	D-20 152mm	TH	(1980)	1981	(100)	
:	D-30 122mm	TH	(1979)	1980-82	(30)	
:	D-30 122mm	TH	(1980)	1980-82	(90)	
:	JSU-122	SPG	(1979)	1979	(100)	
:	JSU-152	SPG	(1980)	1980	(100)	
:	M-1973 152mm	SPG	(1979)	1980-82	(30)	
:	M-1973 152mm	SPG	(1981)	1981	(20)	
:	M-1973 152mm	SPG	(1982)	1982	(100)	
:	M-1974 122mm	SPH	(1979)	1980-82	(30)	

Recipient code/ Recipient	Supplier	No. ordered	Weapon designation	Weapon description	Year of order	Year(s) of delivery	Total delivered	Comments
		..	M-1974 122mm	SPH	(1981)	1981	(100)	
		..	S-23 180mm	TG	(1982)	1983	(100)	
		(4)	SA-13 TELAR	AAV(M)	(1984)	1984-85	(4)	
		100	T-54	MBT	(1970)	1970-71	(100)	
		100	T-55	MBT	(1970)	1970-71	(100)	
		(300)	T-55	MBT	1974	1975	(300)	Unconfirmed
		(2 000)	T-55	MBT	1976	1977-78	2 000	
		(300)	T-62	MBT	1974	1975	(300)	Received Sep 1975; acc to US sources
		(1 500)	T-62	MBT	(1975)	1976	(1 500)	Unconfirmed
		(400)	T-62	MBT	1976	1976-78	400	
		250	T-62	MBT	1978	1978	250	
		(500)	T-64	MBT	(1975)	1976	(500)	Unconfirmed
		(200)	T-64	MBT	1976	1976-77	(200)	
		(30)	T-72	MBT	(1978)	1979	(30)	Unknown number received
		(60)	ZSU-23-4 Shilka	AAV	(1977)	1978	(60)	
			FROG L	Mobile SSM system	(1978)	1979-82	(16)	
		(20)	SA-2 SAMS	Mobile SAM system	1974	1975	(20)	
		(45)	SA-3 SAMS	Mobile SAM system	(1974)	1974-76	(45)	
		(12)	SA-5 SAMS	Mobile SAM system	(1985)	1985	(12)	
		..	SA-6 SAMS	Mobile SAM system	1974	1975-78	(35)	
		..	SA-8 SAMS	Mobile SAM system	(1980)	1981-82	(20)	
		4	SA-N-4 L	ShAM launcher	1980	1981-85	4	Arming Nanuchka Class corvettes
		(12)	SS-12 L	Mobile SSM system	(1980)	1980-81	(12)	
		12	SSN-2 Styx L	ShShM launcher	1975	1976-80	12	
		4	SSN-2 Styx L	ShShM launcher	1980	1981-85	4	Arming Nanuchka Class corvettes
			SSN-2 Styx L	ShShM launcher	(1982)	1983-85	(12)	Land-based version
		(25)	Scud-B L	Mobile SSM system	(1975)	1976	(25)	
		(45)	Scud-B L	Mobile SSM system	(1980)	1981-82	(45)	
		..	AA-2 Atoll	AAM	1974	1975	(500)	Arming MIG-23s
		..	AA-2 Atoll	AAM	(1975)	1976-82	(420)	Arming MiG-23s
		..	AA-6 Acrid	AAM	(1978)	1979-82	(160)	Arming MiG-25s
		(36)	AS-4 Kitchen	ASM	1975	1977-78	(36)	
		..	AT-2 Swatter	ATM	(1984)	1984	(100)	
		..	AT-3 Sagger	ATM	1974	1975	(2 000)	
		..	AT-3 Sagger	ATM	(1977)	1978	(400)	
		12	FROG-7	Landmob SSM	(1978)	1979-80	(12)	
		(288)	SA-13 Gopher	Landmob SAM	(1984)	1984-85	(288)	In service with TELAR launch system
		..	SA-2 Guideline	Landmob SAM	1974	1975	(60)	
		..	SA-3 Goa	Landmob SAM	1974	1974	(100)	

Recipient	Supplier	No.	Weapon designation	Weapon description	Year of order	Year(s) of deliveries	No. delivered	Comments
		(36)	SA-5 Gammon	SAM	(1985)	1985	(36)	
		..	SA-6 Gainful	Landmob SAM	1974	1975	(100)	
		..	SA-7 Grail	Port SAM	(1977)	1978-82	(150)	
		..	SA-8 Gecko	Landmob SAM	(1980)	1981-82	(120)	
		..	SA-9 Gaskin	Landmob SAM	(1979)	1979	(100)	
		(12)	SA-N-4	ShAM	1980	1981-85	(12)	Arming Nanuchka Class corvettes
		..	SCUD-B	Landmob SSM	(1980)	1980-82	(45)	
		(25)	SCUD-C	Landmob SSM	(1975)	1976	25	
		..	SSN-2 Styx	ShShM	1975	1976-80	(144)	Arming Osa-2 Class FACs
		(48)	SSN-2 Styx	ShShM	1980	1981-85	(48)	Arming Nanuchka Class corvettes
		..	SSN-2 Styx	ShShM	(1982)	1983-85	(108)	Land-based version for protection of Gulf of Sirte
		12	Scaleboard	Landmob SSM	(1980)	1980-81	(12)	
		3	Foxtrot Class	Submarine	1975	1976-78	3	In addition to 3 in service
		3	Foxtrot Class	Submarine	1978	1982-83	3	
		4	Nanuchka Class	Corvette	1980	1981-85	4	
		2	Natya Class	MSO	(1980)	1981	2	
		4	Natya Class	MSO	(1982)	1983-84	4	In addition to 2 delivered 1981
		1	Natya Class	MSO	1984	1985	1	In addition to 6 in service
		12	Osa-2 Class	FAC	1975	1976-80	12	
		4	Polnocny Class	LS	(1977)	1977-79	4	
	Yugoslavia	50	G-2AE Galeb	Jet trainer	1975	1976-80	(50)	Unspecified number ordered
		..	G-2AE Galeb	Jet trainer	(1983)	1984-85	(12)	
		4	Koncar Class	FAC	1981	1984-85	(12)	Based on Swedish Spica design
4 Madagascar	France	1	AS-350 Ecureuil	Hel	(1984)	1984	(3)	
		(3)	Model F337	Trainer	(1973)	1974	(10)	
		(10)	M-3	APC	(1972)	1973		Ex-French L-9082
		1	EDIC/EDA Type	LC	(1984)	1985	1	
	Korea, North	(8)	MiG-17F	Fighter	(1978)	1979	(8)	
		(8)	MiG-21FL	Fighter	(1978)	1979	(8)	
		..	M-46 130mm	TG	(1983)	1983	(20)	
		..	Type 59/1 130mm	TG	(1982)	1982	(6)	
		..	Type-60 122mm	TG	(1982)	1982	(10)	
		4	Nampo Class	LC	(1978)	1979	4	
	Poland	2	Mi-2 Taurus-2	Hel	(1979)	1979	2	Supplier unconfirmed
	UK	1	BN-2A Defender	Lightplane	(1979)	1979	1	
		1	HS-748-2	Transport	(1979)	1980	1	
	USA	6	Model 172	Trainer	(1975)	1975	6	
	USSR	1	An-24 Coke	Transport	(1978)	1978	(1)	Also reported as An-12
		..	An-26 Curl	Lightplane	(1978)	1978-80	(5)	
		2	Yak-40 Codling	Transport	(1979)	1979-80	2	

Recipient code/ Recipient	Supplier	No. ordered	Weapon designation	Weapon description	Year of order	Year(s) of delivery	Total delivered	Comments
		..	BMP-1	MICV	1980	1981	(25)	Designation unconfirmed; deal incl MiG-21s and An-24s
		..	BRDM-2	SC	(1985)	1983	(20)	
		..	BRDM-2	SC	(1985)	1985	(5)	
		(10)	BRDM-2 Gaskin	AAV(M)	(1983)	1984	(10)	
		..	D-30 122mm	TH	(1983)	1983	(20)	
		..	PT-76	LT	(1983)	1983	(6)	
		(50)	SA-9 Gaskin	Landmob SAM	(1983)	1984	(50)	
4 Malawi	France	1	AS-350 Ecureuil	Hel	(1985)	1985	1	
		1	AS-365	Hel	(1985)			For VIP use
		1	SA-316B	Hel	(1978)	1978	1	
		(6)	SA-330L Puma	Hel	(1978)	1978–80	(6)	
	Germany, FR	3	Do-228-200	Transport	1985	1986	(3)	Ex-Belgian Army; refurbished in FR Germany
		6	Do-27	Transport	(1978)	1979–80	6	
	South Africa	6	Do-28D-2	Transport	(1975)	1976–78	6	
		6	Do-28D-2	Transport	1979	1980–81	(6)	Ordered Apr 1979
		9	Ferret FV-703	Recce AC	(1970)	1972	9	
	UK	1	HS-125/700	Transport	1983	1983	(1)	Ordered Dec 1979; for police
		1	Skyvan-3M	Transport	(1979)	1980	1	
		(22)	Fox FV-721	AC	(1981)	1981	(22)	
	USA	..	M-101-A1 105mm	TH	(1978)	1978	(10)	
	USSR	20	BRDM-2	SC	(1983)	1983	(20)	Supplier unconfirmed
11 Malaysia	Australia	6	CA-27 Sabre	Fighter	(1970)	1971	6	Ex-RAAF
	Belgium	186	Sibmas	APC	1982	1983–86	(186)	162 APCs (AFSV-90) and 24 ARVs
	Canada	2	Challenger-600	Transport	(1981)	1982	2	For VIP transport
		14	DHC-4 Caribou	Transport	1968	1969–72	14	4 supplied under MAP agreement
	France	(70)	AML-60	AC	1971	1973–74	(70)	
		(70)	AML-90	AC	1971	1973–74	(70)	
		44	M-3	APC	(1971)	1974	44	
		(4)	MM-38 L	ShShM launcher	1970	1973	(4)	On Combattante-2 (Perdana) Class FACs
		(4)	MM-38 L	ShShM launcher	1976	1979	(4)	Arming 4 Spica Class FACs
		(2)	MM-38 L	ShShM launcher	1981	1984	2	On 2 FS-1500 Class frigates
		(24)	MM-38 Exocet	ShShM	1970	1973	(24)	On 4 Combattante-2 (Perdana) Class FACs
		(48)	MM-38 Exocet	ShShM	1976	1979	(48)	Arming 4 Spica Class FACs
		(24)	MM-38 Exocet	ShShM	1981	1984	(24)	Arming 2 FS-1500 Class frigates
		..	SS-11	ATM	1979	1979	(20)	Unconfirmed; unknown number; for Army

	No.	Designation	Type	(Order)	Delivery	(No.)	
	(96)	SS-12	ShShM	(1970)	1971	(96)	On 4 Soloven Class FACs delivered 1967
Germany, FR	4	Combattante-2	FAC	1970	1973	4	Called Perdana Class
	459	Condor	APC	1981	1982-84	(459)	Not classified as arms sale
	2	FS-1500 Type	Frigate	1981	1984	2	Similar to frigates sold to Colombia
	1	Sri Indera	Support ship	1979	1980	1	
Indonesia	4	CN-212	Transport	(1986)			Re-negotiating original order from 1981
	4	CN-235	Transport	(1986)			Negotiating
	10	NBo-105	Hel	1980	1982-83	(10)	
Italy	5	AB-212	Hel	1974	1978	5	Order number: 3-6
	12	MB-339A	Jet trainer	1982	1983	12	Option on 14 more
	1	MB-339K	Fighter/trainer	(1985)			Replacing lost aircraft
	12	Model 56 105mm	TH	(1978)	1979	12	Different engines and armament than version produced for Italian Navy
	4	Lerici Class	Minehunter	1981	1986	4	Similar to West German-built Sri Indera
Korea, South	2	Mahawangsa	Support ship	1981	1983-84	2	Negotiating
	1	Mash Class	OPV	(1983)	1985	1	
Netherlands	2	Tacoma Type	LS	(1986)			
	2	F-27 Mk-1000	Transport	1974	1975	2	Ordered via Indonesian oil-company
Singapore	7	Alouette-3	Hel	(1981)	1982	7	Sold by AF
	1	Duyong	Support ship	(1969)	1971	1	Gun-armed diving tender
Sweden	4	Spica-2 Class	FAC	1976	1979	4	
Switzerland	44	PC-7	Trainer	1981	1983-84	(44)	
UK	1	BN-2A Defender	Lightplane	1974	1974	1	Unconfirmed
	15	Bulldog-120	Trainer	1971	1972	15	
	40	AT-105 Saxon	APC	1977	1979	40	
	26	Scorpion 90	LT/TD	1982	1983-84	(26)	Total cost incl 25 Stormer APCs: $40 m
	(20)	Shorland SB-301	APC	(1977)	1978	(20)	Unconfirmed
	25	Stormer	APC	1982	1983-84	(25)	Ordered Jan 1982
	(5)	Sultan FV-105	CPC	(1982)	1983	(5)	Unconfirmed
	3	S-600	Air defence radar	(1970)	1971	(3)	Out of service from 1985
	(1)	Seacat L	ShAM launcher	1966	1971	(1)	On 1 Yarrow Type frigate
	(128)	Blowpipe	Port SAM	1976	1979	(128)	For Army
	(12)	Seacat	ShAM/ShShM	1966	1971	(12)	On 1 Yarrow Type frigate
	1	Mermaid Class	Frigate	(1975)	1977	1	
	1	Yarrow Type	Frigate	1966	1971	(40)	
USA	40	A-4E Skyhawk	Fighter/bomber	1981	1984-85	(40)	Seacat ShAMs replaced with gun in 1983; 63 A-4Ls and 25 A-4Cs; 40 A-4Ls to be refurbished by Grumman; remaining 23 A-4Cs to be stored in USA; the A-4Cs to be used for spares
	6	C-130H Hercules	Transport	1974	1976	6	Total cost: $48 m incl spares
	3	C-130H-MP	Mar patrol	1979	1980	3	Total cost: $27.5 m
	2	F-5B	Fighter/trainer	1972	1974	2	
	14	F-5E Tiger-2	Fighter	1972	1975-76	(14)	

Recipient code/ Recipient	Supplier	No. ordered	Weapon designation	Weapon description	Year of order	Year(s) of delivery	Total delivered	Comments
		1	F-5E Tiger-2	Fighter	(1980)	1981	1	
		4	F-5F Tiger-2	Jet trainer	(1980)	1981	4	
		2	HU-16B Albatros	Mar patrol/ASW	1985	1985	2	Refurbished by Grumman; unit cost: $4 m
		4	Model 205 UH-1H	Hel	(1978)	1979	(4)	
		5	Model 206B	Hel	1975	1978	5	Ordered Aug 1975
		12	Model 402B	Lightplane	1974	1975	12	
		6	Model 47G	Hel	1974	1974	6	
		2	RF-5E Tigereye	Recce	1980	1983	2	
		6	S-61A-4 Nuri	Hel	1971	1971	6	In addition to 10 in use
		6	S-61A-4 Nuri	Hel	1976	1977	(6)	
		16	S-61A-4 Nuri	Hel	1977	1978	16	
		100	V-100 Commando	APC	1971	1971	100	Ordered Jul 1971
		130	V-150 Commando	APC	1977	1978–79	(130)	
		(..)	HADR	Air defence radar	(1982)	1986	(1)	
		(84)	AIM-9J	AAM	(1972)	1976	(84)	Arming 14 F-5Es
		(30)	AIM-9L	AAM	(1980)	1981	(30)	Arming 1 F-5E and 4 F-5Fs
		1	LST 511-1152	LS/minelayer	(1970)	1971	1	Loaned 1971;purchased 1974
		2	LST 511-1152	LS/minelayer	(1975)	1976	2	In addition to 1 in service
3 Mali	China	(6)	T-62	LT	(1977)	1977	(6)	
	France	1	SN-601 Corvette	Transport	(1983)	1983	(1)	
	USSR	..	M-8 Greyhound	AC	(1982)	1982	(10)	Unconfirmed
		..	An-2	Transport	(1975)	1975	(3)	
		(2)	An-24 Coke	Transport	(1980)	1980	(2)	
		1	Mi-8 Hip	Hel	(1983)	1983	(1)	
		..	Yak-18	Trainer	(1977)	1977	(6)	
		(6)	BM-21 122mm	MRS	(1981)	1982	(6)	Deal incl 8 D-30s
		..	BRDM-2	SC	(1975)	1975	(3)	
		(10)	BTR-152	APC	(1975)	1975	(10)	
		..	BTR-60P	APC	(1982)	1982	(10)	
		..	D-30 122mm	TH	(1981)	1981	(10)	Unconfirmed
		8	D-30 122mm	TH	(1983)	1984	8	
		..	M-46 130mm	TG	(1982)	1982	(10)	Unconfirmed
		..	T-34	MT	(1981)	1981	(20)	
		(5)	SA-3 SAMS	Mobile SAM system	(1981)	1981	(5)	
		..	SA-3 Goa	Landmob SAM	(1981)	1981	(3)	Unconfirmed
4 Mauritania	Canada	2	DHC-5D Buffalo	Transport	1977	1978	2	
	France	1	C-54 Skymaster	Transport	(1975)	1976	1	

Supplier	No. ordered	Designation	Description	Year of order	Year(s) of delivery	No. delivered	Comments
Spain	4	Model F337	Trainer	(1977)	1978	4	
	(10)	AML-90	AC	1978	1979	(10)	Arms: 40mm Bofors gun
	(14)	M-3	APC	(1980)	1980	(14)	
	1	Patra Class	PC/FAC	1980	1982	1	Ordered Jul 1976
UK	3	Barcelo Class	PC	1976	1979-82	3	
	9	BN-2A Defender	Lightplane	1975	1976-78	9	
USA	2	Skyvan-3M	Transport	(1977)	1978	2	For coastal patrol
	2	PA-31 Cheyenne	Mar patrol	(1980)	1981	2	
	..	M-3	APC	(1979)	1980	(40)	Supplier unconfirmed

4 Mauritius	No. ordered	Designation	Description	Year of order	Year(s) of delivery	No. delivered	Comments
France	(11)	VAB	APC	(1979)	1979	(11)	
India	1	Abhay Class	PC	(1974)	1974	1	
UK	4	Shorland	AC	1970	1971	4	
USSR	..	BRDM-2	SC	(1984)	1985	(10)	Supplier unconfirmed

4 Mexico	No. ordered	Designation	Description	Year of order	Year(s) of delivery	No. delivered	Comments
Canada	3	DHC-5D Buffalo	Transport	(1980)	1981	3	
France	10	SA-330L Puma	Hel	(1977)	1979	10	
	(40)	ERC-90 Lynx	AC	1981	1982	40	Unconfirmed
	(40)	VBL	Recce AC	1984	1985-86	(40)	Also designated Ultrav; some reportedly armed with Milan ATMs
	(40)	VBL-M11	AC	1984	1985-86	(40)	Unspecified number ordered; arming M-11 VBL vehicles
	(120)	Milan	ATM	1984	1985-86	(120)	
Germany, FR	6	Bo-105	Hel	(1985)	1986	6	
	6	Bo-105C	Hel	(1980)	1982-83	6	On 6 Halcon Class PCs
Israel	5	IAI-201 Arava	Transport	(1972)	1973-74	(5)	
	5	IAI-201 Arava	Transport	(1974)	1976	5	
Singapore	10	B-737-100	Transport	1981	1981	1	For VIP transport
Spain	6	C-212-200	Transport	1985	1982-83	6	For Navy
	(6)	Halcon Class	OPV	1980	1979-83	6	Last of 6 commissioned Mar 1983
Switzerland	55	PC-7	Trainer	1978	1980-81	(55)	47 of which armed
	25	PC-7	Trainer	(1985)			Reportedly ordered
UK	6	BN-2A Islander	Transport	(1970)	1971	6	
	36	BN-2A Islander	Transport	1980	1971	(36)	Most of which also for civilian use
	1	HS-125	Transport	(1970)	1974-76	1	For VIP use
	21	Azteca Class	PC	1973	1974-76	21	For fishery protection duties
USA	2	B-727	Transport	(1981)	1981	2	
	1	B-737-100	Transport	(1982)	1983	1	
	3	C-118A	Transport	(1974)	1975	3	
	20	Commander 500	Lightplane	(1972)	1974	(20)	
	5	Commander 680	Transport	(1974)	1975	5	Possibly version 690
	20	F-33C Bonanza	Trainer	1974	1974-75	20	
	4	F-33C Bonanza	Trainer	(1984)	1984	4	For training

Recipient code/Recipient	Supplier	No. ordered	Weapon designation	Weapon description	Year of order	Year(s) of delivery	Total delivered	Comments
		21	F-33C Bonanza	Trainer	1985	1986	(21)	
		10	F-5E Tiger-2	Fighter	1980	1982	10	Total cost incl 2 F-5Fs: $115 m
		2	F-5F Tiger-2	Jet trainer	1980	1982	2	
		2	FH-227	Transport	(1978)	1978	2	
		4	HU-16B Albatros	Mar patrol/ASW	(1974)	1975	4	For Navy
		8	HU-16D Albatros	Mar patrol/ASW	1976	1977	8	
		3	HU-16D Albatros	Mar patrol/ASW	1979	1980	3	Ordered Nov 1979
		1	Jetstar-1	Transport	(1970)	1971	1	
		1	Learjet 24D	Transport	(1974)	1975	1	
		1	MU-2J	Transport	1973	1974	1	Bought new from US importer
		1	Merlin-3A	Transport	(1982)	1983	1	
		5	Model 205 UH-1D	Hel	(1970)	1972	5	
		5	Model 206A	Hel	(1971)	1973	5	For Navy
		2	Model 212	Hel	(1970)	1971	2	For Navy
		1	Model 402A	Lightplane	(1970)	1971	1	
		1	Admirable Class	MSO	(1972)	1973	1	
		19	Auk Class	Minelayer	(1972)	1973	19	
		2	Buckley Class	Frigate	1970	1971	2	Also designated Rudderow Class
		1	Edsall Class	Frigate	(1972)	1973	1	
		2	Gearing Class	Destroyer	(1981)	1982	2	Sold at scrap value: $362 000 each
		2	LST 511-1152	LS/minelayer	(1971)	1971-72	2	
15 Morocco	Argentina	(20)	IA-58A Pucara	COIN	(1985)			
	Austria	121	Cuirassier	LT/TD	(1978)	1979	121	
	Brazil	..	Steyr-4K 7FA	APC	(1980)	1981	(10)	
		60	EE-11 Urutu	APC	(1985)			17 on loan from Libya for training prior to delivery from Brazil
	Canada	5	C-119 Packet	Transport	(1971)	1973	5	Ex-CAF; refurbished in Italy
	Egypt	..	BRDM-2 Sagger	TD(M)	(1984)	1984	(5)	Unconfirmed
		..	M-46 130mm	TG	(1980)	1981	(12)	Supplier unconfirmed
		..	OT-62	APC	(1980)	1980	(25)	Supplier unconfirmed
		..	AT-3 Sagger	ATM	(1984)	1984	(60)	
	France	1	AS-365N	Hel	(1982)	1983	1	
		24	Alpha Jet	Jet trainer/strike	1978	1979-81	(24)	
		1	Falcon-50	Transport	1980	1980	1	
		25	Mirage F-1A	Fighter/grd attack	1975	1977	25	
		25	Mirage F-1C	Fighter/interceptor	1977	1979	25	
		24	Mirage-2000	Fighter/strike	1986			
		(2)	Mystere-20	Transport	(1982)	1982	(2)	

	Designation		Year order	Year delivery		Comments
(29)	SA-330 Puma	Hel	1975	1978-79	(29)	
12	SA-342K Gazelle	Hel	1976	1978	(12)	6 for police
12	SA-342K Gazelle	Hel	(1980)	1982-83	12	6 for police
:	AML-90	AC	(1978)	1981-85	(140)	
108	AMX-10RC	Recce AC	1978	1982-84	(40)	Delivery halted due to funding problems
(3)	AMX-13 ARV	ARV	1981	1982-83	(3)	Saudi funding
12	AMX-13 DCA	AAV	1981	1981-82	12	Saudi funding
:	AMX-155 Mk-F3	SPH	(1981)	1981-83	(50)	
:	M-3	APC	(1979)	1979	(100)	
423	VAB	APC	1975	1979-84	(391)	Several versions; last 32 held up for financial reasons
15	Crotale SAMS	Mobile SAM system	1975	1979	15	
4	MM-38 L	ShShM launcher	(1978)	1981-82	4	Arming 4 Lazaga Class FACs
1	MM-40 L	ShShM launcher	1980	1983	1	Arming F-30 Class frigate
:	Entac	ATM	(1980)	1980	(100)	Unconfirmed
:	HOT	ATM	(1982)	1982	(60)	Arming M-125-A1; unconfirmed
48	MM-38 Exocet	ShShM	(1978)	1981-82	(48)	Arming 4 Lazaga Class FACs
(12)	MM-40 Exocet	ShShM/SShM	(1980)	1983	(12)	Arming F-30 Class frigate
32	R-440 Crotale	Landmob SAM	1975	1979	32	
300	R-550 Magic	AAM	1975	1977	(300)	Arming F-1s
300	R-550 Magic	AAM	1976	1978-79	(300)	Arming Mirage F-1s
3	Batral Class	LC	1975	1977-78	3	
2	PR-72 Type	PC	1973	1976-77	2	
1	Sirius Class	MSC/PC	1974	1974	1	On loan
Germany, FR						
(10)	Do-28D-2	Transport	(1979)	1981-82	(10)	
:	UR-416	APC	1978	1978	(30)	Supplier unconfirmed
:	Cobra-2000	ATM	(1978)	1978	(30)	Arming UR-416s; supplier unconfirmed
:	AMX-10P	MICV	(1980)	1981	(20)	
	RAM V-1	Recce AC	1983	1983	(3)	Unconfirmed
Italy						
12	AB-205	Hel	(1973)	1974	12	In addition to 12 delivered mid-1960s
8	AB-206B	Hel	1975	1976	8	
(5)	AB-212	Hel	(1975)	1976	(5)	
	AL-60	Lightplane	(1970)	1971	1	
6	C-119 Packet	Transport	(1973)	1974	6	Ex-Canadian; ex-IAF
6	CH-47C Chinook	Hel	1977	1980	6	In addition to 6 in service
6	CH-47C Chinook	Hel	1981	1982	6	
1	Aspide/Albatros	ShAM/ShShM launcher	1977	1983	1	Arming F-30 Class frigate
(24)	Aspide	AAM/SAM/ShAM	1977	1983	(24)	Arming F-30 Class frigate
South Africa						
(150)	Eland-60	AC	(1979)	1980-84	(150)	
(100)	Eland-90	AC	(1979)	1980-84	(100)	
(80)	Ratel-20	ICV	(1979)	1980-81	(80)	
Spain						
1	F-30 Class	Frigate	1977	1983	1	Reportedly delivered as of early 1980s
4	Lazaga Class	PC/FAC	1977	1981-82	4	Armed with Exocet ShShMs

Recipient code/Recipient	Supplier	No. ordered	Weapon designation	Weapon description	Year of order	Year(s) of delivery	Total delivered	Comments
		6	Vigilance Class	PC	1985		10	Development of Lazaga Class; for fishery protection
	Switzerland	10	AS-202 Bravo	Trainer	1976	1978	10	
	UK	:	Light Gun 105mm	TG	(1980)	1981	(30)	Supplier unconfirmed
	USA	1	B-707-320C	Transport	1983	1983	1	For VIP use
		6	C-130H Hercules	Transport	1973	1975	6	
		6	C-130H Hercules	Transport	1976	1977-78	(6)	
		6	C-130H Hercules	Transport	(1981)	1981-82	(6)	Ordered Jun 1981
		1	C-47	Transport	1971	1971	1	MAP
		(24)	F-5E Tiger-2	Fighter	1980	1980-81	(24)	Incl in $245 m aid package financed by Saudi Arabia; 20 F-5Es and 4 F-5Fs
		1	Gulfstream-2	Transport	(1977)	1977	1	
		1	HH-43F Huskie	Hel	(1976)	1976	1	MAP
		3	KC-130H	Tanker/transport	1980	1981	3	
		1	KC-130H	Tanker/transport	1982	1983	1	
		:	KC-130H	Tanker/transport	(1985)			In addition to 4 in service
		6	King Air A-100	Transport	1973	1975	6	
		24	Model 500MD	Hel	1980	1980-81	24	Financed by Saudi Arabia
		6	OV-10A Bronco	Trainer/COIN	1979	1981	6	
		3	Super King Air	Transport	(1981)	1982-83	3	
		1	Super King Air	Transport	(1983)	1984	1	
		12	T-34C-1	Trainer	1975	1977	12	
		:	M-101-A1 105mm	TH	(1981)	1981	(30)	Supplier unconfirmed
		334	M-113-A1	APC	1975	1978-79	334	
		:	M-114 155mm	TH	(1976)	1976	(14)	
		:	M-125-A1	APC	(1982)	1982	(20)	Armed with HOT ATMs; unconfirmed
		40	M-163 Vulcan	AAV	(1979)	1981-82	(40)	
		25	M-48 Patton	MBT	(1973)	1974	25	Order expected for 100 more
		100	M-48 Patton	MBT	1975	1977	100	
		100	M-48 Patton	MBT	1978	1978-79	100	
		37	M54 Chaparral	Mobile SAM system	1976	1979-80	(37)	
		381	AGM-65B	ASM	1982	1983	(381)	To arm F-5Es; delivery unconfirmed
		(1 000)	BGM-71A TOW	ATM	1975	1977-78	(1 000)	
		:	BGM-71A TOW	ATM	1980	1981-82	(192)	Arming 24 Model 500MD helicopters
		:	FGM-77A Dragon	ATM	(1977)	1978	(2 000)	
		504	MIM-72C	Landmob SAM	1976	1979-80	(504)	
		:	D-30 122mm	TH	(1980)	1981	(10)	Supplier unconfirmed; possibly taken from Sahauri guerrilla
	USSR	:	SA-7 Grail	Port SAM	(1978)	1978	(100)	Unconfirmed

4 Mozambique	Portugal	(5)	C-47	Transport	(1974)	1975	(5) Handed over at independence
		(4)	Model 182	Lightplane	(1974)	1975	(4) Handed over at independence
		7	Noratlas 2501	Transport	1978	1978	7
		(4)	PA-28 Cherokee	Lightplane	(1974)	1975	(4) Handed over at independence
		(4)	SA-316B	Hel	(1974)	1975	(4) Handed over at independence
		(15)	T-6 Harvard	Trainer	(1974)	1975	(15) Handed over at independence
		(30)	M-18	TD	(1974)	1975	(30)
	USSR	1	Alfange Class	LC	(1975)	1975	1
		2	An-26 Curl	Lightplane	(1981)	1981-82	2
		1	An-26 Curl	Lightplane	(1982)	1983	1 Handed over at independence
		(3)	Mi-8 Hip	Hel	1978	1978	(3)
		(24)	MiG-17	Fighter/strike	(1977)	1977-78	(24)
		(24)	MiG-17	Fighter/strike	(1981)	1983-84	(24)
		(44)	MiG-21MF	Fighter	1976	1977-78	(44)
		(48)	MiG-21MF	Fighter	(1981)	1984	(48)
		1	Tu-134	Transport	(1982)	1982	1
		(7)	Zlin-226	Trainer	(1979)	1979	(7)
		(30)	BM-21 122mm	MRS	(1977)	1978-79	(30)
		(20)	BRDM-1	SC	1976	1977	(20)
		:	BRDM-1	SC	(1979)	1979-80	(31)
		:	BRDM-2	SC	(1979)	1979-81	(56)
		:	BTR-152	APC	(1977)	1977	(6)
		:	BTR-152	APC	(1980)	1980-83	(100)
		:	BTR-60P	APC	1977	1977	(30)
		:	BTR-60P	APC	1979	1981-85	(50)
		:	D-1 152mm	TH	(1979)	1979	(20)
		:	D-30 122mm	TH	(1981)	1981	(20)
		:	M-1938 122mm	TG	(1977)	1977	(20)
		:	M-1944 100mm	TG	(1979)	1979	(20)
		:	M-46 130mm	TG	(1979)	1979	(20)
		(5)	PT-76	LT	(1977)	1977	(5)
		(50)	PT-76	LT	(1980)	1980	(50)
		(40)	T-34	MT	1976	1977	(40)
		(100)	T-34	MT	(1980)	1980-84	(100) Unconfirmed
		:	T-54	MBT	1978	1978	(100)
		:	T-54	MBT	(1980)	1980-82	(60)
		:	T-55	MBT	(1978)	1978	(50)
		:	T-55	MBT	(1982)	1983-85	(60)
		(24)	ZSU-23-4 Shilka	AAV	(1983)	1983	(6)
		(24)	SA-6 SAMS	Mobile SAM system	(1978)	1978	(24) Unconfirmed
		(2)	SA-8 SAMS	Mobile SAM system	(1983)	1983	(2) Unconfirmed
		:	AT-3 Sagger	ATM	(1977)	1977	(300) Unconfirmed

Recipient code/ Recipient	Supplier	No. ordered	Weapon designation	Weapon description	Year of order	Year(s) of delivery	Total delivered	Comments
		..	SA-6 Gainful	Landmob SAM	(1977)	1978	(216)	24 launch systems in operation
		..	SA-7 Grail	Port SAM	(1976)	1977	(300)	
		(6)	SA-8 Gecko	Landmob SAM	(1983)	1983	(6)	Unconfirmed
		2	SO-1 Class	PC	(1984)	1985	2	
11 Nepal	France	(2)	C-47	Transport	(1970)	1971	(2)	Unconfirmed
		2	SA-316B	Hel	(1971)	1972	2	
		2	SA-330J Puma	Hel	1975	1975	2	
	India	2	SA-316B Chetak	Hel	(1974)	1974	2	Pilots trained in India
		1	HS-748-2	Transport	(1975)	1975	1	
		3	Skyvan-3M	Transport	(1969)	1970-72	3	
	UK	1	Skyvan-3M	Transport	1984	1984	1	In addition to 3 in service
12 Nicaragua	Algeria	30	T-55	MBT	(1980)	1981	(30)	Unconfirmed
	Bulgaria	(25)	BRDM-2	SC	(1982)	1983	(25)	
	Cuba	(6)	An-26 Curl	Lightplane	(1980)	1982	(6)	Delivered via Cuba; unconfirmed
	France	2	Alouette-3	Hel	1981	1982	2	Ordered Dec 1981; deal incl 2 patrol boats and a training programme
	Israel	14	IAI-201 Arava	Transport	(1973)	1974	(14)	Eight in service by 1984
		(3)	M-4 Sherman	MT	(1974)	1975	(3)	
		4	Dabur Class	PC	(1976)	1978	4	
		2	Sin Hung Class	FAC	(1983)	1983	2	Unconfirmed
	Korea, North	(6)	L-39 Albatross	Jet trainer	(1983)	1984	(6)	Unconfirmed
	Libya	..	MB-326K	Jet trainer	1984	1984	(3)	Unconfirmed; acc to US intelligence
		1	Mystere-20	Transport	(1983)	1983	(1)	For VIP use
		4	SF-260M	Trainer	1982	1982	4	
		(10)	T-54	MBT	(1981)	1982	(10)	Seller unconfirmed
		(10)	T-55	MBT	(1981)	1982	(10)	Seller unconfirmed
		(2)	SA-8 SAMS	Mobile SAM system	(1981)	1982	(2)	
		(100)	SA-7 Grail	Port SAM	(1981)	1982-83	(100)	
		..	SA-8 Gecko	Landmob SAM	..	1982	(24)	
	Poland	(2)	Mi-2 Taurus-2	Hel	1985	1985	(2)	
	Spain	5	C-212A Aviocar	Transport	(1975)	1977	5	
	USA	5	C-47	Transport	(1975)	1976-78	5	
		6	DHC-3 Otter	Transport	(1976)	1976	6	
		2	Model 185	Lightplane	(1971)	1972	2	
		1	Model 204 UH-1B	Hel	1986	1986	1	For Contras; delivered by private US organization after official approval
		5	Model 205 UH-1H	Hel	1977	1978	5	

Recipient	Supplier	Qty	Designation	Type	Year of order	Year of delivery	No. delivered	Comments
4 Niger	USSR	10	Model 337	Trainer	1975	1976	10	
		1	Model 35	Lightplane	1976	1976	1	
		7	OH-6A Cayuse	Hel	1970	1971	7	
		(12)	S-58	Hel	(1971)	(1972-73)	(12)	
		6	An-2	Transport	(1983)	1984	(6)	Unconfirmed
		(10)	Mi-24 Hind-C	Hel	(1984)	1984-85	(10)	
		2	Mi-8 Hip	Hel	(1980)	1981	2	
		(12)	Mi-8 Hip	Hel	(1981)	1981-84	(12)	
		(24)	BM-21 122mm	MRS	(1982)	1983-85	(24)	
		(26)	BRDM-2	SC	(1983)	1984	(26)	Unconfirmed; possibly with Sagger ATMs
		(140)	BTR-152	APC	(1982)	1982-84	(140)	
		(20)	BTR-40	APC	(1980)	1981-82	(20)	
		(24)	BTR-60P	APC	(1981)	1983-84	(24)	Designation unconfirmed
		(24)	D-20 152mm	TH	(1981)	1981-84	(24)	According to US DoD
		(24)	D-30 122mm	TH	(1981)	1981-84	(24)	According to US DoD
		(24)	M-1938 122mm	TG	1983	1984-85	(24)	
		(28)	PT-76	LT	(1983)	1984	(28)	Unconfirmed
		(35)	T-54	MBT	(1984)	1985	(35)	Unconfirmed
		(66)	T-55	MBT	(1984)	1984	(66)	Unconfirmed
		..	ZSU-57-2	AAV	(1982)	1983	(10)	Seller unconfirmed
		(100)	AT-3 Sagger	ATM	(1983)	1984	(100)	Unconfirmed
		(300)	SA-7 Grail	Port SAM	(1983)	1984-85	(300)	Seller unconfirmed
		2	Yevgenia Class	MSC	(1983)	1984	(2)	Unconfirmed
	France	3	C-47	Transport	(1971)	1972	3	
		2	Model F337	Trainer	(1970)	1971	2	
		(1)	Noratlas 2501	Transport	(1979)	1980	(1)	Ex-French AF
		18	AML-60	AC	1981	1983	(18)	Also reported as ERC-60
		..	AML-90	AC	1981	1983	(12)	Also reported as ERC-90
		(14)	M-3	APC	(1979)	1980	(14)	
		3	M-3	AC	(1983)	1983	3	Unconfirmed; possibly modified as AAV
	Germany, FR		VBL-M11	AC	1986	1986	3	
		1	Commander 500	Lightplane	(1970)	1972	1	French MAP
		2	DC-6	Transport	1970	1971	2	Ex-Luftwaffe
		1	Do-228-200	Transport	1985	1986	(1)	
		3	Do-28D-1	Transport	(1979)	1980	3	Ex-Luftwaffe
		4	Noratlas 2501	Transport	(1970)	1971	4	
		20	UR-416	APC	1984	1984	20	
	USA	1	B-737-200C	Transport	(1978)	1978	1	
		2	C-130H Hercules	Transport	1979	1979	2	
		1	Model 337	Trainer	(1973)	1973	1	
7 Nigeria	Austria	1	Cuirassier	LT/TD	1979	1981	1	For evaluation

Recipient code/Recipient	Supplier	No. ordered	Weapon designation	Weapon description	Year of order	Year(s) of delivery	Total delivered	Comments
	Brazil	23	Steyr-4K 7FA	APC	(1980)	1981	23	In addition to 23 delivered 1981
		70	Steyr-4K 7FA	APC	1982	1982-83	70	Option on 1 more; may be for civilian use
		1	EMB-121 Xingu	Transport	1982	1983	1	Negotiating
	France	40	EMB-312 Tucano	Trainer	(1986)			Ongoing negotiations since 1981 after demonstration of vehicle
		(100)	EE-9 Cascavel	AC	(1986)			
		13	SA-330 Puma	Hel	1977	1977-78	13	Deal incl trade-in of 9 old Pumas
		12	SA-330L Puma	Hel	1985	1986-87	(12)	All delivered by Jan 1981
		54	AML-60	AC	1979	1980-81	(54)	
		70	AML-60	AC	1981	1982	70	
		16	AMX-30 Roland	AAV(M)	1982	1984-85	(16)	
		40	ERC-90 Lynx	AC	(1986)	1986	(10)	
		40	ERC-90 Sagaie	AC	(1986)	1986	(10)	Several versions
		18	M-3	APC	1979	1980-81	(18)	
		12	MM-38 L	ShShM launcher	1977	1981-82	(12)	Arming Combattante-3 Class FACs
		36	MM-38 Exocet	ShShM	1977	1981-82	36	Unspecified number of missiles and launchers ordered
		..	Milan	ATM	(1983)			
	Germany, FR	595	Roland-2	Landmob SAM	1982	1984-85	(595)	Total value incl launchers: $170 m
		3	Combattante-3B	FAC	1977	1981-82	3	
		12	Alpha Jet	Jet trainer/strike	1979	1981-82	(12)	
		12	Alpha Jet	Jet trainer/strike	1983	1985-86	(12)	
		4	Bo-105	Hel	1973	1974	4	In addition to 12 in service
		20	Bo-105	Hel	1978	1978-79	(20)	
		16	Do-128-6	Transport	1982	1982-85	16	
		3	Do-228-200	Transport	1983	1984	3	Delivered Sep 1984
		3	Do-228-200	Transport	(1985)	1985-86	(3)	In addition to 3 delivered 1984
		(20)	Do-28D-2	Transport	(1973)	1974	(20)	
		..	UR-416	APC	(1974)	1974	(10)	
		..	FPB-57	FAC	1977	1981	3	Armed with 4 Otomat ShShMs
		1	Meko-360 Type	Destroyer	1977	1981	1	
		2	RoRo-1300	LS	1976	1979	2	
	Italy	4	G-222	Transport	1982	1984	(4)	
		12	MB-339A	Jet trainer	1983	1985	12	Replacing L-29 Delfins; cost: $82 m
		25	Palmaria 155mm	SPH	1982	1983-86	(25)	
		..	Aspide/Albatros	ShAM/ShShM launcher	(1978)	1981	1	Arming Meko-360 destroyer
		(3)	Otomat-1 L	ShShM launcher	1977	1981	(3)	Arming 3 FPB-57 Class FACs
		2	Otomat-1 L	ShShM launcher	(1978)	1981	2	Arming Meko-360 destroyer

	Qty	Item	Type	(Ordered)	Delivered	(No.)	Comments
	(32)	Aspide	AAM/SAM/ShAM	(1978)	1981	(32)	Arming Meko-360 destroyer
	(16)	Aspide	AAM/SAM/ShAM	1982	1983	(16)	Second order; arming Meko-360 destroyer
	(36)	Otomat-1	ShShM	1977	1981	(36)	Arming 3 FPB-57 Class FACs
	(24)	Otomat-1	ShShM	(1978)	1981	(24)	Arming Meko-360 destroyer
	2	Lerici Class	Minehunter	1983			Ordered Jun 1983; for delivery 1986; option for second ship taken up 1984
Netherlands	2	F-27 Maritime	Mar patrol	(1982)	1985	2	For VIP use
	1	F-27 Mk-1000	Transport	(1971)	1973	1	
	3	F-27 Mk-500	Transport	1977	1978	3	
	6	F-27 Mk-600M	Transport	(1970)	1972	6	
Sweden	42	FH-77 155mm	TH	1982	1983-85	(42)	
UK	20	Bulldog-120	Trainer	(1971)	1973	20	
	12	Bulldog-120	Trainer	1977	1978	12	
	5	Bulldog-120	Trainer	1980	1982	5	
	18	Jaguar	Fighter	1983	1984-85	(18)	Option on 18 more
	3	Lynx	Hel	1981	1984	3	
	(4)	AT-105 Saxon	APC	(1980)	1980	(4)	
	50	FV-101 Scorpion	LT	1975	1977-78	(50)	
	75	Fox FV-721	AC	1975	1977-79	(75)	
	..	Light Gun 105mm	TG	(1975)	1976	(50)	
	36	MBT Mk-3	MBT	1981	1983-85	(36)	Order incl 6 ARVs and 5 BLs
	(50)	MBT Mk-3	MBT	1984	1985	(12)	In addition to 47 ordered 1981
	6	MBT-3 ARV	ARV	1981	1983-85	(6)	
	5	MBT-3 BL	BL	1981	1983-84	(5)	
	49	Stormer	APC	(1982)	1982-83	(49)	Reportedly also Scorpion, Spartan and Samaritan versions
	2	Seacat L	ShAM launcher	1975	1979-80	2	For Erinmi Class corvettes
	(24)	Seacat	ShAM/ShShM	1975	1979-80	24	For Erinmi Class corvettes
	2	Bulldog Class	OPV	1973	1976	2	Used as survey ship
	2	Dorina Class	Corvette	(1968)	1972	2	Refitted 1975
	2	Erinomi Class	Corvette	1975	1979-80	2	
USA	4	Type 32m	PC	1971	1974-77	4	
	6	C-130H Hercules	Transport	1974	1975-76	6	Total cost: $47 m
	3	C-130H-30	Transport	(1982)	1983-84	(3)	
	5	CH-47C Chinook	Hel	(1987)			Ordered Feb 1983; delivery halted due to funding problems; being re-negotiated
	1	DC-6	Transport	1970	1971	1	
	1	FH-1100	Hel	(1970)	1972	1	
	(1)	Gulfstream-2	Transport	1978	1978	(1)	For army and AF training
	(15)	Model 300C	Hel	(1983)	1983	(15)	Sold by Piper International, Geneva
	3	Navajo	Lightplane	1971	1973	3	Delivered via Switzerland
	(4)	Navajo	Lightplane	(1974)	1974	(4)	
USSR	(20)	MiG-21F	Fighter	(1975)	1976	(20)	Arms: Atoll AAM

Recipient code/ Recipient	Supplier	No. ordered	Weapon designation	Weapon description	Year of order	Year(s) of delivery	Total delivered	Comments
		18	MiG-21MF	Fighter	1984	1985	(18)	In exchange for 17 MiG-21Fs in service but not in operational condition; order incl 6 MiG-21UTIs
		12	MiG-21MF	Fighter	1984			Agreed late 1984
		2	MiG-21UTI	Jet trainer	(1975)	1976	2	
		6	MiG-21UTI	Jet trainer	1984	1985	(6)	Agreed late 1984
		..	MiG-21UTI	Jet trainer	1984			
		(10)	BM-21 122mm	MRS	(1976)	1977-78	(10)	
		..	M-46 130mm	TG	(1976)	1976	(100)	Supplier unconfirmed
		(55)	T-55	MBT	(1979)	1981	(55)	
		(30)	ZSU-23-4 Shilka	AAV	(1980)	1980	(30)	
		..	AA-2 Atoll	AAM	(1973)	1975		Arming MIG-21S
4 Oman	Canada	1	DHC-4 Caribou	Transport	(1972)	1973	1	
		1	DHC-5D Buffalo	Transport	(1978)	1979	1	
	China	(12)	Type 59/1 130mm	TG	(1981)	1983	(12)	Unconfirmed
	France	2	AS-332	Hel	(1980)	1984	(2)	
		16	VAB	APC	(1981)	1982-83	(16)	
		6	VBC-90	AC	(1983)	1984-85	(6)	
		1	MM-38 L	ShShM launcher	(1976)	1978	1	Arming 'Al Mansur' FAC
		3	MM-40 L	ShShM launcher	1980	1982-84	3	Arming 3 Province Class FACs
		(1)	MM-40 L	ShShM launcher	1986			To arm fourth Province Class FAC
		(24)	AM-39 Exocet	AShM	(1981)	1982-83	(24)	Unconfirmed
		(6)	MM-38 Exocet	ShShM	(1976)	1978	(6)	Arming 'Al Mansur' FAC
		(66)	MM-40 Exocet	ShShM/SShM	1981	1982-84	(66)	Arming 3 Province Class FACs
		(24)	MM-40 Exocet	ShShM/SShM	1986			To arm fourth Province Class FAC
		(72)	R-550 Magic	AAM	1975	1977-78	(72)	
	Iran	5	AB-205	Hel	(1971)	1972	5	
	Italy	8	AB-205	Hel	(1970)	1971	8	
		(10)	AB-205	Hel	(1972)	1974-75	(10)	
		4	AB-206A	Hel	(1970)	1971	4	
		3	AB-212	Hel	1976	1976-80	3	
		..	Palmaria 155mm	SPH	(1983)			Undisclosed number on order
	Jordan	31	Hunter FGA-74	Fighter	1975	1975	31	Originally intended for Rhodesia; incl 2 T-66 trainers and 16 spare engines
	Kuwait	2	Hunter T-66	Fighter/trainer	(1980)	1980	2	
	Netherlands	2	Dokkum Class	MSC	1974	1974	2	
	Saudi Arabia	2	AB-205	Hel	(1971)	1972	2	
	Singapore	1	Saba al Bahr	LC	(1980)	1981	1	
		2	Saba al Bahr	LC	1982	1983	2	

Switzerland	2	AS-202 Bravo	Trainer	(1976)	1976	2	
	1	PC-6	Lightplane	(1973)	1974	1	
UK	3	BAC-111	Transport	1973	1974-75	3	
	8	BAC-167	Trainer/COIN	(1971)	1973	8	
	4	BAC-167	Trainer/COIN	1974	1976	4	
	1	BAC-167	Trainer/COIN	(1985)	1985	1	Attrition replacement
	8	BN-2A Defender	Lightplane	(1973)	1974	8	
	12	Jaguar	Fighter	1974	1977-78	(12)	Ordered Jul 1980; in addition to 12 in service
	12	Jaguar	Fighter	1980	1983	12	One out of 18 on loan to India sold to Oman
	1	Jaguar	Fighter	1982	1982	1	Replacing lost aircraft
	1	Jaguar	Fighter	(1985)	1985	1	Deliveries postponed until 1991 for lack of funding
	8	Skyvan-3M	Transport	(1969)	1970-71	(8)	Some bought in Australia and Ireland for refurbishment in UK
	8	Skyvan-3M	Transport	(1971)	1972-75	(8)	
	8	Tornado ADV	Fighter/MRCA	1985	1985	6	
	6	VC-2 Viscount	Transport	(1971)	1971-73	6	
	(25)	AT-105 Saxon	APC	(1980)	1982	(25)	Unconfirmed
	12	Chieftain-5	MBT	1981	1982	12	On lease
	(15)	Chieftain-5	MBT	1983	1984-85	(15)	12-15 in addition to 12 in service
	(30)	FV-101 Scorpion	LT	1980	1980	(30)	
	(40)	Light Gun 105mm	TG	(1974)	1975-76	(40)	
	(10)	Sultan FV-105	CPC	(1980)	1981	(10)	Unconfirmed
	28	Rapier SAMS	Mobile SAM system	1974	1976-77	(28)	Upgraded by 1980 order for 28 Blindfire radar units
	4	S-723 Martello	3-D radar	(1984)	1985-86	(4)	
	1	Watchman	Surveillance radar	1986	1986	1	
	(200)	Blowpipe	Port SAM	1982	1984-85	(200)	Ordered Dec 1982
	(728)	Rapier	Landmob SAM	1974	1976-77	(728)	
	48	Sky Flash	AAM	1985	1985		Arming 8 Tornado ADV fighters
	1	Al Said	OPV/training ship	1969	1971	1	Yacht converted to naval use 1983
	1	Ardennes Class	LS	1977	1979	1	Greatly modified; large helicopter deck; ship named 'Al Munassir'
	1	Brooke Logistic	LS	1982	1985	1	Ship named 'Nasr Al Bahr'
	1	Province Class	FAC	1980	1982	1	Ordered Mar 1980
	2	Province Class	FAC	1981	1984	2	In addition to 1 delivered 1982; to be armed with MM-40 Exocet ShShMs
	1	Province Class	FAC	1986	1986	1	In addition to 3 in service
	2	Type 37.5M	FAC	1970	1973	2	MM-38 Exocet ShShMs fitted on 1 1977-78
	4	Type 37M	PC	1974	1977	4	Omani designation: Al Wafi Class; similar to 'Al Mansur'

Recipient code/ Recipient	Supplier	No. ordered	Weapon designation	Weapon description	Year of order	Year(s) of delivery	Total delivered	Comments
	USA	1	C-130H Hercules	Transport	1980	1981	1	Delivered Mar 1981
		2	C-130H Hercules	Transport	1981	1982-83	2	
		(1)	C-130H Hercules	Transport	(1985)	1986	(1)	In addition to 3 in service
		1	DC-8	Transport	(1981)	1983	1	
		1	DHC-2 Beaver	Lightplane	(1971)	1973	1	
		(5)	Model 205 UH-1A	Hel	1975	1975	(5)	In return for base rights
		5	Model 214B	Hel	1974	1975	5	
		6	Model 214ST	Hel	1983	1983-84	6	
		(10)	M-109-A1 155mm	SPH	(1980)	1981-82	(10)	
		6	M-60-A1	MBT	(1979)	1980	6	
		250	AIM-9P	AAM	1979	1982-83	(250)	Arming Jaguar fighters
		300	AIM-9P	AAM	1985			To arm Jaguar and Hunter fighters
		120	BGM-71A TOW	ATM	1975	1975	120	Including 10 launchers and some helicopters in return for base rights
	USSR	(15)	M-46 130mm	TG	1978	1979-80	(15)	Seller unconfirmed
	United Arab Emirates	28	Saladin FV-601	AC	(1973)	1974	28	
3 Pakistan	China	(24)	F-4	Fighter	(1978)	1978	(24)	Unconfirmed
		(80)	F-6	Fighter	(1969)	1971-72	(80)	Incl some FT-5 trainers
		(15)	F-6	Fighter	(1972)	1974	(15)	
		(20)	F-6	Fighter	1979	1980-81	(20)	Probably FT-6 trainers
		(60)	F-7	Fighter	(1986)			Negotiating
		(42)	Q-5 Fantan-A	Fighter/grd attack	1982	1983-85	(42)	
		(100)	Q-5 Fantan-A	Fighter/grd attack	1984	1986	(50)	For delivery 1986-88
		210	T-59	MBT	(1968)	1970-72	(210)	
		159	T-59	MBT	(1973)	1974	159	
		..	T-59	MBT	(1975)	1978-86	(675)	
		(50)	T-60	LT	(1980)	1981-82	(50)	
		(50)	T-63	LT	(1971)	1972-73	(50)	
		(200)	Type 531	APC	1972	1973-76	(200)	
		(50)	Type 54 122mm	SPH	(1977)	1978-79	(50)	
		(200)	Type 59/1 130mm	TG	1974	1976-80	(200)	
		(50)	Type-81 122mm	MRS	(1981)	1982-83	(50)	Seller unconfirmed
		(2)	CSA-1 SAMS	Mobile SAM system	(1985)	1985	(2)	Unconfirmed
		4	Hai Ying-2 L	ShShM launcher	1980	1981	4	Arming 4 Hegu Class FACs
		4	Hai Ying-2 L	ShShM launcher	1983	1984	4	Arming 4 Huangfen (Osa-2) Class FACs
		(6)	SA-2 SAMS	Mobile SAM system	1979	1980	(6)	Unconfirmed; copy of SA-2 SAM
		(20)	CSA-1	SAM	(1985)	1985	(20)	
		(8)	Hai Ying-2	ShShM/SShM	1980	1981	(8)	Arming 4 Hegu Class FACs

Supplier	No. ordered	Designation	Description	Year of order	Year(s) of deliveries	No. delivered	Comments
	(16)	Hai Ying-2	ShShM/SShM	1983	1984	(16)	Arming 4 Huangfen (Osa-2) Class FACs
	(54)	SA-2 Guideline	Landmob SAM	(1979)	1980	(54)	SAMs deployed Jul 1980; designation unconfirmed
	2	Hainan Class	PC	1975	1976	2	
	2	Hainan Class	PC	1979	1980	2	In addition to 2 delivered 1976
	4	Hegu Class	FAC	(1980)	1981	4	
	4	Huangfen Class	FAC	(1983)	1984	4	Chinese-built version of Osa-2 Class
	4	Huchuan Class	Hydrofoil FAC	1972	1973	4	
	12	Shanghai Class	PC	(1970)	1972-73	(12)	
France	3	Breguet-1150	Mar patrol/ASW	1974	1975-76	3	
	2	Mirage-5DP	Jet trainer	1970	1971	2	
	2	Mirage-5DP	Jet trainer	1979	1980	2	
	28	Mirage-5P	Fighter	1970	1971-72	(28)	
	30	Mirage-5P	Fighter	1979	1980-83	(30)	
	10	Mirage-5R	Recce	1975	1977	10	
	1	Mystere-20	Transport	(1970)	1972	1	For VIP transport
	36	SA-316B	Hel	(1972)	1972-75	(36)	For AF and Army
	35	SA-330L Puma	Hel	1977	1978-79	(35)	For Army
	4	Super Frelon	Hel	(1975)	1975	(4)	Unconfirmed
	(36)	Crotale SAMS	Mobile SAM system	1975	1977-78	(36)	6 btys with 6 launchers each
	(36)	AM-39 Exocet	AShM	(1980)	1982-83	(36)	Arming some of 32 Mirage-5s delivered 1980-83
	(432)	R-440 Crotale	Landmob SAM	(1975)	1977-78	(432)	
	(216)	R-530	AAM	(1967)	1968-72	(216)	Arming Mirage-3/5s
	(128)	R-530	AAM	1979	1980-83	(128)	Arming 32 Mirage-5s
	(60)	R-550 Magic	AAM	(1975)	1977	(60)	Arming Mirage-5s
	(192)	R-550 Magic	AAM	1979	1980-83	(192)	Arming 32 Mirage-5s
	2	Agosta Class	Submarine	1978	1979-80	2	Built for South Africa but embargoed Jan 1978
Germany, FR	(50)	UR-416	APC	(1972)	1975-76	(50)	
Iran	5	C-130E Hercules	Transport	(1974)	1974	5	
Jordan	10	F-104A	Fighter	(1970)	1971	10	Reportedly returned after 1971 war
Netherlands	1	F-27 Maritime	Mar patrol	(1984)	1985	1	Refurbished by Fokker for Navy use for mar patrol and navigation training
Portugal	4	Daphne Class	Submarine	1975	1975	1	
Romania	15	SA-316B	Hel	(1982)	1983	4	
Sweden	..	Supporter	Trainer/strike	1974	1974-76	(15)	Ordered with RBS-70 SAMs
	..	Giraffe	Fire control radar	(1986)			Version RBS-70+; total value incl Giraffe radars: SEK 700 m
	..	RBS-70	Port SAM	(1986)			
UK	6	SH-3D Sea King	Hel	(1973)	1975	6	For Navy
	2	Seacat L	ShAM launcher	(1981)	1982	2	Arming County Class destroyer
	3	Seawolf L-1	ShAM/PDM launcher	1986			To arm 3 Amazon Class frigates

Recipient code/ Recipient	Supplier	No. ordered	Weapon designation	Weapon description	Year of order	Year(s) of delivery	Total delivered	Comments
	USA	(24)	Seacat	ShAM/ShShM	(1981)	1982	(24)	Arming County Class destroyer
		(54)	Seawolf-1	ShAM/PDM	1986			To arm 3 Amazon Class frigates
		2	Amazon Class	Frigate	(1985)			One more ship to be built in Pakistan
		1	County Class	Destroyer	1981	1982	1	Ex-RN 'HMS London'
		(5)	Bird Dog	Lightplane	(1971)	1972	(5)	Assembled from parts
		2	C-130B Hercules	Transport	(1973)	1974-75	2	
		3	C-130B Hercules	Transport	(1979)	1979-81	3	
		34	F-16A	Fighter/strike	1981	1984-86	(34)	Total cost incl 6 trainers: $1.1 b; may be 28 fighters and 12 trainers
		(6)	F-16B	Fighter/trainer	1981	1982-84	6	
		4	G-134 Mohawk	Recce	1984			US LoO Aug 1984
		1	King Air C-90	Trainer	(1978)	1979	1	
		6	Model 205 UH-1H	Hel	(1976)	1977	6	For Army
		5	Model 206A	Hel	1975	1976	5	For Army
		12	Model 209 AH-1S	Hel	1981	1984-85	(12)	Deal incl TOW missiles, MBTs, ARVs, anti-tank vehicles and howitzers
		12	Model 209 AH-1S	Hel	1982	1986	(12)	In addition to 12 ordered 1981
		2	PA-34 Seneca-2	Lightplane	(1977)	1978	2	
		4	T-37C	Jet trainer	(1970)	1971	4	
		30	T-37C	Jet trainer	1977	1978	30	On loan; unconfirmed whether returned
		64	M-109-A2 155mm	SPH	1981	1983-84	(64)	
		36	M-109-A2 155mm	SPH	1982	1984-85	(36)	In addition to 64 ordered 1981
		88	M-109-A2 155mm	SPH	(1985)			US LoO Sep 1985; total value: $78 m
		40	M-110-A2 203mm	SPH	1981	1984-85	(40)	
		300	M-113	APC	(1972)	1973	300	
		110	M-113-A2	APC	(1985)			US LoO Sep 1985; total value: $25 m
		75	M-198 155mm	TH	1981	1984-86	(75)	
		100	M-48-A5	MBT	1981	1982-83	(100)	
		35	M-48-A5	MBT	(1984)	1985	35	
		35	M-88-A1	ARV	1981	1984-85	(35)	
		24	M-901 TOW	TD(M)	(1982)	1984-85	(24)	
		..	AN/TPQ-36	Tracking radar	(1981)	1982	(9)	
		4	AN/TPQ-37	Tracking radar	(1981)	1982	(4)	
		4	AN/TPQ-37	Tracking radar	(1985)			US LoO
		(2)	RGM-84A L	ShShM launcher	1986			Arming 1 Gearing Class destroyer
		3	RGM-84A L	ShShM launcher	1986			To arm 3 Amazon Class frigates
		(500)	AIM-9B	AAM	1974	1974	(500)	Converted to AIM-9J standard in Pakistan
		500	AIM-9L	AAM	1985	1985	100	Arming F-16 fighters; total cost: $50m; quick delivery of 100

Recipient	Supplier	No.	Weapon designation	Weapon description	Year of order	Year of delivery	No. delivered	Comments
		1 005	BGM-71A TOW	ATM	1981	1983-86	(1 005)	Arming Model-209 helicopters and M-901 AVs
		2 030	BGM-71C 1-TOW	ATM	1986	1985	(100)	Total cost: $20 m
		(100)	FIM-92A Stinger	Port SAM	1985	1986	(16)	Undisclosed number delivered
		16	RGM-84A Harpoon	ShShM	(1985)			To arm 1 Gearing Class destroyer; also planned for other 5 ships of same type
		(36)	RGM-84A Harpoon	ShShM	1986			To arm 3 Amazon Class frigates
		2	Gearing Class	Destroyer	1976	1977	2	
		2	Gearing Class	Destroyer	1980	1980	2	In addition to 2 delivered 1977
		2	Gearing Class	Destroyer	(1982)	1982-83	2	In addition to 4 in service
	USSR	12	Mi-8 Hip	Hel	(1967)	1968-71	(12)	For Army
15 Panama	Argentina	(60)	TAM	MT	(1985)			
	Canada	3	DHC-6	Transport	(1969)	1970-75	3	
	France	1	Mystere-20	Transport	(1978)	1979	1	
		2	Batral Class	LC	1978	1980	2	
	Spain	3	C-212-200	Transport	1981	1981-82	3	
		7	C-212-200	Transport	(1986)			Negotiating
	UK	2	BN-2A Islander	Transport	(1974)	1975	2	
		1	Skyvan-3M	Transport	1978	1978	1	
		2	Vosper 103 Type	PC	(1969)	1971	2	
	USA	..	A-37B Dragonfly	Fighter/COIN	(1984)	1984	(5)	First combat aircraft in AF
		1	B-727	Transport	(1981)	1983	1	
		1	DC-6	Transport	(1970)	1971	1	
		6	DHC-3 Otter	Transport	1971	1972	6	
		1	L-188 Electra	Transport	(1973)	1974	1	
		2	Model 172	Trainer	(1976)	1977	2	
		12	Model 204 UH-1B	Hel	1975	1976-77	12	2 re-transferred to Costa Rica 1979
		7	Model 205 UH-1H	Hel	(1970)	1971	7	
		(3)	Model 205 UH-1H	Hel	1972	1973	3	
		1	Model 207	Lightplane	(1984)	1984	(1)	
		5	Model 212	Hel	(1974)	1975	5	
		2	Model 212	Hel	(1984)	1985	2	Replacing Skyhawk
		1	Model 412	Hel	(1984)	1984	(1)	
		2	PA-31 Cheyenne	Mar patrol	(1977)	1978	2	
		(16)	V-150 Commando	APC	(1972)	1973	(16)	
		12	V-300 Commando	APC	1982	1983	(12)	
		1	LSMR Type	LS	1975	1975	1	
11 Papua New Guinea	Australia	3	N-22B Nomad	Mar patrol	1977	1978	3	
		2	N-22L Nomad	Mar patrol	1980	1981	(2)	
		1	N-22L Nomad	Mar patrol	(1983)	1984	(1)	
		3	ASI-315	PC	1985			

Recipient code/ Recipient	Supplier	No. ordered	Weapon designation	Weapon description	Year of order	Year(s) of delivery	Total delivered	Comments
	Israel	3	IAI-201 Arava	Transport	1984	1984-85	(3)	Total cost: $10 m
15 Paraguay	Argentina	1	C-47	Transport	1979	1979	1	Military assistance
	Brazil	1	DHC-3 Otter	Transport	(1970)	1972	1	Military aid
		8	122A Uirapuru	Trainer/COIN	1972	1976	8	
		2	C-47	Transport	(1984)	1984	2	
		5	DC-6	Transport	1975	1975	5	
		(10)	EMB-110	Transport	(1985)	1985	(4)	
		10	EMB-326 Xavante	Trainer/COIN	1979	1980-82	(10)	
		2	HB-350M Esquilo	Hel	1985	1985	2	Total cost: $2.7 m
		8	S-11	Trainer	1975	1975	8	
		10	T-6 Texan	Trainer	1975	1975	10	
		..	EE-11 Urutu	APC	(1984)			Unspecified number ordered
		..	EE-9 Cascavel	AC	(1984)			Unspecified number ordered
		1	Roraima Class	PC	1982	1985	1	Paraguayan designation: P-2 Itaipu
	Chile	2	UH-12	Hel	(1980)	1981	2	
		2	UH-12	Hel	(1982)	1983	2	
		5	Universal-1	Trainer	(1983)	1983	5	Brazil delivered to Chile 1975
	Israel	..	IAI-201 Arava	Transport	(1985)		(2)	Unconfirmed
	Spain	2	C-212-200	Transport	1984	1985		Original order for 4
	USA	6	A-37B Dragonfly	Fighter/COIN	1978	1978	6	Instead of EMB-326Gs
		1	Model 210T	Lightplane	(1974)	1975	1	
		12	Model 47	Hel	(1970)	1972	12	
		10	T-41D Mescalero	Lightplane	(1968)	1970-71	10	
15 Peru	Argentina	16	TAM	MT	(1980)	1981	16	
		80	TAM	MT	(1986)			Negotiating
	Brazil	3	EMB-111	Mar patrol	(1984)			
	Canada	14	DHC-5 Buffalo	Transport	(1970)	1971-72	14	
		14	DHC-5D Buffalo	Transport	(1976)	1978-80	(14)	
		8	DHC-6	Transport	1982	1983	(8)	Total cost: $21.1 m
		8	DHC-6	Transport	1985			
	Cuba	12	MiG-21F	Fighter	1976	1976-77	12	Ex-Cuban AF;
	France	12	Mirage-2000	Fighter/strike	1982	1985-86	(12)	Order reduced from 26 for financial reasons; option on 2 more; armed with AM-39 Exocets
		(26)	Mirage-5	Fighter	(1981)	1984-85	(26)	Possibly Mirage-50
		8	Mirage-5P	Fighter	1973	1974	8	
		4	Mirage-5P	Fighter	(1975)	1976	4	

Country	No.	Designation	Type	Order	Delivery	No.	Comments
	1	Mystere-20	Transport	1982	1983	1	Gift; equipped for air surveillance
	10	AMX-13	LT	(1980)	1981	10	
	4	MM-38 L	ShShM launcher	(1970)	1973	4	Arming 2 Daring Class destroyers
	(12)	MM-38 L	ShShM launcher	1977	1979-80	12	Arming PR-72P Class FACs
	(8)	MM-38 L	ShShM launcher	(1980)	1980-81	(8)	
	(24)	AM-39 Exocet	AShM	1982	1986	(24)	Ordered Dec 1982; arming Mirage-2000s
	(30)	AS-11	ASM	1974	1975	(30)	Arming 9 SH-3D Sea King helicopters
	(30)	AS-11	ASM	(1977)	1979-85	(30)	Arming SH-3D Sea King helicopters
	(30)	AS-30	ASM	1973	1977	(30)	Arming Mirage-5s
	(16)	MM-38 Exocet	ShShM	(1970)	1973	(16)	Arming 2 Daring Class destroyers
	(48)	MM-38 Exocet	ShShM	1977	1979-80	(48)	Arming PR-72P Class FACs
	48	MM-38 Exocet	ShShM	(1980)	1980-81	48	Arming 4 Friesland Class destroyers
		PR-72P Type	FAC	1976	1980-81	6	Arms: MM-38 Exocet ShShMs
Germany, FR	9	Bo-105CB	Hel	(1981)	1982-83	(9)	Armed with Cobra ATMs
	10	UR-416	APC	(1974)	1975	(10)	In addition to 10 delivered 1975
	100	UR-416	APC	(1976)	1977-78	100	
	(28)	Cobra-2000	ATM	(1981)	1982-83	(28)	Arming Bo-105 helicopters
	2	Type 209/1	Submarine	1970	1974-75	2	In addition to 2 delivered 1974-75; also designated Type 1200
	4	Type 209/1	Submarine	1977	1980-83	4	
Italy	6	AB-212	Hel	1976	1977-78	6	For ASW duties
	16	MB-339A	Jet trainer	1981	1981-82	(16)	
	6	SH-3D Sea King	Hel	1977	1979	6	In addition to 6 in service
	7	SH-3D Sea King	Hel	(1984)	1985	7	
	10	Type 6614	APC	1980	1981	10	Arms: 81mm mortar
	15	Type 6616	AC	1981	1981	(15)	
	4	Aspide/Albatros	ShAM/ShShM launcher	1975	1979-85	(4)	1 octuple launcher/ship on 4 Lupo Class frigates
	8	Otomat-1 L	ShShM launcher	1974	1979-85	(8)	Arming Lupo Class frigates
	96	Aspide	AAM/SAM/ShAM	1975	1979-85	(96)	Arming Lupo Class frigates
	96	Otomat-1	ShShM	1974	1979-85	(96)	Prior to licensed production of 2
Netherlands	2	Lupo Class	Frigate	1974	1979	2	
	2	F-27 Maritime	Mar patrol	1976	1977	2	
	4	F-27 Mk-1000	Transport	(1975)	1976	4	
	2	De Ruyter Class	Cruiser	1973	1973-76	2	Terrier SAMs returned to USA before sale
	6	Friesland Class	Destroyer	1980	1981-82	6	
	1	Holland Class	Destroyer	1978	1978-79	1	Ex-Netherlands
Portugal	(40)	Chaimite	APC	(1976)		(40)	Unconfirmed
Spain	(24)	BMR-600	ICV	(1985)		(24)	
	2	DC-8	Transport	(1980)	1981	2	For VIP transport
Switzerland	18	PC-6	Lightplane	(1973)	1975-76	19	
	(15)	Roland	APC	(1981)	1983-84	(15)	

Recipient code/ Recipient	Supplier	No. ordered	Weapon designation	Weapon description	Year of order	Year(s) of delivery	Total delivered	Comments
	UK	11	Canberra B-I-8	Bomber/interdictor	1974	1976-77	11	
	USA	36	A-37B Dragonfly	Fighter/COIN	1973	1975-76	(36)	
		5	C-130H-30	Transport	1980	1981	5	
		6	L-100-20	Transport	1972	1973-76	6	
		2	L-100-20	Transport	1979	1980	2	
		3	L-100-30	Transport	(1985)			Delivery delayed for financial reasons
		2	Learjet 25B	Transport	(1973)	1974	2	
		2	Learjet-35A	Mar patrol/trpt	(1983)	1983	2	
		1	Model 182	Lightplane	(1983)	1983	1	
		17	Model 212	Hel	(1972)	1974-76	(17)	
		6	Model 214ST	Hel	1983	1983-84	(6)	
		1	Queen Air A65	Transport	(1983)	1983	1	
		(9)	S-2E Tracker	Fighter/ASW	(1976)	1976	(9)	
		6	T-34C-1	Trainer	1977	1978	6	
		18	T-37B	Jet trainer	1980	1980	18	
		5	UH-60A	Hel	(1984)			Barter deal; unconfirmed
		(50)	M-101-A1 105mm	TH	1974	1976	(50)	
		40	M-101-A1 105mm	TH	(1976)	1977-78	(40)	
		..	M-101-A1 105mm	TH	(1980)	1981-82	80	
		200	M-113	APC	(1978)	1978-79	(200)	
		(75)	M-113	APC	1980	1983-86	75	
		50	M-114 155mm	TH	(1974)			
		50	M-48-A2	MBT	(1981)			
		(25)	M-8 Greyhound	AC	(1980)	1982	(25)	
		2	Guppy-2 Class	Submarine	1974	1975	2	Purchased from civilian firm
		1	LST 511-1152	LS/minelayer	(1977)	1977	1	
		16	An-26 Curl	Lightplane	1976	1977-78	16	Unconfirmed; reportedly traded against older helicopters from Peruvian inventory
		..	Mi-17 Hip-H	Hel	(1985)	1985	(6)	
	USSR	16	Mi-24 Hind-D	Hel	(1984)	1978	6	
		6	Mi-6 Hook	Hel	1977	1976-77		
		31	Mi-8 Hip	Hel	1976	1978-79	31	Order extended from 14 helicopters
		(17)	Mi-8 Hip	Hel	1978	1977-78	17	
		36	Su-22 Fitter-J	Fighter/grd attack	1976	1977-78	36	Total cost: $250 m
		16	Su-22 Fitter-J	Fighter/grd attack	1980	1980-81	16	
		(250)	T-55	MBT	1976	1976-78	(250)	
		200	T-55	MBT	(1978)	1979-80	(200)	In addition to 250 T-54/55s in service
		(10)	ZSU-23-4 Shilka	AAV	(1976)	1977	(10)	

Recipient	Supplier	No.	Designation	Description	(Order)	Delivery	No.	Comments
		(4)	SA-2 SAMS	Mobile SAM system	(1974)	1975	(4)	Incl 10 SA-3 Goa SAMs
		(2)	SA-3 SAMS	Mobile SAM system	1976	1977	(2)	Arming Su-22s
		(108)	AA-2 Atoll	AAM	(1976)	1977-78	(108)	
		(20)	SA-2 Guideline	Landmob SAM	(1974)	1975	(20)	Mounted on ZIL-151 trucks
		(10)	SA-3 Goa	Landmob SAM	1976	1977	10	
		100	SA-7 Grail	Port SAM	(1978)	1980-81	(100)	
11 Philippines	Australia	12	N-22B Nomad	Mar patrol	(1974)	1975-76	(12)	Prior to local assembly
	Germany, FR	5	Bo-105	Hel	1974	1974	5	Prototypes; licensed production planned
		2	Katapangan Cl	PC	(1977)	1979	2	For COIN duties
	Italy	16	SF-260 Warrior	Trainer/COIN	1972	1973-74	(16)	Order incl 16 SF-260 Warrior
		27	SF-260M	Trainer	(1972)	1973-74	(27)	Number and delivery schedule uncertain
		(100)	Model 56 105mm	TH	(1980)	1982-83	(100)	
	Netherlands	(3)	F-27 Maritime	Mar patrol	1980	1982	(1)	Last 2 probably cancelled
		(7)	F-27 Mk-100	Transport	1971	1972-73	(7)	
		(2)	F-27 Mk-100	Transport	(1974)	1975	(2)	
	Portugal	(20)	Chaimite	APC	(1978)	1979-80	(20)	
		2	Bataan Class	PC	(1973)	1975	2	
	Singapore	28	FV-101 Scorpion	LT	1976	1977	28	
	UK	11	AC-47	Transport	(1972)	1973	11	Transferred from USAF in S. Vietnam
	USA	15	C-123 Provider	Transport	(1972)	1973-74	(15)	
		4	C-130H Hercules	Transport	1976	1977-78	4	
		18	C-47	Transport	(1968)	1970-71	18	USAF surplus from S. Vietnam
		10	DHC-2 Beaver	Lightplane	(1972)	1973	10	Preferred over F-5Es; 35 aircraft bought for $11.7 m; 25 refurbished for $23 m; 10 for spares
		25	F-8H Crusader	Fighter	1977	1978	25	
		4	HU-16B Albatros	Mar patrol/ASW	1975	1976-77	4	Purchased from US dealer; ex-USAF stocks
		4	L-100-20	Transport	(1972)	1973	4	
		1	L-100-20	Transport	(1974)	1975	1	
		13	Model 185	Lightplane	(1964)	1965-71	13	U-17A/B Skywagon
		12	Model 205 UH-1D	Hel	(1966)	1968-71	12	
		(10)	Model 205 UH-1D	Hel	(1972)	1973	(10)	
		28	Model 205 UH-1H	Hel	(1970)	1971	28	
		17	Model 205 UH-1H	Hel	1976	1977	17	
		18	Model 205 UH-1H	Hel	1980	1980	(18)	Part of base facility agreement
		15	Model 205 UH-1H	Hel	1982	1983	15	For Army
		12	Model 205 UH-1H	Hel	1983	1983	12	For Army
		3	Model 210T	Lightplane	(1981)	1982	(3)	
		8	Model 500MD	Hel	1979	1981-82	(8)	Ordered Aug 1979
		18	OV-10A Bronco	Trainer/COIN	1980	1983	(18)	
		(2)	RT-33A	Fighter/recce	(1976)	1977	(2)	
		2	S-70C	Hel	(1985)		2	Unconfirmed

Recipient code/ Recipient	Supplier	No. ordered	Weapon designation	Weapon description	Year of order	Year(s) of delivery	Total delivered	Comments
		17	S-76 Spirit	Hel	1983	1983	17	Total cost incl 2 UH-60As: $60 m
		8	T-28D Trojan	Trainer/COIN	(1969)	1970-71	(8)	
		4	T-28D Trojan	Trainer/COIN	(1971)	1972	4	
		(20)	T-28D Trojan	Trainer/COIN	(1978)	1979-81	(20)	
		7	T-33A	Jet trainer	(1971)	1972	7	
		2	UH-60A	Hel	1983	1985	(2)	
		45	AIFV	MICV	(1978)	1979	45	
		(30)	LVTP-5	Amph ASSV	(1978)	1979	(30)	For Marine Corps
		55	LVTP-7A1	Amph ASSV	1982	1984-85	(55)	For Marine Corps; total cost: $64 m
		(15)	M-113-A1	APC	(1972)	1973	(15)	
		20	M-113-A1	APC	1976	1976	20	
		(25)	M-113-A1	APC	(1977)	1978	(25)	
		20	M-113-A1	APC	(1980)	1981	(20)	
		(6)	M-114 155mm	TH	(1971)	1972	(6)	Delivery year and number uncertain
		10	V-150 Commando	APC	1982	1982	10	
		100	V-150 Commando	APC	1983	1984-85	(100)	
		24	M-167 Vulcan	Mobile AA-system	(1984)			
		4	Series-3200	3-D radar	(1984)	1984-85	(4)	
		1	Admirable Class	MSO	1975	1975	1	Acquired from S. Vietnam; minesweeping gear removed
		2	Aggressive Cl	MSO	(1971)	1972	2	Ex-US MSOs built 1953-54
		4	Barnegat Class	Support ship	1975	1975	4	Acquired from S. Vietnam
		3	Cannon Class	Frigate	(1977)	1980	3	Refurbished in S. Korea before delivery
		1	Edsall Class	Frigate	1975	1975	1	Acquired from S. Vietnam
		3	LCU 1466 Class	LC	(1975)	1975	3	
		4	LSIL Type	LC	(1975)	1975	4	Acquired from S. Vietnam
		2	LSM Type	LC/minelayer	1975	1975	2	Acquired from S. Vietnam
		6	LST 1-510	LS	(1971)	1972-78	6	
		18	LST 511-1152	LS/minelayer	1968	1969-76	18	
		1	PC-452 Type	PC	(1975)	1975	1	Acquired from Cambodia
		3	PCE-827 Class	Corvette	1975	1975-76	3	
		1	PGM-71 Class	PC	1975	1975	1	Acquired from S. Vietnam
15 Qatar	Brazil	(20)	EE-9 Cascavel	AC	1978	1979	(20)	Possibly more
	Egypt	..	Fahd	APC	(1984)	1985	(10)	
	France	6	Alpha Jet	Jet trainer/strike	1979	1980-81	6	First sale in Middle East
		2	Mirage F-1B	Jet trainer	1980	1984	2	
		12	Mirage F-1C	Fighter/interceptor	1980	1984-85	(12)	
		6	SA-330 Puma	Hel	1980	1983-84	(6)	

	No.	Designation	Type	Order	Delivered	No.	Comments
	2	SA-341H Gazelle	Hel	(1973)	1974	2	Possibly for police
	30	AMX-10P	MICV	1975	1977-78	30	
	6	AMX-155 Mk-F3	SPH	(1979)	1980	6	
	24	AMX-30B	MBT	1975	1977	24	
	(180)	VAB	APC	(1979)	1980-82	(180)	Several versions
	(6)	MM-40 L	ShShM launcher	1980	1982-83	6	Arming 3 Combattante-3 FACs
	..	MM-40 L-2	SShM launcher	1980	1983-84	(3)	For coastal defence
	..	AM-39 Exocet	AShM	(1983)	1984	(20)	Unspecified number reportedly ordered for Commando Mk-2 helicopters
UK	..	HOT	ATM	1982			Total cost incl Milan ATMs: $20 m
	(24)	MM-40 Exocet	ShShM/SShM	1980	1982-83	(24)	Arming 3 Combattante-3 Class FACs
	(50)	MM-40 Exocet	ShShM/SShM	1980	1983-84	(50)	3 coastal defence systems ordered
	..	Milan	ATM	(1982)			Unconfirmed
	3	Combattante-3	FAC	1980	1982-83	3	Armed with 8 Exocet MM-40 ShShMs
	1	BN-2A Islander	Transport	1975	1976	1	
	4	Commando Mk-2	Hel	(1974)	1975-76	4	
	8	Commando Mk-3	Hel	1981	1983-84	(8)	One for VIP, 3 for troop transport
	3	Hunter FGA-74	Fighter	(1969)	1971-72	3	For ASW duties
	1	Hunter T-7	Fighter/trainer	(1969)	1971	1	
	3	Lynx	Hel	1976	1977	3	
	6	Saracen FV-603	APC	(1985)	1985	6	Part of deal incl 10 patrol craft, rifles and grenades; UK military aid
	(4)	Rapier SAMS	Mobile SAM system	1981	1983-84	(4)	Reportedly on order
	..	Blowpipe	Port SAM	(1984)			
	..	Rapier	Landmob SAM	(1981)	1983-84	(48)	1 bty ordered; option on more
	6	Type 33M	PC	1972	1975-76	6	Qatari designation: Barzan Class
4 Rwanda							
France	2	C-47	Transport	(1974)	1975	2	
	3	Magister	Jet trainer	(1973)	1975	3	
	2	Noratlas 2501	Transport	(1984)			
	2	Rallye-235GT	Lightplane	1983	1983-84	(2)	
	(4)	SA-316B	Hel	1971	1973	(4)	
	6	SA-342L Gazelle	Hel	(1982)	1983	6	
Germany, FR	..	M-3	APC	(1983)	1983	(10)	
Italy	1	Do-27	Transport	(1974)	1975	1	In addition to 1 previously acquired
Romania	3	AM-3C	Lightplane	1970	1972	3	
UK	1	BN-2A Defender	Lightplane	(1974)	1975	1	From licensed production in Romania
	1	BN-2A Defender	Lightplane	1978	1979	1	
11 Samoa							
Australia	1	ASI-315	PC	1985			
7 Saudi Arabia							
Austria	(400)	Cuirassier	LT/TD	(1986)			Discussing purchase of up to 400; status of deal uncertain

Recipient code/ Recipient	Supplier	No. ordered	Weapon designation	Weapon description	Year of order	Year(s) of delivery	Total delivered	Comments
	Brazil	(30)	EE-11 Urutu	APC	(1982)	1985	(30)	
		2	EE-9 Cascavel	AC	1984	1984	(2)	For evaluation
		(1 000)	EE-T2 Osorio	MBT	(1986)			
	France	1	AS-365	Hel	(1985)	1986	1	For VIP use
		24	AS-365F	Hel	1980	1983-86	(24)	20 armed with AS-15TT; some to arm 4 F-2000 Class frigates
		(2)	ATL-2	Mar patrol	(1983)			Unconfirmed
		4	Model 172	Lightplane	(1973)	1975	4	
		(350)	AMX-10P	MICV	1974	1975-78	(350)	
		(60)	AMX-10P	MICV	(1982)	1983-84	(60)	
		(36)	AMX-30 Shahine	AAV(M)	1974	1980-82	(36)	
		(80)	AMX-30 Shahine	AAV(M)	1984			Improved version to be developed with Saudi financial assistance; part of 'Al Thakeb' contract
		51	AMX-30-155 GCT	SPG	1975	1978	(51)	Delivered from first production run; number unconfirmed
		53	AMX-30-30mm	AAV	1975	1979-82	(53)	
		30	AMX-30B	MBT	(1970)	1972-73	30	
		359	AMX-30B	MBT	1975	1976-82	(359)	Incl 57 AMX-30D and 12 BL versions
		600	ERC-90 Sagaie	AC	(1986)			Negotiating; deal incl modernization of French vehicles in Saudi arsenal
		4	Crotale Naval L	ShAM launcher	1980	1985-86	(4)	1x4 launchers on 4 F-2000 Class frigates
		8	Otomat-2 L	ShShM launcher	1980	1985-86	(8)	On F-2000 frigates
		..	Otomat-2 L	ShShM launcher	1984			Coastal defence btys; 'Al Thakeb' deal
		(54)	Shahine shelter	Mobile SAM system	1984			'Al Thakeb' deal; launch canisters for defence of fixed installations; 134 launch systems of which rest are AMX-30s
		221	AS-15TT	AShM	1980	1983-86	(221)	Arming SA-365F helicopters
		104	Crotale Naval	ShAM	1980	1985-86	(104)	First export order of naval version; arming F-2000 Class frigates
		(2 000)	Harpon	ATM	(1975)	1977-78	(2 000)	
		(96)	Otomat-2	ShShM	1980	1985-86	(96)	Arming 4 F-2000 Class frigates
		..	Otomat-2/Teseo	SShM	1984			'Al Thakeb' deal; for coastal defence
		(280)	R-550 Magic	AAM	(1974)	1975-76	(280)	Arming F-5Es
		(2 000)	SS-11	ATM	(1973)	1975-76	(2 000)	
		(216)	Shahine	Landmob SAM	1974	1980-82	(216)	
		(1 000)	Shahine-2	Landmob SAM	1984	1984-85		Total value of 'Al Thakeb' deal: $4.1 b
		2	Durance Class	Support ship	1980	1984-85	2	Fuel supply ship; displacement: 10 000t
		4	F-2000 Class	Frigate	1980	1985-86	(4)	Part of 'Sawari' naval deal

	No. ordered	Designation	Description	Year of order	Year of deliveries	No. delivered	Comments
Germany, FR	(300)	Gepard	AAV	(1986)			Ongoing negotiations
	(60)	Wildcat	AAV	(1986)			Unconfirmed
Indonesia	40	CN-212	Transport	1979	1983-85	(15)	One in VIP configuration from USA, rest from Italy; unconfirmed
Italy	(30)	AB-212	Hel	1977	1977-79	(30)	
	3	S-61A-4	Hel	1977	1978	3	
	1	SH-3D Sea King	Hel	(1985)	1985	1	
	200	VCC-1	APC	1982	1984-85	(100)	Some armed with TOW ATMs
Japan	6	KV-107/2A	Hel	1977	1979	6	For rescue missions and fire fighting
	10	KV-107/2A	Hel	1982	1984-86	(10)	Order may be increased to 10
	6	KV-107/2A-1	Hel	1976	1978	6	
Spain	4	CN-235	Transport	(1985)	1986	(1)	Total cost: $62 m; UK workshare: 10%
	140	BMR-600	ICV	1984			
Switzerland	30	PC-9	Trainer	1986			
UK	10	BAC-167	Trainer/COIN	(1971)	1973	10	
	21	BAC-167	Trainer/COIN	1976	1977	21	Replacing losses; unconfirmed
	30	Hawk	Jet trainer/strike	(1986)			Negotiating
	2	Jetstream-31	Transport	(1986)			
	24	Tornado ADV	Fighter/MRCA	1986	1986	(2)	Total value incl 72 Tornados, 30 Hawks, 30 PC-9s and missiles: approx $5.5 b
	48	Tornado IDS	Fighter/MRCA	1986	1986	(4)	Unit cost: $0.75 m
	72	FH-70 155mm	TH	1982	1983-85	(72)	
	(50)	Ferret FV-703	Recce AC	1974	1977-78	(50)	
	(50)	Fox FV-721	AC	1974	1977-78	(50)	
	..	SSR	Surveillance radar	(1984)	1985-86	(20)	
	..	ALARM	ARM	(1986)			Arming Tornado fighters
	..	Sea Eagle	AShM	(1986)			Arming Tornado fighters
	..	Sky Flash	AAM	(1986)			Arming Tornado fighters
USA	2	B-707-320C	Transport	(1977)	1980	2	Some equipped for tanker operations
	1	B-737-200C	Transport	(1976)	1979	1	
	1	B-747-100B	Transport	(1984)	1984	1	
	1	B-747-131	Transport	1977	1980	1	2 bought on behalf of N. Yemen
	14	C-130H Hercules	Transport	(1971)	1974-75	14	
	17	C-130H Hercules	Transport	1976	1977-78	17	
	5	C-130H Hercules	Transport	(1979)	1980	5	
	3	C-130H Hercules	Transport	(1981)	1982	3	
	4	C-130H Hercules	Transport	(1984)	1984	(4)	
	5	E-3A Sentry	AEW	1981	1981	5	4 USAF AWACS in Saudi Arabia until 1986
	45	F-15C Eagle	Fighter	1978	1981-83	(45)	Order incl 15 F-15D trainers
	2	F-15C Eagle	Fighter	1980			
	15	F-15D Eagle	Jet trainer	1978	1981-83	(15)	
	20	F-5B	Fighter/trainer	(1971)	1972-73	20	Retained until needed as replacement
	70	F-5E Tiger-2	Fighter	1974	1974-76	70	Of which first 30 ordered 1971

Recipient code/ Recipient	Supplier	No. ordered	Weapon designation	Weapon description	Year of order	Year(s) of delivery	Total delivered	Comments
		4	F-5E Tiger-2	Fighter	1982	1984	(4)	Cost incl 10 RF-5Es and 1 F-5F: $350 m
		20	F-5F Tiger-2	Jet trainer	1974	1977-78	20	
		4	F-5F Tiger-2	Jet trainer	1976	1979	4	
		1	F-5F Tiger-2	Jet trainer	1982	1984	(1)	
		1	Gulfstream-3	Transport	(1983)	1985	1	For VIP use
		1	KC-10A Extender	Tanker/transport	1984	1984	1	Delivered along with 200 Stinger SAMs
		4	KC-130H	Tanker/transport	(1973)	1973-74	4	
		3	KC-130H	Tanker/transport	1975	1977	3	
		2	KC-130H	Tanker/transport	(1979)	1980	2	Delivered Dec 1980
		8	KC-135	Tanker/transport	1981			Order increased from 6 to 8 in 1984; total cost: $2.4 b; for delivery 1987-88
		(1)	Learjet 25C	Transport	(1979)	1980	1	At least 1 delivered
		1	Learjet-35A	Mar patrol/trpt	(1980)	1981	1	
		10	RF-5E Tigereye	Recce	1982	1984-85	(10)	
		12	UH-60A	Hel	(1986)			
		3	M-1 Abrams	MBT	(1983)	1983	3	For evaluation
		(100)	M-101-A1 105mm	TH	1976	1977-78	(100)	Incl some M-102 155mm guns
		12	M-106-A1	APC	1979			Replacing 12 sent to N. Yemen
		(20)	M-109-A1 155mm	SPH	(1976)	1978-79	(20)	
		18	M-109-A2 155mm	SPH	1983	1984-85	(18)	
		50	M-110-A1 203mm	SPH	(1980)	1981-82	(50)	
		(200)	M-113-A1	APC	1976	1976-79	(200)	
		26	M-113-A1	APC	1979	1979	26	Armed with TOW ATMs
		(505)	M-113-A2	APC	1983	1984-86	(505)	Also incl M-578s, M-992s, M-106s, M-577s and M-88/125s; total cost: $271 m
		(50)	M-114 155mm	TH	(1976)	1977-78	(50)	
		(43)	M-198 155mm	TH	(1978)	1979-80	(43)	
		18	M-198 155mm	TH	1981	1982	(18)	
		42	M-198 155mm	TH	1983	1984-85	(42)	
		(20)	M-56	TD	(1974)	1976	(20)	
		6	M-577-A1	CPC	1979	1979	6	Unconfirmed
		(150)	M-60-A1	MBT	1976	1977-79	(150)	Replacing 6 sent to N. Yemen
		32	M-60-A1	MBT	1979	1980	32	Replacing 32 sent to N. Yemen
		100	M-60-A3	MBT	1983	1984-85	(100)	
		6	M-88	ARV	1979	1979	6	Replacing several sent to N. Yemen
		(214)	M-88-A1	ARV	(1985)			Unconfirmed
		579	V-150 Commando	APC	(1980)	1981-86	(579)	For modernization of National Guard
		..	AN/TPQ-36	Tracking radar	(1982)	1984-85	(10)	
		..	AN/TPS-32	3-D radar	(1984)			

No.	Weapon designation	Weapon description	Year of order	Year(s) of deliveries	No. delivered	Comments
: :	AN/TPS-43	3-D radar	(1977)	1978-80	(9)	
: :	AN/TPS-43	3-D radar	1985		(6)	
6	I-Hawk SAMS	Mobile SAM system	1974	1974	(4)	
: :	Phalanx	CIWS	(1979)	1980-82	(9)	On Badr Class corvettes
4	Phalanx	CIWS	(1980)	1980-82	9	On Al Siddiq Class FACs
6	RGM-84A L	ShShM launcher	1977	1980-82	4	Arming 9 Al Siddiq Class FACs
4	RGM-84A L	ShShM launcher	1978	1980-83		Arming 4 Badr Class corvettes
(140)	AGM-45A Shrike	ARM	(1974)	1975-76	(140)	
1 650	AGM-65A	ASM	(1974)	1975-78	(1 650)	
916	AGM-65A	ASM	1979	1979	(916)	Arming F-15s
1 600	AGM-65D	ASM	(1984)			To arm F-15s
100	AGM-84A Harpoon	AShM	1986	1986		
(1 000)	AIM-7F Sparrow	AAM	1978	1981-85	(1 000)	Arming F-15 fighters
400	AIM-9J	AAM	1975	1976-77	(400)	
1 177	AIM-9L	AAM	1981	1982-85	(750)	
995	AIM-9L	AAM	1986	1986		
(660)	AIM-9P	AAM	1979	1980-81	(660)	
671	AIM-9P	AAM	1986	1986		For delivery 1989-91
(4 000)	BGM-71C I-TOW	ATM	1983	1984	(4 000)	Some replacing SS-11/Harpoon on AMX-30s
1 000	BGM-71A TOW	ATM	1976	1977-78	(1 000)	Incl 50 M-110-A1 vehicles
2 500	BGM-71C I-TOW	ATM	1979	1979-80		Probably not delivered; not identical with US LoO for 2538 TOWs in 1983
2 538	BGM-71C I-TOW	ATM	1977	1978-81		Total cost: $26 m
(400)	FGM-77A Dragon	ATM	1976	1976-79	(400)	
1 292	FGM-77A Dragon	ATM	1979	1980	1 292	On order
: :	FIM-43A Redeye	Port SAM	1977	1977-78		
400	FIM-92A Stinger	Port SAM	1984	1984	(400)	Incl 200 launchers
(1 458)	MIM-23B Hawk	Landmob SAM	1974	1978-81	(1 458)	Replacing old Hawk systems
(108)	RGM-84A Harpoon	ShShM	1977	1980-82	(108)	Arming 9 Al Saddiq Class FACs
(96)	RGM-84A Harpoon	ShShM	1978	1980-83	96	Arming 4 Badr Class corvettes
4	Adjutant Class	MSC	1975	1978-79		Also designated MSC 322 Class
9	Al Siddiq Class	FAC	1977	1980-82	9	Ordered Feb 1977
4	Badr Class	Corvette	1977	1980-83	4	Ordered Sep 1977
4	LCU 1610 Class	LC	(1975)	1976	4	

4 Senegal

Canada

No.	Weapon designation	Weapon description	Year of order	Year(s) of deliveries	No. delivered	Comments
1	DHC-6 Srs-300	Transport	1981	1982	1	

France

No.	Weapon designation	Weapon description	Year of order	Year(s) of deliveries	No. delivered	Comments
6	F-27 Mk-600	Transport	1977	1978-79	6	Military aid; including 4 Rallyes
4	Magister	Jet trainer	(1983)	1984	4	
1	Model F337	Trainer	1970	1971	1	
2	Rallye-180T	Lightplane	(1981)	1982	2	
2	Rallye-235CA	Lightplane	(1981)	1982	2	
4	Rallye-235CA	Lightplane	(1982)	1984	4	
4	Rallye-235GT	Lightplane	1984	1985	4	For fire support and COIN duties; gift

Recipient code/ Recipient	Supplier	No. ordered	Weapon designation	Weapon description	Year of order	Year(s) of delivery	Total delivered	Comments
		(3)	SA-330 Puma	Hel	(1980)	1980	(3)	
		1	SA-341H Gazelle	Hel	(1977)	1977	(1)	
		..	AML-90	AC	(1975)	1975	(20)	
		3	AML-90	AC	1984	1984	3	Unconfirmed
		..	M-20	AC	(1982)	1982	6	Military aid
		(12)	M-3	APC	(1978)	1978	(12)	Delivery schedule unconfirmed
		..	M-3	APC	(1981)	1981	(6)	Unconfirmed
		..	Model-50 155mm	TH	(1980)	1981	(6)	Unconfirmed
		(12)	VXB-170	APC	(1978)	1978	(12)	Delivery schedule unconfirmed
		..	Milan	ATM	(1978)	1979	(50)	
		1	EDIC/EDA Type	LC	(1973)	1974	1	
		2	EDIC/EDA Type	LC	1985			EDIC-3 version
	USA	3	P-48 Type	PC/FAC	(1970)	1971-77	3	
		1	PR-72 Type	PC	1979	1982	1	Supplier unconfirmed
		1	B-727-200	Transport	(1980)	1980	(1)	
4 Seychelles	France	1	Sirius Class	MSC/PC	(1978)	1979	1	Handed over Apr 1979; ex-French Navy; minesweeping gear removed
		1	Sirius Class	MSC/PC	(1979)	1979	1	French gift
	India	2	SA-316B Chetak	Hel	1982	1982	2	
	Italy	(1)	Type 42M	PC	1981	1983	1	Follow-on order expected
	Libya	2	Rallye-235GT	Lightplane	1980	1980	2	Gift
	UK	1	BN-2A Defender	Lightplane	1980	1980	1	Gift
		1	BN-2A Islander	Transport	1979	1979	1	
	USSR	..	BRDM-2	SC	(1979)	1980	(20)	Shown in military parade
		..	SA-7 Grail	Port SAM	(1983)	1984	(50)	Designation unconfirmed
3 Sierra Leone	China	3	Shanghai Class	PC	(1973)	1973	3	
	France	2	AS-350 Ecureuil	Hel	(1984)	1985	(2)	
	Germany, FR	1	Bo-105CB	Hel	1978	1978	1	For VIP use
	Sweden	4	MFI-15 Safari	Lightplane	(1971)	1973	4	
	Switzerland	..	Piranha	APC	(1978)	1978	(3)	Delivery schedule unconfirmed
	UK	1	Saladin FV-601	AC	(1982)	1983	(3)	Unconfirmed
	USA	1	Model 300	Hel	(1971)	1973	1	
		2	Model 500	Hel	1972	1972	2	
4 Singapore	Canada	2	Model 205A-1	Hel	(1983)	1983-84	(2)	Probably attrition aircraft
	France	22	AS-332	Hel	1984	1985	(5)	Five delivered early 1985; 17 to be assembled by Samaero; option on 12 more for Navy (missile-armed)

Country	No.	Designation	Description	Order year	Delivery year	No.	Comments
Germany, FR	6	AS-350 Ecureuil	Hel	1982	1984	(6)	For Navy
	24	T-33A	Jet trainer	1979	1980-82	24	Ex-French AF
	150	AMX-13	LT	1978	1980-84	(150)	
Israel	2	TNC-45	FAC	1970	1972	2	Prior to licensed production of 4
	:	M-68 155mm	TH	(1972)	1972	(20)	Unconfirmed
	(20)	M-71 155mm	TH	1976	1977	(20)	Unconfirmed number and delivery year
	(6)	Gabriel L	ShShM launcher	1972	1972-75	(6)	For 6 TNC-45 FACs
	90	Gabriel-1	ShShM	(1972)	1972-75	(90)	Arming 6 TNC-45 FACs
Italy	30	S-211	Trainer	1983	1984-86	(30)	First 6 to be delivered directly; last 24 to be assembled in Singapore; total cost approx $60 m
	6	SF-260 Warrior	Trainer/COIN	1979	1980	6	Follow-on order to 16 purchased in 1971
	6	SF-260 Warrior	Trainer/COIN	1982	1983	(6)	
	16	SF-260M	Trainer	(1969)	1971	16	
Jordan	2	C-130B Hercules	Transport	(1976)	1977	2	
New Zealand	4	Airtourer-150	Lightplane	(1972)	1973	4	Option for 2 more not taken
Oman	5	BAC-167	Trainer/COIN	(1976)	1977	5	
Sweden	300	RBS-70	Port SAM	(1978)	1980	300	Order incl 25 aiming units; total value: SEK 60 m
Switzerland	550	RBS-70	Port SAM	(1980)	1982	550	Order incl 50 aiming units
	150	AMX-13	LT	1979	1979	150	Old type reportedly purchased
UK	12	Hunter FGA-74	Fighter	(1969)	1970-71	12	
	22	Hunter FGA-74	Fighter	1971	1972-73	22	
	4	Hunter FR-11	Recce	(1969)	1970-71	(4)	
	5	Hunter T-75	Fighter	(1971)	1973	5	
	6	Skyvan-3M	Transport	1969	1973-74	6	Three special version for Singapore AF
	28	Bloodhound-2	Mobile SAM system	1981	1971	28	Ex-RAF; refurbished
	:	DN-181 Rapier	Mobile SAM system	1972	1984-85	(2)	
	(3)	Rapier SAMS	Mobile SAM system	1969	1977	(3)	
	(312)	Bloodhound-2	Landmob SAM	1972	1977	(312)	Ex-RAF; total cost: $24 m
	(120)	Rapier	Landmob SAM	1981	1984-85	(120)	Incl 6 launchers
	(96)	Rapier	Landmob SAM	1972	1977	(96)	
USA	40	A-4S Skyhawk-2	Fighter/bomber	1972	1975-76	40	From surplus US Navy stocks
	2	C-130B Hercules	Transport	(1977)	1978	2	
	4	C-130B Hercules	Transport	(1978)	1980	4	
	4	E-2C Hawkeye	AEW	1983	1986	(2)	
	8	F-16A	Fighter/strike	1985			Order changed from F-16/79s to F-16A/Bs; contract value unchanged at $280 m
	18	F-5E Tiger-2	Fighter	1976	1979	18	Total cost: $601 m
	6	F-5E Tiger-2	Fighter	1980	1981	6	Total cost including 3 F-5F trainers and 200 Sidewinder AAMs; Sidewinder AAMs: $110 m
	3	F-5F Tiger-2	Jet trainer	1976	1979	3	Total cost: $34 m; Armed with Sidewinder AAMs

Recipient code/ Recipient	Supplier	No. ordered	Weapon designation	Weapon description	Year of order	Year(s) of delivery	Total delivered	Comments
		(20)	Model 204 UH-1B	Hel	(1980)	1981	(20)	20 or more transferred from US Army
		17	Model 205A-1	Hel	1976	1977	17	Bought new from factory
		3	Model 212	Hel	1977	1977	3	For VIP transport
		7	TA-4S Skyhawk-2	Jet trainer	1972	1975–77	7	From US Navy stocks
		8	TA-4S Skyhawk-2	Jet trainer	1983	1984	(8)	
		(250)	M-113-A1	APC	(1974)	1975–76	(250)	
		(250)	M-113-A1	APC	(1978)	1979–80	(250)	In addition to 250 in service
		(200)	M-113-A1	APC	(1981)	1982–83	(200)	
		(20)	M-114 155mm	TH	(1976)	1977	(20)	
		(40)	V-150 Commando	APC	(1974)	1975–76	(40)	
		250	V-200 Commando	APC	(1969)	1970–74	(250)	
		3	I-Hawk SAMS	Mobile SAM system	1979	1981	3	Unconfirmed
		(3)	I-Hawk SAMS	Mobile SAM system	(1982)	1985	(3)	3 systems ordered Jul 1979
		24	M-167 Vulcan	Mobile AA-system	(1984)			
		200	AGM-65A	ASM	1981	1981	(200)	Total cost: $30 m
		31	AGM-84A Harpoon	AShM	1985			Arming F-5Es; cost: $26 m
		200	AIM-9J	AAM	1976	1979	200	Arming AS-332s
		200	AIM-9P	AAM	1978	1979–80	200	For 21 F-5E/F fighters
		(200)	AIM-9P	AAM	(1982)	1983	(200)	Total cost: $12 m
		(162)	MIM-23B Hawk	Landmob SAM	1979	1981	(162)	3 systems ordered Jul 1979
		(162)	MIM-23B Hawk	Landmob SAM	(1982)	1985	(162)	
		2	Bluebird Class	MSC	(1974)	1975	2	
	Yemen, South	6	LST 511-1152	LS/minelayer	(1970)	1971–75	(6)	
		4	BAC-167	Trainer/COIN	(1974)	1975	4	
		4	Jet Provost T52	Jet trainer	(1974)	1975	4	Order also incl 4 Jet Provost T-52s
11 Solomon Islands	Australia	1	ASI-315	PC	1985			
3 Somalia	China	20	F-6	Fighter	(1979)	1980–81	(20)	Unconfirmed
		(4)	F-7	Fighter	(1986)			Negotiating
		:	Type 59/1 130mm	TG	(1982)	1982	(10)	Unconfirmed
		:	Type-60 122mm	TG	(1982)	1982	10	Unconfirmed
	Egypt	:	M-46 130mm	TG	1978	1979	(10)	Supplier unconfirmed
		(35)	T-54	MBT	1977	1977	(35)	Unconfirmed
		:	T-54	MBT	(1980)	1981	(50)	Delivered Jan 1981
		20	T-55	MBT	(1982)	1982	20	
		:	SA-3 SAMS	Mobile SAM system	1977	1978	2	
		:	SA-3 Goa	Landmob SAM	(1977)	1978	(20)	
	France	50	VLRA	Recce AC	(1983)			Designation unconfirmed

Supplier	No. ordered	Weapon designation	Weapon description	Year of order	Year of delivery	No. delivered	Comments
Germany, FR	:	Milan	ATM	(1978)	1979	(100)	Supplier unconfirmed
Iran	1	Do-28D-1	Transport	(1979)	1979	(1)	For paramilitary police
Italy	4	SA-7 Grail	Port SAM	1978	1978	(100)	Unconfirmed
	4	AB-212	Hel	1980	1982	(4)	First 2 delivered Feb 1982
	(4)	G-222	Transport	1979	1980-82	4	
	(4)	P-166	Transport	(1979)	1981	(4)	Unconfirmed
	(6)	S-211	Trainer	(1985)			
	(14)	SF-260 Warrior	Trainer/COIN	1978	1979-80	(14)	
	6	SM-1019E	Lightplane	1980	1982	6	
	(40)	Centurion	MBT	(1979)	1980	(40)	Supplier unconfirmed
	100	M-47 Patton	MBT	(1983)	1985	(100)	All of Italy's 500 M-47s to be returned to USA for refurbishing before transfer to Third World countries
Saudi Arabia	(50)	M-47 Patton	MBT	(1985)			In addition to 100 delivered earlier
	(270)	Type 6614	APC	1977	1978-79	(270)	Unspecified number reportedly delivered
	30	Type 6616	AC	1977	1978-79	(30)	
Spain		AML-90	AC	(1984)	1984	(20)	Unspecified number reportedly delivered
	6	C-212-200	Transport	1984			
	:	BMR-600	ICV	(1984)			Unspecified number reportedly ordered
	:	M-41E Cazador	TD	(1984)			Unspecified number reportedly ordered
USA	(1)	Model 150	Lightplane	(1981)	1981	(1)	
	24	M-113-A1	APC	(1981)	1982	24	Armed with TOW ATMs
	(12)	M-163 Vulcan	AAV	1981	1983	(12)	Order incl 3 TPS/43 defence radars; in exchange for US base rights in Berbera and Mogadishu
	:	AN/TPS-43	3-D radar	(1979)	1980	(3)	
	:	I-Hawk SAMS	Mobile SAM system	1982	1982-83	(8)	
	431	BGM-71A TOW	ATM	(1981)	1982	431	Arming M-113-A1 APCs
	:	MIM-23B Hawk	Landmob SAM	1982	1982-83	(48)	Began arriving Aug 1982 as part of US emergency aid
USSR	(2)	An-24 Coke	Transport	1972	1973	(2)	
	(2)	An-26 Curl	Lightplane	(1971)	1973	(2)	
	(2)	Il-18	Transport	(1973)	1973	(2)	
	(3)	Il-28	Bomber	(1971)	1973	(3)	
	(6)	Mi-4 Hound	Hel	1971	1973	(6)	
	(5)	Mi-8 Hip	Hel	1971	1973	(5)	
	6	MiG-15	Fighter/grd attack	1971	1973	6	
	7	MiG-15UTI	Fighter/trainer	1973	1974	7	
	(18)	MiG-17	Fighter/strike	(1972)	1973	18	
	13	MiG-17	Fighter/strike	1973	1974	13	
	(6)	MiG-19	Fighter/grd attack	(1972)	1974	(6)	
	7	MiG-21F	Fighter	1973	1974	7	Bringing total to 25
	(30)	BM-13-16 132mm	MRS	(1973)	1974	(30)	

Recipient code/Recipient	Supplier	No. ordered	Weapon designation	Weapon description	Year of order	Year(s) of delivery	Total delivered	Comments
		(60)	BRDM-2	SC	(1972)	1973	(60)	
		:	BRDM-2 Gaskin	AAV(M)	(1974)	1974	(10)	
		:	BRDM-2 Sagger	TD(M)	(1975)	1975	(10)	
		(200)	BTR-152	APC	(1972)	1972-73	(200)	
		(30)	BTR-50P	APC	(1971)	1973	(30)	
		:	BTR-60P	APC	(1976)	1976	(10)	
		:	M-1931 122mm	TG	(1972)	1973	(70)	
		:	M-1938 122mm	TG	(1973)	1973	(60)	
		:	M-1944 100mm	TG	(1974)	1974	(25)	
		:	M-1955 100mm	TG	(1974)	1974	(25)	
		100	T-54	MBT	(1972)	1973-74	(100)	
		:	T-55	MBT	(1973)	1975	(50)	
		(10)	ZSU-23-4 Shilka	AAV	(1976)	1976	(10)	
		:	SA-2 SAMS	Mobile SAM system	(1973)	1974	(3)	
		(2)	SA-3 SAMS	Mobile SAM system	(1973)	1973	(2)	
		4	SSN-2 Styx L	ShShM launcher	1975	1975	4	
		:	AT-3 Sagger	ATM	(1975)	1975	(60)	
		:	SA-2 Guideline	Landmob SAM	(1973)	1974	(30)	
		:	SA-3 Goa	Landmob SAM	(1973)	1974	(10)	
		:	SA-9 Gaskin	Landmob SAM	(1974)	1974	(60)	On BRDM-2 vehicles
		(48)	SSN-2 Styx	ShShM	(1975)	1975	(48)	Arming 2 Osa-2 Class FACs
		4	Mol Class	FAC	(1976)	1976-77	4	
		2	Osa-2 Class	FAC	(1975)	1975	2	
		7	P-6 Class	FAC	(1972)	1972	7	
	United Arab Emirates	(4)	BN-2A Islander	Transport	(1983)	1983	(4)	Possibly some from Oman
		(8)	Hunter FGA-9	Fighter/grd attack	(1983)	1983	(8)	Possibly some from Oman
4 South Africa	Belgium	(7)	Merlin-3A	Transport	(1975)	1976	(7)	Unconfirmed
	Canada	(3)	CL-215	Amphibian	(1975)	1977	(3)	Replacement
	France	1	Mirage-3C	Fighter	1970	1971	1	
		(10)	Mirage-3D	Jet trainer	1972	1973-74	(10)	Supplementary deliveries
		(12)	Mirage-3E	Fighter/bomber	1972	1973	(12)	Supplementary deliveries
		(2)	SA-316B	Hel	(1983)	1983-84	(2)	For Bophuthatswana AF
			SA-330 Puma	Hel	(1973)	1975-76	(40)	
		54	Crotale SAMS	Mobile SAM system	(1970)	1972-74	(54)	
		30	AM-39 Exocet	AShM	1976	1980	(30)	Reportedly offered to Argentina during Falkland/Malvinas war; possibly clandestinely acquired
		..	AS-12	ASM/AShM	1974	1975-77	(768)	Arming Mirages

Supplier	No. ordered	Weapon designation	Weapon description	Year of order	Year(s) of deliveries	No. delivered	Comments
	...	Milan	ATM	1973	1974	(10)	Confirmed by Aerospatiale
	(486)	R-440 Crotale	Landmob SAM	(1970)	1972-74	(486)	Developed with South African financing
	..	R-550 Magic	AAM	1972	1975	(100)	Arming Mirage F-1s
	..	SS-11	ATM	(1976)	1976	(100)	Unconfirmed; sometimes also reported as Milan ATM
Germany, FR	3	Daphne Class	Submarine	(1968)	1970-71	3	
	2	BK-117	Hel	(1984)	1984	2	Origin unconfirmed; for Ciskei defence force
India	2	BK-117	Hel	(1984)	1985	2	For Ciskei and Venda
	100	Centurion	MBT	1978	1978-79	(100)	Sold to private company; delivered via Spain and Jordan; refurbished in South Africa; called Oliphant
Israel	6	Mooney-201	Lightplane	(1983)	1983	6	For Ciskei defence force
	1	Westwind 1124	Transport	(1983)	1983	1	For Ciskei defence force
		Gabriel L	ShShM launcher	1974	1978-86	9	Arming Reshef Class FACs
	(162)	Gabriel-2	ShShM	1974	1978-86	(162)	Arming Reshef Class FACs
	3	Reshef Class	FAC	1974	1978	3	South African designation: MOD Class
Italy	40	AM-3C	Lightplane	1971	1973	40	
	50	MB-326K	Jet trainer	(1974)	1974	50	
	9	P-166	Transport	1971	1973-74	(9)	
	(2)	P-68 Victor	Lightplane	(1982)	1982-83	2	For Bophuthatswana AF
	(15)	M-108 105mm	SPH	(1979)	1979	(15)	Unconfirmed; also reported as M-109s and incl M-113 APCs
Jordan	(14)	Tigercat SAMS	Mobile SAM system	(1973)	1974	(14)	Via private company; total value: $17 m
	(555)	Tigercat	Landmob SAM	(1973)	1974	(555)	Some possibly shipped on to Rhodesia
Spain	(1)	C-212-200	Transport	(1984)	1985	1	For Bophuthatswana AF
	(3)	C-212-200	Transport	(1986)			For Bophuthatswana AF
UK	2	BN-2A Islander	Transport	(1983)	1984	2	For Ciskei
	3	HS-125	Transport	1970	1971	3	
	6	Wasp	Hel	1971	1973	(6)	To replace 3 lost in accidents; 7th ordered embargoed March 1974
	1	Hecla Class	OPV	1969	1972	1	
USSR	10	T-55	MBT	1979	1979	10	Destined for Uganda but seized in South African port Apr 1979
3 Sri Lanka							
China	5	Shanghai Class	PC	(1971)	1972	5	Possibly Taiwanese Hai Ou Class
	2	Shanghai Class	PC	(1979)	1980	2	
France	2	AS-365	Hel	1977	1978	2	
Israel	(2)	Dvora Class	FAC	(1985)			
Italy	(6)	SF-260TP	Trainer	1985			Number ordered also reported to be 8
Singapore	3	Abheetha Class	Support ship	(1984)	1984	(3)	Former Ro-Ro ships used as command ships
	3	Mahawele Class	Support ship	(1984)	1984	(3)	Classified as surveillance command tenders; supplier unconfirmed
	2	Type 30M	LC	(1985)	1986	2	200t mechanized-infantry landing craft; ordered from Vosper Aug 1985

Recipient code/Recipient	Supplier	No. ordered	Weapon designation	Weapon description	Year of order	Year(s) of delivery	Total delivered	Comments
	South Africa	6	Samil-100	APC	(1985)	1985	6	Via a third country
	UK	(15)	Ferret FV-703	Recce AC	(1970)	1971	(15)	
		18	Saladin FV-601	AC	(1970)	1971	18	
	USA	6	Model 150	Lightplane	(1972)	1972	6	
		4	Model 206A	Hel	(1971)	1971	4	
		2	Model 206B	Hel	(1983)	1983	2	
		(4)	Model 206B	Hel	(1983)	1984	(4)	Seller unconfirmed
		2	Model 212	Hel	(1983)	1983	2	Via Singapore
		6	Model 212	Hel	(1984)	1985	6	Sold via Bell Asia in Singapore
		4	Model 212	Hel	1985	1985-86	(4)	For COIN duties; via Singapore
		4	Model 337	Trainer	(1971)	1972	4	
		4	Model 412	Hel	(1986)	1986	4	
		6	Model 47G	Hel	(1970)	1971	6	Paid for by the UK
		1	Super King Air	Transport	(1985)	1986	1	
	USSR	2	Ka-26	Hel	(1970)	1971	2	
		1	MiG-15UTI	Fighter/trainer	(1970)	1971	1	
		5	MiG-17	Fighter/strike	(1970)	1971	5	
		20	BTR-152	APC	(1970)	1971	20	
		1	Mol Class	FAC	(1975)	1975	1	
4 Sudan	Canada	4	DHC-5D Buffalo	Transport	1977	1977-78	4	
		1	DHC-6	Transport	1976	1977	1	
	China	4	F-4	Fighter	(1973)	1974	4	
		(10)	T-59	MBT	(1971)	1972	(10)	
		20	T-62	LT	(1970)	1972	20	
		:	T-63	LT	(1978)	1978	(10)	
		:	Type 531	APC	(1981)	1981	(10)	
		:	Type 54 122mm	SPH	(1980)	1981	(20)	
		:	Type 59/1 130mm	TG	(1980)	1981	(20)	
		:	BRDM-1	SC	(1980)	1981	(50)	
		:	BRDM-2	SC	(1980)	1981	(50)	
		:	D-30 122mm	TH	(1982)	1981	(20)	
		:	M-46 130mm	TG	(1983)	1982	(20)	
		:	Type-60 122mm	TG	(1982)	1982	(20)	
	Egypt	(40)	Walid	APC	(1981)	1981	(40)	Dates and number ordered unconfirmed
		20	Walid	APC	(1986)	1986	20	MAP: further deliveries planned
			I-Hawk SAMS	Mobile SAM system	(1981)	1981	(2)	Reportedly delivered
		(8)	SA-2 SAMS	Mobile SAM system	1984	1984	(8)	Designation and number unconfirmed; left behind by Egypt; MAP

Supplier	No.	Weapon designation	Weapon description	Year of order	Year(s) of delivery	No. delivered	Comments
	:	MIM-23B Hawk	Landmob SAM	(1981)	1981	(12)	Unspecified number reportedly delivered
	:	SA-2 Guideline	Landmob SAM	1984	1984	(24)	Unspecified number delivered Mar 1984; for launchers delivered in 1971
France	:	SA-7 Grail	Port SAM	(1981)	1981	(20)	
	(50)	SA-7 Grail	Port SAM	1984	1984	(50)	
	6	Swingfire	ATM	(1982)		6	Reportedly on order
	50	AML-90	AC	(1980)	1981	50	Unconfirmed
	11	AMX-10RC	Recce AC	1977	1978	(11)	Unconfirmed
	15	AMX-155 Mk-F3	SPH	1980	1983-84	15	
		ERC-120 Guepard	AC	(1982)	1982	(20)	Unconfirmed
	15	M-3	APC	1980	1983	(4)	
Germany, FR	20	Bo-105C	Hel	1977	1979-80	12	Some for police force
Italy	(4)	AB-212	Hel	(1982)	1982-83	10	
	12	AB-212	Hel	1984	1984	(10)	Designation unconfirmed
Romania	10	SA-330 Puma	Hel	1981	1984-85	55	
Saudi Arabia	55	M-41	LT	1981	1981	17	
	17	M-47 Patton	MBT	1984	1981	(6)	
Spain	6	C-212-200	Transport	(1984)	1985-86	3	
	:	M-41E Cazador	TD	(1983)	1984	6	Unconfirmed
UK	10	BAC-167	Trainer/COIN	1976	1976	2	
USA	6	C-130E Hercules	Transport	1984	1984	2	Delivery halted for financial reasons
	2	F-5E Tiger-2	Fighter	1980	1982	12	
	2	F-5F Tiger-2	Jet trainer	1980	1981	80	
	12	M-101-A1 105mm	TH	1981	1981-82	8	
	80	M-113-A2	APC	1980	1981	50	Delivered to AF Oct 1982
	8	M-163 Vulcan	AAV	1980	1981-82	2	Part of $100 m MAP package
	50	M-60-A1	MBT	1979	1982	(50)	
	2	V-150 Commando	APC	1982	1983	2	Ordered Feb 1979
	(54)	V-150 Commando	APC	1984	1984	(54)	
	24	M-1944 100mm	TG	(1986)		(40)	Total cost: $10.7 m
USSR	:	SA-2 SAMS	Mobile SAM system	(1973)	1974	1	
	1	SA-2 Guideline	Landmob SAM	1970	1971	(10)	
	:			1970	1971		

Recipient	Supplier	No.	Weapon designation	Weapon description	Year of order	Year(s) of delivery	No. delivered	Comments
15 Suriname	Brazil	(10)	EE-11 Urutu	APC	(1983)	1984	(10)	Part of $15 m aid programme
	UK	4	BN-2A Islander	Transport	(1981)	1982	4	
		3	Type 32m	PC	1975	1977	3	Crashed on arrival
	USA	1	Model 500MD	Hel	1981	1981	1	
8 Swaziland	Israel	2	IAI-201 Arava	Transport	(1979)	1979	(2)	
		1	IAI-201 Arava	Transport	(1981)	1981	1	Replacement for 1 crashed aircraft

Recipient code/ Recipient	Supplier	No. ordered	Weapon designation	Weapon description	Year of order	Year(s) of delivery	Total delivered	Comments
5 Syria	Czechoslovakia	(60)	L-29 Delfin	Jet trainer	(1965)	1966-72	(60)	
		(40)	L-39 Albatross	Jet trainer	(1980)	1980-84	(40)	
	France	(300)	OT-64	APC	(1976)	1977-79	(300)	
		2	Mystere-20	Transport	(1975)	1976	2	For VIP transport
		50	SA-342K Gazelle	Hel	1976	1977-81	(50)	
		15	SA-342K Gazelle	Hel	1984			Armed with HOT ATMs
		16	SA-342L Gazelle	Hel	1979	1980-81	(16)	Arming Gazelle helicopters
		(216)	HOT	ATM	1978	1980-81	(216)	Arming 15 Gazelle helicopters
		(180)	HOT	ATM	1984			
		(1 000)	Milan	ATM	1978	1978-79	(1 000)	
	Italy	18	AB-212ASW	Hel	(1986)			Order pending
		6	CH-47C Chinook	Hel	(1986)			Order pending
		12	SH-3D Sea King	Hel	(1986)			Order pending
	Libya	(20)	MiG-21F	Fighter	1982	1982	(20)	
		(15)	MiG-23	Fighter/interceptor	1982	1982	(15)	
		(500)	T-62	MBT	1978	1979	(500)	Gift
	Poland	3	Polnocny Class	LS	(1983)	1984-85	3	
	Switzerland	32	MBB-223K	Trainer	(1975)	1976-77	(32)	
	USSR	(2)	An-24 Coke	Transport	(1973)	1974	(2)	In civilian markings
		4	An-26 Curl	Lightplane	(1977)	1979-80	(4)	In civilian markings
		2	Il-76 Candid	Transport	(1981)	1982	2	
		9	Ka-25 Hormone	Hel	(1973)	1974	9	
		(35)	Mi-24 Hind-D	Hel	(1983)	1983-85	(35)	
		2	Mi-4 Hound	Hel	(1970)	1971	2	
		(10)	Mi-6 Hook	Hel	(1973)	1975	(10)	
		(30)	Mi-8 Hip	Hel	(1969)	1971-72	(30)	
		(15)	Mi-8 Hip	Hel	(1973)	1973	(15)	War replacements
		(25)	Mi-8 Hip	Hel	(1978)	1979-83	(25)	
		(20)	MiG-17	Fighter/strike	(1969)	1971-72	(20)	
		(40)	MiG-17	Fighter/strike	(1973)	1973	(40)	War replacements
		(110)	MiG-21F	Fighter	(1965)	1967-71	(110)	
		(175)	MiG-21F	Fighter	(1973)	1973	(175)	War replacements
		(25)	MiG-21MF	Fighter	(1970)	1972	(25)	
		54	MiG-21MF	Fighter	(1973)	1973	54	
		30	MiG-21MF	Fighter	1975	1977	30	
		(25)	MiG-21UTI	Jet trainer	1965	1967-71	(25)	
		(20)	MiG-21bis	Fighter	(1983)	1983	(20)	As attrition aircraft
		25	MiG-23	Fighter/interceptor	(1973)	1974	25	
		(45)	MiG-23BN	Fighter/grd attack	(1978)	1979-81	(45)	

Qty	Designation	Role	In svc	Delivered	No.	Notes
(·)	MiG-23M	Fighter/interceptor	1981	1982-85	(105)	Incl some MiG-23BNs (grd attack version)
(20)	MiG-23U	Jet trainer	1973	1974	(20)	
(20)	MiG-25	Fighter/interceptor	(1979)	1980	(20)	
(·)	MiG-25 Foxhound	Fighter	(1984)		(8)	Unconfirmed
(8)	MiG-25RE	Recce	1981	1984	3	Order earlier reported as being larger
3	MiG-27	Fighter/strike	(1978)	1979	(36)	
(·)	MiG-27	Fighter/strike	(1980)	1980-85	(15)	
(80)	MiG-29	Fighter	(1984)	1986	(3)	
(3)	Su-11 Flagon	Fighter/interceptor	(1974)	1975	(30)	Unconfirmed
(30)	Su-22 Fitter-J	Fighter/grd attack	(1976)	1978-79	(60)	4 squadrons
(60)	Su-22 Fitter-J	Fighter/grd attack	1981	1982-83	(20)	
(20)	Su-7 Fitter	Fighter	(1968)	1969-71	(20)	War replacements
(20)	Su-7 Fitter	Fighter	(1973)	1969-74	(15)	
(15)	Su-7U Moujik	Jet trainer	(1968)			Unconfirmed
2	Tu-126	AEW	(1981)			
7	Yak-40 Codling	Transport	(1972)	1973-74	(7)	In civilian markings
(200)	BM-21 122mm	MRS	(1972)	1972-73	(200)	
(150)	BM-21 122mm	MRS	(1979)	1980-82	(150)	
(100)	BMP-1	MICV	(1976)	1977-80	(100)	
(800)	BMP-1	MICV	1981	1982-85	(400)	
(40)	BMP-1 Spigot	TD(M)	(1980)	1981-82	(40)	
(100)	BRDM-1	SC	(1970)	1970-71	(100)	
(4)	BRDM-2 Gaskin	AAV(M)	1974	1975	(4)	
(36)	BRDM-2 Gaskin	AAV(M)	1978	1980-85	(36)	
(200)	BRDM-2 Sagger	TD(M)	1980	1981-82	(200)	
(2 000)	BRDM-2 Sagger	TD(M)	1980	1981-82	(2 000)	On BRDM-2s
(300)	BTR-152	APC	(1968)	1969-71	(300)	
(150)	BTR-50P	APC	(1970)	1970-71	(150)	
(400)	BTR-50P	APC	(1973)	1973-75	(400)	
(150)	BTR-60P	APC	(1970)	1970-71	(150)	
(500)	BTR-60P	APC	(1973)	1973-75	(500)	
(200)	D-1 152mm	TH	(1973)	1973-76	(200)	
(300)	D-30 122mm	TH	(1972)	1973-76	(300)	
(200)	JSU-122	SPG	1967	1967-73	(200)	
(200)	JSU-152	SPG	1967	1967-73	(200)	
(200)	M-1973 152mm	SPG	1981	1982-85	(200)	Designation unconfirmed
(500)	M-1974 122mm	SPH	1981	1982-85	(400)	Designation unconfirmed
(200)	M-46 130mm	TG	(1973)	1974-75	(200)	
80	PT-76	LT	(1971)	1972-73	(80)	
(200)	S-23 180mm	TG	(1970)	1971-72	(200)	
(6)	SA-13 TELAR	AAV(M)	(1984)	1985-86	(6)	
(50)	SM-4-1 130mm	TG	(1973)	1974-75	(50)	
(100)	T-34	MT	1973	1973-74	(100)	Version T-34/85

Recipient code/ Recipient	Supplier	No. ordered	Weapon designation	Weapon description	Year of order	Year(s) of delivery	Total delivered	Comments
		(300)	T-54	MBT	(1967)	1967-72	(300)	
		(400)	T-54	MBT	1973	1973-78	(400)	
		(300)	T-55	MBT	(1968)	1969-72	(300)	
		(400)	T-55	MBT	1973	1973-78	(400)	
		(600)	T-55	MBT	(1978)	1979-81	(600)	
		(500)	T-62	MBT	1973	1973-74	(500)	
		(300)	T-62	MBT	1982	1982-84	(300)	
			T-72	MBT	1980	1980-85	(1 050)	
		(250)	T-74	MBT	(1985)	1986	(250)	Up to 250; unconfirmed
		(250)	ZSU-23-4 Shilka	AAV	1981	1982-85	(100)	
			ZSU-57-2	AAV	(1966)	1967-73	(250)	
		(18)	FROG L	Mobile SSM system	(1970)	1973	(18)	Frog-7
		(4)	FROG L	Mobile SSM system	1979	1980-81	(4)	
			SA-11 SAMS	Mobile SAM system	(1984)	1984	(1)	Unconfirmed
		(10)	SA-11 SAMS	Mobile SAM system	(1985)	1986	(10)	Unconfirmed
		(18)	SA-2 SAMS	Mobile SAM system	(1970)	1971-73	(18)	
		(18)	SA-3 SAMS	Mobile SAM system	1971	1971-73	(18)	
		(4)	SA-5 SAMS	Mobile SAM system	(1981)	1982	(10)	
		(20)	SA-6 SAMS	Mobile SAM system	1982	1983	(4)	
		(40)	SA-6 SAMS	Mobile SAM system	(1973)	1973	(20)	
		(24)	SA-8 SAMS	Mobile SAM system	1978	1978-81	(40)	
			SA-8 SAMS	Mobile SAM system	1977	1979-81	(24)	
			SS-21 L	Mobile SSM system	(1982)	1982-85	(32)	
		(6)	SS-21 L	Mobile SSM system	(1983)	1983	(2)	Unconfirmed
			SS-21 L	Mobile SSM system	(1984)	1985	(6)	
		9	SSN-2 Styx L	ShShM launcher	1962	1963-74	(9)	Arming 9 Komar Class FACs
		9	SSN-2 Styx L	ShShM launcher	1969	1972-73	(9)	Arming 10 Osa-2 Class FACs
		10	SSN-2 Styx L	ShShM launcher	1977	1978-84	(10)	Arming 2 Osa-2 Class FACs
		2	SSN-2 Styx L	ShShM launcher	(1985)	1985	2	
		(6)	Scud-B L	Mobile SSM system	(1973)	1974	(6)	Scud launcher
		(2 500)	AA-2 Atoll	AAM	(1967)	1967-74	(2 500)	Arming MiG-21s
		180	AA-2 Atoll	AAM	1975	1977	180	Arming MiG-21s
		(360)	AA-2 Atoll	AAM	(1977)	1978-83	(360)	Arming Su-22s
		(1 380)	AA-2 Atoll	AAM	(1979)	1979-85	(1 380)	Arming MiG-23/-25/-27s
			AA-6 Acrid	AAM	(1984)	1984-85	(100)	Unconfirmed; arming MiG-25s
			AA-7 Apex	AAM	(1984)	1984-85	(100)	Unconfirmed; arming MiG-21s and MiG-23s
			AA-8 Aphid	AAM	(1984)	1984-85	(40)	Unconfirmed; arming MiG-21s and MiG-23s
		(200)	AT-1 Snapper	ATM	(1971)	1972-73	(200)	
		(200)	AT-2 Swatter	ATM	(1973)	1973-74	(200)	

No. ordered	Weapon designation	Weapon description	Year of order	Year of delivery	No. delivered	Comments
(300)	AT-3 Sagger	ATM	(1971)	1972-73	(300)	
(6 000)	AT-3 Sagger	ATM	1973	1974-75	(6 000)	
(1 200)	AT-3 Sagger	ATM	1978	1978	(1 200)	Captured by Israeli forces in Lebanon
..	AT-4 Spigot	ATM	1980	1981-85	(400)	Unconfirmed
..	AT-5 Spandrel	ATM	(1984)	1984-85	(200)	Unconfirmed
(30)	FROG-7	Landmob SSM	(1970)	1973	(30)	
(20)	FROG-7	Landmob SSM	1979	1980-81	(20)	Ordered Nov 1979; version unconfirmed
(12)	SA-11	Landmob SAM	(1984)	1984	(12)	Unconfirmed
(30)	SA-11	Landmob SAM	(1985)	1986	(30)	Unconfirmed
(432)	SA-13 Gopher	Landmob SAM	(1984)	1985-86	(432)	
(162)	SA-2 Guideline	Landmob SAM	(1970)	1971-73	(162)	
(162)	SA-3 Goa	Landmob SAM	(1971)	1972-73	(162)	
..	SA-3 Goa	Landmob SAM	(1981)	1982	(90)	
(24)	SA-5 Gammon	SAM	1982	1983	(24)	
(180)	SA-6 Gainful	Landmob SAM	(1973)	1973	(180)	
(360)	SA-6 Gainful	Landmob SAM	1978	1978-81	(360)	
(500)	SA-7 Grail	Port SAM	(1971)	1972-73	(500)	
(100)	SA-7 Grail	Port SAM	(1973)	1974	(100)	
..	SA-7 Grail	Port SAM	1978	1979-85	(250)	
(192)	SA-8 Gecko	Landmob SAM	1978	1979-81	(192)	
..	SA-8 Gecko	Landmob SAM	1982	1982-85	(256)	
(32)	SA-9 Gaskin	Landmob SAM	1974	1975	(32)	
..	SA-9 Gaskin	Landmob SAM	1978	1980-85	(288)	
(20)	SCUD-C	Landmob SSM	(1973)	1974	(20)	
..	SS-21	SSM	(1983)	1983	(10)	Unconfirmed
(18)	SS-21	SSM	(1984)	1985	(18)	
(54)	SSN-2 Styx	ShShM	(1962)	1963-74	(54)	Arming Komar Class FACs
(108)	SSN-2 Styx	ShShM	(1969)	1972-73	(108)	Arming 9 Osa-1 Class FACs
(120)	SSN-2 Styx	ShShM	(1977)	1978-84	(120)	Arming 10 Osa-2 Class FACs
(12)	SSN-2 Styx	ShShM	(1985)	1985	(12)	Arming 2 Osa-2 Class FACs
3	Komar Class	FAC	1973	1974	3	Replacing war losses
1	Natya Class	MSO	(1984)	1985	1	
9	Osa-1 Class	FAC	(1969)	1972-73	(9)	
10	Osa-2 Class	FAC	(1977)	1978-84	10	Armed with 4 SSN-2 Styx ShShMs
2	Osa-2 Class	FAC	(1985)	1985	2	
17	P-4 Class	FAC	(1956)	1957-74	17	1974 delivery replacing 1 lost in October War 1973

10 Taiwan

No. ordered	Weapon designation	Weapon description	Year of order	Year of delivery	No. delivered	Comments
2	Petya-2 Class	Frigate	(1974)	1975	2	
2	Vanya Class	MSC	(1972)	1973	2	
2	Yevgenia Class	MSC	1977	1978-81	2	

Indonesia

No. ordered	Weapon designation	Weapon description	Year of order	Year of delivery	No. delivered	Comments
(15)	AS-332	Hel	(1986)			Negotiating

Israel

No. ordered	Weapon designation	Weapon description	Year of order	Year of delivery	No. delivered	Comments
(450)	Shafrir-2	AAM	(1973)	1975-77	(450)	Arming F-104 and F-5E fighters

Recipient code/ Recipient	Supplier	No. ordered	Weapon designation	Weapon description	Year of order	Year(s) of delivery	Total delivered	Comments
	Netherlands	2	Zwaardvis Class	Submarine	1981		2	Request for 2 more turned down by Dutch Government 1983; for delivery 1986-87
	Singapore	2	Type 32M	LC	(1984)	1985	2	Modified design; licensed production of 20-24 more planned
	USA	1	B-720-047B	Transport	(1971)	1971	1	Ex-Northwest Airlines; for VIP
		16	C-123 Provider	Transport	(1971)	1972-73	16	C-123K
		12	C-130H Hercules	Transport	1984	1986	(12)	Total cost: $325 m
		5	C-54 Skymaster	Transport	(1972)	1973-74	5	One VC-54D and four C-54D
		3	CH-47D Chinook	Hel	1983	1984	(3)	
		26	F-100A	Fighter	(1970)	1970-71	26	US excess stocks; refurbished
		6	F-104D	Fighter/trainer	(1974)	1975	6	From West German surplus; incl 25 TF-104 trainers; total cost: $31 m
		66	F-104G	Fighter	(1979)	1982-83	66	In addition to 66 received 1982-83
		20	F-104G	Fighter	(1985)	1985	(20)	
		45	F-5A	Fighter	(1968)	1969-71	45	
		9	F-5B	Fighter/trainer	(1968)	1969-71	9	Delivered prior to licensed production
		60	F-5E Tiger-2	Fighter	1973	1974-76	60	For Army
		50	Model 205 UH-1H	Hel	1976	1977-78	50	
		12	Model 500MD	Hel	(1978)	1979	12	Torpedo-armed; for operation from Gearing Class destroyers
		18	S-2E Tracker	Fighter/ASW	(1977)	1978-79	(18)	Approved
		9	S-2G Tracker	Mar patrol/ASW	(1985)	1985	9	From US Navy surplus stocks
		14	S-70C	Hel	1984	1986	(14)	Option on 10 more
		1	Super King Air	Transport	(1983)	1984	(1)	
		42	T-34C-1	Trainer	1984			
		20	T-38 Talon	Jet trainer	(1971)	1972-73	(30)	Delivered in the early 1970s
		(25)	LVT-4	Amph ASSV	(1970)	1971	(25)	For Marines
		(20)	LVTP-5	Amph ASSV	(1982)	1983-84	(20)	For Marines
		(225)	M-109 155mm	SPH	(1978)	1980-82	(225)	
		25	M-109-A2 155mm	SPH	1980	1983	(25)	Total cost: $18 m
		50	M-110-A2 203mm	SPH	1980	1981-82	(50)	Total cost: $37 m
		(100)	M-110-A2 203mm	SPH	(1982)	1983-84	(100)	
		357	M-113-A2	APC	1982	1983-85	(357)	140 APCs, 90 M-106-A2 and 72 M-125-A2 mortar carriers, 31 CPCs and 24 of the ambulance version
		100	M-48 Patton	MBT	1977	1978-79	(100)	Total cost: $8.54 m
		(75)	M-60-A3	MBT	1984			For local assembly; hulls to be fitted with locally produced engines and equipment; some sources report 215 on order and 140 more on option

No.	Designation	Description	Year of order	Year(s) of delivery	No. delivered	Comments
33	M-88-A1	ARV	1983	1985-86	(33)	
(150)	V-150 Commando	APC	(1983)	1983	(150)	
:	AN/PPS-15	Surveillance radar	(1975)	1976-77		
(1)	AN/TPQ-37	Tracking radar	1986		(40)	
(4)	I-Hawk SAMS	Mobile SAM system	1980	1981	(4)	
(1)	M54 Chaparral	Mobile SAM system	1976	1977	(1)	
(12)	M54 Chaparral	Mobile SAM system	1983	1985-86		
(8)	M54 Chaparral	Mobile SAM system	(1985)			
(10)	RIM-66A L	ShAM launcher	(1983)	1985-86	(10)	For corvettes under construction
500	AGM-65A	ASM	1979	1980-82	(500)	Arming F-5E fighters; cost: $25 m
(100)	AIM-7M Sparrow	AAM/SAM	1983	1986-87	(100)	Arming F-5E/F Tiger-2 fighters
(1 850)	AIM-9J	AAM	1973	1974-83	(1 850)	Arming F-5E/F fighters
(216)	AIM-9J	AAM	1982	1983-85	(216)	Total cost incl 49 launchers: $11.5 m
1 013	BGM-71A TOW	ATM	1980	1981-83	(1 013)	Total cost: $167 m (incl 27 launchers)
280	MIM-23B Hawk	Landmob SAM	1980	1981	(280)	Reserve missiles; total cost: $16 m
90	MIM-23B Hawk	Landmob SAM	1981	1982	(90)	
20	MIM-72C	Landmob SAM	1976	1977	20	
384	MIM-72F	SAM/ShAM	1983	1985-86	(300)	US LoO Jul 1983; total cost incl 120 Chaparral ShAMs, 170 SM-1 Standard ShAM/ShShMs, 18 extra MIM-72Fs, 100 AIM-7F Sparrow SAMs, 33 M-88-A1 AVs and 309 M-48-A5 conversion kits: $ 530 m
(18)	MIM-72F	SAM/ShAM	(1984)	1985	(18)	In addition to 384 missiles ordered 1983
262	MIM-72F	SAM/ShAM	(1985)	1985-86		For Army; cost incl launchers: $94 m
170	RIM-66A/SM-1	ShAM/ShShM	1983		(170)	To arm 4 Fletcher Class Destroyers
284	Sea Chaparral	ShAM	1980	1981-82	(284)	
120	Sea Chaparral	ShAM	1983	1985	(120)	
1	Amphion Class	Support ship	(1973)	1974	1	Ex-US Navy
(3)	Asheville Class	Frigate	(1985)			Unconfirmed
1	C1-M-AV1 Type	Support ship	(1971)	1972	1	Former merchant ship
1	Diver Class	Support ship	(1976)	1977	1	
4	Fletcher Class	Destroyer	(1966)	1967-71	4	Ex-US Navy
6	Gearing Class	Destroyer	(1970)	1971-73	6	Ex-US Navy
4	Gearing Class	Destroyer	(1976)	1977-78	4	One more transferred for spares in 1977; armed with 3 Gabriel ShShMs after sale
2	Gearing Class	Destroyer	(1980)	1980	2	Two more purchased for spares 1980-81
2	Guppy-2 Class	Submarine	(1972)	1973	1	Ex-US Navy
1	LSD-13 Class	AALS	(1973)	1974	1	Ex-US Navy
1	Liberty Type	Support ship	(1971)	1972	1	Gun-armed cargo ship
1	Mark Class	Support ship	(1970)	1971	1	
1	PSMM-5 Type	FAC	1977	1978	1	Prior to local production of 1
3	Patapsco Class	Support ship	(1960)	1961-72	3	Gun-armed tankers

Recipient code/ Recipient	Supplier	No. ordered	Weapon designation	Weapon description	Year of order	Year(s) of delivery	Total delivered	Comments
4 Tanzania	Canada	8	Sumner Class	Destroyer	(1968)	1969-74	8	Ex-US Navy; 3 armed with Gabriel ShShMs
	China	8	DHC-4 Caribou	Transport	(1970)	1971	8	
		4	DHC-5D Buffalo	Transport	1977	1979	4	
		2	DHC-5D Buffalo	Transport	1980	1981	2	Ordered Mar 1980
		12	F-4	Fighter	(1971)	1973	12	Incl 2 trainer version
		12	F-6	Fighter	(1972)	1973	12	Pilots trained in China
		..	F-6	Fighter	1973	1974	8	
		(10)	F-6	Fighter	(1982)	1984	(10)	
		16	F-7	Fighter	1973	1974	(16)	Displayed in military parade in 1974
		(20)	BRDM-2	SC	1980	1981	(20)	
		(50)	D-30 122mm	TH	(1981)	1981	(50)	Supplier unconfirmed
		(18)	M-1931 122mm	TG	(1973)	1973-75	(18)	Supplier unconfirmed
		20	T-59	MBT	(1970)	1971	20	
		(35)	T-63	LT	(1979)	1980	(35)	
		(20)	Type 531	APC	(1976)	1977	(20)	
		..	Type 531	APC	(1979)	1980	(30)	Designation unconfirmed
		(100)	Type 54 122mm	SPH	(1982)	1982	(100)	
		..	Type 55	APC	(1977)	1977	(10)	Unconfirmed
		..	Type 56	APC	(1977)	1977	(10)	Unconfirmed
		(100)	Type-60 122mm	TG	(1982)	1982	(100)	
		4	Huchuan Class	Hydrofoil FAC	1975	1975	4	
		(6)	Shanghai Class	PC	(1971)	1971-72	(6)	
	Italy	(6)	AB-205	Hel	(1979)	1980	(6)	
		2	AB-206A	Hel	(1972)	1973	2	
		2	CH-47C Chinook	Hel	1980	1982	2	
		2	Model 47G-3B	Hel	(1972)	1973	2	
	Korea, North	4	Nampo Class	LC	(1979)	1979-81	(4)	
	UK	1	HS-748-2	Transport	1973	1974	1	For VIP use
		3	HS-748M	Transport	1976	1977-78	3	
		6	FV-101 Scorpion	LT	1978	1979	(6)	Ordered Sep 1978
	USA	(6)	Model 310	Lightplane	(1977)	1977	(6)	
		2	Model 402A	Lightplane	(1981)	1981	2	
		5	PA-28 Cherokee	Lightplane	(1970)	1972	5	
		1	PA-28 Cherokee	Lightplane	(1972)	1972	1	
	USSR	(50)	BM-21 122mm	MRS	(1976)	1977-78	(50)	
		..	BRDM-2	SC	(1978)	1978	(20)	
		..	T-54	MBT	1977	1978	(50)	
		..	SA-6 SAMS	Mobile SAM system	(1978)	1979	(4)	

	..	SA-6 Gainful	Landmob SAM	(1978)	1979	(20)	Unconfirmed
11 Thailand							
Australia	20	N-22B Nomad	Mar patrol	1981	1982-84	(20)	For COIN duties
	4	N-22B Nomad	Mar patrol	1983	1984	(4)	For maritime patrol in piracy areas; financed by UN High Commission for Refugees
	1	N-22B Nomad	Mar patrol	1984	1985	(1)	
	4	N-24A Nomad	Transport	(1985)	1985	4	Military aid
Austria	12	GHN-45 155mm	TH/TG	(1979)	1981	12	Originally ordered from SRC, Canada
Brazil	56	EE-9 Cascavel	AC	1982	1984-85	(56)	
Canada	2	CL-215	Amphibian	1977	1978	2	
	20	DHC-1 Chimunk	Trainer	(1973)	1974	(20)	Delivery year uncertain
China	24	T-59	MBT	(1985)	1985	24	Gift
	18	Type 59/1 130mm	TG	(1985)	1985	18	Gift
France	16	T-33A	Jet trainer	(1982)	1983	16	Refurbished before delivery
	(3)	MM-38 L	ShShM launcher	1976	1979-80	(3)	On 3 MV-250 (Ratcharit Class) FACs
	..	MM-40 LAUNCH-2	SShM launcher	(1983)			For coastal defence; unconfirmed
	(36)	MM-40 Exocet	ShShM	1976	1979-80	(36)	Arming 3 MV-250 (Ratcharit Class) FACs
	..	MM-40 Exocet	ShShM/SShM	(1983)			For coastal defence; unconfirmed
Germany, FR	2	RFB Fantrainer	Trainer	1982	1984	2	Delivered prior to licensed production
	(2)	M-41	LT	1984	1984	1	Refurbished; for trials
	1	M-40 Type	MSC/PC	1986			Option on 3-5 more; unit cost: $18 m
	1	M-40 Type	MSC/PC	(1978)			In addition to 2 ordered 1984
Indonesia	1	CN-212	Transport	1985			In addition to 4 ordered from Spain
	3	CN-212	Transport	(1979)	1980	1	In addition to 5 in service (4 from Spain and 1 from Indonesia)
Israel	(25)	NBo-105	Hel	1980	1983-85	(10)	For survey and ECM missions
	3	IAI-201 Arava	Transport	(1974)	1980-82	3	Unconfirmed
	(20)	M-68 155mm	TH	1973	1975	(20)	
	(3)	Gabriel L	ShShM launcher	(1972)	1976-77	3	On 3 TNC-45 FACs
	(15)	Gabriel-1	ShShM	(1981)	1976-77	(15)	Arming 3 Luerssen TNC-45 FACs
Italy	12	SF-260M	Trainer	1984	1973-74	12	Delivery year uncertain
	6	SF-260M	Trainer	1984	1982	6	
	(2)	Aspide/Albatros	ShAM/ShShM launcher	1976			To arm 2 corvettes ordered from USA
	(48)	Aspide	AAM/SAM/ShAM	1979			To arm 2 corvettes ordered from USA
Malaysia	3	MV-250 Type	FAC		1979-80	3	Thai designation: Ratcharit Class
	3	MV-400 Class	FAC	1982	1983	3	Thai designation: Dhonburi Class
Netherlands	2	F-5B	Fighter/trainer		1982	2	From surplus
	3	F-27 Maritime	Mar patrol		1984	3	For Navy; pylons for AShMs
	1	F-27 Maritime	Mar patrol	1985			In addition to 3 in service
New Zealand	24	CT-4 Airtrainer	Trainer	1972	1973-74	24	
Singapore	3	TNC-45	FAC	1973	1976-77	3	Built under licence in Singapore; armed with 5 Gabriel ShShMs and 2 Bofors guns

Recipient code/ Recipient	Supplier	No. ordered	Weapon designation	Weapon description	Year of order	Year(s) of delivery	Total delivered	Comments
	Spain	4	C-212-100	Transport	(1978)	1979-80	4	
	Switzerland	5	PC-7	Trainer	1976	1977	5	
	UK	1	BN-2A Islander	Transport	(1974)	1976	1	
		1	HS-748-2	Transport	(1971)	1972	1	
		2	HS-748-2	Transport	1974	1974	2	
		3	Shorts 330-UTT	Transport	1984	1984	3	Two aircraft for Army, one for police
		144	FV-101 Scorpion	LT	1977	1978-84	(144)	
		..	MBT Mk-3	MBT	(1986)			Unconfirmed
		20	Saracen FV-603	APC	(1976)	1977	(20)	
		32	Shorland	AC	1970	1971-72	32	
		(1)	Seacat L	ShAM launcher	1969	1973	(1)	On one Yarrow Type frigate
		(100)	Blowpipe	Port SAM	1981	1982	(100)	Requested after US refusal to sell Redeye SAMs
		(50)	Blowpipe	Port SAM	1982	1984	(50)	Additional batch ordered
		(12)	Seacat	ShAM/ShShM	1969	1973	(12)	Arming one Yarrow type frigate
		1	Yarrow Type	Frigate	1969	1973	1	
	USA	16	A-37B Dragonfly	Fighter/COIN	(1973)	1974	(16)	Delivery year uncertain
		8	AC-47	Transport	(1972)	1973	8	
		14	AU-23A	Transport	(1971)	1973-74	14	USAF military aid; for COIN duties
		20	AU-23A	Transport	1974	1975-76	20	Total cost: $12 m; incl 5 for police
		58	Bird Dog	Lightplane	(1970)	1971-72	58	For Army; also designated O-1A
		7	C-123 Provider	Transport	(1969)	1972	7	
		3	C-130H Hercules	Transport	1979	1980	3	Total cost: $48 m
		3	C-130H-30	Transport	1981	1982-83	3	Two ordered Nov 1981, one 1982
		4	C-47	Transport	(1971)	1972-73	4	C-47D
		4	CH-47A Chinook	Hel	1978	1979	4	For Army
		4	CH-47C Chinook	Hel	(1971)	1972	4	For Army
		4	EC-47	ECM	(1974)	1975	4	
		8	F-16A	Fighter/strike	1985			Number reduced from 16 for cost reasons; for delivery 1988-89; total cost incl 4 F-16Bs: $378 m
		(4)	F-16B	Fighter/trainer	1985			
		9	F-5A	Fighter	(1970)	1971-73	9	
		17	F-5E Tiger-2	Fighter	1976	1978	17	Armed with Sidewinder AAMs
		15	F-5E Tiger-2	Fighter	1979	1981	15	
		3	F-5F Tiger-2	Jet trainer	1976	1978	3	
		3	F-5F Tiger-2	Jet trainer	1979	1981	3	Delivered May 1981
		25	F-8H Crusader	Fighter	(1979)	1979	(25)	From US Navy surplus stocks
		2	LA-4-200	Amphibian	(1982)	1983	(2)	Delivery year uncertain; for Navy

	Model	Type				Comments
2	Merlin-4	Transport	1977	1977-78	2	
3	Merlin-4	Transport	1978	1979	3	
3	Model 185	Lightplane	(1972)	1973	3	
14	Model 205 UH-1A	Hel	1977	1981	14	For Army; also called U-17B
19	Model 205 UH-1D	Hel	(1968)	1969-71	19	For Army
120	Model 205 UH-1H	Hel	(1968)	1969-73	120	
13	Model 205 UH-1H	Hel	(1976)	1977	13	For Army
12	Model 205 UH-1H	Hel	1982	1982	12	For AF
4	Model 206B	Hel	(1971)	1972	4	For Army; total cost: $30 m
7	Model 206B	Hel	1985	1985	7	For Army
10	Model 208	Lightplane	1985	1986-87	(10)	For Army VIP transport
2	Model 212	Hel	1977	1977	2	For Army VIP transport
(8)	Model 212	Hel	(1984)	1985	(8)	For border surveillance; delivered via Bell, Singapore
2	Model 214B	Hel	1978	1978	2	For Army
2	Model 214ST	Hel	1984	1984	2	
23	Model 269A	Hel	(1973)	1974	23	Ex-US Army TH-55A
(24)	Model 300C	Hel	(1986)	1986-87	(24)	
6	Model 337	Trainer	1980	1981	6	For Navy
4	Model 337	Trainer	(1984)	1984	4	For Navy
2	Model 412	Hel	1981	1982	2	
1	Model 99A	Transport	(1979)	1980	1	For Army transport
16	OV-10C Bronco	Trainer/COIN	1969	1971	16	Provision for 2 Sidewinder AAMs on each
6	OV-10C Bronco	Trainer/COIN	(1973)	1973-74	16	Provision for 2 Sidewinder AAMs on each
6	OV-10C Bronco	Trainer/COIN	1977	1981	(6)	Attrition replacement; unconfirmed
2	PL-2	Lightplane	(1971)	1972	2	Built for evaluation
2	Queen Air A65	Transport	(1980)	1981	(2)	
18	S-58	Hel	1977	1978	18	Converted to S-58T standard by Thai-Am
1	Super King Air	Transport	(1983)	1984	1	
6	T-37B	Jet trainer	1979	1979	6	Surplus
4	T-37B	Jet trainer	(1983)	1983	4	
6	T-41D Mescalero	Lightplane	1971	1974	6	
14	U-10A Courier	Lightplane	1969	1970-71	14	
21	LVTP-7A1	Amph ASSV	1984	1984-85	(21)	
24	M-101-A1 105mm	TH	1979	1981	(24)	
47	M-108 105mm	SPH	1978	1979	47	
34	M-109-A2 155mm	SPH	1978	1980-81	(34)	
(16)	M-109-A2 155mm	SPH	(1983)	1983	(16)	
30	M-113-A1	APC	(1979)	1979	30	
40	M-113-A1	APC	1980	1980	40	In addition to 30 delivered 1979
148	M-113-A2	APC	1982	1984-85	(80)	Total cost incl 40 trucks: $33 m
34	M-114 155mm	TH	1979	1980-81	(34)	
34	M-114 155mm	TH	1982	1983-84	(34)	

Recipient code/Recipient	Supplier	No. ordered	Weapon designation	Weapon description	Year of order	Year(s) of delivery	Total delivered	Comments
		24	M-163 Vulcan	AAV	1980	1980-81	(24)	Ordered Feb 1980
		18	M-198 155mm	TH	1982	1983	18	Total cost: $17 m
		44	M-198 155mm	TH	(1983)	1984	(44)	
		(20)	M-198 155mm	TH	1984	1985	(20)	
		(50)	M-48-A5	MBT	(1979)	1979-80	50	
		40	M-48-A5	MBT	1984	1984-85	(40)	
		(164)	V-150 Commando	APC	1978	1980-85	(120)	
		..	AN/MPQ-4	Tracking radar	(1986)			
		..	AN/TPQ-36	Tracking radar	1982	1984-85	(9)	
		2	AN/TPQ-37	Tracking radar	1985			
		2	AN/TPS-43	3-D radar	(1980)	1980	(2)	
		..	AN/TPS-70	Air defence radar	1985	1986-87	(3)	
		24	M-167 Vulcan	Mobile AA-system	1982	1982	24	
		(4)	RGM-84A L	ShShM launcher	1983			Arming 2 corvettes on order from USA
		(192)	AIM-9D	AAM	(1970)	1971-74	(192)	To arm 32 OV-10 Bronco
		(120)	AIM-9J	AAM	1976	1978	(120)	Arming 20 F-5 fighters
		206	AIM-9P	AAM	(1979)	1980	206	Arming F-5E/F fighters
		215	BGM-71A TOW	ATM	1978	1980	215	Delivered with 12 launchers
		600	FGM-77A Dragon	ATM	(1979)	1980	600	
		20	FIM-43A Redeye	Port SAM	(1981)	1982	20	Order first rejected but later approved
		..	FIM-43A Redeye	Port SAM	1983	1983	(50)	Large number supplied in Apr 1983
		(48)	RGM-84A Harpoon	ShShM	1983			Arming 2 corvettes on order from USA
		4	LST 511-1152	LS/minelayer	(1961)	1962-75	4	
		2	PF-103 Class	Corvette	1969	1971-74	2	Second ordered 1971; called Tapi Class
		2	Tacoma Type	Corvette	1983			Ordered May 1983; for delivery 1986-87; similar to Badr Class for Saudi Arabia
15 Togo	Brazil	3	EMB-326 Xavante	Trainer/COIN	1976	1976	3	
		3	EMB-326 Xavante	Trainer/COIN	(1977)	1977	3	
		(36)	EE-9 Cascavel	AC	(1982)	1983	(36)	
	Canada	2	DHC-5D Buffalo	Transport	(1976)	1976	(2)	
	Egypt	(7)	T-34	MT	(1982)	1982	(7)	Supplier unconfirmed
		(1)	T-54	MBT	(1982)	1982	(1)	Supplier unconfirmed
		..	T-55	MBT	(1982)	1982	(1)	Supplier unconfirmed
	France	5	Alpha Jet	Jet trainer/strike	1977	1980-81	5	
		(1)	DC-8	Transport	(1984)	1984	(1)	
		(5)	Magister	Jet trainer	(1975)	1975	(5)	
		2	Model F337	Trainer	(1970)	1971	2	
		1	SA-315B Lama	Hel	1981	1981	1	

Supplier / Country	No.	Designation	Type	Year ordered	Year delivered	No. delivered	Comments
	1	SA-330 Puma	Hel	(1977)	1978	1	First export order
	3	TB-30 Epsilon	Trainer	1984	1985	(3)	
	(3)	AML-60	AC	(1978)	1978	(3)	
	(7)	AML-90	AC	(1978)	1978	(7)	
	(4)	M-2 105mm	TH	(1980)	1980	(4)	
	(3)	M-20	AC	(1980)	1980	(3)	
	..	M-3	APC	(1978)	1978	(3)	
Germany, FR	(5)	M-3	APC	(1978)	1978	(5)	Supplier unconfirmed
	(1)	Do-27	Transport	(1971)	1971	(1)	
	(30)	UR-416	APC	(1977)	1977	(30)	
Netherlands	1	F-27 Mk-1000	Transport	(1976)	1976	(1)	Supplier unconfirmed
USA	1	B-720-047B	Transport	(1979)	1980	1	VIP configuration
	(1)	C-130H Hercules	Transport	(1985)			Reportedly ordered
	1	Model 337	Trainer	(1970)	1971	1	
4 Trinidad & Tobago							
France	2	SA-341H Gazelle	Hel	(1977)	1978-79	3	
Sweden	2	Spica-2 Class	FAC	1978	1980	2	For Coast Guard
UK	4	Vosper 103 Type	PC	(1963)	1965-72	4	For Coast Guard
	1	Model 402A	Lightplane	(1978)	1978	1	
USA	2	S-76 Spirit	Hel	(1979)	1981	2	In service for internal security duties
7 Tunisia							
Austria	45	Cuirassier	LT/TD	1976	1979	45	
	..	Steyr-4K 7FA	APC	(1980)	1980	(30)	
Brazil	..	EE-11 Urutu	APC	1982	1983	(24)	
	..	EE-3 Jararaca	SC	(1984)			Unconfirmed
	(18)	EE-9 Cascavel	AC	1982	1983	(18)	
China	2	Shanghai Class	PC	1976	1977	2	
France	1	AS-365N	Hel	(1983)	1984	1	
	2	SA-318C	Hel	(1977)	1978	2	
	(1)	SA-330 Puma	Hel	(1974)	1974	(1)	
	..	VXB-170	APC	(1982)	1982	(10)	Unconfirmed
	(6)	MM-40 L	ShShM launcher	1981	1984	6	Arming 3 Combattante Class FACs
	(4)	SS-12M L	ShShM launcher	1973			Arming third P-48 Class
	(24)	MM-40 Exocet	ShShM/SShM	1981	1984	(24)	Arming 3 Combattante-3 Class FACs
	..	Milan	ATM	(1981)	1981	(100)	Unconfirmed
	(48)	SS-12	ShShM	1970	1971	(48)	To arm 2 P-48 Class; military aid
	(24)	SS-12	ShShM	1973	1975	(24)	Arming third P-48 Class
	2	Adjutant Class	MSC	1976	1976-77	2	
	3	Combattante-3	FAC	1981	1984	(3)	Armed with Exocet ShShMs
	1	P-48 Type	PC/FAC	1973	1975	1	
Italy	18	AB-205	Hel	1979	1979-80	18	In addition to 2 delivered 1970
	(1)	AL-60	Lightplane	(1971)	1971	(1)	
	12	MB-326K	Jet trainer	(1975)	1977	12	8 single seat and 4 two-seat version

Recipient code/ Recipient	Supplier	No. ordered	Weapon designation	Weapon description	Year of order	Year(s) of delivery	Total delivered	Comments
		12	SF-260 Warrior	Trainer/COIN	1974	1975	12	In addition to 12 in service
		6	SF-260C	Trainer/COIN	1977	1978	6	
		(100)	Type 6614	APC	1979	1980	(100)	
	Sweden	..	RBS-70	Port SAM	1979	1979-81	750	
	UK	2	Tazarka Class	PC	1975	1977	2	
	USA	2	C-130H Hercules	Transport	1975	1977	2	To replace old transport aircraft
		(8)	F-5E Tiger-2	Fighter	1984	1985	(2)	Number increased from 6
		2	F-5F Tiger-2	Jet trainer	1982	1984-85	(8)	Number reduced from 6
		4	Model 205 UH-1H	Hel	(1977)	1980	6	MAP
		6	Model 212 UH-1N	Hel	1980	1981	(10)	
		..	M-101-A1 105mm	TH	(1981)	1981	(10)	Supplier unconfirmed
		..	M-108 105mm	SPH	(1981)	1984	(10)	
		19	M-109-A2 155mm	SPH	1981	1984	(19)	
		(30)	M-113	APC	(1973)	1973	(30)	
		60	M-113-A1	APC	1978	1980-81	(60)	
		26	M-163 Vulcan	AAV	1978	1981-82	(26)	
		(14)	M-48-A3	MBT	(1982)	1982	(14)	Supplier unconfirmed
		(20)	M-577-A1	CPC	1979	1979	(20)	Ordered Jun 1979
		54	M-60-A3	MBT	1982	1984	54	
		(14)	V-150 Commando	APC	(1981)	1981	(14)	Supplier unconfirmed
			M54 Towed	Mobile SAM system	(1980)	1980	(10)	
		454	BGM-71A TOW	ATM	1978	1981-82	(454)	
		(62)	MIM-72A	Landmob SAM	(1980)	1980	(62)	Supplier unconfirmed
		(300)	MIM-72C	Landmob SAM	1980	1981-82	(328)	Supplier unconfirmed
		1	Edsall Class	Frigate	(1973)	1973	1	Called 'President Bourguiba'
8 Uganda	Iraq	(6)	MiG-17	Fighter/strike	1976	1976	(6)	Ex-Iraqi; surplus; replacing MiG-17/21s lost during Israeli raid at Entebbe
	Israel	(6)	MiG-19	Fighter/grd attack	1976	1976	(6)	Ex-Iraqi
	Italy	1	Westwind 1124	Transport	(1971)	1971	(1)	
		6	AB-205	Hel	(1972)	1973	6	
		2	AB-206A	Hel	(1971)	1973	2	
		6	AB-412 Griffon	Hel	1982	1985	(2)	Held in storage due to funding problems; at least 2 delivered late 1985
	Libya	8	F-5A	Fighter	(1971)	1973	8	Possibly only loaned
		(12)	Mirage-5	Fighter	1974	1974	12	Possibly only loaned; agreed March 1974
		40	Mirage-5	Fighter	(1976)	1976-77	40	Ex-Libyan AF; possibly on loan only; to replace aircraft lost in Israeli raid
		..	M-1938 122mm	TG	(1975)	1975	(20)	

Supplier	No.	Weapon designation	Type	Year of order	Year of delivery	No. delivered	Comments
Switzerland	..	Saladin FV-601	AC	(1976)	1976	(10)	Supplier unconfirmed
	..	Saracen FV-603	APC	(1976)	1976	(10)	Supplier unconfirmed
	(10)	T-34	MT	(1976)	1976	(10)	Supplier unconfirmed
USA	6	AS-202 Bravo	Trainer	1977	1977	6	
	..	Gulfstream-2	Transport	1975	1976	1	
	7	Model 205A-1	Hel	1970	1971	(7)	
	3	Model 206B	Hel	(1982)	1982-83	(3)	
	4	Model 212	Hel	(1970)	1972	4	Police Air Wing
	1	Model 212	Hel	1975	1976	1	
	3	Model 214B	Hel	(1981)	1982-83	(3)	
USSR	..	Mi-4 Hound	Hel	1971	1973	7	Reportedly gift
	12	MiG-17	Fighter/strike	1973	1974	12	Assembled by Soviet technicians at Gulu AF base; arms Atoll AAM
	8	MiG-21F	Fighter	(1974)	1975	8	Acc to Uganda Radio replacing MiGs lost during Israeli raid at Entebbe
	12	MiG-21F	Fighter	1976	1976	12	
	62	BRDM-1	SC	(1971)	1973	62	
	36	BRDM-1	SC	1973	1974	36	
	(100)	BRDM-2	SC	(1974)	1975	(100)	
	..	K-61	APC	(1974)	1975	58	Delivered through Kenya
	58	PT-76	LT	(1972)	1973	58	Delivered through Kenya
	16	T-54	MBT	1974	1975	16	Reportedly delivered
	15	T-55	MBT	1976	1976	15	Arming MiG-21s
	..	AA-2 Atoll	AAM	1974	1975	(100)	
	200	AT-3 Sagger	ATM	(1974)	1975	200	Mounted on BRDM vehicles displayed in military exercise
15 United Arab Emirates							
Brazil	66	EE-11 Urutu	APC	1982	1982-83	(66)	For Dubai
	30	EE-11 Urutu	APC	(1983)	1985	30	
Canada	1	DHC-4 Caribou	Transport	1970	1971	1	For Abu Dhabi; replacing lost aircraft
	(6)	DHC-5D Buffalo	Transport	1977	1978-79	(6)	
	1	DHC-5D Buffalo	Transport	(1981)	1982	1	
Egypt	..	Fahd	APC	(1984)	1985	(10)	Unconfirmed order for unspecified number
France	8	AS-332	Hel	1982	1982-84	(8)	
	18	Mirage-2000	Fighter/strike	1983	1985-87	(18)	For Abu Dhabi
	(20)	Mirage-2000	Fighter/strike	1984	1986	(5)	For Abu Dhabi
	12	Mirage-5	Fighter	1971	1973-74	12	
	14	Mirage-5	Fighter	1975	1976-77	(14)	
	2	Mirage-5DP	Jet trainer	(1972)	1973-74	2	
	1	Mirage-5DP	Jet trainer	1975	1976	1	
	3	Mirage-5R	Recce	(1975)	1976-77	3	
	5	SA-316B	Hel	(1971)	1972	5	For Abu Dhabi

Recipient code/ Recipient	Supplier	No. ordered	Weapon designation	Weapon description	Year of order	Year(s) of delivery	Total delivered	Comments
		5	SA-316B	Hel	(1974)	1975	5	For Abu Dhabi
		3	SA-330 Puma	Hel	(1971)	1972	3	For Abu Dhabi
		(4)	SA-330 Puma	Hel	(1972)	1973-74	4	For Abu Dhabi
		5	SA-330L Puma	Hel	1977	1978	5	For Abu Dhabi
		(12)	SA-342K Gazelle	Hel	(1980)	1981-83	(12)	
		(150)	AML-90	AC	(1975)	1976-78	(150)	
		(23)	AMX-10P	MICV	1976	1977-79	(23)	
		(20)	AMX-155 Mk-F3	SPH	(1976)	1977-79	(20)	
		(100)	AMX-30B	MBT	(1978)	1980-82	(100)	
		(10)	AMX-VCI	MICV	(1974)	1975-76	(10)	
		(200)	M-3	APC	(1974)	1975-78	(200)	
		(48)	M3-VDA	AAV	(1977)	1978	48	
		20	VAB	APC	1979	1980	20	VTT-version for Abu Dhabi
		(10)	VBC-90	AC	(1983)	1983-84	(10)	
		(10)	Crotale SAMS	Mobile SAM system	1976	1978	(10)	
		6	MM-40 L	ShShM launcher	(1977)	1980-81	6	Arming 6 TNC-45 FACs
		(24)	AM-39 Exocet	AShM	(1982)	1983-84	(24)	Unconfirmed
		(1 000)	AS-11	ASM	1974	1975	(1 000)	Arming Alouette-3s
		(1 000)	AS-12	ASM/AShM	(1974)	1975	(1 000)	Arming Alouette-3s
		(1 825)	Harpon	ATM	(1974)	1975	(1 825)	Unconfirmed
		(72)	MM-40 Exocet	ShShM/SShM	1977	1980-81	(72)	Arming 6 TNC-45 FACs
		(40)	Martel	ASM	(1974)	1974	(40)	Arming Mirage-5s; unconfirmed
		(50)	R-440 Crotale	Landmob SAM	1976	1978	(50)	
		(200)	R-550 Magic	AAM	(1975)	1976-77	(200)	Arming Mirage-5s
		(1 825)	SS-11	ATM	1974	1975	(1 825)	Unconfirmed
	Germany, FR	4	Bo-105CB	Hel	1974	1975	4	For Dubai Police Air Wing
		3	Bo-105L	Hel	(1981)	1981	3	For SAR duties in Dubai
		6	TNC-45	FAC	1977	1980-81	6	Armed with Exocet ShShMs
	Italy	(30)	A-129 Mangusta	Hel	(1986)			Negotiating
		6	AB-205	Hel	(1972)	1972-76	6	For Dubai
		2	AB-206A	Hel	(1971)	1971	2	For Abu Dhabi; transferred to Dubai 1972
		1	AB-212	Hel	1981	1982	1	
		1	G-222	Transport	1975	1976	1	For Dubai
		4	MB-326K	Jet trainer	1975	1978-79	(4)	For Dubai; incl 1 trainer
		4	MB-326L	Jet trainer	1974	1976-77	(4)	For Dubai; incl 1 trainer
		4	MB-339A	Jet trainer	(1984)	1984-86	(4)	For Dubai; unconfirmed
		1	SF-260 Warrior	Trainer/COIN	(1973)	1974	1	For Dubai
		(6)	SF-260TP	Trainer	1982	1984-85	(6)	For Dubai
		(20)	Model 56 105mm	TH	(1981)	1981-82	(20)	For Dubai

Country	Quantity	Designation	Type	(Order)	Delivery	(Number)	Comment
Spain	18	OF-40	MBT	1981	1982-83	(18)	For Dubai; option on more
	(21)	OF-40	MBT	(1982)	1984-85	(21)	Mk-2 version incl some ARVs; for Dubai
Sweden	4	C-212-200	Transport	1981	1982	4	For Abu Dhabi
	143	RBS-70	Port SAM	(1978)	1980	143	Total cost incl 13 aiming units: SEK 27 m; purchased by Unicorn International in Singapore on behalf of Dubai
Switzerland	14	PC-7	Trainer	(1981)	1982	14	For Abu Dhabi
	10	PC-7	Trainer	1984	1985-86	(10)	In addition to 14 delivered 1982
UK	1	AS-350 Ecureuil	Hel	(1985)	1985	(1)	Ex-civilian
	4	BN-2A Islander	Transport	(1967)	1968-72	(4)	For Abu Dhabi; re-sold to Somalia 1973
	1	BN-2A Islander	Transport	(1983)	1983	1	Turbo version; for Dubai
	24	Hawk	Jet trainer/strike	1983	1984-86	(24)	Ordered Jan 1983; Mk 61
	12	Hunter FGA-9	Fighter/grd attack	(1968)	1970-71	12	For Abu Dhabi
	1	Model 206A	Hel	(1985)	1985	(1)	Ex-civilian
	3	Skyvan-3M	Transport	(1972)	1974	3	Transferred to N. Yemen
	1	Skyvan-3M	Transport	(1985)	1986	1	For Sharyah
	36	FV-101 Scorpion	LT	1978	1980-81	(36)	
	(44)	FV-101 Scorpion	LT	(1983)	1984-86	(44)	Unconfirmed
	(65)	Ferret FV-703	Recce AC	(1968)	1968-71	(65)	
	(50)	Light Gun 105mm	TG	(1976)	1976-77	(50)	
	(125)	Saladin FV-601	AC	(1968)	1968-71	(125)	
	(30)	Saracen FV-603	APC	(1968)	1969-71	(30)	
	6	Shorland	AC	(1970)	1971	6	
	(10)	Sultan FV-105	CPC	(1983)	1985	(10)	Unconfirmed
	(2)	Tracked Rapier	AAV(M)	1976	1978	(2)	
	2	Rapier SAMS	Mobile SAM system	1976	1978	2	
	(50)	Rapier	Landmob SAM	1976	1978	(50)	
	:	Rapier	Landmob SAM	(1984)			For Dubai; unconfirmed
	159	Vigilant	ATM	(1970)	1972-73	(159)	
USA	6	P-1101 Class	PC	(1973)	1975-76	6	For Abu Dhabi
	2	C-130H Hercules	Transport	(1973)	1975	2	For Abu Dhabi
	2	C-130H Hercules	Transport	(1980)	1981	2	For Abu Dhabi
	1	C-130H-30	Transport	(1982)	1983	1	For Dubai
	1	L-100-30	Transport	(1980)	1981	1	For Dubai
	1	LA-4	Amphibian	(1970)	1971	1	For VIP transport
	3	Model 212	Hel	(1974)	1975	3	For Police Air Wing
	4	Model 214B	Hel	(1980)	1981	4	
	7	I-Hawk SAMS	Mobile SAM system	1981	1983-84	(7)	Order incl 343 missiles
	1 085	BGM-71A TOW	ATM	1981	1984-85	(1 085)	Total cost incl 54 launchers and 101 practice missiles: $28 m
	343	MIM-23B Hawk	Landmob SAM	1981	1983-84	(343)	Total cost incl 7 launch units, support equipment and training: $800 m
	45	MIM-23B Hawk	Landmob SAM	(1985)	1985	(45)	Replacing missiles used for practice

Recipient code/Recipient	Supplier	No. ordered	Weapon designation	Weapon description	Year of order	Year(s) of delivery	Total delivered	Comments
15 Uruguay	Argentina	8	IA-58A Pucara	COIN	1980	1981	8	
		9	T-28	Trainer	1978	1979	9	
		9	T-28	Trainer	1980	1981	9	
	Belgium	(30)	FN-4RM/62F	AC	1980	1982	(30)	Refurbished in Belgium
		15	FV-101 Scorpion	LT	1980	1982	(15)	
	Brazil	5	EMB-110	Transport	1975	1976	5	Including 10 Ipanema agricultural planes
		1	EMB-110	Transport	1978	1978	1	Attrition aircraft
		(15)	EE-11 Urutu	APC	(1986)			Unconfirmed
		(16)	EE-3 Jararaca	SC	(1982)	1983	(16)	
	Chile	4	T-34A Mentor	Trainer	(1980)	1981	4	
	France	3	Vigilante Class	PC	1978	1981	3	
		1	Vigilante Class	PC	1979	1981	1	
	Germany, FR	(55)	Condor	APC	(1976)	1977–78	(55)	
	Korea, South	32	M-101-A1 105mm	TH	1981	1982	(32)	
	Spain	5	C-212-200	Transport	1981	1982–83	(5)	
	USA	8	A-37B Dragonfly	Fighter/COIN	(1976)	1977	8	Delivered when USA embargoed 12 F-86s from Argentina
		3	FH-227	Transport	1971	1971	3	
		2	FH-227	Transport	(1972)	1973	2	
		2	Hiller 360	Hel	(1970)	1971	(2)	
		1	Learjet-35A	Mar patrol/trpt	(1979)	1981	1	
		6	Model 204 UH-1B	Hel	(1973)	1974	6	Surplus
		6	Model 205 UH-1H	Hel	(1974)	1975	6	Surplus
		2	Model 212	Hel	(1979)	1981	2	
		2	Queen Air A65	Transport	(1973)	1974	2	
		5	Queen Air A65	Transport	1979	1979	5	
		5	RT-33A	Fighter/recce	(1974)	1975	5	
		1	Super King Air	Transport	(1980)	1981	1	For maritime patrol
		20	T-34B Mentor	Trainer	(1976)	1977–78	20	
		3	T-34C-1	Trainer	(1980)	1981	3	
		(10)	T-41D Mescalero	Lightplane	(1970)	1972	(10)	
		(20)	M-3	APC	(1971)	1972–73	(20)	
		1	Dealey Class	Frigate	1972	1972	1	Ex-US Navy
		1	Gearing Class	Destroyer	1983	1983	1	
		2	LCI Type	LC	1972	1972	2	Ex-US Navy
11 Vanuatu	Australia	1	ASI-315	PC	1985			

No.	Recipient	Supplier	No. ordered	Weapon designation	Weapon description	Year of order	Year of delivery	No. delivered	Comments
15	Venezuela	Brazil	30	EMB-312 Tucano	Trainer	(1985)	1986	30	Total cost: $50 m; option on 14 more
			4	HB-350M Esquilo	Hel	(1981)	1982	4	
			(30)	EE-11 Urutu	APC	(1984)	1984	(30)	
			..	EE-3 Jararaca	SC				
		Canada	(20)	CF-5A	Fighter	1971	1972	(20)	
			19	CF-5A	Fighter	1982	1983	19	15 fighters and 4 two-seat trainers
			1	DHC-7	Transport	(1981)	1982	1	
		France	2	Mirage-3D	Jet trainer	1971	1973-74	2	
			7	Mirage-3E	Fighter/bomber	1971	1973-74	7	
			1	Mirage-3E	Fighter/bomber	1977	1977	1	Replacement
			6	Mirage-5	Fighter	1971	1973-74	6	
			(10)	AML-60	AC	(1975)	1976	10	
			(10)	AML-90	AC	(1974)	1975	10	
			(10)	AMX-105 Mk-50	SPH	(1980)	1982	(10)	
			(20)	AMX-13	LT	(1972)	1974	(20)	In addition to 20 received 1954
			(50)	AMX-13-90	LT	(1986)			Advanced negotiations
			20	AMX-155 Mk-F3	SPH	(1972)	1972-73	(20)	
			20	AMX-155 Mk-F3	SPH	(1973)	1975	20	
			120	AMX-30B	MBT	(1972)	1973	120	
			22	AMX-30B	MBT	(1975)	1976	22	In addition to 120 in service
			25	AMX-VCI	MICV	(1980)	1981-82	(25)	
			(80)	AS-11	ASM	(1977)	1979-81	(80)	Arming S-2Es and AB-212 helicopters
			(30)	R-530	AAM	(1972)	1974	(30)	Arming Mirage-3s
			(30)	R-550 Magic	AAM	(1972)	1974	(30)	Arming Mirage-3s
			(300)	SS-11	ATM	(1976)	1976-78	(300)	
		Germany, FR	10	Tpz-1	APC	(1983)	1983-84	(10)	
			20	UR-416	APC	(1976)	1978	20	For Army and paramilitary forces
		Israel	2	Type 209/2	Submarine	1971	1976-77	2	Ships named 'Sabalo' and 'Cariba'
			3	IAI-201 Arava	Transport	1979	1980	3	
			2	IAI-201 Arava	Transport	(1981)	1983	2	
			(4)	IAI-202 Arava	Transport	(1978)	1980	(4)	
		Italy	25	LAR-160	MRS	(1980)	1981-82	(25)	On AMX-13 chassis
			(10)	A-109 Hirundo	Hel	(1984)	1985	(10)	
			10	AB-212ASW	Hel	1977	1980-81	(10)	For use on Lupo Class frigates; some equipped to launch Sea Killer ShShMs
			8	G-222	Transport	(1982)	1984-85	(8)	6 for AF, 2 for Army
			4	S-61R	Hel	1984	1984-85	(4)	
			6	Aspide/Albatros	ShAM/ShShM launcher	1975	1980-82	6	Arming 6 Lupo Class frigates
			(12)	Otomat-1 L	ShShM launcher	1975	1980-82	(12)	
			6	Otomat-2 L	ShShM launcher	1972	1975	6	Arming 3 Constitution Class FACs
			(144)	Aspide	AAM/SAM/ShAM	1975	1980-82	(144)	Arming 6 Lupo Class frigates
			(48)	Otomat-1	ShShM	1975	1980-82	(48)	Arming 6 Lupo Class frigates
			18	Otomat-2	ShShM	1972	1975	18	Arming 3 of 6 Constitution Class FACs

Recipient code/ Recipient	Supplier	No. ordered	Weapon designation	Weapon description	Year of order	Year(s) of delivery	Total delivered	Comments
	Korea, South	6	Lupo Class	Frigate	1975	1980-82	6	Armed with Otomat and Aspide ShShM/ShAMs
		4	Tacoma Type	LS	1982	1984	4	
	Spain	2	C-212-200	Transport	1980	1981	2	
		4	C-212-200	Transport	1981	1983	4	
		4	C-212-200	Transport	(1984)	1985-86	(4)	For Navy
	UK	2	BN-2A Islander	Transport	(1978)	1979	2	
		12	Canberra PR-3	Bomber/recce	1974	1975	12	For repairing and refurbishing; guess version PR-3
		1	HS-748-2	Transport	(1974)	1976	1	In addition to 1 delivered 1966
		6	Constitucion Cl	PC/FAC	1973	1974-75	6	In gun- and missile versions; 3 ships armed with Otomat ShShMs
	USA	1	B-737-100	Transport	(1974)	1976	1	For VIP transport
		4	C-130E Hercules	Transport	1971	1971	4	
		2	C-130H Hercules	Transport	1974	1974	2	
		1	C-130H Hercules	Transport	1978	1979	1	
		2	C-130H Hercules	Transport	1981	1983	(2)	Total cost: $40 m
		1	Citation-1	Transport	(1972)	1973	1	
		1	Citation-2	Transport	(1979)	1979	1	
		1	DC-9	Transport	(1979)	1981	1	
		18	F-16A	Fighter/strike	1981	1983-85	(18)	Total cost incl 6 F-16Bs: $500 m
		6	F-16B	Fighter/trainer	1981	1983-84	(6)	
		14	F-5E Tiger-2	Fighter	1975	1978	14	
		3	Falcon-20G	Mar patrol	(1985)	1985	3	Bought from civilian airline
		1	Gulfstream-3	Transport	(1980)	1981	1	
		(4)	King Air C-90	Trainer	(1970)	1972	(4)	
		2	Merlin-4	Transport	(1979)	1979	2	
		12	Model 182	Lightplane	1971	1971	12	
		12	Model 205 UH-1D	Hel	(1968)	1969-72	12	
		2	Model 205 UH-1H	Hel	(1979)	1981	2	
		8	Model 205 UH-1H	Hel	(1982)	1984	8	
		6	Model 206B	Hel	1976	1976-77	6	
		1	Model 206L	Hel	1976	1977	1	
		1	Model 206L	Hel	(1983)	1984	1	
		3	Model 214ST	Hel	1981	1982	2	Total cost: $13 m
		1	Model 310	Lightplane	(1980)	1981-82	3	
		1	Model 402A	Lightplane	(1969)	1971	1	
		2	Model 412	Hel	(1980)	1981	2	
		16	OV-10A Bronco	Trainer/COIN	1971	1973-75	(16)	
		7	Queen Air B-80	Transport	(1964)	1966-71	7	

(10)	S-2E Tracker	Fighter/ASW	(1968)	1970-71	(10)	Ex-US Navy
6	Super King Air	Transport	(1981)	1981-83	7	3 for AF, 3 for Army
12	T-2D Buckeye	Jet trainer	1971	1973	12	
12	T-2D Buckeye	Jet trainer	1975	1976-77	12	
(10)	LVTP-7	Amph ASSV	(1971)	1973	10	
50	V-150 Commando	APC	(1974)	1976	50	
(48)	AGM-65A	ASM	1975	1978	(48)	Arming 14 F-5Es
100	AIM-9E	AAM	(1972)	1972	100	Arming CF-5s
(48)	AIM-9E	AAM	1975	1978	(48)	Arming 14 F-5Es
1	Guppy-2 Class	Submarine	(1973)	1973	1	Ex-US Navy; refitted in Argentina
2	LCU	LC	(1980)	1984	2	Displ: 390t
1	LST-1173 Class	LS	1973	1977	1	Ex-US; on loan 1973, purchased 1977
1	Parish Class	LS	1973	1973	1	Ex-US Navy
2	Sumner Class	Destroyer	1973	1973-74	2	Ex-US Navy

2 Viet Nam

USSR

12	An-12 Cub-A	Transport	(1979)	1979	12	Delivered Jul 1979
10	An-26 Curl	Lightplane	(1984)	1985	10	
(12)	Be-12 Chaika	Mar patrol/amphibian	(1981)	1982-84	(12)	For ASW
(15)	Ka-25 Hormone	Hel	1979	1979-81	(15)	Unspecified number delivered 1979-81
2	Ka-25 Hormone	Hel	(1984)	1984	(2)	Unconfirmed
30	Mi-24 Hind-D	Hel	(1984)	1984-85	(30)	Unconfirmed
11	Mi-6 Hook	Hel	1979	1979-80	(11)	
(30)	Mi-8 Hip	Hel	1979	1979-80	(30)	
30	Mi-8 Hip	Hel	(1982)	1982-84	(30)	
55	MiG-17PF	Fighter	(1979)	1979	55	Unconfirmed
60	MiG-19P	Fighter	(1979)	1979	60	Delivered Feb 1979
120	MiG-21F	Fighter	(1979)	1979-81	(120)	Delivered Feb 1979
(51)	MiG-21F	Fighter	(1982)	1983	(51)	
(60)	MiG-21bis	Fighter	(1979)	1979-81	(60)	
..	MiG-23	Fighter/interceptor	(1984)	1985	(6)	Unconfirmed
30	MiG-27	Fighter/strike	(1979)	1979	(30)	Unconfirmed; could be Su-22s
..	Su-20 Fitter-C	Fighter/grd attack	(1980)	1981	(70)	Delivered Feb 1979
60	Su-7 Fitter	Fighter	(1979)	1979	60	
(100)	BM-21 122mm	MRS	(1973)	1974-75	(100)	
(1 000)	BTR-60P	APC	(1979)	1979	1 000	Unconfirmed
(500)	D-20 152mm	TH	(1978)	1978-79	(500)	Unconfirmed number and year of delivery
(200)	T-62	MBT	(1978)	1979	(200)	Number and designation unconfirmed
(100)	ZSU-23-4 Shilka	AAV	(1978)	1978	(100)	Number and designation unconfirmed
90	SA-2 SAMS	Mobile SAM system	(1978)	1978-79	(90)	
20	SA-3 SAMS	Mobile SAM system	(1978)	1979	(20)	
(10)	SA-6 SAMS	Mobile SAM system	(1979)	1979-80	(10)	
(50)	SSN-2 Styx L	ShShM launcher	(1978)	1978	(50)	Coastal defence version
(8)	SSN-2 Styx L	ShShM launcher	(1979)	1979-81	(8)	On 8 Osa-2 Class FACs

Recipient code/ Recipient	Supplier	No. ordered	Weapon designation	Weapon description	Year of order	Year(s) of delivery	Total delivered	Comments
		..	AS-7 Kerry	ASM	1982	1983-85	(60)	
		(900)	SA-2 Guideline	Landmob SAM	(1978)	1978-79	(900)	Designation unconfirmed; 360 delivered Sep 1978 and 500 Feb 1979
		(360)	SA-3 Goa	Landmob SAM	(1978)	1979	(360)	
		(200)	SA-6 Gainful	Landmob SAM	(1979)	1979-80	(200)	
		(1 500)	SA-7 Grail	Port SAM	(1978)	1978	(1 500)	Designation and number unconfirmed
		(1 000)	SSN-2 Styx	ShShM	(1978)	1978	(1 000)	For coastal defence; number unconfirmed
		(48)	SSN-2 Styx	ShShM	(1979)	1979-81	(48)	Arming 8 Osa-2 Class FACs
		8	Osa-2 Class	FAC	(1979)	1979-81	8	Armed with SSN-2 Styx ShShMs
		2	Petya-2 Class	Frigate	1978	1978	2	Gift
		3	Petya-2 Class	Frigate	1983	1983-84	3	In addition to 2 in service
		3	Polnocny Class	LS	(1979)	1979-80	3	Ex-Soviet landing ships
		8	SO-1 Class	PC	(1979)	1980-83	8	
		14	Shershen Class	FAC	(1979)	1979-83	14	In addition to 2 delivered 1973
		6	Shershen Class	FAC	(1984)	1985	(6)	Unconfirmed
		(2)	Turya Class	Hydrofoil FAC	(1984)	1985	(2)	Unconfirmed
		1	Yurka Class	MSO	(1979)	1979	1	Unconfirmed
3 Vietnam, North	China	(35)	F-6	Fighter	(1966)	1967-72	(35)	Including some Soviet-built MiG-19s
		(20)	MiG-17	Fighter/strike	(1968)	1970-72	(20)	
		(100)	T-60	LT	(1970)	1971-72	(100)	
		(100)	Type-60 122mm	TG	(1970)	1971	(100)	Unconfirmed
		..	Teamwork	Air defence radar	(1971)	1971-72	(100)	Unconfirmed
		..	Wuchang Class	MSC	(1972)	1973	1	Unconfirmed
		1	Wusung Class	MSO	(1973)	1974	1	Unconfirmed
	USSR	(40)	MiG-17	Fighter/strike	(1968)	1969-72	(40)	
		(95)	MiG-21F	Fighter	(1966)	1968-72	(95)	Armed with AA-2 Atoll AAMs
		(40)	Yak-11 Moose	Trainer	(1970)	1971-72	(40)	Delivery year uncertain
		(300)	BM-21 122mm	MRS	(1968)	1969-71	(300)	
		(50)	BTR-50P	APC	(1969)	1970-71	(50)	
		(50)	D-1 152mm	TH	(1972)	1972	(50)	Unconfirmed number and year of delivery
		(50)	D-30 122mm	TH	(1974)	1974	(50)	Unconfirmed number and year of delivery
		(200)	D-74 122mm	TG	(1970)	1970-71	(200)	Unconfirmed number and year of delivery
		75	T-54	MBT	(1969)	1970-72	75	Designation, number and delivery year unconfirmed
		(500)	T-54	MBT	(1973)	1974-75	(500)	
		(50)	ZSU-57-2	AAV	(1972)	1972	(50)	Unconfirmed number and delivery year
		(170)	SA-2 SAMS	Mobile SAM system	(1968)	1969-72	(170)	Unconfirmed number and delivery year
		(10)	SA-3 SAMS	Mobile SAM system	(1971)	1972	(10)	Unconfirmed number and delivery year

	Weapon designation	Weapon type	(Order)	Delivery	No.	Comments
4	SSN-2 Styx L	ShShM launcher	(1971)	1972	4	On 4 Komar Class FACs
(690)	AA-2 Atoll	AAM	(1965)	1966-72	(690)	To arm MiG-21
(500)	AT-3 Sagger	ATM	(1971)	1972	(500)	
(3 400)	SA-2 Guideline	Landmob SAM	(1968)	1969-72	(3 400)	Including launchers
(180)	SA-3 Goa	Landmob SAM	(1971)	1972	(180)	Unconfirmed number and delivery year
(1 000)	SA-7 Grail	Port SAM	(1971)	1972	(1 000)	
(12)	SSN-2 Styx	ShShM	(1971)	1972	(12)	To arm 4 Komar Class FACs
4	Komar Class	FAC	(1971)	1972	4	Ex-Soviet FACs armed with 2 SSN-2 Styx ShShMs (single launchers)
(6)	P-6 Class	FAC	(1966)	1967-72	6	In addition to 6 received from China
2	Shershen Class	FAC	(1972)	1973	2	Torpedo-armed
10 Vietnam, South — **Korea, South**, **USA**						
45	F-5A	Fighter	(1972)	1972	45	Delivery incl F-5B and RF-5A versions
67	A-1 Skyraider	Fighter	(1969)	1970-72	67	Military aid
198	A-37B Dragonfly	Fighter/COIN	(1969)	1970-72	198	Military aid
225	Bird Dog	Lightplane	(1963)	1964-71	225	Military aid
34	C-119 Packet	Transport	(1967)	1968-72	34	Military aid
20	C-119 Packet	Transport	(1971)	1972	20	Gunship version
66	C-123 Provider	Transport	(1969)	1971	66	Military aid
34	C-130A Hercules	Transport	(1971)	1972	34	Delivered in Nov 1972 airlift
(40)	C-47	Transport	(1966)	1967-72	40	D version
6	C-47	Transport	(1968)	1969-71	6	A version
30	CH-47A Chinook	Hel	(1970)	1971-72	30	Some delivered in Nov 1972 airlift
20	CH-47A Chinook	Hel	(1972)	1973	20	
36	DHC-4 Caribou	Transport	(1971)	1972	36	
27	EC-47	ECM	(1971)	1972-73	27	For electronic warfare
120	F-5A	Fighter	(1971)	1972	120	Delivered in Nov airlift; 20 from USA, 30 from Iran, 70 from S. Korea/Taiwan
125	F-5E Tiger-2	Fighter	1972	1973-74	47	47 delivered probably to Thailand 1975
80	Model 185	Lightplane	(1961)	1963-71	80	
350	Model 205 UH-1H	Hel	(1967)	1969-71	350	Both new and ex-US Army
549	Model 205 UH-1H	Hel	(1971)	1972	549	279 from departing US units; rest direct
34	Model 321	Lightplane	(1972)	1973	34	Also called Birddog O-2A
1	PL-2	Lightplane	1970	1971	1	
7	RF-5A	Fighter/recce	(1969)	1970-71	7	Military aid
42	T-41D Mescalero	Lightplane	(1967)	1968-71	42	Military aid
(600)	M-101-A1 105mm	TH	(1967)	1968-72	(600)	Delivery year uncertain
(600)	M-102 105mm	TH	(1969)	1970-73	(600)	Delivery year uncertain
24	M-107 175mm	SPG	(1970)	1971	24	
(150)	M-107 175mm	SPG	(1972)	1972	(150)	Delivery year uncertain
24	M-109 155mm	SPH	(1970)	1971	24	
1 100	M-113-A1	APC	(1968)	1969-72	1 100	
235	M-113-A1	APC	(1972)	1973-74	235	Both new and US army

Recipient code/ Recipient	Supplier	No. ordered	Weapon designation	Weapon description	Year of order	Year(s) of delivery	Total delivered	Comments
		(100)	M-114 155mm	TH	(1972)	1972	(100)	Delivery year uncertain
		(350)	M-41	LT	(1968)	1969-72	(350)	
		107	M-48 Patton	MBT	(1970)	1971-72	(107)	Some refurbished in Japan
		300	M-48 Patton	MBT	(1972)	1974	300	
		(85)	M-60	MBT	(1971)	1972-73	(85)	
		(1 000)	BGM-71A TOW	ATM	(1971)	1972	(1 000)	
		7	Barnegat Class	Support ship	(1970)	1971-72	7	Ex-US Navy
		2	Edsall Class	Frigate	(1971)	1971	2	Ex-US Navy
		15	LCU 1466 Class	LC	(1957)	1958-71	(15)	Ex-US Navy
8 Yemen, North	Egypt	(20)	Walid	APC	(1974)	1975	(20)	Dates and number ordered unconfirmed
	Italy	2	AB-204	Hel	(1973)	1974	2	
		1	AB-212	Hel	(1980)	1981	1	For VIP use
	New Zealand	(5)	F-27 Mk-400	Transport	(1984)	1984-85	5	Supplier unconfirmed for last 2 aircraft
	Saudi Arabia	4	F-5B	Fighter/trainer	1977	1977	4	
		(20)	Vigilant	ATM	1977	1977	(20)	
	USA	2	C-130H Hercules	Transport	1979	1979	2	
		12	F-5E Tiger-2	Fighter	1979	1979	12	Saudi funding
		(50)	M-101-A1 105mm	TH	(1979)	1980-81	(50)	
		12	M-106-A1	APC	1979	1979	12	
		50	M-113-A1	APC	1979	1979	50	Saudi funding
		(34)	M-163 Vulcan	AAV	(1979)	1979	(34)	
		6	M-577-A1	CPC	1979	1979	6	
		64	M-60-A1	MBT	1979	1979	64	Saudi funding
		6	M-88	ARV	1979	1979	6	
		(40)	M-167 Vulcan	Mobile AA-system	(1979)	1979	(40)	
		(72)	AIM-9E	AAM	1979	1979	(72)	Arming F-5Es
		(250)	BGM-71A TOW	ATM	1979	1979	(250)	Saudi funding; 12 launchers
		(1 500)	FGM-77A Dragon	ATM	1979	1979	(1 500)	Transferred Mar 1979
	USSR	1	An-12 Cub-A	Transport	(1984)	1985	(1)	
		(2)	An-24 Coke	Transport	(1984)	1984	(2)	
		(2)	An-26 Curl	Lightplane	(1979)	1981	(2)	
		1	Il-18	Transport	(1979)	1980	1	
		..	Mi-4 Hound	Hel	(1980)	1981	(2)	
		(25)	Mi-8 Hip	Hel	(1984)	1984-85	(25)	
		(30)	MiG-21F	Fighter	(1979)	1979-80	(30)	
		(24)	MiG-21F	Fighter	(1985)	1985	(24)	
		(5)	MiG-21UTI	Jet trainer	(1979)	1979-80	(5)	Unconfirmed
		(15)	Su-22 Fitter-J	Fighter/grd attack	(1980)	1980	(15)	

(70)	BM-21 122mm	MRS	(1979)	1980-81	(70)	
(50)	BRDM-2	SC	(1979)	1980	(50)	
150	BTR-60P	APC	1979	1980	150	Designation unconfirmed
(100)	M-1938 122mm	TG	(1979)	1979-80	(100)	
(70)	T-34	MT	(1979)	1980	(70)	
(200)	T-54	MBT	1979	1979-80	(200)	
(200)	T-55	MBT	1979	1979-80	(200)	
(12)	T-62	MBT	(1985)	1985	(12)	Unconfirmed
(40)	ZSU-23-4 Shilka	AAV	1979	1979-80	(40)	
(3)	SA-2 SAMS	Mobile SAM system	(1979)	1981	(3)	12 launchers in 3 btys
2	SSN-2 Styx L	ShShM launcher	(1981)	1982	(2)	
(90)	AA-2 Atoll	AAM	(1980)	1980	(90)	Arming 16 Su-22 fighters reportedly flown by Cuban pilots
(108)	SA-2 Guideline	Landmob SAM	(1979)	1981	(108)	
(200)	SA-7 Grail	Port SAM	1979	1980-81	(200)	
(8)	SSN-2 Styx	ShShM	(1981)	1982	(8)	Arming 2 Osa-2 Class FACs
2	Ondatra Class	LC	(1982)	1983	2	
2	Osa-2 Class	FAC	(1981)	1982	2	
2	Yevgenia Class	MSC	(1982)	1982	2	
3	Skyvan-3M	Transport	1974	1974	3	

United Arab Emirates

5 Yemen, South   Poland   USSR

(50)	T-54	MBT	1978	1979	(50)	
(2)	An-12 Cub-A	Transport	(1985)	1985	(2)	
3	An-24 Coke	Transport	1972	1974	3	
(4)	An-26 Curl	Lightplane	(1984)	1984-86	(4)	
4	Il-14	Transport	1972	1974	4	
6	Mi-4 Hound	Hel	1973	1974	6	
(8)	Mi-8 Hip	Hel	(1973)	1974	(8)	
(7)	Mi-8 Hip	Hel	1979	1979	(7)	
(36)	MiG-17	Fighter/strike	(1968)	1969-71	(36)	
(12)	MiG-21F	Fighter	1969	1972	(12)	
(36)	MiG-21F	Fighter	(1979)	1979-81	(36)	
(4)	MiG-21UTI	Jet trainer	(1979)	1979	(4)	
(15)	MiG-23	Fighter/interceptor	(1978)	1979	(15)	
(5)	MiG-27	Fighter/strike	(1979)	1979	(5)	
(30)	Su-22 Fitter-J	Fighter/grd attack	(1979)	1979-80	(30)	Unconfirmed
(12)	Su-7 Fitter	Fighter	(1979)	1979	(12)	Unconfirmed
(150)	BM-21 122mm	MRS	(1972)	1973-75	(150)	
(20)	BM-25 250mm	MRS	(1979)	1980	(20)	
(100)	BMP-1	MICV	(1983)	1983-84	(100)	
(100)	BRDM-2	SC	(1979)	1979-80	(100)	
(6)	BRDM-2 Gaskin	AAV(M)	1979	1979-80	(6)	
(100)	BTR-152	APC	(1979)	1979-80	(100)	

Recipient code/ Recipient	Supplier	No. ordered	Weapon designation	Weapon description	Year of order	Year(s) of delivery	Total delivered	Comments
		(100)	BTR-60P	APC	(1981)	1981-82	(100)	
		(100)	D-30 122mm	TH	(1982)	1982-84	(100)	
		(75)	M-1938 122mm	TG	(1974)	1975-76	(75)	
		(100)	M-1955 100mm	TG	(1982)	1982-84	(100)	
		(75)	M-46 130mm	TG	(1975)	1976-77	(75)	
		(20)	SM-4-1 130mm	TG	(1980)	1980-81	(20)	
		(50)	T-34	MT	(1972)	1973	(50)	
		(20)	T-54	MBT	(1971)	1972-73	(20)	
		(20)	T-55	MBT	(1972)	1973-74	(20)	
		(200)	T-55	MBT	(1980)	1980-81	(200)	Following Polish T-55 deliveries
		(50)	T-62	MBT	1979	1979	(50)	
		(100)	T-62	MBT	1980	1981-82	(100)	Ordered Jun 1980
		(100)	ZSU-23-4 Shilka	AAV	(1979)	1979-80	(100)	In service
		(2)	FROG L	Mobile SSM system	(1979)	1979	(2)	Unconfirmed
		(6)	SA-2 SAMS	Mobile SAM system	(1979)	1979-80	(6)	
		6	SA-3 SAMS	Mobile SAM system	1979	1979-80	(6)	
		(6)	SA-6 SAMS	Mobile SAM system	1979	1979-80	(6)	
		(8)	SSN-2 Styx L	ShShM launcher	(1979)	1979-83	(8)	Arming 8 Osa-2 Class FACs
		(2)	Scud-B L	Mobile SSM system	1979	1979-80	(2)	Unconfirmed
		(288)	AA-2 Atoll	AAM	(1972)	1972-81	(288)	Arming MiG-21s
		(12)	FROG-7	Landmob SSM	(1979)	1979	(12)	Unconfirmed
		(60)	SA-2 Guideline	Landmob SAM	(1979)	1979-80	(60)	
		..	SA-3 Goa	Landmob SAM	(1979)	1979-80	(100)	
		(54)	SA-6 Gainful	Landmob SAM	1979	1979-80	(54)	
		(600)	SA-7 Grail	Port SAM	(1979)	1979-81	(600)	
		(72)	SA-9 Gaskin	Landmob SAM	(1979)	1979-80	(72)	
		(6)	SCUD-B	Landmob SSM	1979	1979-80	(6)	Unconfirmed
		96	SSN-2 Styx	ShShM	(1979)	1979-83	(96)	Arming 8 Osa-2 Class FACs
		2	Mol Class	FAC	(1977)	1978	2	
		8	Osa-2 Class	FAC	(1979)	1979-83	8	
		2	P-6 Class	FAC	(1972)	1973	2	
		2	Polnocny Class	LS	(1972)	1973	2	
		1	Polnocny Class	LS	(1976)	1977	1	
		1	Ropucha Class	LS	(1978)	1979	1	
		2	SO-1 Class	PC	(1971)	1972	2	
		1	T-58 Class	MSO	(1977)	1978	1	Minesweeping gear removed
4 Zaire	Canada	3	DHC-5D Buffalo	Transport	1974	1976	3	Order reduced from 6, of which 2 delivered to Togo instead

Country	No.	Designation	Type	(Year of order)	Year of delivery	No. delivered	Comments
China	60	T-62	LT	1977	1977	60	
	(50)	Type 59/1 130mm	TG	(1982)	1982	(50)	Unconfirmed
	(100)	Type-60 122mm	TG	(1981)	1981	(20)	
	:	Type-63 107mm	MRS	(1972)			Unconfirmed
	:	Type-66 152mm	TH	(1982)	1982	(20)	
	4	Huchuan Class	Hydrofoil FAC	1978	1978-79	(4)	Unconfirmed
	4	Shanghai Class	PC	(1975)	1976-78	4	
France	1	AS-332	Hel	(1982)	1984	1	
	(4)	AS-350 Ecureuil	Hel	(1981)	1982	(4)	Unconfirmed
	(10)	Mirage-5	Fighter	1973	1974-75	(10)	Order reduced from 17 for financial reasons
	1	Mystere-20	Transport	(1980)	1980	(1)	
	7	SA-316B	Hel	1972	1972	7	
	(1)	SA-321	Hel	(1978)	1978	(1)	
	7	SA-330 Puma	Hel	1970	1971	7	
	(30)	AML-60	AC	(1969)	1971	(30)	In addition to 60 previously acquired; some given to FNLA in Angola
	(95)	AML-60	AC	(1974)	1975	(95)	
	(30)	AML-90	AC	(1969)	1971	(30)	In addition to 60 previously acquired; some possibly given to FNLA in Angola
	(95)	AML-90	AC	(1974)	1975	(95)	
Italy	(60)	M-3	APC	(1970)	1972-73	(60)	
	:	AS-30	ASM	1973	1976	(50)	Arming Mirages
	6	MB-326KG	Jet trainer	1979	1979-80	(6)	
	12	SF-260M	Trainer	1969	1971	12	
	12	SF-260M	Trainer	1972	1973	12	
	9	SF-260M	Trainer	(1982)	1982	9	
Japan	2	MU-2J	Transport	1974	1974	2	Replacing 9 previously delivered
Korea, North	:	BTR-60P	APC	(1980)	1980	(10)	For VIP use; via USA
	(50)	D-30 122mm	TH	(1981)	1981	(50)	Supplier and designation unconfirmed
	(100)	M-1938 122mm	TG	(1978)	1978	(100)	Supplier unconfirmed
	:	Type 531	APC	(1982)	1982	(10)	Unconfirmed
	3	P-4 Type	FAC	(1973)	1974	3	
UK	1	HS-146	Transport	(1983)	1983	(1)	Unconfirmed; for VIP use
USA	3	C-130E Hercules	Transport	1971	1971	3	For paratroop lifting
	3	C-130H Hercules	Transport	1974	1975	3	In addition to 3 previously acquired
	1	C-130H Hercules	Transport	1977	1977	1	
	15	Model 150	Lightplane	1976	1976	15	
	15	Model 310	Lightplane	1974	1975	15	
	:	M-113-A1	APC	1976	1977		
	:	M-3	APC	(1981)	1981	(10)	Supplier unconfirmed
Zambia	4						
Canada	1	DHC-4 Caribou	Transport	(1970)	1971	1	

Recipient code/ Recipient	Supplier	No. ordered	Weapon designation	Weapon description	Year of order	Year(s) of delivery	Total delivered	Comments
	China	8	DHC-5D Buffalo	Transport	1974	1976	8	
		:	BT-6	Trainer	(1977)	1978	(10)	
		12	F-6	Fighter	(1977)	1977–78	(12)	
		(4)	T-34	MT	(1983)	1983	(4)	Unconfirmed
	France	(4)	Type 59/1 130mm	TG	(1983)	1983	(4)	Unconfirmed
		8	SA-316B	Hel	(1980)	1980	(8)	Unconfirmed
			Tiger	Point defence radar	(1978)	1979	(3)	
	Germany, FR	10	Do-28D-2	Transport	1973	1974	10	
	Italy	25	AB-205	Hel	(1972)	1973	25	
		7	AB-205	Hel	1980	1981	7	
		1	AB-212	Hel	(1970)	1971	1	
		1	AB-212	Hel	(1977)	1978	1	
		(6)	AB-47G	Hel	1978	1978	(6)	
		(18)	MB-326GB	Jet trainer	1973	1974	(18)	Replacement for losses
		3	MB-326GB	Jet trainer	(1982)	1982	(3)	
		8	SF-260M	Trainer	(1971)	1972	8	
	Sweden	20	Supporter	Trainer/strike	1975	1976–77	20	
	UK	1	HS-748-2	Transport	(1970)	1971	1	Unconfirmed
		:	Tracked Rapier	AAV(M)	(1970)	1971	(3)	
		10	Rapier SAMS	Mobile SAM system	(1970)	1971	10	
		:	Tigercat SAMS	Mobile SAM system	1978	1978	(5)	
		(100)	Rapier	Landmob SAM	(1970)	1971	(100)	
		:	Tigercat	Landmob SAM	(1978)	1978	(100)	
	USA	(10)	M-101-A1 105mm	TH	(1982)	1982	(10)	Unconfirmed
	USSR	6	Mi-8 Hip	Hel	(1975)	1976	6	
		16	MiG-21F	Fighter	1980	1981	16	Incl 2 trainers
		3	Yak-40 Codling	Transport	(1982)	1982	3	
		(50)	BM-21 122mm	MRS	(1980)	1981–82	(50)	Unconfirmed
		(20)	BRDM-1	SC	(1975)	1976	(20)	
		:	BRDM-2	SC	(1978)	1978	(40)	
		:	BTR-60P	APC	(1980)	1980–81	(100)	Designation unconfirmed
		:	BTR-60P	APC	(1984)	1984	(30)	Unspecified number of armoured vehicles delivered Mar 1984; designation unconfirmed
		:	D-30 122mm	TH	(1983)	1983	(10)	
		(100)	PT-76	LT	(1983)	1984	(100)	
		:	T-54	MBT	1975	1976	8	
		:	T-55	MBT	1980	1980–81	(60)	Ordered Feb 1980
		:	SA-3 SAMS	Mobile SAM system	1980	1980	(10)	Delivered Dec 1980

Country		Designation	Type				Comments
Yugoslavia	:	AT-3 Sagger	ATM	(1980)	1980-81	(50)	Designation unconfirmed
	:	SA-3 Goa	Landmob SAM	1980	1980	(20)	
	2	G-2A Galeb	Jet trainer	1970	1971	2	
	:	G-4 Super Galeb	Jet trainer	(1984)		4	Unconfirmed
	4	J-1 Jastreb	Fighter	1970	1971	4	
15 Zimbabwe Brazil	90	EE-9 Cascavel	AC	1983	1983-84	(90)	Option on 60 more
China	(12)	F-7	Fighter	(1983)		(10)	Supplier unconfirmed
	(10)	T-34	MT	(1981)	1981	(10)	Supplier unconfirmed
	(10)	T-54	MBT	(1981)	1981		Unconfirmed
	(35)	T-59	MBT	(1984)		(20)	Designation unconfirmed
	20	T-63	LT	(1983)	1984	(20)	
	:	Type-60 122mm	TG	(1983)	1983	(20)	
France	(14)	Model F337	Trainer	1976	1977	(14)	Illegally acquired via private company
	4	OV-10F Bronco	Trainer/COIN	1976	1977	4	Acquired illegally via private source
Indonesia	(11)	Model 205A-1	Hel	1978	1978	(11)	Smuggled by private company
Israel	10	AB-412 Griffon	Hel	1984	1986-87	(10)	Acquired illegally
Italy	(22)	SF-260 Warrior	Trainer/COIN	(1978)	1978	(22)	Designation unconfirmed
	5	SF-260 Warrior	Trainer/COIN	(1982)	1983	5	
Korea, North	(20)	BRDM-1	SC	(1984)	1984	(20)	Designation unconfirmed
	:	BRDM-2	SC	(1983)	1983	(10)	Supplier unconfirmed
	:	BTR-152	APC	(1983)	1983	10	Supplier unconfirmed
	(12)	T-55	MBT	(1981)	1981	(12)	
South Africa	20	AM-3C	Lightplane	(1970)	1972-74	(20)	Unconfirmed
	(10)	C-47	Transport	(1976)	1976-78	(10)	
	(1)	Canberra B-2	Bomber	(1975)	1976	(1)	Ex-SAAF; for recce
	(6)	Mirage-3B	Jet trainer	(1975)	1976	(6)	Ex-SAAF
	(12)	Model 185	Lightplane	(1976)	1977	(12)	
	(45)	SA-316B	Hel	(1975)	1975-77	(45)	Designation unconfirmed
	(2)	SA-330 Puma	Hel	(1971)	1973	(2)	
	(7)	AML-60	AC	(1970)	1971	(7)	
	(30)	AML-60	AC	(1971)	1972	(30)	
	:	Buffel	AC	(1978)	1979	(20)	Unconfirmed
	:	Casspir	AC	(1976)	1976-78	(100)	Unconfirmed
	:	Eland-60	AC	(1975)	1976	(10)	Unconfirmed
	(30)	Eland-90	AC	(1974)	1975	(30)	Dates and number ordered unconfirmed
	:	UR-416	APC	(1975)	1975	(20)	Unconfirmed
Spain	6	C-212-200	Transport	1982	1982-84	6	
UK	4	BN-2A Defender	Lightplane	(1976)	1977	(4)	Acquired illegally; reportedly delivered via Botswana
	1	Canberra B-2	Bomber	1981	1981	1	Surplus
	1	Canberra T-4	Jet trainer	1981	1981	1	Surplus
	8	Hawk	Jet trainer/strike	1980	1982	8	1 destroyed and 3 damaged in terrorist attack; Mk-60

Recipient code/ Recipient	Supplier	No. ordered	Weapon designation	Weapon description	Year of order	Year(s) of delivery	Total delivered	Comments
		4	Hunter FGA-9	Fighter/grd attack	1981	1981	4	Surplus
		5	Hunter FGA-9	Fighter/grd attack	1983	1984	5	Replacing aircraft destroyed in sabotage attack 1982
		1	Hunter T-7	Fighter/trainer	1981	1981	1	Surplus
		1	Falconer	PAR	(1984)	1984	(1)	
	USSR	..	BRDM-2	SC	(1980)	1980	(3)	Supplier unconfirmed

Appendix 2. Register of licensed production of major conventional weapons in Third World countries, 1971–85

The sources and methods for the data collection are explained in appendix 9, and the conventions, abbreviations and acronyms used are given in the front of the book. The entries are made alphabetically, by recipient and licenser, in chronological order by year of licence and, finally, alphabetically by weapon designation.

Region code/ Country	Licenser	No. ordered	Weapon designation	Weapon description	Year of licence	Year(s) of production	Total produced	Comments
5 Algeria	Bulgaria	..	Kebir Type	Corvette	1983			Unconfirmed whether licensed production, assembly or sale
	UK	4	Kebir Class	PC	1981			In addition to 2 delivered from UK
		3	Kebir Class	PC	1985	1985	(3)	For delivery by 1987
4 Argentina	Germany, FR	(300)	TAM	MT	1976	1981-85	(230)	220 for Argentina plus for export; developed by Thyssen (FRG)
		300	VCTP	ICV	1976	1981-85	(300)	Similar to Marder MICV
		6	Meko-140 Type	Frigate	1980	1985-86	(4)	
		4	Type TR-1700	Submarine	1977			In addition to 2 delivered directly
	Switzerland	(80)	Roland	APC	1970	1974-79	(80)	
	UK	1	Type 42	Destroyer	1970	1981	1	In addition to 1 ship acquired directly
	USA	120	Model 500D	Hel	1972	1974-84	(57)	Assembly of knocked-down components
7 Brazil	Austria	..	GC-45 155mm	TH/TG	(1985)			Unconfirmed
	France	6	HB-350M Esquilo	Hel	(1985)			Requirement for 40 more
	Germany, FR	(300)	Cobra-2000	ATM	1973	1976-81	(300)	Pre-production; production unconfirmed
		1	Type 209/3	Submarine	1982			Hull and some components to be built in Brazil; barter agreement for iron ore
	Italy	166	EMB-326 Xavante	Trainer/COIN	1970	1972-83	(166)	AF designation: AT-26 Xavante; initial licence-production contract for 112; later increased to a total of 166
	UK	2	Niteroi Class	Frigate	1970	1979-80	2	In addition to 4 built in UK
		1	Niteroi Class	Frigate	1981	1986	(1)	Ordered Jun 1981; training ship; completion delayed

4 Chile	France	3 Batral Type	LS	1980	1982-84	3	
	Spain	(20) T-36 Halcon	Jet trainer	1984	1986-87	(8)	In addition to 16 delivered 1982-83; at least 1 armed with Sea Eagle AShMs
	Switzerland	(150) Piranha	APC	1980	1981-85	(90)	
	USA	(17) PA-28 Dakota	Trainer	1980	1981-82	(17)	
		(120) T-35 Pillan	Trainer	1980	1985	(10)	Developed from Piper PA-28 by US and Chilean engineers; 80 for Chile, 40 for Spain
		3 PC-1638 Type	PC	(1970)	1971-81	(3)	Chilean designation: Papudo Class
15 Egypt	Brazil	110 EMB-312 Tucano	Trainer	1983	1985-86	(60)	30 for Egypt, 80 for Iraq
	France	·· AS-332	Hel	1983			Ordered Dec 1983; mainly assembly
		37 Alpha Jet	Jet trainer/strike	1981	1982-85	(37)	Following delivery of 8; local component share increased from 10% (1982) to 48% (1984); last 15 NG-version (MS2)
		15 Alpha Jet	Jet trainer/strike	(1986)			Negotiating
		36 SA-342L Gazelle	Hel	1981	1983-86	(36)	
		·· SA-342L Gazelle	Hel	(1986)			
	UK	(5 000) Swingfire	ATM	1977	1979-85	(3 250)	Negotiating continued production
4 India	France	(140) SA-315B Lama	Hel	1971	1973-85	(140)	First 40 assembly only, then licensed production of 100 from local raw materials; also for civilian use
		·· SA-316B Chetak	Hel	(1962)	1964-85	(277)	Also for civilian use; some production of parts for French AS-316s
		(10 000) Milan	ATM	1982	1985-86	(600)	First missile completed early 1985
		(10 400) SS-11	ATM	(1970)	1971-83	(10 400)	70% indigenous
	Germany, FR	(150) Do-228	Transport	1982	1986	(3)	Complementing HS-748 aircraft produced in India; production for AF, Navy and Coast Guard began 1986
		4 Type 1500	Submarine	1984			Option from 1981 taken up Feb 1984
	Switzerland	215 Fledermaus II	Mobile AA-system	(1967)	1970-80	(44)	
	UK	·· Gnat	Fighter/bomber	1956	1963-74	(215)	
		·· HS-748	Transport	(1960)	1964-84	(64)	
		45 Jaguar	Fighter	1978	1982-87	(45)	Local production of components; in addition to 40 purchased directly
		31 Jaguar	Fighter	1982			
		(1 425) Vijayanta	MBT	1961	1965-84	(1 425)	
		6 Nilgiri Class	Frigate	1964	1972-81	6	Similar to British Leander Class; arms: Seacat ShShM/ShAMs
	USSR	140 MiG-21FL	Fighter	(1962)	1967-74	(140)	First MiG version produced in India
		(150) MiG-21MF	Fighter	1972	1973-81	(150)	
		(220) MiG-21bis	Fighter	1976	1979-87	(220)	

Region code/ Country	Licenser	No. ordered	Weapon designation	Weapon description	Year of licence	Year(s) of production	Total produced	Comments
		(165)	MiG-27	Fighter/grd attack	1983	1984-86	(32)	Agreement signed July 1983; first flight Nov 1984
			BMP-1	APC/ICV	1983			Prototype ready Mar 1984; for entry into service 1987; production initially 10% indigenous; Indian designation: T-72M; possibly similar to Soviet T-74
		(1 000)	T-72	MBT	(1980)			
		(2 200)	AA-2 Atoll	AAM	(1963)	1968-87	(2 200)	Arming MiG fighters
4 Indonesia	France	(56)	AS-332	Hel	(1982)	1985-86	4	Production switched from Puma to Super Puma 1983; total orders by end-1984: 69; military orders: 56
	Germany, FR	7	SA-330 Puma	Hel	1980	1981-83	(7)	
		(100)	BK-117	Hel	1982	1984	2	Total production schedule: 100; 2 pre-production aircraft delivered 1984
	Spain	(50)	NBo-105	Hel	1976	1976-86	(39)	Military order for approx 50 helicopters
		6	PB-57 Type	PC	1982	1985	(1)	Probably 4 for Coast Guard
		(80)	CN-212	Transport	1976	1978-86	(20)	For civil and military use; 18 delivered to armed forces by early 1986
	USA	(28)	Model 412	Hel	1982	1986	1	More than 100 to be assembled from 1985; military orders by 1986: 28
1 Israel	USA	..	Westwind 1124	Transport	1968	1976-85	(20)	Production transferred to Israel 1968
		(24)	Dabur Class	PC	1973	1977-82	(24)	
		9	Flagstaff-2 Cl	Hydrofoil FAC	1981	1983-85	2	In addition to 1 directly; remaining 8 may not all be built for cost reasons
3 Korea, North	China	8	Romeo Class	Submarine	1973	1975-82	(8)	In addition to 7 directly from China
	USSR	(6)	MiG-19	Fighter	(1972)	1976	(6)	Unconfirmed; probably trial production
		..	T-54	MBT	1967	1969-74	(300)	Unconfirmed
		..	T-55	MBT	(1973)	1975-79	(500)	Unconfirmed; also reported as T-59 (Chinese version of T-55)
4 Korea, South	Italy	(350)	Type 6614	APC	1976	1977-83	(350)	
	USA	(68)	F-5E Tiger-2	Fighter	1979	1982-86	(68)	Incl 36 F-5Es and 32 F-5Fs; local assembly of aircraft, incl engines
		(139)	Model 500MD	Hel	1976	1978-85	(110)	
		4	PL-2	Lightplane	1975	1975-76	4	Built for evaluation as trainers

Recipient	Supplier	No. ordered	Designation	Type	Year of order	Year(s) of delivery	No. delivered	Comments
		..	M-101-A1 105mm	TH	(1971)	1977-85	(90)	Possibly without US consent
		..	M-109-A2 155mm	SPH	1983	1978-85	(80)	Possibly without US consent
		..	M-114-A1	TH	(1971)	1979	5	
		5	CPIC Type	PC/FAC	1977	1979-81	(6)	
		6	LCU-1610 Type	LC	(1977)	1977-80	8	4 for S. Korea; rest for Indonesia and the Philippines
		..	PSMM-5 Type	FAC	(1974)			
4 Madagascar	France	1	EDIC/EDA Type	LC	(1977)	1979	1	
4 Malaysia	Germany, FR	6	Jerong Class	PC	1973	1976-77	6	Luerssen-designed FPB-45 Type
	Germany, FR	1	Mutiara	Survey ship	1975	1978	1	
	Korea, South	1	Mash Class	OPV	(1983)	1986	(1)	In addition to 1 delivered directly
4 Mexico	UK	(10)	Azteca Class	PC	1975	1976-82	10	In addition to 31 in service
	UK	5	Azteca Class	PC	1983			
7 Nigeria	Austria	(200)	Steyr-4K 7FA	APC	(1981)			Various versions to be built; possibly also Curassier LT/TD; status uncertain due to financial problems
4 Pakistan	Germany, FR	..	Cobra-2000	ATM	1963	1978-79	(200)	West German Government claims no licence-production contract exists
	Sweden	..	Supporter	Trainer	1974	1977-86	(130)	Assembly of 90 from imported kits began 1976; from 1982 with local raw material; production transferred to Kamra 1981
	UK	1	Amazon Class	Frigate	(1985)			In addition to 2 from UK
4 Peru	Italy	2	Lupo Class	Frigate	1974	1984-85	2	In addition to 2 delivered directly
	USA	1	PGM-71 Class	PC	(1971)	1972	1	MAP financed
4 Philippines	Germany, FR	(..)	Bo-105C	Hel	1974	1976-85	(13)	Approx 15 in service incl 5 from FRG
	UK	(100)	BN-2A Islander	Lightplane	1974	1974-85	(60)	
4 Singapore	Germany, FR	3	PB-57 Type	PC/FAC	1980			Luerssen design; status unclear
	Germany, FR	4	TNC-45	FAC	1970	1974-75	4	In addition to 2 delivered directly from Luerssen 1972; armed with 5 Gabriel ShShMs
	UK	3	Type 27M	LC	1970	1971-75	3	Built for Kuwait by Vosper, Singapore
	UK	3	Type 32M	LC	(1978)	1979	3	Built for Kuwait by Vosper, Singapore
	UK	4	Type A/B	PC	1968	1971	4	In addition to 2 delivered from UK

Region code/Country	Licenser	No. ordered	Weapon designation	Weapon description	Year of licence	Year(s) of production	Total produced	Comments
4 South Africa	France	3	Waspada Class	FAC	(1976)	1978-79	3	For Brunei
		32	Mirage F-1A	Fighter	1971	1973-76	(32)	
		16	Mirage F-1C	Fighter	1971	1976-77	(16)	
		(400)	AML-60	AC	1962	1966-72	(400)	Based on French AML 245
		(400)	AML-90	AC	1962	1966-72	(400)	Based on French AML 245
	Israel	..	Reshef Class	FAC	1974	1978-86	6	In addition to 3 previously acquired; armed with 6 Scorpioen ShShMs derived from Israeli Gabriel ShShM
	Italy	(151)	Impala-1	Jet trainer	1966	1966-74	151	
		(100)	Impala-2	Jet trainer	1974	1974-82	100	Also designated MB-326K
8 Taiwan	Israel	..	Gabriel L	ShShM/SShM launcher	(1978)	1980-85	(48)	Taiwanese designation: Hsiung Feng
		..	Gabriel-2	ShShM/SShM	(1978)	1980-85	(375)	Developed from Israeli Dvora Class; armed with 2 Hsiung Feng (Gabriel-2) ShShMs; more than 50 planned
		..	Hai Ou Class	FAC	(1979)	1980-85	(41)	
	USA	212	F-5E Tiger-2	Fighter	1973	1974-83	(212)	
		30	F-5E Tiger-2	Fighter	1982	1983-85	(18)	Total cost incl 30 F-5Fs: $620 m; for delivery 1983-87
		36	F-5F Tiger-2	Jet trainer	1973	1974-83	(36)	
		30	F-5F Tiger-2	Jet trainer	1982	1983-85	(18)	
		118	Model 205 UH-1H	Hel	1969	1969-76	(118)	Original contract for 50 1969; 68 more ordered 1972
		56	PL-1B Chienshou	Lightplane	1968	1968-74	56	Modified version of US Pazmany PL-1
		(1)	Lung Chiang Cl	FAC	1977	1979	1	Two more possibly laid down 1981; armed with 4 Gabriel ShShMs
4 Thailand	France	1	PS-700 Class	LS	1984			To be built by Ital Thai Ltd
	Germany, FR	45	Fantrainer	Trainer	1983			After 2 from FRG; local assembly and some component manufacture
		1	Thalang Type	MCM	(1978)	1980	1	

Appendix 3. Register of major conventional weapons exported to Third World countries, 1971–85, by supplier and recipient

(l) = licensed production (s) = second-hand

Supplier	Weapon designation	Acquired by
Algeria	Nord-262A	Angola(s)
	T-55	Nicaragua(s)
Angola	Do-27	Guinea Bissau(s)
	HS-748	Guinea Bissau(s)
	Mystere	Guinea Bissau(s)
	Noratlas 2501	Congo(s)
	Yak-40	Guinea Bissau(s)
Argentina	C-47	Paraguay(s)
	DHC-3 Otter	Paraguay(s)
	IA-58A Pucara	Central African Republic; Iraq; Kuwait; Morocco; Uruguay
	IA-63 Pampa	Bolivia
	T-28 Trojan	Uruguay(s)
	TAM	Jordan; Panama; Peru
Australia	ASI-315	Papua New Guinea; Samoa; Solomon Islands; Vanuatu
	Attack Class	Indonesia
	C-130 Hercules	Colombia(s)
	C-47	Indonesia(s); Kampuchea(s); Laos(s); Nepal(s)
	CA-27 Sabre	Indonesia; Malaysia
	Ikara	Brazil
	Model 47	Indonesia(s)
	N-22 Nomad	Indonesia; Papua New Guinea
	Nomad	India; Indonesia; Papua New Guinea; Philippines; Thailand
Austria	Cuirassier	Argentina; Bolivia; Morocco; Nigeria; Saudi Arabia; Tunisia
	GC-45 155mm	Brazil(l)
	GHN-45 155mm	Jordan; Libya; Thailand
	S-65A	Israel(s)

	Steyr-4K 7FA	Bolivia; Morocco; Nigeria; Tunisia
Belgium	BDX	Argentina
	FN-4RM/62F	Uruguay
	FV-101 Scorpion	Uruguay(s)
	Merlin	South Africa(s)
	Sibmas	Malaysia
Brazil	122A Uirapuru	Bolivia; Paraguay
	Astros	Iraq; Libya
	C-47	Paraguay(s)
	Cobra-2000	Iraq
	DC-6	Paraguay(s)
	EE-11 Urutu	Bolivia; Chile; Colombia; Egypt; Gabon; Guyana; Iraq; Libya; Morocco; Paraguay; Saudi Arabia; Suriname; Tunisia; United Arab Emirates; Uruguay; Venezuela
	EE-3 Jararaca	Gabon; Iraq; Tunisia; Uruguay; Venezuela
	EE-9 Cascavel	Algeria; Argentina; Bolivia; Burkina Faso; Chile; Colombia; Ecuador; Egypt; Gabon; Guyana; Iraq; Libya; Nigeria; Paraguay; Qatar; Saudi Arabia; Thailand; Togo; Tunisia; Zimbabwe
	EE-T1 Osorio	Libya
	EE-T2 Osorio	Saudi Arabia
	EMB-110	Chile; Gabon; Guyana; Paraguay; Uruguay
	EMB-111	Argentina; Chile; Gabon; Libya; Peru
	EMB-120	Chile
	EMB-121 Xingu	Libya; Nigeria
	EMB-312 Tucano	Argentina; Egypt; Honduras; Libya; Nigeria; Venezuela
	EMB-326 Xavante	Argentina; Paraguay; Togo
	HB-315B Gaviao	Bolivia
	HB-350M Esquilo	Paraguay; Venezuela
	Model 412	Guyana(s)
	Roraima Class	Paraguay
	S-11	Bolivia; Paraguay
	T-37	Korea, South(s)
	T-6 Texan	Paraguay(s)
	Universal	Chile
Bulgaria	BRDM-2	Nicaragua(s)
	Kebir Type	Algeria(l)
	SA-7	Argentina(s)
Canada	C-119 Packet	Morocco(s)
	CF-5A	Venezuela

Supplier	Weapon designation	Acquired by
	CL-215	Algeria; South Africa; Thailand
	Challenger	Malaysia
	DHC-1 Chipmunk	Thailand
	DHC-2 Beaver	Haiti
	DHC-4 Caribou	Cameroon; Kenya; Malaysia; Oman; Tanzania; United Arab Emirates; Zambia
	DHC-5 Buffalo	Cameroon; Chile; Ecuador; Egypt; Kenya; Mauritania; Mexico; Oman; Peru; Sudan; Tanzania; Togo; United Arab Emirates; Zaire; Zambia
	DHC-6	Botswana; Chile; Ecuador; Ethiopia; Haiti; Panama; Peru; Senegal; Sudan
	DHC-7	Venezuela
	Model 205	Singapore(s)
	T-33A	Bolivia(s); Ethiopia(s)
Chile	T-34 Mentor	Uruguay(s)
	UH-12	Paraguay(s)
	Universal	Paraguay(s)
China	BRDM-1	Kampuchea(s)
	BRDM-2	Tanzania(s)
	BT-6	Bangladesh; Korea, North; Zambia
	BTR-60P	Congo(s)
	CSA-1	Iran; Pakistan
	Crow Slot	Korea, North
	D-30 122mm	Tanzania(s)
	F-4	Kampuchea; Pakistan; Sudan; Tanzania
	F-6	Bangladesh; Egypt; Iran; Kampuchea; Pakistan; Somalia; Tanzania; Vietnam, North; Zambia
	F-7	Egypt; Pakistan; Somalia; Tanzania; Zimbabwe
	Hai Ying-2	Bangladesh; Egypt; Pakistan
	Hainan Class	Bangladesh; Egypt; Korea, North; Pakistan
	Hegu Class	Bangladesh; Egypt; Pakistan
	Hong Jian-73	Kampuchea
	Hong Ying-5	Iran
	Huangfen Class	Pakistan
	Huchuan Class	Pakistan; Tanzania; Zaire(s)
	Jianghu Class	Egypt
	Luda Class	Egypt
	M-1931 122mm	Tanzania(s)
	M-1938 122mm	Congo(s); Guinea(s)
	M-1944 100mm	Congo(s)

M-46 130mm	Guinea(s)
MiG-15	Bangladesh
MiG-17	Vietnam, North(s)
P-4 Class	Bangladesh(s)
PT-76	Congo(s)
Q-5 Fantan-A	Korea, North; Pakistan
Romeo Class	Bangladesh; Egypt; Korea, North
SA-2	Pakistan(s)
Shanghai Class	Angola; Bangladesh; Cameroon; Cape Verde; Guinea; Korea, North; Pakistan; Sierra Leone; Sri Lanka; Tanzania; Tunisia; Zaire
	Zambia(s); Zimbabwe(s)
	Zimbabwe(s)
T-34	Angola; Bangladesh; Congo; Iran; Iraq; Korea, North; Pakistan; Sudan; Tanzania;
T-54	Thailand; Zimbabwe
T-59	Kampuchea; Pakistan; Vietnam, North
T-60	Congo; Korea, North; Mali; Sudan; Zaire
T-62	Guinea; Pakistan; Sudan; Tanzania; Zimbabwe
T-63	Iraq
T-69	Vietnam, North
Teamwork	Korea, North
Type 63 130mm	Iraq; Korea, North; Pakistan; Sudan; Tanzania
Type-531	Bangladesh; Guinea; Korea, North; Pakistan; Sudan; Tanzania
Type-54 122mm	Congo; Tanzania
Type-55	Congo; Guinea Bissau; Tanzania
Type-56	Iran; Korea, North; Oman; Pakistan; Somalia; Sudan; Thailand; Zaire; Zambia
Type-59/1 130mm	Iran; Somalia; Tanzania; Vietnam, North; Zaire; Zimbabwe
Type-60 122mm	Iran; Zaire
Type-63 107mm	Korea, North; Zaire
Type-66 152mm	Pakistan
Type-81 122mm	Vietnam, North
Wuchang Class	Vietnam, North
Wusung Class	

Cuba	An-26	Nicaragua(s)
	MiG-15	Congo(s)
	MiG-17	Congo(s)
	MiG-21	Peru(s)

Czechoslovakia	Dana 152mm	Libya
	L-29 Delfin	Afghanistan; Iraq; Syria
	L-39 Albatross	Afghanistan; Congo; Cuba; Ethiopia; Guinea; Guinea Bissau; Iraq; Syria
	L-39Z Albatross	Libya
	Let L-410	Libya
	M-51 130mm	Libya

Supplier	Weapon designation	Acquired by
	M-53/59	Libya
	OT-62	Angola; India; Libya
	OT-64	India; Iraq; Libya; Syria
	RM-70 122mm	Libya
	T-54	India(s)
Denmark	Caravelle	Central African Republic(s)
Egypt	AT-3	Iraq(s); Morocco(s)
	BRDM-1	Sudan(s)
	BRDM-2	Central African Republic(s); Morocco(s); Sudan(s)
	D-30 122mm	Sudan(s)
	EMB-312 Tucano	Iraq(s)
	F-6	Iraq(s)
	F-7	Iraq(s)
	Fahd	Bahrain; Jordan; Qatar; United Arab Emirates
	M-46 130mm	Cameroon(s); Morocco(s); Somalia(s); Sudan(s)
	MIM-23 Hawk	Sudan(s)
	OT-62	Morocco(s)
	SA-2	Sudan(s)
	SA-3	Somalia(s)
	SA-7	Sudan(s)
	Swingfire	Sudan
	T-34	Togo(s)
	T-54	Somalia(s); Togo(s)
	T-55	Iraq(s); Somalia(s); Togo(s)
	Type-60 122mm	Sudan(s)
	Walid	Algeria; Burundi; Guinea; Iraq; Sudan; Yemen, North
Ethiopia	F-5	Iran(s)
France	A-1 Skyraider	Chad(s)
	AM-39 Exocet	Argentina; Brazil; Egypt; India; Iraq; Kuwait; Oman; Pakistan; Peru; Qatar; South Africa; United Arab Emirates
	AML-60	Burundi; Chad; Ecuador; Ethiopia; Gabon; Kenya; Malaysia; Niger; Nigeria; South Africa; Togo; Venezuela; Zaire
	AML-90	Argentina; Bahrain; Chad; Djibouti; Ecuador; El Salvador; Gabon; Kenya; Malaysia; Mauritania; Morocco; Niger; Senegal; South Africa(l); Sudan; Togo; United Arab Emirates; Venezuela; Zaire

AML/D-90 Lynx	Burundi
AMX-10	Indonesia; Iraq; Morocco; Qatar; Saudi Arabia; Sudan; United Arab Emirates
AMX-10 PAC-90	Indonesia
AMX-105	Venezuela
AMX-13	Argentina; Chile; Ecuador; El Salvador; Guatemala; Indonesia; Kuwait; Lebanon; Morocco; Peru; Singapore; Venezuela
AMX-155	Argentina; Chile; Ecuador; Kuwait; Morocco; Qatar; Sudan; United Arab Emirates; Venezuela
AMX-30	Chile; Iraq; Qatar; Saudi Arabia; United Arab Emirates; Venezuela
AMX-30 Roland	Argentina; Brazil; Iraq; Nigeria
AMX-30 Shahine	Saudi Arabia
AMX-30-155 GCT	Iraq; Saudi Arabia
AMX-30-30mm	Saudi Arabia
AMX-VCI	Ecuador; Indonesia; United Arab Emirates; Venezuela
ARMAT	Egypt; Iraq; Kuwait
AS-11	Argentina; Brazil; Chile; Colombia; Iraq; Peru; United Arab Emirates; Venezuela
AS-12	Argentina; Brazil; Cameroon; Chile; Colombia; Egypt; Iran; Iraq; South Africa; United Arab Emirates
AS-15TT	Saudi Arabia
AS-30	Egypt; Iraq; Peru; Zaire
AS-332	Argentina; Brazil; Cameroon; Chile; Egypt(l); Indonesia(l); Kuwait; Oman; Singapore; United Arab Emirates; Zaire
AS-350 Ecureuil	Benin; Botswana; Brazil; Central African Republic; Djibouti; Gabon; Madagascar; Malawi; Sierra Leone; Singapore; Zaire
AS-365	Angola; Burkina Faso; Cote d'Ivoire; Dominican Republic; India; Malawi; Morocco; Saudi Arabia; Sri Lanka; Tunisia
ATL-2	Tunisia(s)
Adjutant Class	Pakistan
Agosta Class	Pakistan
Alouette	Angola; Argentina; Cameroon; Chad; Chile; Djibouti; Ecuador; Gabon; Ghana; Guinea; Guinea Bissau; India(l); Iraq; Lebanon; Libya; Malawi; Nepal; Nicaragua; Pakistan; Rwanda; South Africa; Tunisia; United Arab Emirates; Zaire; Zambia
Alpha Jet	Cameroon; Cote d'Ivoire; Egypt; Iraq; Morocco; Qatar; Togo
BRDM-1	Algeria(s)
Batral Class	Cote d'Ivoire; Gabon; Morocco; Panama
Batral Type	Chile(l)
Breguet Alize	India
Breguet-1150	Pakistan
C-130 Hercules	Chad(s)
C-160 Transall	Indonesia
C-212	Chad(s)
C-47	Benin(s); Chad(s); Niger(s); Rwanda(s)
C-54 Skymaster	Mauritania(s)

Supplier	Weapon designation	Acquired by
	Caravelle	Chad
	Combattante	Iran; Libya; Malaysia; Nigeria; Qatar; Tunisia
	Crotale	Chile; Egypt; Libya; Morocco; Pakistan; Saudi Arabia; South Africa; United Arab Emirates
	D'Orves Class	Argentina
	D-74 122mm	Algeria(s)
	DC-8	Togo(s)
	DHC-4 Caribou	Chad(s)
	Daphne Class	South Africa
	Durance Class	Saudi Arabia
	EDIC/EDA Type	Ethiopia; Lebanon; Madagascar(l); Senegal
	ERC-120 Guepard	Sudan
	ERC-20 Kriss	Gabon
	ERC-90 Lynx	Argentina; Chad; Mexico; Nigeria
	ERC-90 Sagaie	Argentina; Cote d'Ivoire; Gabon; Iraq; Nigeria; Saudi Arabia
	Entac	Morocco
	F-2000 Class	Saudi Arabia
	F-27	Senegal(s)
	Falcon-50	Jordan; Morocco
	HB-350M Esquilo	Brazil(l)
	HOT	Angola; Argentina; Cameroon; Egypt; Gabon; Iraq; Kuwait; Morocco; Qatar; Syria
	Harpon	Kuwait; Saudi Arabia; United Arab Emirates
	M-2 105mm	Togo(s)
	M-20	Benin(s); Cameroon(s); Senegal(s); Togo(s)
	M-3	Niger(s); Senegal(s); Togo(s)
	M-3 Panhard	Algeria; Bahrain; Burkina Faso; Burundi; Chad; Cote d'Ivoire; Gabon; Iraq; Kenya; Lebanon; Madagascar; Malaysia; Mauritania; Morocco; Niger; Nigeria; Rwanda; Senegal; Sudan; Togo; United Arab Emirates; Zaire
	M-3 VDA	Cote d'Ivoire; United Arab Emirates
	M-7 105mm	Mali(s)
	M-8 Greyhound	Argentina; Bahrain; Brazil; Brunei; Chile; Cote d'Ivoire; Ecuador; India; Indonesia; Korea, South; Malaysia; Morocco; Nigeria; Oman; Peru; Thailand
	MM-38 Exocet	Argentina; Brazil; Cameroon; Colombia; Ecuador; Kuwait; Morocco; Oman; Qatar; Thailand; Tunisia; United Arab Emirates
	MM-40 Exocet	Libya
	MS-880 Rallye	India
	Magic-2	Rwanda; Senegal; Togo
	Magister	United Arab Emirates
	Martel	Algeria; Cameroon; Chile; Egypt; Gabon; India; Kenya; Lebanon; Libya; Mexico;
	Milan	Nigeria; Qatar; Senegal; Somalia; South Africa; Syria; Tunisia

Mirage F-1	Ecuador; Iraq; Jordan; Kuwait; Libya; Morocco; Qatar; South Africa(l)
Mirage-2000	Egypt; India; Morocco; Peru; United Arab Emirates
Mirage-3	Argentina; Brazil; Chile; Gabon; Libya; South Africa; Venezuela
Mirage-5	Bolivia; Colombia; Ecuador; Egypt; Gabon; Iraq; Libya; Pakistan; Peru; United Arab Emirates; Venezuela; Zaire
Mirage-50	Chile
Model 150	Burundi
Model 172	Djibouti; Saudi Arabia
Model 337	Chad(s)
Model 50 155mm	Senegal
Model F337	Cote d'Ivoire; Guinea; Guinea Bissau; Madagascar; Mauritania; Niger; Senegal; Togo; Zimbabwe
Mystere	Egypt; Gabon; Iran; Iraq; Libya; Morocco; Pakistan; Panama; Peru; Syria; Zaire
Noratlas 2501	Chad; Congo; Djibouti; Niger; Rwanda
Nord-262A	Burkina Faso; Congo
Omar Bongo	Gabon
Otomat	Egypt; Kenya; Saudi Arabia
P-400 Class	Gabon
P-48 Type	Cameroon; Cote d'Ivoire; Senegal; Tunisia
PBY-5A Catalina	Chile(s)
PC-7	Chad(s)
PR-72 Type	Morocco; Peru; Senegal
PS-700 Class	Libya; Thailand(l)
Patra Class	Cote d'Ivoire; Mauritania
R-440 Crotale	Chile; Egypt; Libya; Morocco; Pakistan; South Africa; United Arab Emirates
R-530	Argentina; Brazil; Chile; Colombia; Egypt; Iraq; Jordan; Kuwait; Libya; Pakistan; Venezuela
R-550 Magic	Argentina; Ecuador; Egypt; India; Iraq; Jordan; Kuwait; Libya; Morocco; Oman; Pakistan; Saudi Arabia; South Africa; United Arab Emirates; Venezuela
Rallye	Central African Republic; Djibouti; El Salvador; Rwanda; Senegal
Roland	Argentina; Brazil; Iraq; Nigeria
S-58	Chad(s)
SA-315B Lama	Argentina; Bolivia; Chile; Colombia; Ecuador; India(l); Togo
SA-319B	Chile; Ecuador; Guyana
SA-321	Zaire
SA-330 Puma	Algeria; Argentina; Brazil; Cameroon; Chad; Chile; Congo; Cote d'Ivoire; Ecuador; Gabon; Guinea; Indonesia; Iraq; Kenya; Kuwait; Lebanon; Malawi; Mexico; Morocco; Nepal; Nigeria; Pakistan; Qatar; Senegal; South Africa; Togo; Tunisia; United Arab Emirates; Zaire
SA-341 Gazelle	Chad; Qatar; Senegal; Trinidad & Tobago
SA-342 Gazelle	Angola; Burundi; Cameroon; Ecuador; Egypt; Gabon; Guinea; Iraq; Kenya; Kuwait; Lebanon; Libya; Morocco; Rwanda; Syria; United Arab Emirates

Supplier	Weapon designation	Acquired by
	SA-360 Dauphin	Congo
	SATCP Mistral	Jordan
	SN-601 Corvette	Benin; Central African Republic; Mali
	SS-11	India(l); Iran; Iraq; Kuwait; Lebanon; Libya; Malaysia; Saudi Arabia; South Africa; United Arab Emirates; Venezuela
	SS-12M	Brunei; Ethiopia; Gabon; Iran; Lebanon; Libya; Malaysia; Tunisia
	Shahine	Saudi Arabia
	Sirius Class	Morocco; Seychelles
	Super Etendard	Argentina; Iraq
	Super Frelon	Iran; Iraq; Libya; Pakistan
	Super Magister	Bangladesh; Cameroon; Ecuador; El Salvador; Guatemala; Lebanon; Libya
	Super-530	Ecuador; Egypt; India; Kuwait
	T-33A	Bolivia(s); Singapore(s); Thailand(s)
	TB-30 Epsilon	Togo
	TRS-2052/3/6	Brazil
	TRS-2230/15	Indonesia
	Tiger	Egypt; Zambia
	UH-12	Guinea(s)
	VAB	Central African Republic; Cote d'Ivoire; Lebanon; Mauritius; Morocco; Oman; Qatar; United Arab Emirates
	VBC-90	Argentina; Oman; United Arab Emirates
	VBL	Mexico; Niger
	VCR-6	Gabon; Iraq
	VLRA	Comoros; Djibouti; Somalia
	VP-2000	Algeria; Gabon
	VPX-110	Indonesia
	VXB-170	Gabon; Senegal; Tunisia
	Vigilante Class	Uruguay
Gabon	Leon M'Ba Class	Cameroon
German DR	T-55	Iraq(s)
Germany, FR	Alpha Jet	Nigeria
	BK-117	Indonesia(l); Iraq; South Africa
	Bandar Abbas Cl	Iran
	Bo-105	Bahrain; Brunei; Chile; Colombia; Indonesia(l); Iraq; Lesotho; Mexico; Nigeria; Peru; Philippines; Sierra Leone; Sudan; United Arab Emirates

Cobra-2000	Brazil(l); Morocco; Pakistan(l); Peru
Commander 500	Niger(s)
Condor	Malaysia; Uruguay
DC-6	Niger(s)
Dela Class	Ghana
Do-128-6	Cameroon; Nigeria
Do-228	Cameroon; India(l); Malawi; Niger; Nigeria
Do-27	Israel; Lesotho; Malawi; Rwanda; Togo
Do-28	Cameroon; Ethiopia; Israel; Kenya; Malawi; Morocco; Niger; Nigeria; Somalia; Zambia
Do-28B-1	Lesotho
FPB-38	Bahrain
FPB-45	Ghana
FPB-57	Nigeria
FS-1500 Type	Colombia; Malaysia
Fantrainer	Thailand(l)
Gepard	Saudi Arabia
Jerong Class	Malaysia(l)
Katapangan Cl	Philippines
M-40 Type	Thailand
M-41	Thailand(s)
Mamba	Chile
Meko Type	Argentina; Nigeria
Model F337	Ethiopia(s)
Mutiara	Malaysia(l)
Noratlas 2501	Niger(s)
PB-57 Type	Ghana; Indonesia; Kuwait; Singapore(l)
RFB Fantrainer	Thailand
RoRo-1300	Nigeria
Schuetze Class	Brazil
Sri Indera	Malaysia
TAM	Argentina(l)
TNC-36	Ecuador
TNC-45	Argentina; Bahrain; Ecuador; Kuwait; Singapore; United Arab Emirates
Thalang Type	Thailand(l)
Tpz-1	Venezuela
Type 1500	India
Type 209	Argentina; Brazil; Chile; Colombia; Ecuador; Indonesia; Iran; Korea, South; Peru; Venezuela
Type 62-001	Bahrain
Type TR-1700	Argentina
UR-416	Ecuador; Kenya; Morocco; Niger; Nigeria; Pakistan; Peru; Togo; Venezuela
VCTP	Argentina(l)

Supplier	Weapon designation	Acquired by
	Wildcat	Saudi Arabia
Greece	Steyr-4K 7FA	Libya
Hungary	Fug-70	Iraq
India	Abhay Class	Bangladesh; Mauritius
	Alouette	Bangladesh; Ethiopia; Liberia; Nepal; Seychelles
	An-12	Bangladesh(s)
	Centurion	South Africa(s)
	DHC-3 Otter	Bangladesh(s)
	DHC-4 Caribou	Bangladesh(s)
	HJT-16 Kiran-2	Liberia
	HTT-34	Ghana
	Model 56 105mm	Bangladesh(s)
Indonesia	AS-332	Taiwan
	Bo-105	Malaysia; Thailand
	CN-212	Malaysia; Saudi Arabia; Thailand
	CN-235	Korea, South; Malaysia
	F-27	Benin(s)
	OV-10 Bronco	Zimbabwe(s)
Iran	AB-205	Oman(s)
	AGM-12B Bullpup	Ethiopia(s)
	C-130 Hercules	Pakistan(s)
	F-5	Jordan(s)
	SA-7	Somalia(s)
Iraq	An-12	Jordan(s)
	BRDM-2	Djibouti(s)
	BTR-60P	Djibouti(s)
	M-60	Jordan(s)
	MiG-17	Uganda(s)
	MiG-19	Uganda(s)
	Mystere	Djibouti(s)
Israel	A-4 Skyhawk	Indonesia(s)
	AMX-10	Morocco(s)

Arava	Bolivia; Cameroon; Colombia; Ecuador; El Salvador; Guatemala; Honduras; Liberia; Mexico; Nicaragua; Papua New Guinea; Paraguay; Swaziland; Thailand; Venezuela
B-707	Argentina(s)
Dabur Class	Argentina; Nicaragua
Dvora Class	Sri Lanka
Gabriel	Chile; Ecuador; Kenya; Singapore; South Africa; Taiwan(l); Thailand
Hai Ou Class	Taiwan(l)
Kfir	Colombia
LAR-160	Venezuela
M-4 Sherman	Chile(s); Nicaragua(s)
M-68 155mm	Singapore; Thailand
M-71 155mm	Singapore
MD-450 Ouragan	El Salvador(s)
Magister	El Salvador
Mirage-3	Argentina(s)
Model 205	Brazil(s); Zimbabwe(s)
Mooney-201	South Africa(s)
Mystere	El Salvador(s); Honduras(s)
Nesher	Argentina
RAM V-1	Morocco
RBY-1	Guatemala; Honduras
Reshef Class	Chile; South Africa
Shafrir	Argentina; Chile; Honduras; Taiwan
Shoet	Argentina
TA-4 Skyhawk	Indonesia(s)
Westwind 1124	Honduras; South Africa; Uganda

Italy	A-109 Hirundo	Argentina; Iraq; Venezuela
	A-129 Mangusta	United Arab Emirates
	AB-204	Yemen, North
	AB-205	Iran; Morocco; Oman; Tanzania; Tunisia; Uganda; United Arab Emirates; Zambia
	AB-206	Iran; Morocco; Oman; Tanzania; Uganda; United Arab Emirates
	AB-212	Bahrain; Iran; Iraq; Lebanon; Libya; Malaysia; Morocco; Oman; Peru; Saudi Arabia; Somalia; Sudan; Syria; United Arab Emirates; Venezuela; Yemen, North; Zambia
	AB-412 Griffon	Lesotho; Uganda; Zimbabwe
	AB-47G	Libya; Zambia
	AL-60	Morocco; Tunisia
	AM-3C	Rwanda; South Africa
	ATR-42	Gabon
	Aspide	Argentina; Colombia; Ecuador; Egypt; Iraq; Jordan; Libya; Morocco; Nigeria; Peru; Thailand; Venezuela
	C-119 Packet	Morocco(s)
	CH-47 Chinook	Egypt; Iran; Libya; Morocco; Syria; Tanzania

Supplier	Weapon designation	Acquired by
	Centurion	Somalia(s)
	EMB-326 Xavante	Brazil(l)
	Esmeraldas Cl	Ecuador
	G-222	Argentina; Libya; Nigeria; Somalia; United Arab Emirates; Venezuela
	Impala	South Africa(l)
	Lerici Class	Malaysia; Nigeria
	Lion	Libya
	Lupo Class	Iraq; Peru; Venezuela
	M-108 105mm	South Africa(s)
	M-113	Libya(s)
	M-47 Patton	Somalia(s)
	MB-326	Argentina; Ghana; South Africa; Tunisia; United Arab Emirates; Zaire; Zambia
	MB-339	Argentina; Malaysia; Nigeria; Peru; United Arab Emirates
	MV-250 Type	Thailand
	MV-400 Class	Thailand
	Model 47	Tanzania(s)
	Model 56 105mm	India; Malaysia; Philippines; United Arab Emirates
	OF-40	United Arab Emirates
	Otomat	Egypt; Iraq; Libya; Nigeria; Peru; Venezuela
	P-166	Somalia; South Africa
	P-68 Victor	South Africa
	Palmaria 155mm	Argentina; Libya; Nigeria; Oman
	S-211	Haiti; Singapore; Somalia
	S-61	Argentina; Egypt; Iran; Iraq; Libya; Saudi Arabia; Venezuela
	SF-260	Bolivia; Brunei; Burma; Burundi; Comoros; Ecuador; Ethiopia; Ghana; Haiti; Libya; Philippines; Singapore; Somalia; Sri Lanka; Thailand; Tunisia; United Arab Emirates; Zaire; Zambia; Zimbabwe
	SH-3D Sea King	Argentina; Brazil; Iran; Peru; Saudi Arabia; Syria
	SH-4	Brazil
	SHORAR	Argentina
	SM-1019E	Somalia
	Sea Killer	Iran
	Seakiller	Iran
	Skyguard SAMS	Egypt
	Spada	Jordan
	Stromboli Class	Iraq
	Type 42M	Seychelles
	Type-6614	Korea, South(l); Peru; Somalia; Tunisia
	Type-6616	Libya; Peru; Somalia

	VCC-1	Saudi Arabia
	Wadi Class	Iraq; Libya
Japan	Aiyar Maung Cl	Burma
	KV-107/2	Saudi Arabia
	MU-2J	Zaire
	Shamjala Class	Bangladesh
	Sinde Class	Burma
Jordan	C-130 Hercules	Singapore(s)
	F-104	Pakistan(s)
	F-6	Iraq(s)
	GHN-45 155mm	Iraq(s)
	Hunter	Oman(s)
	Khalid	Iraq(s)
	M-109 155mm	Iraq(s)
	M-114 155mm	Iraq(s)
	M-48 Patton	Lebanon(s)
	Tigercat	South Africa(s)
Korea, North	BRDM-1	Zimbabwe(s)
	BRDM-2	Zimbabwe(s)
	BTR-152	Zimbabwe(s)
	BTR-60P	Zaire(s)
	D-30 122mm	Zaire(s)
	F-6	Iran(s)
	M-1938 122mm	Zaire(s)
	M-46 130mm	Madagascar(s)
	MiG-17	Madagascar(s)
	MiG-21	Madagascar(s)
	Nampo Class	Madagascar; Tanzania
	P-4 Class	Benin(s)
	P-4 Type	Zaire
	SA-2	Iran(s)
	Sin Hung Class	Guyana; Nicaragua
	T-55	Zimbabwe(s)
	T-62	Iran(s)
	Type-531	Zaire(s)
	Type-59/1 130mm	Madagascar(s)
	Type-60 122mm	Madagascar(s)
Korea, South	F-5	Vietnam, South(s)
	F-5 Tiger-2	Brazil(s)

Supplier	Weapon designation	Acquired by
	LC-3800 Type	Argentina
	M-101-A1 105mm	Uruguay(s)
	M-44 155mm	Brazil(s)
	Mahawangsa	Malaysia
	Mash Class	Malaysia
	PSMM-5 Type	Indonesia
	Tacoma Type	Argentina; Indonesia; Malaysia; Venezuela
Kuwait	Chieftain	Iraq(s)
	Hunter	Oman(s)
Libya	BM-13-16 132mm	Chad(s)
	BM-21 122mm	Chad(s)
	BRDM-2	Chad(s)
	BTR-152	Central African Republic(s)
	D-30 122mm	Chad(s)
	EE-9 Cascavel	Iran(s); Iraq(s)
	F-27	Chad(s)
	F-5	Uganda(s)
	Falcon-50	Benin(s)
	Ferret	Central African Republic(s)
	L-39 Albatross	Nicaragua(s)
	M-1938 122mm	Uganda(s)
	MB-326	Nicaragua(s)
	MiG-21	Syria(s)
	MiG-23	Syria(s)
	Mirage-5	Uganda(s)
	Mystere	Nicaragua(s)
	Rallye	Seychelles(s)
	SA-7	Argentina(s); Nicaragua(s)
	SA-8	Nicaragua(s)
	SF-260	Chad(s); Nicaragua(s)
	Saladin	Uganda(s)
	Saracen	Uganda(s)
	Scaleboard	Iran(s)
	T-34	Uganda(s)
	T-54	Iran(s); Nicaragua(s)
	T-55	Central African Republic(s); Ethiopia(s); Iran(s); Nicaragua(s)
	T-62	Iran(s); Syria(s)

Country	Equipment	Recipients
Malaysia	F-5	Thailand(s)
	Pioneer	Indonesia(s)
Morocco	T-28 Trojan	Honduras(s)
Netherlands	Alkmaar Class	Egypt; Indonesia
	De Ruyter Class	Peru
	Dokkum Class	Ethiopia; Oman
	F-27	Algeria; Angola; Argentina; Bolivia; Chile; Colombia; Congo; Cote d'Ivoire; Gabon; Ghana; Indonesia; Iran; Malaysia; Nigeria; Pakistan; Peru; Philippines; Thailand; Togo
	F-28	Algeria; Argentina; Ecuador; Ghana
	Fatahillah Cl	Indonesia
	Flycatcher	India
	Friesland Class	Peru
	Holland Class	Peru
	Kimbla Class	Guyana
	Van Speijk Cl	Indonesia
	Wasp	Indonesia(s)
	Zwaardvis Class	Taiwan
New Zealand	Airtourer-150	Indonesia; Singapore
	CT-4 Airtrainer	Thailand
	F-27	Yemen, North(s)
Oman	BAC-167	Singapore(s)
Pakistan	M-24 Chaffee	Bangladesh(s)
	Town Class	Bangladesh(s)
Panama	Model 204	Costa Rica(s)
Peru	Mirage-5	Argentina(s)
Poland	Mi-2	Cuba; Lesotho; Madagascar; Nicaragua
	Polnocny Class	India; Syria
	SA-6	Iraq(s)
	T-54	India(s); Yemen, South(s)
	T-55	Iraq(s)
	TS-11 Iskra	India
Portugal	AML-90	Angola(s)

Supplier	Weapon designation	Acquired by
	AOP-9	Angola(s)
	Alfange Class	Angola; Mozambique
	Alouette	Angola(s); Guinea Bissau(s); Mozambique(s)
	Argos Class	Angola
	C-45 Expeditor	Angola(s)
	C-47	Angola(s); Guinea Bissau(s); Mozambique(s)
	Chaimite	Libya; Peru; Philippines
	DC-6	Ecuador(s)
	Daphne Class	Pakistan(s)
	Do-27	Angola(s); Guinea Bissau(s)
	Flower Class	Angola(s)
	G-91	Angola(s)
	M-18	Mozambique(s)
	M-3 Panhard	Angola(s)
	Model 182	Mozambique(s)
	Noratlas 2501	Angola(s); Mozambique(s)
	PA-28 Cherokee	Mozambique(s)
	T-6 Harvard	Mozambique(s)
Romania	Alouette	Algeria; Angola; Ethiopia; Pakistan
	BN-2A	Angola; Rwanda
	SA-330 Puma	Sudan
	T-55	Egypt
Saudi Arabia	AB-205	Oman(s)
	AML-90	Somalia(s)
	C-123 Provider	Egypt(s)
	F-5	Yemen, North(s)
	M-41	Sudan(s)
	M-47 Patton	Sudan(s)
	Vigilant	Yemen, North(s)
Senegal	Manga Class	Gabon
Singapore	Abheetha Class	Sri Lanka
	Alouette	Malaysia(s)
	B-737	Mexico(s)
	Bataan Class	Philippines
	Duyong	Malaysia

Mahawele Class	Sri Lanka(s)
PB-46 Type	Bangladesh
Saba al Bahr	Oman
TNC-45	Thailand
Type 27M	Kuwait
Type 30M	Sri Lanka
Type 32M	Kuwait; Taiwan
Waspada Class	Brunei

South Africa	AM-3C	Zimbabwe(s)
	AML-60	Zimbabwe(s)
	Alouette	Zimbabwe(s)
	Buffel	Zimbabwe
	C-47	Zimbabwe(s)
	Canberra	Zimbabwe(s)
	Casspir	Zimbabwe
	Eland	Gabon; Morocco; Zimbabwe
	Ferret	Malawi(s)
	Mirage-3	Zimbabwe(s)
	Model 185	Zimbabwe(s)
	Ratel-20	Morocco
	SA-330 Puma	Zimbabwe(s)
	Samil-100	Sri Lanka
	UR-416	Zimbabwe(s)

Spain	BMR-600	Egypt; Iraq; Peru; Saudi Arabia; Somalia
	Barcelo Class	Mauritania
	Bo-105	Iraq(s)
	C-101 Aviojet	Chile; Honduras; Jordan
	C-212	Angola; Argentina; Chile; Colombia; Costa Rica; Djibouti; Equatorial Guinea; Guinea; Jordan; Mexico; Nicaragua; Panama; Paraguay; Somalia; South Africa; Sudan; Thailand; United Arab Emirates; Uruguay; Venezuela; Zimbabwe
	CN-212	Indonesia(l)
	CN-235	Jordan; Saudi Arabia
	CV-440	Bolivia(s)
	F-30 Class	Egypt; Morocco
	Halcon Class	Argentina; Mexico
	Lazaga Class	Morocco
	M-41E Cazador	Somalia; Sudan
	Pelicano Class	Gabon
	Piranha Class	Congo
	S-70 Class	Egypt; Libya
	T-36 Halcon	Chile(l)

Supplier	Weapon designation	Acquired by
	Vigilance Class	Morocco
Sudan	MiG-21	Iraq(s)
Sweden	BOFI 40mm	Brazil
	FH-77 155mm	India; Nigeria
	Giraffe	Brazil; Pakistan
	MFI-15 Safari	Sierra Leone
	RB-53 Bantam	Argentina
	RBS-70	Argentina; Bahrain; Indonesia; Pakistan; Singapore; Tunisia; United Arab Emirates
	Spica-2 Class	Malaysia; Trinidad & Tobago
	Supporter	Pakistan; Zambia
	Tre Kronor Cl	Chile
Switzerland	AMX-13	Singapore(s)
	AS-202 Bravo	Indonesia; Iraq; Morocco; Oman; Uganda
	BN-2A	Cameroon(s); Gambia(s)
	DC-8	Peru(s)
	Fledermaus II	India(l)
	MBB-223K	Syria
	MR-8	Chile
	PC-6	Angola; Argentina; Burma; Cameroon; Chad; Colombia; Ecuador; Iran; Oman; Peru
	PC-7	Angola; Bolivia; Burma; Cameroon; Chile; Guatemala; Iran; Iraq; Malaysia; Mexico; Thailand; United Arab Emirates
	PC-9	Burma; Saudi Arabia
	Piranha	Chile(l); Ghana; Sierra Leone
	Roland	Argentina(l); Iraq; Peru
	Skyvan 3M	Colombia
Syria	BMP-1	Iran(s)
	D-74 122mm	Lebanon(s)
	M-1938 122mm	Lebanon(s)
	M-46 130mm	Lebanon(s)
	SCUD	Iran(s)
	Scud	Iran(s)
	T-54	Lebanon(s)
	T-55	Iran(s)
	T-62	Iran(s)

Taiwan	C-47	Bolivia(s)
	T-6 Harvard	Bolivia(s)
Turkey	C-107 Class	Libya
	SAR-33	Libya
UK	ALARM	Saudi Arabia
	AS-350 Ecureuil	United Arab Emirates(s)
	AT-104	Brunei
	AT-105 Saxon	Bahrain; Kuwait; Malaysia; Nigeria; Oman
	Abbot 105mm	India
	Al Said	Oman
	Amazon Class	Pakistan
	Ardennes Class	Oman
	Azteca Class	Mexico
	B-727	Ecuador(s)
	BAC-111	Brazil; Oman
	BAC-167	Ecuador; Kenya; Kuwait; Oman; Saudi Arabia; Sudan
	BN-2A	Belize; Botswana; Ghana; Guyana; Haiti; India; Iraq; Israel; Jamaica; Madagascar; Malaysia; Mauritania; Mexico; Oman; Panama; Philippines(l); Qatar; Rwanda; Seychelles; South Africa; Suriname; Thailand; United Arab Emirates; Venezuela; Zimbabwe
	Baron	Central African Republic(s)
	Beeswing	Egypt
	Bloodhound	Singapore
	Blowpipe	Chile; Ecuador; Jordan; Malaysia; Oman; Qatar; Thailand
	Brooke Logistic	Oman
	Bulldog	Botswana; Ghana; Jordan; Kenya; Lebanon; Malaysia; Nigeria
	Bulldog Class	Nigeria
	Canberra	Argentina; Chile; India; Peru; Venezuela; Zimbabwe
	Centurion	Israel; Jordan
	Chieftain	Iran; Kuwait; Oman
	Commando	Egypt; Qatar
	Constitucion Cl	Venezuela
	County Class	Chile; Pakistan
	Dorina Class	Nigeria
	Erinomi Class	Nigeria
	FH-70 155mm	Saudi Arabia
	FV-101 Scorpion	Brunei; Honduras; Indonesia; Iran; Kuwait; Nigeria; Oman; Philippines; Tanzania; Thailand; United Arab Emirates
		Zimbabwe
	Falconer	Bahrain; Burkina Faso; Central African Republic; Iran; Kenya; Libya; Saudi Arabia; Sri Lanka;
	Ferret	United Arab Emirates

Supplier	Weapon designation	Acquired by
	Fox	Iran; Kenya; Malawi; Nigeria; Saudi Arabia
	Gnat	India(l)
	Guardian Class	Bahrain
	HS-125	Argentina; Brazil; Malawi; Mexico; South Africa
	HS-146	Zaire
	HS-748	Brazil; Brunei; Burkina Faso; Cameroon; Colombia; Ecuador; India(l); Korea, South; Madagascar; Nepal; Tanzania; Thailand; Venezuela; Zambia
	Hawk	Algeria; Indonesia; Kenya; Kuwait; Saudi Arabia; United Arab Emirates; Zimbabwe
	Hecla Class	South Africa
	Hengam Class	Iran
	Hermes Class	India
	Hunter	Chile; India; Kenya; Lebanon; Qatar; Singapore; United Arab Emirates; Zimbabwe
	Jaguar	Ecuador; India; Nigeria; Oman
	Javelin	Jordan
	Jetstream-31	Honduras; Saudi Arabia
	Kebir Class	Algeria
	Khalid	Jordan
	Kharg Type	Iran
	Leander Class	Chile
	Leopard Class	Bangladesh
	Light Gun 105mm	Kenya; Morocco; Nigeria; Oman; United Arab Emirates
	Loadmaster Type	Kuwait
	Lynx	Argentina; Brazil; Nigeria; Qatar
	MBT Mk-1	Kuwait
	MBT Mk-3	Kenya; Nigeria; Thailand
	MBT-3 ARV	Nigeria
	MBT-3 BL	Nigeria
	Mermaid Class	Malaysia
	Model 206	United Arab Emirates(s)
	Nilgiri Class	India(l)
	Niteroi Class	Brazil
	Oberon Class	Brazil; Chile
	P-1101 Class	United Arab Emirates
	Protector Class	Bahamas
	Province Class	Oman
	Ramadan Class	Egypt
	Rapier	Brunei; Indonesia; Iran; Oman; Qatar; Singapore; United Arab Emirates; Zambia
	S-600	Malaysia
	S-723 Martello	Oman

Supplier	Weapon designation	Acquired by
	VC-2 Viscount	Oman
	Vigilant	United Arab Emirates
	Vijayanta	India(l)
	Vosper 103 Type	Bahamas; Panama; Trinidad & Tobago
	Wasp	Brazil; South Africa
	Waspada Class	Singapore(l)
	Watchman	Oman
	Wessex	Bangladesh
	Yarrow Type	Malaysia; Thailand
USA	A-1 Skyraider	Gabon; Vietnam, South
	A-37B Dragonfly	Chile; Colombia; Ecuador; El Salvador; Guatemala; Honduras; Kampuchea; Korea, South; Panama; Paraguay; Peru; Thailand; Uruguay; Vietnam, South
	A-4 Skyhawk	Argentina; Indonesia; Israel; Kuwait; Malaysia; Singapore
	AC-47	El Salvador; Kampuchea; Philippines; Thailand
	AGM-12B Bullpup	Israel
	AGM-45 Shrike	Israel; Saudi Arabia
	AGM-65	Brazil; Chile; Egypt; Iran; Israel; Korea, South; Morocco; Saudi Arabia; Singapore; Taiwan; Venezuela
	AGM-65 Maverick	Saudi Arabia
	AGM-84A Harpoon	Iran; Saudi Arabia; Singapore
	AIFV	Philippines
	AIM-54A Phoenix	Iran
	AIM-7 Sparrow	Colombia; Egypt; Iran; Israel; Korea, South; Saudi Arabia; Taiwan
	AIM-9	Bahrain; Brazil; Chile; Egypt; Indonesia; Iran; Israel; Jordan; Korea, South; Kuwait; Malaysia; Oman; Pakistan; Saudi Arabia; Singapore; Taiwan; Thailand; Venezuela; Yemen, North
	AN/MPQ-4	Thailand
	AN/PPS-15	Argentina; Israel; Taiwan
	AN/TPQ-36	Jordan; Korea, South; Lebanon; Pakistan; Saudi Arabia; Thailand
	AN/TPQ-37	Egypt; Pakistan; Taiwan; Thailand
	AN/TPS-32	Jordan; Kuwait; Saudi Arabia
	AN/TPS-43	Argentina; Saudi Arabia; Somalia; Thailand
	AN/TPS-44	Argentina
	AN/TPS-70	Thailand
	AS-365	Israel(s)
	AU-23A	Thailand
	Adjutant Class	Saudi Arabia
	Admirable Class	Mexico; Philippines

Aggressive CI	Philippines
Al Siddiq Class	Saudi Arabia
Amphion Class	Iran; Taiwan
Arcadia Class	Indonesia
Asheville Class	Colombia; Korea, South; Taiwan
Asroc	Brazil
Auk Class	Mexico
B-26	Indonesia
B-707	Brazil; Indonesia; Iran; Israel; Korea, South; Morocco; Saudi Arabia
B-720	Ecuador; Egypt; Taiwan; Togo
B-727	Cameroon; Chile; Ecuador; Mexico; Panama; Senegal
B-737	Brazil; Ecuador; Egypt; India; Indonesia; Mexico; Niger; Saudi Arabia; Venezuela
B-747	Iran; Saudi Arabia
BGM-71 TOW	Bahrain; Egypt; Iran; Israel; Jordan; Kenya; Korea, South; Kuwait; Lebanon; Morocco; Oman; Pakistan; Saudi Arabia; Somalia; Taiwan; Thailand; Tunisia; United Arab Emirates; Vietnam, South; Yemen, North
Badr Class	Saudi Arabia
Balao Class	Argentina
Barnegat Class	Philippines; Vietnam, South
Baron	Haiti
Bird Dog	Kampuchea; Pakistan; Thailand; Vietnam, South
Bluebird Class	Indonesia; Korea, South; Singapore
Buckley Class	Mexico
C-118A	El Salvador; Guatemala; Mexico
C-119 Packet	Ethiopia; Jordan; Vietnam, South
C-123 Provider	El Salvador; Kampuchea; Korea, South; Philippines; Taiwan; Thailand; Vietnam, South
C-130 Hercules	Algeria; Angola; Argentina; Bolivia; Brazil; Cameroon; Chad; Chile; Colombia; Cote d'Ivoire; Ecuador; Egypt; El Salvador; Gabon; Honduras; Indonesia; Iran; Israel; Jordan; Korea, South; Libya; Malaysia; Morocco; Niger; Nigeria; Oman; Pakistan; Peru; Philippines; Saudi Arabia; Singapore; Sudan; Taiwan; Thailand; Togo; Tunisia; United Arab Emirates; Venezuela; Vietnam, South; Yemen, North; Zaire
C-47	Bolivia; Cameroon; Comoros; El Salvador; Haiti; Indonesia; Kampuchea; Laos; Liberia; Morocco; Nicaragua; Philippines; Thailand; Vietnam, South
C-54 Skymaster	Korea, South; Taiwan
C1-M-AV1 Type	Taiwan
CH-47 Chinook	Argentina; Iran; Korea, South; Nigeria; Taiwan; Thailand; Vietnam, South
CPIC Type	Korea, South
Cannon Class	Philippines
Citation	Argentina; Burma; Chile; Ecuador; Venezuela
Claud Jones CI	Indonesia
Cohoes Class	Dominican Republic
Commander 500	Mexico
Commander 680	Iran, Mexico

Supplier	Weapon designation	Acquired by
	Commando	Botswana; Cameroon; Chad; Dominican Republic; Ethiopia; Gabon; Guatemala; Haiti; Indonesia; Jamaica; Kuwait; Malaysia; Panama; Philippines; Saudi Arabia; Singapore; Sudan; Taiwan; Thailand; Tunisia; Venezuela
	Commando Ranger	Indonesia
	Commando Scout	Indonesia
	Commuter-1900	Egypt
	DC-6	Argentina; Chile; Nigeria; Panama
	DC-7	Colombia
	DC-8	Oman
	DC-9	Kuwait; Venezuela
	DHC-2 Beaver	Oman(s); Philippines(s)
	DHC-3 Otter	Costa Rica(s); Ethiopia(s); Kampuchea(s); Nicaragua(s); Panama(s)
	DHC-4 Caribou	Vietnam, South(s)
	Dabur Class	Israel
	Dealey Class	Colombia; Uruguay
	Diver Class	Korea, South; Taiwan
	Duke B60	Jamaica
	E-2C Hawkeye	Egypt; Israel; Singapore
	E-3A Sentry	Saudi Arabia
	EC-47	Thailand; Vietnam, South
	Edsall Class	Mexico; Philippines; Tunisia; Vietnam, South
	F-100	Taiwan
	F-104	Jordan; Taiwan
	F-14A Tomcat	Iran
	F-15 Eagle	Israel; Saudi Arabia
	F-16 Falcon	Egypt; Indonesia; Israel; Korea, South; Pakistan; Singapore; Thailand; Venezuela
	F-27	Guatemala(s)
	F-33C Bonanza	Cote d'Ivoire; Haiti; Iran; Mexico
	F-4 Phantom	Bahrain; Egypt; Iran; Israel; Korea, South
	F-5	Ethiopia; Iran; Malaysia; Saudi Arabia; Taiwan; Thailand; Vietnam, South
	F-5 Tiger-2	Bahrain; Brazil; Chile; Ethiopia; Indonesia; Iran; Jordan; Kenya; Korea, South; Malaysia; Mexico; Morocco; Saudi Arabia; Singapore; Sudan; Taiwan; Thailand; Tunisia; Venezuela; Vietnam, South; Yemen, North
	F-51 Mustang	Honduras; Indonesia
	F-86 Sabre	Bolivia; Honduras
	F-8H Crusader	Philippines; Thailand
	FGM-77A Dragon	Iran; Israel; Jordan; Morocco; Saudi Arabia; Thailand; Yemen, North
	FH-1100	Chile; Costa Rica; El Salvador; Nigeria
	FH-227	Burma; Mexico; Uruguay

FIM-92A Stinger	Afghanistan; Angola; Chad; Korea, South; Pakistan; Saudi Arabia
FS-330 Type	Korea, South
Falcon-20G	Venezuela(s)
Flagstaff-2 Cl	Israel
Fletcher Class	Argentina; Brazil; Taiwan
G-134 Mohawk	Israel; Pakistan
Gearing Class	Argentina; Brazil; Ecuador; Iran; Korea, South; Mexico; Pakistan; Taiwan; Uruguay
Gulfstream	Cameroon; Cote d'Ivoire; Egypt; Gabon; Ghana; Morocco; Nigeria; Saudi Arabia; Uganda; Venezuela
Guppy-2 Class	Brazil; Peru; Taiwan; Venezuela
HADR	Malaysia
HH-13	Brazil
HH-43F Huskie	Morocco
HS-748	Colombia(s)
HU-16 Albatros	Argentina; Indonesia; Malaysia; Mexico; Philippines
Hiller 360	Uruguay
Honest John	Korea, South
Jetfoil	Indonesia
Jetstar	Libya; Mexico
KC-10A Extender	Saudi Arabia
KC-130H	Argentina; Brazil; Israel; Morocco; Saudi Arabia
KC-135	Saudi Arabia
King Air	Algeria; Argentina; Bolivia; Chile; Colombia; Guyana; Indonesia; Jamaica; Libya; Morocco; Pakistan; Venezuela
L-100	Algeria; Argentina; Bolivia; Ecuador; Gabon; Indonesia; Kuwait; Peru; Philippines; United Arab Emirates
L-188 Electra	Argentina; Bolivia; Ecuador; Honduras; Panama
LA-4	Thailand; United Arab Emirates
LCI Type	Uruguay
LCU	Venezuela
LCU 1466 Class	Philippines; Vietnam, South
LCU 1610 Class	Brazil; Saudi Arabia
LCU-1610 Type	Korea, South(l)
LCU-501 Class	Brazil; Kampuchea
LSD-13 Class	Taiwan
LSIL Type	Philippines
LSM Type	Argentina; Israel; Philippines
LSMR Type	Panama
LST 1-510	Philippines
LST 511-1152	Brazil; Ecuador; Indonesia; Malaysia; Mexico; Peru; Philippines; Singapore; Thailand
LST-1173 Class	Venezuela
LVT-4	Taiwan

Supplier	Weapon designation	Acquired by
	LVTP-5	Philippines; Taiwan
	LVTP-7	Brazil; Korea, South; Philippines; Thailand; Venezuela
	Lance SAM	Israel
	Learjet	Argentina; Chile; Ecuador; Mexico; Peru; Saudi Arabia; Uruguay
	Liberty Type	Taiwan
	Lung Chiang Cl	Taiwan(l)
	M-1 Abrams	Saudi Arabia
	M-101 105mm	Korea, South(l)
	M-101-A1 105mm	Argentina; Bangladesh; Brazil; Ecuador; Ethiopia; Honduras; Indonesia; Israel; Lebanon; Liberia; Malawi; Morocco; Peru; Saudi Arabia; Sudan; Thailand; Tunisia; Vietnam, South; Yemen, North; Zambia
	M-102 105mm	El Salvador; Honduras; Indonesia; Jordan; Vietnam, South
	M-106	Egypt; Saudi Arabia; Yemen, North
	M-107 175mm	Iran; Israel; Korea, South; Vietnam, South
	M-108 105mm	Brazil; Thailand; Tunisia
	M-109 155mm	Egypt; Ethiopia; Iran; Israel; Jordan; Kampuchea; Kenya; Korea, South; Oman; Pakistan; Saudi Arabia; Taiwan; Thailand; Tunisia; Vietnam, South
	M-110 203mm	Iran; Israel; Jordan; Korea, South; Pakistan; Saudi Arabia; Taiwan
	M-113	Argentina; Brazil; Chile; Costa Rica; Egypt; El Salvador; Ethiopia; Guatemala; Haiti; Indonesia; Iran; Israel; Jordan; Kampuchea; Korea, South; Kuwait; Laos; Lebanon; Morocco; Pakistan; Peru; Philippines; Saudi Arabia; Singapore; Somalia; Sudan; Taiwan; Thailand; Tunisia; Vietnam, South; Yemen, North; Zaire
	M-114 155mm	Argentina; Brazil; El Salvador; Ethiopia; Jordan; Korea, South(l); Lebanon; Morocco; Peru; Philippines; Saudi Arabia; Singapore; Thailand; Vietnam, South
	M-115 203mm	Jordan; Korea, South
	M-125	Egypt; Lebanon; Morocco
	M-163 Vulcan	Ecuador; Jordan; Morocco; Somalia; Sudan; Thailand; Tunisia; Yemen, North
	M-167 Vulcan	Jordan; Korea, South; Philippines; Singapore; Thailand; Yemen, North
	M-18	Argentina
	M-198 155mm	Ecuador; Egypt; Lebanon; Pakistan; Saudi Arabia; Thailand
	M-3	Cameroon; Ecuador; Liberia; Mauritania; Uruguay; Zaire
	M-3-A1 Stuart	Brazil; Colombia; El Salvador
	M-4 Sherman	Brazil
	M-41	Dominican Republic; Vietnam, South
	M-44 155mm	Jordan
	M-46 130mm	Libya(s)
	M-48 Patton	Israel; Jordan; Kampuchea; Korea, South; Lebanon; Morocco; Pakistan; Peru; Taiwan; Thailand; Tunisia; Vietnam, South
	M-5 Stuart	Argentina

M-52 105mm	Jordan
M-548	Egypt; Israel
M-56	Burkina Faso; Ecuador; Saudi Arabia
M-577	Egypt; Israel; Korea, South; Lebanon; Saudi Arabia; Tunisia; Yemen, North
M-578	Lebanon
M-59 155mm	Jordan
M-60	Bahrain; Egypt; Ethiopia; Israel; Jordan; Korea, South; Lebanon; Oman; Saudi Arabia; Sudan; Taiwan; Tunisia; Vietnam, South; Yemen, North
M-7 105mm	Brazil; Gabon
M-728	Israel
M-8 Greyhound	Peru
M-88	Egypt; Israel; Korea, South; Pakistan; Saudi Arabia; Taiwan; Yemen, North
M-901 TOW	Egypt; Kuwait; Pakistan
MGM-52C Lance	Israel
MIM-23 Hawk	Brazil; Chad; Egypt; Israel; Jordan; Korea, South; Kuwait; Saudi Arabia; Singapore; Somalia; Taiwan; United Arab Emirates
MIM-72	Egypt; Israel; Morocco; Taiwan; Tunisia
MU-2J	Mexico(s)
Mark Class	Taiwan
Merlin	Argentina; Mexico; Thailand; Venezuela
Metro-2	Chile
Model 150	Ecuador; Haiti; Somalia; Sri Lanka; Zaire
Model 152	Botswana
Model 172	Laos; Liberia; Madagascar; Panama
Model 182	Argentina; Peru; Venezuela
Model 185	Argentina; Bolivia; Guyana; Kampuchea; Liberia; Nicaragua; Philippines; Thailand; Vietnam, South
Model 204	Ecuador; Honduras; Nicaragua; Panama; Singapore; Uruguay
Model 205	Argentina; Bolivia; Brazil; Brunei; Burma; Chile; Colombia; Dominican Republic; El Salvador; Guatemala; Honduras; Indonesia; Jordan; Kampuchea; Korea, South; Malaysia; Mexico; Nicaragua; Oman; Pakistan; Panama; Philippines; Singapore; Taiwan(l); Thailand; Tunisia; Uganda; Uruguay; Venezuela; Vietnam, South
Model 206	Bangladesh; Botswana; Brazil; Brunei; Guatemala; Guyana; Indonesia; Israel; Jamaica; Korea, South; Malaysia; Mexico; Pakistan; Sri Lanka; Thailand; Uganda; Venezuela
Model 207	Argentina; Bolivia; Indonesia; Liberia; Panama
Model 208	Thailand
Model 209	Iran; Israel; Jordan; Korea, South; Pakistan
Model 210	Bolivia; Paraguay; Philippines
Model 212	Argentina; Bangladesh; Brunei; Colombia; Ecuador; Ghana; Guatemala; Guyana; Indonesia; Israel; Jamaica; Korea, South; Mexico; Panama; Peru; Singapore; Sri Lanka; Thailand; Tunisia; Uganda; United Arab Emirates; Uruguay
Model 214	Iran; Iraq; Oman; Peru; Thailand; Uganda; United Arab Emirates; Venezuela
Model 269	Bahrain; Thailand

Supplier	Weapon designation	Acquired by
	Model 300	Colombia; El Salvador; Haiti; Honduras; India; Indonesia; Iraq; Korea, North; Nigeria; Sierra Leone; Thailand
	Model 310	Chile; Indonesia; Tanzania; Venezuela; Zaire
	Model 321	El Salvador; Korea, South; Vietnam, South
	Model 337	Bangladesh; Benin; Chile; Haiti; Jamaica; Liberia; Nicaragua; Niger; Sri Lanka; Thailand; Togo
	Model 35	Nicaragua
	Model 402	Comoros; Haiti; Malaysia; Mexico; Tanzania; Trinidad & Tobago; Venezuela
	Model 412	Brazil; Colombia; Guatemala; Honduras; Indonesia; Korea, South; Panama; Sri Lanka; Thailand; Venezuela
	Model 414	Bolivia
	Model 421	Bolivia; Libya
	Model 47	Indonesia; Malaysia; Paraguay; Sri Lanka
	Model 500	Argentina; Bahrain; Colombia; Costa Rica; Dominican Republic; El Salvador; Haiti; Honduras; Iraq; Israel; Jordan; Kenya; Korea, North; Korea, South; Morocco; Philippines; Sierra Leone; Suriname; Taiwan
	Model 530	Colombia; Iraq
	Model 99	Thailand
	Model R172K	Chile
	Musketeer Sport	Indonesia
	Navajo	Argentina; Chile; Ecuador; Kenya; Nigeria
	Nike Hercules	Korea, South
	OH-6 Cayuse	Brazil; Nicaragua
	OV-10 Bronco	Indonesia; Korea, South; Morocco; Philippines; Thailand; Venezuela
	Osprey Class	Dominican Republic
	P-3 Orion	Iran
	PA-28 Cherokee	Costa Rica; Jordan; Tanzania
	PA-28 Dakota	Chile(l)
	PA-31 Cheyenne	Mauritania; Panama
	PA-34 Seneca-2	Jordan; Pakistan
	PA-38 Tomahawk	Indonesia
	PC-1638 Type	Chile(l)
	PC-452 Type	Philippines
	PCE-827 Class	Philippines
	PF-103 Class	Thailand
	PGM-71 Class	Peru(l); Philippines
	PL-1B Chienshou	Taiwan(l)
	PL-2	Korea, South; Thailand; Vietnam, South
	PSMM-5 Type	Korea, South; Taiwan

Parish Class	Brazil; Venezuela
Patapsco Class	Taiwan
Phalanx	Saudi Arabia
Queen Air	Algeria; Argentina; Ecuador; Israel; Peru; Thailand; Uruguay; Venezuela
RC-47 Skytrain	Argentina
RF-4 Phantom	Iran; Israel
RF-5 Tigereye	Malaysia; Saudi Arabia, Vietnam, South
RGM-84A Harpoon	Egypt; Iran; Israel; Korea, South; Pakistan; Saudi Arabia; Thailand
RH-53D	Iran
RIM-66 Standard	Iran; Korea, South; Taiwan
RT-33A	Philippines; Uruguay
RU-21E	Israel
Redeye FIM-43A	Chad; Israel; Jordan; Saudi Arabia; Thailand
S-2 Tracker	Argentina; Korea, South; Peru; Taiwan; Venezuela
S-55 Chickasaw	Argentina; Chile; Haiti; Indonesia; Korea, South
S-58	Argentina; Brazil; Costa Rica; Haiti; Laos; Nicaragua; Thailand
S-61	Argentina; Brazil; Israel; Libya; Malaysia
S-62A	Iran
S-65A	Israel
S-70C	Philippines; Taiwan
S-76 Spirit	Brunei; Honduras; Jordan; Philippines; Trinidad & Tobago
SA-366	Israel(s)
SH-3D Sea King	Brazil
SP-2 Neptune	Argentina
Sabreliner	Argentina; Bolivia; Jordan
Sea Chaparral	Taiwan
Seasparrow	Colombia
Series-3200	Philippines
Sewart Type	Jamaica
Sierra	Algeria
Stallion	Kampuchea; Laos
Stratofreighter	Israel
Sumner Class	Argentina; Brazil; Chile; Colombia; Iran; Korea, South; Taiwan; Venezuela
Super King Air	Algeria; Argentina; Bolivia; Ecuador; Israel; Morocco; Sri Lanka; Taiwan; Thailand; Uruguay; Venezuela
Swift Type	Costa Rica; Ethiopia; Gabon; Honduras
T-2 Buckeye	Venezuela
T-28 Trojan	Kampuchea; Philippines
T-33A	Burma; Colombia; Ecuador; Ethiopia; Indonesia; Korea, South; Philippines
T-34 Mentor	Algeria; Argentina; Colombia; Dominican Republic; Ecuador; Gabon; Indonesia; Morocco; Peru; Taiwan; Uruguay
T-35 Pillan	Chile(l)
T-37	Brazil; Burma; Chile; Jordan; Pakistan; Peru; Thailand

Supplier	Weapon designation	Acquired by
	T-38 Talon	Colombia; Taiwan
	T-41 Mescalero	Argentina; Bolivia; Costa Rica; Ecuador; El Salvador; Honduras; Indonesia; Kampuchea; Korea, South; Paraguay; Thailand; Uruguay; Vietnam, South
	T-54	Chile(s)
	TA-4 Skyhawk	Israel; Kuwait; Singapore
	Tacoma Type	Thailand
	Tonti Class	Korea, South
	Turbo Centurion	Bolivia
	Turbo Porter	Argentina; Bolivia
	U-10A Courier	Thailand
	UH-12	Egypt
	UH-60A	Brazil; Peru; Philippines; Saudi Arabia
	VC-60 Lodestar	Brazil
	Westwind 1124	Israel(l)
	YO Type	Korea, South
USSR	AA-2	Afghanistan; Algeria; Angola; Bangladesh; Cuba; Egypt; India(l); Iraq; Korea, North; Laos; Libya; Nigeria; Peru; Syria; Uganda; Vietnam, North; Yemen, North; Yemen, South
	AA-5	India
	AA-6	Libya; Syria
	AA-7	India; Syria
	AA-8	Cuba; India; Syria
	AS-4	Iraq; Libya
	AS-5	Egypt
	AS-6	Iraq
	AS-7	Viet Nam
	AT-1	Egypt; Syria
	AT-2	Libya; Syria
	AT-3	Afghanistan; Algeria; Angola; Cuba; Egypt; Ethiopia; India; Iraq; Libya; Mozambique; Nicaragua; Somalia; Syria; Uganda; Vietnam, North; Zambia
	AT-4	Algeria; Angola; Syria
	AT-5	Algeria; Syria
	AT-6	Algeria
	An-12	Angola; Ethiopia; Iraq; Viet Nam; Yemen, North; Yemen, South
	An-2	Angola; Korea, North; Laos; Mali; Nicaragua
	An-24	Bangladesh; Congo; Guinea; Iraq; Laos; Madagascar; Mali; Somalia; Syria; Yemen, North; Yemen, South

An-26	Afghanistan; Angola; Bangladesh; Benin; Cape Verde; Cuba; Ethiopia; Guinea Bissau; Iraq; Laos; Libya; Madagascar; Mozambique; Peru; Somalia, Syria; Viet Nam; Yemen, North; Yemen, South
An-32	Angola; Cuba; India
BM-13-16 132mm	Somalia
BM-21 122mm	Algeria; Angola; Congo; Egypt; Ethiopia; India; Iraq; Korea, North; Mali; Mozambique; Nicaragua; Nigeria; Syria; Tanzania; Viet Nam; Vietnam, North; Yemen, North; Yemen, South; Zambia
BM-25 250mm	Yemen, South
BMD-20 200mm	Ethiopia
BMP-1	Afghanistan; Algeria; Cuba; Egypt; Ethiopia; India; Iraq; Korea, North; Libya; Madagascar; Syria; Yemen, South
BRDM-1	Afghanistan; Burundi; Cuba; Ethiopia; Guinea; Libya; Mozambique; Syria; Uganda; Zambia
BRDM-2	Algeria; Angola; Benin; Cape Verde; Congo; Cuba; Equatorial Guinea; Ethiopia; Guinea; Guinea Bissau; India; Iraq; Jordan; Libya; Madagascar; Malawi; Mali; Mauritius; Mozambique; Nicaragua; Seychelles; Somalia; Syria; Tanzania; Uganda; Yemen, North; Yemen, South; Zambia; Zimbabwe
BTR-152	Cuba; Equatorial Guinea; Ethiopia; India; Korea, North; Mali; Mozambique; Nicaragua; Somalia; Sri Lanka; Syria; Yemen, South
BTR-40	Algeria; Korea, North; Nicaragua
BTR-50P	Algeria; Guinea; India; Iraq; Libya; Somalia; Syria; Vietnam, North
BTR-60P	Afghanistan; Algeria; Angola; Cuba; Egypt; Ethiopia; Guinea; India; Iraq; Laos; Lebanon; Libya; Mali; Mozambique; Nicaragua; Somalia; Syria; Viet Nam; Yemen, North; Yemen, South; Zambia
Be-12	Viet Nam
C-123 Provider	Laos(s)
D-1 152mm	Cuba; Mozambique; Syria; Vietnam, North
D-20 152mm	Algeria; Cuba; Ethiopia; Libya; Nicaragua; Viet Nam
D-30 122mm	Afghanistan; Algeria; Angola; Cuba; Ethiopia; India; Iraq; Laos; Libya; Madagascar; Mali; Morocco; Mozambique; Nicaragua; Syria; Vietnam, North; Yemen, North; Yemen, South; Zambia
D-74 122mm	Algeria; Vietnam, North
FROG	Algeria; Egypt; India; Korea, North; Kuwait; Libya; Syria; Yemen, South
Foxtrot Class	Cuba; India; Libya
Il-14	Congo; Yemen, South
Il-18	Congo; Somalia; Yemen, North
Il-20	India
Il-28	Somalia
Il-38	India
Il-76	India; Iraq; Libya; Syria
JSU-122	Algeria; Ethiopia; Libya; Syria
JSU-152	Algeria; Libya; Syria

Supplier	Weapon designation	Acquired by
	K-61	Egypt; Uganda
	Ka-25	India; Syria; Viet Nam
	Ka-26	Sri Lanka
	Ka-27	India
	Kashin Class	India
	Komar Class	Korea, North; Syria; Vietnam, North
	Koni Class	Algeria; Cuba
	Kresta-2 Class	India
	M-1931 122mm	Somalia
	M-1938 122mm	Mozambique; Nicaragua; Somalia; Yemen, North; Yemen, South
	M-1944 100mm	Mozambique; Somalia; Sudan
	M-1955 100mm	Iraq; Somalia; Yemen, South
	M-1973 152mm	Iraq; Libya; Syria
	M-1974 122mm	Algeria; Angola; Iraq; Libya; Syria
	M-46 130mm	Algeria; Angola; Cuba; Ethiopia; India; Iran; Laos; Mali; Mozambique; Nigeria; Oman; Syria; Yemen, South
	M-47 Patton	Ethiopia(s)
	Mi-14	Cuba; Ethiopia; Libya
	Mi-17	Cuba; India; Peru
	Mi-24	Afghanistan; Algeria; Cuba; Ethiopia; India; Iraq; Kampuchea; Libya; Nicaragua; Peru; Syria; Viet Nam
	Mi-26	India
	Mi-4	Algeria; Iraq; Somalia; Syria; Uganda; Yemen, North; Yemen, South
	Mi-6	Algeria; Egypt; Ethiopia; Iraq; Peru; Syria; Viet Nam
	Mi-8	Afghanistan; Algeria; Angola; Bangladesh; Cuba; Egypt; Ethiopia; Guinea Bissau; India; Iraq; Kampuchea; Laos; Libya; Mali; Mozambique; Nicaragua; Pakistan; Peru; Somalia; Syria; Viet Nam; Yemen, North; Yemen, South; Zambia
	MiG-15	Angola; Egypt; Somalia; Sri Lanka
	MiG-17	Angola; Burkina Faso; Egypt; Ethiopia; Mozambique; Somalia; Sri Lanka; Syria; Uganda; Viet Nam; Vietnam, North; Yemen, South
	MiG-19	Afghanistan; Egypt; Korea, North(0); Somalia; Viet Nam
	MiG-21	Afghanistan; Algeria; Angola; Bangladesh; Cuba; Egypt; Ethiopia; Guinea; Guinea Bissau; India; Iraq; Korea, North; Laos; Mozambique; Nigeria; Somalia; Syria; Uganda; Viet Nam; Vietnam, North; Yemen, North; Yemen, South; Zambia
	MiG-23	Afghanistan; Algeria; Angola; Cuba; Egypt; Ethiopia; India; Iraq; Korea, North; Libya; Syria; Viet Nam; Yemen, South
	MiG-25	Algeria; India; Iraq; Libya; Syria
	MiG-27	India(0); Syria; Viet Nam; Yemen, South
	MiG-29	India; Syria

Mol Class	Ethiopia; Somalia; Sri Lanka; Yemen, South
Nanuchka Class	Algeria; India; Libya
Natya Class	India; Libya; Syria
Ondatra Class	Yemen, North
Osa Class	Algeria; Angola; Cuba; Ethiopia; India; Iraq; Korea, North; Libya; Somalia; Syria; Viet Nam; Yemen, North; Yemen, South
P-4 Class	Syria
P-6 Class	Equatorial Guinea; Guinea; Guinea Bissau; Somalia; Vietnam; North; Yemen, South
PT-76	Afghanistan; Angola; Cuba; Egypt; Guinea; Iraq; Kampuchea; Madagascar; Mozambique; Nicaragua; Syria; Uganda; Zambia
Petya-2 Class	Ethiopia; India; Syria; Viet Nam
Polnocny Class	Algeria(s); Angola(s); Cuba(s); Egypt(s); Ethiopia(s); Iraq(s); Libya(s); Viet Nam(s); Yemen, South
Romeo Class	Algeria
Ropucha Class	Yemen, South(s)
S-23 180mm	Ethiopia; India; Libya; Syria
SA-11	Syria
SA-13	Angola; Libya; Syria
SA-2	Angola; Cuba; Egypt; India; Iraq; Korea, North; Laos; Libya; Peru; Somalia; Sudan; Syria; Viet Nam; Vietnam, North; Yemen, North; Yemen, South
SA-3	Afghanistan; Angola; Cuba; Egypt; Ethiopia; India; Iraq; Korea, North; Laos; Libya; Mali; Peru; Somalia; Syria; Viet Nam; Vietnam, North; Yemen, South; Zambia
SA-5	Libya; Syria
SA-6	Algeria; Angola; Cuba; Egypt; India; Iraq; Kuwait; Libya; Mozambique; Syria; Tanzania; Viet Nam; Yemen, South
SA-7	Angola; Botswana; Cuba; Egypt; Ethiopia; Guinea Bissau; Guyana; India; Iran; Jordan; Korea, North; Kuwait; Laos; Libya; Morocco; Mozambique; Nicaragua; Peru; Seychelles; Syria; Viet Nam; Vietnam, North; Yemen, North; Yemen, South
SA-8	Algeria; Angola; India; Iraq; Jordan; Kuwait; Libya; Mozambique; Syria
SA-9	Algeria; Angola; Benin; Guinea; Guinea Bissau; India; Iran; Iraq; Jordan; Libya; Madagascar; Somalia; Syria; Yemen, South
SA-N-1	India
SA-N-4	Algeria; Cuba; India; Libya
SCUD	Egypt; Iraq; Korea, North; Libya; Syria; Yemen, South
SM-4-1 130mm	Syria; Yemen, South
SO-1 Class	Egypt; Mozambique; Viet Nam; Yemen, South
SS-21	Iraq; Syria
SSN-2 Styx	Algeria; Angola; Cuba; India; Iraq; Korea, North; Libya; Somalia; Syria; Viet Nam; Vietnam, North; Yemen, North; Yemen, South
SU-100	Angola; Cuba
Samlet	Korea, North
Scaleboard	Libya
Scud	Egypt; Iraq; Korea, North; Libya; Syria; Yemen, South

Supplier		
Weapon designation		**Acquired by**
Shershen Class		Angola; Cape Verde; Congo; Guinea; Guinea Bissau; Korea, North; Viet Nam; Vietnam, North
Sonya Class		Cuba
Straight Flush		Egypt
		Syria
Su-11		Afghanistan
Su-17		Algeria; Egypt; Ethiopia; Iraq; Viet Nam
Su-20		Angola; Libya; Peru; Syria; Yemen, North; Yemen, South
Su-22		Afghanistan; Algeria; Egypt; Iraq; Korea, North; Syria; Viet Nam; Yemen, South
Su-7		Afghanistan; Angola; Ethiopia; Mali; Mozambique; Syria; Yemen, North; Yemen, South
T-34		Egypt
T-43 Class		Afghanistan; Angola; Bangladesh; Egypt; Ethiopia; Iraq; Kampuchea; Korea, North(l);
T-54		Laos; Libya; Mozambique; Nicaragua; Somalia; Syria; Tanzania; Uganda; Vietnam, North; Yemen, North; Yemen, South; Zambia
T-55		Afghanistan; Algeria; Bangladesh; Cuba; Egypt; Ethiopia; Guinea; India; Iraq; Korea, North; Laos; Libya; Mozambique; Nicaragua; Nigeria; Peru; Somalia; South Africa; Syria; Uganda; Yemen, North; Yemen, South; Zambia
T-58 Class		Guinea; India; Yemen, South
T-62		Afghanistan; Algeria; Angola; Cuba; Egypt; Ethiopia; Iraq; Korea, North; Libya; Syria; Viet Nam; Yemen, North; Yemen, South
T-64		Libya
T-72		Algeria; Ethiopia; India; Iraq; Libya; Syria
T-74		Syria
Tarantul Class		India
Tu-124		Iraq
Tu-126		Syria
Tu-134		Iraq; Mozambique
Tu-142		India
Tu-16B		Egypt
Tu-22		Iraq; Libya
Turya Class		Cuba; Kampuchea; Viet Nam
Vanya Class		Syria
Whiskey Class		Cuba; Egypt
Yak-11		Vietnam, North
Yak-18		Guinea; Mali
Yak-40		Angola; Bangladesh; Equatorial Guinea; Ethiopia; Guinea; Laos; Madagascar; Syria; Zambia
Yevgenia Class		Cuba; India; Iraq; Nicaragua; Syria; Yemen, North
Yurka Class		Egypt; Viet Nam

Country	Weapon	Recipients
	ZSU-23-4 Shilka	Afghanistan; Algeria; Angola; Congo; Cuba; Egypt; Ethiopia; India; Iran; Iraq; Jordan; Korea, North; Libya; Mozambique; Nigeria; Peru; Somalia; Syria; Viet Nam; Yemen, North; Yemen, South
	ZSU-57-2	Algeria; Angola; Ethiopia; Iraq; Laos; Nicaragua; Syria; Vietnam, North
	Zlin-226	Mozambique(s)
United Arab Emirates	BN-2A	Somalia(s)
	Hunter	Somalia(s)
	Saladin	Oman(s)
	Skyvan-3M	Yemen, North(s)
Venezuela	F-86 Sabre	Bolivia(s)
Yemen, South	BAC-167	Singapore(s)
	Jet Provost	Singapore(s)
Yugoslavia	CL-13 Sabre	Honduras(s)
	Frigate	Indonesia; Iraq
	G-2 Galeb	Libya; Zambia
	G-4 Super Galeb	Algeria; Zambia
	J-1 Jastreb	Zambia
	Koncar Class	Libya
	Kraljevica Cl	Bangladesh; Ethiopia
	M-47 Patton	Ethiopia(s)
	M-56 105mm	El Salvador

Appendix 4A. Values of exports of major weapons to the Third World, 1951–70, by supplier[a]

Figures are US $m., at constant (1985) prices.

Country	1951	1952	1953	1954	1955	1956	1957	1958	1959
Canada	18	1	–	2	2	101	9	9	238
China	40	–	–	–	–	–	8	505	439
Czechoslovakia	–	–	–	–	37	87	21	64	114
France	21	18	144	169	109	199	235	201	204
Germany, FR	0	–	–	6	9	10	6	0	82
Iran	–	–	–	–	–	–	–	–	–
Italy	28	–	–	–	0	88	88	129	–
Japan	–	–	–	2	2	2	62	9	26
Netherlands	51	15	1	1	0	2	26	2	2
Poland	–	–	–	–	–	–	0	–	179
Sweden	4	42	16	19	12	12	–	265	4
UK	195	214	531	443	455	645	616	879	743
USA	1 259	457	467	581	941	1 013	1 144	898	834
USSR	96	73	338	50	146	561	646	448	314
Yugoslavia	–	–	–	–	–	101	–	60	–
Total[b]	1 711	821	1 530	1 284	1 724	2 828	2 879	3 480	3 197

[a]Suppliers with export value ≥0.1 per cent of total for 1951–70.
[b]Items do not add up to totals due to omission of suppliers with low export values, see a.
. . Not applicable.
– Nil.
0 < $0.5 million.

1960	1961	1962	1963	1964	1965	1966	1967	1968	1969	1970
24	24	4	17	10	18	16	20	39	95	60
406	0	19	19	16	74	233	214	162	86	101
109	10	10	8	25	1	83	120	163	137	143
91	109	245	278	316	189	345	274	580	274	693
100	15	5	8	42	43	60	66	36	56	3
–	–	1	–	–	–	295	26	–	–	20
7	–	9	0	1	26	37	96	121	85	37
–	41	5	6	4	5	8	43	28	12	–
3	7	12	–	47	68	6	–	29	58	7
–	–	–	0	–	–	23	6	–	1	–
4	1	–	–	–	–	1	–	–	–	–
877	555	262	251	300	338	315	478	518	1 038	472
1 210	1 591	855	960	1 073	1 424	1 511	1 816	2 215	3 118	3 551
403	912	2 236	1 009	1 255	1 356	2 597	4 317	3 787	2 164	4 110
–	–	21	21	8	38	–	–	–	6	–
3 247	3 272	3 726	2 590	3 110	3 658	5 560	7 509	7 721	7 238	9 212

Appendix 4B. Values of exports of major weapons to the Third World, 1971–85, by supplier[a]

Figures are US $m., at constant (1985) prices.

Country	1971	1972	1973	1974	1975	1976	1977	1978	1979
Australia	32	2	72	3	24	24	13	33	–
Austria	–	–	–	–	–	4	4	–	179
Brazil	–	–	–	11	25	154	130	120	112
Canada	95	257	12	10	3	113	88	220	78
China	321	417	232	382	320	211	114	459	412
Czechoslovakia	60	46	30	19	–	10	31	141	100
Egypt	–	–	–	–	4	–	9	17	2
France	677	786	1 643	1 263	1 144	1 398	2 147	2 406	3 264
Germany, FR	86	108	–	408	261	166	204	258	162
Israel	1	34	4	67	121	59	55	470	228
Italy	95	137	148	268	139	163	294	323	975
Jordan	38	–	–	45	55	–	13	–	–
Korea, South	–	101	–	–	–	–	–	–	30
Libya	–	–	18	38	2	4	128	–	330
Netherlands	93	63	169	65	131	357	94	172	196
Poland	–	26	26	–	23	53	46	–	24
Spain	–	10	–	–	5	7	17	30	21
Sweden	137	–	2	6	6	24	10	13	184
Switzerland	5	5	7	5	10	19	17	23	73
UK	1 212	1 195	1 307	1 071	1 196	834	1 641	1 200	773
USA	3 830	5 924	6 264	4 481	7 074	7 257	9 465	6 852	4 052
USSR	4 956	5 874	7 025	4 732	2 874	4 875	7 231	9 035	10 118
Yugoslavia	7	–	–	–	8	16	40	16	16
Total[b]	**11 659**	**15 023**	**16 974**	**12 982**	**13 571**	**15 921**	**21 892**	**21 921**	**21 502**

[a]Suppliers with export value ≥0.1 per cent of total for 1971–85.
[b]Items do not add up to totals due to omission of suppliers with low export values, see a.
. . Not applicable.
– Nil.
0 < $0.5 million.

1980	1981	1982	1983	1984	1985
–	11	18	24	29	8
28	90	35	154	–	96
268	273	202	298	269	152
100	79	201	150	23	33
484	328	675	878	1 296	767
129	99	68	77	78	–
24	92	44	478	176	147
2 356	3 134	2 892	2 771	3 476	3 531
283	931	320	1 169	1 819	479
209	277	441	386	145	122
653	1 332	1 347	1 000	1 068	987
–	12	42	214	94	–
30	116	3	52	140	36
26	69	210	85	77	–
115	189	154	–	52	32
–	82	–	1	5	42
9	97	373	538	530	256
140	8	72	20	29	37
65	127	69	108	154	15
703	1 161	1 648	900	1 434	888
5 664	6 131	7 121	6 346	5 108	4 380
9 085	7 992	7 777	7 164	8 382	7 315
36	100	2	–	60	10
20 513	**22 908**	**23 978**	**23 035**	**24 713**	**19 474**

Appendix 5A. Values of imports of major weapons by the Third World, 1951–70, by region

Figures are in US $m., at constant (1985) prices.

Five-year moving averages are calculated as a more stable measure of the trend in arms imports than the often erratic year-to-year figures; A = yearly values, B = five-year moving averages.

Recipient region		1951	1952	1953	1954	1955	1956	1957	1958	1959
Middle East	A	94	32	149	115	371	957	644	389	496
	B	. .	. .	152	325	447	495	571	552	415
South Asia	A	164	113	265	305	225	420	765	895	565
	B	. .	. .	215	266	396	522	574	632	682
Far East and	A	404	356	651	382	843	731	1 075	1 612	1 359
Oceania	B	. .	. .	527	593	737	929	1 124	1 245	1 257
North Africa	A	–	–	–	–	–	18	16	8	15
	B	. .	. .	–	4	7	8	11	20	23
Sub-Saharan	A	10	9	33	29	20	3	5	10	135
Africa	B	. .	. .	20	19	18	13	35	62	94
Central	A	47	49	49	32	30	54	15	31	11
America	B	. .	. .	42	43	36	32	28	36	87
South	A	991	201	370	405	178	476	261	464	479
America	B	. .	. .	429	326	338	357	371	482	567
South Africa	A	–	61	13	15	57	170	98	71	137
	B	. .	. .	29	63	70	82	107	98	90
Total[a]	A	1 711	821	1 530	1 284	1 724	2 828	2 879	3 480	3 197
	B	. .	. .	1 414	1 637	2 049	2 439	2 822	3 126	3 215

[a]Items may not add up to totals due to rounding.

. . Not applicable.

– Nil.

0 < $0.5 million.

1960	1961	1962	1963	1964	1965	1966	1967	1968	1969	1970
274	271	1 393	809	1 400	1 072	1 397	3 228	3 634	3 240	4 893
565	649	830	989	1 214	1 581	2 146	2 514	3 278	4 199	4 541
515	672	280	299	232	397	1 108	758	817	865	798
585	466	400	376	463	559	662	789	869	889	1 085
1 448	790	749	723	754	1 021	1 756	2 328	2 392	1 935	2 238
1 191	1 014	893	807	1 001	1 316	1 650	1 886	2 130	2 410	3 064
41	35	79	68	106	331	385	354	167	343	185
36	48	66	124	194	249	269	316	287	255	258
156	162	85	108	189	183	221	198	161	126	357
110	129	140	145	157	180	190	178	213	247	260
69	311	844	340	190	165	202	28	51	60	181
253	315	351	370	348	185	127	101	105	91	138
729	903	191	118	133	277	264	305	330	601	285
553	484	415	324	197	219	262	355	357	472	643
16	128	104	125	107	212	226	310	169	67	275
91	102	96	135	155	196	205	197	209	185	181
3 247	3 272	3 726	2 590	3 110	3 658	5 560	7 509	7 721	7 238	9 212
3 384	3 206	3 189	3 271	3 729	4 485	5 511	6 337	7 448	8 668	10 171

Appendix 5B. Values of imports of major weapons by the Third World, 1971–85, by region

Figures are in US $m., at constant (1985) prices.

Five-year moving averages are calculated as a more stable measure of the trend in arms imports than the often erratic year-to-year figures; A = yearly values, B = five-year moving averages.

Recipient region		1971	1972	1973	1974	1975	1976	1977	1978
Middle East	A	5 601	5 339	10 269	6 760	7 248	7 398	9 833	7 605
	B	5 868	6 572	7 043	7 403	8 302	7 769	7 619	7 902
South Asia	A	1 208	1 734	1 049	936	573	1 044	1 957	1 789
	B	1 131	1 145	1 100	1 067	1 112	1 260	1 309	1 612
Far East and Oceania	A	3 155	5 601	1 825	1 786	1 451	1 468	1 976	3 497
	B	2 951	2 921	2 764	2 426	1 701	2 036	2 804	3 097
North Africa	A	224	373	340	591	1 747	2 629	2 595	3 702
	B	293	342	655	1 136	1 580	2 253	3 297	3 580
Sub-Saharan Africa	A	393	266	468	841	645	968	2 523	2 532
	B	322	465	523	638	1 089	1 502	1 519	1 659
Central America	A	135	261	309	299	201	234	557	202
	B	189	237	241	261	320	299	286	283
South America	A	840	1 156	2 255	1 235	1 473	1 809	2 279	2 251
	B	1 028	1 154	1 392	1 586	1 811	1 810	1 884	1 998
South Africa	A	104	292	459	533	232	371	171	343
	B	240	333	324	378	353	330	244	219
Total[a]	A	11 659	15 023	16 974	12 982	13 571	15 921	21 892	21 921
	B	12 021	13 170	14 042	14 894	16 268	17 257	18 961	20 350

[a]Items may not add up to totals due to rounding.

. . Not applicable.

– Nil.

0 < $0.5 million.

1979	1980	1981	1982	1983	1984	1985
6 010	8 665	9 557	11 996	11 408	12 881	10 670
8 334	8 766	9 527	10 901	11 302	. .	. .
1 181	2 088	2 202	2 449	2 616	2 574	2 707
1 843	1 942	2 107	2 386	2 510	. .	. .
5 627	2 916	2 831	1 604	2 431	2 353	2 472
3 370	3 295	3 082	2 427	2 338	. .	. .
5 810	3 164	2 646	3 047	1 673	1 556	1 013
3 583	3 674	3 268	2´417	1 987	. .	. .
929	1 341	1 872	1 511	1 145	1 930	1 212
1 839	1 637	1 360	1 560	1 534	. .	. .
238	185	650	1 055	888	518	271
366	466	603	659	676	. .	. .
1 605	2 045	3 146	2 311	2 640	2 897	1 124
2 265	2 272	2 350	2 608	2 424	. .	. .
102	109	4	4	232	5	6
146	112	90	71	50	. .	. .
21 502	**20 513**	**22 908**	**23 978**	**23 035**	**24 713**	**19 474**
21 747	**22 164**	**22 387**	**23 029**	**22 822**	. .	. .

Appendix 6A. Values of imports of major weapons by the Third World, 1951–70, by country[a]

Figures are in US $m., at constant (1985) prices.

Recipient	1951	1952	1953	1954	1955	1956	1957	1958	1959
Afghanistan	–	–	–	–	–	2	36	37	55
Algeria	–	–	–	–	–	–	–	–	–
Argentina	348	106	58	3	15	20	36	34	79
Bolivia	–	7	3	–	0	6	–	0	–
Brazil	279	8	47	47	25	53	82	80	255
Burma	–	–	–	9	12	5	4	69	15
Chile	279	25	28	85	9	3	2	–	4
Colombia	29	26	12	7	6	24	4	268	17
Cuba	7	9	21	1	10	13	1	15	1
Dominican Republic	7	39	24	1	11	12	1	8	2
Ecuador	3	1	–	–	52	–	8	–	12
Egypt	18	–	56	39	121	600	169	89	35
Ethiopia	4	8	16	13	1	1	–	8	13
Ghana	–	–	–	–	–	–	–	–	1
India	52	52	202	244	133	202	595	637	468
Indonesia	64	28	18	15	46	13	35	254	391
Iran	3	0	1	4	46	72	58	55	262
Iraq	2	–	20	18	31	27	19	45	90
Israel	43	24	56	14	116	158	38	38	85
Jordan	–	0	2	13	19	20	15	21	2
Kampuchea	–	–	–	2	6	9	4	2	5
Korea, North	136	73	338	53	96	102	177	688	551
Korea, South	115	118	52	10	201	315	175	91	77
Kuwait	–	–	0	1	1	4	–	3	–
Lebanon	–	2	3	5	4	–	16	45	–
Libya	–	–	–	–	–	–	3	–	1
Malaysia	–	–	–	–	–	–	–	4	2
Mexico	27	–	4	–	–	13	5	–	0
Morocco	–	–	–	–	–	18	5	6	7
Nigeria	–	–	–	–	–	–	–	–	0
Pakistan	112	62	61	61	90	215	135	212	27
Paraguay	–	1	1	–	2	–	–	–	–
Peru	21	8	0	27	35	46	28	15	96
Philippines	0	0	13	2	7	18	22	52	37
Saudi Arabia	0	4	1	0	3	16	44	18	4
Singapore	–	–	–	–	–	3	–	–	–
Somalia	–	–	–	–	–	–	–	–	–
South Africa	–	61	13	15	57	170	98	71	137
Sudan	–	–	–	–	–	0	1	2	2
Syria	28	–	11	21	31	60	265	51	12
Taiwan	15	57	226	248	440	226	603	437	255
Thailand	74	79	4	10	6	2	46	3	11
Tunisia	–	–	–	–	–	–	7	3	7
Uruguay	26	14	4	–	2	5	3	1	6
Venezuela	6	5	217	236	32	318	99	65	10
Vietnam, North	–	–	–	2	4	2	10	2	2
Vietnam, South	–	–	–	30	22	35	1	7	9
Yemen, North	–	2	–	–	0	–	20	24	4
Yemen, South	–	–	–	–	–	–	–	–	–
Zaire	–	–	–	–	–	–	–	–	–
Zimbabwe	6	1	17	17	19	2	3	–	112
Total[b]	1 711	821	1 530	1 284	1 724	2 828	2 879	3 480	3 197

[a]Recipients with import value ≥ 0.1 per cent of total for 1951–70.
[b]Items do not add up to totals due to omission of recipients with low import values, see a.
. . Not applicable.
– Nil.
0 < $0.5 m.

1960	1961	1962	1963	1964	1965	1966	1967	1968	1969	1970
80	82	21	17	32	33	164	148	106	101	5
–	–	43	53	65	295	318	251	48	7	27
128	339	20	9	9	21	80	109	133	127	110
5	3	2	–	2	1	6	9	33	2	6
128	295	73	31	38	58	79	69	103	153	70
13	14	15	15	6	16	–	7	34	–	–
244	72	19	6	40	21	27	13	2	55	42
65	11	9	3	18	7	3	6	15	54	–
26	279	712	305	165	118	171	16	30	35	30
–	9	8	3	2	20	3	0	9	4	0
21	–	1	–	–	6	6	16	1	–	3
45	125	805	251	361	279	422	1 518	1 010	395	2 205
47	27	4	4	1	17	69	17	26	9	15
8	90	20	2	17	17	7	22	–	1	–
369	542	136	214	145	300	460	435	510	673	658
306	316	414	162	389	141	3	0	40	9	24
31	36	37	35	588	508	437	511	993	598	327
76	55	188	157	202	127	107	128	172	183	196
68	20	275	255	199	57	66	299	585	1 041	1 431
12	9	52	12	9	20	24	42	61	186	125
2	1	11	8	35	68	15	8	37	26	9
453	38	30	31	–	91	438	120	247	145	184
16	72	8	230	22	271	237	169	224	345	115
20	–	11	28	36	23	3	–	38	47	46
1	2	17	18	–	22	44	40	0	–	9
3	5	2	1	18	4	26	8	47	301	99
10	3	6	35	65	5	44	85	49	78	5
33	22	117	30	16	22	10	10	1	–	131
12	29	34	10	22	6	39	96	62	15	29
1	1	3	6	5	70	44	53	59	15	2
62	47	124	66	54	59	484	176	199	90	130
3	1	21	3	4	63	5	1	3	–	1
95	182	36	38	11	35	19	2	35	182	28
34	24	10	1	3	60	36	30	11	30	9
8	8	–	–	3	34	230	101	257	312	85
–	–	–	0	0	0	0	–	2	24	75
8	3	1	20	–	20	29	15	7	–	–
16	128	104	125	107	212	226	310	169	67	275
16	8	21	7	40	12	7	–	10	27	277
11	2	9	52	–	–	58	516	445	393	370
584	127	30	119	110	178	212	380	171	352	388
5	84	95	17	10	12	22	54	36	56	108
26	1	–	4	2	26	1	–	11	20	29
20	0	2	1	5	10	7	4	–	9	11
19	2	8	28	6	47	30	76	6	19	14
14	30	6	–	67	93	667	1 274	1 348	399	506
9	77	109	93	40	82	74	187	187	464	801
–	14	0	0	–	–	–	49	50	3	–
–	–	–	–	–	–	–	19	4	55	28
18	7	9	39	90	12	14	50	–	22	15
6	–	23	19	7	–	–	6	0	–	–
3 247	3 272	3 726	2 590	3 110	3 658	5 560	7 509	7 721	7 238	9 212

Appendix 6B. Values of imports of major weapons by the Third World, 1971–85, by country[a]

Figures are in US $m., at constant (1985) prices.

Recipient	1971	1972	1973	1974	1975	1976	1977	1978	1979
Afghanistan	57	48	–	–	50	69	2	335	392
Algeria	–	113	46	84	22	109	188	1 195	1 291
Angola	–	–	–	2	52	227	363	254	18
Argentina	406	337	151	413	278	172	485	397	410
Bahrain	0	4	0	1	–	–	4	9	24
Bangladesh	6	19	53	21	146	136	25	22	2
Bolivia	–	10	21	20	74	20	23	28	39
Brazil	35	401	918	145	498	539	686	683	251
Cameroon	4	12	5	5	10	9	15	18	29
Chile	181	17	215	360	86	283	86	96	89
Colombia	9	61	229	8	147	–	10	12	–
Cuba	30	234	206	204	14	134	484	140	142
Ecuador	85	29	43	17	50	126	237	398	81
Egypt	2 581	2 105	2 056	419	215	493	222	166	773
El Salvador	3	–	–	7	49	–	–	2	2
Ethiopia	42	16	3	125	44	19	1 456	632	102
Gabon	8	–	28	8	25	63	19	70	–
India	712	1 239	882	665	242	737	1 483	938	497
Indonesia	64	10	103	77	67	120	35	433	567
Iran	1 266	1 282	1 554	2 026	3 615	3 232	4 774	2 390	47
Iraq	233	106	659	744	300	792	1 008	1 218	806
Israel	666	1 031	2 561	826	1 284	1 291	1 081	877	520
Jordan	21	27	90	211	213	312	738	615	135
Kampuchea	9	41	140	51	–	–	–	163	–
Kenya	13	6	9	32	15	1	71	163	130
Korea, North	277	126	160	361	200	144	85	147	113
Korea, South	128	392	96	207	363	208	889	529	817
Kuwait	90	21	–	69	164	367	497	429	275
Laos	2	8	17	5	13	22	126	2	–
Lebanon	7	21	15	7	47	30	9	–	36
Libya	220	259	273	473	1 578	2 492	1 713	2 128	3 302
Malaysia	177	17	232	41	80	216	105	173	275
Mexico	51	18	61	30	61	22	16	5	76
Morocco	0	–	10	29	130	25	646	374	1 157
Mozambique	–	–	–	–	9	–	99	645	15
Nicaragua	4	4	4	29	1	7	13	13	–
Nigeria	3	134	31	44	58	278	47	123	139
Oman	29	11	76	54	131	142	241	100	27
Pakistan	404	412	114	249	109	101	447	489	289
Peru	77	78	229	88	171	467	550	491	696
Philippines	34	55	99	25	166	86	104	280	55
Qatar	3	4	–	2	21	11	65	8	10
Saudi Arabia	–	83	154	244	589	500	713	1 053	725
Singapore	373	160	60	106	245	225	123	35	278
Somalia	–	29	197	209	80	18	35	45	58
South Africa	104	292	459	533	232	371	171	343	102
Sudan	6	16	–	15	–	–	24	160	12
Syria	640	515	2 984	1 978	397	75	338	488	1 330

1980	1981	1982	1983	1984	1985
132	25	48	71	455	384
562	290	550	358	603	276
132	213	233	420	448	319
119	786	584	1 281	964	432
15	19	12	119	119	40
13	22	53	108	65	16
96	41	7	38	2	8
388	63	37	24	25	30
2	3	60	37	95	43
208	240	360	130	409	25
18	18	152	473	551	20
72	442	590	632	307	133
130	203	298	264	234	–
1 265	816	2 745	2 419	2 504	1 700
15	20	44	24	91	48
239	73	192	19	99	105
72	31	41	12	70	43
1 440	1 872	1 746	2 107	1 343	1 589
490	485	350	173	193	142
31	231	408	374	477	377
1 734	2 314	1 837	2 809	4 718	3 492
1 170	1 741	1 008	357	290	441
107	260	774	878	201	251
12	–	–	4	8	8
157	113	49	27	22	12
68	47	123	32	410	519
578	275	174	270	240	356
94	–	9	163	595	560
–	16	3	67	60	41
71	13	44	86	315	23
2 090	1 693	2 124	839	419	645
148	37	54	270	526	145
41	119	358	121	0	12
435	622	322	458	82	8
20	16	22	46	421	12
–	24	38	26	80	31
104	704	356	145	392	585
25	30	148	279	226	199
495	282	602	326	669	689
712	831	270	121	302	355
78	20	40	165	56	75
72	69	139	318	291	118
1 228	1 585	1 997	1 118	918	1 529
175	244	107	71	72	204
112	108	140	223	2	47
109	4	4	232	5	6
12	141	87	11	87	21
1 810	1 834	2 590	2 145	1 882	1 579

Appendix 6B. (Continued)

Figures are in US $m., at constant (1985) prices.

Recipient	1971	1972	1973	1974	1975	1976	1977	1978	1979
Taiwan	359	154	174	383	166	351	420	352	272
Tanzania	20	5	90	137	10	–	35	41	103
Thailand	139	83	146	137	22	84	88	197	445
Tunisia	3	–	10	4	18	3	48	5	60
Uganda	13	6	36	63	111	84	129	–	–
United Arab Emirates	35	22	66	81	244	143	125	227	33
Venezuela	44	190	446	176	141	173	162	112	31
Viet Nam	–	–	–	20	20	–	–	1 121	2 726
Vietnam, North	650	1 654	14	73	64	–	–	–	–
Vietnam, South	933	2 888	584	286	–	–	–	–	–
Yemen, North	–	–	–	4	4	–	9	–	528
Yemen, South	28	109	54	95	24	9	11	25	740
Zaire	100	11	8	45	146	45	39	28	24
Zambia	104	3	12	53	–	74	46	78	12
Zimbabwe	1	5	5	1	19	29	26	17	4
Total[b]	**11 741**	**15 023**	**16 974**	**12 982**	**13 571**	**15 921**	**21 892**	**21 921**	**21 502**

[a]Recipients with import value ≥ 0.1 per cent of total for 1971–85.
[b]Items do not add up to totals due to omission of recipients with low import values, see *a*.
. . Not applicable.
– Nil.
0 < $0.5 m.

1980	1981	1982	1983	1984	1985
351	614	525	658	347	520
27	32	86	–	47	–
357	221	145	359	208	148
75	41	51	18	452	85
–	–	8	4	–	1
229	431	161	266	265	217
286	869	577	257	393	227
651	849	72	344	228	309
–	–	–	–	–	–
–	–	–	–	–	–
479	65	32	1	42	131
337	146	95	76	38	14
15	9	20	13	8	–
160	170	33	2	34	–
0	23	63	23	72	–
20 513	22 908	23 978	23 035	24 713	19 474

Appendix 7. Shares of major suppliers in Third World imports of major conventional weapons, 1951–85, by region and country

Total imports of major conventional weapons for each five-year period are given in US $m., at constant (1985) prices. Imports from each of the major suppliers are given as a percentage of the total for each period[a]

| Recipient region/country | Period | Supplier | | | | | | | | | Total in 1985 US $m. |
		USSR	USA	France	UK	FR Germany	Italy	China	Third World	Other	
Middle East	1951-55	5	15	20	43	0	4	–	3	8	761
	1956-60	48	14	11	7	1	–	–	1	17	2 760
	1961-65	49	29	11	9	1	0	–	0	0	4 946
	1966-70	49	35	4	8	1	0	–	0	3	16 392
	1971-75	45	41	3	9	0	0	–	0	0	35 217
	1976-80	27	54	10	3	0	1	1	1	1	39 510
	1981-85	33	32	16	4	1	2	5	4	3	56 510
South Asia	1951-55	0	15	20	65	–	–	–	–	0	1 073
	1956-60	7	13	14	66	–	–	–	0	0	3 160
	1961-65	39	22	5	28	0	–	2	0	4	1 880
	1966-70	58	0	9	13	1	–	8	7	3	4 347
	1971-75	54	1	8	13	0	0	16	2	4	5 501
	1976-80	63	4	14	8	0	–	8	0	2	8 058
	1981-85	54	12	9	17	–	–	7	0	1	12 548
Far East and Oceania	1951-55	24	64	2	1	1	–	3	0	5	2 636
	1956-60	12	50	1	1	3	2	22	0	10	6 225
	1961-65	36	51	2	4	0	0	2	0	4	4 037
	1966-70	46	45	0	2	–	–	4	0	2	10 649
	1971-75	23	62	2	5	2	0	3	2	2	13 818
	1976-80	33	48	7	2	1	1	2	3	4	15 485
	1981-85	25	46	3	3	5	3	2	8	4	11 691
North Africa	1956-60	–	6	83	6	–	–	–	3	2	98
	1961-65	75	8	10	1	–	3	–	3	0	619
	1966-70	46	15	8	24	1	0	–	2	4	1 434
	1971-75	62	6	28	2	–	2	–	–	0	3 274
	1976-80	70	6	15	0	0	3	0	3	3	17 900
	1981-85	46	14	20	1	0	12	–	2	5	9 936
Sub-Saharan Africa	1951-55	–	25	–	61	–	–	–	–	13	101
	1956-60	16	23	5	46	–	2	–	2	6	309
	1961-65	21	23	7	22	4	2	–	1	21	727
	1966-70	44	20	10	5	0	8	1	1	11	1 063
	1971-75	27	18	13	12	3	3	12	4	9	2 613
	1976-80	59	8	7	7	2	2	3	4	7	8 293
	1981-85	40	10	15	8	9	5	4	5	5	7 671
Central America	1951-55	–	71	–	–	–	–	–	–	29	208
	1956-60	14	58	3	8	0	–	–	–	17	180
	1961-65	84	12	1	0	1	–	–	–	2	1 850
	1966-70	54	41	1	–	1	–	–	1	2	523
	1971-75	57	27	0	6	–	–	–	9	0	1 205
	1976-80	69	12	6	4	–	–	–	5	4	1 416
	1981-85	66	17	1	1	0	0	–	3	11	3 382

[a]Percentages may not add up to 100 per cent due to rounding.

Recipient region/country	Period	Supplier									Total in 1985 US $m.
		USSR	USA	France	UK	FR Germany	Italy	China	Third World	Other	
South America	1951-55	–	69	0	29	–	1	–	–	0	2 143
	1956-60	–	42	2	36	–	7	–	0	12	2 408
	1961-65	–	86	5	7	–	–	–	0	1	1 622
	1966-70	–	48	11	19	4	1	–	0	16	1 785
	1971-75	0	52	17	10	6	3	–	1	10	6 959
	1976-80	11	22	15	23	6	10	–	5	9	9 990
	1981-85	1	11	20	6	23	21	–	8	10	12 118
South Africa	1951-55	–	7	–	93	–	–	–	–	–	145
	1956-60	–	4	–	76	0	–	–	–	20	492
	1961-65	–	17	30	43	–	–	–	2	8	676
	1966-70	–	10	61	7	–	22	–	–	–	1 046
	1971-75	–	–	77	6	–	15	–	3	–	1 621
	1976-80	0	–	49	–	–	2	–	46	2	1 097
	1981-85	–	–	1	0	2	3	–	92	1	251
Afghanistan	1956-60	100	–	–	–	–	–	–	–	0	210
	1961-65	100	–	–	–	–	–	–	–	–	186
	1966-70	100	–	–	–	–	–	–	–	–	523
	1971-75	100	–	–	–	–	–	–	–	–	155
	1976-80	96	–	–	–	–	–	–	–	4	931
	1981-85	98	–	–	–	–	–	–	–	2	984
Algeria	1961-65	95	0	2	–	–	–	–	3	0	455
	1966-70	95	–	4	–	–	–	–	0	–	651
	1971-75	92	–	8	–	–	–	–	–	0	266
	1976-80	96	1	–	–	–	–	–	0	3	3 346
	1981-85	52	24	19	4	–	–	–	–	0	2 078
Angola	1971-75	–	–	–	–	–	–	33	–	67	53
	1976-80	94	2	1	–	–	–	–	1	2	995
	1981-85	98	–	–	–	–	–	–	–	2	1 635
Argentina	1951-55	–	76	–	20	–	4	–	–	0	530
	1956-60	–	75	3	22	–	–	–	–	0	297
	1961-65	–	94	5	1	–	–	–	–	0	397
	1966-70	–	46	12	21	0	2	–	–	19	559
	1971-75	–	66	16	2	12	1	–	–	2	1 584
	1976-80	–	29	23	22	–	5	–	13	8	1 582
	1981-85	–	3	26	8	47	3	–	7	7	4 047
Bahamas	1976-80	–	–	–	100	–	–	–	–	–	8
Bahrain	1961-65	–	–	–	100	–	–	–	–	–	1
	1966-70	–	–	–	100	–	–	–	–	–	1
	1971-75	–	25	–	75	–	–	–	–	–	5
	1976-80	–	2	59	–	7	–	–	–	32	51
	1981-85	–	52	11	2	35	1	–	–	0	309
Bangladesh	1971-75	29	–	–	1	–	–	54	14	2	246
	1976-80	–	10	3	19	–	–	67	1	0	198
	1981-85	1	8	1	8	–	–	76	4	3	264
Belize	1981-85	–	–	–	100	–	–	–	–	–	2
Benin	1956-60	–	–	100	–	–	–	–	–	–	1
	1961-65	–	–	100	–	–	–	–	–	–	1
	1966-70	–	49	51	–	–	–	–	–	–	2
	1971-75	–	100	–	–	–	–	–	–	–	0
	1976-80	15	–	24	–	–	–	–	61	–	8
	1981-85	26	–	52	–	–	–	–	22	–	13

Recipient region/country	Period	USSR	USA	France	UK	FR Germany	Italy	China	Third World	Other	Total in 1985 US $m.
Bolivia	1951-55	–	100	–	–	–	–	–	–	–	10
	1956-60	–	73	–	–	–	–	–	27	–	11
	1961-65	–	100	–	–	–	–	–	–	–	7
	1966-70	–	96	–	–	–	–	–	–	4	57
	1971-75	–	60	–	–	–	–	–	25	16	125
	1976-80	–	34	–	–	–	2	–	20	45	206
	1981-85	–	4	53	–	–	–	–	7	36	97
Botswana	1976-80	–	0	–	100	–	–	–	–	–	23
	1981-85	23	51	11	10	–	–	–	–	5	15
Brazil	1951-55	–	83	–	17	–	–	–	–	–	405
	1956-60	–	68	5	25	–	–	–	–	2	600
	1961-65	–	92	1	5	–	–	–	–	2	496
	1966-70	–	58	1	12	–	–	–	–	29	473
	1971-75	–	76	6	9	3	7	–	–	0	1 996
	1976-80	–	27	7	62	0	4	–	–	1	2 547
	1981-85	–	14	36	–	0	35	–	9	6	178
Brunei	1961-65	–	–	–	100	–	–	–	–	–	3
	1966-70	–	22	–	78	–	–	–	–	0	19
	1971-75	–	66	5	28	–	–	–	–	–	27
	1976-80	–	9	26	8	–	–	–	58	–	116
	1981-85	–	56	–	24	18	2	–	–	–	42
Burkina Faso	1956-60	–	–	100	–	–	–	–	–	–	3
	1961-65	–	–	100	–	–	–	–	–	–	1
	1966-70	–	10	51	–	–	–	39	–	–	4
	1971-75	–	–	84	16	–	–	–	–	0	7
	1976-80	–	–	–	100	–	–	–	–	–	8
	1981-85	33	5	13	30	–	–	–	19	0	26
Burma	1951-55	–	–	–	80	–	–	–	20	–	21
	1956-60	–	23	–	28	–	–	–	1	48	106
	1961-65	2	64	20	8	–	–	–	–	6	66
	1966-70	–	88	–	–	–	–	–	–	12	41
	1971-75	–	86	–	–	–	5	–	–	8	58
	1976-80	–	38	–	–	–	15	–	–	47	44
	1981-85	–	17	–	–	–	14	–	–	69	8
Burundi	1961-65	–	–	100	–	–	–	–	–	–	1
	1966-70	–	–	98	–	2	–	–	–	0	3
	1971-75	–	–	100	–	–	–	–	–	–	0
	1976-80	100	–	–	–	–	–	–	–	–	2
	1981-85	–	–	55	5	–	11	–	29	–	15
Cameroon	1961-65	–	19	55	26	–	–	–	–	0	2
	1966-70	–	22	54	–	24	–	–	–	–	4
	1971-75	–	38	50	–	–	–	–	2	11	36
	1976-80	–	54	13	21	3	–	8	–	0	74
	1981-85	–	14	48	–	4	–	–	1	33	240
Cape Verde	1971-75	–	–	–	–	–	–	100	–	–	3
	1976-80	100	–	–	–	–	–	–	–	–	21
	1981-85	100	–	–	–	–	–	–	–	–	1
Central African Republic	1961-65	–	19	81	–	–	–	–	–	–	2
	1966-70	–	–	98	–	–	2	–	–	–	9
	1971-75	–	–	–	100	–	–	–	–	–	1
	1976-80	–	–	11	–	–	–	–	3	86	11
	1981-85	–	–	57	–	–	–	–	43	0	7

Recipient region/country	Period	Supplier									Total in 1985 US $m.
		USSR	USA	France	UK	FR Germany	Italy	China	Third World	Other	
Chad	1956-60	–	–	100	–	–	–	–	–	–	1
	1966-70	–	–	100	–	–	–	–	–	–	0
	1971-75	–	–	100	–	–	–	–	–	–	30
	1976-80	–	–	96	–	–	–	–	–	4	34
	1981-85	–	30	55	–	–	–	–	15	0	39
Chile	1951-55	–	99	–	1	–	–	–	–	0	425
	1956-60	–	5	–	95	–	–	–	–	0	254
	1961-65	–	76	7	9	–	–	–	–	8	157
	1966-70	–	39	–	43	–	–	–	–	18	140
	1971-75	–	24	16	37	–	–	–	0	24	858
	1976-80	–	25	30	13	6	–	–	16	10	762
	1981-85	–	8	15	38	15	–	–	14	9	1 164
Colombia	1951-55	–	96	–	–	–	–	–	–	4	80
	1956-60	–	25	–	–	–	–	–	–	75	378
	1961-65	–	100	–	–	–	–	–	–	–	47
	1966-70	–	74	–	–	–	–	–	1	25	78
	1971-75	–	22	39	7	31	–	–	–	1	453
	1976-80	–	84	–	–	–	–	–	16	0	40
	1981-85	–	14	8	1	44	1	–	19	12	1 215
Comoros	1976-80	–	33	–	–	–	67	–	–	–	4
	1981-85	–	–	100	–	–	–	–	–	–	1
Congo	1956-60	–	–	100	–	–	–	–	–	–	0
	1961-65	–	–	100	–	–	–	–	–	–	2
	1966-70	100	–	–	–	–	–	–	–	–	7
	1971-75	39	–	–	–	–	–	18	–	43	32
	1976-80	42	–	11	–	–	–	22	25	–	53
	1981-85	3	–	19	–	–	–	11	–	67	35
Costa Rica	1951-55	–	100	–	–	–	–	–	–	–	1
	1956-60	–	–	–	–	100	–	–	–	–	0
	1961-65	–	100	–	–	–	–	–	–	–	0
	1966-70	–	100	–	–	–	–	–	–	–	0
	1971-75	–	100	–	–	–	–	–	–	–	3
	1976-80	–	76	–	–	–	–	–	24	–	6
	1981-85	–	100	–	–	–	–	–	–	–	10
Côte d'Ivoire	1961-65	–	–	100	–	–	–	–	–	–	2
	1966-70	–	24	76	–	–	–	–	–	–	52
	1971-75	–	–	56	–	–	–	–	–	44	26
	1976-80	–	1	71	–	–	–	–	–	27	144
	1981-85	–	23	77	–	–	–	–	–	–	81
Cuba	1951-55	–	100	–	–	–	–	–	–	–	47
	1956-60	45	30	–	24	–	–	–	–	1	57
	1961-65	98	–	–	–	–	–	–	–	2	1 579
	1966-70	100	–	–	–	–	–	–	–	0	282
	1971-75	100	–	–	–	–	–	–	–	–	689
	1976-80	100	–	–	–	–	–	–	–	–	972
	1981-85	99	–	–	–	–	–	–	–	1	2 105
Djibouti	1976-80	–	–	33	–	–	–	–	67	–	9
	1981-85	–	–	100	–	–	–	–	–	–	33

Recipient region/country	Period	Supplier									Total in 1985 US $m.
		USSR	USA	France	UK	FR Germany	Italy	China	Third World	Other	
Dominican Republic	1951-55	–	45	–	–	–	–	–	–	55	82
	1956-60	–	20	26	–	–	–	–	–	54	22
	1961-65	–	92	7	–	–	–	–	–	1	42
	1966-70	–	61	39	–	–	–	–	–	–	17
	1971-75	–	100	–	–	–	–	–	–	–	4
	1976-80	–	92	8	–	–	–	–	–	–	33
	1981-85	–	100	–	–	–	–	–	–	–	22
Ecuador	1951-55	–	34	–	66	–	–	–	–	–	56
	1956-60	–	100	–	–	–	–	–	–	–	40
	1961-65	–	100	–	–	–	–	–	–	–	7
	1966-70	–	100	–	–	–	–	–	–	–	26
	1971-75	–	22	19	25	25	–	–	8	3	223
	1976-80	–	25	23	20	28	0	–	0	3	971
	1981-85	–	9	35	1	–	47	–	3	6	999
Egypt	1951-55	5	14	3	50	0	–	–	10	19	233
	1956-60	79	–	–	0	–	–	–	–	21	938
	1961-65	99	–	–	0	–	–	–	–	1	1 821
	1966-70	94	–	–	–	–	–	–	0	6	5 550
	1971-75	96	0	4	0	–	–	–	–	–	7 376
	1976-80	13	37	30	2	–	2	15	–	0	2 918
	1981-85	–	64	9	5	–	2	12	0	8	10 182
El Salvador	1956-60	–	100	–	–	–	–	–	–	–	8
	1961-65	–	100	–	–	–	–	–	–	–	2
	1966-70	–	83	–	–	17	–	–	–	–	29
	1971-75	–	7	3	–	–	–	–	90	–	59
	1976-80	–	81	19	–	–	–	–	–	0	18
	1981-85	–	82	1	–	–	–	–	15	1	227
Equatorial Guinea	1976-80	100	–	–	–	–	–	–	–	–	7
	1981-85	11	–	–	–	–	–	–	–	89	9
Ethiopia	1951-55	–	59	–	11	–	–	–	–	31	41
	1956-60	–	96	–	–	–	–	–	–	4	69
	1961-65	30	55	7	–	–	–	–	–	8	53
	1966-70	–	88	1	7	2	2	–	–	0	136
	1971-75	–	89	5	–	1	–	–	0	4	230
	1976-80	97	2	0	–	0	–	–	0	1	2 447
	1981-85	88	–	–	–	–	–	–	7	5	488
Gabon	1961-65	–	–	100	–	–	–	–	–	–	3
	1966-70	–	9	47	–	–	–	–	–	44	36
	1971-75	–	76	24	–	–	–	–	–	–	70
	1976-80	–	46	39	–	–	–	–	4	12	225
	1981-85	–	31	51	–	–	–	–	16	3	197
Gambia	1981-85	–	–	–	76	–	–	–	–	24	3
Ghana	1956-60	–	–	–	69	–	–	–	11	21	9
	1961-65	48	–	–	44	–	–	–	–	9	144
	1966-70	–	9	4	36	–	51	–	–	–	30
	1971-75	–	7	5	29	13	–	–	–	48	106
	1976-80	–	10	–	–	39	16	–	–	35	121
	1981-85	–	–	–	–	–	100	–	–	–	6

Recipient region/country	Period	Supplier									Total in 1985 US $m.
		USSR	USA	France	UK	FR Germany	Italy	China	Third World	Other	
Guatemala	1951-55	–	100	–	–	–	–	–	–	–	7
	1956-60	–	73	–	–	–	–	–	–	27	14
	1961-65	–	100	–	–	–	–	–	–	–	10
	1966-70	–	100	–	–	–	–	–	–	–	10
	1971-75	–	74	3	–	–	–	–	23	0	64
	1976-80	–	63	4	–	–	–	–	18	16	49
	1981-85	–	83	–	–	–	–	–	5	12	45
Guinea	1956-60	87	–	–	–	–	–	–	–	13	38
	1961-65	98	2	–	–	–	–	–	–	0	17
	1966-70	97	–	3	–	–	–	–	–	0	17
	1971-75	24	–	6	–	–	–	42	–	27	41
	1976-80	79	–	4	–	–	–	17	–	0	62
	1981-85	63	–	0	–	–	–	24	10	3	41
Guinea Bissau	1971-75	100	–	–	–	–	–	–	–	–	4
	1976-80	90	–	0	–	–	–	–	8	1	98
	1981-85	21	–	1	–	–	–	3	–	75	49
Guyana	1966-70	–	100	–	–	–	–	–	–	–	0
	1971-75	–	22	27	51	–	–	–	–	–	7
	1976-80	–	51	–	29	–	–	–	20	–	24
	1981-85	4	–	–	13	–	–	–	70	13	20
Haiti	1951-55	–	100	–	–	–	–	–	–	–	1
	1956-60	–	100	–	–	–	–	–	–	–	7
	1966-70	–	100	–	–	–	–	–	–	–	1
	1971-75	–	100	–	–	–	–	–	–	–	8
	1976-80	–	86	–	–	–	–	–	–	14	4
	1981-85	–	6	–	5	–	79	–	–	10	13
Honduras	1951-55	–	100	–	–	–	–	–	–	–	9
	1956-60	–	100	–	–	–	–	–	–	–	16
	1961-65	–	100	–	–	–	–	–	–	–	5
	1966-70	–	27	–	–	–	–	–	73	0	8
	1971-75	–	100	–	–	–	–	–	–	–	23
	1976-80	–	39	–	–	–	–	–	41	21	96
	1981-85	–	65	–	9	–	–	–	12	14	93
India	1951-55	0	9	31	60	–	–	–	–	0	683
	1956-60	–	0	19	81	–	–	–	–	0	2 272
	1961-65	41	9	7	38	–	–	–	0	5	1 337
	1966-70	68	–	6	21	1	–	–	–	4	2 735
	1971-75	73	0	2	19	–	0	–	–	6	3 740
	1976-80	82	1	4	11	–	–	–	–	2	5 094
	1981-85	68	1	10	22	–	–	–	–	0	8 657
Indonesia	1951-55	–	37	–	4	6	–	–	–	53	172
	1956-60	11	11	–	2	16	13	–	–	47	999
	1961-65	78	11	1	3	–	–	–	0	7	1 422
	1966-70	–	73	14	10	–	–	–	–	3	76
	1971-75	–	56	–	–	–	–	–	0	44	321
	1976-80	–	24	46	3	1	–	–	6	20	1 645
	1981-85	–	36	13	14	15	–	–	8	14	1 343
Iran	1951-55	–	99	–	–	–	–	–	–	1	54
	1956-60	–	52	–	0	–	–	–	–	48	478
	1961-65	–	100	0	–	–	–	–	–	–	1 203
	1966-70	12	85	1	2	–	1	–	–	–	2 866
	1971-75	–	67	2	28	1	1	–	–	1	9 744
	1976-80	2	89	4	1	–	3	–	0	0	10 473
	1981-85	–	–	7	10	–	3	58	18	3	1 868

Recipient region/country	Period	Supplier									Total in 1985 US $m.
		USSR	USA	France	UK	FR Germany	Italy	China	Third World	Other	
Iraq	1951-55	–	–	–	100	–	–	–	–	0	71
	1956-60	78	4	–	10	–	–	–	8	0	257
	1961-65	75	–	–	25	–	–	–	–	–	729
	1966-70	88	–	4	2	–	–	–	0	6	787
	1971-75	97	–	2	0	–	–	–	–	–	2 042
	1976-80	85	–	10	–	0	–	–	3	2	5 559
	1981-85	55	1	22	0	0	6	2	12	3	15 170
Israel	1951-55	–	9	54	31	–	–	–	–	6	253
	1956-60	–	2	78	11	10	–	–	–	–	387
	1961-65	–	21	66	7	6	–	–	–	0	807
	1966-70	–	81	13	5	1	0	–	0	0	3 423
	1971-75	–	96	–	4	0	–	–	–	–	6 368
	1976-80	–	99	–	1	0	–	–	–	0	4 938
	1981-85	–	100	–	–	–	–	–	–	0	3 837
Jamaica	1961-65	–	38	–	62	–	–	–	–	–	2
	1966-70	–	–	–	–	–	–	–	–	100	1
	1971-75	–	99	–	1	–	–	–	–	0	22
	1976-80	–	64	–	36	–	–	–	–	0	6
	1981-85	–	100	–	–	–	–	–	–	–	2
Jordan	1951-55	–	–	–	99	–	–	–	–	1	34
	1956-60	–	22	–	69	–	–	–	9	0	71
	1961-65	–	16	5	79	–	–	–	–	–	101
	1966-70	–	46	3	48	–	–	–	3	0	438
	1971-75	–	75	–	11	–	–	–	14	1	562
	1976-80	–	99	–	0	–	–	–	1	0	1 908
	1981-85	8	33	31	17	–	–	–	1	10	2 363
Kampuchea	1951-55	–	–	87	–	–	–	–	–	13	8
	1956-60	–	67	33	–	–	–	–	–	0	21
	1961-65	24	14	28	–	–	–	6	–	27	123
	1966-70	8	13	7	–	–	–	73	–	–	95
	1971-75	–	99	–	–	–	–	–	–	1	241
	1976-80	7	–	–	–	–	–	93	–	–	175
	1981-85	100	–	–	–	–	–	–	–	–	20
Kenya	1961-65	–	–	–	100	–	–	–	–	–	9
	1966-70	–	16	33	44	–	–	–	–	7	7
	1971-75	–	1	5	91	–	–	–	–	3	76
	1976-80	–	21	13	45	4	–	–	–	17	521
	1981-85	–	23	23	33	–	–	–	21	–	223
Korea, North	1951-55	89	1	–	–	–	–	10	–	–	696
	1956-60	32	–	–	–	–	–	68	–	–	1 972
	1961-65	80	–	–	–	–	–	20	–	0	190
	1966-70	97	–	–	–	–	–	3	–	–	1 133
	1971-75	77	–	–	–	–	–	23	–	–	1 124
	1976-80	72	–	–	–	–	–	28	–	–	556
	1981-85	82	3	–	–	–	–	15	–	0	1 130
Korea, South	1951-55	–	99	–	–	–	–	–	–	1	496
	1956-60	–	100	–	–	–	–	–	–	–	675
	1961-65	–	100	–	–	–	–	–	–	–	603
	1966-70	–	100	–	–	–	–	–	–	0	1 091
	1971-75	–	98	2	–	–	–	–	–	–	1 185
	1976-80	–	95	3	1	–	1	–	–	–	3 020
	1981-85	–	97	–	–	–	1	–	1	0	1 314

Recipient region/country	Period	Supplier									Total in 1985 US $m.
		USSR	USA	France	UK	FR Germany	Italy	China	Third World	Other	
Kuwait	1951-55	–	–	–	100	–	–	–	–	–	1
	1956-60	–	–	–	100	–	–	–	–	–	27
	1961-65	–	–	–	100	–	–	–	–	–	98
	1966-70	–	–	1	95	–	2	–	–	2	134
	1971-75	–	55	27	17	–	–	–	1	–	345
	1976-80	11	42	29	17	–	–	–	0	–	1 663
	1981-85	5	30	36	7	22	–	–	–	0	1 327
Laos	1951-55	–	–	100	–	–	–	–	–	–	4
	1956-60	13	67	20	–	–	–	–	–	0	8
	1961-65	8	80	11	–	–	–	–	–	–	36
	1966-70	–	81	–	–	–	–	–	19	–	29
	1971-75	51	47	–	–	–	–	–	–	1	46
	1976-80	100	–	–	–	–	–	–	–	–	150
	1981-85	100	–	–	–	–	–	–	–	–	186
Lebanon	1951-55	–	–	–	99	–	1	–	–	1	13
	1956-60	–	34	26	38	–	–	–	0	2	63
	1961-65	–	48	16	25	–	–	–	11	–	59
	1966-70	–	10	90	–	–	–	–	–	0	93
	1971-75	6	46	29	14	–	5	–	–	0	96
	1976-80	–	25	23	49	–	4	–	–	–	146
	1981-85	–	63	30	–	–	–	–	6	–	480
Lesotho	1976-80	–	–	–	83	17	–	–	–	–	6
	1981-85	–	–	–	–	–	76	–	–	24	2
Liberia	1956-60	–	95	–	–	–	–	–	5	0	4
	1966-70	–	100	–	–	–	–	–	–	–	0
	1971-75	–	100	–	–	–	–	–	–	–	1
	1976-80	–	100	–	–	–	–	–	–	–	5
	1981-85	–	4	–	–	–	–	–	96	–	13
Libya	1956-60	–	11	–	86	–	–	–	3	0	7
	1961-65	–	77	8	15	–	–	–	–	0	30
	1966-70	6	21	1	72	–	–	–	1	–	481
	1971-75	64	2	31	2	–	2	–	–	0	2 804
	1976-80	79	1	9	0	–	4	–	5	2	11 725
	1981-85	61	1	13	–	–	21	–	2	3	5 721
Madagascar	1961-65	–	–	100	–	–	–	–	–	–	5
	1966-70	–	–	95	5	–	–	–	–	–	12
	1971-75	–	21	79	–	–	–	–	–	–	1
	1976-80	23	–	5	6	–	–	–	62	4	66
	1981-85	78	–	7	–	–	–	–	16	–	36
Malawi	1966-70	59	–	–	41	–	–	–	–	0	3
	1971-75	–	–	–	–	–	–	–	100	–	1
	1976-80	–	2	71	5	23	–	–	–	–	55
	1981-85	9	–	4	68	19	–	–	–	–	21
Malaysia	1956-60	–	–	–	100	–	–	–	–	–	16
	1961-65	–	–	14	81	–	–	–	–	4	114
	1966-70	–	22	5	37	–	–	–	–	36	262
	1971-75	–	22	48	18	–	–	–	0	12	547
	1976-80	–	49	7	9	17	1	–	–	17	918
	1981-85	–	19	3	4	41	7	–	11	15	1 031

Recipient region/country	Period	Supplier									Total in 1985 US $m.
		USSR	USA	France	UK	FR Germany	Italy	China	Third World	Other	
Mali	1961-65	95	4	–	–	–	–	–	–	1	13
	1966-70	100	–	–	–	–	–	–	–	–	9
	1971-75	100	–	–	–	–	–	–	–	–	1
	1976-80	78	–	–	–	–	–	22	–	0	5
	1981-85	97	–	3	–	–	–	–	–	–	78
Mauritania	1956-60	–	–	100	–	–	–	–	–	–	1
	1961-65	–	–	100	–	–	–	–	–	–	3
	1971-75	56	–	44	–	–	–	–	–	–	9
	1976-80	–	4	6	37	–	–	–	–	54	63
	1981-85	–	8	57	–	–	–	–	–	35	17
Mauritius	1966-70	–	100	–	–	–	–	–	–	–	0
	1971-75	–	–	–	22	–	–	–	78	–	2
	1976-80	–	–	100	–	–	–	–	–	–	3
	1981-85	100	–	–	–	–	–	–	–	–	1
Mexico	1951-55	–	100	–	–	–	–	–	–	–	30
	1956-60	–	72	–	–	–	–	–	–	28	51
	1961-65	–	82	6	0	9	–	–	–	2	207
	1966-70	–	95	–	–	–	–	–	–	5	152
	1971-75	–	67	–	29	–	–	–	5	0	221
	1976-80	–	17	39	29	–	–	–	7	8	160
	1981-85	–	37	5	2	1	–	–	2	53	611
Morocco	1956-60	–	–	94	–	–	–	–	6	0	48
	1961-65	32	22	41	–	–	–	–	4	0	101
	1966-70	6	39	17	–	7	2	–	8	21	241
	1971-75	–	81	2	–	–	11	–	–	6	169
	1976-80	0	34	59	–	0	1	–	1	5	2 638
	1981-85	0	34	35	1	1	2	–	6	21	1 491
Mozambique	1971-75	–	–	–	–	–	–	–	–	100	9
	1976-80	99	–	–	–	–	–	–	–	1	779
	1981-85	100	–	–	–	–	–	–	–	–	517
Nepal	1961-65	95	–	–	5	–	–	–	–	0	2
	1966-70	–	–	–	36	–	–	–	33	31	7
	1976-80	–	–	52	39	–	–	–	7	2	27
	1981-85	–	–	–	100	–	–	–	–	–	3
Nicaragua	1951-55	–	39	–	–	–	–	–	–	61	30
	1956-60	–	100	–	–	–	–	–	–	–	5
	1961-65	–	100	–	–	–	–	–	–	–	1
	1966-70	–	100	–	–	–	–	–	–	–	21
	1971-75	–	27	–	–	–	–	–	73	–	41
	1976-80	–	44	–	–	–	–	–	17	39	33
	1981-85	71	–	1	–	–	–	–	26	2	200
Niger	1961-65	–	–	100	–	–	–	–	–	–	7
	1966-70	–	–	100	–	–	–	–	–	–	1
	1971-75	–	3	5	–	91	–	–	–	–	13
	1976-80	–	90	4	– .	5	–	–	–	–	70
	1981-85	–	–	58	–	42	–	–	–	0	12
Nigeria	1956-60	–	–	–	100	–	–	–	–	–	1
	1961-65	–	–	–	9	10	–	–	–	81	83
	1966-70	50	1	2	12	–	13	–	3	20	173
	1971-75	–	24	–	41	12	–	–	–	23	269
	1976-80	33	10	10	34	11	–	–	–	3	691
	1981-85	6	4	28	17	29	10	–	0	6	2 182

Recipient region/country	Period	Supplier									Total in 1985 US $m.
		USSR	USA	France	UK	FR Germany	Italy	China	Third World	Other	
Oman	1956-60	–	–	–	100	–	–	–	–	–	2
	1961-65	–	–	–	89	–	–	–	–	11	4
	1966-70	–	9	–	83	–	–	–	–	8	48
	1971-75	–	12	–	59	–	3	–	23	3	301
	1976-80	0	1	4	92	–	0	–	1	2	535
	1981-85	–	18	20	61	–	–	1	0	0	883
Pakistan	1951-55	–	27	–	73	–	–	–	–	–	385
	1956-60	–	61	–	39	–	–	–	–	–	650
	1961-65	–	87	–	4	1	–	8	–	0	350
	1966-70	13	1	23	1	1	–	31	30	1	1 079
	1971-75	1	5	26	0	0	–	58	6	2	1 288
	1976-80	–	15	53	–	0	–	30	–	2	1 821
	1981-85	–	54	9	8	–	–	27	–	1	2 569
Panama	1961-65	–	100	–	–	–	–	–	–	–	0
	1966-70	–	78	–	–	–	–	–	–	22	3
	1971-75	–	85	–	13	–	–	–	–	2	71
	1976-80	–	34	57	9	–	–	–	–	0	30
	1981-85	–	84	–	–	–	–	–	–	16	52
Papua New Guinea	1976-80	–	–	–	–	–	–	–	–	100	6
	1981-85	–	–	–	–	–	–	–	46	54	14
Paraguay	1951-55	–	100	–	–	–	–	–	–	–	3
	1956-60	–	33	–	–	–	–	–	67	0	3
	1961-65	–	93	–	–	–	–	–	7	–	90
	1966-70	–	72	–	–	–	–	–	20	7	10
	1971-75	–	10	–	–	–	–	–	90	–	25
	1976-80	–	65	–	–	–	–	–	35	–	27
	1981-85	–	–	–	–	–	–	–	85	15	36
Peru	1951-55	–	100	–	–	–	–	–	–	0	92
	1956-60	–	36	1	63	–	–	–	–	–	280
	1961-65	–	78	17	5	–	–	–	–	0	301
	1966-70	–	22	42	35	–	–	–	–	0	266
	1971-75	3	38	15	–	0	–	–	–	43	643
	1976-80	37	9	15	1	3	19	–	2	14	2 914
	1981-85	7	11	30	–	9	25	–	1	17	1 879
Philippines	1951-55	–	100	–	–	–	–	–	–	–	23
	1956-60	–	81	–	–	–	–	–	–	19	163
	1961-65	–	76	–	–	–	8	–	–	16	99
	1966-70	–	85	–	–	–	–	–	–	15	117
	1971-75	–	78	–	2	2	5	–	3	11	379
	1976-80	–	90	–	3	3	–	–	–	3	603
	1981-85	–	82	–	7	2	6	–	–	3	355
Qatar	1966-70	–	–	–	100	–	–	–	–	–	25
	1971-75	–	–	7	93	–	–	–	–	–	30
	1976-80	–	–	77	17	–	–	–	6	–	166
	1981-85	–	–	89	11	–	–	–	0	0	934
Rwanda	1961-65	–	7	–	–	16	–	–	–	77	1
	1966-70	–	–	100	–	–	–	–	–	–	1
	1971-75	–	–	85	–	2	8	–	–	5	10
	1976-80	–	–	–	100	–	–	–	–	–	2
	1981-85	–	–	100	–	–	–	–	–	–	8

Recipient region/country	Period	Supplier									Total in 1985 US $m.
		USSR	USA	France	UK	FR Germany	Italy	China	Third World	Other	
Saudi Arabia	1951-55	–	74	–	26	–	–	–	–	0	9
	1956-60	–	92	–	2	–	–	–	6	–	90
	1961-65	–	93	–	7	–	–	–	–	0	45
	1966-70	–	35	6	53	5	1	–	0	0	984
	1971-75	–	86	12	2	–	–	–	–	–	1 070
	1976-80	–	75	22	2	–	1	–	–	1	4 218
	1981-85	–	73	25	1	–	0	–	1	0	7 147
Senegal	1956-60	–	–	100	–	–	–	–	–	–	1
	1961-65	–	–	100	–	–	–	–	–	–	6
	1966-70	–	–	100	–	–	–	–	–	–	3
	1971-75	–	–	100	–	–	–	–	–	–	23
	1976-80	–	16	84	–	–	–	–	–	–	60
	1981-85	–	–	94	–	–	–	–	–	6	31
Seychelles	1976-80	28	–	48	21	–	–	–	3	–	7
	1981-85	11	–	–	–	–	67	–	22	–	16
Sierra Leone	1971-75	–	7	–	–	–	–	70	–	23	7
	1976-80	–	–	–	–	55	–	–	–	45	3
	1981-85	–	–	60	40	–	–	–	–	–	3
Singapore	1956-60	–	–	–	100	–	–	–	–	–	3
	1961-65	–	–	–	96	–	–	–	4	0	1
	1966-70	–	11	8	71	–	–	–	8	3	102
	1971-75	–	19	–	47	24	1	–	9	0	943
	1976-80	–	76	2	12	–	0	–	3	6	836
	1981-85	–	73	13	4	–	2	–	–	8	699
Somalia	1956-60	–	–	–	–	–	80	–	20	–	8
	1961-65	90	–	–	9	–	1	–	0	–	44
	1966-70	95	3	–	–	–	2	–	–	–	52
	1971-75	100	–	–	–	–	–	–	–	–	516
	1976-80	17	11	1	–	0	47	15	10	0	268
	1981-85	–	59	–	–	–	16	19	7	0	521
Sri Lanka	1951-55	–	–	–	100	–	–	–	–	–	6
	1956-60	–	–	–	48	–	–	–	52	–	29
	1961-65	–	3	–	97	–	–	–	–	–	6
	1966-70	–	100	–	–	–	–	–	–	–	2
	1971-75	59	12	–	10	–	–	19	–	–	45
	1976-80	–	–	37	–	–	–	63	–	0	14
	1981-85	–	45	–	–	–	–	–	55	–	72
Sudan	1956-60	11	–	–	72	–	–	–	17	–	22
	1961-65	–	14	–	22	17	10	–	–	37	87
	1966-70	87	2	–	1	–	–	–	–	10	322
	1971-75	27	–	–	–	–	–	73	–	–	37
	1976-80	–	48	15	–	12	–	3	–	22	209
	1981-85	–	45	4	1	–	1	3	35	11	347
Suriname	1976-80	–	–	–	100	–	–	–	–	–	15
	1981-85	–	20	–	34	–	–	–	46	–	8
Swaziland	1976-80	–	–	–	–	–	–	–	100	–	4
	1981-85	–	–	–	–	–	–	–	100	–	2

Recipient region/country	Period	Supplier									Total in 1985 US $m.
		USSR	USA	France	UK	FR Germany	Italy	China	Third World	Other	
Syria	1951-55	30	3	3	27	–	38	–	–	–	91
	1956-60	95	1	–	2	–	–	–	–	2	399
	1961-65	100	–	–	–	–	–	–	–	–	63
	1966-70	93	–	–	0	–	–	–	1	6	1 783
	1971-75	100	–	–	–	–	–	–	–	0	6 514
	1976-80	87	–	2	–	–	–	–	8	3	4 041
	1981-85	97	–	0	–	–	–	–	2	1	10 030
Taiwan	1951-55	–	98	–	–	–	–	–	–	2	987
	1956-60	–	97	–	–	–	–	–	–	3	2 106
	1961-65	–	100	–	–	–	–	–	–	–	566
	1966-70	–	98	–	–	–	–	–	–	2	1 503
	1971-75	–	99	–	–	–	–	–	1	–	1 236
	1976-80	–	95	–	–	–	–	–	5	–	1 745
	1981-85	–	77	–	–	–	–	–	23	–	2 665
Tanzania	1961-65	–	–	–	–	12	–	–	–	88	7
	1966-70	10	–	–	–	–	–	67	–	23	10
	1971-75	–	0	–	2	–	0	94	–	4	263
	1976-80	47	1	–	13	–	1	15	1	22	206
	1981-85	–	1	–	–	–	5	81	0	13	165
Thailand	1951-55	–	98	–	2	–	–	–	–	0	172
	1956-60	–	100	–	–	–	–	–	–	–	66
	1961-65	–	91	–	2	6	–	–	–	1	219
	1966-70	–	96	–	–	–	–	–	–	4	276
	1971-75	–	81	–	15	–	1	–	2	1	527
	1976-80	–	69	4	1	1	12	–	11	2	1 171
	1981-85	–	50	1	8	0	24	2	5	10	1 082
Togo	1961-65	–	–	100	–	–	–	–	–	–	2
	1966-70	–	–	100	–	–	–	–	–	–	1
	1971-75	–	16	81	–	2	–	–	–	0	3
	1976-80	–	23	35	–	3	–	–	9	31	115
	1981-85	–	–	66	–	–	–	–	34	–	59
Trinidad & Tobago	1966-70	–	–	–	100	–	–	–	–	–	8
	1971-75	–	–	–	100	–	–	–	–	–	8
	1976-80	–	0	4	–	–	–	–	–	96	83
	1981-85	–	100	–	–	–	–	–	–	–	6
Tunisia	1956-60	–	12	84	–	–	–	–	–	4	43
	1961-65	–	15	18	9	–	53	–	–	4	33
	1966-70	–	36	57	–	7	–	–	–	–	61
	1971-75	–	29	53	–	–	18	–	–	–	35
	1976-80	–	23	4	5	–	36	2	–	30	191
	1981-85	–	49	48	–	–	–	–	3	0	646
Uganda	1961-65	–	–	–	85	11	–	–	4	–	6
	1966-70	25	9	–	–	–	–	–	10	56	46
	1971-75	65	8	–	–	–	1	–	26	0	228
	1976-80	20	7	–	–	–	–	–	72	1	213
	1981-85	–	89	–	–	–	11	–	–	0	14
United Arab Emirates	1966-70	–	0	–	84	–	1	–	–	16	53
	1971-75	–	11	73	13	1	0	–	–	1	447
	1976-80	–	–	68	7	12	5	–	–	8	757
	1981-85	–	38	27	10	13	6	–	3	3	1 340

Recipient region/country	Period	Supplier									Total in 1985 US $m.
		USSR	USA	France	UK	FR Germany	Italy	China	Third World	Other	
Uruguay	1951-55	–	100	–	–	–	–	–	–	0	45
	1956-60	–	100	–	–	–	–	–	–	–	35
	1961-65	–	100	–	–	–	–	–	–	–	18
	1966-70	–	75	10	–	–	–	–	–	15	31
	1971-75	–	100	–	–	–	–	–	–	–	37
	1976-80	–	35	–	–	34	–	–	31	–	55
	1981-85	–	37	20	–	–	–	–	23	20	144
Venezuela	1951-55	–	10	1	89	–	–	–	–	–	497
	1956-60	–	18	–	48	–	35	–	–	0	511
	1961-65	–	44	–	56	–	–	–	–	–	92
	1966-70	–	34	12	9	44	–	–	–	0	144
	1971-75	–	33	35	9	–	6	–	–	17	997
	1976-80	–	35	8	1	19	35	–	3	0	765
	1981-85	–	25	1	–	0	62	–	5	7	2 324
Viet Nam	1971-75	100	–	–	–	–	–	–	–	–	40
	1976-80	100	–	–	–	–	–	–	–	–	4 499
	1981-85	100	–	–	–	–	–	–	–	–	1 801
Vietnam, North	1951-55	100	–	–	–	–	–	–	–	–	6
	1956-60	72	–	–	–	–	–	28	–	–	30
	1961-65	73	–	–	–	–	–	27	–	–	197
	1966-70	92	–	–	–	–	–	8	–	0	4 194
	1971-75	92	–	–	–	–	–	8	–	0	2 456
Vietnam, South	1951-55	–	28	71	–	–	–	–	–	1	52
	1956-60	–	39	57	–	–	–	–	–	4	61
	1961-65	–	98	–	–	–	–	–	–	2	399
	1966-70	–	100	–	–	–	–	–	–	–	1 713
	1971-75	–	98	–	–	–	–	–	2	0	4 690
Yemen, North	1951-55	–	92	–	–	–	–	–	8	0	2
	1956-60	37	–	–	–	–	–	–	–	63	49
	1961-65	96	3	–	–	–	1	–	–	–	15
	1966-70	93	–	–	7	–	–	–	–	0	101
	1971-75	–	–	–	–	–	11	–	89	–	8
	1976-80	60	39	–	–	–	–	–	1	–	1 016
	1981-85	95	1	–	–	–	0	–	–	4	271
Yemen, South	1966-70	77	–	–	22	–	–	–	–	1	105
	1971-75	100	–	–	–	–	–	–	–	–	310
	1976-80	98	–	–	–	–	–	–	–	2	1 123
	1981-85	100	–	–	–	–	–	–	–	–	369
Zaire	1956-60	72	–	–	–	–	–	–	–	28	18
	1961-65	–	79	8	5	1	1	–	2	4	155
	1966-70	–	53	8	–	0	37	–	–	2	102
	1971-75	–	36	59	–	–	3	–	0	1	310
	1976-80	–	13	8	–	–	15	34	8	22	151
	1981-85	–	1	22	25	–	7	30	14	0	50
Zambia	1961-65	–	–	–	12	–	–	–	6	82	24
	1966-70	–	–	–	72	–	28	–	–	0	8
	1971-75	–	–	–	55	8	32	–	–	5	171
	1976-80	49	–	4	8	–	1	22	–	16	370
	1981-85	95	0	–	–	–	4	0	–	–	239

Recipient region/country	Period	Supplier									Total in 1985 US $m.
		USSR	USA	France	UK	FR Germany	Italy	China	Third World	Other	
Zimbabwe	1951-55	–	–	–	100	–	–	–	–	–	59
	1956-60	–	–	–	97	–	–	–	–	3	123
	1961-65	–	–	16	84	–	–	–	–	0	49
	1966-70	–	5	–	–	–	36	–	59	–	6
	1971-75	–	–	–	–	–	–	–	100	–	30
	1976-80	0	–	0	7	–	6	–	86	–	77
	1981-85	–	–	–	55	–	1	6	28	9	182

Appendix 8. The SIPRI price system

I. Introduction

The aggregation of disparate data requires a common unit of measurement. Only one such unit is available for weapon systems—monetary value. Despite many efforts there is no measure of military-use value as such.[1]

The purpose of SIPRI's valuation method for the arms trade is to measure changes in the total flow of weapons and its geographical pattern. In order to do this, the prices used by SIPRI cannot always be equal to the prices actually paid, since these vary considerably from case to case (see also appendix 9, section III). The price of an F-16 fighter aircraft, for example, varied in the mid-1980s from zero (when supplied as military aid to Egypt), to $9.7 million (US Navy fly-away cost for a simplified version), to $15 million (US Air Force fly-away cost), to $21 million (US Air Force average unit programme acquisition cost) to $35 million (average unit cost for the Singaporean Air Force, including spares and support).[2]

Matters are further complicated by inflation, currency conversion problems, training costs and the wide range of weapon types available. How, for example, can a reasonable price relation be established between a US nuclear-powered aircraft carrier and a Chilean armoured personnel carrier?

SIPRI has designed its own price system for the valuation of the flow of major conventional weapons. This price system was first introduced in 1968 and has since undergone a major revision. The purpose of this appendix is to describe this revision.

II. SIPRI rules

One assumption and one convention constitute the core of the SIPRI price system. The assumption is that there is a competitive global market for armaments and that—over a wide range of arms deals—actual prices paid approximate to the military-use value of the weapons. The convention is that among the various prices of a weapon system—including or excluding R&D outlays, support, spares and so on—the unit production cost is chosen. To the cost of producing one unit as part of a long production run is then added a percentage to represent the average cost of armaments (unless separately priced), spares, support and so on.

There are problems both with the assumption and the convention. There is in many areas and sectors no competitive arms market. Often the distinction between unit production cost and other cost levels is impossible to make. These two basic rules are only guidelines.

The 1968 prices

The original price system was constructed from a long list of comparable prices in 1968 US dollars.[3] These prices were then grouped into four weapon categories and 27 sub-categories. Within each sub-category, the prices obtained were compared with such performance criteria as weight, speed and role of the weapon. A price reflecting these criteria was set, both for weapons for which prices were available and for those weapons for which no price figure existed. A percentage was added to reflect costs for spare parts, and so on. The percentage varied with different weapon types. Ships were valued differently: for each sub-category a 1968 US dollar price per ton was estimated. In addition, a technical improvement factor of 3.5 per cent per year was assumed. Each ship traded thus received an individual price depending on sub-category, displacement and year of transfer. Second-hand and refurbished ships were treated separately. An exponential depreciation was assumed, with different time lengths for different sub-categories. For the other weapon categories, blanket percentage assumptions were used in determining prices for second-hand and refurbished weapons.

Later additions

Prices for weapon systems introduced into SIPRI's arms trade data collection after 1968 were estimated in the same way as for the original price system. Existing prices were continuously updated as new data became known. In order to get more recent base years, the total price system was updated by applying a weighted average of British, French and US wholesale price indexes, first to 1973 and then to 1975.

With the computerization of the data base, the special valuation of ships was changed. Ships were grouped into individual ship classes and these classes received new, second-hand and refurbished prices. These prices were calculated using the 1968 prices per ton, multiplied by the appropriate technical improvement factor.

III. Price system revision

The main reason why a revision was necessary was the constantly changing relations between prices, often caused by changes in the mix of inputs of labour, capital and pre-products. New production technologies also affect input mixes and prices. Another very important factor is the embodiment of new technologies and materials, particularly for weapon systems. An example is given in figure 8A.1, showing the high and increasing share of electronics in the cost of military aircraft.

Additional reasons for the price system revision were the introduction of a new weapon category (see appendix 9) and a wish to use the same valuation method for all weapon categories.

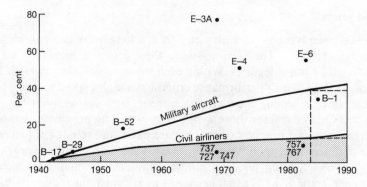

Figure 8A.1. Electronics as a percentage of total programme costs

Source: Aviation Week and Space Technology, 2 Dec. 1985, p. 96 (based on Boeing Aircraft Company data).

Some early decisions had to be made concerning the collection and systematization of the data. A first decision concerned deflation and currency conversion; another concerned the choice of estimation method.

Currency conversion

The prices for weapon systems quoted in government papers, journals and so on, are normally expressed in current prices and national currencies. They have to be converted into a common currency and deflated to an appropriate base year.

The rule used for currency conversion follows from the basic assumption mentioned above. The conversion is made for the year to which the quoted price refers. The US dollar was chosen as the standard currency—it is the most frequently used currency in arms sales. The ordinary exchange rate (average market rate) is used.

The choice of the US dollar has another advantage. It allows for the use of special military price deflators for the different SIPRI weapon categories. Such deflators are only available for a few countries, but they are to be preferred to other price deflators such as consumer price index or GNP deflators.[4]

Deflation

The variation in price over time of a unit such as one ton of a weapon system (or a succession of weapon systems performing similar tasks) can be attributed to three components of change: (*a*) changes in the input mix, (*b*) changes in the production process and (*c*) changes in the military-use value of the product.

The first component concerns changes in the prices of raw materials, preproducts and labour as well as changing profit margins and interest rates. To the extent that the input mix in the production of weapon systems is different from the inputs used to calculate other available deflators, military price deflators will vary. This difference varies from one weapon category to another—and within weapon categories—with the use of specialized labour, special materials and costly pre-products, such as advanced electronics.

The second component that changes over time—the production process—tends in most cases to lower prices. The introduction of better tools and machinery and the growing experience of workers all make production progressively more efficient and thus less expensive. Another element influencing the production cost is the number of items produced in a given time period. Differences in the price of a weapon system owing to varying lengths of production runs can be quite substantial.[5] Since the number of items produced varies from year to year, the influence of this factor on a deflator is erratic and not representative of changes in production costs. Its effects should therefore be eliminated to the largest possible extent in the construction of a deflator.

The US military price deflators are designed to capture these two types of effect, thus eliminating them from the measurement of real price changes of weapon systems.

The third influence on prices remains outside the deflator, since it reflects real changes in the product. The extent to which the US authorities are able to distinguish between the various components of price change is a matter of debate. However, the military price deflators are not very different from the broader ones mentioned, and they are much lower than the increases of prices quoted for individual weapon systems.[6] This third factor was called the technical improvement factor in the 1968 SIPRI price system. Deflating quoted prices with the US military price deflator implies the assumption that price increases to a considerable extent result from qualitative improvements.

Parametric costing

A second decision referred to the extent to which the revision of the price system should be based on the use of statistical estimation techniques. In the 1960s, the use of mathematical equations for estimating the cost of weapon systems became widespread in the US Department of Defense. There were two main reasons: the availability of computers and the general trend to introduce more systematic judgement in procurement decisions. The main use of the various models, developed by the RAND Corporation and other 'braintrust' contractors, was in the projection of costs of future weapons. With the help of these models, unknown future costs could be estimated and, for example, used to judge tenders by prospective contractors.[7] Such models are probably also in wide use in order to estimate prices of weapon systems in the Soviet Union and in other countries.

In most models, physical parameters of weapon systems—such as weight, speed and thrust of engines or the extent of high-cost materials embodied—are used as independent variables in a regression analysis, with the known price as a dependent variable. The resulting coefficients for the various parameters can then be multiplied by the physical parameters of a weapon system for which the price is unknown.

Regression equations using only the two parameters weight and speed have been found to give a good fit for weapon systems such as fighter aircraft. The introduction of more complex equations has not added to the confidence in the price estimates.

Parametric costing is a very mechanistic pricing method. The more that is known about a weapon system—its characteristics, uses and prices involved—the less relevant parametric costing becomes. It can therefore only be used as a guideline: it cannot substitute for examination of the specific weapon system. For the purpose of SIPRI's price system revision, it was decided to estimate equations, but to use them prudently, that is, only as a basis for further judgement of individual weapon prices.

Intra- and inter-generational price changes

It is widely believed that there is a distinct difference between the technical improvement during the life-cycle of a weapon system and the embodiment of technological improvements in new generations of weapon systems. While in the second case there is ample evidence of large improvement and thus real price increases, in the first case opinions are divided as to the level of improvement that takes place.[8]

With the SIPRI price system there is no problem in identifying improvements in successive generations since each weapon system becomes a separate entry in the register and, thus, gets its own price. Questions arise with respect to incorporations of new technology during the life-cycle of a weapon system. The SIPRI rule is a compromise: on the one hand, no technical improvement is automatically assumed for a weapon system within its life-cycle: on the other hand, whenever actual improvements do take place, a new version—or model—of the weapon system is introduced into the register. Each version has a different price. Substantial improvements can result from design changes, incorporation of different sub-systems or improved component performance. Often, such improvements are reflected in slightly different weapon designations given by the producer of the weapon system. There are, however, many borderline cases. Sometimes, differing designations do not reflect different capabilities and, sometimes, substantial improvements are made without any change in the weapon designation.

Procedures

As a first step, prices were collected from a large number of open sources over a period of more than two years. These were converted into dollars and deflated as described above. After examination and elimination of several prices for the same weapon system, newly-collected prices were available for approximately 550 weapon systems. These were then compared to the prices for the same weapons from the updated 1968 price system. After further detailed examination a final price for these weapons was determined.

Next. a regression analysis was performed. The weapon categories were divided into two groups of sub-categories (with a total of 16 and 90 weapon types, respectively) reflecting physical capabilities. Average prices were estimated for these weapon types on the basis of weight and first production year. Separate estimates were made for the 5 weapon categories and the two groups of sub-categories. In the end, average prices per unit of weight were taken from the sample with 90 weapon types. The technical improvement factor was taken from the most detailed categorization yielding significant results (see table 8A.1).

Prices were then estimated for those weapons that had not been included in the regression analysis. These estimates were compared with the price in the updated 1968 system. After case by case examination considering technical characteristics, military use value, market response and so on, the final price was settled. A complete set of new prices was sent to reviewers at the Swedish Defence Material Administration (FMV). Their comments are fully integrated in the new price system.

Table 8A.1. Percentage product improvement rates calculated from SIPRI arms production data base (rounded to next 0.5 per cent)

5 weapon categories		16 weapon types		90 weapon types[a]	
Aircraft	3.0	Fighter aircraft	3.5	Fighters	4.5
		Helicopters	5.5	Fighters/	
		Patrol aircraft	3.0	Interceptors	6.5
		Utility aircraft	4.5	Jet trainers	5.5
				Helicopters	5.5
				Trainers	2.5
				Transports	5.0
Armour and artillery	3.5	Light vehicles	1.5	APCs	0.5
		Artillery	5.0	MBTs	3.5
		Special vehicles	6.5		
		Tanks	4.0		
Guidance and radar systems	4.0	Ground radar, etc	4.0		
Missiles	5.5	Anti-air	4.5	AAMs	5.5
		Anti-surface	3.5	Landmob SAMs	6.0
		Anti-ship	7.0		
		Anti-tank	10.0		
Ships	3.0	Major ships	3.5	Destroyers	2.0
		Small combatants	2.0	Fast attack	
		Support ships	0.0	craft	3.0

[a]Only statistically significant results are given.
Source: SIPRI data base.

Mark-up for weapons, spares and initial support

Information was gathered on the cost of actual arms deals including goods and services in addition to the weapon system. The range of these additional costs is a wide one, ranging from less than 1 per cent and up to more than 100 per cent. An average mark-up of 25 per cent was decided upon.

Second-hand and refurbished weapons

The SIPRI data base has separate prices for second-hand and refurbished weapons. Again, the data collected showed a wide range of prices. It is doubtful whether the introduction of a depreciation procedure would improve the estimate of second-hand prices; in the case of refurbished weapons this is highly unlikely. Depreciation is highly dependent on the assumption made about depreciation rates and the form of depreciation (see table 8A.2). Not enough information on second-hand prices could be collected to make an empirically-based choice of depreciation form or rates. For reasons of simplicity in the calculation of second-hand values, it was decided to set all second-hand values at 40 per cent of the value of a new weapon system. With respect to refurbished weapons—where it is even more difficult to establish an empirical basis because of varying degrees of refurbishment—a blanket assumption of a value of 66 per cent of the new price was made.

IV. Effects of the new price system

The new price system re-establishes a comprehensive set of prices. Prices are now in 1985 US dollars. Some earlier estimating errors have been corrected. All

Table 8A.2. Average time span between introduction of major weapon systems and trade as second-hand or refurbished weapons and examples in implied rest values with different depreciation formulae

Weapon category	Refurbished (years)	Second-hand (years)	Implied rest values (%)					
			a	b	c	d	e	f
Aircraft	11.4	14.7	44	62	65	4	13	39
Armour and artillery	16.3	17.9	19	46	51	1	5	26
Missiles	Not applicable							
Ground radar, etc	Not available							
Ships	14.4	18.0	29	52	57	1	7	30

Implied rest values:
a) Life span 20 years, scrap value 1%, linear depreciation.
b) Life span 30 years, scrap value 1%, linear depreciation.
c) Life span 30 years, scrap value 10%, linear depreciation.
d) Life span 20 years, scrap value 1%, exponential depreciation.
e) Life span 30 years, scrap value 1%, exponential depreciation.
f) Life span 30 years, scrap value 10%, exponential depreciation.
Source: SIPRI data base.

prices are now based on the same deflators and currency conversion methods. As with all base year revisions, the change of base year from 1968 to 1985 created new price relations between years. In comparison with the old price system, the new system makes weapons produced in the 1970s and 1980s appear 'cheaper' than those produced earlier. This is not surprising since the 1985 prices better reflect the input mixes used for the production of weapons in the 1970s and 1980s. As a result, growth rates in the arms trade are reduced or, to put it differently, some of the increase in the arms trade (at constant prices) using the old price system resulted from inflation.

The relations between the prices of different weapon categories or of weapons from different producer/supplier countries have not changed much. The ratios between prices of weapons produced in NATO countries and WTO countries are approximately the same. Some types of ship have received higher prices since the technical improvement factor used earlier was too low. Other types have received lower prices.

Notes and references

[1] See Sköns, E., 'Military prices', in *World Armaments and Disarmament, SIPRI Yearbook 1983* (Taylor & Francis: London, 1983), pp. 195–211; and *GAO, Measures of Military Capability: a Discussion of their Merits, Limitations and Interrelationships*, GAO/NSIAD–85–75, 13 June 1985 (US General Accounting Office: Washington, DC, 1985).

[2] Fly-away costs are quoted from:
Department of Defense Appropriations for 1986, Hearings before a Subcommittee of the Committee on Appropriations, House of Representatives, 99th Congress (US Government Printing Office: Washington, DC, 1985), Part 2, p. 336; programme acquisition costs from: *Programme Acquisition Costs by Weapon System*, Department of Defense Budget for Fiscal Year 1986 (US Department of Defense: Washington, DC, 1985), p. 39; the price for the Singaporean Air Force from: Chanda, N., 'For you, US $280 million', *Far Eastern Economic Review*, 1 Aug. 1985, p. 31.

[3] The procedures involved in the production of the original price system are described in: SIPRI, *The Arms Trade with the Third World* (Almqvist & Wiksell: Stockholm, 1971), pp. 789–92; the procedures used to update the information thereafter is described in the appendices to the arms trade chapters in all *SIPRI Yearbooks*.

[4] A detailed analysis of military prices used in various countries is given in Sköns (note 1); the various aspects involved in constructing a military price deflator are described in: US Department of Commerce, Bureau of Economic Analysis, *Measuring Price Changes of Military Expenditures, Prepared for the US Arms Control and Disarmament Agency* (US Government Printing Office: Washington, DC, 1975). See also: US Congress, Congressional Budget Office, *Budgeting for Defense Inflation* (CBO: Washington, DC, 1986) and the various published deliberations of the UN expert group on the measurement and limitation of military expenditures, e.g., United Nations, Department of Disarmament Affairs, Report of the Secretary General, *Reduction of Military Budgets: Construction of Military Price Indexes and Purchasing-Power Parities for Comparison of Military Expenditures* (United Nations: New York, 1986), UN document A/40/421.

[5] Such differences were at the bottom of much political debate in the USA in the early 1980s. US procurement agencies had paid outrageous prices for single items, such as a $9609 wrench. The same wrench was quoted to cost only 12 cents when supplied from mass production, see Comeau, L., *Nuts and Bolts at the Pentagon: A Spare Parts Catalogue* (Defense Budget Project, Center on Budget and Policy Priorities: Washington, DC, 1974).

[6] See Sköns (note 1); also Maisonneuve, P., 'Prix des materiels d'armement', *Défense Nationale*, July 1980, pp. 65–80.

[7] A short overview can be found in: Large, J. P., *Development of Parametric Cost Models for Weapon Systems*, Rand Corporation, P–6604, Santa Monica, CA, Apr. 1981.

[8] See Sköns (note 1); Maisonneuve (note 6); Albrecht, U., 'Rüstung und Inflation' in Sonntag, P. (ed.), *Rüstung und Ökonomie* (Haag + Herchen: Frankfurt, 1982), pp. 209–36.

Appendix 9. Sources and methods

I. Introduction

When compared to earlier SIPRI assessments of the volume changes in the global flow of major conventional weapons, the methods employed in the preparation of this book incorporate two important changes. First, SIPRI has adopted a new price system. The reasons for this revision and the nature and methodology of the current system are described separately in appendix 8. Second, SIPRI has introduced a fifth weapon category—guidance and radar systems—in addition to those used earlier. This marks an attempt to adapt to the changing nature of the arms market so as to be able to cover as much as possible of the arms transfers that occur—especially in the field of electronics (see below).

II. Selection criteria

The SIPRI arms trade data cover five categories of 'major' weapons: aircraft, armour and artillery, guidance and radar systems, missiles and warships. The statistics presented refer to the value of the trade in these five categories only.

There are two criteria for the selection of major weapon items. The first is that of military application. The *aircraft* category excludes aerobatic aeroplanes, remotely piloted vehicles, drones and gliders. The *armour and artillery* category includes all types of tank, tank destroyer, armoured car, armoured personnel carrier, infantry combat vehicle as well as multiple rocket launchers and self-propelled and towed guns and howitzers with a calibre equal to or above 100 millimetres. Military trucks, lorries and jeeps are not included. The category *guidance and radar systems* is a residual category for electronic acquisition, launch and guidance systems that are either (*a*) deployed independently of a weapon system listed under another weapon category (e.g., certain ground-based SAM launch systems) or (*b*) shipborne missile launch or point defence (CIWS) systems. The values of acquisition, launch and guidance systems on aircraft and armoured vehicles are included in the value of the respective aircraft or armoured vehicle. The reason for treating shipborne systems separately is that a given type of ship is often equipped with numerous combinations of different acquisition, launch and guidance systems. The *missile* category includes only guided missiles; unguided rockets are excluded. The *ship* category excludes some types of ship, such as small patrol craft (with a displacement of less than 100t, unless they carry missiles or torpedoes), research vessels, tugs and ice-breakers.

The second criterion for selection of major weapon items is the identity of the buyer—that is, items either destined for or purchased by the armed forces of the buyer country are included. Arms supplies to guerrilla forces pose a problem. For example, if weapons are delivered to the Afghani resistance they are listed as imports to Afghanistan with a comment in the arms trade register indicating the local recipient. Weapons for police and para-military forces are as a rule not included.

The entry of any arms transfer is made according to the five categories listed above. This means that when, for example, a missile-armed ship is purchased, the missiles and the launch and guidance equipment are entered separately under their respective category in the arms trade register.

Both the order dates and the delivery dates for arms transactions are continuously revised in the light of new information. The *order date* should ideally be the date on which the sales contract was signed. The exact number of weapons ordered as well as the number of weapons delivered may not always be known and is sometimes estimated.

III. The value of the arms trade

The SIPRI system for evaluating the arms trade (described more fully in appendix 8) was designed as a *trend-measuring device*, to enable the measurement of changes in the total flow of major weapons and its geographic pattern. Expressing the evaluation in monetary terms reflects both the quantity and the quality of the weapons transferred. Aggregate values and shares are based only on *actual deliveries* during the year or years covered in the relevant tables and figures.

The SIPRI valuation system is not comparable to official economic statistics such as gross domestic product, public expenditure and export/import figures. The monetary values chosen do not correspond to the actual prices paid, which vary considerably depending on different pricing methods, the length of production runs and the terms involved in individual transactions. For instance, a deal may or may not cover spare parts, training, support equipment, compensation and offset arrangements for the local industries in the buying country, and so on. Furthermore, to use only actual sales prices—even assuming that the information were available for all deals, which it is not—military aid and grants would be excluded, and the total flow of arms would therefore not be measured.

Production under licence is included in the arms trade statistics in such a way that it should reflect the import share embodied in the weapon. In reality, this share is normally high in the beginning and then it gradually decreases over time. SIPRI has attempted to estimate an average import share for each weapon produced under licence.

IV. The SIPRI sources

The sources of the data presented in the registers are of five general types: official national documents; journals and periodicals; newspapers; books, monographs and annual reference works; and documents issued by international and intergovernmental organizations. These are all open sources, available to the general public. The total number of sources regularly perused for data is at present about 200. The sources listed below represent a selection of the first-priority sources of the arms trade and arms production data.

Journals and periodicals

Afrique Défense (Paris)
Air et Cosmos (Paris)
Air Force Magazine (Washington)
Antimilitarismus Information (Frankfurt/M)
Armed Forces Journal (Washington)
Asia Monitor (Hong Kong)
Asian Defence Journal (Kuala Lumpur)
Aviation Week & Space Technology (New York)
Beiträge zur Konfliktforschung (Cologne)
Campaign against Arms Trade (London)
Current News (Washington)
Defence Journal (Karachi)
Defence Today (Rome)
Defensa (Madrid)
Defense & Economy World Report and Survey (Washington)
Defense & Foreign Affairs Daily (Washington)
Defense & Foreign Affairs Digest (Washington)
Defense Daily (Washington)
Defense Electronics (Palo Alto)
Défense & Armement (Paris)
DMS Intelligence (Greenwich)
Far Eastern Economic Review (Hong Kong)
Flight International (Sutton, UK)
IDF Journal (Jerusalem)
Interavia (Geneva)
Interavia Airletter (Geneva)
International Defense Review (Geneva)
Jane's Defence Weekly (London)
Keesing's Contemporary Archives (Bristol)
Latin America Weekly Report (London)
Marine-Rundschau (Stuttgart)
Maritime Defence International (London)
Middle East Review (New York)
Milavnews (Stapleford)
Military Electronics & Countermeasures (Santa Clara, CA)
Military Technology (Cologne)
NACLA Report on the Americas (New York)
NATO's Sixteen Nations (Brussels)

Naval Forces (Aldershot, UK)
Navy International (Dorking, UK)
News Review (Institute for Defense Studies & Analyses, New Delhi)
Pacific Defence Reporter (Victoria)
Soldat und Technik (Frankfurt/M)
Der Spiegel (Hamburg)
Technología Militar (Bonn)
Wehrtechnik (Bonn)
World Missile Forecast (Ridgefield)

Newspapers

Dagens Nyheter (Stockholm)
Daily Telegraph (London)
Financial Times (London)
Frankfurter Rundschau (Frankfurt/M)
Hsin Hua News (London)
International Herald Tribune (Paris)
Izvestia (Moscow)
Jerusalem Post (Jerusalem)
Le Monde (Paris)
Le Monde Diplomatique (Paris)
Neue Zürcher Zeitung (Zürich)
New York Times (New York)
Pravda (Moscow)
Svenska Dagbladet (Stockholm)
The Guardian (London)
The Times (London)
Washington Post (Washington)

Annual reference publications

Aerospace Forecast and Inventory, annually in *Aviation Week & Space Technology* (McGraw-Hill: New York)
Combat Fleets of the World (Naval Institute Press: Annapolis, MD)
Defense and Foreign Affairs Handbook (Copley & Associates: Washington, DC)
Interavia Data: Air Forces of the World (Interavia: Geneva)
Interavia Data: Aircraft Armament (Interavia: Geneva)
Interavia Data: World Aircraft Production (Interavia: Geneva)
Interavia Data: World Helicopter Systems (Interavia: Geneva)
International Air Forces and Military Aircraft Directory (Aviation Advisory Services: Stapleford, UK)
Jane's All the World's Aircraft (Macdonald: London)
Jane's Fighting Ships (Macdonald: London)
Jane's Weapon Systems (Macdonald: London)

Jane's Armour and Artillery (Macdonald: London)

Labayle Couhat, J. (ed.), *Flottes de Combat* (Editions Maritimes et d'Outre Mer: Paris)

'Military Aircraft of the World' and 'Missile Forces of the World', annually in *Flight International* (IPC Transport Press: Sutton, UK)

The Military Balance (International Institute for Strategic Studies: London)

Other reference books

Conway's All the World's Fighting Ships 1922–1946 (Conway Maritime Press: London, 1980)

Conway's All the World's Fighting Ships 1947–1982 (Conway Maritime Press: London, 1983)

Hewish, M. et al., *Air Forces of the World* (Salamander Books: London, 1979)

Keegan, J. (ed.), *World Armies*, second edition (Macmillan: London, 1983).

Appendix 10. Some notes on the comparison of arms trade statistics

SIPRI's arms trade statistics are based on various conventions and restrictions—these are described in appendices 8 (the price system) and 9 (sources and methods). Two basic features are that the information is collected deal by deal from open sources and that the statistics cover transfers of major weapons only. How reliable, then, are SIPRI's statistics and how big a share of the total arms trade do they measure?

I. Primary arms trade sources

There are two types of primary source on the arms trade. The first type is represented by national state authorities—such as customs services and statistical offices—which are authorized to collect information on foreign trade activities. Such official bodies register all goods legally traded, both on the export and the import side. The information is then aggregated into foreign trade statistics.

The other primary source comprises reports on weapons and weapon deals. Such reports originate from a multitude of sources including governments, arms manufacturers, armed forces, journalists and intelligence agencies.

Theoretically, the first type of primary source is preferable to the second, since it would seem to be more reliable and more comparable with foreign trade statistics in general. But in practice, it is not possible to compile world-wide statistics on the arms trade from the first type of primary source. This is because most governments in the world are reluctant to publish such information. This reticence is detectable in foreign trade publications. A survey of foreign trade statistics carried out in the late 1960s revealed that the level of omission, under-reporting and the absence of clear separation from civilian goods was such that the official trade statistics were inadequate for registration work and research.[1] A study made in the early 1980s found that these problems had not lessened but, on the contrary, increased. Even fewer countries than before published information on the arms trade in their foreign trade statistics. Data which were published tended to be highly aggregated and often irreconcilable with other information on the arms trade.[2] In addition, the systems used for classification of foreign trade statistics (the Standard International Trade Classification and systems based on the Brussels Tariff Nomenclature) are of little use in distinguishing between military and civilian goods. While they clearly separate military guns, armoured vehicles and warships, such separation is generally not possible for aircraft and electronics. Even if governments are prepared to publish arms trade data in their foreign trade statistics, they cannot simply put weapons in some standard classification category, but have to separate some more recently introduced types of weapon system, such as radars or helicopters, into specifically designed categories. Only the US Government does this thoroughly.

Although foreign trade statistics do not reveal much about the arms trade, data disseminated by other governmental bodies can be useful. In a number of West European countries—such as the UK, France and Sweden—aggregate statistical data are published by the government on a regular basis. In other West European countries and in some Third World countries, such as Israel and Brazil, such data have been published irregularly. One major problem with such data is the absence of standardization. Governmental bodies use their own definitions of weapons and in many countries, for example Brazil or FR Germany, various figures are available reflecting different definitions.[3] Compilations of such figures are not reliable.

II. Secondary arms trade sources

Many organizations and individuals collect information about arms transfers to or from a specific country or region. They use the second type of primary source. Some of them—such as the British Campaign against the Arms Trade or the Israeli Jaffee Centre for Strategic Studies—publish data regularly. Others publish from time to time in articles for journals and newspapers. Such data tend to be comprehensive and are used by SIPRI as much as possible.

There are only two institutions which try to collate all available data on the arms trade annually and on a world-wide basis: SIPRI and the London-based International Institute for Strategic Studies (IISS).[4] Comparisons of SIPRI and IISS data show that SIPRI's data are much more detailed and extensive. The IISS annual publication *The Military Balance* is used as one source for the SIPRI arms trade registers. The IISS does not attempt to aggregate its arms trade registers. The SIPRI aggregated arms trade statistics are the only available monetary-statistical series based on a detailed examination of open sources.

There are other statistical series on the arms trade, but they are not based on open sources. They arise from the data base on world-wide arms transfers maintained by the US Government and are published in excerpt form, for example by the US Arms Control and Disarmament Agency (ACDA)[5] and the Congressional Research Service.[6] These data are collected from many sources, including US intelligence agencies. Neither the data base as such, nor the valuation method, are available to the general public. Checks on reliability can therefore only be performed on the aggregate data.

US government data are preferred by many researchers and journalists because their coverage extends beyond major weapons and includes small arms, ammunition, machinery for arms production, military clothing, and so on. This concept is obviously more useful, but it cannot be reliably used if only open sources are available for data collection. On the other hand, concerns have been raised that the US Government data may not be entirely reliable.[7] As indicated above, no real test of this hypothesis is possible, given the restrictions on public availability. ACDA data differ from national figures on arms transfers for a number of reasons, such as different definitions, different valuation methods and problems of currency conversion.

III. Comparing SIPRI and other sources

There are large differences between SIPRI-figures and those published by governments (table 10A.1). This should be no surprise, given the differences in coverage. There is a pattern of divergence ranging from countries which mostly

Table 10A.1. Comparison of figures on arms exports

Figures are in US $m. at constant (1980) prices.

Country	Source	1977	1978	1979	1980	1981	1982	1983
Canada	A	654	538	551	617	892	780	853
	B	55	139	50	62	60	135	141
	C	90	150	200	90	90	215	150
France	A	2 376	3 618	3 089	4 756	5 606	5 008	4 840
	B	1 966	2 606	2 790	1 938	2 451	2 180	2 183
	C	1 520	2 130	1 630	2 800	4 020	3 090	3 540
FRG	A	1 039	1 021	1 023	897	1 471	1 176	2 302
	B	366	659	447	411	841	457	1 078
	C	1 140	1 150	1 310	1 400	1 280	770	1 480
Sweden	A	213	274	449	363	361	300	282
	B	106	8	147	92	19	51	20
	C	63	130	130	120	90	155	30
Switzerland	A	322	277	266	203	288	259	206
	B	17	22	55	55	90	48	69
	C	393	343	381	650	311	309	271
UK	A	1 942	2 435	2 196	2 767	2 896	3 148	2 914
	B	1 149	911	531	601	890	1 277	807
	C	1 110	1 645	1 300	1 900	1 560	1 717	1 318
USA	A = C	8 500	7 680	6 500	6 500	7 990	7 990	8 730
	B	8 122	8 485	4 765	6 616	7 351	7 924	7 520
USSR	B	4 888	6 132	9 448	7 223	6 612	6 537	5 549
	C	8 380	9 090	13 600	11 600	10 250	9 700	8 070
Total	B	17 437	20 371	20 358	18 620	20 968	21 441	20 321
	C	25 020	27 500	29 860	29 530	33 400	32 720	30 760

A: Official figures.
B: SIPRI figures for exports of major weapons.
C: ACDA figures.
Sources:
Official sources:
Canada: data supplied by the Department of External Affairs Information.
France: data supplied by the Ministry of Defence, Service of Information and Public Relations.
FRG: data taken from Foreign Trade Statistics, residual category.
Sweden: data from the Swedish War Materials Inspectorate, as published in Regeringens skrivelse 1984/85: 223.
Switzerland: Kreigsmaterial-Exportstatistik; mimeo, supplied by Swiss Embassy in Stockholm.
USA and ACDA: *World Military Expenditures and Arms Trade*, US Arms Control and Disarmament Agency, Washington, DC, annual.

export major weapons (such as France and the USA) to those which mainly export ammunition, small arms and parts for weapon systems (such as Belgium, Czechoslovakia, Canada, Sweden or Switzerland). In the latter cases, this means that SIPRI figures systematically underrepresent total arms exports from these countries.

ACDA figures should be closer to national data since the definition used by ACDA is wider. While this holds in some cases, in other cases there are large discrepancies between ACDA data and national data resulting from differences in definition, unreliable national data or unreliable ACDA data. In general, ACDA data seem to underestimate the arms exports of some countries, which export mainly weapon components, production technology, small arms and ammunition.

The uncertain nature of the data means that it is difficult to estimate what proportion of the whole arms market—however this is defined—is covered by SIPRI. The ratio could be as low as 1:2 or as high as 2:3. For reasons given

Table 10A.2. Comparison of SIPRI and ACDA statistics on the number of arms delivered to developing regions, 1979–83, selected categories[a]

Weapon category		Total	USSR	USA	France	UK	China
Land armaments							
Tanks	A	13 654	6 540	1 829	115	365	670
	B	13 404	6 061	1 349	792	1 095	1 015
Field	A	20 404	5 545	3 874	325	140	980
artillery[b]	B	6 165	2 409	1 644	178	75	891
Armoured	A	21 281	8 615	6 171	1 955	545	150
personnel carriers	B	19 099	4 578	4 855	2 539	492	140
Warships							
Surface[d]	A	800	206	103	63	55	35
combatants	B	532	150	73	46	35	30
Submarines[d]	A	39	8	0	2	0	2
	B	22	8	0	2	0	6
Aircraft							
Combat	A	4 306	2 275	706	330	125	320
aircraft	B	3 736	1 675	768	339	127	264
Helicopters[c]	A	2 145	1 065	165	405	20	0
	B	2 120	479	696	560	17	0
Other	A	2 043	340	93	120	55	125
aircraft[c]	B	1 911	172	485	105	127	12

A: ACDA.
B: SIPRI.
[a]SIPRI includes licensed production; weapon systems may be judged to be in different categories.
[b]ACDA includes mortars, guns and howitzers below 100-mm calibre, etc., which are excluded by SIPRI.
[c]The inclusion or exclusion of aircraft used both in military and civilian roles may be different between SIPRI and ACDA.
[d]SIPRI excludes ships of less than 100t displacement.
Source: SIPRI data base; US ACDA, *World Military Expenditures and Arms Transfers*, Washington, DC, 1985, p. 137.

elsewhere (see chapter 4) the share of major weapons in the total arms trade has probably declined since the mid-1970s, as more technology, components and upgrading kits are traded now than before. As explained in appendix 9, some measures have been taken to broaden the scope of the SIPRI arms trade statistics in order to keep pace with the changing pattern.

IV. The reliability of SIPRI's statistics

SIPRI's arms trade statistics are compiled from open sources by a small research staff. This obviously means that there are reliability problems. There are large discrepancies between SIPRI and ACDA figures for arms deliveries (table 10A.2). The specific details of these particular differences cannot be checked since ACDA data are not available for detailed inspection. All the detailed information available is used as source material by SIPRI. SIPRI aims at reflecting the state of collective public knowledge of individual arms deals. This information is published—in the form of registers and valuation statistics—in the *SIPRI Yearbook* as well as in other SIPRI publications. Errors, both omissions and wrong inclusions, are unavoidable. Additional reliability problems arise from the price system used. SIPRI's data provide, at best, a reasonable approximation of the truth.

Notes and references

[1] SIPRI, *The Arms Trade with the Third World* (Almqvist & Wiksell: Stockholm, 1971), pp. 798–804.
[2] IFSH-Arbeitsgruppe Rüstung und Unterentwicklung, 'Data in the socio-military field: Report to the UN expert commission on Disarmament and Development', mimeo, Hamburg 1980.
[3] For FR Germany, licences for exports of 'weapons of war' amounted to 1540 m. DM in 1983 while licences for exports of 'arms and strategic material' amounted to 8610 m. DM; see *Frankfurter Rundschau*, 18 Feb. 1985; in Brazil, at a time when government and industrial officials were judging arms exports to be around $2000m., the central bank figures were less than half that, see *Latin America Regional Report Brazil*, 18 Oct. 1985.
[4] IISS, *Military Balance* (IISS: London, annual).
[5] US Arms Control and Disarmament Agency, *World Military Expenditures and Arms Transfers* (Government Printing Office: Washington, DC, annual).
[6] See, e.g., Grimmett, R., *Trends in Conventional Arms Transfers to the Third World by Major Supplier* (US Congressional Research Service: Washington, DC, Apr. 1985).
[7] See Kolodziej, E., 'Measuring French arms transfers', *Journal of Conflict Resolution*, vol. 23, no. 2 (1979).

Appendix 11. Selective bibliography

I. Overview

Harkavy, R. E., *The Arms Trade and International Systems* (Ballinger: Cambridge, MA, 1975).

Harkavy, R. E. and Neuman, S. G. (eds), *Arms Transfers in the Modern World* (Praeger Special Studies: New York, 1979).

Klare, M. T., 'The unnoticed arms trade: exports of conventional arms-making technology', *International Security*, vol. 8, no. 2 (Fall 1983).

Leiss, A., Kemp, G., *et al.*, *Arms Transfers to Less Developed Countries*, Center for International Studies, Massachusetts Institute of Technology, Cambridge, MA, 1970.

Ra'anan, U., Pfalzgraff Jr., R. L. and Kemp, G. (eds), *Arms Transfers to the Third World: The Military Buildup in Less Industrial Countries* (Westview Press: Boulder, CO, 1978).

Pierre, A. J., *The Global Politics of Arms Sales* (Princeton University Press: Princeton, NJ, 1982).

SIPRI, *The Arms Trade with the Third World* (Almqvist & Wiksell: Stockholm, 1971).

Öberg, J., 'Arms trade with the Third World as an aspect of imperialism', *Journal of Peace Research*, vol. 12, no. 3 (1975).

II. Arms transfer data

Blackaby, F. and Ohlson, T., 'Military expenditure and the arms trade: problems of data', *Bulletin of Peace Proposals*, vol. 13, no. 4 (1982).

Brzoska, M., 'Arms transfer data sources', *Journal of Conflict Resolution*, vol. 26, no. 1 (Mar. 1982).

Central Intelligence Agency, *Communist Aid to Less Developed Countries of the Free World, 1976* (ER 77–10296U), and *1977* (ER 78–10478U); *Communist Aid Activities in Non-Communist Less Developed Countries, 1978* (ER 79–10412U); and *Communist Aid Activities in Non-Communist Less Developed Countries, 1979 and 1954–79* (ER 80–10318U), (Washington, DC, 1977, 1978, 1979 and 1980).

Grimmett, R. F., *Trends in Conventional Arms Transfers to the Third World by Major Supplier*, Congressional Research Service, Library of Congress, Washington, DC, annual (CRS 82–08–12 for 1974–81, CRS 84–82 for 1976–83, CRS 85–86F for 1977–84 and CRS 86–99F for 1978–85).

Kolodziej, E. A., 'Measuring French arms transfers: a problem of sources and some sources of problems with ACDA data', *Journal of Conflict Resolution*, vol. 23, no. 2 (June 1979).

SIPRI, *Arms Trade Registers: The Arms Trade with the Third World* (Almqvist & Wiksell: Stockholm, 1975).

US Arms Control and Disarmament Agency, ACDA, *World Military Expenditures and Arms Transfers* (Washington, DC, annual).

III. Suppliers

General

Ball, N. and Leitenberg, M. (eds), *The Structure of the Defense Industry* (Croom Helm: London and Canberra, 1983).

Cannizzo, C. (ed.), *The Gun Merchants: Politics and Policies of the Major Arms Suppliers* (Pergamon Press: New York, 1980).

Copper, J. F. and Papp, D. S. (eds), *Communist Nations' Military Assistance* (Westview Press: Boulder and London, 1983).

Harkavy, R. E., 'Arms resupply during conflict: a framework for analysis', *The Jerusalem Journal of International Relations*, vol. 7, no. 3 (1985).

Neuman, S., 'Coproduction, barter and countertrade: offsets in the international arms market, *Orbis*, vol. 29, no. 1 (Spring 1985).

Smith, R., Humm, A. and Fontanel, J., 'The economics of exporting arms', *Journal of Peace Research*, vol. 22, no. 3 (1985).

USSR

Albrecht, U., 'Soviet arms exports', in SIPRI, *World Armaments and Disarmament, SIPRI Yearbook 1983* (Taylor & Francis: London, 1983).

Cassen, R., *Soviet Interest in the Third World* (SAGE Publications and RIIA: London, 1985).

Efrat, M., 'The economics of Soviet arms transfers to the Third World', in Wiles, P. and Efrat, M., (eds), *The Economics of Soviet Arms*, STICERD Occasional Paper no. 7, London School of Economics and Political Science, London, 1985.

Holloway, D., *The Soviet Union and the Arms Race* (Yale University Press: New Haven, 1983).

Kozyrev, A., *The Arms Trade: A New Level of Danger* (Progress Publishers: Moscow, 1985).

Krause, J., *Sowjetische Militärhilfe an die Dritte Welt* (Nomos: Baden-Baden, 1985).

Menon, R., *Soviet Power and the Third World* (Yale University Press: New Haven and London, 1986).

Pajak, R. F., 'Soviet arms transfers as an instrument of influence', *Survival*, vol. 23, no. 4 (1981).

Wharton Econometric Forecasting Associates, *Soviet Arms Trade with the Non-Communist Third World in the 1970s and 1980s*, Special Report, Washington, DC, 1984.

USA

Farley, P. J., Kaplan, S. S. and Lewis, W. H., *Arms Across the Sea* (Brookings Institution: Washington, DC, 1978).

Gansler, J., *The Defence Industry* (MIT Press: Cambridge, MA, 1980).

Gervasi, T., *The Arsenal of Democracy*, editions I and II (Grove Press: New York, 1977 and 1981).

Green, A. and Janik, M., 'The law and politics of foreign arms sales', *The George Washington Journal of International Law and Economics*, vol. 16, no. 3 (1982).

Grimmett, R., *Arms Sales: US Policy*, Congressional Research Services report no. IB77079, US Library of Congress, Washington, DC, 1981.

Hammond, P., Louscher, D., Salomone, M. and Graham, N., *The Reluctant Supplier: US Decisionmaking for Arms Sales* (OGH Publishers: Cambridge, MA, 1983).

Klare, M., *American Arms Supermarket* (University of Texas Press: Austin, 1984).

Moodie, M., 'Arms transfer policy: a national dilemma', *Washington Quarterly*, Spring 1982.

Pierre, A. J. (ed.), *Arms Transfers and American Foreign Policy* (New York University Press: New York, 1979).

Sorley, L., *Arms Transfers under Nixon: A Policy Analysis* (University Press of Kentucky: Lexington, MA, 1983).

US Congressional Research Service, *US Military Sales and Assistance Programs: Laws, Regulations and Procedures*, Report to the Committee on Foreign Affairs, US House of Representatives, 99th Congress (US Government Printing Office: Washington, DC, July 1985).

France

Collet, A., 'Le régime des matériels de guerre, armes et munitions', *Défense Nationale*, vol. 41, no. 6 (1985).

Dubos, J.-F., *Ventes d'Armes: une Politique* (Gallimard: Paris, 1974).

Dussauge, P., *L'Industrie Francaise de l'Armement* (Economica: Paris, 1985).

Gerdan, E., *Dossier a.... commes Armes* (Alain Moreau: Paris, 1975).

Klein, J., 'Commerce des armes et politique: la cas française', *Politique Etrangère*, vol. 41, no. 5 (1976).

Kolodziej, E. A., *Making and Marketing of Arms: The French Experience and the International System* (Princeton University Press: Princeton, 1986).

The United Kingdom

Edmonds, M., 'The British government and arms sales', *ADIU-report*, vol. 4, no. 6 (1982).

Freedman, L., *Arms Production in the United Kingdom: Problems and Prospects* (Royal Institute for International Affairs: London, 1978).

Pearson, F. S., 'The question of control in British defence sales policy', *International Affairs*, vol. 28, no. 2 (1983).

Italy

Battistelli, F., *Armi: Nuovo Modello di Sviluppo? L'Industria Militaire in Italia* (Einaudi: Torino, 1980).
Rossi, S. A., 'The Italian defence industry with respect to international competition', *Defence Today*, no. 77–78, 1984.

China

Gilks, A. and Segal, G., *China and the Arms Trade* (Croom Helm: London and Sydney, 1985).
Tow, W., 'Arms Sales', in Segal, G. and Tow, W. (eds), *Chinese Defence Policy* (MacMillan: London, 1984).

FR Germany

Albrecht, U., Lock, P. and Wulf, H., *Mit Rüstung gegen Arbeitslosigkeit?* (Rowohlt: Reinbek, 1982).
Ehrenberg, E., *Der Deutsche Rüstungsexport: Beurteilungen und Perspektiven* (Bernhard & Graefe: Munich, 1981).
Pearson, F., 'Of Leopards and Cheetahs', *Orbis*, vol. 29, no. 1 (Spring 1985).
Krause, J., *Die Rüstungsexportpolitik der Bundesrepublik Deutschland*, Arbeitspapier 2286, Stiftung Wissenschaft und Politik, Ebenhausen, 1981.

Other suppliers

Brzoska, M. and Ohlson, T., (eds) *Arms Production in the Third World* (Taylor & Francis: London and Philadelphia, 1986).
Colijn, C. and van der Mey, L. (eds), *De Nederlandse Wapenexport: Beleid en Praktijk, Indonesie, Iran, Taiwan* (Statsutgiverij: 's-Gravenhage, 1984).
Hagelin, B. *Kulorna Rullar* (Ordfront: Stockholm, 1985).
Katz, J. E. (ed.), *Arms Production in Developing Countries* (Lexington Books: Lexington, MA, 1984).
Klieman, A. S., *Israel's Global Reach: Arms Sales as Diplomacy* (Pergamon, Brassey's: Washington et al., 1985).
Pilz, P., *Die Panzermacher: Die Österreichische Rüstungsindustrie und ihre Exporte* (Verlag für Gesellschaftskritik: Wien, 1982).

IV. Recipients

General

Bertram, C., *Third World Conflict and International Security* (IISS and MacMillan: London and Basingstoke, 1982).

Brzoska, M., 'Research communication: the military related external debt of Third World countries', *Journal of Peace Research*, vol. 20, no. 3 (1983).

Deger, S., *Military Expenditure in Third World Countries: The Economic Effects* (Routledge and Kegan Paul: London, Boston and Henley, 1986).

Foster, J., *New Conventional Weapons Technologies: Implications for the Third World*, RAND paper 5965, Santa Monica, CA, 1978.

Kaldor, M. and Eide, A. (eds), *The World Military Order: The Impact of Military Technology on the Third World* (MacMillan: London et al, 1979).

Kolodziej, E. and Harkavy, R. (eds), *Security Policies for Developing Countries* (D. C. Heath and Co., Lexington Books: Lexington, MA, 1982).

Wolpin, M. D., *Militarization, Internal Repression and Social Welfare in the Third World* (Croom Helm: London and Sydney, 1986).

Middle East

Cordesman, A. H., *The Gulf and the Search for Strategic Stability: Saudi Arabia, the Military Balance in the Gulf and Trends in the Arab-Israeli Military Balance* (Westview Press and Mansell Publishing Ltd: Boulder, CO, and London, 1984).

Heller, M., Levran, A. and Eytan, Z., *The Middle East Military Balance* (The Jerusalem Post and Westview Press: Jerusalem and Boulder, CO, annual).

Karsh, E., *Soviet Arms Transfers to the Middle East in the 1970s*, Tel Aviv University, Jaffee Center for Strategic Studies, paper no. 22, Dec. 1983.

Korany, B. and Dessouki, A. (eds), *The Foreign Policies of Arab States* (Westview Press: Boulder, CO, 1984).

Leitenberg, M. and Scheffer, G. (eds), *Great Power Intervention in the Middle East* (Pergamon Press: New York, 1979).

Roberts, C. A., 'Soviet arms transfer policy and the decision to upgrade Syrian air defenses', *Survival*, vol. 35, no. 4 (July/Aug. 1983).

Africa

Akehurst, F. S. (ed.) *Arms and African Development* (Praeger: New York, 1972).

Arlinghaus, B. E., *Military Development in Africa: The Political and Economic Risks of Arms Transfers* (Westview Press: Boulder, CO, and London, 1984).

Arlinghaus, B. E. (ed.), *Arms for Africa: Military Assistance and Foreign Policy in the Developing World* (Lexington Books: Lexington, MA, 1983).

Luckham, R., 'Militarization in Africa', in SIPRI, *World Armaments and Disarmament: SIPRI Yearbook 1985* (Taylor & Francis: London, 1985).

Smaldone, J. P., 'Soviet and Chinese military aid and arms transfers to Africa: a contextual analysis', in Weinstein, W. and Henrikson, T. H. (eds), *Soviet and Chinese Aid to African Nations* (Praeger: New York, 1980).

Latin America

Ball, N., Carranza, M. E., Cordero, F., Encinas del Pando, J. A., Portales, C. and Varas, A., *Ibero Americana, Nordic Journal of Latin American Studies*, The Institute of Latin American Studies, Stockholm, vol. 12, no. 1–2 (1983).

Brigagão, Clóvis, *O Mercado da Segurança* (Editoria Nova Fronteira: Rio de Janeiro, 1984).

Brigagão, C., Herrera, A. Q., Dagnino, R. P., Dos Santos, L. G. and Pinguelli Rosa, L., *O Armamentismo e o Brasil: A Guerra Deles* (Editoria Brasiliense: São Paulo, 1985).

Einaudi, L., et al., *Arms Transfers to Latin America, Toward a Policy of Mutual Respect*, RAND, R-1173-DOS, June 1973.

Varas, A., *Militarization and the International Arms Race in Latin America* (Westview Press: Boulder, CO, and London, 1985).

South and East Asia

Gregor, A. J. and Chang, M. H., 'Military power, the Taiwan Relations Act and US interests in East Asia', *Journal of Strategic Studies*, vol. 8, no. 3 (Sep. 1985).

Huisken, R., *Defence Resources of Southeast Asia and the Southwest Pacific: A Compendium of Data* (Australian National University: Canberra, 1980).

Makeig, D., 'War, no-war and the India-Pakistan negotiating process', *Defence Journal*, vol. 12, no. 7 (1986).

Subrahmanyam, K., *Perspectives in Defense Planning* (Abhinav Publications: New Delhi, 1972).

Terhal, P., 'Foreign exchange costs of the Indian military, 1950–72', *Journal of Peace Research*, vol. 19, no. 3 (1982).

Thomas, R. G. C., *The Defence of India: A Budgetary Perspective of Strategy and Politics* (MacMillan of India: New Delhi, 1978).

V. Bibliographies

Ball, N., 'Bibliography', in Harkavy, R. F. and Neuman, S. G. (eds), *Arms Transfers in the Modern World* (Praeger: New York, 1979).

Belgian Parliament Library, *Wapenhandel* (Brussels, 1973). (Also in French: *Le Commerce des Armes*.)

Burns, R. D., *Arms Control and Disarmament: A Bibliography* (ABC-Clio: Santa Barbara, 1977).

Conventional Arms Transfers: A Bibliography, the Arms Control Association, Washington, DC, 1979.

Gillingham, A., 'Arms traffic: an introduction and bibliography', Center for the Study of Armament and Disarmament, California State University, Los Angeles, *Political Issues Series*, vol. 4, no. 2 (1976).

'Selected Bibliography', in Kaldor, M. and Eide, A. (eds), *The World Military Order* (MacMillan: London et al., 1979).

Index

A-7 aircraft 56
Aeritalia 80, 81
Aermacchi 80
Aérospatiale 62, 64, 65, 66
Afghanistan 33, 34, 35, 36, 39, 44, 58, 130
Africa:
    arms imports 2, 4, 6, 8, 9, 11, 21–7, 60, 76,
        83, 97, 101, 114, 117, 118
    conflicts in 21, 23
    military aid to 23
Agusta 80, 81
aircraft:
    trade in 2, 6, 8–9, 11
Algeria 4, 7, 22, 23–4, 39, 40, 60
Alpha jet 62, 92
America see Canada; Central America; South
        America; United States of America
Angola 7, 22, 26, 39, 40, 44, 101
Arab arms industry 19, 118
Arab–Israeli Wars 6, 15, 19, 20, 23, 47, 55,
        60, 128; see also Camp David peace
        agreement
Argentina:
    arms embargoes 31, 66, 67
    arms imports 6, 7, 30, 31, 47, 75, 89, 94,
        114
    arms production 112
    see also Falklands/Malvinas War
armour:
    trade in 2, 8, 9, 11
Armscor 117
arms trade:
    commercialization of 28, 46
    conflicts and 6, 14, 36, 134
    debts and 134
    decline and 126–7, 132
    demand patterns 15–37
    domestic procurement costs and 126
    economic factors 11, 14, 126–7, 129, 132–4
    export weapons 131
    financing 36, 131
    forces propelling 125–7
    future developments 134–5
    growth 1, 15, 128
    historical analysis 127–32
    influence and 126
    monopoly supply, decline in 11
    new weapons 10, 11, 14
    offset deals 131, 134
    oil revenues, recycling of and 128
    phases of 127
    political fragmentation 11, 14
    politics and 1, 126, 127, 130

proliferation and diversification 11–14
    recipients 3–6, 131
    second-hand weapons 10, 11, 14
    shares of 2, 4
    size of 2
    structural analysis 127–32
    suppliers 1–3
    trends 1–14
    value 1
    weapon categories 6–9
    weapon status 10–11
artillery:
    trade in 2, 8, 9
ASEAN (Association of South-East Asian
        Nations) 28, 29, 30, 94
Australia 56, 95, 96, 101
Austria 105, 106, 107, 108, 129
Avions Marcel 65
AWACS (airborne warning and control
        system) aircraft 15, 20, 52, 56, 58

Bahrain 16, 21, 109, 116
Bangladesh 34, 36
Bazán 100
Belgium 95–7, 108
Bell helicopters 47
Bell Textron 53
Blohm & Voss 93
BMP-1/2 vehicles 35
Boeing 53
Bofors 108, 109, 116
Bolivia 30, 106
Brazil:
    arms exports 3, 5, 17, 23, 112, 115
    arms imports 7, 30, 31, 32, 47, 109
    arms industry 6, 32
    arms production 112, 114–15
    Engesa 23
    USA and 115–16
Britain see United Kingdom
British Aerospace 72, 73
British Shipbuilders 72, 73
Brunei 29
Bulgaria 102, 103, 104, 105

CACEX 115
Cambodia see Kampuchea
Cameroon 22
Camp David peace agreement 19, 21, 47, 56,
        118
Canada 4, 95, 96, 97–8
Canadair 97